THE WILEY BICENTENNIAL—KNOWLEDGE FOR GENERATIONS

*E*ach generation has its unique needs and aspirations. When Charles Wiley first opened his small printing shop in lower Manhattan in 1807, it was a generation of boundless potential searching for an identity. And we were there, helping to define a new American literary tradition. Over half a century later, in the midst of the Second Industrial Revolution, it was a generation focused on building the future. Once again, we were there, supplying the critical scientific, technical, and engineering knowledge that helped frame the world. Throughout the 20th Century, and into the new millennium, nations began to reach out beyond their own borders and a new international community was born. Wiley was there, expanding its operations around the world to enable a global exchange of ideas, opinions, and know-how.

For 200 years, Wiley has been an integral part of each generation's journey, enabling the flow of information and understanding necessary to meet their needs and fulfill their aspirations. Today, bold new technologies are changing the way we live and learn. Wiley will be there, providing you the must-have knowledge you need to imagine new worlds, new possibilities, and new opportunities.

Generations come and go, but you can always count on Wiley to provide you the knowledge you need, when and where you need it!

WILLIAM J. PESCE
PRESIDENT AND CHIEF EXECUTIVE OFFICER

PETER BOOTH WILEY
CHAIRMAN OF THE BOARD

STUDY GUIDE

Katharine Rockett
University of Essex, England

Microeconomics

Third Edition

David Besanko
Northwestern University

Ronald R. Braeutigam
Northwestern University

John Wiley & Sons, Inc.

Dedication

To Pierre, Laurel, and Ioline

Cover Photo: Eastcott Momatiuk/Stone/Getty Images

Bicentennial Logo Design: Richard J. Pacifico

To order books or for customer service, please call 1-800-CALL-WILEY (225-5945).

ISBN-13   978- 0-470-23333-7
ISBN-10   0-470-23333-8

Printed in the United States of America

10 9 8 7 6 5 4 3 2 1

Printed and bound by Bind-Rite Graphics, Inc.

Preface

This Study Guide accompanies *Microeconomics, 3rd Edition* by David Besanko and Ron Braeutigam. Each chapter of the guide re-summarizes the theory and techniques covered in the corresponding chapter of the book. <u>Exercises</u> embedded within each summary build a working knowledge of the material. <u>Chapter Review Questions</u> at the end of the summaries provide practice of this knowledge. The <u>Problem Sets</u> aim to build and deepen your understanding. An <u>Exam</u> concludes each chapter. The exam allows you to consolidate your knowledge of the concepts, techniques, and definitions. Complete and detailed <u>Answers</u> for all exercises, problems and exam questions are provided at the end of each chapter. These answers are written so as to teach: students who have gotten an answer wrong should be able to understand why once they have read the answer.

Students of all levels should find material here that suits and extends their abilities. For beginners, the exercises in the text and chapter review questions are appropriate. For students ready for more of a challenge, the problem sets are appropriate. The exams are at the level of a standard intermediate microeconomics end-of-term test.

Wherever possible, the material is covered from three different approaches: verbally, graphically, and algebraically. The verbal explanation presents the intuition and the logic of the theory. The graphs are useful to capture the essence of the problem. The algebra allows you to explore the finer points that the graphs cannot capture simply. Students should be able to find aspects of the summaries that use their preferred perspective, as well as the opportunity to broaden their appreciation of all three approaches and how they can be used together to analyze economic problems fully.

The best way to use the guide is to work through the material weekly, as it is covered in your course, rather than waiting until the end of term to review it all at once. Later chapters are easier to understand if you are very comfortable with earlier chapters, as certain concepts and techniques introduced early are fundamental to understanding the entire course. I would suggest that you read the summary and work through the Exercises and Chapter Review Questions each week. Use selected problems from the Problem Set and the Exams to review the material periodically during term.

Contents

Chapter 1: Analyzing Economic Problems

Microeconomics is the study of the economic behavior of individual economic decision makers such as consumers, workers, firms, or managers. It analyzes both the individual behavior of these economic agents and the way they interact to form larger units such as markets or industries. Understanding the economic behavior of individual agents is important for many types of professionals. For example, policy makers need to know how consumers, workers, and investors will react to economic reforms (such as tax relief) in order to know how the performance of the national economy will be affected. Business managers need to know how individual agents, such as consumers and rival companies, will react to changes in business policy (such as pricing) in order to know how the firm's profits will change. Chapter 1 introduces you to the basic tools that you will need to analyze the microeconomic problems facing such individuals.

In reality, the world is extremely complex. Economics usually bases its analysis on abstractions of reality called "models". These models are simplifications of the real world that help the economist understand the fundamental forces that determine movement of an economic variable she is interested in, without getting bogged down in the details of the everyday functioning of the economy.

Exercise 1: *The following is a model of the market for cars. There are four possible types of cars: brand-new good cars, brand-new lemon cars (bad cars), used good cars, and used lemon cars. All individuals in the economy have the same preferences for all the four types of cars. That is:*

1. *New and old lemon cars have a value of zero for all consumers*
2. *New good cars are preferable to used good cars, and both have a value greater than zero*

Suppose that half of all cars (new and old) are lemons and half are good cars, and this is known to all individuals; however, it is not possible to perform a test on any car to know if that specific car is good or bad before purchasing it.

There are four types of agents in the economy: (1) dealers who sell new cars for a given uniform price, (2) buyers of cars who do not currently own cars, (3) sellers of good used cars (who may also buy cars), and (4) sellers of lemon used cars (who may also buy cars). Buyers purchase so as to maximize the expected value of a car minus its price. If sellers choose to sell their used car and buy a new car, their payoff is the expected value of a new car minus its price plus the price their used car commands in the market. Sellers may also choose to keep their old car. Sellers decide whether to sell or not based on which choice maximizes their expected payoff.

How has reality been simplified in this model?

    a. In reality, many consumers can figure out the true quality of a used car to some degree.
    b. In reality, there are more than four possible types of car.
    c. In reality, all individuals in the economy do not have the same preferences.

   d. In reality the sales tax on new cars might not be the same as the sales tax on used cars.

   e. All of the above.

To the extent that complexity is added to the model, it can be introduced in a step-by-step manner after the simplest representation of reality is fully understood so that the effects of each element can be seen more clearly. For example, if we were to solve a mathematical representation of the model described in Exercise 1, we would find that good used cars are never sold (lemon used cars drive good used cars out of the market). If we change the model to suppose that consumers can distinguish between good and bad cars, this is no longer true. Comparing the two versions of our model suggests that the type of uncertainty we assumed may be a key reason why good cars never are sold in this market. Similarly, it is often useful to determine how a market operates in the absence of any government intervention, such as indirect taxes, in order to see more clearly how market behavior changes once government policies are introduced.

We all perform such abstractions as a matter of course in our lives. For example, when you calculate how early you need to leave your house in order to arrive at school in the morning, you ignore many of life's uncertainties. You might include in your calculations the possibility that you might forget something and have to return to your house, but you might not include the possibility that you witness an accident and be called upon to remain at the scene of the accident until the police arrive. The economic models studied in this book proceed in a similar way, eliminating details that are unlikely to affect significantly the aspect of reality we care about. Economic models are more formal than the simplifications you perform in everyday life, but are the same in spirit.

Most microeconomic problems deal with the allocation of limited resources to satisfy (unlimited) human wants. In other words, a consumer may want more satisfaction from her consumption of goods, but may have only a limited amount of money to make these purchases. A manager may want more profit from sales, but may only have a limited capacity to make products that can be sold and may encounter consumers who have a limited ability to pay for the products. This means that most microeconomic problems deal with resolving tradeoffs. If the consumer purchases more of good A, he must purchase less of good B. If the manager wants to build a new plant in Europe, she might have to give up plans to build a new factory in Texas. Therefore, one of the important concepts underlying economic models is that of the choice set. In fact, one of the most important simplifications of the models we study is the description of the alternatives facing the economic agent. How we specify these alternatives determines the possible choices faced by the agent and can therefore influence our conclusions about economic behavior. We will describe this in detail when we cover opportunity costs in chapter 7.

Once the alternatives facing the agent have been described, our models must specify what the agent cares about and what constraints the agent faces in making his choice. Here again, how we simplify reality can affect the conclusions we draw from studying economic behavior. For example, it might be reasonable to assume that the manager making the investment choice between facilities and R&D cares about earning the most profits possible for the firm as a result of his decision. In this case, the choice could very well be as we have specified it in the preceding paragraph. Alternatively, it might be the case that the manager cares solely about improving his own power within the firm. If power depends primarily on how many workers the manager has under his command, then the relevant aspect of the choice is the number of workers that each strategy allows the manager to hire and not how much the profits of the firm increase. This changes the specification of the problem considerably. As a result, when specifying the alternatives facing the agent, account should be taken of what the agent cares about.

Exercise 2: *What are the choices available to the agent in exercise 1? How does this implicit choice set affect the sort of answer you would expect to obtain from the model?*

We usually refer to the representation of what an economic agent wants as the **objective function** of the agent. In our example of the manager above, we suggested two possible objective functions for the agent. In one case, we supposed that the objective function was the profits of the firm. In the second case, we supposed that the objective function was "power", which we suggested might be proxied by the number of workers under the manager's command. In either case, the manager tried to make the best – or "optimal" – choice, according to this objective function. Further, in each case, the manager faced a **constraint**: he did not have unlimited resources to invest in improving profits or in hiring workers. Rather, he had a budget ($100) that he could allocate to different investment projects. In other words, an economic agent's behavior can be modeled as optimizing the objective function subject to the various constraints that the agent faces. In much of what follows we will represent this objective function and the constraints algebraically. However we will also represent the objective function and constraints graphically, or simply in words, when this helps us to obtain a solution more easily or to understand the workings of the model in more depth. In some cases, in fact, we will interpret the agent's problem verbally, graphically, and algebraically in order to understand the problem as thoroughly as possible.

Let us return to the example of the manager who has a given budget of size $B to allocate between new facilities and R&D investment. We have described this example verbally already. We will now represent this problem algebraically and graphically as well. Suppose that the manager cares about power. If he invests in facilities, he must spend $100 on the expansion and can then hire workers at $25 each in order to operate the new facilities. If he invests in R&D, say that he can hire workers at $50 each. We can then write the number of workers, N, he could hire under each alternative, if he were willing to spend $R, as:

Invest in facilities: N = ($R - $100)/$25 if $R > $100, otherwise N = 0
Invest in R&D: N = $R/$50.

We could then write his objective function and constraints under the two investment alternatives as

Maximize   N
(facilities, R&D)

Subject to: 1. $R ≤ $B

2. N = Max{($R - $100)/$25, 0}   if invest in facilities

3. N = $R/$50 if invest in R&D

Where the notation "(facilities, R&D)" refers to the choices over which the manager chooses.

In Figure 1.1, we have represented graphically his problem as choosing the alternative that maximizes N (i.e., is the highest on the graph) subject to the three constraints:

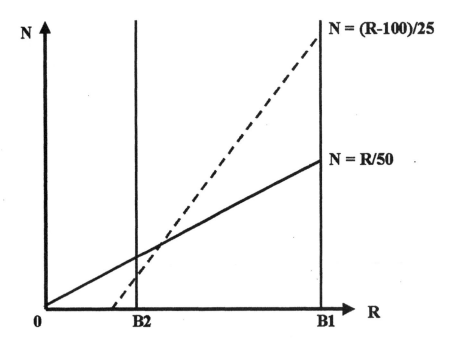

Figure 1.1

The two vertical lines represent two possible values for the budget available to the manager. Let's suppose for the moment that the budget, B, equals the lower value, B2. The dashed line represents the number of workers obtained with investment in new facilities. Clearly, this number is maximized by spending the whole budget, as this is the highest point on the constraint. The flatter, sloped, line represents the number of workers hired under the R&D policy. Again this number is maximized by spending the whole budget. We can conclude, then, that the manager would prefer to invest in R&D if his budget were B2. On the other hand, if we choose a different value for the budget, say B1, we can see that investing in new facilities is the manager's optimal choice.

Exercise 3: *An individual's enjoyment from consumption increases as the curve drawn below shifts right. The individual 's budget is represented by the straight line in the graph: a higher line corresponds to a higher budget. Assume that the individual tries to obtain the highest possible enjoyment from consumption but has a fixed budget. Which line/curve represents the objective function and which represents the constraint?*

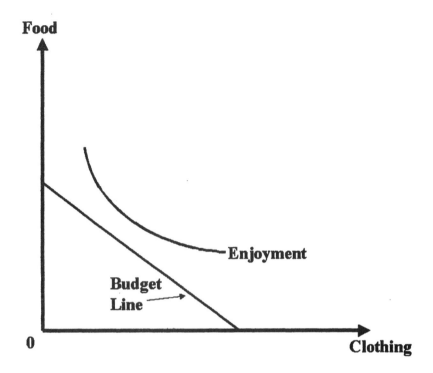

a. The straight line is the objective function; the curve is the constraint
b. The curve is the objective function; the straight line is the constraint
c. The curve is the objective function; the horizontal axis is the constraint
d. The curve is the objective function; the vertical axis is the constraint

Suppose now that the individual would like to reach a given level of enjoyment from consumption but with the lowest possible total budget. Which line/curve represents the objective function and which represents the constraint?

a. The straight line is the objective function; the curve is the constraint
b. The curve is the objective function; the straight line is the constraint
c. The curve is the objective function; the horizontal axis is the constraint
d. The curve is the objective function; the vertical axis is the constraint

Not only do economic models deliberately ignore certain elements of economic life, they also specify which of the variables considered have values that are set outside the model (such as the amount of the budget that the manager can spend on R&D or on new facilities) and which variables are going to have values that are set within the model (such as the investment decision of the manager and the resulting number of workers employed). Variables that have values that are taken as given in the analysis are called **exogenous variables**. Variables that have values that are determined as a result of the workings of our economic model are called **endogenous variables**. What aspect of an economic problem we wish to study determines which variables we take as endogenous and which we take as exogenous. Consider for example how one might want to set up models of "global warming". A meteorologist might analyze how given volumes of emission of CO_2 (carbon dioxide) resulting from economic activities would affect worldwide temperatures. She might also be interested in predicting the effects of such temperatures on weather patterns. In her model, the level of CO_2 emissions is an exogenous variable while the levels of temperatures and other aspects of the weather pattern determined by the meteorologist's model are endogenous variables. An agricultural engineer would be more interested in the effects of climatic changes on the world's ability to feed itself. He would then take weather predictions as given and build a model explaining how these would affect the yields of various crops in various regions. In his study, all aspects of climatic changes would be exogenous variables while crop yields would be endogenous variables. Finally, an economist might want to study the likely effect of policy measures such an emissions tax on the levels of CO_2 emissions and on economic activity. She would then take weather patterns and policy measures as exogenous variables and build a model that endogenously determines the resulting levels of CO_2 and national product.

Exercise 4: *When NASA sent Apollo XI to the moon, it relied on complex models of its flight in order to make crucial decisions. Explain whether each of the following factors was likely to be an exogenous or an endogenous variable in NASA 's flight model and why.*

a. The amount of oxygen loaded aboard Apollo
b. The amount and types of radiation emitted by the sun
c. The times at which Apollo's rockets would have to be fired
d. The number of times that Apollo would circle the moon before the beginning of the landing phase
e. The distance between the earth and the moon

So far, we have said that economic models must clearly state the set of possible choices facing the agent, what the agent cares about and any constraints that the agent faces in making her choice. In addition, we have said that the economic issue we wish to study determines what we specify as endogenous to the model and what we take as exogenous. We must also specify *what state of behavior* we wish to study. This can be understood by drawing an analogy to models of physical phenomena. Suppose that we wish to study the behavior of bowling pins. We begin our study with the ten pins standing in their usual formation. Unless some external force perturbs them, the ten pins will remain in this position. We say that the ten pins are *in a state of rest* or, equivalently, that they are in a *static equilibrium*. We now let one player roll a ball toward the pins. If well thrown, the ball hits some pins, starting a chain reaction that leaves many pins on the floor. After a while the pins stop moving and we are in another state of rest (i.e. in another static equilibrium characterized by the number of pins still standing and their positions). A static equilibrium, then, is a state that will perpetuate itself as long as it is not further disturbed by external forces. Using the terms that we defined above, we can rephrase this by saying that we have a static equilibrium when the values of the endogenous variables (e.g., the position of the pins) will remain unchanged as long as exogenous variables (i.e., whether or not a ball is thrown) remain unchanged. Instead of focusing on static equilibria, one could also take an interest in the process of adjustment from one state of rest to the other (e.g., one could study the trajectory of the ball and the movement of all ten pins once they are struck). Such an analysis of the *process of adjustment* from one static equilibrium to another is referred to as *dynamic analysis*. Although such dynamics can be very interesting and important, a large part of economics and all the material included in this book is concerned with the description of static equilibria.

Exercise 5: *The equilibrium market price is the price at which demand equals supply in the graph below (i.e., the point where the two lines cross). This equilibrium price is $P^e = \$5$ and the associated equilibrium output is $Q^e = 10$.*

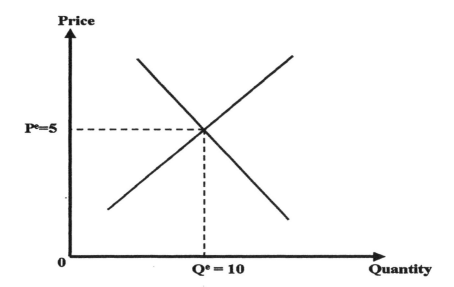

Now, we conduct an experiment in this market. We artificially and temporarily set the price at P = \$10. We then observe the following behavior: initially, a supply of 20 units is offered, but only 5 units are demanded. We then observe that suppliers gradually reduce the price at which they offer to supply output and demanders gradually raise the price they say they are willing to pay so that the excess supply is gradually eliminated. Once the price offered by both demanders and suppliers equals \$5, we observe that no further change occurs in the market. Graphically, our experiment results in price offers that gradually fall from point C (for suppliers) and point B (for demanders) toward point E.

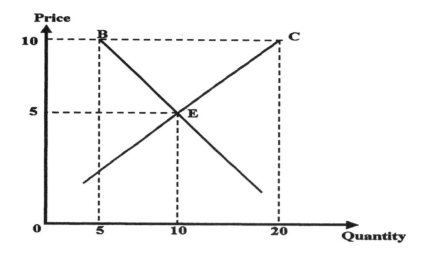

An equilibrium analysis of the market we just described focuses on which of the following issues?

a. Identifying the price and quantity at which the system is "at rest" (i.e., where no further change occurs).
b. Identifying the amount of excess supply and the amount of insufficient demand associated with price P = $10.
c. Identifying the pattern of offers made by demanders and suppliers as the market adjusts toward its final state of rest.
d. All of the above.

An **equilibrium** analysis is an analysis of the system in a state that will continue indefinitely as long as the exogenous factors remain unchanged. When we change some of the exogenous factors, the system eventually reaches another static equilibrium. By comparing the equilibrium state of the system before and after the changes in exogenous factors we can determine the effect of such exogenous perturbations on the values of the state of the system (i.e., on the values of the endogenous variables). We could, for example, conclude that a bowling ball thrown strongly right at the center pin leaves the player with a "split" (i.e., with one pin left on each side of the lane). The change in exogenous conditions is the throw of the ball. The resulting change in the endogenous variables is the change in the position of the pins (eight fell down, the two extreme ones remained standing).
Similar experiments can be conducted by the meteorologist who wants to determine the change in world temperatures (endogenous variables in her model)) resulting from a 10 % increase in CO_2 emissions (exogenous variables) or by an economist who wants to determine the decrease in CO_2 emissions (endogenous variables) that would be induced by a doubling of emission taxes (exogenous variables). In order to do this, the economist would determine the *equilibrium* level of CO_2 emissions under the original tax, solve again for the equilibrium level of CO_2 emissions with a tax twice as high, and then compare these two equilibrium levels. Such comparisons are examples of **comparative statics**, since they compare two static equilibria.

Exercise 6: *The demand for apartments, Q^d is represented by $Q^d = 100 - P + .5I$, where P is the price of apartments and I is income. short-term supply is represented by Q = 50. Let I = 10. Demand and supply are depicted below as the solid lines with P on the vertical axis and Q on the horizontal axis. The point of intersection of these lines is the market equilibrium, at point A*

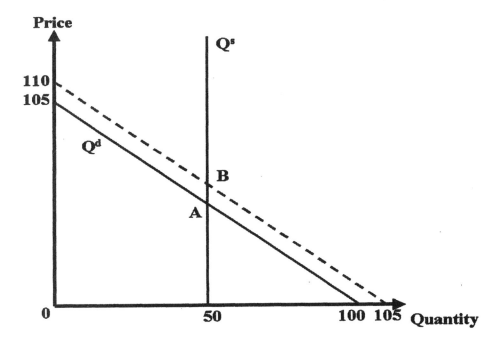

Now, suppose that income rises from I = 10 to I = 20. The new demand curve is depicted by the dashed line, above, and the new equilibrium point is shown as point B in the graph.

Which variables are exogenous and which are endogenous in this problem?

a. Price and income are exogenous; the demand for apartments is endogenous
b. Price and income are exogenous; the demand and supply for apartments is endogenous
c. Income is exogenous; the price, demand, and supply of apartments is endogenous
d. None of the above

Exercise 7: *In Exercise 6, what would a comparative statics analysis study?*

a. The change in equilibrium price that results from the change in income
b. The change in equilibrium quantity that results from the change in income
c. (a) and (b)
d. None of the above

It is important to understand what economic models can and cannot do. The reason why we use formal models rather than simply informally talking through problems is that often the formality reveals that the "obvious" answer to a problem is not the correct answer. In other words, by analyzing problems very carefully, we can often see effects that were not obvious and are important to resolving the problem or predicting behavior. We will see many examples of this throughout the textbook, but one example is that of the importance of **marginal** reasoning in solving constrained optimization problems.

In microeconomics "marginal" refers to how an endogenous variable changes as a result of adding one unit or taking away one unit of an exogenous variable. In other words, the marginal impact of a change in the exogenous variable is the incremental impact of the last unit of the exogenous variable on the endogenous variable. When we study how an economic agent allocates resources among various choices, we need to know not just whether a particular allocation is good, but whether the agent could do better by readjusting the allocation "marginally" or "incrementally". In other words, we care not only about the total impact of an exogenous variable on the endogenous variable, but on the marginal impact of a change in the exogenous variable on the endogenous variable. If the agent can do better with a marginal reallocation, then the agent cannot be optimizing his objective function. In the example given in the text, the "obvious" answer comes from observing that the total impact of TV advertising is higher than radio advertising. The obvious answer is not correct because the marginal impact of TV advertising is actually lower than radio advertising at the obvious solution, so that it pays the agent to reallocate the advertising dollars away from this solution.

Getting the right answer to such a constrained optimization problem can be important for policy makers and managers. For a manager, getting the right answer makes the difference between earning more or less money for her firm. For a policy maker, getting the right answer makes the difference between correctly or incorrectly predicting the behavior of an economic agent (and so correctly or incorrectly interpreting the impact of a change in economic policy). In both cases, the difference can be quite significant in economic terms.

Exercise 8: *A consumer wishes to maximize her satisfaction from eating French pastries. The total satisfaction she receives from eating pastries is listed below along with the marginal satisfaction she receives from each additional pastry consumed:*

Number of Pastries Consumed	Total Satisfaction (Cumulative)	Marginal Satisfaction
1	5	5
2	7	2
3	9	2
4	10	1
5	9	-1
6	5	-4
7	-3	-8

How many pastries should the consumer eat if they are free?

a. 1
b. 7
c. 4
d. 6

Exercise 9: *Suppose that the price of French pastries is 3 (in units measured the same way as satisfaction) in Exercise 8. How many pastries should the consumer eat now?*

a. 1
b. 4
c. 3
d. 0

Finally, while economic analysis can help you to think logically and precisely about the impact of various policy options or various economic choices, it cannot make value judgments about what the goals of economic policy or the preferences of economic agents ought to be. Economics can perform **positive analysis** in the sense that it can explain what has happened due to an economic policy or it can predict what might happen due to a policy, but it can only perform **normative analysis** (analysis of what should be done) if the goals to be achieved and their relative weights have already been determined. For example, suppose that a policy maker has decided that it would be desirable to reduce pollution up to a given level but at the lowest possible economic cost. Economic analysis can help the policy maker to decide the best method (taxes, subsidies, tradable emission permits, and so on) to achieve this goal. Economics cannot, however, say whether reducing pollution is a desirable goal or whether the pollution level targeted by the policy maker is "appropriate".

Exercise 10: *Asking how much economic growth would result from adopting a policy of export promotion is a question of:*

a. normative economics
b. positive economics
c. a value judgment that is outside of economic analysis

Exercise 11: *Asking whether economic growth can best be achieved by following a policy of export promotion or a policy of protectionism is a question of:*

a. normative economics
b. positive economics
c. a value judgment that is outside of economic analysis

Chapter Review Questions

1. Suppose that individuals hold their savings in a bank. If all individuals keep their money in the bank, then the bank continues to have enough funds to pay interest on the accounts. If many individuals withdraw their money, those that remain with the bank lose all their funds, as the bank goes bankrupt and is unable to return any money to its depositors. Suppose each individual can choose, on his or her own, between continuing to hold his/her money at the bank and removing it, knowing what all other individuals have chosen. Each individual wishes to keep as much money as possible. Can it be an equilibrium for all individuals to leave their money in the bank?

Answer:

It is an equilibrium for everyone to stay with the bank: given that everyone else stays with the bank, there is no reason to wish to withdraw all funds. Hence, the system is "stable" with no incentive to change unless outside circumstances change. Suppose for a moment that outside circumstances do, in fact, change. For example, suppose that for some reason a certain number of depositors withdraw money from the bank. What happens now? It may no longer be an equilibrium for the remaining depositors to keep their money in the bank, as each would anticipate that the bank would go bankrupt. Hence, each prefers to withdraw his funds. This can cause a "run" where all depositors rush to withdraw money.

2. You are asked to build a model to investigate the effect of growth in world population on the number of yearly hunger-related deaths. For each of the following variables, say whether it should be exogenous or endogenous and why.

   a. The amount of food produced in various regions of the world

   b. Population growth

   c. The frequency of droughts and floods in various regions

   d. Farming technology

Answer:

a. Endogenous. The level of food production cannot be controlled directly (even in planned economies!) as it depends on the decision of a multitude of individuals. Moreover it will clearly be affected by population growth and be crucial in determining the effect of such growth on hunger-related deaths. Its value should, therefore, be determined *within* the model.

b. Exogenous. The purpose of the study is not to determine whether world population will grow and by how much but to determine the *consequences* of population growth. One should therefore take population growth as given. Of course, this does not prevent the consideration of various scenarios for population growth; that is, one can still solve the model repeatedly for different given values of the exogenous variable.

c. Exogenous, unless one believes that population growth can itself modify the frequency of floods and droughts. For example, one could think that faster population growth leads to faster deforestation and therefore to a larger risk of floods and mudslides. The variable would be treated as endogenous if such linkages were deemed to be important enough to be specified in the model.

d. It would be a good idea to treat farming technology as endogenous. As population pressure increases, the reward to investment in technologies that increase food production also tends to increase. This means that the consequences of population growth on famine are likely to be much less drastic than if technology were assumed to remain unchanged. Indeed, failure to account for changing investment incentives and their effects on the pace of technological change explain why doomsday scenarios, like the one presented in the famous report on "limits to growth" by the "Roma Club", have repeatedly been widely off the mark.

3. Whether policy-makers should foster economic growth regardless of the consequences for short term income inequality is a question of positive economics, normative economics, or a value judgment outside of economic analysis?

Answer:

This is a question about what the goals or objectives of economic policy ought to be. It is, therefore, a value judgment that is outside of economic analysis. Normative economics could examine how growth can best be fostered given that one is willing to disregard income inequalities. Positive economics could try to explain how different policies affect growth and inequality or even why policy makers decide to pursue certain policy goals, but it has nothing to say about what these goals ought to be.

Problem Set

1. Refer back to Exercise 1 in this summary and think about buying a used car. Do you think that there is important information about the used car market that the model has left out? Write down another possible model of the used car market. In other words, simplify reality in a different way from the model in the exercise.

2. Farmer Marge uses land that she owns in her production of maple syrup. What value do you think she should attribute to the land for the purpose of computing her true costs of production? What was the implicit alternative you were presenting to Marge when you constructed your answer?

3. A consumer's satisfaction, S, when she purchases F units of food and C units of clothing is measured by the function $S = (FC)^{1/2}$. Her monthly budget is income I and she faces price p_f for food and price p_c for clothing. She must achieve a level of satisfaction of 10 to survive. She seeks to minimize the expenditure she makes in order to achieve this survival level of satisfaction. What is the objective function and what is the constraint in this problem? State the constrained optimization problem algebraically.

4. Suppose that output is the following function of labor:

$$Q = L^2 - (1/36)L^3$$

Graph this function with Q on the vertical axis and L on the horizontal axis. Now, suppose that L must not exceed 6. Graph this constraint. Suppose that an agent wishes to maximize her output subject to the constraint that labor cannot exceed 6. Write down her maximization problem. Can you see from your graph where the agent would choose to produce?

5. Students are willing to pay more for an apartment located close to the campus than for one that is located far away from the campus, all else equal. Further, for the same location and quality of apartment, they prefer to rent a cheaper apartment. As the rental price for apartments falls in the vicinity of the campus, more students are willing to move out of campus housing or move away from their parents' houses and rent apartments on their own.

Builders face the same cost of building apartments no matter where they are located. On the other hand, the higher are rental prices, the more apartments builders are willing to build or convert from units that are owner-occupied. It takes time to build or convert apartments, however, so that the supply of apartments is fixed at any point in time. Over time, the supply of apartments is able to respond to price, however.

a. Write down the factors that affect the demand for rental apartments by students.

b. Write down the factors that affect the supply of rental apartments by builders at any point in time.

c. Write down the factors that affect the supply of rental apartments over a longer time horizon.

6. Let us return to Exercise 5 of the summary. Suppose that we had performed the same experiment on this market as before (we temporarily set the price at $10), but now we observed the following path of adjustment of the market back toward a state of rest. First, a large excess supply appeared, as before. In an effort to eliminate this excess supply, suppliers lowered the price a lot (to $3) and an excess demand appeared. Next, as buyers rushed into the market, price

rose to $6 and an excess supply appeared again. Finally, price was set at $5 by buyers and sellers and no excess supply or demand occurred. No further changes were observed in this market.

    a. Has the equilibrium behavior changed in this problem from that of Exercise 6?

    b. Has the dynamic behavior changed?

7. Go out and perform some economic action (buy an apple, for example). What factors do you weigh when you make this decision? What aspects of reality do you leave out? Try to describe your objective function and constraint(s) in words.

Exam *(60 minutes: Closed book, closed notes)*

1. Distinguish between positive and normative economics, giving an example of each type of analysis.

2. A firm's production of output from the inputs K and L is represented by the curves in the graph, below. For example, the curve labeled Q* represents all the combinations of L and K that result in output Q*. Output increases as the curve shifts right so that higher curves represent higher output levels. The cost of production, on the other hand, is represented by the straight lines in the graph below. Each straight line represents a higher level of cost. Show on the graph the combination of inputs, (L, K) that *minimizes* the firm's cost subject to the fact that it must produce at output level Q*. Which line represents the objective function? Which line represents the constraint? Where would the equilibrium combination of inputs be?

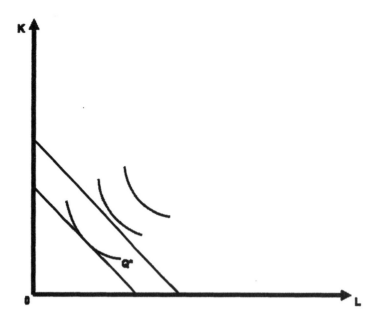

3. The price of rental apartments tends to adjust to eliminate excess demand and excess supply. In other words, the price tends to rise when there is excess demand and tends to fall when there is excess supply. When there is no excess demand or supply, then there is no tendency for price to change.

    a. Under what demand and supply conditions is the market price in equilibrium?

    b. Under what conditions is the market price out of equilibrium?

    c. Which variables are exogenous in this model and which variables are exogenous, assuming that price is determined by the conditions for equilibrium?

4. A presidential candidate on the campaign trail declares "We must reduce public expenditures on welfare while, at the same time, improving the health and education of poor children. Given an opportunity to work and for training, most welfare recipients can become financially independent. When I am president I will pass legislation forcing welfare recipients to work. Part of the public funds that such a policy would save will then be used to finance education and health clinics in poor neighborhoods. This is the best way to solve our problem." In this statement, distinguish the elements that belong to positive economic analysis, those that refer to a normative economic analysis, and those that cannot be addressed by economic analysis.

Answers to Exercises

1. The correct answer is (e), all of the above. First, there are several ways for consumers to figure out the true quality of a used car. They can, for

example, have it examined by an independent mechanic before purchase, or they can buy second-hand cars from friends or family who would be candid about the true condition of the car. Warranties also play a role, as car dealers are less likely to offer a one-year warranty on cars they know to be of bad quality. Second, there are more than four categories of cars: the probability of being a lemon is not the same for certain makes of car as for others. In fact, other things equal, the longer a (still running) car has been on the road, the lower the probability that it is a lemon. Third, not everybody cares equally about the quality of a car. Someone who is handy with cars might be more willing to take the chance on buying a lemon than someone who needs help to find the gas tank. Finally, the relative prices of new and used cars might be affected by taxes. This is, for example, the case in England, where there is a 25% VAT tax on a new car but no sales tax on used cars.

2. In the first question, it is implicit that the customers only choose between buying or not buying the car. Testing it, leasing it towards purchase and other common purchase options are not possible. Nor are creative pricing options available such as pricing contingent on experience or price rebates based on service records.

3. The correct answer to the first part of the question is (b). An objective function is a description of what the agent is trying to achieve. Since the individual is trying to "obtain the highest possible level of enjoyment", his objective function is represented by the curve. A constraint represents limits on what the agent can do. Here the limits come from the finite size of the budget at the individual 's disposal. The constraint is therefore represented by the straight line.

The correct answer to the second part of the question is (a). The level of enjoyment (the curve) limits what the agent can do, the straight line (the level of expenditure) represents what the agent is trying to achieve.

4. Endogenous variables are likely to be variables that are, directly or indirectly, under NASA's control and are important to the mission's success. Exogenous variables are variables outside NASA's control that still influence the chances of success of the mission. The amount of oxygen on board is an endogenous variable: it is in NASA's hands and affects the number of days the astronauts can survive in space, the weight of the Apollo capsule, and the risk of fire. Solar radiation can affect the health of the astronauts and the performance of onboard electronics, as well as transmissions between Earth and Apollo. It is, therefore, an important factor in determining many variables that NASA does control such as the type of clothing worn by the astronauts or the thickness and composition of Apollo's walls. Still, the amount and type of radiation emitted by the sun is itself out of NASA's control. It is, therefore, an exogenous variable. The times at which the rockets are fired are determined by NASA and are crucial to put the craft on the correct trajectory. It is an endogenous variable. Similarly, the number of circles around the moon affects the craft's velocity and can be decided by NASA: it is another

endogenous variable. Finally, the distance between Earth and Moon would probably be included as an exogenous variable since it is clearly important to the mission but is not something that NASA engineers can modify. However, since the distance between the earth and the moon is not constant over time, one could also argue that the actual distance to be traveled is itself determined by the time chosen for the launch. In that sense it would be an endogenous variable since its value would only be known after NASA has chosen the value of the other variable that it controls directly.

5.   The correct answer is (a). Answers (b) and (c) refer to aspects of the market *out of equilibrium* (i.e. to states of the market that would not perpetuate themselves). If there is an excess supply, consumers and seller will change their behavior. Similarly a process of *adjustment* cannot, by definition, correspond to a state of rest.

6.   The correct answer is (c). The income level is clearly exogenous as its value is *given* to you. On the other hand, you can only determine the equilibrium price level and the equilibrium quantities supplied and demanded by *using the model* of the market for apartments represented in the graph. In other words, these three variables are *endogenously* determined.

7.   The correct answer is (c). Comparative statics analysis looks at the change in the value of some endogenous variable(s) induced by a given change in the value of an exogenous variable. Since income is exogenous and the equilibrium price and quantity are each endogenous, both (a) and (b) are true.

8.   The correct answer is (c). The goal is to maximize total satisfaction. This is clearly achieved with four pastries since they provide the highest possible satisfaction of 10. Alternatively one can say that one should keep eating more pastries as long as the additional satisfaction that it provides is not smaller than the cost of the pastry. Since pastries are free, this means that one should keep eating as long as the *marginal* satisfaction is non-negative, that is, until four pastries are consumed.

9.   The correct answer is (a). Since pastries cost 3 apiece one should only consume additional pastries if they provide a marginal satisfaction of at least 3. Hence one should stop after eating a single pastry.

10.   The correct answer is (b). This is a question measuring the actual consequences of a policy.

11.   The correct answer is (a): this is a prescription as to how a given objective (i.e., economic growth) can be achieved most efficiently.

Answers to Problem Set

1.   There are, of course, many possibilities. We will just mention two interesting alternatives. The first one would be to develop a little bit more (i.e., simplify less) the behavior of car manufacturers. In Exercise 1 we just assumed that a *given* proportion of their cars were "lemons", that is, we took that proportion as exogenous. This is a simplification since car manufacturers can decrease the proportion of lemons by investing more in quality control. One could therefore modify the model to account for the manufacturers' choice of quality control. One could for example assume that the proportion of lemons is a decreasing function of the amount invested in quality control. In other words, the proportion of lemons would become an endogenous variable. Another interesting modification of the model would be to allow consumers to differ in their willingness to pay for higher expected quality. One could, for example, assume that some consumers get zero satisfaction from buying a lemon while others do get some positive enjoyment from buying a lemon, albeit less than they get from getting a good car. We could, in fact, combine the two modifications that we have suggested. We could then ask whether all car manufacturers would invest equally in quality or whether some would specialize in serving the "quality conscious" consumers while the others have little quality control and sell mostly to consumers who care less about quality.

2.   The alternative for using the land for producing maple syrup is probably using it for other purposes, such as logging or recreation. If this is the case, then Marge should use the potential (net) revenues from logging or recreation as the "value" her land.

3.   The constraint is that the individual must achieve a level of satisfaction of at least ten, otherwise she dies. Algebraically, this constraint can be written as

$$(FC)^{1/2} \geq 10$$

The objective function is a representation of what the consumer tries to achieve. In this case she is trying to minimize her total expenditure on F and C (i.e., she wants to minimize $p_cC + p_fF$). The variables under the consumer's control are the amounts of each good that she purchases. We can therefore write the constrained optimization problem as

$$\underset{\text{wrt } C,F}{\text{Min}} \quad p_cC + p_fF$$

$$\text{Subject to } (FC)^{1/2} \geq 10$$

4.

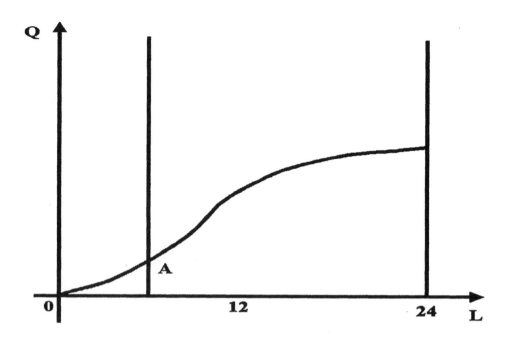

The maximization problem is

$$\underset{\text{wrt L}}{\text{Max}} \quad L^2 - (1/36)L^3$$

Subject to $L \le 6$

The solution to this problem is at point A on the graph, where the vertical line intersects the horizontal axis at $L = 6$. In other words, the vertical line represents the constraint while the curve represents the objective. Point A corresponds to the highest level of output that can be achieved given that total daily work time cannot exceed 6 hours.

5.

  a. Students' demand for apartments is affected by the rental price of apartments, their quality and their location.

  b. At any given point in time the supply of rental apartments only depends on the number of rental units that are already available.

  c. Over a longer time horizon, the supply of rental apartments also depends on the cost of building apartments and the rental price of apartments.

6.

  a. No. At equilibrium we still have a price equal to $5 and an output of 10.

  b. Yes. The process of adjustment towards the (unchanged) equilibrium is not the same as in Exercise 6.

Answers to Exam

1. Positive analysis asks *explanatory* or *predictive* questions, whereas normative analysis asks *prescriptive* questions. An explanatory question asks why something has happened. For example, we can analyze past price movements as the result of changes in exogenous variables that affect the equilibrium of a demand and supply system. This explains why price might have shifted in a simple story, attributing the price change to a specific "shock" on an equilibrium system. A predictive question asks what will result from a specific event. For example, we can analyze the likely effect of a policy change on price in a simple equilibrium system. Here, the object is not to explain so much as to put a particular explanation to work in forecasting the future. Hence, an example of positive analysis might be a description of the probable effects of a change in income levels on the price of corn. Such an analysis might first propose a particular explanation for price movements and then use the explanation to forecast future price movements in the corn market. A prescriptive question asks whether something should be done. For example, using some criterion for what is a "good" policy, we could evaluate the effects of a price change on the well-being of the citizens of a country. Notice that this assumes that a criterion for "good" and "bad" is established. Economics cannot, by itself, establish such a criterion. We need the input of other fields of study, such as philosophy, to do this. Rather, taking the criterion as given, normative analysis in economics measures how well alternative policies do at fulfilling this criterion.

2. The firm has a constraint that it must produce Q* units, so the curve labeled Q* is the constraint in this case. The firm wishes to minimize the cost of producing the Q* units, so its objective function is represented by the straight lines. In order to minimize the cost of production of the Q* units, then, we must find the *lowest* straight line that still allows points on the curve labeled Q* to be reached. This is the point where the Q* line and the straight line just touch. This will also be the equilibrium combination of inputs for the firm, as it is doing the best it can at obtaining its objective within the constraints it faces. Only if its objective changes or if its constraints change will the equilibrium change.

3.

    a. Equilibrium occurs at the price for which the number of rental apartments demanded is equal to the number of rental apartments supplied. In other words, equilibrium occurs at the price for which the excess supply of rental apartments is equal to zero.

    b. Whenever the number of rental apartments demanded at this price is not equal to the number of rental apartments offered at this price.

    c. The market price and the number of rental apartments demanded and supplied at this price are endogenous variables. The cost of building or converting rental apartments is an exogenous variable.

4.   "We must reduce public expenditures on welfare while, at the same time, improving the health and education of poor children" is a statement about goals that are deemed to be socially desirable. As such, it lies outside of the scope of economics. "Given an opportunity to work and training, most welfare recipients can become financially independent" is a hypothesis about the behavior of welfare recipients. Studying such hypotheses is the province of positive economic analysis. The rest of the quote is a claim about what the best way of achieving the stated goals is. This is the domain of normative economic analysis.

Chapter 2: Supply and Demand Analysis

Chapter 2 develops tools that can help you answer questions about the equilibrium behavior of **competitive markets**. By competitive markets we mean markets where sellers and buyers are all small and numerous enough that they take the market price as given when they decide how much to buy or sell. The main tools that economists use to analyze the behavior of such markets are the **demand curve**, the **supply curve**, and the notion of **market equilibrium**. The chapter also introduces the concept of *elasticity* that helps us describe the shape of demand and supply curves. We will see that these shapes differ according to the type of goods and the length of the period of time considered.   Finally, the chapter presents several "back of the envelope" methods that allow us to obtain demand and supply curves for specific markets based on a minimum of information about their past behavior.

The market *demand curve* tells us how the quantity of a good demanded by the sum of all consumers depends on the price of the good. In other words, a market demand curve answers the question, "What will consumers be willing to pay if Q units of the good are put up for sale?" or, alternatively, "How many units of the good will consumers be willing to acquire if the good is for sale at a price P?" As the price of the good changes, the quantity demanded also changes. Such changes correspond to moves *along* the demand curve. According to the **law of demand**, the quantity of a good demanded decreases when the price of this good increases. This means that, for example, an increase in the price of bread corresponds to a move upward along the demand curve for bread while a decrease in the price of bread would result in a move downward along the demand curve.

The **market demand curve** only relates quantity to the price of a good. In other words, it is drawn under the assumption that all the other factors that can affect the demand for that good remain unchanged. What happens to the demand curve when one of these other factors does change? Suppose, for example, that the income of consumers increases from I_1 to I_2 and that this makes them want to purchase more of the good. This means that, *for any given price of the good*, consumers are now willing to purchase greater quantities than before so that their behavior is now represented by a new demand curve that lies *to the right* of the initial demand curve. In other words, the increase in consumer income has *shifted* the market demand curve to the right. The effect of a change in any of the factors other than the price of the good included in the demand function can be obtained in a similar manner. If the change increases the consumers' willingness to acquire the good, then the demand curve for this good shifts to the right. If, on the other hand, the change decreases the consumers' willingness to purchase the good, then the demand curve shifts to the left. This is illustrated in Figure 2.1, below.

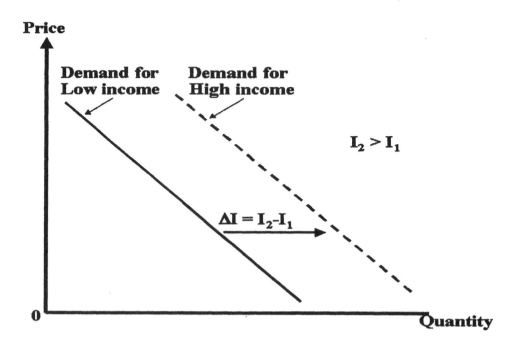

Figure 2.1

To summarize, moves *along* the demand curve and shifts *of* the demand curve are easily distinguished by applying a simple rule: *A move along the demand curve for good X can only be triggered by a change in the price of good X. On the other hand, any change in another factor that affects the consumers' willingness to pay for good X results in a shift in the demand curve for good X.* In the language of Chapter 1, this means that changes in the endogenous variables (Q and P) correspond to changes along the curve while changes in the exogenous variables cause shifts in the curve.

Other Representations of the Demand Relationship

Economists are not always interested in the role of prices. For example, some researchers study the relationship between the level of income and the pattern of consumption. In that case, quantity Q and income I are the variables of greater interest. It therefore makes sense to draw demand – income curves where Q is on the vertical axis and I is on the horizontal axis. An upward sloping curve indicates that the quantity of the good demanded increases as the level of income rises, while a downward sloping curve would imply that the demand for the good is greater at lower levels of income. In other words, changes in Q resulting from changes in I correspond to *moves along* the curve. What, then, would shift this curve to the left or to the right ? Any factor *other than income* that is likely to affect demand. One such factor is the price of the good. An increase in this price would now decrease Q for any level of I (i.e. it would shift the curve down). Why does a change in price now *shift* the curve? Because the graph now depicts a relationship between Q and I, while price is now just one of many factors that affects this relationship. This is illustrated in Figure 2.2, below, for $P_2 > P_1$.

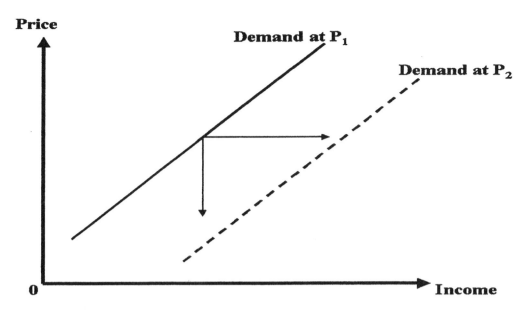

Figure 2.2

Exercise 1: *Which (perhaps more than one) of the following demand curves obeys the law of demand?*

    a. Q = 100 - 50P
    b. Q = 100 + 50P
    c. Q = 10/P

Exercise 2: *Which of the following causes a shift in the demand curve for gasoline?*

    a. A change in weather.
    b. A change in the price of cars
    c. A change in the price of gasoline
    d. A $1 tax, paid by consumers, per gallon of gasoline

      The **market supply curve** plots the aggregate quantity of a good that will be offered for sale at different prices. This supply curve refers to the quantity of a good supplied by all sources, when taken together as a group, and not to the supply provided by one of the sellers. As the price of the good changes, the quantity offered moves along this curve. Supply curves typically slope upwards: as price rises, quantity offered rises. This upward slope is referred to as the **law of supply**.

      As before, the supply curve only relates the quantity of a good to its price. We draw a supply curve assuming that all these other factors are fixed. Hence any change in these other factors causes a shift in the supply curve. Changes that make sellers willing to accept a lower price for given quantities of the good shift the supply curve downward (or, equivalently, to the right). Changes that lead sellers to demand a higher price for given quantities of the good shift the supply curve upward (or, equivalently, to the left). As in the case of demand, a change in the price of the good is the *only* possible cause of movements along the supply curve. Any other change causes the supply curve to shift.

Up, Down, Left, or Right ?

Refer to Figure 2.3. We have seen that any change in factors other than the price shift the demand curve <u>to the right</u> (from A to B on the graph) if this change increases the consumers' desire to acquire the good. This is because, <u>for a given price</u>, consumers are now willing to acquire more units of the product. <u>Equivalently</u> we could say that the demand curve is shifted <u>up</u> (from A to C on the graph below). This is because consumers are now willing to pay more <u>for a given quantity</u> of the good. In the same manner, any change in factors other than price that decreases the consumers' willingness to purchase the good can be seen as shifting the demand curve to the <u>left</u> (from A to D on the graph) or, equivalently, as shifting the demand curve <u>down</u> (from A to E). A shift to the left reflects the fact that consumers will now purchase smaller quantities of the good at a given price. The equivalent shift down reflects the fact that consumers are willing to pay less for a given quantity of the good.

The same logic applies to the supply curve. Any change in factors other than price that increases the willingness to sell (e.g., decreases in costs of production) shifts the supply curve <u>to the right</u>, or equivalently <u>down</u>. Any change in factors other than price that decreases the willingness to sell shifts the supply curve to the left or, equivalently <u>up</u>.

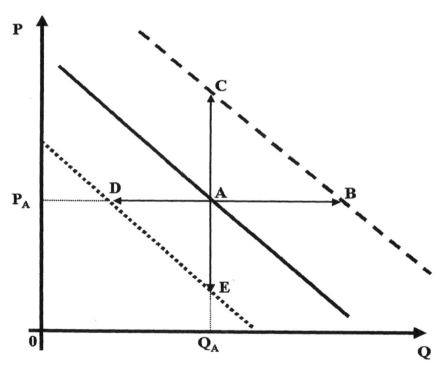

Figure 2.3

Exercise 3: *Which of the following supply functions obeys the law of supply, where Q is quantity, P is price, and I is income?*

        a. $Q = 100 + 50P$
        b. $Q = 100 - 50P$
        c. $Q = 100P$
        d. $Q = 100 - 50P + 20I$

Exercise 4: *Which of the following will cause a shift in the supply curve of sofa beds?*

        a. A change in the price of living space (such as apartments)
        b. A change in the price of mattresses
        c. A change in the price sofa beds
        d. A 10% subsidy (paid to producers) on the sales price of sofa beds

     A **market equilibrium** is a price such that, at this price, the quantities demanded and supplied are the same. On a graph, market equilibrium occurs at the point where the demand curve and the supply curve cross. Hence, the market equilibrium point lies on both the demand and the supply curves. The market equilibrium is the price and the corresponding quantity that we would expect to prevail if market conditions remained unchanged for a long enough period of time. What are these "market conditions"? They are just the "exogenous" variables of Chapter 1, that is, the factors other than the price of the good that appear in the demand and supply functions.

     There is a tendency for markets to move toward equilibrium. If the price is higher than the equilibrium price, then the quantities supplied exceed the quantities demanded. In other words, there is **excess supply**: sellers do not sell as much as they would like at this price and we would expect this to put downward pressure on the price. If the price is lower than the equilibrium price, then quantities supplied fall short of quantities demanded. There is then **excess demand**: buyers cannot purchase as much as they want at this price and we would expect this to put upward pressure on price.

Exercise 5: *Which of the following is true at equilibrium?*

        a. Quantity demanded equals quantity supplied
        b. There is no excess demand or excess supply
        c. There is no pressure for prices to change
        d. Demanders can buy as much as they wish at the prevailing price, and
           sellers can sell as much as they wish at the prevailing price.
        e. The best price is being offered from the point of view of consumers and
           the best price is being tendered from the point of view of producers.

Exercise 6: *Suppose that demand and supply are as follows (with price measured in dollars):*

        $Q^d = 200 - 50P$ (demand)

        $Q^s = 50 + 100P$ (supply)

Which of the following statements is true?

a. Equilibrium price is $2.
b. Equilibrium price is $1.
c. At a price of $.50, there is excess supply.
d. At a price of $.50, there is excess demand.
e. At a price of $.50, consumers cannot buy as much as they want.

When a change in an exogenous variable causes demand or supply to shift, the equilibrium point shifts as well. The analysis of how this shift affects the equilibrium price and quantity is called **comparative statics** because we compare two static equilibrium points. For example, if bad weather causes the supply of strawberries to shift down, we can compute the new equilibrium point where the new supply curve crosses the demand curve. We can then compare this new equilibrium to the point where the old supply curve crossed the demand curve in order to determine whether bad weather would lead to an increase or a decrease in the equilibrium price of strawberries and in the quantities of strawberries that are bought and sold in the market.

Exercise 7: *Suppose that demand and supply for tea can be written as follows (where quantities are in ounces):*

$$Q^d = 100 - 5P$$

$$Q^s = 10 + 10P$$

a. *Now, suppose that a change in the price of coffee causes demand to become:*

$$Q^d = 70 - 5P$$

   i. *Compute the old equilibrium price and quantity.*

   ii. *Compute the new equilibrium price and quantity. What has changed?*

b. *Now, suppose that a 20% (of sales price) tax is levied on consumers. In other words, consumers must pay 20% more than the asking price per ounce of tea.*

   i. *Compute the new equilibrium price and quantity and compare it to the old equilibrium. What has changed?*

Exercise 8: *Suppose that demand is Q = 500 - 10P. Suppose that supply is Q = 100.*

a. *Graph the curves and show the equilibrium point.*

b. *Now, suppose that a subsidy of $1 per unit is given to suppliers. What happens to equilibrium price and quantity?*

c. *Suppose that supply is horizontal at P = $10. Graph the new equilibrium. If a subsidy of $1 per unit is given to suppliers, what happens to equilibrium price and quantity?*

We know that an increase in the price of a good leads to a decrease in the quantity of the good demanded. But how strong is this effect? Does a change in price lead to a big or a small change in demand? To answer such questions economists rely on the concept of **elasticity**. The own price elasticity of demand is the percentage change in quantity demanded brought about by a 1% change in the price of the good. Mathematically, it is expressed as the ratio between the relative change in the quantity demanded, $\Delta Q/Q$, and the relative change in the price of the good, $\Delta P/P$, that is,

$$\varepsilon_{Q,P} = (\Delta Q/Q)/(\Delta P/P)$$

When a 1% change in price leads to a change in quantity demanded in excess of 1% the price elasticity of demand is less than −1 (e.g., −2). In such a case one says that the demand is **elastic** meaning that the quantity demanded is rather sensitive to prices. When a 1% change in price leads to a change in quantity demanded of less than 1%, the elasticity is greater than −1 (e.g., −0.5) and the demand curve is referred to as **inelastic**. When the elasticity is equal to −1, the demand curve is referred to as **unit elastic**. Because elasticities are expressed as ratios of *relative* changes (e.g., percentage changes), they do not depend on the units used to measure either Q or P. In other words, the value of the elasticity does not change if prices are measured in dollars rather than pounds or if quantities are measured in gallons rather than in quarts. This makes it possible to compare elasticities across very different markets. For example, if the elasticity of demand for cars in Malaysia is −2.1 and the elasticity of demand for coffee in the U.S. is −0.6 one can meaningfully say that the demand for cars in Malaysia is more price-sensitive than the demand for coffee in the U.S.

A **linear demand curve** can be written as $Q^d = a - bP$, where −b is the (negative) slope of the demand curve. The **choke price** is the value of the price at which the quantity demanded is zero. For a linear demand curve, the choke price is equal to a/b. Although the slope of a linear demand curve is constant, its elasticity changes from -∞ to 0 as one moves down the demand curve from the choke price to a price of zero. To the contrary, **log-linear demand curves** have the same elasticity everywhere. Such demand curves are written as $Q^d = P^{-b}$, where -b is the price-elasticity of demand.

Exercise 9: *Which of the following statements is/are correct?*

    a. If supply is unit elastic, a 1% change in price will elicit a 1% change in the same direction in the quantity supplied.
    b. If demand is inelastic, a 1% change in price will elicit a 1% change of the opposite sign in the quantity demanded.
    c. If demand is elastic, a 1% change in price will elicit a greater than 1% change of the opposite sign in quantity demanded.
    d. At the choke price, a linear demand curve is elastic.
    e. A linear demand is unit elastic when Q = bP.

Exercise 10: *What is the elasticity of the following demand curve?*

$$QP = 100$$

    a. -2.5
    b. 0

c. 1.5

d. -1

Anything that tends to make quantity demanded more responsive to price tends to make demand more elastic. For example, the demand for Exxon gasoline will be more elastic in a large town where gasoline of another brand can always be found across the street than in a small village where the nearest gas station is 60 miles down the road. This is because consumers tend to move their consumption to the substitute good more readily when price rises if the substitutes are more readily available. Similarly, demand at the brand level tends to be more elastic than demand at the market level simply because substitution across brands tends to occur more readily than substitution to different categories of goods. For example, you might be more willing to switch from Minute Maid to Tropicana orange juice than from orange juice to grape juice. Finally, demand for non-durable goods will tend to less elastic in the **short-run**, when consumers can only partially adapt their behavior to the new price than in the **long-run**, when all adjustments can take place. For example, if the relative price of diesel versus unleaded gas increases, then there will be more substitution away from diesel fuel in the long-run because consumers will eventually buy cars that run on unleaded fuel in order to take full advantage of the relative price advantage of unleaded gas. In the short-run, when no significant adjustments in the stock of cars have occurred, the switch to unleaded fuel may be relatively modest. On the other hand, demand for durable goods can be more elastic in the short-run than in the long-run. This is because consumers can react *immediately* to a price increase by delaying the purchase of a new item and simply keeping the old one for a longer period of time. This leads to a brusque decrease in the rate of purchase of the product. After a while, however, the old product breaks down or deteriorates so much that consumers can no longer delay, and the rate of purchase picks up. Similarly, a lower price will incite many consumers to immediately replace their old product, creating a large increase in the rate of purchase. Once this "replacement frenzy" is over, the rate of purchase of the good will return closer to its initial level.

Exercise 11: *Which of the following goods might have relatively inelastic demand and which might have relatively elastic demand? Justify your choices.*

a. Life-saving drugs

b. Arrow brand plain white paper

c. Current demand for videocassettes

d. Demand for videocassettes over a ten-year horizon

Exercise 12: *Would you guess that the long-run elasticity of demand is higher or lower than the short-run elasticity for the following goods?*

a. the supply of newsprint

b. the demand for telephones

c. the demand for apples

The concept of elasticity is quite general. The elasticity of any variable X with respect to another variable Y can be computed as $\varepsilon_{X,Y} = (\Delta X/X)/(\Delta Y/Y)$. One can, for example, compute the elasticity of one's weight to one's daily intake of calories. In the short-run, the value of this elasticity is likely to be close to zero: an increase of 1% in the calorie intake for one day will likely have little effect on one's weight. At the end of a year, however, such an increase in calories might well result in a 2% increase in weight, that is, the long-run value of the weight/calorie intake elasticity would be 2. Economics makes great use of all kinds of elasticities. One can, for example, consider the price elasticity of supply, which describes the responsiveness of quantity supplied to a change in price. Further, one can use the concept of elasticity to describe the responsiveness of demand to other variables than a good's own price. For example, the **income elasticity of demand** measures the responsiveness of the quantity demanded to changes in income. Similarly, the **cross price elasticity of demand** measures the responsiveness of demand to the price of another good.

Exercise 13: *What would be the formula for the elasticity of demand with respect to wealth, where Q is quantity and W is wealth?*

a. $\Delta Q/\Delta W$
b. $(\Delta Q/W)(Q/W)$
c. $(\Delta Q/\Delta W)(W/Q)$
d. $\Delta W/\Delta Q$
e. $(\Delta Q/W)(\Delta W/Q)$

We have seen that **comparative statics** allow us to say whether a change in an exogenous variable will increase or decrease the equilibrium price and the equilibrium quantity in the market. In many cases it is also useful to know *by how much* prices and quantities are likely to change. To do this, we need to "estimate" both the supply and the demand curve. If data are abundant, precise estimates can be obtained through the use of statistical techniques. Often, however, the cost of gathering the data required for such statistical procedures is prohibitive. One can then use "back of the envelope" computations. The first step consists of choosing the general shape of the demand and supply functions. A log-linear supply or demand curve is simplest since one only needs information about the respective price elasticities. Linear demand and supply curves require more information, as we must obtain numbers for their respective slopes and vertical intercepts. Consider the case of a linear demand curve $Q^d = a - bP$. Since $-b = \Delta Q/\Delta P$, the own price elasticity of demand can be written as $\varepsilon_{Q,P} = -b(P/Q)$. This means that we can determine the numerical value of both a and b if we know E, as well as a market equilibrium (P,Q). We can then solve for $b = -\varepsilon_{Q,P}(Q/P)$ and then, using this information, we can solve for $a = Q + bP$. One can then estimate the supply function in a similar fashion, provided that one also knows the value of the elasticity of supply $\sigma_{Q,P}$.

One can also estimate linear demand and supply curves when information on elasticities is not easily available, provided that one has some knowledge about the past behavior of the market. The key to this approach is to realize that *a shift in the supply curve reveals the slope of the demand curve while a shift in the demand curve reveals the slope of the supply curve*. To see this, assume that we know that the market equilibrium price and quantity were P_1 and Q_1. We also know that this equilibrium was disturbed by a change in supply conditions that shifted the supply curve to the right. Demand conditions, on the other hand, were essentially unchanged. This means that the new equilibrium price and quantity P_2 and Q_2 lie at the intersection of the old demand curve with the new supply curve. Hence, both (P_1,Q_1) and (P_2,Q_2) lie on the same linear demand curve. We can, therefore, compute $-b = \Delta Q/\Delta P = (Q_2 - Q_1)/(P_2 - P_1)$. Once we have determined b we can obtain a as before by computing $a = Q_1 + bP_1$. In order to determine the slope of the supply curve we would need to know about a shift in the demand curve that occurred at a time when supply conditions were essentially unchanged. The equilibrium prices and quantities before and after the shift would then both be on the old supply curve and we could use them to obtain its slope.

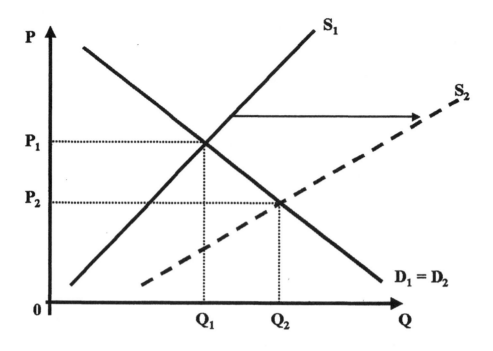

Figure 2.4

Chapter Review Questions

1. Let the demand curve be Q = A - BP, where A and B are positive constants.

    a. What is the price elasticity of demand at Q = 0?

    b. What is the price elasticity of demand at P = 0?

    c. What is the price elasticity of demand at P = A/(2B)?

    d. What is the slope of demand at each of these points?

    e. What can you say about elasticity along this curve? What can you say about the slope along this curve?

    Answer: This is an application of the formula $\varepsilon_{Q,P} = (\Delta Q/\Delta P)(P/Q)$.

    a. At Q = 0, P/Q goes to infinity. Since $\Delta Q/\Delta P = -B < 0$, the price elasticity of demand goes to minus infinity.

b. Now $P/Q = 0$ so $\varepsilon_{Q,P} = 0$.

c. If $P = A/2B$, then $Q = A - B(A/2B) = A - (A/2) = A/2$ so that $P/Q = (A/2B)/(A/2) = (1/B)$. Since $\Delta Q/\Delta P = -B$, we have $\varepsilon_{Q,P} = (-B)(1/B) = -1$.

d. $\Delta Q/\Delta P = -B$ at all points.

e. The elasticity changes over the entire curve, while the slope remains constant.

2. Suppose that the government wishes to encourage the manufacture and sale of small cars. The current supply and demand of small cars are:

$Q^s = -(10/9) + (1/9)P$

$Q^d = 100 - P$

where Q is in millions of cars and P is in hundreds of dollars.

   a. What is the current equilibrium price and quantity of cars sold? Graph the curves and show the solution on the graphs, as well as solving algebraically.

   b. Calculate the price elasticity of demand and the price elasticity of supply at the equilibrium.

   c. The government is considering two alternative plans for encouraging small car sales. Under Plan A, every car manufacturer will receive a $500 rebate from the government for each car sold. What would the equilibrium price and quantity of small cars be under this plan? Relative to the old equilibrium how much more or less do consumers pay? How much more or less do manufacturers receive per car? Graph the new situation.

   d. Under Plan B, every purchaser of a small car will receive a $500 rebate from the government. What would the equilibrium price received by sellers and the quantity sold under this plan be? What, on net, do consumers pay per car? Plot this on your graph from (c).

   e. Which plan, A or B, is more effective? Why?

Answer:

   a. At the market equilibrium the quantity demanded must be equal to the quantity supplied, that is, $-(10/9) + (1/9)P = 100 - P$, implying that $P = 91$. Plugging this value of P in the demand curve gives us the equilibrium quantity $Q = 100 - 91 = 9$. Alternatively we could also use the equilibrium value of P in the equation for the supply curve to get $Q = -(10/9) + 91/9 = 81/9 = 9$.

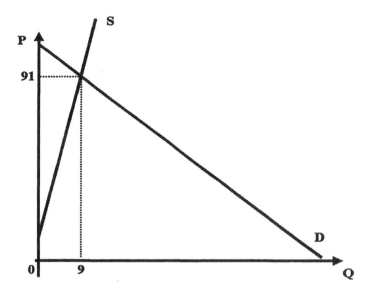

b. The price elasticity of demand is $(\Delta Q/\Delta P)$ (P/Q). From (a) we know that $P/Q = 91/9$. With a linear demand curve we also know that $\Delta Q/\Delta P$ is equal to the coefficient of P in the equation of the demand curve, that is, $\Delta Q/\Delta P = -1$. Hence the elasticity of demand is $\varepsilon_{Q,P} = -1(91/9) = -91/9$. The elasticity of supply is obtained in a similar manner but we now replace $\Delta Q/\Delta P$ by the value of the coefficient of P in the supply curve, that is, by $(1/9)$. This gives us $\sigma_{Q,P} = (1/9)(91/9) = 91/81$.

c. We must now distinguish between P^d, the price paid by consumers, and P^s, the price collected by sellers. The demand and supply curves can be rewritten as $Q^s = -(10/9) + (1/9)P^s$ and $Q^d = 100 - P^d$. Since car manufacturers receive \$500 from the government for every car they sell, the price they receive is higher than the price paid by consumers by \$500. Since the prices are expressed in hundreds of dollars, this means that $P^s = P^d + 5$. Using this relationship we can now rewrite the supply curves in terms of P^d as $Q^s = -(10/9) + (1/9)(P^d + 5) = -(5/9) + (1/9)P^d$. Hence, if we draw both supply and demand curves in terms of P^d, the rebate paid to the manufacturer shifts their supply curve down by 5 to S'. This is as expected. What determines the number of cars that manufacturers are willing to sell is the total amount of money that they get for each car. Since they are getting 5 from the government, they are willing to supply the same number of cars as before if they get exactly 5 less from the consumers.

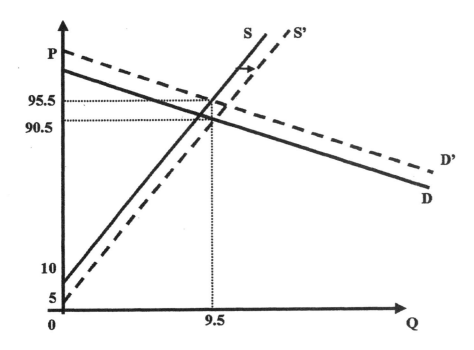

We can then determine the price paid by consumers in the new equilibrium by setting Q^s equal to Q^d, that is, $100 - P^d = -(5/9) + (1/9) P^d$ so that we get $P^d = 90.5$, $P^s = 90.5 + 5 = 95.5$, and $Q = 100 - 90.5 = 9.5$. Compared to the situation in (a), consumers pay 0.5 (i.e., $50) less per car and sellers get $P^s = 90.5 + 5 = 95.5$, that is, they get $450 more per car. In other words, 10% of the rebate offered to manufacturer has been passed on to consumers.

d. Since the rebate now goes to buyers we have $P^d = P^s - 5$ where P^d is the amount of money buyers effectively pay to buy a car. Hence we can write the demand curve in terms of P^s as $Q^d = 100 - (P^s - 5) = 105 - P^s$. Intuitively, the rebate of 5 has shifted market demand up by 5 (to D') because it has increased consumers' willingness to pay for a car by 5. Equating the quantities demanded and supplied we have $105 - P^s = -(10/9) + (1/9) P^s$ so that $P^s = 95.5$, $P^d = 90.5$, and $Q = 100 - 90.5 = 9.5$, just as in c (see graph above).

e. Under both plans, car sales increase by 500,000 cars. Since the goal of the government is to increase the sales of small cars, both plans can be said to be equally effective.

3. The demand and supply curves for good X are both linear. The quantity sold of good X is 100 and the price is $100.

   a. Now, suppose that supply of X is restricted to 50 units and the price rises to $200. What is the equation of demand?

   b. Now suppose that supply is no longer restricted, but demand jumps due to an influx of new consumers. Now, quantity sold is 150 and price rises to $150. What is the equation of supply?

Answer:

We have $Q^d = A - BP$ and $Q^s = C + DP$. Since Q = 100 and P = 100 is a market equilibrium, the point (100,100) must lie on both the supply and the demand curves. Hence, we know that 100 = A − 100B and 100 = C + 100D so that A= 100(1 + B) and C = 100(1 − D).

a. Since the supply is restricted to a level that is smaller than in the market equilibrium, there must be excess demand. This means that the price at which the 50 units are sold is determined by the demand curve. Hence, we know that Q = 50 and P= 200 is a point on the demand curve, that is, 50 = A − 200B. Since we already know that A = 100 (1+B) we can solve for B as 50 = 100(1+B) − 200 B so that B = ½. This in turn implies that A = 100 (1 + ½) = 150. The demand curve can, therefore, be written as Q^d = 150- ½ P.

b. After the shift in demand, the market equilibrium obtains at a point that is both on the new demand curve and on the old supply curve. Since Q = 150 and P = 150 is a point on the original supply curve, we can write that 150 = C + 150D. But we already know that C = 100(1 − D). Hence, we can write 150 = 100(1 − D) + 150D, which implies that D = 1. Therefore, C = 100 (1 − 1) = 0 and we can write the supply curve as Q^s = P. We can now quickly check our answer by determining the market equilibrium implied by our equations for demand and supply. Setting the quantities demanded and supplied equal to each other, we get P = 150 − ½ P, implying P = 100. Plugging this value of P in either the supply or the demand curve gives us Q = 100. This is indeed the market equilibrium that we started with!

Problem Set

1. The following equations represent *demand curves* for a commodity, q:

a. q = 300 - P

b. q = 10 + 10p

c. q = 50

i. Draw these demand curves on a graph. For which of these demands does the *law of demand* hold?

ii. What is the *choke price* for each of the demands?

iii What is the *slope* of each of the demands?

iv. What are the *price elasticities of demand* in the neighborhood of q = 100?

v. What are *the price elasticities of demand* in the neighborhood of q = 50?

vi. Can you think of examples of goods that might have demands that look like these?

2. Suppose that disposable personal income for an average person in the U.S. and *the per capita* (i.e., per person) consumption of salmon are as follows:

	Year 1	Year 2
Income ($000's)	12	13
Salmon (lbs.)	1	1.1

a. Assuming that the price of salmon remained the same over the two years, what is the *income elasticity of demand* for salmon in the U.S. for these years and in the neighborhood of 12.5 in income and a quantity of 1 pound of fish?

b. Based on the information that you have been given here, what are the variables that affect the demand for salmon?

3. In the town of Terrassa, there are 1000 apartments currently available for rental. Maintenance costs are $10 per month for each occupied apartment and $0 if an apartment is not occupied. Any apartment currently on the market that rents for more than $10 per month is, therefore, profitable for the landlord. We will assume that landlords only make apartments available for rental if it is profitable to do so.

a. Draw the *short-run supply curve* for apartments in Terrassa, that is, the curve showing how many of the 1000 currently available apartments landlords are willing to rent as a function of the rental price. What is the *price elasticity* of this short-run supply curve for prices greater than $10 per month?

b. Now, suppose that apartments that are not currently available for rental can be converted into rental apartments in the medium-term so that, as the rental price rises, more apartments become available to rent. Suppose that we can write the supply curve in the medium-term as:

Q = 1000 + P   when price is greater than or equal to $10

Q = 0   when price is less than $10

What is the price elasticity of supply in the neighborhood of P = $50? Is the elasticity of supply of this medium-term supply curve greater or less than the elasticity of the short-run supply curve of part (a)? Does this supply curve obey the *law of supply*?

4. The current (short-run) demand for apartments in Terrassa can be written as:

$$Q = 2000 - P$$

The supply curves for rental apartments in the short-term and medium-term are as in question (3).

 a. Solve for the *equilibrium* price and quantity.

 b. Assume that the medium-run demand curve is the same as the short-run demand curve. What are the equilibrium quantity and price in the medium-run? How do they compare to the short-run equilibrium ?

 c. Now, suppose that Terrassa places a limit on the rental price of $400. At this price, will there be *excess demand, excess supply,* or neither?

 d. Suppose that the limit on rental price is changed to $600. At this price, will there be excess demand, excess supply, or neither? In what sense is this new price limit "better" or "worse" than a price limit of $400?

 e. Now, suppose that there is no rent control; however, a new state college opens in Terrassa, causing an influx of students from out of town who need apartments. The new demand curve is:

$$Q = 3000 - P$$

 Draw the new short-run demand and the short-run supply on the same graph and solve for the new equilibrium price and quantity in the short-term and medium-term. How have equilibrium price and quantity changed in the short-term and medium-term?

5. The current price in the market for gourmet ice-cream bars is $5 per unit. At this price, 1000 units are sold. The price elasticity of demand is -.5 and the price elasticity of supply is 1 at the current price.

 a. Solve for the equations of demand and supply, assuming that they are both linear.

 b. Now, suppose that the current price is $1 and, at this price, 2000 units are sold. The price elasticities are -.05 for demand and 0.1 for supply. What has happened to the supply and demand curves? What kind of changes in the market environment could explain such changes ?

6. Suppose that demand for housing and food can be written as follows:

 $Q^h = (1/3)(I/P^h)$, where Q^h refers to the number of housing units and P^h refers to price per unit.

 $Q^f = (2/3)(I/P^f)$, where Q^f refers to quantity of food in pounds and P^f refers to price per pound.

 a. Which of the two commodities accounts for the greater part of consumers' budgets?

b. What are the price elasticities of demand for the housing and food?

c. Is it the case that the commodity that accounts for the greater portion of the budget has higher price elasticity of demand?

d. Suppose that housing is now free and consumers only spend money on food (so that food expenditure always accounts for 100% of income.) What is the price elasticity of demand for food? What is the income elasticity of demand for food?

Exam *(60 minutes: Closed book, closed notes)*

1. Suppose that the *demand* for pizza in the U.S. is as follows:

$$Q = 200 - .5P^p - .25P^b + 50D + .01I$$

where: P^p is the average price in dollars per medium-sized pizza, P^b is the average price of beer in dollars per six pack, D is a variable which takes the value 1 when it is football season and takes the value 0 otherwise, and I is disposable personal income.

a. What is the *price elasticity of demand* for pizza in the neighborhood of P^p = $8, P^b = $4, D = 1, and I =$10,000?

b. What is the *cross price elasticity of demand* for pizza with respect to beer in the neighborhood of P^p = $8, P^b = $4, D = 1, and I = $10,000?

c. What is the *income elasticity of demand* for pizza in the neighborhood of I = $10,000, D = 1, P^p = $8, and P^b = $4?

d. Draw the *demand curve* for pizza supposing that P^b = $4, D=1, and I = $10,000.

   i. Now, draw the *demand curve* for pizza supposing that all the values of the variables are the same except that D = 0. Compare the two demand curves. What has changed?

   ii. Now, draw the *demand curve* for pizza supposing that P^b = $4, D=1, and I = $12,000. Compare this to the first demand curve in d. What has changed?

   iii. Now, draw the *demand curve* for pizza supposing that P^b = $4, D=0, and I=$12,000. Compare this to the first demand curve in (d). What has changed?

2. Indicate whether each of the following events will shift the monthly demand curve for the Ford Taurus (a midsize car) to the right, left, or not at all.

   a. GM introduces a new line of small, fuel-efficient cars.

   b. Following an agreement between the U.S. and Japan, Japanese car manufacturers will "voluntarily" reduce their exports of medium-sized cars to the U.S.

   c. The cost of steel increases.

    d. Ford offers a discount on all Taurus purchases and

        i. Consumers expect this discount to be temporary.

        ii. Consumers expect the discount to be permanent.

    e. *Consumer Reports* does a cover story favorable to the Taurus.

    f. The U.S. government announces that it will significantly increase its investment in public transportation.

    g. There are persistent rumors of war coming from the Middle East.

3. Most Californians use cars daily to commute to work and for their transportation needs. The increasing price of auto insurance, however, has led to consumer discontent. In order to hold costs down the auto insurance industry has promoted tort law reform which would reduce insurers' costs by limiting when and for how much people can sue each other after an accident. An alternative proposal by a pro-consumer group is to limit the price insurers can charge to 75% of the current price. The current demand and supply curves for auto insurance (before any program is enacted) are:

$$Q^d = 100 - 0.04P$$

$$Q^s = 0.06P - 20$$

where P is the price of auto insurance and Q is the quantity, in millions.

    a. What are the current market price and quantity in the market?

    b. Under the pro-consumer plan, a price ceiling is imposed where the new maximum price is 75% of the equilibrium price obtained in (a). What are the new price and quantity in the market?

    c. The reduction in insurers' cost under the industry-sponsored plan will change the supply curve to

$$Q^s = 0.06P$$

What is the new price and quantity in the market under this proposal?

4. Suppose that consumers all spend exactly one third of their income on housing. There are N identical consumers, each with an income of I_o.

    a. Write the market demand curve for housing.

    b. What is the price elasticity of market demand for housing?

    c. What is the income elasticity of market demand for housing?

d. Suppose that disposable personal income of all consumers rises by 10%. Write the equation for the new market demand curve. Graph the old demand curve and the new demand curve. Has the price elasticity or the income elasticity changed?

5. The current price in the market for bananas is $0.50 per pound. At this price, 1 million pounds are sold per year in Smalltown, U.S.A. Suppose that the price elasticity of demand is -4 and the short-run price elasticity of supply is 0.01. Solve for the equations of demand and supply, assuming that demand and supply are linear.

Answers to the Exercises

1. (a) and (c) obey the law of demand. Functions that obey the law of demand have negative slopes. In other words the quantity demanded decreases when the price of the good increases. The slope of function (a) is -50. The slope of function (b) is +50. Both functions (a) and (b) are linear demands and have, therefore, constant slopes. The slope of function (c) is not constant. You can see that this function is downward-sloping, however, by first rewriting it with Q on the left-hand side of the equals sign and P on the right-hand side, that is, as $Q = 100P^{-1}$. You see later in the summary that this is a "constant elasticity" demand curve. Now, graph the function and you will notice that it is downward-sloping.

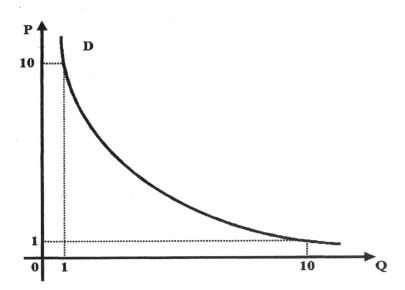

2. For the demand curve of any good (call the good X), only changes in the price of X will cause movements along the demand curve. *Any* other change affecting the market for good X will cause a shift in the curve. Hence, (c) corresponds to a move along the curve while (a), (b), and (d) will shift the demand curve if they affect it at all. The weather pattern clearly affects the demand for gasoline. For example, rainy weather might increase the use of cars and hence the quantity of gasoline demanded at any given price. This would shift the demand curve for gasoline to the right. The price of cars also matters. If, for example, the price of cars goes up, there will be fewer cars and thus a lesser demand for gasoline at any price. Hence, the demand for gasoline would shift to the left. Finally, a tax paid by consumers

means that they are now willing to pay $1 less *to the sellers* in order to get any given quantity of gasoline.

Note: Why is it that a tax is different from an increase in the price of the gasoline? The reason is that the tax is paid *whatever* the price of gasoline: whatever the asking price, consumers will behave as if price were higher by $1. This drives a wedge between demand without the tax and demand with the tax.

3. (a) and (c) obey the law of supply. Functions that obey the law of supply are upward-sloping in price. In other words, the quantity supplied increases when the price increases. Function (a) has a slope of 50. Function (b) has a slope of -50 and so violates the law of supply. Function (c) has a slope of 100. The slope of function (d) with respect to price is –50, which violates the law of supply.

4. Only (b) and (d). Since only a change in the price of sofa beds can cause movements along the supply curve, (a), (b), and (d) *potentially* shift the supply curve while (c) corresponds to a move along the supply curve. Do the changes mentioned in (a), (b), and (d) actually shift the supply curve? It depends on whether or not they are likely to affect the conditions of supply. As sofa beds contain mattresses, a change in the price of mattresses is a change in the cost of making sofa beds and this does affect the conditions of supply. Similarly, a production subsidy makes producers willing to accept a lower price from consumers and shifts the supply curve down. On the other hand a change in the price of living space affects the <u>demand</u> for sofa beds: the lower the price of living space, the more living space people rent and hence the higher their demand for bulky items such as sofa beds (alternatively one could think that the need for sofa beds decreases as people have more space where they can use regular beds and couches).

5. (a), (b), (c), and (d) are true at equilibrium. At equilibrium, the demand and supply curves cross so that the equilibrium point is on both the demand curve and the supply curves. This implies that (a) is true. It also implies that (d) is true since "being on the demand (supply) curve" means that buyers (sellers) buy (sell) as much as they want at the prevailing price. If both sellers and buyers are satisfied, then (c) must be true as well. Since excess supply is the difference between quantity supplied and demanded, the fact that (a) is true implies that (b) must also be true. On the other hand, (e) is incorrect. Saying that we are at equilibrium is a descriptive statement only: it carries no value judgment about the desirability of being at such a price or having a certain number of units sold.

6. Statements (b), (d), and (e) are correct. Solving the two equations simultaneously to obtain the equilibrium point we have:

    200 - 50P = 50 + 100P (setting quantity demanded equal to quantity supplied)

    150 = 150P (rearranging terms), so that P* = 1 (i.e., equilibrium price, indicated by the "*", is 1).

    Therefore, statement (b) is correct, and statement (a) is incorrect. At a price of $.50, we have quantity demanded = 200 - 50(0.50) = 175 and quantity supplied = 50 + 100(0.50) = 100 so that quantity demanded exceeds quantity supplied, that is, we have excess demand. This means that (d) is correct, and (c) is incorrect; (e) simply states that there is excess demand, which we know to be true from (d).

7.

    a. The equilibrium price and quantity at the original levels of demand and supply can be computed as follows:

$100 - 5P = 10 + 10P$ (setting demand equal to supply)

$90 = 15P$ (rearranging terms) so that $P^* = 6$ (solving for equilibrium price, P^*)

Turning now to equilibrium quantity:

$Q = 100 - 5(6)$ (substituting P^* into the equation of demand)
$Q^* = 70$ (solving for equilibrium quantity, Q^*)

Now, we compute the new equilibrium price and quantity as follows:

$70 - 5P = 10 + 10P$ (setting demand equal to supply)

$60 = 15P$ (rearranging terms) so $P^{**} = 4$ (solving for the new equilibrium price, P^{**})

and:

$Q = 70 - 5(4)$ (substituting the new equilibrium price into the new demand)

$Q^{**} = 50$ (solving for the new equilibrium quantity, Q^{**})

Graphically, we have:

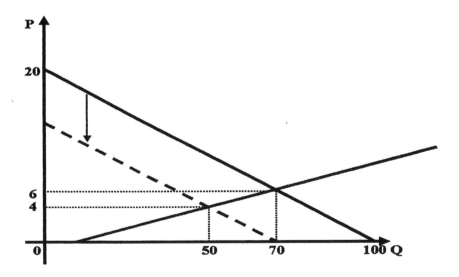

    There has been a downward shift in demand. This has caused both equilibrium price and quantity to fall.

    b. With a 20% tax on consumers, we have the following demand:

Q = 100 - 6P (in other words, consumers pay 20% more than before for their tea)

Combining this with the original supply curve (Q = 10 + 10P) and solving for the equilibrium prices and quantities we have:

100 - 6P = 10 + 10P (setting the new demand equal to supply)

90 = 16P (rearranging terms) so that P*** = 5.625 (solving for the new equilibrium price, P***) and:

100 - 6(5.625) = 66.19 = Q*** (substituting the new equilibrium price into new demand)

Graphically, we have:

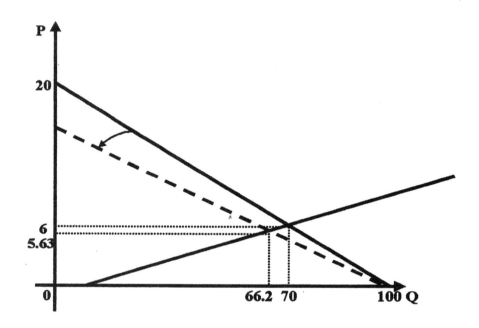

so that both quantity and price have fallen compared to the original amount.

8.
    a. Graphically, we have:

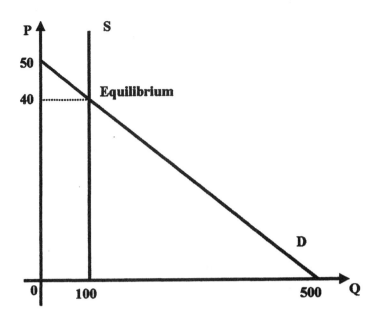

The equilibrium point is at the intersection of the demand and supply curves.

b. When a subsidy of $1 is given to suppliers, there is no change since supply is fixed at Q = 100. In other words, the supply curve "shifts down" by $1, but shifting down a vertical curve does not change the equilibrium point. It follows that consumers pay the same price as before so that the entire benefit of the subsidy goes to suppliers.

c. Suppose that supply is horizontal at P = 10, as shown below:

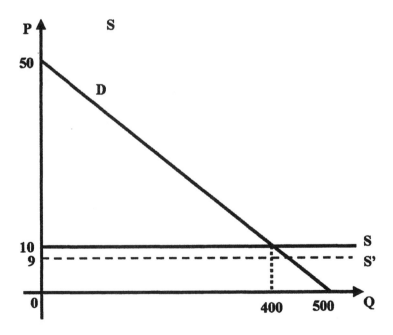

The new equilibrium point is at the intersection of demand and supply. If a $1 subsidy is given to suppliers now, the supply curve shifts down by $1 since sellers are now willing to accept a lower price from buyers. Hence, the equilibrium price falls by $1 and quantity increases. Consumers pay $1 less per unit than before while sellers receive the same amount of money per unit as before (i.e., the old price - $1 plus the $1 of subsidy received from the government). In other words, the entire benefit of the subsidy goes to buyers.

9. Statements (a), (c), (d), and (e) are correct. Analogously to the case of demand, a supply curve can be elastic, unit-elastic, or inelastic. Statement (a) is, in fact, the definition of unit elasticity and so is correct. If demand is inelastic, a 1% change in price will elicit a change in quantity demanded of *less than 1%*, so (b) is incorrect. Statement (c) is the definition of elastic demand, and so is correct. At the choke price, $Q = 0$ so that the elasticity of a linear demand curve $Q = a - bP$ is given by $\varepsilon_{Q,P} = -b (P/0)$, so that the demand is infinitely elastic and (d) is correct. At $Q = bP$ we have $P/Q = (1/b)$, so that $\varepsilon_{Q,P} = -b(1/b) = -1$ and (e) is correct.

10. (d) is correct. This is a constant elasticity demand curve. Rewriting the demand in the exercise, we have $Q = 100P^{-1}$ so that the elasticity is given by -1.

11.

   a. We might suppose that, for several reasons, life-saving drugs might have relatively inelastic demand (in other words, quantity demanded is relatively unresponsive to changes in price). First, when faced with a life-or-death choice, both patients and doctors tend to be willing to undertake the treatment which saves the patient's life, whatever the cost. Often, too, insurance covers much of the cost of the drug so that patients do not feel the effect of price changes as strongly as if they were not insured.

   b. To the extent that a single brand of white paper might have many close substitutes, we might expect that *Arrow* brand white paper might have a relatively elastic demand.

   c. Current demand for videocassettes might be relatively responsive to price, to the extent that videocassettes have close substitutes in the form of television or movies shown in theaters. On the other hand, switching to other close substitutes of videocassettes (such as videodisks or CD-ROMS) involves the cost of buying a different machine to play the disk, which would tend to make demand less price elastic.

   d. The long-term demand for videocassettes would tend to be more elastic than the short-term demand because people could switch out of videocassettes and into emerging technologies such as videodisks at little cost as the video machines they own start breaking down and need to be replaced anyway. On the other hand, an argument in favor of long-run elasticity being less elastic than short-run demand is that, in the short-run, people can adjust to a price increase by simply replaying videocassettes that they currently own rather than buy new ones. This effect occurs because videocassettes are durable products.

12. Newsprint is a recyclable good, so that one might expect the long-run market supply to be less elastic than the short-run supply. Telephones are a durable good, and for this reason, one might expect long-run market demand to be less elastic than short-run demand. On the other hand, in the very long-run, substitutes to the telephone may exist (such as electronic mail) so that very long-run demand may, in fact, be more elastic than short-run demand. Apples would tend to have higher elasticity of demand in the long-run than in the short-run, as

consumers (including producers that use apples as an intermediate product) switch from apple consumption and into the consumption of other fruits.

13. Expressions (a) and (c) are correct. We would define this elasticity as any other elasticity: the percentage change in quantity with respect to a percentage change in (whatever). In this case, "whatever" is wealth. Expression (c) uses the definition of percentage change %ΔX= $\Delta X/X$. Note that if Q is expressed in percents, then (a) would be correct as well.

Answers to Problems

1. This question reviews a series of definitions from the text.

   i.   The law of demand holds for demand (a). Demand (b) slopes upward and demand (c) is vertical at 50.

   ii.   The choke price for demand (a) is 300 since 0 = 300 – 300x1. For demands (b) and (c), there is no price at which quantity demanded is zero.

   iii.   The slope of demand (a) is –1 (the coefficient of price). The slope of demand (b) is 10, and the slope of demand (c) is zero.

   iv.   (a) $\varepsilon_{Q,P} = (\Delta Q/\Delta P)(P/Q) = (-1)(200/100) = -2$
           (b) $\varepsilon_{Q,P} = (\Delta Q/\Delta P)(P/Q) = (10/1)(9/100) = 0.9$
           (c) $\varepsilon_{Q,P} = (\Delta Q/\Delta P)(P/Q) = 0$ (since $\Delta Q = 0$ for any price and quantity)

   v.   (a) $\varepsilon_{Q,P} = (\Delta Q/\Delta P)(P/Q) = (-1)(250/50) = -5$
           (b) $\varepsilon_{Q,P} = (\Delta Q/\Delta P)(P/Q) = (10/1)(4/50) = 0.8$
           (c) $\varepsilon_{Q,P} = (\Delta Q/\Delta P)(P/Q) = 0$

   vi.   An example of (a) might be apples: as the price rises, people would buy less.

           It is not clear that any good examples of demands such as (b) exist. In the text, it was pointed out that status goods are not a good example of demands of type (b) because here, consumers' perceptions of the good actually change as price rises. In other words, price is a characteristic of the good so that the characteristics of the good change as we move along the demand curve. Usually, economists define the demand curve for a good whose characteristics do not change. In other words, economists usually assume that price is not a characteristic of the good. It has been claimed that, during periods of extreme poverty, staples such as potatoes or bread violate the law of demand. Such goods are referred to as *Giffen goods*. A more detailed treatment of these goods will follow in Chapter 5.

           An example of a demand such as (c) might be a life-saving drug: those who consume it would do so almost irrespective of price.

2.

   a. The income elasticity of demand is defined as: $\varepsilon_{Q,I} = (\Delta Q/\Delta I)(I/Q) = (.1/1)(12.5/1) = 1.25$

   b. We would certainly want income and quantity. Actually, we have no information on price, but presumably, price would affect demand as well.

3.

   a. The supply curve is vertical at 1000 apartments as long as price is greater than or equal to $10 per month, and vertical at zero if price is less than $10 per month, as shown below. The price elasticity of the short-run supply curve for prices higher than $10 per month is 0 since ΔQ is zero.

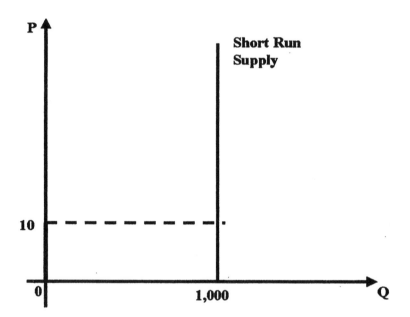

   b. The medium-term supply curve is upward sloping at price greater than or equal to $10 and vertical at zero for price less than $10. In the neighborhood of P = $50, $\varepsilon_{Q,P} = (\Delta Q/\Delta P)(P/Q) = (1/1)(50/1050) = 1/21$. This elasticity is clearly greater than the elasticity of part (a). The supply curve obeys the law of supply in the medium-term as long as price is at least $10.

4.

   a. In the short-run, equilibrium price and quantity can be obtained by setting quantity demanded equal to quantity supplied: 2000 − P = 1000, so that P* = $1000 and Q* = 1000, where * indicates the equilibrium quantity.

   b. In the medium-term, equilibrium quantity and price can be obtained as follows: 1000 + P = 2000 − P, so that P* = $500 and Q* = 1500. Clearly, quantity is greater and price lower in the medium-term than in the short-term.

c. If the rental price is limited to $400, then demand will be 1600 and supply will be 1400 in the medium-term. In the short-term, demand will be 1600 and supply will be 1000. Therefore, in the medium-term, there is a 200 unit excess demand and in the short-term there is a 600 unit excess demand.

d. If the limit on the rental price is changed to $600, then there will still be a short-term excess demand, since short-term demand will be 1400 and short-term supply will be 1000 (creating an excess demand of 400 units); however, in the medium-term, equilibrium rental price will be below the limit so that there will be no excess demand or supply. While we can say, based on what we have studied so far, that the new price might result in a more stable situation in the medium-term (since price and quantity can attain their equilibrium levels), we cannot say that the equilibrium price and quantity are "better" or "worse" than any other price or quantity. This issue will be revisited in Chapter 10.

e. Here, demand has shifted up by 1000 units. The new short-term equilibrium can be computed as: 3000 - P = 1000 so that P* = $2000 and Q* = 1000. In the medium-term, we have: 3000 − P = 1000 + P so that P* = $1000 and Q* = 2000. Price has risen dramatically in the short-term and price and quantity have risen in the medium-term.

In Chapter 9, we will revisit the issue of the relative slopes of short-run and long-run demand and supply!

5.

a. We know that elasticity at P = $5 and Q = 1000 is -.5. In other words, $\varepsilon_{Q,P}$ =$(\Delta Q/\Delta P)(P/Q) = (\Delta Q/\Delta P)(5/1000) = -.5$. Solving for the slope of demand, we have slope = $(\Delta Q/\Delta P) = -100$. Now, substituting this slope into the equation for a linear demand and solving for the intercept we have: $1000 = A - 100(\$5)$ or A = 1500. Therefore, the equation for demand is $Q^d = 1500 - 100P$.

Similarly, we can solve for the slope of supply using elasticity of supply since $\sigma_{Q,P}$ =$(\Delta Q/\Delta P)(P/Q) = 1$. Solving for the slope of supply at P = $5 and Q = 1000 we have slope = $(\Delta Q/\Delta P) = 200$. Substituting slope into the equation for a linear supply and solving for the intercept term (using P = $5 and Q = 1000, as before), we have: $1000 = A + 200P$ or A = 0. Therefore, the equation for supply is Q = 200P.

b. At the new values, we have $\varepsilon_{Q,P}$ =$(\Delta Q/\Delta P)(P/Q) = (\Delta Q/\Delta P)(1/2000) = -.05$ so that the slope of demand is -100. Solving for the intercept of demand, as before, we have A = 2100 so that the new equation for demand is Q = 2100 − 100P.

Similarly, using the elasticity of supply and solving for the slope of supply, we have slope = 200. The new intercept of supply is A = 1800. Therefore, the new equation of supply is Q = 1800 + 200P.

We can conclude that demand and supply have shifted up. A condition that could cause demand to shift up might be a change in the weather, making it generally warmer. A condition that could cause the supply curve to shift up is a decrease in the price of inputs to ice- cream bars (such as the price of milk or chocolate or the price of labor).

6.

a. Food accounts for 2/3 of the consumers' budget (income), since $Q^f P^f$ is the expenditure on food and, expressed as a proportion of income, expenditure on food is $Q^f P^f / I = (2/3)(I/P^f)(P^f/I) = 2/3$.

b. Both housing and food have constant price elasticity demands at price elasticity of demand = –1. In the case of food, for example, we can rewrite demand in the constant elasticity form $(2/3)I \times P^{f-1}$. $(2/3)I$ is just the coefficient of price.

c. Since both commodities have the same elasticity, it is not the case that the commodity that accounts for the greater portion of the budget has a higher elasticity.

d. If consumers only spend on food, their demand can be rewritten as $Q^f = I/P^f$. Again, this is a constant elasticity demand function, so the price elasticity is –1.

Writing the demand for food in the same form as the constant elasticity demand function in the text, we have: $Q^f = I^1 P^{f-1}$. Recall that the *price* elasticity of demand is simply the exponent of price (here, -1). Similarly, we can infer that the *income* elasticity of demand is the exponent of income. Here, the exponent of income is 1.

Answers to the Exam

1.

a. First, solving for demand at the values of the variables that we are given, we have: $Q = 200 - 0.5P^p -0.25(4) + 50 + 0.1(10000) = 349 - 0.5P^p$. Now, substituting into the formula for the price elasticity of demand, we have: $\varepsilon_{Q,P} = (\Delta Q/\Delta P)(P/Q) - 0.5(8/345) = -4/345$.

b. Similarly, using the values of the variables we are given, we have: $Q = 200 - 0.5(8) - 0.25P^b + 50 + 0.01(10000) = 346 - 0.25P^b$. Substituting into the formula for the cross price elasticity of demand, we have $\varepsilon_{Q,P} = (\Delta Q/\Delta P)(P/Q) = -0.25(4/345) = -1/345$.

c. Using the values of the variables we are given, we have: $Q = 200 - 0.5(8) - 0.25(4) + 50 + 0.01I = 245 + 0.01I$. Substituting into the formula for the income elasticity of demand, we have $\varepsilon_{Q,P} = (\Delta Q/\Delta I)(I/Q) = 0.01(10,000/345) = 100/345$.

d. The demand curves for this case are depicted below. In each case, the demand curve shifts as shown. The equations for the demands in the cases are as follows:

Initial demand: $Q = 200 - 0.5P^p - 0.25(4) + 50 + 0.01(10,000) = 349 - 0.5P^p$
Case d.i. $\quad Q = 200 - 0.5P^p - 0.25(4) + 0 + 0.01(10,000) \quad = 299 - 0.5P^p$
Case d.ii. $\quad Q = 200 - 0.5P^p - 0.25(4) + 50 + 0.01(12,000) = 369 - 0.5P^p$
Case d.iii. $\quad Q = 200 - 0.5P^p - 0.25(4) + 0 + 0.01(12,000) \quad = 319 - 0.5P^p$

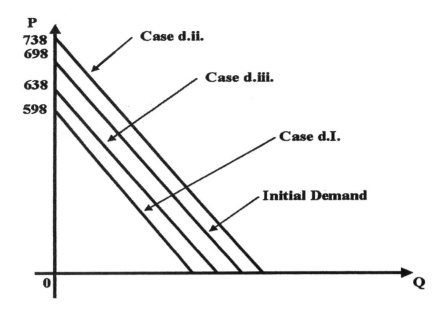

2.

a. To the left: at a given price for the Ford Taurus, some of its potential buyers will now purchase the new model.

b. To the right: as the price of Japanese imports increases more people are willing to purchase U.S.-made cars.

c. This does not affect the demand curve.

d. Let us begin with the case of a permanent discount. If the demand curve is represented on a graph with the list price on the vertical axis, then demand shifts to the right because the quantity demanded when the list price is p is actually the larger quantity that would be demanded when the effective price is p minus the discount. If on the other hand the demand curve is drawn on a graph with the effective price on the vertical axis, then the demand curve does not shift at all: the permanent discount only corresponds to a move along the demand curve.

If the discount is expected to be temporary, then the demand curve shifts to the right even if the graph uses the effective price on the vertical axis. This is because some consumers will decide to purchase the car earlier than they had planned in order to take advantage of the temporary discount.

e. This raises consumers' valuation of the Taurus and thus shifts the demand curve to the right.

f. This makes public transportation more attractive. Since cars and public transportation are substitutes, this shifts the demand for the Taurus to the left.

g. The net effect is not clear. The rumors increase the probability that the price of oil will go up. This has a negative effect on the demand for cars in general but it also shifts demand for cars toward more fuel-efficient models. Hence, if the Taurus is not very fuel efficient, the demand for Taurus shifts to the left. If, on the other hand, the Ford

Taurus is one of the most efficient cars in the market, the second effect discussed above might be strong enough so that the net effect would be a shift of the demand curve for Taurus to the right.

3.

a. Setting quantity demanded equal to quantity supplied, we obtain that P = 1200 and Q = 52.

b. The price ceiling is set at P = 900 so that quantity supplied equals 34 and quantity demanded equals 64. The new equilibrium quantity under the consumer group's proposal is the smaller of these two, or Q = 34.

c. The equilibrium under the industry's proposal is P = 1000 and Q = 60.

4.

a. Define D^h as the number of units of housing demanded by an individual consumer. since this consumer spends one third of her income I_0 on housing, we have $PD^h = I_0/3$, where P is the price of a unit of housing. This equality can be rewritten as

$$D^h = I_0/3P$$

which is the demand curve for housing of an individual. Market demand is then obtained as the sum of the quantities of housing demanded at this price by all N consumers, that is, $Q^h = ND^h = NI_0/3P$. Constructing market demand from individual demands is explored in more detail in Chapter 5.

b. The market demand function can be rewritten as $Q^h = (1/3)NI\ P^{-1}$, which is a log-linear demand curve of elasticity −1. Here, I is a variable representing any value that disposable income might take.

c. The income elasticity of the market demand for housing is 1. This can be seen in the equation of demand where I has an exponent of 1. The same answers can also be obtained by simple reasoning. Since consumers always spend one third of their income on housing, every 1% increase in income triggers new expenditure of housing equal to 0.33% of income, which is a 1% increase in housing expenditures since these represent one third of income.

d. If I_0 stands for the initial value of disposable income then the new demand curve is $Q^h = (1/3)NI_0(1.1)P^{-1}$. As shown on the graph, this new demand curve lies everywhere above the old demand curve. However, its price elasticity is still −1 and its income elasticity is still equal to 1.

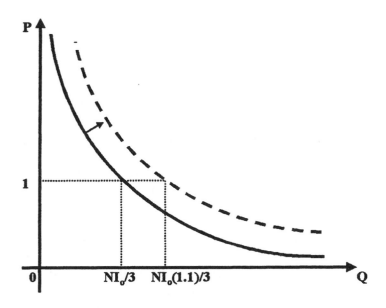

5. We will express quantities in millions of pounds and the price in dollars.

The equation for demand is $Q = A - BP$ and the equation for supply is $Q = C + DP$. The current market equilibrium is $Q = 1$ and $P = 0.5$. Since the equilibrium lies on both the demand and the supply curve, this implies that $1 = A - 0.5B$ and $1 = C + 0.5D$ or, equivalently that $A = 1 + 0.5B$ and $C = 1 - 0.5D$. At the market equilibrium we also know that $P/Q = 0.5/1 = 0.5$ so that the elasticity of demand can be written as $(\Delta Q/\Delta P)(P/Q) = -0.5B$ and the elasticity of supply can be written as $(\Delta Q/\Delta P)(P/Q) = 0.5D$. Since the elasticity of demand is equal to -4 we have $-0.5B = -4$ or $B = 8$ and $A = 1 + (0.5)(8) = 5$. As the elasticity of supply is equal to 0.01 we have $0.5D = 0.01$ or $D = .02$ and $C = 1 - (0.5)(.02) = 0.99$. Hence the equation of demand is $Q^d = 5 - 8P$ and the equation of supply is $Q^s = 0.99 + .02P$. As a check, setting the quantity supplied equal to the quantity demanded, one immediately recovers the equilibrium price $P = 0.5$.

Chapter 3: Preferences and Utility

In Chapter 2, we took the existence of market demand and supply functions for granted and analyzed their characteristics. Chapters 3 through 5 examine the individual consumption behavior that underlies market demand. This will help us understand how changes in public policy (e.g., taxes) and corporate policy (such as pricing decisions) affect both individual consumer behavior and aggregate demand. The theory of consumer choice will be developed in three steps: a theory and analysis of consumer preferences (Chapter 3), a description and analysis of the constraints on consumption due to consumers' limited budgets (Chapter 4), and an analysis of how consumers make consumption choices given their preferences and budgets (Chapter 5).

Suppose that there are only two commodities, food and housing. If we are to describe how a consumer allocates her budget between these two products we need some way to describe her preferences for these two goods. In other words, we must specify the *objective function* of the consumer. We will do this by assuming three rules for the way consumers rank, by preference, various combinations or allotments (called **baskets**) of these goods. Before reviewing these rules, note that since preferences can change over time (e.g., preferences often change with age) and also change with place or other physical circumstances (most people have stronger preferences for an umbrella on a rainy than on a sunny day), these baskets contain allotments of food and housing to be consumed at a particular time, place, and under particular circumstances. For example, basket A may include a certain amount of food today in the city where the consumer lives and basket B might include the same amount of food, to be available tomorrow in the same city.

The first rule is that consumers' preferences are **complete** in the sense that, for any baskets of these two goods that she could be offered, a consumer should be able to say whether she prefers basket A to basket B, prefers B to A, or is indifferent between the two. The second rule is that consumers who prefer basket A to B and basket B to C must also prefer basket A to C. This is called **transitivity**. The third rule is that "**more is better**" (often called **monotonicity**). This means that a consumer will always prefer a basket that contains at least as much of every good and strictly more of at least one good.

Except for certain life and death situations, the assumption of completeness usually holds. More to the point, it holds for most economic decisions that we will be concerned with. The assumption of transitivity is more controversial: for example, laboratory experiments indicate that the assumption does not hold very well for children. On the other hand, the assumption is satisfied for most adults. This suggests that people might "learn" transitivity as they progress in life. Moreover, it seems that people attempt to be transitive in the sense that, when some intransitivity in their choices is pointed out, they try to "correct" their behavior. The last assumption, that more is better, can be justified in two ways. First, over the range that is relevant for many people's choices, it is often true that more really is better: most of us never reach the point where we would not be happy to travel more, have a bigger house, or have more CDs. Second, if one assumes that consumers can dispose of excess at no cost then a basket with "more" can, at worst, be just as good as a basket with "less".

Exercise 1: *Ted can choose among four baskets of goods. Basket A contains 10 of good X and 1 of good Y. Basket B contains 10 of good X and 0 of good Y. Basket C contains 5 of good X and 5 of good Y. Basket D contains 0 of good X and 10 of good Y. He prefers basket A to B, B to C, C to D, A to C, A to D, and B to D. Ted's preferences are:*

a. complete
b. transitive
c. monotonic (more is better)

Exercise 2 : *In the exercise above, suppose now that Ted prefers basket B to basket A. Ted's preferences are:*

a. complete
b. transitive
c. monotonic (more is better)

Now, suppose that basket A contains some quantity of food and housing for the consumer. Let us take all other baskets (i.e., all other combinations of food and housing) for which the consumer is indifferent between these baskets and basket A. This set of baskets forms the **indifference set** or **indifference curve** of the consumer. If the consumer is not indifferent between basket A and basket B, then A and B will be on different indifference curves. A set of indifference curves representing the consumer 's preference with respect to all possible baskets of goods is called an **indifference map**.

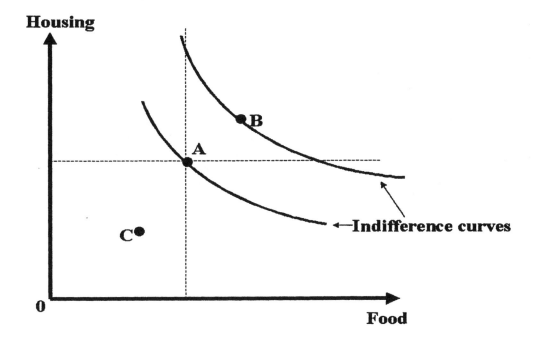

Figure 3.1

Indifference curves are usually drawn as negatively-sloping curves that are convex to the origin and do not cross or touch, as those in the graph above. This conventional shape is linked to assumptions about consumer preferences. If more really is better, then the indifference curves must have a **negative slope**. This is because any basket, such as B, that lies to the northeast of basket A has more of both goods and must therefore be preferable to A. Conversely, any basket, such as C, that lies to the southwest of basket A has less of both goods and must be less desirable than A. Hence, the only remaining areas where the baskets may be indifferent to A lie to the northwest and southeast, resulting in a negative slope to the curve. The assumption of transitivity means that the **indifference curves cannot cross**. Suppose that basket B is preferable to basket A, but the indifference curves going through A and B respectively cross at D, as shown on Figure 3.2. This leads us to a contradiction. On the one hand B is preferable to A. On the other hand the consumer must be indifferent between B and D since they are on the same indifference curve. Similarly, the consumer must be indifferent between A and D since D is also on the indifference curve going through A. By transitivity then, the consumer should be indifferent between A and B, which contradicts our initial assumption.

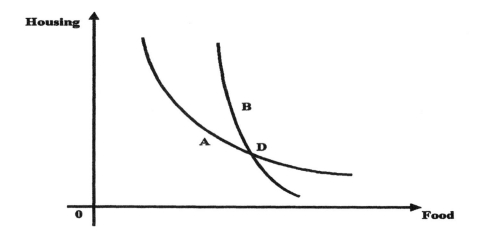

Figure 3.2

Since indifference curves cannot cross, *every basket has only one indifference curve that passes through it:* indifference curves *cannot be "thick"* (see Figure 3.3). If they were, we could find two points A and B so that B lies to the northeast of A and the consumer is indifferent between A and B since they are on the same indifference curve. Since "more is (strictly) better", B must be preferable to A and cannot therefore lie on the same indifference curve.

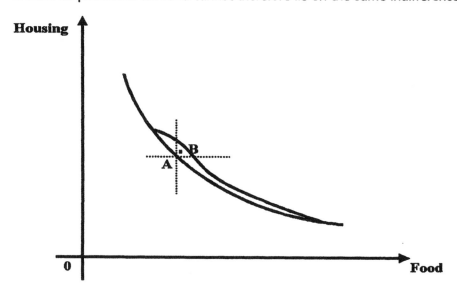

Figure 3.3

Combining transitivity and monotonicity also allows us to conclude that **higher indifference curves correspond to higher levels of satisfaction.** Consider A and B on the following graph. B lies on a higher indifference curve than A. Is it preferable to A? Yes, because we can always find a point such as C that lies to the northeast of A and is on the same indifference curve as B. Monotonicity implies that C is preferable to A. But, since the consumer is indifferent between B and C, transitivity then implies that B is also preferable to A.

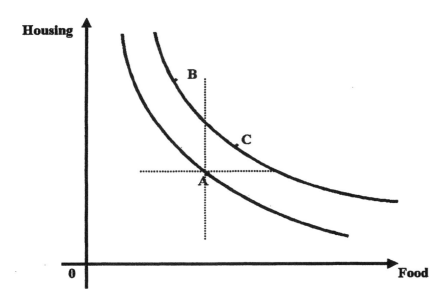

Figure 3.4

Finally, if "averages are preferable to extremes" then a balanced basket will be preferable to a very unbalanced basket, for the same total amount of goods consumed. This means that the curves are bowed in toward the origin (or convex to the origin). This is seen on the graph below where A, which is made up of half of B's content and half of C's content lies on a higher indifference curve than either B or C if the indifference curve is convex (but not if it is concave)

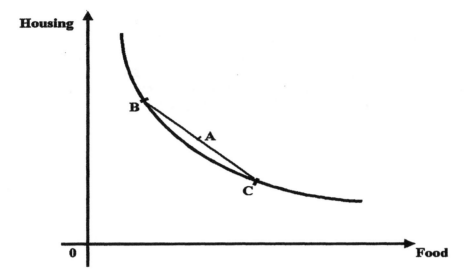

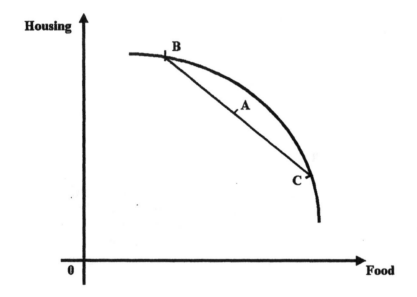

Figure 3.5

Exercise 3: *For the indifference curves that are graphed below, are the underlying preferences:*

    a. transitive?
    b. monotonic?
    c. such that averages are preferable to extremes?
    d. complete?

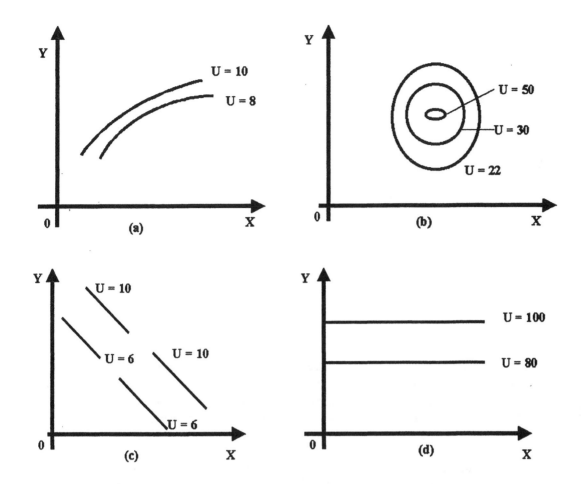

The **marginal rate of substitution** (between food and housing) is the rate at which the consumer would be willing to substitute a little more food for a little less housing. If the consumer is currently consuming at basket A, the marginal rate of substitution is the increase in housing that he would require in exchange for a small decrease in food to leave him just indifferent between consuming basket A and the new basket that lies very close by. Formally, the marginal rate of substitution is defined as the negative of the slope of the indifference curve:

$$MRS_{f,h} = -\Delta housing/\Delta food \text{ (for a constant level of preference)}$$

Depending on which basket the consumer is now consuming, the marginal rate of substitution can change. For example, in order to compensate for a small loss of housing at basket B, below, the consumer needs a much larger increase in food than at basket A.

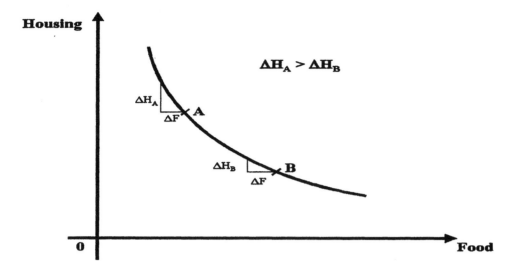

Figure 3.6

For preferences such as those pictured in Figure 3.6, we have a **diminishing marginal rate of substitution**. In other words, the more food you have, the more food you are willing to give up to get a little housing. This, again, reflects the consumer 's preference for variety. Graphically, this means that the indifference curves get flatter as we go toward the extremes on the horizontal axis and steeper as we go toward the extremes on the vertical axis.

The rate of substitution that leaves the consumer on the same indifference curve can be quite different for large changes than for very small changes. This is shown Figure 3.7, where the rate of substitution for small changes would be x/a and the rate of substitution for large changes would be (x+y)/b.

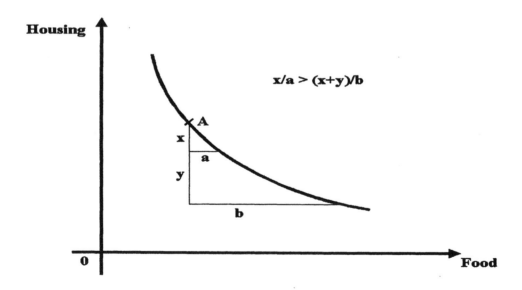

Figure 3.7

To avoid such ambiguity, the rate of substitution on which we focus refers to only very small (or "marginal") changes in consumption and so is called the "marginal" rate of substitution.

Exercise 4: *For the following indifference curves, the marginal rate of substitution between food and clothing is:*

a. 1
b. .5
c. 2
d. 5
e. diminishing

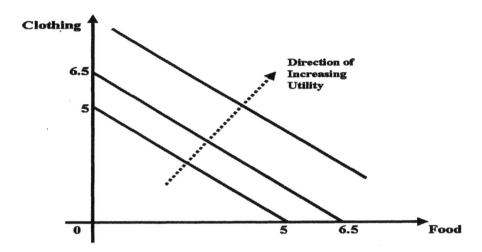

Exercise 5: *For the following indifference curves, the marginal rate of substitution between food and clothing at point A is:*

a. 0
b. ∞
c. undefined
d. diminishing
e. all of the above

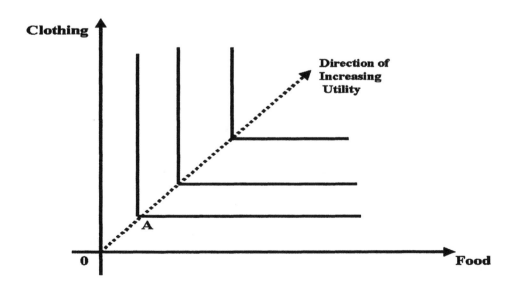

As you can see, the indifference map summarizes a great deal of information about consumer preferences and so is a powerful tool for analysis. However, in order to go farther in our discussion, it will be convenient to describe preferences in an alternative shorthand way with a **utility function**. The utility function simply assigns a number to each possible basket of goods so that more preferable baskets get a higher number than less preferable baskets. Hence every point on a single indifference curve must get the same number assigned to it from the utility function, but points that lie on a higher indifference curve must correspond to higher numbers. Utility functions are simply a way to order, or rank, baskets: the precise magnitude of the number that the function assigns to a basket generally is thought to have no significance, and any function that ranks the baskets in the same order represents the same preferences. In other words, whether I assign basket A the number "5" and basket B the number "10" or I assign basket A the number "1" and basket B the number "2", these utility functions still rank B as preferable to A, and that is all that counts in describing preferences. Restating this differently, utility is generally thought of as an **ordinal** and not a **cardinal** concept.

It is generally possible to find a utility function that represents consumer preferences that follow the rules we described above. Conversely, you can also check whether the preferences that underlie a utility function satisfy the assumptions of completeness, transitivity, "more is better", and any other assumptions that you might wish to add (such as "averages are better than extremes"). For example, suppose that we have a utility function of $U = xy$, where x and y are the quantities of housing and food. The preferences that underlie this function are complete (since the function assigns a value to any conceivable level of x or y), more is better (since the larger is either x or y, the larger is the value of U), and the preferences are transitive. (Take any baskets of x and y, labeled basket A, basket B, and basket C. Each of these baskets is assigned a value by the utility function of U_A, U_B, and U_C, where $U_A > U_B$ and $U_B > U_C$ so that basket A is preferable to basket B and basket B is preferable to basket C. Clearly, then, it is the case that basket A is preferable to basket C as well, since $U_A > U_C$.) It is also the case that averages are better than extremes for this function since you can check that, for the same total quantity of x and y, the total value of the utility function is higher when the quantities of x and y are equal than when they are very unequal. (For example, if $x = 5$ and $y = 5$, $U = 25$; whereas if $x = 10$ and $y = 0$, $U = 0$.)

Exercise 6: *A,B, and C are the only three possible bundles of good x and y. A utility function assigns utility to these bundles as follows:*

> *Bundle A (x = 10, y = 5)   receives U = 5*
> *Bundle B (x = 7.5, y = 7.5)   receives U = 4*
> *Bundle C (x = 5, y = 10)   receives U = 5*

A set of preferences that is consistent with this utility function must be:

  a. complete, transitive (only)
  b. complete (only)
  c. complete, transitive, averages are preferable to extremes (only)
  d. complete, transitive, monotonic, averages are preferable to extremes

Since the indifference curve is simply the set of baskets that all yield the same utility value, an example of an indifference curve based on utility function $U = xy$ might look like $10 = xy$. In other words, all baskets that yield a utility value of 10 lie on the curve $10 = xy$ and belong to the indifference curve. The graph of this curve is plotted below:

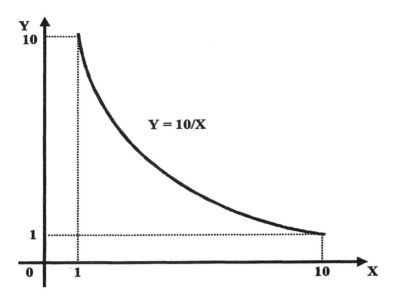

Figure 3.8

Not surprisingly, since we already know that the preferences represented by our example utility function are complete, transitive, monotonic, and averages are better than extremes, the indifference curves that are based on this function will look just like those in Figure 3.6, above.

The **marginal utility** of a good, x, is the additional utility that you get from consuming a little more of x when the consumption of all the other goods in the consumer's basket remains constant. The marginal utility of y, similarly, would be the additional utility obtained from consuming a little more of y when the consumption of all other goods in the consumer's basket remains constant. In the case of two goods, x and y, the marginal utilities of x and y can be written:

$$\Delta U/\Delta x \text{ (for y held constant)} = MU_x$$
$$\Delta U/\Delta y \text{ (for x held constant)} = MU_Y$$

Stated differently, the marginal utility of x is simply the slope of the utility function with respect to x. Similarly, the marginal utility of y is simply the slope of the utility function with respect to y. The principle of **diminishing marginal utility** states that the marginal utility often falls as we consume more of a good (so that MU_x falls as x rises).

The marginal utility is related to the marginal rate of substitution. A move along the indifference curve is defined by compensating changes in x and y that leave total utility unchanged. Mathematically, a small change in x will result in a total change in utility of $MU_x(\Delta x)$ (i.e., the change in x times the utility that a small change in x generates) and a small change in y will result in a total change in utility of $MU_y(\Delta y)$. In order to stay on the indifference curve, we want the sum of these changes in utility to be zero or, mathematically:

$$MU_x(\Delta x) + MU_y(\Delta y) = 0$$

Rearranging terms, we see that the ratio of the marginal utilities must equal the ratio of the changes in x and y:

$$MU_x/MU_y = -\Delta y/\Delta x = MRS_{x,y}$$

But the ratio of changes in x and y which leaves utility unchanged is just the slope of the indifference curve, or the (negative of the) marginal rate of substitution!

You can see from the above equation that, when both marginal utilities are positive, the indifference curve must have a negative slope. If both marginal utilities are positive, then the consumer would prefer to have more of any of the two goods rather than less. Hence, in order to leave the consumer at the same preference level, we must compensate a slight decrease in one good with a slight increase in the other.

Exercise 7: *Suppose that U = x + 10y*

   a.   *The marginal utility of x is:*

   i.   10
   ii.   1
   iii.   1/10

   b.   *The marginal utility of y is:*

   i.   10
   ii.   1
   iii.   1/10

   c.   *Which of the following is true?*

   i.   The marginal utility of x is decreasing, the marginal utility of y is increasing
   ii.   The marginal utility of x and y are increasing
   iii.   The marginal utility of x and y are constant
   iv.   The marginal utility of x and y are positive

   d.   *The marginal rate of substitution between x and y is:*

   i.   10
   ii.   −10
   iii.   1/10

e. *Graph two indifference curves for this function, showing which indifference curve has a higher level of utility. Are the preferences that underlie this function complete, transitive, and monotonic? Are averages preferable to extremes?*

Some particularly useful functional forms of utility are the following:

1. **Cobb-Douglas,** generally represented as $U = Ax^\alpha y^\beta$. A special case of this is the example we have used in this summary, $U = xy$ (i.e., both exponents equal 1 in this case and the constant,

A, equals 1 as well). The indifference curves for this type of function are negatively-sloped and bowed toward the origin, as in the graphs we have shown in much of this summary.

2. **Perfect Substitutes**, represented as $U = x + Ay$. In this case, the consumer cares only about the weighted total amount of x and y he consumes: one unit more of x would be exchanged against A units of y in order to leave the consumer at the same preference level. In this sense, x and y are perfect substitutes. The indifference curves for this type of function are negatively-sloped (as long as A is positive) and straight.

3. **Perfect Complements**, represented as $U = min(x,y/A)$. In this case, the consumer cares about one good only to the extent that she has the other good as well. In other words, the only units of y that are valuable to the consumer are those that can be paired with units of x in a proportion of A units of y to one unit of x. In this sense, x and y are perfect complements. The indifference curves for this type of function are right angles to the origin (or, put differently, are "L" shaped). With y on the vertical axis, the right angles lie on a ray of slope A going through the origin.

4. **Quasi-Linear Preferences**, represented as $U = v(x) + Ay$, where $v(x)$ is an increasing function and A is a positive constant. The indifference curves for this type of function have the same marginal rate of substitution as one moves due North on the indifference map with y on the vertical axis. To see this, notice that $MU_x = v'(x)$ and $MU_y = A$ so that the marginal rate of substitution is equal to $v'(x)/A$. Since this expression is independent of y, the MRS is constant for any given value of x. Because of their convenient and yet somewhat general form, such preferences will be used extensively in later chapters of the textbook.

Exercise 8: *Which of these four special types of preferences could represent preferences for the following goods? Justify your answer.*

    a. bicycle seats, bicycle handle bars
    b. umbrellas and raincoat
    c. bread and pasta

Chapter Review Questions

1. Basket A consists of 5 units of X and 3 units of Y. Basket B consists of 10 units of X and 0 of Y. Basket C consists of 5 units of X and 1 unit of Y. You prefer X to Y and like more rather than less of each good. Write a preference ordering for these three baskets. Are the preferences transitive and is more better?

Answer:

A possible ordering would be: A is preferable to B, C is preferable to A, and C is preferable to B. This ordering is transitive since C preferable to A and A preferable to B implies C preferable to B. However this ordering violates the assumption that "more is better": since A includes more Y and as much X as C, A should be preferable to C.

2. $U = x+y^2+z$. What do the indifference curves between x and z look like? What do the indifference curves between x and y look like?

Answer:

An indifference curve between x and z will be drawn for a given amount of y defined as y_0 and a given level of utility U_0. The equation of such a curve is $U_0 = x + y_0^2 + z$ or $z = (U_0 - y_0^2) - x$. It is drawn on the graph below.

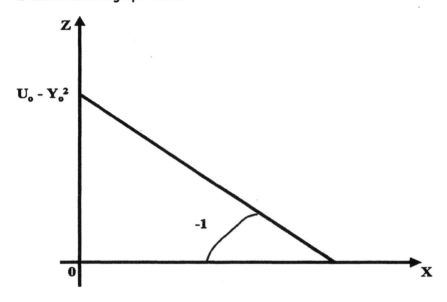

Similarly, an indifference curve between x and y will be drawn for a given level of z defined as z_0 and a given level of utility U_0. The equation of such a curve is $U_0 = x + y^2 + z_0$ or $y = [U_0 - z_0 - x]^{1/2}$. It is drawn on the graph below.

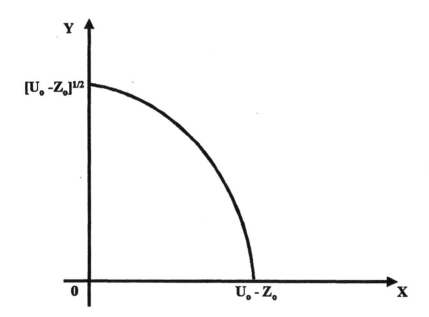

3. $U = \min(x,y)$. What is the marginal utility of x? What is the marginal utility of y? Is marginal utility decreasing in x or y?

Answer:

Suppose that $y = y_0$. For $x < y_0$ we have $U = x$ so that the marginal utility of x is 1. For $x \geq y_0$, however, we have $U = y_0$ so that the marginal utility of x is zero. Intuitively, the consumer only likes more of the two goods if she can get them in a proportion of 1 to 1. In other words she only care about *pairs* of x and y. If there is already more of x than of y, larger quantities of x do not increase the number of pairs available to the consumers and, therefore, do not increase her satisfaction. The marginal utility of x is constant for all x smaller than y. At $x = y_0$, the marginal utility of x suddenly decreases to zero and stays there for all $x > y_0$:

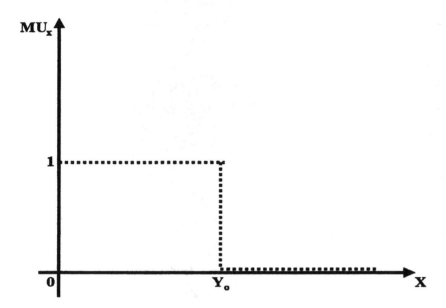

Problem Set

1. Draw indifference curves (over baseball and football) to represent the following descriptions of consumer preferences:

   a. I don't care whether I watch football or baseball: I just like to watch sports.

   b. I only watch football: baseball is boring.

   c. I don't like to watch football: it is too violent. I don't like to watch baseball either: it is too dull.

   d. I like to watch a little football and a little baseball more than a lot of either: while I like sports, I enjoy variety as well.

e. My friend and I only like to watch sports together, but since I like football and he likes baseball, we always watch equal amounts of each.

f. I like watching baseball and football, although I enjoy baseball somewhat more than football. Unfortunately, after an hour of watching TV, my eyes get tired and I don't enjoy it anymore.

2. Eva likes to take medicine when she is sick since it makes her feel better; however, she tells her doctor that she does not care whether she gets a prescription for generic or brand name drugs since they both contain the same amount of the important active ingredients. For Eva, prescription and brand name drugs are:

   a. perfect substitutes

   b. perfect complements

3. On Saturday, Jane and Michael go to a seaside restaurant called The Salty Dog. Jane orders fish. The next evening, Michael makes dinner for Jane at his apartment in the city. He would like to prepare a meal that Jane enjoys. Should he prepare fish? Why or why not?

4. Which of the following represents the same preferences as $U = xy$?

   a. $U = x^4 y^4$

   b. $U = \ln x + \ln y$

   c. $U = 100 - xy$

   d. $U = 25x + xy$

   e. $U = xy - 100$

5. Jane's utility function over cake and fruit salad is $U = F + C$ (where F is measured in cups of fruit salad and C is measured in pieces of cake). Michael's utility function is $U = 5(F + C)$. Who likes fruit salad more?

6. Suppose that $U = x^2 y^3$. For this function, $MU_x = 2xy^3$ and $MU_y = 3x^2 y^2$.

   a. Is marginal utility decreasing?

   b. Is the marginal rate of substitution between x and y decreasing?

   c. Draw indifference curves for this utility function. What properties do the underlying preferences obey?

7. Refer to the list of four "special forms" of utility in the summary. Which form(s) would best describe the following pairs of goods? Why?

   a. mittens and gloves

   b. different brands of white paper

   c. left and right gloves

8. Questionnaires indicate that absolute income and life satisfaction are related as follows in Europe:

GNP per capita	"Satisfaction" score
< $2000	5.5
$2000-$4000	6.6
$4000-$8000	7.0
$8000-$16,000	7.4

   (Taken from Hirshleifer, J. and D. Hirshleifer, <u>Price Theory and Applications</u>. Sixth Edition. Prentice Hall: Upper Saddle River, NJ. 1998.)

   Graph the marginal utility of income. Is it diminishing?

Exam *(60 minutes: Closed book, closed notes)*

1. Let us consider a "map" where North is on the vertical axis and East is on the horizontal axis. The origin represents the center of town. The university campus is located at a point corresponding to 2 miles north of the origin and three miles east. Draw indifference curves representing students' preferences for the location for the following cases:

   a. Students want to live as close to the campus as possible

   b. There is a straight road joining the campus to the center of town. Students prefer to live along this road, irrespective of the relative distance from the town and the campus. If they cannot live on this road, they want to live as close to it as possible.

   c. There is a straight road between the center of town and the campus. This road is served by a bus that stops at either end of the road as well as halfway between town and campus. The students' only concern is to be as close as possible to one of these three stops

2. What assumptions guarantee that indifference curves have the following "standard" shape, where the axes in the diagram measure the quantities of Y and X consumed? Interpret each of these assumptions, stating what its implications are for the shape of the indifference curves and commenting on how realistic you think each assumption is in practice.

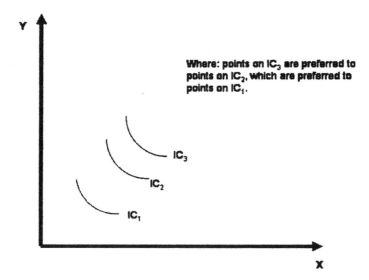

Now, suppose that indifference curves for the individual are as pictured below in the diagram. Which of your assumptions in (a) are satisfied for these curves and which are violated? Interpret the shape of the indifference curves, commenting on how realistic this type might be in practice.

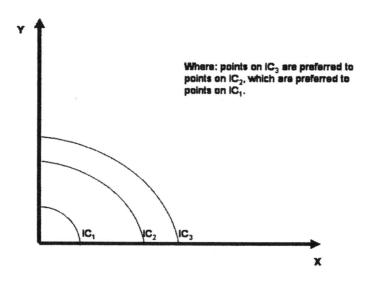

3. Suppose that U = 2x + 5y + xy and MU$_x$ = 2+y while MU$_y$ = 5+x.

   a. Is marginal utility constant, diminishing, or increasing?

   b. Is the marginal rate of substitution between x and y increasing, constant, or decreasing?

   c. Draw indifference curves for this utility function. What are the properties of the preferences that underlie this utility function?

4. It is observed that some people give to charity and some do not. Let us examine this by graphing George Banks' indifference curves over his own income and the income of Joe Lowly in the following cases:

   a. George Banks likes more money for himself. He does not care what Joe Lowly's income is.

   b. George Banks likes more money for himself; however, he also likes more money for people who are poorer than himself.

   c. George Banks is a complete egalitarian: he likes more money for himself or others only if total income is equally shared.

   Now, suppose that George Banks' income is $1000 and Joe Lowly's income is $0. In each of the three cases that you just graphed, would George Banks give charity to Joe Lowly?

Answers to Exercises

1. The correct answer is a, b, and c. Ted 's preferences are complete since we know how he would rank any two of the four possible baskets. Ted 's preferences are also transitive. Since he prefers A to B and B to C, transitivity requires that he also prefers A to C, which is the case. Since he prefers C to D, he should also prefer A to D, which is the case. Since he prefers B to C and C to D, he should also prefer B to D, which is true. Finally, Ted 's preference do not violate the assumption of monotonicity: A contains the same amount of X as B but more of Y. Hence monotonicity requires that A be preferable to B, which is the case.

2. Ted 's preferences now violate the assumption of monotonicity since there is the same amount of X in A and B and A contains more of Y. Ted 's preferences are still complete and transitive.

3. (a). These preferences violate the assumption of monotonicity. To see this, start from point A and move horizontally to the right. You are increasing the amount of X consumed and keeping the amount of Y constant, but you move from a utility level of 10 to a utility level of 8. These preferences also fail to reflect a taste for variety: point D corresponds to a lower level of satisfaction than either B or C.

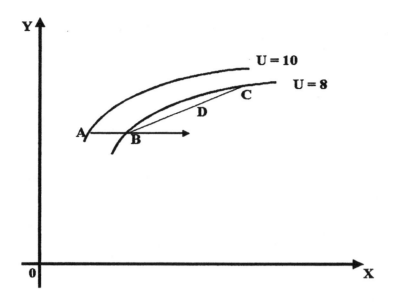

(b). These preferences fail to satisfy the assumption of monotonicity since some points located on the northeast segment of the outer indifference curve yield lower levels of utility than points on the inner curve that contain less of both goods.

(c). These preferences are not complete. There are "holes" in the difference curves. We do not know how baskets of goods corresponding to these holes would be ranked by the consumer.

(d). These preferences violate the assumption of *strict* monotonicity since getting more of X leaves the level of utility of the consumer unchanged.

4. The correct answer is (a). The marginal rate of substitution between food and clothing is the slope of the indifference curve. Since the indifference curves are linear, they have the same slope everywhere. One can then compute the slope as the ratio of the vertical intercept over the horizontal intercept, that is, as MRS $= 5/5 = 6.5/6.5 = 1$.

5. The correct answer is (c), that is, the MRS between food and clothing is undefined since the slope of the indifference curve at A is undefined.

6. The correct answer is (a). The preferences are complete: since each of the three possible bundles is assigned a utility number we can rank any two bundles. Since the ranking of the "utility" number is itself transitive (i.e., $6 > 5$ and $5 > 4$ implies $6 > 4$) the underlying preferences are transitive. Since no bundle has "as much or more" of x and y than any other bundle, we do not know whether the preferences are monotonic. On the other hand, we know that averages are *not* preferable to extremes. Bundles A and C are on the same indifference curve since they are associated with the same level of utility. Bundle B is the exact average of bundles A and C, but corresponds to a lower level of utility.

7. a. The correct answer is (ii): increasing x by one increases U by one.

b. The correct answer is (i): increasing y by one increases U by 10.
c. The correct answer is (iii). The marginal utilities of x and y remain 1 and 10, irrespective of the initial levels of x and y. They are therefore constant.
d. The correct answer is (iii). The MRS is equal to the ratio between the marginal utility of x and the marginal utility of y, that is, to 1/10.

8. a. For most bikers, these are perfect complements as the two goods are only needed in proportions of one to one.
    b. To the extent that umbrellas and raincoats protect equally well from the rain, they would be perfect substitutes and the indifference curves representing the preferences between the two would be straight lines. On the other hand, some people like to wear a raincoat to protect their bodies and use an umbrella to protect their faces. For such people, the two goods would be perfect complements to be used in a proportion of one to one.
    c. Most people think of bread and pasta as alternative sources of starch but do not consider them perfect substitutes. A Cobb Douglas utility function might therefore be appropriate.

Answers to Problem Set

1.

a. This means that football and baseball are perfect substitutes, that is, that consumer satisfaction depends on the total quantity of sports watched, not on which specific sport is being watched.

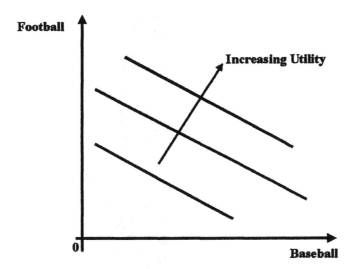

b. This means that the consumer's utility only increases when the amount of football watched increases. The amount of baseball watched is irrelevant. Hence indifference curves are parallel to the baseball axis.

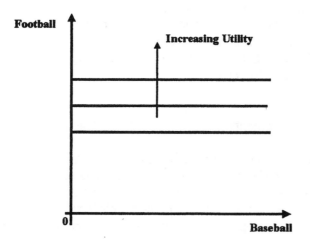

c. The consumer actively dislikes watching either baseball or football. This means that indifference curves must be downward sloping: if the consumer is forced to watch more baseball, she needs to watch less football to remain at the same level of satisfaction. Satisfaction increases as one moves to the southwest, that is, as the consumer watches less of both sports. We do not have enough information to say whether the indifference curves are linear, convex, or concave toward the origin.

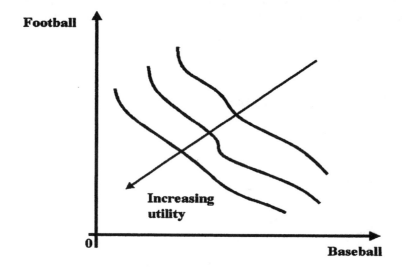

d. This is the "traditional" type of preferences where the consumer likes both goods but also likes variety. Such tastes are represented by downward sloping indifference curves bowed out toward the origin.

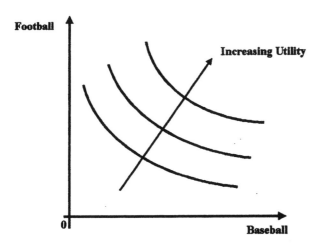

e. The two programs are only watched in a proportion of one to one. The indifference curves are right-angled with the angle lying on a ray of slope 1 going through the origin.

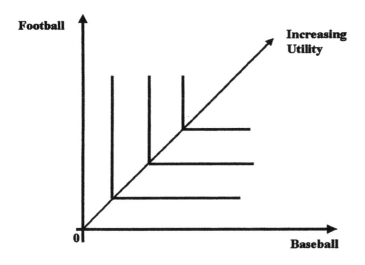

f. Both baseball and football are "goods" so that indifference curves are downward sloping. The relative preference for baseball means that the indifference curves are somewhat "vertical". The downward sloping line represents the combinations of football and baseball that add up to one hour of TV. Let us assume that watching more TV would actually hurt the consumer quite drastically and that the pain would be the same irrespective of the mix of sports watched. Then, our downward sloping indifference curves stop at the "one hour" line. Beyond this line, satisfaction decreases as the number of hours spent in front of the TV increase. This is represented by a set of straight downward sloping lines with utility decreasing as one moves to the northeast. (Arrows in the figure below represent direction of increasing utility.)

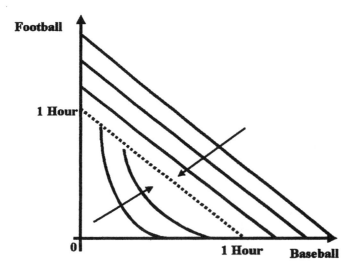

2. The goods are perfect substitutes since Eva is indifferent between any combination of generic and brand name drugs providing the same amount of the active ingredients.

3. By ordering fish, Jane has revealed that it is a type of food that she likes. On the other hand, she might have a "preference for variety" so that she might not enjoy having fish two nights in a row.

4. These utility functions represent the same preferences as $U = xy$ if they can be obtained as an increasing transformation of $U = xy$. This is because an increasing transformation will leave the ranking of any pair of bundles unchanged. $U = x^4y^4$ is obtained by taking the fourth power of xy, which is an increasing transformation. $U = \ln x + \ln y$ is obtained by taking the logarithm of $U = xy$. Since logarithm is an increasing function, the two utility functions represent the same preferences. On the other hand, $U = 25x + xy$ does not represent the same preferences as $U = xy$. To verify this, notice that $U = xy$ would rank (3,6) ahead of (4,3) while $U = 25x + xy$ would yield the reverse ranking with utility levels equal to 93 and 112 respectively. The remaining two versions look similar, but are quite different. $U = xy - 100$ simply changes utility by a constant and so does not change the ranking of bundles at all. It represents the same preferences. $U = 100 - xy$ reverses the preference ordering, and so does not capture the same preferences as the original function.

5. Since $U = 5(F+C)$ is an increasing transformation of $U = (F+C)$, these two utility functions represent *identical* underlying preferences.

6.

    a. No. $MU_x = 2xy^3$ is an increasing function of x and $MU_y = 3x^2y^2$ is an increasing function of y.

    b. The marginal rate of substitution is equal to $MU_x/MU_y = 2y/x$, which decreases as one "moves down" a given indifference curve (i.e., as x increases and y decreases).

    c. The underlying preferences are complete since $U = x^2y^3$ assigns a level of utility to any possible combination of x and y. Since the ranking of numbers is transitive, the preferences are also transitive. Increasing marginal utilities mean that preferences are monotone (i.e., "more is better"). Finally, the indifference curves are convex toward the origin so that the preferences display a taste for variety.

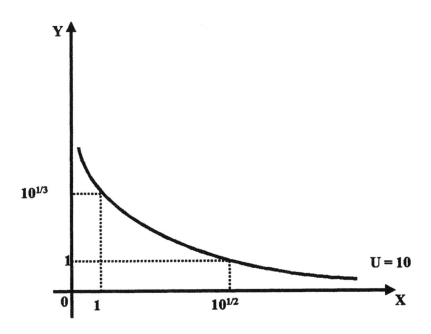

7.

a. Gloves and mittens are substitutes, but not perfect ones. Such preferences could be represented by a Cobb-Douglas utility function.

b. Certainly, many people care little for the brand of white paper they buy. In this case, the two goods would be perfect substitutes and would be captured by a linear utility function.

c. Most people use gloves in a fixed proportion: one to one. Hence, they are represented by L-shaped indifference curves and are perfect complements.

8. The marginal utility of income is the ratio between the increase in the "satisfaction score" and the increase in income. We will assume that each income class is represented by its average. We will assume further that satisfaction with zero income is zero. We have:

GNP Per Capita	Satisfaction	Marginal Satisfaction (ΔSatisfaction/ΔGNP) x 1,000
$ 1,000	5.3	5.3
$ 3,000	6.6	0.65
$ 6,000	7.0	0.13
$ 12,000	7.4	0.07

Hence the marginal utility of income is indeed decreasing. The corresponding graph is:

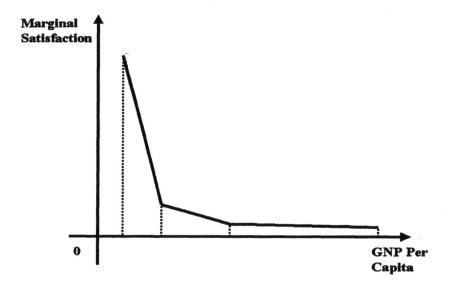

Answers to Exam

1.

a. This means that an indifference curve is the set of points that are equidistant from campus, that is, a circle with the campus at this center. Inner circles correspond to higher level of satisfactions than outer circles.

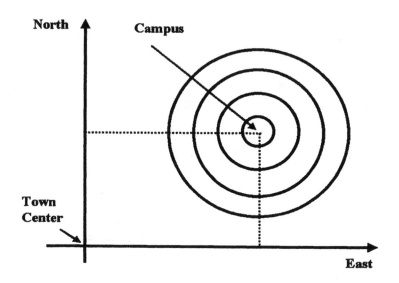

b. The preferable locations are all the points on the straight road between town and campus. This is one indifference curve. Other indifference curves are comprised of all points that are at an equal distance from the road. These points form line segments parallel to the road.

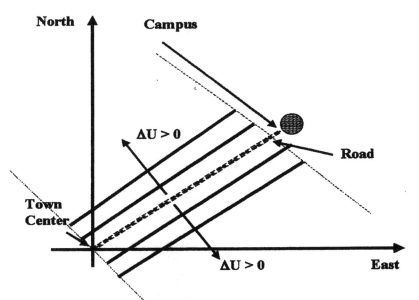

c. The set of points equidistant from any of the three possible bus stops is a circle around this stop. Hence each point in the graph lies on three circles: one centered around the first stop, another one centered around the second stop, and a third one centered around the third stop. For each point we choose the circle with the smallest diameter.

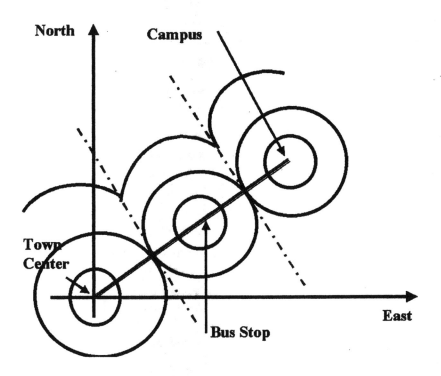

2. Both cases conform to completeness, monotonicity, and transitivity. The definitions of these concepts and discussion are in the text. Finally, one could interpret the first case as a preference for variety and the second as a preference for "lack of variety" ("specialization"). In many cases, the first would be more reasonable, as for most goods people do prefer some degree of variety. For some individuals or certain goods this may not be the case, however. For example, some people prefer to allocate all their time to certain activities at work ("I only like to do research" or "I only like to teach") rather than have a mix, while others prefer a broad variety of responsibilities.

3.

a. MU_x is increasing in y, and MU_y is increasing in x.

b. $MRS = MU_x/MU_y = (2+y)/(5+x)$. For a given y, this decreases in x and for a given x, it increases in y.

c. Using (a) and (b), the underlying preferences are complete, transitive, and monotonic with averages preferable to extremes.

4.

a.

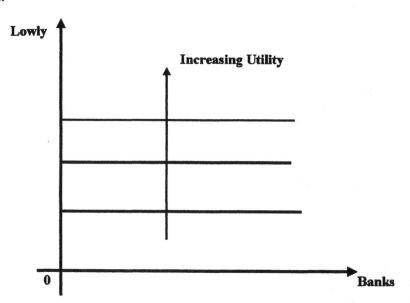

b. This means that the two income levels are (imperfect) substitutes as long as Banks has a higher income than Lowly, i.e., above the 45 degree line. Below that line, Banks, again, only cares about his own income level.

b. This means that the two income levels are (imperfect) substitutes as long as Banks has a higher income than Lowly, i.e., above the 45 degree line. Below that line, Banks, again, only cares about his own income level.

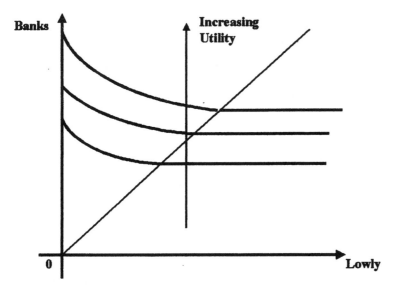

c. Higher income levels are more satisfying to Banks only if both income levels are equal. This means that the two income levels are perfect complements and must be "consumed" in equal proportions.

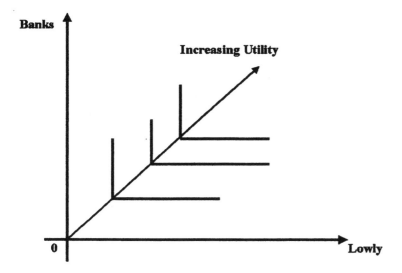

Chapter 4: Consumer Choice

In Chapter 3, we developed tools to describe consumer preferences. Consumer preferences tell us whether a consumer likes one particular basket of goods better than another without considering whether the consumer can actually afford either of these two bundles. However, since consumers have limited resources with which to make their purchases and since goods are costly, consumer preferences alone cannot explain why consumers make the consumption choices that they do. Instead, we must study how consumer choice depends not only on preferences, but also on income constraints and the prices of goods and services.   We will do this in **two steps**. First, we will analyze the constraints on consumption due to consumers' limited budgets. Second, we will combine these constraints with our earlier description of preferences to determine how consumption choices will be made.

Let us return to the example of Chapter 3 where food and housing are the only goods available for consumption. Further, let the price of a "unit" of food be P_f and the price of a "unit" of housing be P_h. For any consumption basket that includes f units of food and h units of housing, the total expenditure required to buy this basket would be:

$$E = P_f f + P_h h$$

In order for the basket to be affordable, this expenditure cannot exceed the income of the consumer. Call this income I. Then this basket is affordable if:

$$E = P_f f + P_h h \leq I$$

The above inequality is the consumer 's **budget constraint**. This constraint determines the consumer's **budget set**, that is, the set of baskets that are affordable. The **budget line** is the set of baskets that are just affordable, that is, the set of baskets that could be purchased if the consumer expended *all* of his income. Mathematically, the budget line is the set of baskets for which the inequality above becomes an equality:

$$P_f f + P_h h = I$$

We can plot the budget line on a graph, such as Figure 4.1, with food on the vertical axis and housing on the horizontal axis by rearranging the equation for the budget line so that we have f on the left-hand side:

$$f = I/P_f - (P_h/P_f)h$$

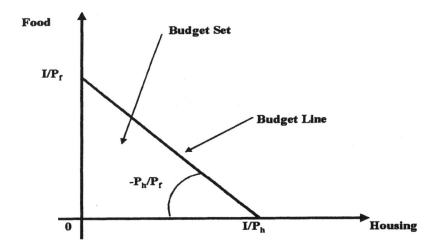

Figure 4.1

If the consumer spent all his income on food, he could buy I/P_f units of food. This is the vertical intercept of the budget line. If the consumer were to spend all his income on housing, he could buy I/P_h units of housing. This is the horizontal intercept of the budget line. By buying one less unit of housing, the consumer saves an amount of income equal to P_h that can be used to buy P_h/P_f additional units of food. This means that the slope of the budget line is equal to $-(P_h/P_f)$. In the language of Chapter 1, the true *economic* cost of consuming housing is, in fact, the loss of the opportunity to consume food. The slope of the budget line measures the magnitude of this **opportunity cost** of consuming housing.

Exercise 1: *Suppose that the consumer's income is $10, which she may split between goods x and y. The price of good x is $1 per unit and the price of good y is $2 per unit. Draw the budget line with x on the horizontal axis and y on the vertical axis.*

   a. What is the slope of the budget line?

      i.   −2
      ii.   −1/2
      iii.   ½
      iv.   2

   b. What is the vertical intercept of the budget line?

      i.   10
      ii.   5
      iii.   2

   c. What is the opportunity cost of x in terms of y?

      i.   1
      ii.   2
      iii.   ½

The position of the budget line depends on the level of income and on the price of both goods. If income changes, the vertical and horizontal intercepts change but the slope of the line remains the same since the prices are still the same. Hence a change in the level of income **shifts the budget line up or down** in a parallel fashion. For example, as income rises, the vertical intercept increases and the set of affordable baskets grows. In other words, the consumer's **purchasing power** increases. If income falls, the vertical intercept falls and the budget line shifts in. The set of affordable baskets, then, shrinks.

A change in the *relative* price of housing, P_h/P_f, changes the slope of the budget line. An increase in the relative price of housing makes the budget line steeper while a decrease makes the budget line flatter. The effect of a price change on the vertical and horizontal intercepts of the budget line depends on the specific change considered. An increase in the price of food reduces the vertical intercept since, for a given income I, a consumer spending all of her income on food could now buy fewer units. Similarly, an increase in the price of housing would reduce the value of the horizontal intercept. Hence, changes in the relative price of the two goods affect both the slope and the intercept(s) of the budget line. Suppose, for example, that the price of food increases while the price of housing stays the same. The budget line becomes flatter as P_h/P_f has decreased and the vertical intercept decreases since fewer units of food can be purchased with the whole income I. On the other hand, the horizontal intercept is unchanged: since the price of housing and the level of income have not changed, the number of units of housing that can be bought with the whole income has not changed either. This means that an increase in P_f with no change in either P_h or I, *rotates* the budget line inward around its horizontal intercept (see Figure 4.2, below) so that the budget set of the consumer shrinks. As a second example, suppose that the price of housing decreases while both P_f and I remain unchanged. The slope of the budget line becomes flatter as P_h/P_f decreases. The horizontal intercept increases since more units of housing can now be obtained by using the whole income I. On the other hand, the vertical intercept is not affected since both I and P_f have not changed. This means that the budget constraint *rotates* outward around its vertical intercept so that the budget set of the consumer expands.

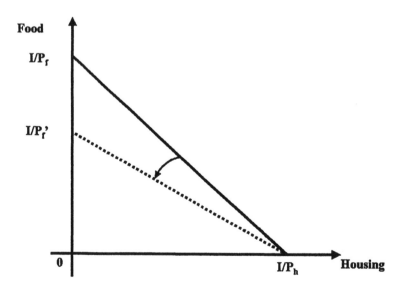

Figure 4.2

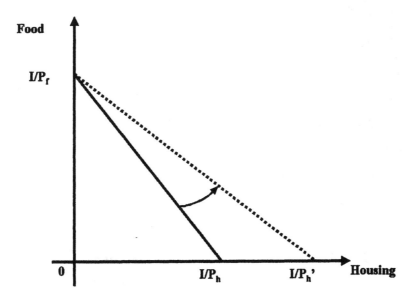

Figure 4.3

Exercise 2: *Plot the budget line of Exercise 1 on a new graph. Now, let income rise to $12, the price of x rise to $2, and the price of y rise to $3. Graph the budget line with these new prices and income. Which of the following statements is true?*

a. The budget line has shifted out
b. Purchasing power has decreased
c. The slope of the budget line has decreased
d. The opportunity cost of x in terms of y has fallen

Are Two Goods Enough?

Before continuing with our analysis of consumer choice, notice that our restriction to two goods may not be as limiting as it initially appears. While consumers typically purchase many goods and services so that their budgeting problem is very complex, we often are interested in the consumer's purchases of a *particular* good. In this case, we can simplify the consumer's choice problem to a decision of how much of the good in question to consume compared to the quantity of expenditures on *all* other goods. We can lump all these other goods into a single **composite good** that represents the collective expenditures on all other goods and place the composite good on one axis, while the good we are interested in analyzing can be placed on the other axis. One convenient way to think of this composite good is that it is simply the money that the consumer can use to spend on other goods. Using this interpretation, the price of the composite good is 1 (since, for example, the "price" of a dollar is simply a dollar). We can, then, rewrite the budget constraint as follows where "c" is the quantity of the composite good and the price of "c" is 1:

$$P_f f + c <= I$$

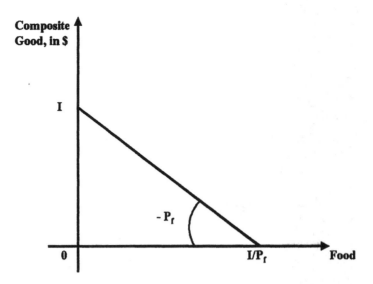

Figure 4.4

The economic model of consumer choice is that a consumer chooses a basket of goods that maximizes her satisfaction while remaining affordable. In other words, a consumer chooses the most preferable basket that lies in her budget set. Graphically then, the consumer chooses the basket within her budget set that lies on the "highest possible" indifference curve. Since the basket must be affordable it must lie on or below the budget line. In fact, because of the assumption of monotonicity (i.e., "more is better") we already know that the best basket that can be chosen by the consumer *must* lie *exactly on* the budget line. If it were to lie anywhere else (e.g., A on Figure 4.5 below) we could always find another bundle (e.g., B) containing at least as much of both goods and strictly more of at least one good. That bundle would provide a higher level of satisfaction to the consumer.

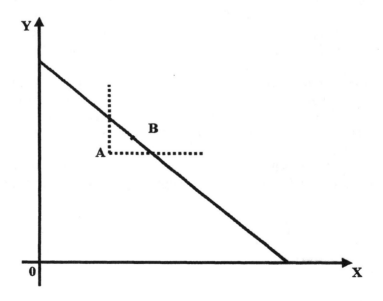

Figure 4.5

The best basket that the consumer can afford is, therefore, the basket on her budget line that lies on the highest possible indifference curve. Two cases can arise. In the first graph in Figure 4.6, the consumer would choose basket A that lies on an indifference curve that is tangent to the budget line at that point. In this case the consumer purchases positive quantities of both goods. We say that she chooses an **interior solution**. In the second graph in Figure 4.6, the highest possible indifference curve still touching the budget line touches it *at a corner*, that is, at a point where the consumer only consumes positive amounts of one of the two goods. We refer to such a situation as a **corner solution**.

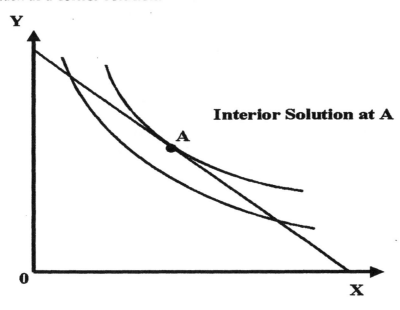

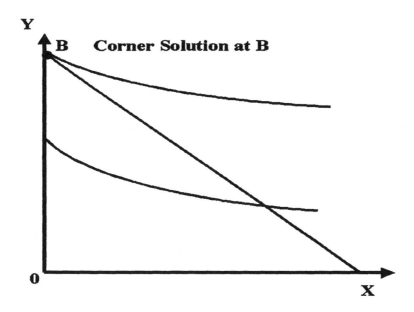

Figure 4.6

At the point of tangency, the slope of the indifference curve and the slope of the budget line must be equal by the definition of tangency. Recalling that the slope of the indifference curve is the (negative of the) marginal rate of substitution, then, we have the following condition for optimal consumer choice in an interior solution:

$$MRS_{f,h} = P_f/P_h$$

In words, at the equilibrium, the rate at which the *consumer* would be willing to exchange food for housing is just equal to the rate at which food and housing are exchanged in the *marketplace* at the optimal basket. To see why this must hold, suppose that this were not the case so that, for example, the marginal rate of substitution was ½ but the price ratio was 1. Here, the *consumer* is willing to "pay" two units of housing in order to obtain one unit of food, but the *market* is willing to let her get the unit of food in exchange for only one unit of housing. This means that the consumer could obtain higher utility by performing such an exchange since she values food much more highly than the market. Therefore, since she is willing to make such a move, the original consumption basket could not have been optimal. Graphically, if this "equal slope" condition were not to hold at point A, A could not be the consumer's best choice: the indifference curves would have to cross the budget line so that other points on the budget line (such as B in Figure 4.7, below) would be preferable.

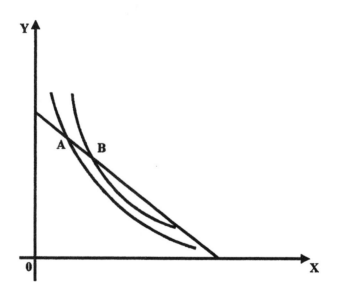

Figure 4.7

Exercise 3: *Suppose that utility is U(f,h) = fh, with marginal utilities $MU_f = h$ and $MU_h = f$. The consumer's income is I = 1000, and prices are $P_f = 50$ and $P_h = 200$. Let basket A contain f = 4 and h = 4.*

At basket A, the marginal rate of substitution between f and h is:

   a. $MRS_{f,h} = 4$
   b. $MRS_{f,h} = 1$
   c. $MRS_{f,h} = ¼$

The negative of the slope of the budget line, where f is on the vertical axis and h is on the horizontal axis is:

a. 4
b. 1
c. ¼

Graph a sample indifference curve for this consumer that passes through basket A. Plot the budget line on the same graph. Is basket A the optimal basket for the consumer to purchase?

a. yes
b. no
c. cannot say from the information given

We can also use the relation between marginal utility and the marginal rate of substitution that we described in Chapter 3 to rewrite this "equal slope" condition as:

$$MU_f/P_f = MU_h/P_h$$

This means that, at the optimal basket, each good gives equal "bang for the buck": the extra satisfaction obtained by spending one more unit of income is the same regardless of the good on which this extra income is spent. If this condition did not hold, then the consumer could reallocate his spending slightly to buy a bit less of the low marginal utility good and a bit more of the high marginal utility good and reach a higher total utility level. Therefore, the original basket could not have been optimal.

In order to solve for the precise basket which the consumer will choose in the "standard" case of an interior solution, we can use the facts that (1) the optimal basket must lie on the budget line and (2) the "equal slope" condition must hold. The budget constraint equation and the slope condition give us two equations, which we may use together to solve for the two "unknowns" that are the quantities consumed of the two goods in the basket.

Exercise 4: *A consumer purchases food and housing and has utility function $U(f,h) = (fh)^2$ with marginal utilities $MU_f = 2fh^2$ and $MU_h = 2f^2h$. Her income is $1000 per month. The price of food is $P_f = \$2$ per unit and the price of housing is $P_h = \$200$ per unit. What is her optimal consumption basket?*

a. f = 200, h = 2
b. f = 250, h = 2.5
c. f = 1, h = 100

If we are not in the standard case, so that the tangency condition does not hold, then we must check all along the budget line to find out where the optimal basket lies. Usually, the easiest way to do this is simply to determine which of the extremes of the budget line (i.e., the *corners*) corresponds to the highest level of satisfaction.

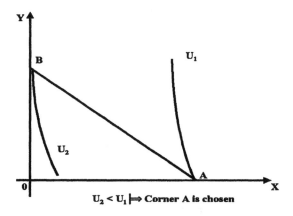

$U_2 < U_1 \Longmapsto$ **Corner A is chosen**

Figure 4.8

Exercise 5: *A consumer purchases food and housing and has utility function U(f,h) = min(f,h). Her income is 1000 and the prices of food and housing are P_f = 50 and P_h=200, respectively. What is her optimal consumption basket?*

   a. f = 4, h = 4
   b. f = 200, h = 50
   c. f = 50, h = 50

Exercise 6: *A consumer purchases food and housing and has utility function U(f,h) = f + h. Her income and the prices of food and housing are the same as in Exercise 5. What is her optimal consumption basket?*

   a. f = 20, h = 0
   b. f = 0, h = 20
   c. f = 4, h = 4

Let us look again at the top graph in Figure 4.6, showing an interior solution at A. At this point, the consumer attains the highest possible utility that can be reached on her budget line. This also implies that A must be *cheapest point* on its indifference curve. If it were not so, then another point on that same indifference curve, say B, would have to correspond to a lower level of expenditure, that is, would have to lie on a parallel line *below* the budget line. But then, one could find points on the budget line, such as C, which are on a higher indifference curve, and A could not have been the optimal choice of the consumer to start with. Intuitively, the difference between income and the expenditure at B could be used to buy a little more of both goods and reach a point preferable to B and, therefore, to A.

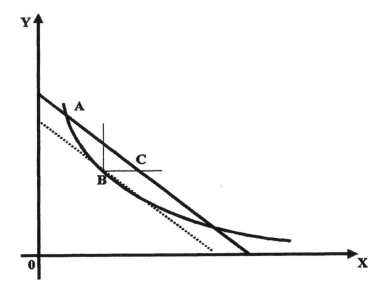

Figure 4.9

In other words, the consumer's optimal choice can be seen as the result of minimizing the expenditure required to attain a given level of satisfaction. In this approach, rather than moving to the highest indifference curve that still allows tangency with the fixed budget line, one moves to the lowest budget line that still allows tangency with a fixed indifference curve. This rephrasing of the problem is called the **expenditure minimization problem** and results in the same optimal basket as the utility maximization problem we have analyzed so far if utility is constrained to be at the optimal level of the utility maximization problem. For example, in Figure 4.10, below, if the given level of utility is constrained to be the same level as was attained in Figure 4.6, then the tangency point in Figure 4.10 will be the same as tangency point A in Figure 4.6. Since expenditure minimization looks at the same problem as utility maximization, only from "the other side", we say that it is the **dual** of the utility maximization problem.

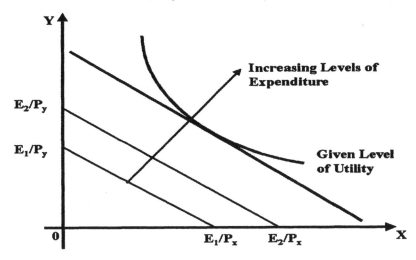

Figure 4.10

Exercise 7: *A consumer purchases food and housing and has utility function U(f,h) = fh. The marginal utility of food is $MU_f = h$ and the marginal utility of housing is $MU_h = f$. Income and* *prices are the same as in Exercise 5. The basket that maximizes utility given the consumer's budget constraint is:*

        a. f = 2.5   h = 10
        b. f = 2.5   h = 2.5
        c. f = 10   h = 2.5

The basket that minimizes expenditure necessary to obtain a utility level of U = 25 is:

        a. f = 2.5   h = 10
        b. f = 2.5   h = 2.5
        c. f = 10   h = 2.5

A Constrained Optimization Interpretation

    Consumer choice is an example of the constrained optimization problems you saw analyzed in Chapter 1. The utility maximization problem of the consumer is simply to choose the basket of goods that maximizes utility given a budget constraint that limits expenditures. In the notation of Chapter 1 we have:

$$\text{Max } U(f,h)$$
$$(f,h)$$

$$\text{subject to } P_f f + P_h h \leq I,$$

where the objective function is the utility function and the constraint is the budget constraint. The endogenous variables are the quantities of food and housing consumed and the exogenous variables are the two prices and income. For an interior optimum, the optimal basket is one where the consumer's money is allocated across the two products in such a way that the additional (or marginal) satisfaction from spending another small amount of money on food is just equal to the additional satisfaction from spending another small amount of money on housing, as the tangency condition suggests.

    If we examine the dual problem of expenditure minimization, we ask what basket the consumer should choose if she wishes to minimize the expenditure necessary to achieve a given level of utility, say U*. In other words, we have:

$$\text{Min } P_f f + P_h h$$
$$(f,h)$$

$$\text{subject to } U(f,h) \geq U^*$$

Here, the objective function is the expenditure of the consumer while the constraint is that the level of satisfaction be at least U*. The endogenous variables are the same as in the initial problem, while the exogenous variables are prices *and the fixed level of utility, U**. As before, the optimal basket at an interior optimum is one where the consumer's money is allocated such that the marginal satisfaction from all products is equalized.

    Until now, we have assumed that the preferences of the consumer were known. This often will not be the case, since preferences are not directly observable. We may, however, use information on observed consumer purchasing decisions to infer what preferences might be. Of course, if we are to use such information, we must assume that the preferences do not change while we are observing behavior. This is a reasonable assumption over short periods of time, but may be less reasonable over longer periods.

Suppose that we observe that, for a given income and for given prices, a consumer purchases basket A. We know that this basket must be preferable to all other baskets that lie on or below the consumer's budget line since these other baskets *were affordable but were not chosen*. In this sense, basket A is "revealed" to be preferable to all other affordable baskets. Further, if we assume that "more is better", then all baskets to the northeast of A must be preferable to A. We know, then, the area of indifference to A must lie to the northwest and/or to the southeast of A (in the shaded areas). Such **revealed preference** does not give us a precise idea of the indifference curve, but it starts to narrow down the possibilities to the shaded area on Figure 4.11, below. Indeed, given more observations on consumer choice, we could narrow down this region of indifference to something that looks like an indifference curve.

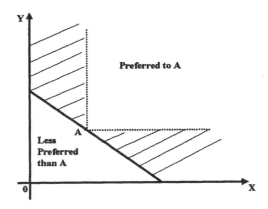

Figure 4.11

A second application of revealed preference is to test whether or not the consumer is actually maximizing utility. For example, suppose that basket A is bought when a set of prices, (P_f, P_h), prevails. If basket B does not cost more than A at these prices, and if the consumer is maximizing her utility, A must be preferable to B. Suppose, now, that prices change to new levels of (P'_f, P'_h) and we observe that basket B is bought at these new prices. Suppose further that A does not cost more than B at these new prices, that is, that A is also affordable. Then we could only conclude that either the preferences of the consumer have changed or the consumer failed to choose her utility maximizing basket in at least one of the two situations observed.

We can also perform such a test of utility maximization by graphically representing the budget lines and the chosen baskets (as in Exercise 8, below) or rewrite it mathematically by using the equations of the budget constraint:

$P_f f + P_h h \geq P_f f' + P_h h'$ says that A and B are affordable at the old prices. But this means that it must not be the case that:

$P'_f f' + P'_h h' \geq P'_f f + P'_h h$. In other words, it must not be the case that A would be affordable at the new prices as well, so that these equations can be used to test for utility maximization (as in Exercise 9 below).

Exercise 8: *A consumer chooses basket A when budget line is BL1 and chooses basket B when the budget line is BL2. Is this behavior consistent with our model of consumer choice (utility maximization subject to a budget constraint)?*

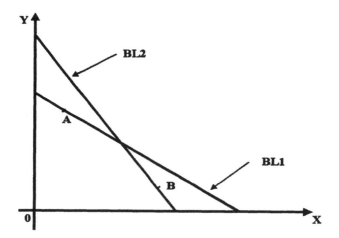

    a. yes
    b. no
    c. cannot tell from the information given

Exercise 9: *A consumer who purchases only food and housing chooses basket A with 100 units of food and 2 units of housing when the price of food is $1 per unit and the price of housing is $200 per unit. When the prices of food and housing change to $2 for food and $100 per unit of housing, the consumer purchases basket B with 50 units of food and 4 units of housing. Is this behavior consistent with our model of consumer choice?*

    a. yes
    b. no
    c. cannot tell from the information given

Chapter Review Questions

1. Illustrate the budget constraint for each case below. For each case, write down relative prices (slope); the maximum amount of X that can be purchased, and the maximum amount of Y that can be purchased.

    a. $P_x = 1$, $P_y = 2$, Income = 50

    b. $P_x = 1$, $P_y = 2$, Income = 80

    c. $P_x = 2$, $P_y = 1$, Income = 50

    d. $P_x = 1$ for the first two units, then $P_x = 0.5$ for each extra unit over 2, , $P_y = 2$, Income = 50

Answer:

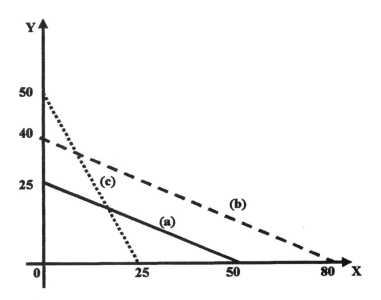

a. The slope is −1/2. The maximum amount of X that can be purchased is $50/P_x = 50$ and the maximum amount of Y that can be purchased is $50/P_y = 25$.

b. The slope is still −1/2. The maximum amount of X that can be purchased is $80/1 = 80$ while the maximum amount of Y that can be purchased is $80/2 = 40$.

c. The slope is −2. The maximum amount of X that can be purchased is $50/2 = 25$. The maximum amount of Y that can be purchased is $50/1 = 1$.

d. If the consumer spends his whole income on Y, he can get 25 units of Y. This gives us the vertical intercept of the budget line. If, on the other hand, he decides to spend everything on X, he can spend 2 to acquire the first two units and have 48 left over to purchase extra units of X at a unit price of 0.5. The consumer can therefore buy a total of 98 units of X. This gives us the horizontal intercept of the budget line. If the consumer buys 2 units of X at a unit price of 1, he has 50-2 = 48 left to spend on Y so that he can buy 24 units of Y. Between the point (0,25) and (2,24) the slope of the budget constraint is −1/2. Between (2,24) and (98,0), the slope is −0.5/2 = −1/4.

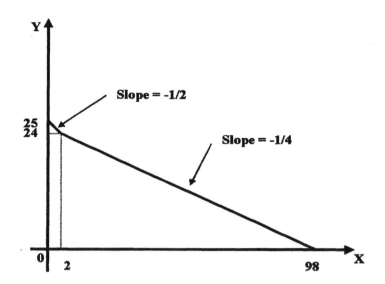

2.

   a. At current consumption levels, Joe's marginal utility from beer is 5 and his marginal utility from Coke is 4. The price of a can of beer is $2 and the price of a can of Coke $1. Is Tony's consumption choice at an "interior" optimum? Explain. If Joe could, would he want to trade beer for Coke, Coke for beer, or stay at the current consumption point?

   b. Suppose that beer and Coke cost the same as they did in part (a). Could Joe be consuming optimally if, for Joe, beer and Coke are perfect substitutes with a marginal rate of substitution constant at 2? If beer and Coke are perfect substitutes for Joe, what mix of beer and Coke would you expect to be consumed?

Answer:

   a. At an interior solution, the slope of the indifference curve must be equal to the slope of the budget line, that is, $MU_{Coke}/MU_{beer} = P_{Coke}/P_{beer}$. At the current levels of consumption and prices we have $MU_{Coke}/MU_{beer} = 4/5 > 1/2 = P_{Coke}/P_{beer}$ so that we cannot be at an interior equilibrium. Joe would benefit from trading beer for Coke. Drinking one less can of beer would decrease Joe's utility by 5 but it would also allow him to buy two more cans of Coke, which would increase his utility by $2 \times 4 = 8$.

   b. Joe's preferences can be represented by linear indifference curves of slope 2. These are always steeper than the slope of the budget constraint (i.e., $1/2$) so that we cannot have an interior solution. Joe 's best choice is a corner solution where he only drinks Coke.

3.

   a. When prices are $(p_1, p_2) = (3, 2)$, a consumer demands $(x_1, x_2) = (0, 6)$ and when prices are $(q_1, q_2) = (2, 3)$, a consumer demands $(y_1, y_2) = (6, 0)$. Can you tell from this information which bundle (X or Y) is preferred by the consumer?

   b. Is the behavior of part (a) consistent with the model of utility maximizing behavior?

c. How would your answers to (a) and (b) change if the bundle consumed at prices (p_1, p_2) were $(x_1, x_2) = (4, 0)$ and the bundle consumed at prices (q_1, q_2) were $(y_1, y_2) = (1,4)$?

Answer:

a. At prices (3,2), the chosen basket X = (0,6) costs (3x0) + (2x6) = 12 while basket Y costs (3x6) + (2x0) = 18. Since Y could not be purchased for the same expenditure as X at these prices we cannot infer anything as to how the consumer would rank X and Y by order of preference. At prices (2,3), Y costs (2x6) + (3x0) = 12 while X costs (2x0) + (3x6) = 18. Again, the discarded basket is not affordable at these prices and we cannot conclude anything about the consumer's preference between X and Y.

b. Since only one of the two baskets is affordable for any of the two sets of prices, the fact that the consumer chose X in one case and Y in the other is not inconsistent with utility maximization.

c. At prices (3,2), the chosen basket X = (4,0) costs (3x4) + (2x0) = 12 while basket Y costs (3x1) + (2x4) = 11. Since Y could be purchased for less than X and is not, it must be the case that X is preferable to Y. At prices (2,3), Y costs (2x1) + (3x4) = 14 while X costs (2x4) + (3x0) = 8. Since X could be purchased for less than Y and is not, it must be the case that Y is preferable to X. Hence, Y is both shown to be preferable to X and not preferable to X. This is inconsistent with maximizing behavior.

Problem Set

1. Suppose that the following graph represents the optimal consumption bundle of a typical consumer, with an income of 80, facing prices of $P_x = 1$, $P_y = 1$ and with utility $U = xy$ (and marginal utility $MU_x = y$ and $MU_y = x$).

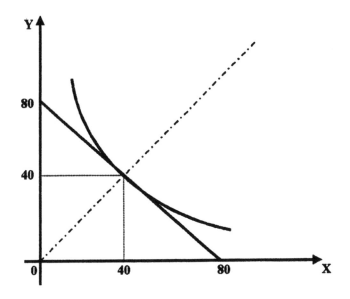

a. Now, let income remain fixed but let prices rise so that the new prices are $P_x = 2$, $P_y = 4$. Illustrate the new budget line and draw a sample indifference curve to show the new optimal bundle.

b. Let income be indexed to the cost of living so that the budget line shifts out just enough that the old bundle (at the original prices, above) is just affordable. In other words, let income increase to 240. Is the old bundle still the optimal choice at this new income level and at the new prices? Has utility increased above that of the original consumption bundle?

c. Suppose that prices are now $P_x = 2$, $P_y = 2$, and income has increased to 160 (so that both prices and income have exactly doubled over their original levels). Is the old bundle optimal now? Has utility increased above that of the original consumption bundle?

2. Let the budget constraint of a consumer be $P_x x + P_y y = I$.

a. Let a consumption tax of t per unit be placed on good x. Write the new budget constraint.

b. Let a subsidy of s% be placed on y. Write the new budget constraint.

c. Let a lump sum tax of t be applied to income. Write the new budget constraint.

3. A consumer has 10 kilos of raspberries and 20 kilos of strawberries. The price of raspberries is $4 per kilo and the price of strawberries is $1 per kilo. Raspberries and strawberries are the only two goods that can be consumed.

a. The consumer can buy or sell the raspberries and strawberries at market prices, write down the budget constraint of this consumer and draw the budget constraint on a graph.

b. Suppose that the price of strawberries increases to $2 per kilo. Draw and interpret the new budget constraint.

c. Assume that the tastes of the consumer can be represented as $U = min(R,S)$, where R is the quantity of raspberries consumed and S is the quantity of strawberries consumed. Is the consumer better off in (a) or (b)? What if his preferences are represented as $U = min(R, 3S)$?

4. Let an individual gain utility from two goods: good X and good Y. The individual's utility function is $U = XY$, where $MU_x = Y$ and $MU_y = X$. Let the individual's income, to be allocated across these two goods, be $24.

a. Suppose that the individual maximized utility by consuming equal quantities of X and Y. Carefully illustrate the consumer's optimal basket in an appropriate diagram, labeling intercepts, slopes and all other relevant items.

b. At the optimal basket, what must the expenditure on good X be?

c. Suppose that, at the optimal basket, the consumer purchases 12 units of X. What must be the prices of the two goods, and the units of good Y consumed? What is the level of utility at this point?

5. Answer both (a) and (b):

a. Kate has $100 today and will receive another $100 tomorrow. She can borrow or lend at a fixed interest rate of 10%. In this situation she chooses to borrow. First, illustrate this choice using an appropriate diagram. Now, suppose that the interest rate rises to 20%. By decomposing the effect of the rise in the interest rate into a substitution effect and an income effect, discuss whether Kate will now choose to borrow more or less than in the previous case. Is it possible that she will now choose to lend? Explain.

b. Pierre also has $100 today and will receive another $100 tomorrow. When the interest rate is 10%, he chooses neither to lend nor to borrow. Explain and illustrate whether he will choose to borrow or to lend when the interest rate rises to 20%.

6. Let income be $I = 80$, $P_x = 1$, $P_y = 3$, and utility $U = x + y$. Compute the optimal consumption bundle for the consumer. Now, suppose that the government is interested in increasing consumption of good y and is considering alternative programs for achieving this objective.

a. Let a subsidy of 1 per unit be introduced on good y. Compute the new optimal consumption bundle and illustrate the change on a graph. How effective has the subsidy been at increasing consumption of y? How costly has the program been to the government?

b. Now, instead of a subsidy a voucher is introduced: the consumer receives $10 that can be spent as the consumer wishes, but the relative prices of the two goods remain the same. Compute the new optimal consumption bundle and illustrate the change on a graph. How effective has the program been at increasing consumption of y? How costly has the program been?

c. Now, instead of the voucher, let a subsidy of 2.5 per unit be introduced on good y. Compute the new optimal consumption bundle. How effective has the program been at increasing the consumption of y? How costly has the program been?

d. Suppose that the government wishes to maintain some consumption of good y as well as some consumption of good x. How do the above subsidies and vouchers compare in their effects of the consumption of good y?

5. A consumer has an income of $10 that he may spend on two goods, x and y. Let price set 1 be ($p_x = \$1$ and $p_y = \$5$) and price set 2 be ($p_x = \$2$ and $p_y = \$4$). Call the budget line under price set 1 "BL1" and the budget line under price set 2 "BL2". Consider the following consumption baskets, where the units of x are listed first and the units of y consumed are listed second:

Case 1: Basket A = (3,1); Basket B = (5, 1); Basket C = (4, 1.2)

Case 2: Basket A = (3,1); Basket B = (5/3,5/3)

Case 3: Basket A = (1,2); Basket B = (5/3,5/3)

Case 4: Basket A = (1,2); Basket B = (5, 1)

    a. Illustrate the baskets of each case in a budget line diagram.

    b. Suppose that, in each case, when the budget line is BL2, the consumer selects basket A. When the budget line is BL1, the consumer selects basket B. What can be said about the way the consumer ranks baskets A and B according to his preferences in each case?

Exam *(60 minutes: Closed book, closed notes)*

1. Will a general rise in prices and income by the same percentage (say, all increase by 10%, for example) make consumers worse off, better off, or is the effect of such a change uncertain? Explain your answer.

2. Suppose that good x is offered with a quantity discount of 25% on the second 10 units purchased and 50% on all units purchased thereafter. The only other good consumed by the consumer is a composite good with a price of 1 for all units consumed. Draw the budget line that the consumer faces.

3. The government must decide how to provide child care to poor families. A child care program could provide a subsidy to lower the hourly rate that a poor family pays for day care. Alternatively, the government could provide an unrestricted lump-sum payment that could be spent on day care or on other goods (such as food and housing).

    a. Illustrate the choice that a consumer faces between hours of day care per day and all other goods consumed per day, as well as the bundle optimally chosen by the consumer.

    b. Consider the price subsidy. Illustrate and analyze how it would affect the consumer's consumption of day care and other goods. Suppose that we measure the value of the program to the consumer as the increase in the amount of other goods that the consumer can now afford along with a given amount of day care. Using this measure, illustrate and discuss the value of the program to the consumer.

    c. Now consider the lump sum payment. Assume that the cost for the government of the lump sum is the same as that for the subsidy of part (b), and makes the consumption point in (b) affordable. Illustrate the two policies on a graph. Which form of payment, subsidy or lump sum provides greater benefits to the recipients? Which increases the demand for day care services by a greater amount?

4. Suppose that, if a family is eligible for food stamps, it pays $100 per month for $200 worth of food. Let the price of food be $P_f = \$5$ per pound and the price of the other good consumed by the family (a composite good) is $P_c = \$3$ per unit. Draw the family's budget constraint on a graph, assuming that the family has an income of $300 per month. Now, draw the family's budget constraint if it does not participate in the food stamps program. Under what circumstances would the family be better off if it were given $100 per month in cash rather than the right to participate in the food stamps program?

Answers to Exercises

1.

   a. The correct answer is (ii.): The slope is given by $-p_x/p_y = -1/2$.

   b. The correct answer is (ii): If the consumer were to spend her whole income of $10 on good y, she could get $I/p_y = 10/2 = 5$ units of y.

   c. The correct answer is (iii): in order to purchase one more unit of x, the consumer needs an extra $1. This can only be obtained by consuming fewer units of y. Since the unit price of y is $2, an extra dollar can only be obtained by decreasing the consumption of y by ½ unit.

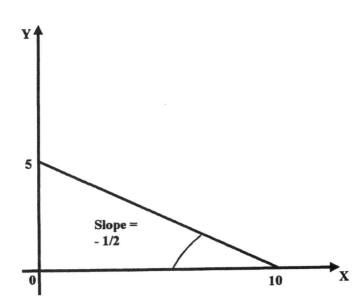

2. The vertical intercept is now $12/3 = 4$ instead of 5, while the horizontal intercept is $12/2 = 6$ instead of 10. We can therefore conclude that the budget line has shifted *in*, that is, (a.) is not correct but (b) is correct. The new slope of the budget line is $-p_x/p_y = -2/3$ so that the budget line has become steeper, that is, (c) is correct. The new slope also means that the opportunity cost of x in terms of y has increased from 1/2 to 2/3 so that (d) is not correct.

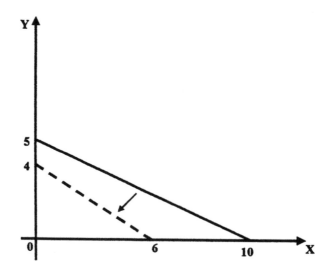

3.

    a. The marginal rate of substitution is $MU_f/MU_h = h/f = 4/4 = 1$, so (b) is correct.

    b. The negative of the slope of the budget line is $p_h/p_f = 200/50 = 4$, that is, (a) is correct.

    c. The correct answer is (b). At A, the MRS is smaller than the (negative of the) slope of the budget line. This means that the consumer could increase his satisfaction by reducing his consumption of housing in order to increase his consumption of food, that is, by moving from point A to a point such as the tangency in the graph below.

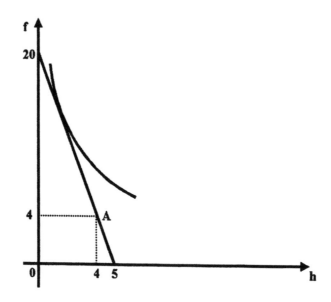

4. In order to be at an interior equilibrium, we need to have $MU_f/p_f = MU_h/p_h$, that is,

$$2fh^2/2 = 2f^2h/200 \Leftrightarrow 200h = 2f \Leftrightarrow f = 100h$$

The budget constraint of the consumer is:

$$1000 = 2f + 200h$$

Combining these two equations, we get $1000 = 200h + 200\,h$ so that $h = 2.5$ and $f = 250$. Hence the correct answer is (b).

5. The two goods are perfect complements, consumed in a proportion of 1 to 1. Hence we must have $f = h$. The budget constraint is $1000 = 50f + 200h$. With $f = h$, this constraint becomes $1000 = 250\,h$ so that $h = 4$ and $f = 4$. The correct answer is (a).

6. This time, the goods are perfect substitutes in the sense that the consumer is always indifferent between one unit of f and one unit of h. Utility will therefore be maximized by buying only the cheaper of the two goods. This is food and the consumer can purchase $1000/50 = 20$ units of it. The correct answer is (a). Graphically, we see that the highest possible indifference curve still touching the budget constraint occurs at the upper corner of the budget constraint because the (linear) indifference curves are always flatter than the budget constraint.

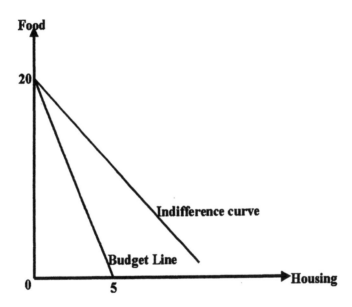

7. At an interior solution we have $MU_f/p_f = MU_h/p_h$ so that $h/50 = f/200$, or $f = 4h$. The budget constraint is $1000 = 50f + 200\,h = 200h + 200h = 400h$ so that $h = 2.5$ and $f = 10$, that is, the correct answer is (c). At this point, utility is $U = (2.5)(10) = 25$. Therefore, the combination of food and housing that minimizes the expense of reaching a utility of 25 is also given by $f = 10$ and $h = 2.5$. The correct answer is again (c).

8. No because both baskets were affordable under both either of the two budget lines. Hence the fact that A was chosen with budget line BL1 should reveal that A is preferable to B, while the fact that B was chosen with budget line BL2 should reveal that B is preferable to A. Such a contradiction could not arise if the consumer was behaving according to our model of consumer choice.

9. The correct answer is (a). At prices ($1,$200) basket A = (100,2) was chosen at a cost of $500 but basket B = (50,4) was not affordable since it would have cost $850. Hence the observed behavior of the consumer did not reveal anything as to his preference ranking of A and B. At prices ($2,$100), B was chosen at a cost of $500, while A would have cost $400. This reveals that B is indeed preferable to A. This is quite compatible with our model of consumer choice: B is preferable to A but A is chosen when B is not affordable.

Answers to Problems

1.

    a.

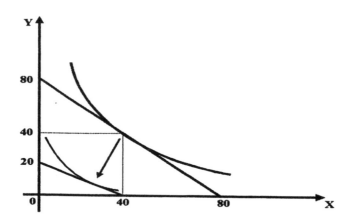

    a.   The new budget line is shown on the graph below. At the original equilibrium point, A, the budget constraint is now flatter than the indifference curve. This means that the consumer can *improve* her satisfaction by increasing her consumption of x and decreasing her consumption of y, that is, by moving to point B.

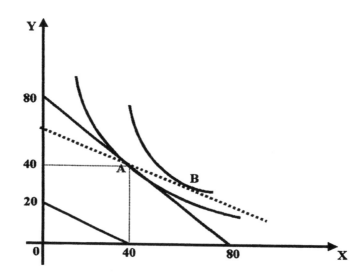

    b.   Since both prices and income have doubled, the budget set of the consumer is exactly the same as in (a). Since the consumer's preferences have not changed either, point A must again be optimal and the consumer's utility is not affected by the joint changes in prices and income.

2.

a. $(P_x + t) x + P_y y = I$

b. Now, purchasing one unit of y only costs $P_y(1-s)$, hence the budget constraint is $P_x x + P_y(1-s)y = I$.

c. The lump sum tax just decreases the amount of income available to spend on x and y. Hence the budget constraint is $P_x x + P_y y = I - t$

3.

a. The consumer can obtain income by selling his endowment of raspberries and strawberries to the tune of $\$4 \times 10 + \$1 \times 20 = \$60$. Hence, the budget constraint of a consumer who can trade these goods freely is $4R + 1S = 60$, where prices and income are measured in dollars, R is the quantity of raspberries and S is the quantity of strawberries.

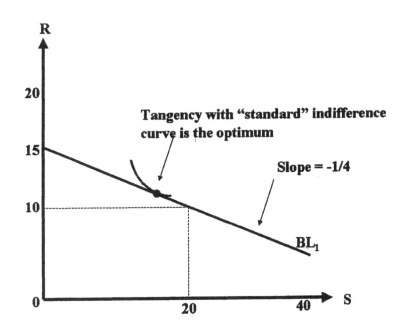

b. If the price of strawberries increases, then the slope of the budget line changes. On the other hand, the consumer always has the choice of not trading any of the goods and simply consuming his original endowment of 10 kilos of raspberries and 20 kilos of strawberries. Hence, the budget line must go through the original endowment point and must change slope as well. This boils down to saying that the budget constraint rotates around the endowment point. The consumer's purchasing power increases in terms of raspberries (in other words he can buy all the bundles he could before and can now buy some bundles he couldn't afford before.) This is because he is a net seller of strawberries, and so benefits from an increase in the price of strawberries. On the other hand, if she is to the right of the endowment point, she is a net buyer of strawberries, so the price rise reduces her purchasing power (Shifting the horizontal intercept in to 40 from its previous location of 60 units of strawberries). A graph representing the old and new budget lines is the following:

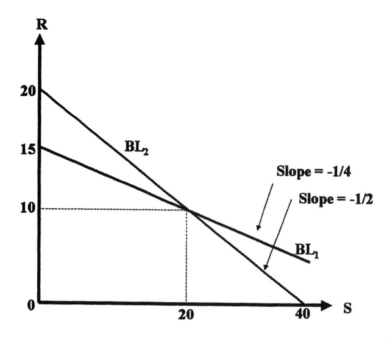

The equation of the new budget line is $4R + 2S = 80$.

c. The indifference curves are as shown below for the two cases. If the consumer has the first set of indifference curves, he is a net seller of strawberries and is made better off by the change. If the consumer has the second set of indifference curves, then he is made worse off by the change.

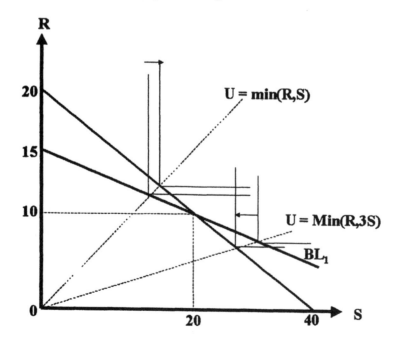

4.

a.

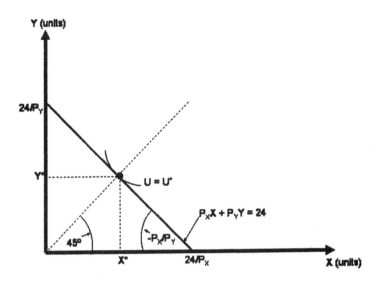

where X* and Y* are the amounts consumed of the two goods at the optimum, which is indicated with the dot. U* is the level of utility at the optimum.

b. We know that $MU_x/P_x = MU_y/P_y$ and $P_xX^* + P_yY^* = 24$ at the optimum. Also, $MU_x = Y$ and $MU_y = X$ so that we have $Y^*/P_x = X^*/P_y$ as a second equation that holds at the optimum. Further, we know that equal quantities of X and Y were consumed, so that $X^* = Y^*$. Putting these together, $X^*/P_x = X^*/P_y$ so that $P_y = P_x$ must hold. Then, from the first equation, we must have $2P_xX^* = 24$. hence, the expenditure on X, $P_xX^* = 24/2$ or $12.

c. When $X^* = 12$ we must have $P_x = P_y = \$1$ for the expenditure to be $12, as it was shown to be in part (b). At this point, utility is $X^*Y^* = 12 \times 12 = 144$.

5.

a. The following is the illustration of Kate's optimal point.

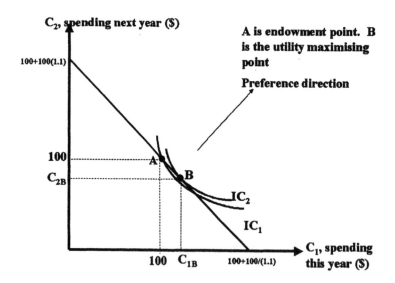

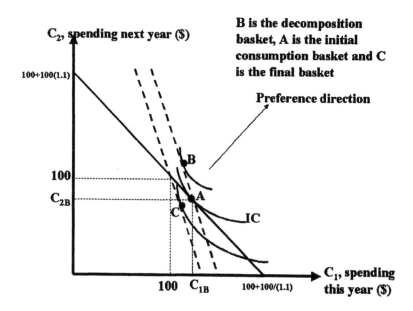

The substitution effect of the change in interest rate is represented by the move from A to B. The income effect is represented by the change from B to C. While the substitution effect reduces C_1 and increases C_2 by making (borrowing in order to) consume today "more expensive" in terms of the alternative, (lending in order to) consumer tomorrow, the income effect can either increase or decrease C_1 depending on whether or not C_1 is a normal or an inferior good. If it is a normal good, C_1 falls from the decomposition basket, B, as income falls. If it is an inferior good, the opposite is the case. If C_1 is so inferior that the income effect outweighs the substitution effect, then C can conceivably fall to the right of the original consumption bundle, A.

If the substitution effect is strong and dominant, then Kate could conceivably lend at the new interest rate. If it is weak, or if C_1 increases strongly as income falls, then Kate will continue to borrow.

Note that the increase in interest rate steepens the budget constraint so that it intersects the horizontal axis at $100 + 100/1.2$ and intersects the vertical axis at $100 + 100(1.2)$. Since the endowment point is still feasible, however, the new budget line goes through the endowment point as well as these two points of intersection of the axes.

b. Pierre must lend when the interest rate rises, since the steeper budget line must now cut the indifference curve at the endowment point. This means that Pierre can always increase utility by decreasing C_1 and increasing C_2. This is because, in essence, the only effect in this case is the substitution effect: no leftward shift of the budget line is occurring when the interest rate changes because no borrowing or lending was occurring at the original consumption point (so the interest rate was "irrelevant" to the level of income, in some sense).

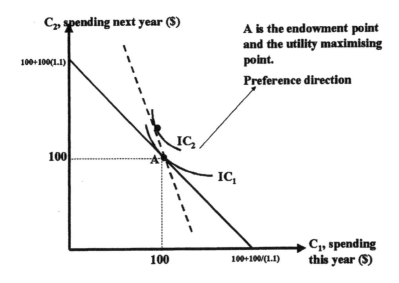

6. The budget constraint is $80 = x + 3y$. The indifference curves have a slope of -1 everywhere. Since the slope of the budget constraint is $-1/3$, the equilibrium occurs at a corner where the consumer only purchases x. Hence we have $x = 80$ and $y = 0$.

a. The effective price of good y is now $3 - 1 = 2$. Hence the new slope of the budget constraint is $-1/2$. This is still flatter than the indifference curves so that the optimal choice remains at the same corner: $x = 80$ and $y = 0$. The subsidy has been completely ineffective in increasing the consumption of y. Since $y = 0$, the total cost of the subsidy to the government is also 0.

b. Since the prices do not change, the slope of the budget line does not change and the consumer still wishes to spend his whole income on x. Since this income has been augmented by a voucher worth \$10 we have $x = 90$ and $y = 0$. The program has increased the consumption of x by 10 units, at a cost of \$10 to the government but has not affected the consumption of y.

c. The effective price of good y is now $3-2.5 = 0.5$ so that the slope of the budget constraint is now -2. This means that the budget constraint is now steeper than the indifference curves so that the new equilibrium is at a corner where the consumer only purchases y. Hence $y = 80/0.5 = 160$ and $x = 0$. This policy is a success since it increases the amount of y consumed. Moreover, this policy costs the government a total of $160 \times 2.5 = 400$.

d. The only policy to achieve an increase in the consumption of y was the policy in (c). Still, it did not help to achieve any balance between the consumption of x and y. The problem is that, as long as the goods are perfect substitutes, the consumer will always wish to be at a "corner solution" (except in the case where the indifference curves have exactly the same slope as the budget constraint). If we were to give an income support, as in (b), but force the consumer to spend it all on good y, then we could perhaps achieve more balance.

7.

  a. This answer assumes standard preferences:

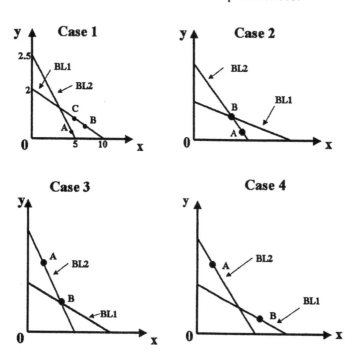

Case 1: B is preferred to A, B is preferred to C as well: in both cases, B is chosen when the alternative bundle (A or C) was affordable as well. When A is chosen, B is not affordable, so we can say nothing.

Case 2: the consumer's choices are inconsistent with utility maximizing behavior. The graph simultaneously implies that B is preferred to A and that A is preferred to B (since, when A is chosen B is affordable and when B is chosen A is affordable). These rankings cannot both be true at the same time.

Case 3: We infer that A is preferred to B since B is chosen when A is not affordable, but when A is chosen, B is affordable.

Case 4: We cannot infer any ranking. Given BL2, the consumer cannot afford B and given BL1, he cannot afford A. Thus, we cannot tell how he ranks the baskets since he cannot afford both with either budget line.

Answers to Exam

1. Such a change will not affect the welfare of the consumer. Before the changes in prices and income, the budget constraint was $I = P_x x + P_y y$. Now assume that all prices and income increase by w%. The budget constraint is now: $I[1 + (w/100)] = P_x[1 + (w/100)]x + P_y[1+(w/100)]y$. Since we can divide both sides of the constraint by $[1 + (w/100)]$, this constraint can be rewritten as $I = P_x x + P_y y$! In other words, the changes have not affected the budget constraint of the consumer.

2. Let us use a graph with x on the horizontal axis and the composite good C, which is measured in $, on the vertical axis. If the consumer spends his whole income on C he can get $I worth of it. This is the vertical intercept of the budget constraint. Let us now imagine that the consumer would prefer to also buy a few units of x. The unit price x is P_x so that the slope of the budget constraint is $-P_x$. This slope remains unchanged as long as the consumer does not want to consume more than 10 units of x, that is, as long as we do not move to the right of the point $(10, I - 10P_x)$. If the consumer wants to buy more than 10 units, the first 10 additional units are priced at $3P_x/4$ so that the slope of this segment of the budget constraint becomes $-3P_x/4$. This slope applies up to the point where the consumer purchases 20 units of x, that is, up to the point of coordinates $(20, I - 10P_x - 7.5P_x)$. Beyond this point, additional units of x can be had for $P_x/2$ apiece so that the slope of the budget constraint is now $-P_x/2$.

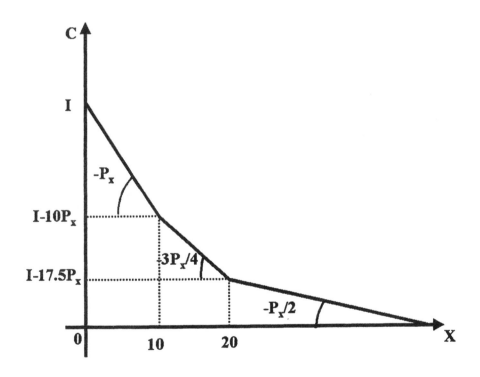

3.

    a. The consumer is able to purchase any combination along the budget constraint under current prices for day care and other goods (normalized to $1 per unit, for simplicity).

If preferences are "well behaved" then one can represent preferences by indifference curves such as the one drawn, below, increasing to the north-east. This means that the optimal choice for the family is at the tangency point, marked with a dot, between the budget constraint and a representative indifference curve. The consumer's pre-program income can be thought of as the point where the budget constraint intersects the vertical axis, as this represents the number of units of goods that the consumer could afford, with each unit valued at exactly \$1. Hence, the amount of goods and the income of the consumer are the same on this graph.

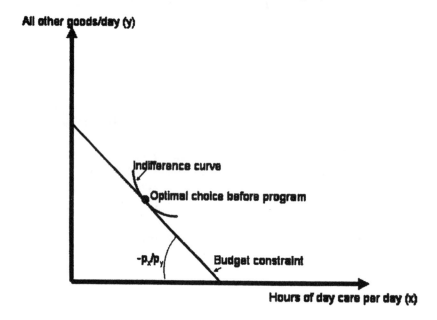

b. The price subsidy would alter the slope of the budget constraint, as it would effectively lower the price of day care. This would swing out the budget constraint, allowing the same vertical intercept (as the income of the consumer has not changed in terms of other goods purchased), but with a horizontal intercept to the right of the current position.

In the graph, the consumer chooses to purchase more day care. In general, it is unclear whether day care consumption increases or not. All we can say is that the maximum will occur somewhere on the new budget line. This issue will be pursued in depth in chapter 5.

One way of measuring the value of the subsidy would be to fix the amount of day care and measure the remaining amount of other goods that the consumer can now afford. For example, if day care consumption were fixed at x_2 in the diagram below, one could say that now y_2 other goods can be consumed along with x_2, whereas before only y_0 could have been purchased. This means that, in terms of income, the consumer essentially has $y_2 - y_0$ more.

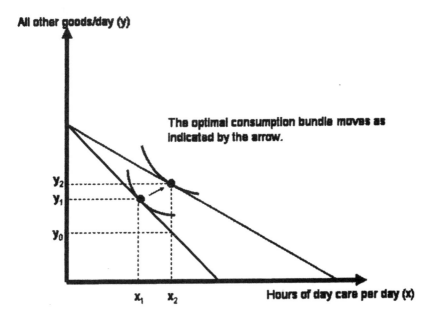

c. Suppose now that a lump sum payment of $y_2 - y_0$ were made to consumers. The new budget constraint has the same slope as the original one, as the price ratio of the two goods is the same as the original one (because the lump sum subsidy does not affect relative prices). Further, the budget constraint with the lump sum must go through the equilibrium derived in (b), as the amount of the lump sum makes the point in (b) affordable by design. On the other hand, one can see that the budget line with the lump sum subsidy is not tangent to the point from (b). In fact, points on higher indifference curves are now available to consumers if they reduce their day care consumption slightly. This is the area of the budget constraint to the left of the point in (b) and above the indifference curve going through (b).

As a result, one can conclude that the family will consume less day care with the lump sum payment than with the subsidy, but is better off in utility terms. Hence, poor consumers who receive the payment prefer the lump sum.

4. If the family decides to purchase no food, then it has $300 to spend on the composite good C so that it can purchase 100 units of C. This vertical intercept is the same whether or not the family participates in the food stamps program. If the family does not participate in the program, it can exchange the composite good for food at a rate of 5 units of C for 3 units of food. In other words, the budget line has a slope of −5/3 and the horizontal intercept is 60. Taking part in the food stamps program is an "all or nothing" deal: if the family pays the $100 but does not use all of its $200 of food stamps, the remaining food stamps are just lost. Therefore, paying $100 allows the family to acquire any bundle on the horizontal line shown on the graph. The vertical intercept of that line corresponds to the number of units of C that can still be purchased once the food stamps have been bought, that is, to (300 − 100)/3 = 66.67. The horizontal segment then extends from F = 0 to F = 40 since, once the $100 is paid, the consumer can obtain any quantity of food between 0 and 40 at no extra charge. Beyond 40, more food can again be obtained by consuming fewer units of C. This exchange occurs at a rate of 1 unit of food for each 5/3 units of C. The budget constraint of a family that has entered the food stamps scheme is therefore represented by the line segments joining

A,B, and C on the graph. If the family were given $100 in cash, its budget line would be parallel to the original budget line but the vertical intercept would be $(300 + 100)/3 = 133.33$. This line goes through the point $(66.67, 40)$ so that this new budget constraint coincides with the constraint with food stamps for $F > 40$ but lies everywhere above the food stamps constraint for $F < 40$. Therefore, the cash scheme is at least as good as the food stamps scheme for any family and is strictly better for families that would consume relatively little food.

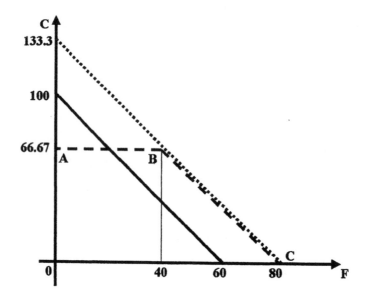

Chapter 5: The Theory of Demand

Chapter 4 showed that a consumer's purchase decisions depend on preferences, income, and the prices of goods and services. This chapter takes the next step: it analyzes how a change in income or the price of a good alters the consumer's purchase decisions. Stated another way, this chapter shows where demand curves come from. In the process of deriving demand curves, the chapter develops the important concepts of income and substitution effects, which can be applied to a wide range of economic problems. Three applications of these concepts are included in this chapter: the labor supply problem of workers, an evaluation of various measures of the benefits that consumers derive from the purchase of goods, and a critique of some commonly used consumer price indices. The chapter concludes by showing how aggregate (market) demand is derived from individual consumer demands.

Individual Demand Curves and Engel Curves

Recall from Chapter 2 that the market demand curve traces out the quantity consumed of a good as the price of that good changes, holding all other variables (including other prices and income) constant. Similarly, the individual demand curve traces out an individual's desired consumption of a good as the price of that good changes *holding income and all other prices constant.* Suppose that, given a set of prices and an income level, the consumer optimally chooses basket B of food and housing in Figure 5.1a. Now, let the price of food increase, *keeping the price of housing and income fixed.* As we saw in Chapter 4, the budget constraint of the consumer rotates in. Given this new budget constraint, basket A is now optimal. If the price of food were to fall from its original level, *while the price of housing and income remained fixed,* the budget constraint of the consumer would rotate out so that basket C would be optimal. In fact, if we could find the optimal basket for every possible price of food, we would trace out a **price consumption curve,** such as the one that would join baskets A, B, and C. This curve would tell us, for each price of food, which basket the consumer would purchase, holding all other prices and income constant.

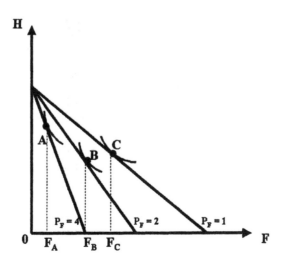

Figure 5.1a

Because we know how much food is contained in each basket that is purchased, we can also read off this graph the quantity of food desired for every price of food that the consumer can face. We can then graph the demand curve of this consumer, as in Figure 5.1b

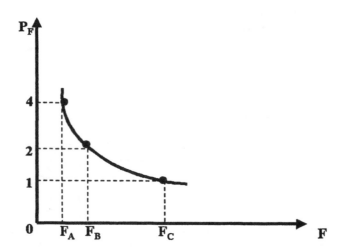

Figure 5.1b

We can make several statements about the individual's demand curve:

- The demand curve is the result of *comparative statics analysis*. From the viewpoint of the individual consumer, the prices of goods and the level of income are treated as exogenous variables. The levels of the goods consumed are endogenous. The demand curve answers the question, "How does a change in an exogenous variable (the price of the good) affect the level of an endogenous variable (the quantity of the good purchased), holding all other exogenous variables constant?"

- At every point along the demand curve the consumer is maximizing utility subject to the budget constraint. As long as the consumer is at an interior optimum this means that, as the price of food changes, the consumer modifies the basket of goods consumed so as to equate the marginal rate of substitution $MRS_{f,h} = MU_f/MU_h$ to the price ratio P_f/P_h. As the price of food falls along the demand curve, $MRS_{f,h}$ also falls so that the relative value that the consumer places on additional consumption of food decreases as the quantity of food consumed increases.

- As the price of food falls, the budget constraint rotates out so that the budget set of the consumer becomes larger and the consumer is able to attain higher levels of utility. In other words, the level of utility attained rises as we move down along the demand curve for food. This increase in utility merely reflects the consumer's increased purchasing power as the price of food falls.

Exercise 1: *Suppose that bananas and coconuts are perfect substitutes for Jane so that her utility can be written $U = x_1 + x_2$, where x_1 is Jane's consumption of bananas and x_2 is Jane's consumption of coconuts. Jane has income, I, which she spends only on bananas and coconuts, and faces prices p_1 for bananas and p_2 for coconuts.*

Draw Jane's price consumption curve for bananas, placing consumption of bananas on the horizontal axis and consumption of coconuts on the vertical axis. When the price of bananas is less than the price of coconuts, the price consumption curve is:

   a. vertical
   b. a 45° line
   c. horizontal

How to Obtain Individual Demand Curves Algebraically

We can solve for an individual's demand curve by using the facts that:

- An optimal basket must be on the budget line, so that $p_x X + p_y Y = I$ must hold at any optimal basket composed of (X,Y).

- At an interior optimum, the tangency condition that we derived in Chapter 4 must hold: $MU_x/MU_y = p_x/p_y$.

These two conditions give us two equations to solve for the two unknowns, X and Y, in terms of their own prices and income. What if the consumer chooses a corner point where only one of the two goods is consumed? Suppose that the consumer decides to spend her entire income on food. The chosen basket must still be on the budget line so that $I = p_f X_f$ or, equivalently, $X_f = I/p_f$, which is the consumer 's demand curve for food for all prices at which she chooses to only consume food.

Exercise 2: *Pierre the Belgian consumes only (Belgian) beer, b, and (Belgian) chocolate, c. His utility function is $U(b,c) = b^{1/2}c^{1/2}$, with marginal utility functions $MU_b = (1/2)b^{-1/2}c^{1/2}$ and $MU_c = (1/2)b^{1/2}c^{-1/2}$. His budget constraint can be written $p_b b + p_c c = I$, where p_b is the price of beer, p_c is the price of chocolate and I is Pierre's income. Pierre's demand for beer is:*

   a. $I/2p_b$
   b. $I/2(p_b+p_c)$
   c. I/p_b

When the price of food changes, the consumer's desired quantity moves *along* the demand curve for food, but what if we change the value of *exogenous variables* such as the price of housing or the consumer's income? A variation in either of these will cause a *shift* in the demand curve. For example, suppose that the prices of food and housing remained fixed, but the income of the consumer decreased. Starting from basket B, as before, the consumer would move to a new optimal basket such as A, in the top panel of Figure 5.2. Similarly, if we were to increase income for the consumer, the consumer would move to a new optimal basket such as C. The curve that connects points A, B, and C is called the **income consumption curve.** The amount of food consumed in each of these baskets is plotted in the lower panel of Figure 5.2 against the (fixed) price of food so that points A', B', and C' correspond to points A, B, and C. For *each* of these levels of income, we can observe the changes in the optimal basket purchased as the price of food changes. We can thereby trace out a demand curve for each of these levels of income through points A', B', and C'. This is shown in the lower panel of Figure 5.2.

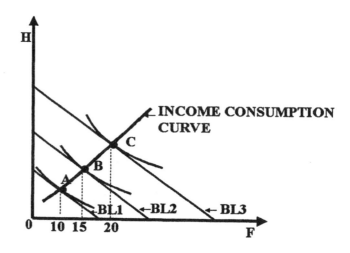

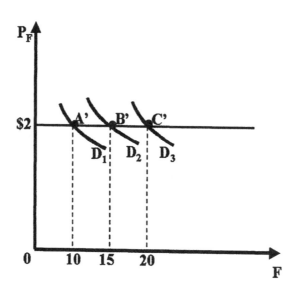

Figure 5.2

Sometimes, it is convenient to relate income to the consumer's desired quantity of food directly. This relation is called an **Engel curve**. As in the case of demand, the Engel curve traces out the result of a comparative statics exercise. This time, the prices of all goods remain fixed, but the income of the consumer changes. As income changes, the optimal consumption basket changes. As in the case of individual demand, utility is maximized along the Engel curve and increases as we move to higher income levels.

Exercise 3: *Michael's utility function can be written $U = min(x_1, x_2)$. Draw an income consumption curve for Michael (where consumption of good 1 is on the horizontal axis and consumption of good 2 is on the vertical axis) and an Engel curve for good 1 (where consumption of good 1 is on the horizontal axis and income is on the vertical axis). Which of the following statements is true?*

    a. The income consumption curve is diagonal, but the Engel curve is vertical.
    b. The income consumption curve and the Engel curve are diagonal.
    c. The income consumption curve is horizontal, but the Engel curve is vertical.
    d. The income consumption curve and the Engel curve are both horizontal.

When the income consumption curve has a positive slope, the optimal consumption of the good increases with income. Such a good is called a **normal** good. If an increase in income causes the optimal consumption level of a good to decrease, that good is called **inferior**. A single good may have ranges of income for which it is normal and other ranges for which it is inferior. This is shown on Figure 5.3, below, where the good is normal until income level I_A, after which it is inferior.

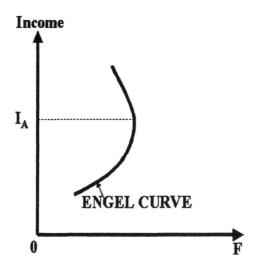

Figure 5.3

Exercise 4: *Goods 1 and 2 in Exercise 3 are:*

a.   normal goods
b.   inferior goods
c.   good 1 is normal, good 2 is inferior

Income and Substitution Effects

A decrease in the price of one good has two effects on the consumer's choice of an optimal basket. First, the real purchasing power of the consumer rises. The effect of this increase in real income on the quantities of each good chosen by the consumer is called an **income effect**. As we just discussed, the income effect may be positive (in the case of a normal good) so that the consumer desires to purchase more of the good as purchasing power rises or negative (in the case of an inferior good) so that the consumer desires to purchase less of the good as purchasing power rises. Second, a decrease in the price of one good makes that good relatively cheaper. This leads the consumer to adjust his/her optimal consumption basket to contain more of the relatively cheaper good. In this sense the change in price also has a **substitution effect**. The sign of the substitution is not ambiguous: it will *always* cause substitution toward the good that has become relatively cheaper. Since these two effects usually occur together in response to a price change, a move *along* the demand curve will be the net result of an income and a substitution effect.

Income Effects versus Changes in Income

Remark: When we refer to an income effect, we are not referring to the effect on demand of a change in the consumer's exogenous income I (which would cause the demand to *shift*). Rather, we are referring to a secondary effect of a change in the price of the good, which affects the purchasing power of the consumer and helps explain moves *along* the demand curve.

More precisely the (own) substitution effect is defined as the change in the amount of a good consumed as the price of that good changes, *holding constant the level of utility*, other prices and the consumer's nominal income. This is illustrated in Figure 5.4., where a decrease in the price of food changes the equilibrium choice of the consumer from A to C. The substitution effect measures the move from A to B *along* the indifference curve that was attainable at the original basket. B must be on the same indifference curve as A in order to *hold the level of utility constant*. B must also be at a point where the slope of that indifference curve is equal to the new relative price of food. In other words, B is the basket that minimizes the expenditure required to remain at the original level of utility under the new price regime.

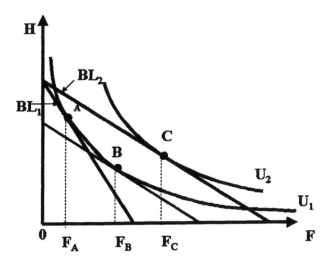

Figure 5.4

Point B is often referred to as the **decomposition basket**: it is a fictitious construction used to analyze the change in demand and not a basket that is on the demand curve of the consumer in reality.

The income effect accounts for move from point B to the new equilibrium position C. It is measured by the shift in purchasing power that would be required to move the budget constraint out from the level that goes though point B to the level that goes through point C. In other words, once the effect of the change in relative prices has been taken into account, we need to take into account the *additional* effect of the change in prices on purchasing power. As we saw above, an increase in purchasing power will cause an increase in consumption of a good if the good is normal, but will cause a decrease in consumption of the good if the good is inferior. If the good is so inferior that the net effect of a price decrease is to decrease the demand for the good, then the good is referred to as a **Giffen** good.

Exercise 5: *Let preferences be $U = x_1 + x_2$ and let the budget constraint be $I = p_1x_1 + p_2x_2$, where x_1 and x_2 are the quantities of two goods, p_1 and p_2 are the prices of the two goods and I is income. At the original price levels, let p_1 exceed p_2. Draw the budget constraint and a sample indifference curve. Now, suppose that the price of good 1 falls to a level that is lower than p_2. Draw the new optimal consumption basket. What effect accounts for the move from the old level of consumption of good 1 to the new level of consumption of good 1?*

    a. A positive income effect and a positive substitution effect.
    b. A positive income effect and a zero substitution effect.
    c. A negative income effect and a positive substitution effect.
    d. A zero income effect and a positive substitution effect.

Exercise 6: *Individual demand for an inferior good that is not a Giffen good is:*

   a. Downward-sloping
   b. Upward-sloping
   c. Flat

Whereas individual demand for a Giffen good is:

   a. Downward-sloping
   b. Upward-sloping
   c. Flat

How to Calculate Income and Substitution Effects Numerically

In order to calculate the income and substitution effects numerically, we must know precisely what income is, what prices were originally and what they are after the change, and what preferences are. If we have this information, we can calculate precisely what baskets A, B, and C are and compare them in order to put numbers on the income and substitution effects. The method we use to calculate income and substitution effects on X due to a change in the price of X from an initial level, P_X, to a final level, P_X', for a given level of income, I, a fixed price of good Y, P_Y, and a utility function, $U(X,Y)$, is the following:

1. Calculate the original optimal consumption basket by solving the original budget constraint, $P_X X + P_Y Y = I$ and the tangency condition at the original prices, $MU_X/MU_Y = P_X/P_Y$ for unknowns X and Y. Call the answer to this calculation the original optimal consumption basket (X_A, Y_A).

2. Substitute (X_A, Y_A) into the utility function to get the utility level at the original optimal basket, (X_A, Y_A). Call this utility level U_A.

3. At the new price for good X, P_X', calculate the tangency condition when the utility is at the original level, U_A by solving equations $MU_X/MU_Y = P_X'/P_Y$ and $U_A = U(X,Y)$. Call the answer to this calculation the decomposition consumption basket (X_B, Y_B).

4. At the new price for good X, P_X', calculate the optimal consumption basket by solving the new budget constraint $P_X'X + P_Y Y = I$ and the tangency condition, $MU_X/MU_Y = P_X'/P_Y$. Call the answer to this calculation the final consumption basket (X_C, Y_C).

5. The substitution effect is the change $X_B - X_A$. The income effect is the change $X_C - X_B$.

Exercise 7: *A consumer's tastes are represented by U = cb, with MU_b = c and MU_c = b. Calculate the income and substitution effects of a move from prices p_b = 1 and p_c = 2 to prices p_b' = 2 and p_c' = 2. Income, I = 20. Which of the following statements are true?*

   a. The decomposition basket contains (approximately) b = 7, c = 7.
   b. The optimal basket at the original prices contains b = 10, c = 5.
   c. The optimal basket at the final prices contains b = 5, c = 5.
   d. The substitution effect on b is -3 while the income effect on b is -2.

Applications of the Decomposition into Substitution and Income Effects

Consider first **the labor-leisure tradeoff**. A consumer consumes only two goods: leisure (L) and a composite good Y. We will measure leisure in units equal to hours of leisure consumed (with a 24-hour maximum each day). Hours worked per day simply equal the total number of hours per day minus the number of hours of leisure consumed. The hourly wage rate is w and the price of the composite good is P_Y. The initial budget constraint is given by:

$$P_Y Y = w(24 - L)$$

In other words, the amount of income that the consumer has to spend on Y depends on how many hours of leisure she chooses to forgo in favor of paid work. The vertical intercept of the budget constraint is Y = $24w/P_Y$: if the wage rate increases, the consumer has a larger income to spend on Y. The horizontal intercept of the budget constraint is L = 24: whatever the wage rate, the maximum amount of leisure that can be consumed in a day is 24 hours. The initial equilibrium position is at point A. Therefore, when the wage increases, the budget line rotates upward around the point (24,0).

Referring to Figure 5.5, let us examine the effect of a wage increase on the consumer's decision of how many hours to work per day. The consumer's purchasing power increases as the wage increases so that the consumer will tend to take *more* leisure (and hence less work) if leisure is a normal good. On the other hand, an increase in the wage rate also represents an increase in the *price of leisure* since the opportunity cost of taking one hour of leisure is the wage that one would have obtained by working. Hence, as the wage increases leisure appears relatively more expensive than before so that the consumer tends to substitute toward more of the composite good and *less* leisure. If the income effect associated with a wage increase outweighs the substitution effect, then the consumer will be observed to desire to work fewer hours at higher wage rates! If we expect that the income effect will only dominate at higher income levels, then we would expect labor supply to increase with the wage at low wage rates, but that labor supplied would *decrease* with the wage at higher wage rates. This leads to a "backward bend" in the labor supply curve. This feature of labor supply may used to explain why a wage increase may not elicit an increase in labor supplied by workers.

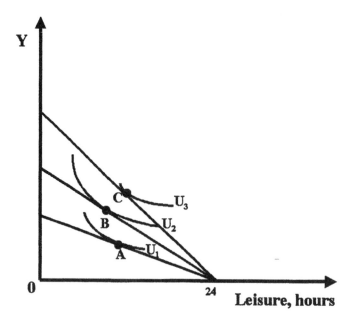

Figure 5.5

Exercise 8: *Laurel works at a desk job that pays her $10 per hour. She currently chooses to work full time (8 hours a day) at that rate. One day, Laurel's grandmother gives her $1,000 as a gift. What is the effect of this gift on Laurel's desired number of hours worked per day?*

    a. Laurel's desired hours of work increase.
    b. Laurel's desired hours of work decrease.
    c. Laurel's desired hours of work do not change.
    d. All of the above are possible.

Income and substitution effects also help us evaluate **measures of consumer welfare**. Consider a proposal for a new government program that changes the relative prices of goods. The government wishes to know whether the benefits to consumers of the program justify its costs. In order to answer this question, we need to have some measure of how much better off consumers are when they make a purchase at the new prices compared to the old prices. We can use the theory of demand that we have developed in order to answer this question.

The net economic benefit to the consumer from a purchase is the difference between the maximum amount the consumer would be willing to pay for a purchase minus the actual amount the consumer does have to pay (the price). For example, if you are willing to pay $10 for a good, but the actual price is only $5.00 you realize a net economic benefit of $5 on the purchase. To compute such a difference we need to know how much the consumer would be willing to pay for a purchase. This information can be obtained from the individual demand curve.

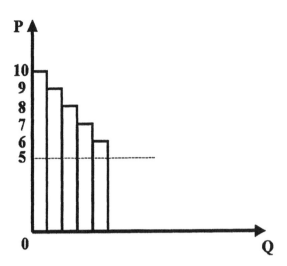

Figure 5.6

Although we usually interpret the demand curve as telling us how many units of the good the consumer would wish to buy at a given price, we can also read it as telling us how much a consumer would be willing to pay to purchase an *additional* unit of the good. For example, in Figure 5.6, the consumer is willing to pay $10.00 for the first unit of the good, but only $9 for the second, $8 for the third, and so on. Notice that the demand curve shows the willingness to pay for *additional* or *marginal* units. This is because the consumer chooses his optimal consumption basket to equate his *marginal* willingness to exchange one good against the other to the market's rate of exchange of one good for the other. In other words, since demand is derived from the consumer's optimization problem, the marginal rate of substitution equals the price ratio all along the demand curve. It follows that the consumer's total willingness to pay for a given quantity Q of a good is equal to the *sum* of her marginal willingness to pay for each individual unit up to Q. In Figure 5.6., for example, the total willingness to pay for five units of the good would be equal to $10 + $9 + $8 + $7 + $6 = $40. This corresponds to the area underneath the demand curve and to the left of the total quantity consumed Q.

Since the consumer pays the same market price for *all* of the units consumed, the actual sum paid is equal to the market price P times Q. In Figure 5.6, the consumer would pay $6 for 5 units. This amounts to an expenditure of 5 x $6 = $ 30 and corresponds to the area underneath the price line and to the left of Q. We can, then, think of the area under an ordinary demand curve and above the price as a measure of the net economic benefit (or **consumer surplus**) of a purchase. In our example, this net benefit would be equal to $40 = $30 = $10.

This benefit can then be used to calculate whether a program that stimulates purchase of a good is worth undertaking by measuring the consumer surplus before and after the change in prices and comparing the increase to the cost of the program.

Exercise 9: *Suppose that demand is $Q^D = 10 - p$. What is the consumer surplus of consuming 5 units?*

   a. $15
   b. $12.5
   c. $10

What is the change in consumer surplus when price rises to $7 per unit?

   a. $8
   b. $7
   c. -$8

But is consumer surplus really the welfare measure that we want? Let us think again about what we would *like* to measure. We would *like* to measure the monetary value a consumer would assign to the change in price that our program would make. In other words, we would like to know the amount of money the consumer would be willing to give up (or the amount of money the consumer would wish to receive) in order to remain as well off with the program as without it. We could calculate this amount of money in two ways. First, we could suppose that the program were actually instituted and then calculate the income transfer necessary to make the consumer as well off as with the old prices. This is called the **compensating variation** (because we *compensate* the consumer for the changes effected by the program). In other words, the compensating variation is the income transfer necessary to maintain the consumer at the *initial* level of utility when facing the *new* prices. Alternatively, we could measure the income that the consumer would be willing to pay to avoid the implementation of the program. In other words, we could assume that the program was not instituted and then give to the consumer (or take from the consumer) enough income to leave him as well off as he would have been with the program. This is called the **equivalent variation** (because we give the consumer enough income to give him utility equivalent to what he would receive with the program when he faces the old prices). We could say that the equivalent variation is the income necessary to maintain the consumer at the *final* level of utility when facing the *old* prices.

Graphically, suppose that the consumer begins by facing budget line BL_1 (with slope $-P_X/P_Y$), optimally consumes at basket A, and attains initial level of utility U_1. The initial level of income is measured by the vertical intercept of BL_1, that is, by OK. The project would decrease the price of good X. After the project is implemented the new budget constraint would be BL_2 (with slope - $(P_X/P_Y)'$) and the consumer would choose to consume at point C, obtaining a level of utility U_2. The level of income of the consumer is measured by the vertical intercept of BL_2, which is still OK.

The compensating variation is the change in income necessary to maintain the consumer at the initial level of utility when facing the new prices. The minimum income required to reach utility U_1 at the new prices is represented by the budget line of slope $-(P_X/P_Y)'$ that is tangent to the initial indifference curve at point B. The level of income associated with this budget constraint is measured by its vertical intercept OL. The compensating variation can then be measured as the difference between OL and OK, that is, by the *negative* income change KL.

The equivalent variation is the change in income necessary to maintain the consumer at the final level of utility U_2 when facing the old prices. The minimum income required to reach utility U_2 at the old prices is represented by the budget line of slope $-(P_X/P_Y)$ that is tangent to the final indifference curve at point E. The level of income associated with this budget constraint is measured by its vertical intercept 0J. The equivalent variation can then be measured as the difference between 0J and 0K, that is, by the *positive* income change KJ.

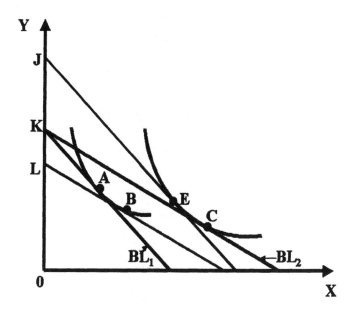

Figure 5.7

As is clear from Figure 5.7., these two measures are not generally the same.

How to Calculate Equivalent Variations and Compensating Variations

We can solve for the compensating variation by calculating the point B in Figure 5.7 as the point where the original indifference curve has a slope equal to the new relative prices. We can then compute the cost of buying basket B at the new prices and compare it to the initial income level I.

(1) Calculate the original optimal consumption basket by solving equations (a) $p_x/p_y =$ MU_x/MU_y and (b) $p_x x + p_y y = I$. Call the original consumption basket (x_A, y_A). Calculate the level of utility at this original consumption basket by plugging (x_A, y_A) into the utility function. This calculation yields U_A.

(2) Calculate the basket that solves the following two equations: (1) $p'_x/p_y = MU_x/MU_y$ and (2) $U(x,y) = U_A$. Call this basket (x_B, y_B). The expenditure that is required to buy this basket at the new prices is $p_x' x_B + p_y y_B$. Call this expenditure I_B.

(3) $I_B - I$ = compensating variation.

(4) Similarly, calculate the final optimal consumption basket by solving equations (a) $p'_x/p_y = MU_x/MU_y$ and (b) $p'_x x + p_y y = I$. Call the final consumption basket (x_C, y_C). Calculate the level of utility at this final consumption basket by plugging (x_C, y_C) into the utility function. This calculation yields U_C.

(5) Calculate the basket that solves the following two equations: (1) $p_x/p_y = MU_x/MU_y$ and (2) $U(x,y) = U_C$. Call this basket (x_E, y_E). The expenditure that is required to buy this basket at the new prices is $p_x x_E + p_y y_E$. Call this expenditure I_E.

(6) $I_E - I$ = equivalent variation.

Exercise 10: *Let a consumer's utility be represented by $U(x,y) = 10x - x^2/2 + y$ and let the consumer's income be $I = 20$. The original prices are $p_x = \$1$, $p_y = \$1$. Suppose now that p_x increases to $p_x' = \$2$. Calculate the compensating variation and the equivalent variation due to this change in prices. Calculate the change in consumer surplus. Which of the following statements are true?*

a. The compensating variation, equivalent variation, and change in consumer surplus are the same magnitudes, although the signs may differ.
b. The demand curve for x is linear.
c. The equivalent variation is -$8.5.

Not only are compensating and equivalent variations not generally the same but, usually, consumer surplus measures neither the equivalent variation nor the compensating variation. This is because the equivalent variation and the compensating variation are measures of the change in income necessary to hold utility *and hence purchasing power* constant when the optimal basket changes due to the change in prices. On the other hand, our measure of consumer surplus is the change in utility holding income *but not necessarily purchasing power* constant when the optimal basket changes due to the change in prices. These measures will be the same only when the change in quantity demanded due to a price change is not affected by changes in purchasing power (since the two measures do not take purchasing power into account in the same way). This is the case when there is no income effect.

Exercise 11: *For the preferences in Exercise 10, which of the following statements are true?*

a. The equivalent variation is the same as the compensating variation.
b. The equivalent variation is larger than the compensating variation.
c. The equivalent variation is smaller than the compensating variation.

A third application of income and substitution effects is the measurement of **consumer price indices**. Price indices that measure the yearly increase in the cost of living are necessary in order to correct various payments made to consumers (such as Social Security benefits or wages) to offset the effects of inflation. Assume that consumers only consume food, F, and a composite good, C. Define (F_1, C_1) as the basket of goods purchased in period 1 when the prices are P_{F1} and P_{C1} and (F_2, C_2) as the basket of goods purchased in period 2 when the prices are P_{F2} and P_{C2}. In some sense, an **ideal index** would be such that consumers whose income is adjusted according to the index would be made neither worse off nor better off by price changes. In practice, simpler indices are used to measure the yearly change in the cost of living. The **Laspeyers index**, L, measures the change in cost of the year 1 basket over the measurement period (two years in our example). For comparison purposes, we will present the **Paasche index**, P, as well. This measures the change in the cost of the year 2 basket over the measurement period. Algebraically, we have:

$$L = (P_{F2}F_1 + P_{c2}C_1)/(P_{F1}F_1 + P_{c1}C_1) \qquad P = (P_{F2}F_2 + P_{c2}C_2)/(P_{F1}F_2 + P_{c1}C_2)$$

In other words, the Laspeyers index uses the quantities of the initial basket to weigh the prices in both periods (while the Paasche index uses the quantity of the period 2 basket to weigh the prices in both periods.)

The problem with both types of indices is that they ignore the fact that consumers are able to change their consumption basket in response to changing prices. In order to be as well off in period 2 as in period 1 a consumer does not need to receive an income that would enable her to keep purchasing the same basket in as in period 1. She could decrease her consumption of the goods that have become relatively more expensive and increase her consumption of the goods that have become relatively less expensive and reach the same level of utility at a lower cost. This is shown in Figure 5.9., where A is the basket chosen in period 1 when the budget line is BL1. Suppose the price of food increases while the price of the composite good remains constant. At these new prices, the cost of purchasing A is given by the level of the budget constraint BL2 going through A at the new prices. However, at the new prices, the consumer can find a new basket of goods, B, that lies on the same indifference curve as A but is less costly to acquire, since it lies on a budget line BL3 that lies below BL2.

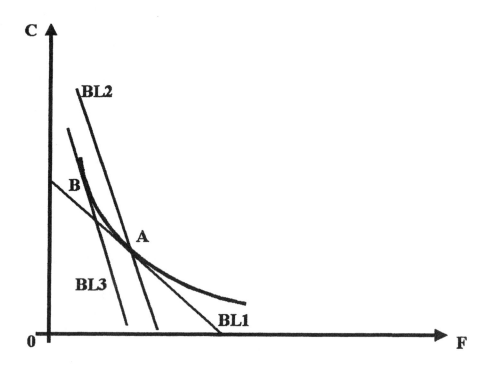

Figure 5.9

This lack of substitution in the baskets means that the numerator of the Laspeyers index *overstates* the expenditure required to keep the consumer as happy as before. (Similarly, you should try as an exercise to understand why the denominator of the Paasche index *overstates* the expenditure that would have been required in period 1 to reach the same utility level as in period 2.) Since L's numerator (and P's denominator) is too high, it follows that the Laspeyers index overstates the increase in the cost of living (while the Paasche index understates it).

Exercise 12: *In year 1, a consumer purchases a basket (x = 9, y = 11) when prices are $p_{x1} = 1$, $p_{y1} = 1$. In year 2, the consumer purchases a basket (x = 8, y = 4) when prices are $p_{x2} = 1$, $p_{y2} = 2$. In order to remain as well off in year (2) as in year (1), the consumer would need to consume (x = 10, y = 10). Calculate the Laspeyers, the Paasche and the ideal consumer price indices for the change in prices over these two years. Which of the following statements is correct?*

    a. L > P > I
    b. L < P < I
    c. L > I > P
    d. P = 1.33

Market Demand

Suppose that a business wishes to sell a product for which there is information on demand from two different market segments. If the business is interested in the total market demand for the product, it must know how to aggregate the information on the individual demands for the market segments into a total market demand curve. The market demand tells us the total quantities demanded for any given price. This total quantity is equal to the quantity demanded by the first segment at this price plus the quantity demanded by the second segment at this price. In other words, the market demand curve is the *horizontal* sum of the individual (or the segment) demands.

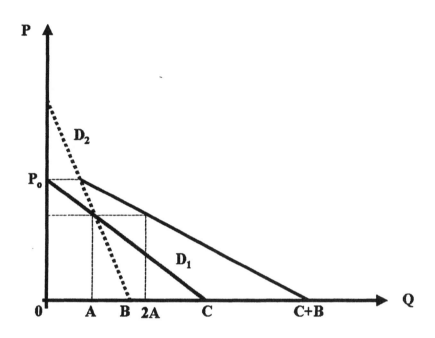

Figure 5.10

For example, in Figure 5.10, market demand coincides with D_2 for prices higher than P_0 and is equal to the horizontal sum of D_1 and D_2 for prices below P_0. Similarly, if we wanted to build aggregate market demand from any number of individual consumer demands, we would want to *horizontally* sum all of the individual demands in the same way as the business horizontally summed the demands in all its segments.

Exercise 13: *Let the demand for market segment 1 be Q = 10 - p and the demand for market segment 2 be Q = 20 - 5p. What is the aggregate demand for this market if there are only two market segments?*

    a. Q = 30 - p
    b. Q = 30 - 6p
    c. Q = 30 - 6p for price no greater than 4 and Q = 10 - p for price greater than 4
    d. Q = 30 - 6p for price greater than 4 and Q = 10 - p for price less than 4

Network Externalities

We say that there are *network externalities* when a consumer's demand for a good depends on the number of other consumers also purchasing the good. There are *positive* network externalities if a consumer's demand *increases* with the number of other buyers and *negative* network externalities if a consumer's demand *decreases* as the number of other buyers increases.

There are three main sources of positive network externalities:

- **Physical network externalities**: these arise mostly in communication and transportation networks such as telephony, the Internet or railroads, where consumers want to be able to reach as many other consumers or destinations as possible.

- **Virtual network externalities** arise because the possibilities of exchange or the quality and variety of complementary products that are available increase with the number of consumers purchasing the good. A typical example is video-game platforms: the more Nintendo consumers there are the better the possibilities of borrowing games and the better the offering of Nintendo-compatible games.

- **Fads**, that is, instances when consumers derive psychological benefits from buying what everyone else buys.

Negative network externalities come mostly from **snob appeal**, that is, situations where consumers derive psychological benefits from purchasing goods that are only bought by very few others.

Positive network externalities make the market demand curve more elastic. As for any non-Giffen good, a decrease in price leads to an increase in the quantity demanded. With positive network externalities, however, this increase itself makes the product more attractive so that sales expand further. This extra positive effect on the quantity demanded is called the **bandwagon effect**. With negative network externalities, the bandwagon effect is negative, making the market demand curve *less* elastic

Exercise 14: *Consider the market demand for Ferraris. Which of the following are sources of network externalities? Are these externalities positive or negative?*

- a. Ferraris are very glamorous cars
- b. Ferraris must be serviced at specialized outlets
- c. Ferrari has recently been quite successful in motor racing events

Chapter Review Questions

1. Let the demand for market segment 1 be $P = 2500 - (Q_1/3)$. The demand for market segment 2 is $P = 5000 - .5Q_2$. Calculate aggregate demand. What is the price elasticity of demand at an output level of 6000 in each of the market segments and for aggregate demand at the same output level?

Answer:

Inverting demand for the two segments, we have $Q_1 = 7500 - 3P$ for segment 1 and $Q_2 = 10000 - 2P$ for segment 2. Adding these two together, we have market demand, $Q = Q_1 + Q_2 = 7500 - 3P + 10000 - 2P = 17500 - 5P$. At $Q = 6000$, price elasticity of demand in segment 1 is $(-3(500/6000)) = -1/4$; for segment 2, elasticity is $(-2)(2000/6000) = -2/3$; for aggregate demand, elasticity is $-5(2300/6000) = -23/12$ so that aggregate demand is more elastic than segment demand at this level of output.

2.

   a. Let a consumer's demand for a good be $q^d = 100 - 5P$. What is the consumer surplus generated at a price of $P = 18$? How much does consumer surplus change when price falls to $P = 16$?

   b. Define "equivalent variation" and "compensating variation". Referring to these concepts, explain in what sense the measure of consumer surplus you used in part (a) is a "good" or "bad" measure of consumer benefit from consumption when price falls.

Answer:

   a. The consumer's surplus, calculated as the triangle below demand and above price, is equal to 10: at a price of 18, 10 units are consumed. Hence, the vertical height of the triangle is the intercept of demand minus the height of the current price, [20-18], while the horizontal length of the triangle is 10. Therefore, the area of the triangle is (20-18)x10/2 = 10. Similarly, when the price is 16, demand is 20. Hence, the area of the triangle is now (20-16)x20/2 = 40. Consumer's surplus has increased by 30 units.

   b. Referring back to the discussion of surplus measures, what we would like to measure when we measure consumer benefit is the monetary value a consumer would assign to a particular purchase or a particular governmental policy (that might affect price, for example). We could measure this in two ways. We could suppose that the change in prices occurred and then calculate the income necessary to make the consumer as well off as he was under the old prices. This is called the compensating variation. We could also assume that the change does not occur and give the consumer enough income to leave him as well off as he would have been with the program. This is called the equivalent variation. Each of these measures holds utility constant (at the level before or after the change). This is not true for consumer's surplus, since utility changes as we move along the individual demand curve. Hence, consumer's surplus does not necessarily reflect either of the other two measures of consumer well-being. In fact, consumer's surplus is the same as the other two only if there are no income effects in the utility function. This is because, when there are no income effects, the change in purchasing power (or utility) that occurs as prices fall does not affect the *pattern* of consumption. Hence, whether utility is held constant or not does not affect the calculation of consumer well-being.

3. For Sally, leisure is a normal good, for George leisure is an inferior good, and for Rudolf leisure is a Giffen good. Suppose that Sally, George, and Rudolf all experience a rise in their wages. Who will increase his or her work hours? Can you tell from the information given?

Answer:

When wages rise, there is a substitution effect toward more hours worked for all three individuals. This is measured by the decrease in leisure that occurs in a move from point A to point B in the graph below. On the graph, note that the slope of the budget line that is tangent to the initial indifference curve at point B is the same as the slope of the new budget line, BL_2. The income effect will determine the direction of the move from the "decomposition basket" B to the final consumption basket on BL_2. If leisure is a normal good, then we know that leisure increases as income increases and the move from point B will be to the northeast. Therefore, the net effect of the substitution effect and the income effect on hours worked is uncertain. If leisure is an inferior good, then we know that consumption of leisure decreases as income increases so that the move from the decomposition basket is to the northwest. Therefore, the income effect reinforces the substitution effect and hours worked increases. If leisure is a Giffen good, then consumption of leisure decreases as income increases and the income effect reinforces the substitution effect in this case as well.

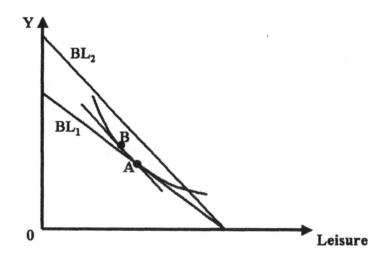

Problem Set

1. An individual consumes two goods, x and y (a composite good), has utility function U = min(x,y), income, I, and faces prices p_x and p_y.

    a. Find the equation of the demand curve for x for this individual.

    b. Is x a normal, inferior of Giffen good?

2. As in problem 1, an individual consumes two goods, x and y (a composite good), has utility function U = min(x,y), income, I, and faces prices p_x and p_y.

   a. Suppose that income is I = $10. Further, let the prices be p_x = $0.5 and p_y = $1. Calculate the optimal consumption basket. Now, suppose that a tax of $0.5 per unit of x purchased is imposed. How does the optimal consumption basket change? What are the substitution and income effects of the change?

   b. Suppose that, instead of taxing each purchase of x the government imposes an income tax of $2.5 on the consumer. What is the new optimal consumption basket? What are the income and substitution effects of the change?

   c. Which plan, the income tax or the per unit tax, is more favorable to the consumer?

   d. Which plan, the income tax or the per unit tax, raises more revenue for the government?

3. Kate has income I and consumes goods x and y. Her utility function is $U(x,y) = x^{1/3}y^{2/3}$ where x is the quantity of good x consumed and y is the quantity of good y consumed. The prices of the two goods are p_x and p_y, and the marginal utilities of the goods are $MU_x = (1/3)x^{-2/3}y^{2/3}$ and $MU_y = (2/3)y^{-1/3}x^{1/3}$

   a. What fraction of her income does Kate spend on each good? Make sure to explain your derivation and reasoning carefully.

   b. Derive and interpret Kate's income elasticity of demand for good x. What might be examples of goods x and y that would fit this model?

4. Suppose that there are three market segments for computers. The first market segment is composed of consumers who buy a single computer each when the price does not exceed $3,000. The next segment is composed of consumers who buy a single computer each when the price does not exceed $2,000. The final market segment is composed of consumers who buy a single computer each when the price does not exceed $1,000.

   a. Construct the aggregate demand for computers.

   b. For each segment separately, calculate the price elasticity of demand for p = $1000.

   c. Calculate the price elasticity of aggregate demand for p = $1000.

5. The "ideal" consumer price index, referred to in the summary, has which of the following characteristics?

   a. It measures both an income effect and a substitution effect of a change in prices.

   b. It measures only a substitution effect of a change in prices.

   c. It compares the change in expenditure required to attain two points along the demand curves for the products.

6. The government considers the following scheme. Unemployed people will receive a lump-sum benefit in cash, but once an individual starts working the benefit will be reduced by the full amount of her earnings (with a minimum total earning of zero).

    a. Discuss the implications for labor supply of introducing this scheme.

    b. What difference would it make if the benefit were to be reduced by only a fraction of the individual's earnings once she started working?

7. A department store currently pays employees $5 per hour. During the Christmas season, the store needs to get employees to work longer hours. Two proposals are being considered:

    a. An overtime premium of double pay (so that wages rise to $10 per hour) for any time worked in excess of 8 hours a day.
    b. An increase in the wage to $5.50.

    Assume that all the employees currently find it optimal to work 8 hours per day when the wage is $5 per hour. Which policy, the overtime wage or the wage increase, is more likely to increase working hours?

8. Suzie purchases two goods, food and clothing. She has the utility function $U(x,y) = xy$, where x denotes the amount of food consumed and y denotes the amount of clothing. The marginal utilities are $MU_x = y$ and $MU_y = x$. The price of food is p_x, the price of clothing is p_y (which you can assume equals $1 per unit) and her income is I.

    a. Derive the equation for the demand curve for food. Is food a normal good?

    b. Now, suppose that Suzie has an income of $70 per week. Suppose that the price of food is initially $p_{x1} = \$9$ per unit, and that the price subsequently falls to $p_{x2} = \$4$ per unit. Find the numerical values of the income and substitution effects on food consumption. Show the income and substitution effects on a carefully labeled graph.

9. Janice consumes only food and housing. She initially faces prices p_f for food and $p_h = 1$ for housing and has income I. Her indifference curves are convex to the origin with utility increasing as the indifference curves move northeast on the indifference map so that her optimal consumption basket is (f_1, h_1). Now, the government imposes a per unit tax on food so that the price of food rises to $p_f + t$. At the same time, the government enacts a rebate program so that Janice's income rises by exactly the amount she pays out in taxes on food.

    a. Write Janice's old (pre-tax) and new (post-tax and rebate) budget constraints. What are the intercepts and slopes of the two budget constraints? By canceling terms, show that her new optimal basket, (f_2, h_2), lies on both budget constraints.

    b. Use revealed preference to show that Janice is worse off under the tax and rebate program than she was before the tax and rebate. Illustrate the old optimal consumption basket and the new optimal basket on a graph with some representative indifference curves.

10. Draw an income consumption curve and an Engel curve for good x for the preferences described below. Also derive algebraically an equation for the income consumption curve and for the Engel curve for good x.

    a. U = xy, where MU_x = y and MU_Y = x

    b. U = min(x,y)

11. A consumer consumes two goods, X and Y. There are two periods. In period 1 prices are P_{X1} and P_{Y1}, while they are equal to P_{X2} and P_{Y2} in period 2. The consumer has the same nominal income I in both periods but chooses different baskets of the two goods in the two periods. Suppose that the Laspeyers price index, L, is less than 1. Is the consumer better off in the first or in the second period? Hint: Use revealed preference.

12. The demand for software has two components. First, consumers value their private use of the product. Their willingness to pay for this private use is represented by the inverse demand curve P = 100 - 5Q, where Q is the total quantity of software sold. Draw this demand curve on a graph. Consumers also value the fact that other consumers are using the same type of software. This "network externality" increases the consumers' willingness to pay by 2Q. Describe this additional benefit on the same graph as above. What does the market demand for software look like? Draw it on the graph and compare it to the P = 100 -5Q curve.

Exam *(60 minutes: Closed book, closed notes)*

1. Let a consumer's preferences be represented by U = min(x,y). The consumer chooses basket A in period 1 and basket B in period 2, as illustrated below:

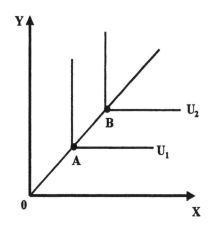

Has the consumer moved along her demand curve or has her demand curve shifted?

2. Let the utility of a consumer be $U(x,y) = 2x^{1/2} + 2y$, where x and y are the quantities consumed of two goods. The marginal utilities are $MU_x = x^{-1/2}$ and $MU_y = 2$. Suppose that a consumer has an income of $20, and the price of good y is p_y = $4 per unit. A proposal is made to impose a price ceiling on good x so that the current price of p_x = $2 would fall to a new price of p_x = $1. Calculate the change in well-being that would accrue to the consumer from this price fall. Discuss your results with reference to measures of consumer's surplus and illustrate with a diagram.

3. The individual demand for books of each consumer, i, is given by Q_i = 10 - P. There are N consumers in the market.

   a. What is the equation of the market demand for books?

   b. Draw an individual demand and the market demand in the same graph. Which one is flatter and why?

   c. What is the elasticity of the market demand for books at P = 5? Is it larger or smaller than the elasticity of an individual demand at the same price?

4. One Monday morning, Melvyn reads in the newspaper that the government estimates that there has been a uniform 5% rise in the general level of prices during the past year. On the other hand, his wages also rose by 5% over the same period. Has Melvyn been made better off or worse off by the change in wages and prices?

5. A politician remarks "The recent increase in the wage rates of teachers has been a total success! The shortage of teachers has been reduced drastically. Another, similar wage increase should eliminate this shortage entirely!". Explain and illustrate how you would model the labor supply decision of a potential teacher. Do you agree that the wage increase will increase the labor supply in this case? Carefully outline the assumptions underlying your argument.

Answers to Exercises

1. The answer is (c). The price consumption curve for bananas is obtained by keeping the price of coconuts fixed at p_2 = $1 and letting the price of bananas vary. As the price of bananas increases, the budget line gets steeper because the slope of the budget line is the price of bananas over the price of coconuts. For example, when the price of bananas is $2, the slope of the budget line is -2. The indifference curves are straight lines with a slope of -1 because the marginal utilities of the goods are each equal to 1 so that the slope of the indifference curve = $-MRS = -MU_{x1}/MU_{x2} = -1/1 = -1$. Therefore, as long as the budget constraint is steeper than the indifference curves, the consumer maximizes utility at the point where the budget constraint touches the vertical, buying only coconuts. In other words, since the consumer views the goods as perfect substitutes, she maximizes utility by consuming whichever is the cheaper of the two products. When the price of bananas is less than the price of coconuts, the consumer maximizes utility by consuming at the point where the budget constraint hits the horizontal axis, buying only bananas. When the prices of the two goods are equal, the budget constraint and the indifference curves have the same slope so that the

consumer maximizes utility at any point along the indifference curve. This means that the consumer is willing to spend her income on bananas and coconuts in any proportion. Therefore, the price consumption curve looks like the line traced out in bold in the graph.

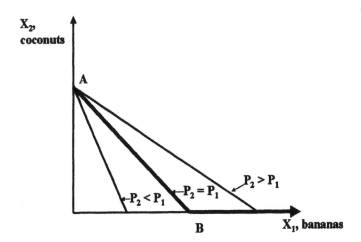

2. The answer is (a). First, calculate the marginal rate of substitution as the ratio of the marginal utilities and then set this equal to the price ratio:

$$MRS_{b,c} = MU_b/MU_c = [(1/2)b^{1/2}c^{1/2}]/[(1/2)b^{1/2}c^{-1/2}] = c/b = p_c/p_b.$$

We can cross multiply to obtain $cp_c = bp_b$. Now, we can solve the budget constraint to obtain $cp_c = I - bp_b$. Setting the right-hand sides of these two equations equal to each other, we obtain $I - bp_b = bp_b$ or $b = I/2p_b$.

3. The answer is (b). Here, the utility function indicates that Michael views goods 1 and 2 as perfect complements and wants to consume them in proportions of 1 to 1. Graphically, the indifference curves for this utility function are at right angles with the corner of the right angle along a 45° line. Therefore, as the income of the consumer increases (so that the budget constraint shifts out) the optimal consumption basket always remains at the point where the corner of the indifference curve just touches the budget constraint. This means that the income consumption curve is the 45° line. We can see that, as income increases, so does the consumption of good 1. Therefore, the Engel curve slopes upward. We can be more precise, however. The budget constraint is $I = p_1x_1 + p_2x_2$, where I is income and p_1 and p_2 are the prices of x_1 and x_2, respectively. Since the consumer always buys equal quantities of the two goods we can write $x_1 = x_2$. Substituting x_1 for x_2 in the budget constraint we get $I = (p_1 + p_2)x1$ which is the equation of the Engel curve for good 1. Similarly, the Engel curve for good 2 is $I = (p_1 + p_2)x_2$. The income consumption curve and the Engel curve are pictured below.

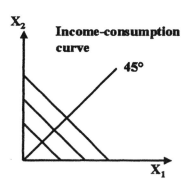

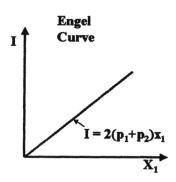

4. The answer is (a). In Exercise (3), we saw that the optimal consumption of both good 1 and good 2 increase as income increases. This was shown graphically by increasing Engel curves. We can, then, conclude that both goods are normal.

5. The new equilibrium position is point B on the graph below. The answer to the second part of the question is (a). First, find the original consumption basket A. When the goods are perfect substitutes and the price of good 1 exceeds that of good 2, the consumer maximizes utility by consuming only good 2. (See Exercise 1.) The decomposition basket is the expenditure minimizing basket on the original indifference curve that is attainable at the new price ratio. In order to find this, we draw a budget line with a slope equal to the new price ratio and shift it in as much as possible while still allowing the consumer to attain the original level of utility. This is a point like C, below. The move from A to C measures the substitution effect, which is positive. Now, we calculate the final optimal basket. This is the utility-maximizing basket using the new prices. This is a point like B in the diagram below. The move from C to B measures the income effect. This is positive as well.

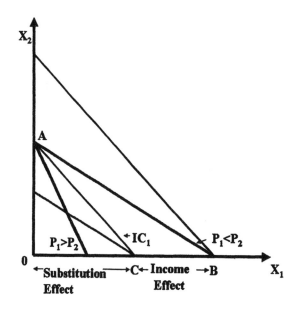

6. The answer to the case of the inferior demand is (a), while the answer to the Giffen good case is (b). As the price of a good falls, there are two effects on demand: the substitution effect tends to increase consumption of the good as it becomes relatively cheaper while the income effect tends to decrease consumption of the good because it is inferior. If the good is inferior, but not a Giffen good, then the substitution effect outweighs the income effect so that the net effect of a price decline is an increase in consumption: demand slopes downward. If the good is a Giffen good, then the income effect outweighs the substitution effect so that the net effect of a price decline is a decrease in consumption: demand slopes upward.

7. All of the statements are correct. We use the method outlined before Exercise 7 to answer the question. The original consumption basket is obtained by simultaneously solving the equations (1) $b + 2c = 20$ and (2) $MU_b/MU_c = p_b/p_c$ or $c/b = 1/2$. Substituting expression (2) into expression (1), we have $2c + 2c = 20$ or $c = 5$. From expression (2), we know that $2c = b$ so that $b = 10$. Therefore, the original consumption basket contains $b = 10$ and $c = 5$. The utility derived from this basket is $5 \times 10 = U_A$. Now, the decomposition basket can be obtained by simultaneously solving the equations (1) $c/b = 2/2$ and (2) $bc = 5 \times 10$. Expression (1) implies that $c = b$ and expression (2) implies that $bc = 50$. Putting these together, we find that the decomposition basket contains $b = 50^{1/2}$ and $c = 50^{1/2}$. The final consumption basket can be obtained by simultaneously solving the equations (1) $c/b = 2/2$ and (2) $2b + 2c = 20$. Expression (1) implies that $c = b$ and, substituting this into expression (2) we obtain that the final consumption basket contains $b = 5$ and $c = 5$.

The substitution effect on b is measured by the difference between the amount of b consumed in the decomposition basket and the amount consumed in the original consumption basket: $\Delta b = 50^{1/2} - 10 = -3$ (approximately). In other words, as the price of b rises, the substitution effect is that the consumer chooses to include less of b in the optimal consumption basket. The income effect on b is measured by the difference between the amount of b consumed in the final consumption basket and the amount consumed in the decomposition basket: $\Delta b = 5 - 50^{1/2} = -2$ (approximately). In other words, as the price of b rises, the income effect is that the consumer chooses to include less of b in the optimal consumption basket. The two effects together add up to -5: the total change in the consumption of b as we move from the original basket to the final consumption basket. As an aside, we can see from the sign of the income effect that b is a normal good.

8. The answer is (d). The gift does not affect the slope of the budget constraint on work and leisure since it does not affect the wage. It does, however, increase the income of Laurel so that she can now purchase more of the composite good no matter how many hours she works. This shifts up her budget constraint at all levels of work. Without knowing more about the shape of utility, we cannot say whether or not this increase in income increases desired working hours since we cannot say whether leisure is a normal good or an inferior good.

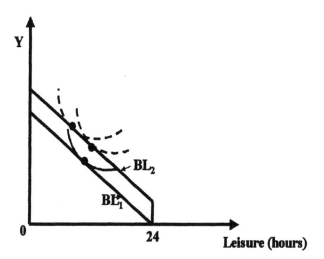

9. The answer to the first part is (b). The answer to the second part is (c). Consumer's surplus is the area under demand and above the unit price. If 5 units are consumed, the unit price is $5 so that the consumer's surplus is the area of triangle ABC in the figure below. This area is equal to 1/2 times the width times the height of the triangle or (1/2)5x5 = $12.5   If the price rises to $7, only three units will be consumed. This changes consumer surplus to the area under demand and above a price of $7 or (1/2)3x3 = $4.5 (area ADE in the figure).   The change in consumer surplus is -$8.

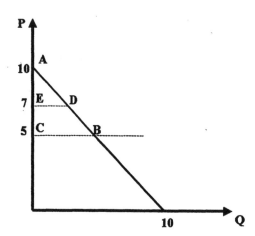

Note that the area ABC is not equal to 15, as it was in the text when a discrete number of units could be consumed. The area is larger when there are a discrete number of units consumed because consumer surplus is computed as the sum of the set of rectangles in the figure below. This is larger than the area under the straight line that represents demand, as you can see from the fact that the rectangles stand up higher than the straight line representing demand. The sum of the small rectangles that "overshoot" demand is $2.5, the difference between the answer to Exercise 9 and the answer for the discrete case in the text.

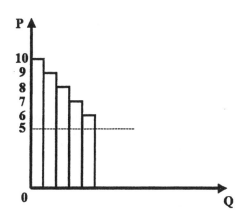

10. The correct answer is that all of the statements are true. To see this, first calculate the original optimal consumption basket, (x_A, y_A) and the associated level of utility, U_A. We do this by solving (a) $p_x/p_y = MU_x/MU_y \Leftrightarrow 1/1 = (10 - x)/1$ and (b) $p_x x + p_y y = 20$. Solving (a) and substituting (a) into (b), we obtain $x_A = 9$ and $9 + y = 20$ or $y_A = 11$. $U_A = 10(9) - 9^2/2 + 11 = 60.5$.

Next, we calculate the expenditure necessary to attain U_A at the new prices by solving (a) $p_x'/p_y = MU_x/MU_y \Leftrightarrow 2/1 = (10 - x)/1$ and (b) $10x - x^2/2 + y = 60.5$ Solving (a) and substituting (a) into (b), we obtain $x_B = 8$ and $10(8) - 8^2/2 + y = 60.5$ or $y_B = 12.5$. The expenditure necessary to purchase (x_B, y_B) at the new prices is $2(8) + 12.5 = 28.5 = I_B$.

The compensating variation is $I_B - I = 8.5$

Now, calculate the final optimal consumption basket, (x_C, y_C) and the associated level of utility, U_c. We do this by solving (a) $p_x'/p_y = MU_x/MU_y \Leftrightarrow 2/1 = (10-x)/1$ and (b) $p_x' x + p_y y = 20$. Solving (a) and substituting (a) into (b) we obtain $x_c = 8$ and $2(8) + y = 20$ or $y_c = 4$. The associated level of utility is $10(8) - 8^2/2 + 4 = 52 = U_c$.

Next, calculate the expenditure necessary to attain U_c at the old prices by solving (a) $p_x/p_y = MU_x/MU_y \Leftrightarrow 1/1 = (10-x)/1$ and (b) $10x - x^2/2 + y = 52$. Solving (a) and substituting into (b), we obtain $x_E = 9$ and $10(9) - 9^2/2 + y = 52$ or $y_E = 2.5$. The expenditure necessary to purchase (x_E, y_E) at the old prices is $9 + 2.5 = 11.5$

The equivalent variation is $I_E - I = -8.5$

To calculate the change in consumer's surplus, we first need to calculate the demand for x and then the change in the area under demand as the price changes. First, we calculate the demand by solving for any arbitrary value of p_x: (a) $p_x/p_y = MU_x/MU_y \Leftrightarrow p_x/p_y = 10 - x$ and (b) $p_x x + p_y y = 20$. Note that, for any given level of p_y, equation (a) implies that demand is linear. For example, suppose that $p_y = 1$, as in the exercise. Demand is linear: $p_x = 10 - x$. In fact, equation (a) completely determines demand since it tells us what x will be demanded for any level of p_x, independent of y.

If $p_x = 1$, then the area under demand curve $p_x = 10 - x$ is $(10 - 1)(9)(1/2) = 40.5$. If $p_x' = 2$, then the new area under the demand curve is $(10-2)(8)(1/2) = 32$. The change in consumer surplus is -8.5. Therefore, the equivalent variation, the compensating variation, and the change in consumer surplus have the same magnitude for this consumer.

11. The correct answer is (a). This utility function has no income effects. As a result, all measures of consumer surplus are the same.

12. The correct answer is that (a) and (d) are correct. Using the formulae in the text that precede the exercise we have: $L = [(9)+2(11)]/[1(9)+1(11)] = 31/20$, $P = [(8)+2(4)]/[1(8)+1(4)] = 16/12 = 1.33$ and, $I = [1(10)+2(10)]/[1(9)+1(11)] = 30/20 = 1.5$.

13. The correct answer is (c). The demand for segment 2 intersects the vertical axis at $p = 4$, while the demand for market segment 1 intersects the vertical axis at $p = 10$. Therefore, for prices between 4 and 10, only consumers from market segment 1 demand positive quantities. Once price falls below 4, consumers from both segments have a positive demand. For each price, then, we must add the two segments' demands together. This yields $Q_1 + Q_2 = 10 - p + 20 - 5p = 30 - 6p$. Graphically, we have:

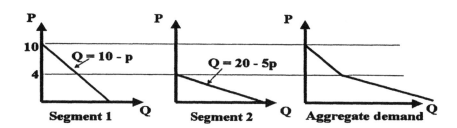

14.

    a. Ferraris are glamorous cars because of their design and the fact that only a limited number of famous and/or rich people own them. In other words, Ferraris have snob appeal, which creates a negative network externality.

b. Since Ferraris can only be serviced by specialists, they are more desirable if the network of Ferrari dealers is extensive. The more Ferrari owners there are, the more extensive the dealer network will be. This is a case where the availability of a complementary good (the servicing) generates a positive network externality.

c. Although one could argue that recent good results in motor racing have made Ferraris more "fashionable", it is still unlikely that Ferrari owners get any satisfaction out of seeing more Ferraris on the road. In other words, the fact that Ferraris might suddenly be "in fashion" amounts to a positive shift in the market demand curve but is not the source of any (positive) network externality.

Answers to Problems

1.

a. The budget constraint is $p_x x + p_y y = I$. We also know from the utility function that there is no benefit to consuming more of one good than the other since the goods are perfect complements in a proportion of one to one. Therefore, $x = y$ must hold at the optimum. Substituting this into the budget constraint, we have $p_x x + p_y x = I$ or $x = I/(p_x+p_y)$. This is the Marshallian demand for good x.

b. X is a normal good, since we can see from the answer to 1(a) that an increase in I leads to an increase in the demand for x.

2.

a. The optimal consumption basket for the original prices, using the demand from 1(a) is $x = \$10/(\$1 + \$0.5) = 6.67 = y$. When the tax is imposed, the price that the consumer pays for x increases to $1 so that the optimal basket changes to $x = y = \$10/(\$1 + \$1) = 5$. There is no substitution effect since any budget line slope yields the same optimal consumption basket for any given level of utility. The entire change in consumption of x and y is due to an income effect equal to $5 - 6.67 = -1.67$.

b. The $2.5 tax reduces the income of the consumer to $7.5 but leaves the prices of the two goods unchanged. Using the demand curve from 1(a), the new optimal consumption basket is $x = \$7.5/(\$0.5 + \$1) = 5 = y$. Again, there is no substitution effect so that the entire change is due to an income effect. This income effect is the same as in 2(a).

c. Both plans result in the same optimal consumption basket and the same level of utility.

d. The income tax raises $2.5 (per consumer) for the government. The unit tax raises $\$0.5 \times 5 = \$2.5$ (per consumer). Therefore, both plans raise the same amount of revenue.

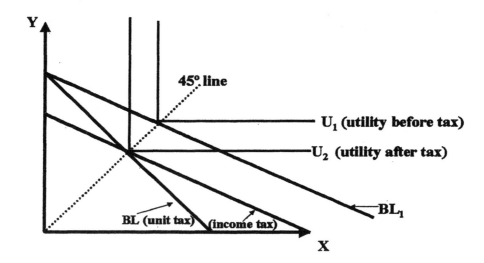

3.

a. We can derive Kate's demand by using two equations: the budget constraint and the tangency condition for the interior optimum for Kate's utility maximization problem:

$p_x x + p_y y = I$ (budget line: constraint)
$MU_x/MU_y = p_x/p_y$ (MRS equals - negative - slope of budget line: tangency)

...so...

$p_x x + p_y y = I$
$y/2x = p_x/p_y$

$y = 2xp_x/p_y$ and substituting into budget line, $p_x x + p_y(2xp_x/p_y) = I$ or $3p_x x = I$ or

$x^d = I/3p_x$

Similarly, $x = yp_y/2p_x$ and substituting into the budget line, $yp_y/2 + yp_y = I$ or $1.5p_y y = I$ or $y^d = I/1.5p_y$ ...or...$y^d = 2I/3p_y$.

The fraction of her income spent on x is $p_x x^d/I = p_x(I/3p_x)/I = 1/3$. Similarly, the fraction of her income spent on y is $p_y y^d/I = p_y(2I/3p_y)/I = 2/3$.

b. The income elasticity of demand for good x is defined as $(\Delta x^d/\Delta I)(I/x^d) = (1/3p_x)(I/(I/3p_x)) = 1$. This measures the degree of shift in demand as income changes (or, as the budget line shifts out). In other words, demand shifts out in a parallel fashion when income increases. Notice that the form of demand is constant elasticity. In this case, a percentage change in income leads to the same percentage increase in demand for good x.

Alternatively, the Engel curve for Kate can be illustrated as a straight line as follows. The line has a positive slope, indicating that x is a normal good for Kate.

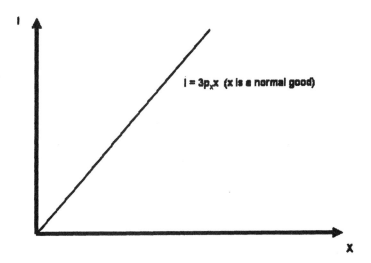

Examples of such goods: Kate's husband would say, uncharitably, that her "x" and "y" are housing and furniture, adding up to a total of her monthly budget. Kate disagrees. She says that housing and purchases for her children would reflect her choice in consumption better. Probably, they are both wrong. Housing and food are better guesses for Kate.

4.

a. Aggregate demand is pictured below, making the assumption that there are N_1 consumers in segment 1, N_2 consumers in segment 2, and N_3 consumers in segment 3.

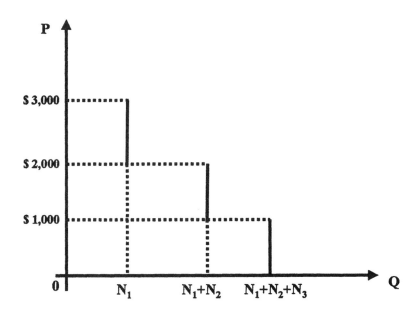

b. The price elasticity of demand for both of these segments is 0 since changing the price for consumers in segment 1 makes no difference to purchase behavior as long as price does not exceed $3,000 (i.e., $\Delta Q/\Delta P = 0$) and the change in price makes no difference to consumers in segment 2 as long as price does not exceed $2,000. For segment 3, a one unit increase in price above $1,000 results in all sales going to zero so that $\Delta Q/\Delta P = -N_3$. Therefore, elasticity for this segment is:

$$\varepsilon = -N_3(1000)/N_3 = -1000$$

c. A one unit increase in price above $1,000 results in a loss of N_3 units purchased. Therefore, since a total of $N_1+N_2+N_3$ units are purchased at a price of $1,000 we have:

$$\varepsilon = -N_3(1000)/(N_1+N_2+N_3)$$

Note that this is a higher elasticity than either of segments 1 or 2 alone but a lower elasticity than for segment three alone.

5. The correct answer is that (b) is true. The ideal consumer price index is the ratio of the expenditure required to attain the initial level of utility at the new prices and the expenditure required to attain the initial level of utility at the old prices. As such, it measures only a substitution effect because the consumer is constrained to remain on the same indifference curve. The point on the curve may change as the prices change, but this simply represents a substitution effect (as the price ratio may change under the new prices). Hence (a) is incorrect. Further, since the baskets must yield the same level of utility in the two periods, statement (c) cannot be correct.

6.

a. This scheme gives a lump sum income to people who are not working. Represent this as a point corresponding to 24 hours of leisure and an amount of the composite good corresponding to the lump sum in the graph below (point A). Now, suppose the wage is such that the budget line without any income support would be BL1. If the lump sum is reduced by exactly the amount of earnings, then the government is essentially guaranteeing that the individual can always earn the same amount as at point A with any amount of work. In other words, the effective budget line is the darkened line, BL2. With standard indifference curves, the individual would always decide not to work.

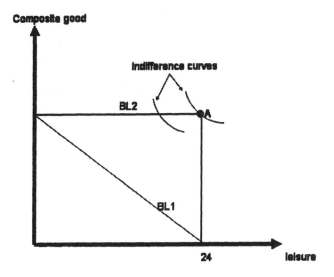

Taking a slightly different case, suppose that the lump sum is relatively small compared to what the individual could earn if she worked all the time. In other words, point A is low compared to the no-support budget line BL1 in the graph below. In this case, the budget line with the program imposed has a kink: it is flat for a low number of hours. Once the individual works a lot, however, the total earnings rise above what she could have earned with the income support. In this case, and with standard indifference curves, it depends on the shape of the curves whether the individual optimizes by choosing not to work or choosing to work a relatively large number of hours. Clearly, as the wage rises and the income support falls, the likelihood increases that this case arises and that the individual chooses to work despite the kink.

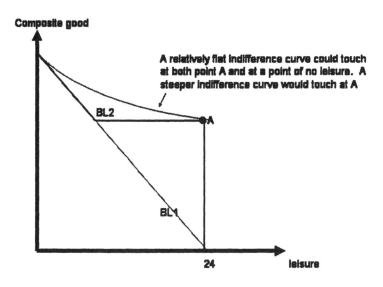

b. If the benefit were reduced by only a fraction of earnings, then the first case in (a) becomes the case depicted below: even if the individual works only a little, the total income rises so that the budget line retains some slope. If the income support is relatively large and wages are relatively low, the budget line has a constant slope throughout, albeit flatter than the slope of the "no support" budget line. If the support is relatively small and the wage relatively large, the budget line has a kink where it becomes steeper, as shown in the second panel, below. In both cases, it is more likely that the individual will optimize by choosing to work some rather than not working at all but the choice of not working remains a good possibility due to the sharp drop at 24 hours of leisure.

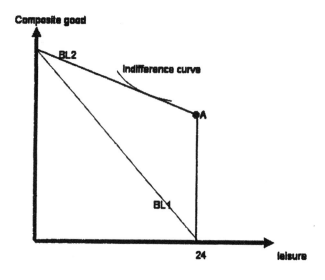

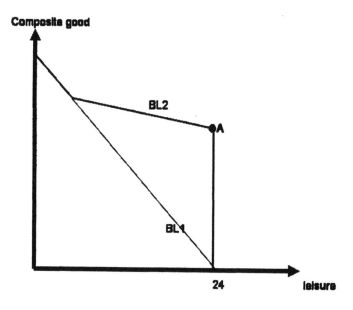

7. The overtime wage only affects the budget constraint for hours worked above 8 hours a day. Therefore, the budget constraint has a kink, becoming steeper once the worker takes less than 16 hours of leisure. The original budget constraint is labeled BL_1 in the diagram below and the budget constraint after the overtime policy is labeled BL_2. After the overtime policy goes into force, the hours of work never decrease because the original indifference curve cuts BL_2 to the left of 8 hours (and does not cut the budget line to the right of 8 hours). The only way to move to a new point of tangency is to move into the overtime region (work more than 8 hours). In fact, since the original indifference curve cuts BL_2, such a move must be utility increasing.

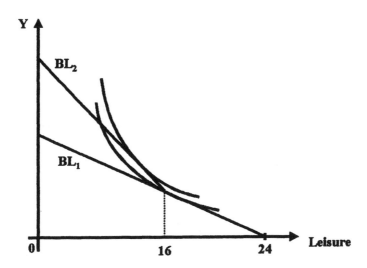

The second wage policy increases the slope of the budget constraint for all hours worked. The shift in the budget constraint is illustrated as BL_3 in the diagram below. Leisure may be an inferior or a normal good and the income effect of a wage increase may or may not outweigh the substitution effect. As a result, the second wage plan may or may not increase hours. Two possibilities are illustrated in panels (a) and (b) of the diagram below.

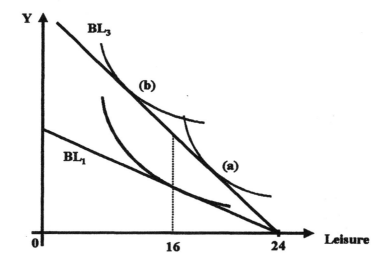

8.

a. The equation for the demand for food is $I/2p_x = x$. Food is a normal good since an increase in income will result in an increase in x consumed. (An income consumption curve for x is upward sloping).

b. $I = \$70$, $p_y = \$1$, $p_{x1} = \$9$: Using the equation for demand, $x = 70/18$ and $y = 35$. $U_1 = 70(35)/18$. This is basket A. $P_{x2} = \$4$: Using the equation for demand, $x = 70/8$ and $y = 35$. $U_2 = 70(35)/8$. This is basket C. The decomposition basket yields the initial level of utility at the new price ratio so that, using the tangency condition, $y = 4x$ and $U = xy = 70(35)/18$, we have $x = 35/6$ and $y = 4(35)/6$ at decomposition basket B. The substitution effect is the change in x from A to B: $(70/18 - 105/18)$. The income effect is the change in x from B to C: $-(140/24 - 210/24)$.

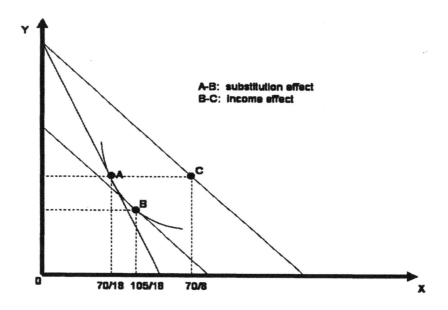

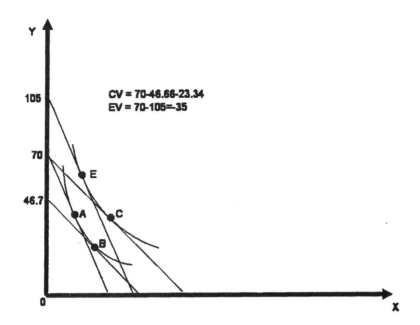

9.

a. The old budget constraint is $p_f f + 1h = I$ and, at the optimal basket, we have $p_f f_1 + h_1 = I$. The intercept is I and the slope is $-p_f$. The new budget constraint is $(p_f+t)f + 1h = I + tf$ and, at the optimal consumption basket, we have $(p_f+t)f_2 + h_2 = I + tf_2$. The intercept is $I + tf_2$ and the slope is $-(p_f+t)$. Canceling the tax terms from the new budget constraint, we have $p_f f_2 + h_2 = I$. This means that the new basket, (f_2, h_2), lies on the old budget constraint as well as on the new budget constraint.

b. Since the new basket, (f_2, h_2), lies on the old budget constraint as well as on the new budget constraint, we know that basket (f_1, h_1) was chosen when (f_2, h_2) was affordable. This means that the old basket must have been revealed preferred to the new basket. We can, then, draw a diagram illustrating the change due to the tax and rebate program as follows:

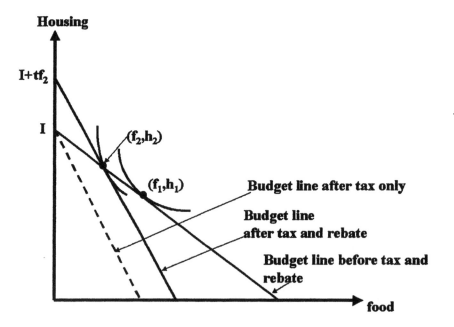

10.

a. The optimal choice of the consumer is determined by $MU_x/MU_Y = P_X/P_Y$, that is, $y/x = P_X/P_Y$ or, equivalently, $P_X x = P_Y y$: the consumer spends the same amount on each good. This is the equation of the income expansion path. We can then write the budget constraint as $I = P_X x + P_Y y = 2P_X x$. We can therefore write the Engel curve for good x as $I = 2P_X x$ and the Engel curve for y as $I = 2P_Y y$.

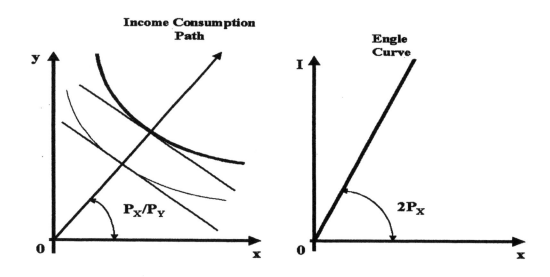

b. The indifference curves are right angles so that the consumer will always choose a consumption basket at the kink, where $x = y$. This is the equation of the income consumption path. Replacing y by x in the budget constraint gives us the Engel curve for good x: $I = P_X x + P_Y x = (P_X + P_Y)x$. Graphically, we have:

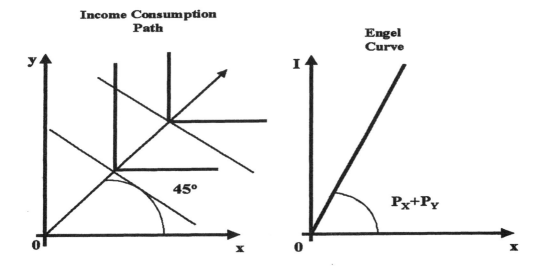

11. Define the basket of goods chosen in period 1 as (X_1, Y_1) and the basket of goods chosen in period 2 as (X_2, Y_2). Since the consumer has the same nominal income in both periods, we know that $P_{X1}X_1 + P_{Y1}Y_1 = I = P_{X2}X_2 + P_{Y2}Y_2$, that is, the consumer spends his whole income in each of the two periods. If the Laspeyers index is less than 1, then L = $[P_{X2}X_1 + P_{Y2}Y_1]/[P_{X1}X_1 + P_{Y1}Y_1] < 1$. This can be rewritten as $P_{X2}X_1 + P_{Y2}Y_1 < P_{X1}X_1 + P_{Y1}Y_1 = I$, which means that the consumer could have purchased (X_1, Y_1) in period 2. Since he did not and chose (X_2, Y_2) instead, he must be better off in period 2 than in period 1.

12. The network externality equal to 2Q must be added to the consumers' willingness to pay for the product, so that the market demand is P = 100 − 5Q + 2Q, or P = 100 − 3Q.

Answers to Exam

1. The consumer may have either moved along her demand curve or may have shifted demand curves. We could think of prices changing, with the price of X falling sufficiently that the budget line swings out to touch indifference curve U_2 at point B (a move along the demand curve) or we could think of income rising with the prices of X and Y unchanged. Either of these would allow the consumer to optimally consume at basket B. The graphs below depict the possibility of income rising with the prices unchanged first.

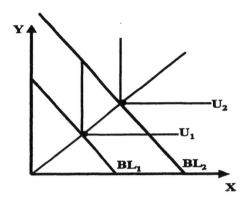

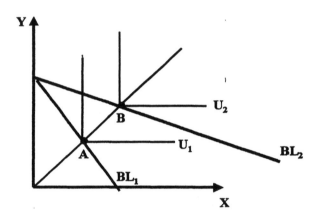

2. This is a quasi-linear utility function, so it does not exhibit income effects. Hence, we know that all measures of consumer's surplus are equal and, in some sense, consumer's surplus would represent our "ideal" measure of consumer well-being as a result of the price change.

More precisely, we can calculate the original, decomposition and new consumption baskets (where A and C denote the old and new consumption baskets, and B and C denote the decomposition baskets) as:

Old: $MU_x/MU_y = p_x/p_y \Leftrightarrow x^{-1/2}/2 = .5$ or $x_A = 1$. Hence, using budget
    constraint $y_A = 4.5$; $U_A = 2(1)^{1/2} + 2(4.5) = 11$
New: $MU_x/MU_y = p_x/p_y \Leftrightarrow x^{-1/2}/2 = .25$ or $x_C = 4$. Hence, $y_c = 4$
    $U_c = 2(4)^{1/2} + 2(4) = 12$
New Price/Old Utility: min $1X + 4Y$ s.t. $11 = 2x^{1/2} + 2Y \rightarrow x^{-1/2}/2 = 1/4$ or $x_B = 4$. Hence, using constraint, $y_B = 3.5$
Old Price/New Utility: min $2X + 4Y$ s.t. $12 = 2x^{1/2} + 2Y \rightarrow x^{-1/2}/2 = 2/4$ or $x_D = 1$. Hence, using constraint, $y_D = 5$.

Therefore, $CV = I - (p_{x2}X_B + p_yY_B) = 20 - [1(4) + 4(3.5)] = 20-4-14 = 2$. In other words, the price fall here is equivalent to gaining two units of income. All other measures of consumer benefit should be the same, but this can be checked by noting that EV = $p_{x1}X_D$ + p_yY_D - I = 2(1)+4(5)-20=2+20-20=2.

3.

a. The equation for market demand is Q = NQ_i = 10N − NP.

b. Market demand is flatter, since each price elicits demand from N consumers instead of only one. This is shown below.

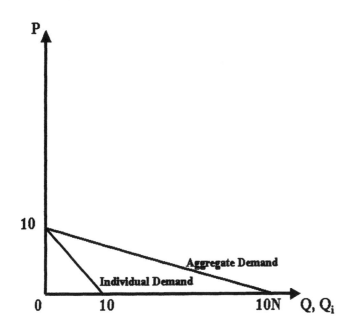

c. At P = 5, the elasticity of market demand is $\varepsilon_{P,Q}$ = (ΔQ/ΔP)(P/Q) = -N(5/5N) = -1. The elasticity of individual demand is (ΔQ_i/ΔP)(P/Q_i) = -1(5/5) = -1. Hence, the elasticity of demand stays the same when we aggregate over identical consumers, even though the slope changes. In this sense, the elasticity preserves the information about the individual consumer's demand better than the slope.

4. If both wages and prices rose by the same amount over the same period, Melvyn's budget constraint representing the tradeoff between consuming a composite good and leisure has not changed slope or intercept. As a result, there is no reason for Melvyn's optimal consumption basket of the composite good and leisure to have changed and he attains the same level of utility as before. Similarly, in terms of Melvyn's consumption of the various goods that make up his composite good (say, goods x and y), the tradeoff among these goods has not changed since the relative prices of goods x and y have not changed and his income has exactly offset the rise in prices of goods since his wages have risen by the same amount -- and we know that his optimal number of hours worked has not changed. Therefore, in terms of his relative consumption of goods x and y, Melvyn attains the same level of utility as before the change and is made no worse off by the change in wages and prices.

5. In this chapter, we modeled the labor supply decision as a "labor-leisure trade-off", where labor included all work hours and leisure included all non-work activities (and so was the complement of "labor" in the day). Utility was a function of a composite good ("y") with a price of $1 and leisure ("l") with a price that is measured by, in effect, the wage rate (w). The budget line gives all the combinations of y and l the consumer/worker can afford. As the wage rate rises, then, the composite good is less expensive in terms of hours of work needed to purchase a unit of y and the budget line rotates. The optimal choice of labor shifts as w changes because a substitution effect leads to less leisure and more labor as w increases, but as w increases, the consumer feels as though he has more income because less work is needed to buy a unit of y. This creates an income effect. If leisure is a normal good, the income effect on leisure is positive (and the effect on labor is negative). If the income effect of a wage increase outweighs the substitution effect, the labor supply curve bends backwards. This politician seems to indicate that, at the lower wage levels, the supply of labor slopes upwards. At higher wage levels, as illustrated above, this need not be the case. The politician's proposed wage increase could possibly make the shortage worse again!

Chapter 6: Inputs and Production Functions

The next few chapters investigate the theory that lies behind the aggregate supply function. The theory of production, set forth in this chapter, is quite similar to the theory of preferences and utility presented in Chapter 3. Therefore, you will already be familiar with the concepts and many of the functional forms described here.

Production transforms a set of productive resources (**inputs**), such as labor, materials, and capital equipment, into a set of goods and services (**outputs**) that may be purchased by consumers or used as inputs by other firms. The technology employed determines the output that can be obtained from a given set of inputs. Different technologies may allow the firm to attain different levels of output for the same levels of input, or may allow the firm to combine inputs differently to obtain the same level of output. The *maximum* possible output that can be attained by the firm for any given quantity of inputs is given by the **production function** of the firm: it is the best the firm can do given the various production methods and technologies available to it at the time. Mathematically, the production function can be written as follows:

$$Q = f(K,L,M,...)$$

Where Q is the output, K is capital input, L is labor input, and M is land input. Of course, other arguments could be included as well. For example, the output, Q, in bushels of corn per year obtained on a farm might be a function of the number of plants, P, per acre planted in that year, pounds of fertilizer, F, used per acre for the year, the man-hours of labor used in that year, L, the fertile acreage during the year, A, and the amount of rainfall R: $Q = f(P,F,L,A,R)$.

- If the firm is producing in a **technically efficient** way, it is attaining the maximum possible output from its inputs. In other words, the production function accurately represents production at the firm. If the firm is technically inefficient, then its output falls short of the level predicted by the production function. The feasible but inefficient points below the production function make up the firm's **production set**. The production function simply describes the upper boundary of the production set. The production function and the production set are pictured in Figure 6.1 for a production function with only a single input labor, L, and an output, Q.

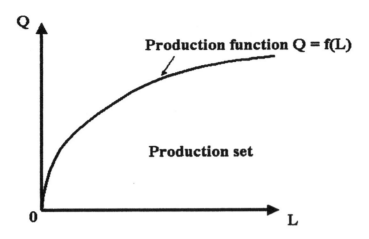

Figure 6.1

- A production function describes the maximum amount of output that can be produced with any given combination of inputs *for a given time period.* Therefore, labor is measured in terms of man-hours used over this period. Similarly, capital is measured as the machine-hours used to produce the output over the same period of time. In short, all variables in the production function are **flows**, not **stocks.** A stock measures the absolute size of something at a point in time. A flow measures the amount of something used over a time interval. For example, the stock of capital available at a factory would include the total factory installation (in square footage, number of machines, and so on), but the flow of capital used in production would be the depreciation in the installation and the machine-hours used per unit of time.

- Capital refers to **physical capital**: goods that are themselves produced goods. It does not refer to **financial capital**, which is the money required to start or maintain production. (In other words, the production function is a purely technological concept.) The issue of how much it costs to produce will be dealt with in the next chapter, while the issue of how to finance an enterprise will not be within the scope of this text.

- If we invert the production function shown on the graph, we get the minimum amount of inputs that are required to produce a given amount of output, Q. For example, if there is only a single input, labor, we obtain the **labor requirement function** by solving for labor as a function of output, L = g(Q).

Exercise 1: *In Joe's office are a box of 15 pencils and a package of 200 sheets of white paper. Joe uses up 1 centimeter of one pencil, one sheet of paper, and 15 minutes of his time to write a letter. Let Joe's pencil use be P (measured in* *centimeters used per day); let his paper use be S (measured in sheets per day); let his labor be L (measured in man-hours per day). The wage he is paid, W, is $5 per hour. Based on this information, which of the following statements is true about Joe's production of letters, measured in quantity of letters produced per day, Q?*

   a. Joe's production function has four inputs: P, S, L, and W.
   b. Joe's flow input of pencils is the amount of pencil used up measured in centimeters per day. His stock of pencils is 15.
   c. A point in the production set would be Q = 2, P = 10, S = 5, and L = 3.
   d. A point on the production function would be Q = 2, P = 2, S = 2, and L = 1.

The production function is, in many ways, analogous to the utility function of the consumer: just as the utility function told us the preference level associated with various combinations of purchases, the production function tells us the level of output associated with various combinations of inputs. The utility function was derived from preferences, and the properties of these preferences determined the properties of the utility functions. Similarly, the production function is derived from technologies and the basic properties of the technologies determine the properties of the production function. For example, the production functions we see in this chapter are based on technologies that are monotonic, so that having at least as much of both inputs allows the firm to produce at least as much output as before.

In consumer theory, an indifference curve was the set of combinations of the goods that resulted in the same level of satisfaction for the consumer. In production theory an **isoquant** tells us the set of all possible combinations of the inputs that are just sufficient to produce a given amount of output. Each point on an isoquant corresponds to a technically efficient combination of inputs, that is, to a point on the production function. Isoquants located farther to the northeast correspond to higher levels of output. Like indifference curves, isoquants are **convex** to the origin, reflecting the fact that average levels of inputs (point C) result in higher levels of output than extremes (points A and B).

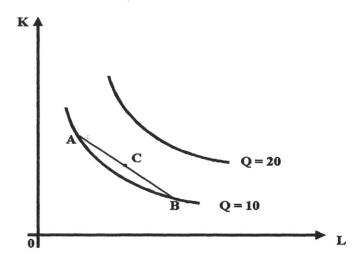

Figure 6.2

Like indifference curves, isoquants cannot cross, since crossing would be in conflict with the assumption that output is produced efficiently. For example, if an isoquant that produced 10 units of output crossed with an isoquant producing only 5 units, then at the point of intersection the same input combination would at the same time produce 5 units of outputs and 10 units! The isoquant representing only 5 units of output could not, then, represent an efficient use of inputs.

There is, however, an important difference. A utility function is an *ordinal* concept: it only helps us *rank* baskets of goods but does not allow us to say by *how much* a basket of goods is preferred to the other. One cannot, for example, say that a consumer likes a basket A that corresponds to a utility of 200 twice as much as a basket B that corresponds to a utility of 100. On the other hand, a production function is a *cardinal* concept: a combination of inputs allowing us to produce 200 cars *does produce twice as much* as a combination of inputs allowing us to produce 100 cars.

Exercise 2: *Consider the graph of the isoquants of a production function for wheat, below. For this isoquant map, which of the following is true?*

a. The underlying technology is convex
b. The underlying technology is monotonic
c. The isoquants do not cross
d. The units we measure output in do not matter

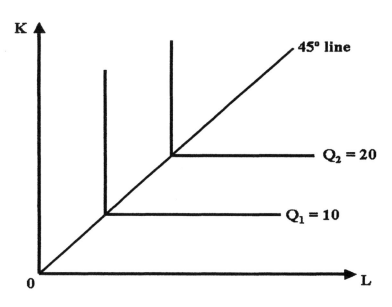

Figure 6.3

The marginal rate of substitution measured the amount of good x the consumer would require in exchange for giving up a small amount of good y to remain just indifferent between the new and the old baskets. Similarly, the **marginal rate of technical substitution** of labor for capital (MRTS) measures the extra amount of input K the firm would require in exchange for using a little less of input L in order to just be able to produce the same output as before. The MRTS is equal to minus the slope of the isoquant in the same way as the marginal rate of substitution was minus the slope of the indifference curve:

$MRTS_{L,K}$ = -$\Delta K/\Delta L$ (for a constant level of output) = - slope of isoquant

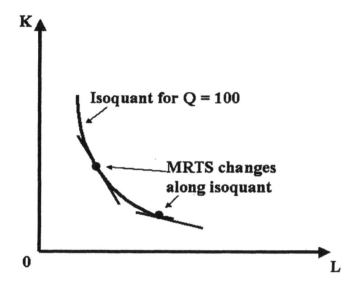

Figure 6.4

The **marginal product** of an input is the change in output that results from a small change in an input, *holding the levels of all other inputs constant.* For example, we have:

Marginal product of labor: MP_L = $\Delta Q/\Delta L$ (holding constant all other inputs)

Marginal product of capital: MP_K = $\Delta Q/\Delta K$ (holding constant all other inputs)

The marginal product of an input must be distinguished carefully from its **average product.** The average product of an input is simply equal to the total output produced divided by the quantity of the input that is used in its production:

Average product of labor: AP_L = Q/L
Average product of capital: AP_K = Q/K

Graphically, the total product, average product, and marginal product can be related as follows for a production function Q = f(L), where Q is output and L is labor:

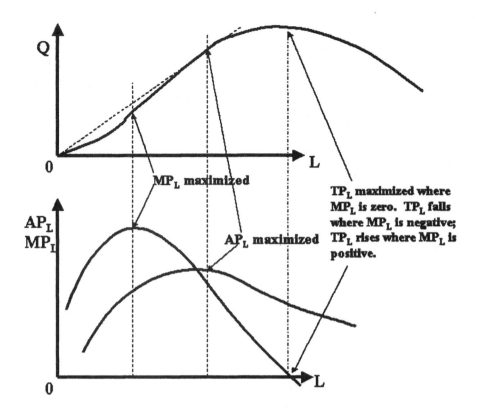

Figure 6.5

Total, Average, and Marginal: The Rough Guide

A meteorologist measures the daily amount of rainfall throughout the year. For the nine days up to January 10, the **total** amount of rain that has fallen is 45 millimeters so that the **average** daily rainfall has been 45/9=5 millimeters. If January 10 is a dry day then the **marginal** amount of rainfall is zero so that the total rainfall remains unchanged. On the other hand, the average rainfall has decreased from 5 mm to 45/10=4.5 mm a day. Suppose now that January 10 is a "typical" day where rainfall is just equal to the daily average of 5 mm. Total rainfall increases to 50 mm and the average rainfall remains unchanged at (45 + 5)/10 = 5 mm. If, on the other hand, January 10 is a very wet day with precipitation of 15 mm then the total rainfall increases by 15 mm, that is, by the amount of the marginal rainfall. Because this marginal rainfall is now greater than the average rainfall so far, the average rainfall also increases to (45 + 15)/10 = 6 mm a day. This example illustrates the following general rules governing the relationship between total, marginal, and average magnitudes:

- The total magnitude increases, decreases, or remains unchanged as the marginal magnitude is positive, negative, or equal to zero.

- The average magnitude increases, decreases, or stays the same as the marginal magnitude is greater, smaller, or equal to the average magnitude.

Exercise 3: *From the information given in the following table concerning the production function Q = f(L,K), fill in the blanks. If you cannot fill in a cell with the information given, leave the cell blank:*

L	K	Q	AP_L	MP_L	AP_K	MP_K
1	3		30			
2	3	60				
3	3			15		
3	2					15
3	1	30				

The marginal product of an input typically declines as we use more and more of this input. For example, the amount of wheat that can be grown on 20 acres of land increases drastically if one employs two workers rather than one, but it would increase very little if the number of workers rises from 50 to 51. This relation is so pervasive that it is referred to as the **law of diminishing marginal returns**, even though it is simply an empirical regularity and not a law based on any theoretical principle. Generally, we will only be concerned with the case of marginal products that remain positive (even if declining). The region where the marginal product becomes negative (so that the total returns to the input are decreasing) is called the **uneconomic region of production.** No rational producer would choose to operate in this region since one could at the same time increase output and decrease cost by using less of the input with a negative marginal product.

Exercise 4: *Consider the following set of isoquants:*

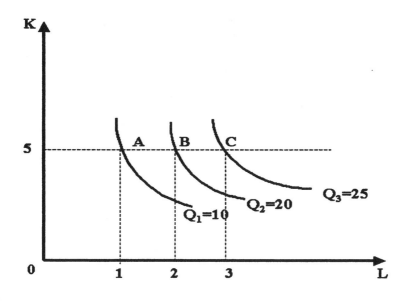

Figure 6.6

Which of the following statements is true?

   a. The marginal product of labor is positive
   b. The marginal product of capital is negative
   c. The marginal product of labor is rising

In the same way as the marginal rate of substitution could be related to the marginal utility, the marginal rate of technical substitution can be related to the marginal product of the inputs. A move along the isoquant is defined by a change in L and K that leaves total output unchanged. Mathematically, a small change in L will result in a total change in output of $MP_L(\Delta L)$ and a small change in K will result in a total change in output of $MP_K(\Delta K)$. In order to stay on the same isoquant, we want the sum of these changes in output to be zero or,

$$MP_L(\Delta L) + MP_K(\Delta K) = 0$$

Rearranging terms, this gives us a relation between the marginal products and the marginal rate of technical substitution that is analogous to our earlier result of Chapter 3:

$$MP_L/MP_K = MRTS_{L,K}$$

We can see from this relation that if the marginal product of both inputs is positive, the slope of the isoquant must be negative. This is the case that we will focus on subsequently in the same way as we focused on the case where indifference curves were negatively sloped in earlier chapters.

Exercise 5: *If the slope of the isoquant is positive, it must be the case that:*

   a. The firm is operating in the uneconomic region of production
   b. The marginal product of both inputs is negative
   c. The marginal product of one of the inputs is negative
   d. The firm is not operating in the uneconomic region of production

Exercise 6: *Consider the production function $Q = 4(KL)^{1/2}$, where Q is output, L is labor, and K is capital. The marginal products of capital and labor are: $MP_K = 2K^{-1/2}L^{1/2}$ and $MP_L = 2K^{1/2}L^{-1/2}$. What is the $MRTS_{L,K}$ at K = 4 and L = 1?*

   a. 1/4
   b. 4
   c. 1
   d. 1/9

What is the $MRTS_{K,L}$ at K = 9 and L = 1?

   a. 9
   b. 1
   c. 1/9
   d. 4

If the marginal products decline as we use more of a single input, then the marginal rate of technical substitution of labor for capital, $MRTS_{L,K}$ *falls* as one moves down along the isoquant: as some capital is replaced by labor, MP_L decreases and MP_K increases so that $MRTS = MP_L/MP_K$ becomes smaller. In other words, isoquants with the convex shape that we often see have a **diminishing rate of technical substitution**. Thus, as we increase the use of labor, we must offset any increase in labor by an ever-smaller decrease in capital in order to keep output constant along the isoquant. As we decrease the use of labor, we must offset any increase in labor by an ever-larger decrease in capital in order to keep output constant along the isoquant.

The **elasticity of substitution**, σ, measures the curvature of the isoquant, that is, how the **capital-labor ratio**, K/L, changes relative to the change in the marginal rate of technical substitution of the labor for capital. It is defined as:

$$\sigma = [\Delta(K/L) / \Delta(MRTS_{L,K})] \times [MRTS_{L,K}/(K/L)]$$

The elasticity of substitution answers the question "How much do you have to change the ratio of inputs in order to get to a flatter part of the isoquant?" or, equivalently, "How much flatter does the isoquant get when I move from one point to another point on the same isoquant?" If the isoquants have fairly little curvature (e.g., they are close to linear), then a large move on the isoquant map is associated with a small change in slope and the elasticity of substitution is large. In such a case labor and capital can be easily substituted for each other: along a linear isoquant, for example, K is completely substitutable for L at a constant rate equal to the slope of the isoquant. In other words, substituting L for K does not become harder as the amount of K already employed increases. Indeed, when the isoquant is perfectly linear, the elasticity of substitution is infinite, reflecting the fact that K and L are perfect substitutes. On the other hand, an elasticity of substitution close to zero corresponds to isoquants that are very convex. This indicates that the firm cannot easily substitute labor for capital. In the extreme case where the two inputs are perfect complements, the isoquants are L-shaped and an increase in one factor has no effect at all on output unless the other factor is increased as well.

Exercise 7: *Two points, A and B, lie on the same isoquant. Suppose that you are told that, at point A, the capital-labor ratio (K/L) equals 4, as does the marginal rate of technical substitution of labor for capital. At a point B, however, the capital-labor ratio equals 1, while the marginal rate of technical substitution is unchanged at 4. What is the shape of the isoquants?*

    a. Cannot tell from the information given
    b. Linear
    c. L-shaped
    d. None of the above

Exercise 8: *You are given the following information about two points A and B that lie on the same isoquant:*

$$MRTS^A_{L,K} = 1.1 \quad K^A/L^A = 11$$
$$MRTS^B_{L,K} = 1 \quad K^B/L^B = 1$$

What is the elasticity of substitution as we move along an isoquant from point A toward point B?

    a. 10
    b. 110
    c. 1
    d. .1

Given this value for elasticity, do you expect the isoquants to be:

    a. relatively linear?
    b. relatively curved?

The production function and its isoquants need not remain fixed over time. In particular, since the properties of the production function depend on the properties of the underlying technology, **technological progress** (or **invention**) can shift the production function by allowing the firm to achieve more output from a given combination of inputs (or the same output with fewer inputs). On the isoquant map, technological progress corresponds to an inward shift of the isoquants: each level of output can now be attained with lower quantities of inputs. We distinguish between three types of technological progress. If the isoquants shift inward, but the marginal rate of technical substitution remains unchanged along any ray from the origin, we have **neutral technological progress**. In other words, while it takes less labor and capital to manufacture the same amount of output, the basic shape of the isoquants has not changed. If technological progress makes the isoquant flatter at any capital/labor ratio, so that the marginal rate of technical substitution of labor for capital ($MRTS_{L,K}$) falls along any ray from the origin, then the technological progress is called **labor saving technological progress**. If the $MRTS_{L,K}$ tends to increase along any ray from the origin when technological progress occurs, then the change is referred to as **capital saving technological progress**.

Exercise 9: *The equation of an isoquant is 100 = 2L + 2K. After a technological change, the equation for an isoquant based on the new technology is 100 = 10L + 2K. Is this technological change?*

    a. Neutral
    b. Labor saving
    c. Capital saving

We have now introduced vocabulary to express how output varies when only a single input is increased (the concept of marginal product) or to express how inputs can be traded off to maintain a given level of output (the concepts of marginal rate of technical substitution or elasticity). These concepts are useful to describe the production plans that are feasible in the relatively short run, defined as the period when at least some of the factors of production will remain fixed. On the other hand, in the longer run, defined as the period for which all the factors of production can be varied, we need a way to express how much output will increase when the use of *all* inputs increases in the same proportion. In other words, we might wish to consider increasing the entire *scale* of operation of the firm rather than increasing the use of just one input. In order to express this relation, we use the concept of **returns to scale**, mathematically written as follows:

Returns to scale (RTS) = %Δ(quantity of output)/%Δ(quantity of all inputs)

We can divide production functions into three categories based on the way returns to scale behave:

- If a 1% increase in all inputs results in a greater than 1% increase in output, then the production function exhibits **increasing returns to scale (IRS)**.
- If a 1% increase in all inputs results in exactly a 1% increase in output, then the production function exhibits **constant returns to scale (CRS)**.
- If a 1% increase in all inputs results in a less than 1% increase in output, then the production function exhibits **decreasing returns to scale (DRS)**.

It is worth noting that a given production function can exhibit increasing, decreasing, or constant returns to scale depending on the level of output considered. Such a possibility is illustrated in Figure 6.7: the returns to scale are constant from Q_1 to Q_2 (since doubling the inputs doubles the output), increasing from Q_2 to Q_3 (since doubling the inputs more than doubles the output) and decreasing from Q_3 to Q_4 since doubling the inputs less than doubles the output).

Algebraically, the nature of returns to scale is determined by multiplying every factor of production by a factor $t > 1$ and determining whether the resulting output has been multiplied by more than t (IRS), less than t (DRS) or exactly t (CRS). For example, $Q = AKL^{0.5}$ exhibits increasing returns to scale because multiplying both L and K by t yields $A(tK)(tL)^{0.5} = t^{1.5}AKL^{0.5}$, which is greater than $tAKL^{0.5}$.

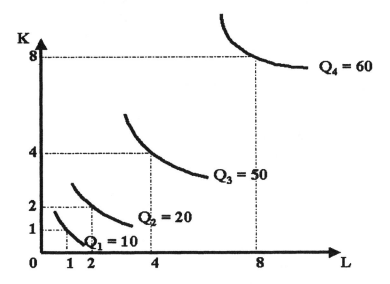

Figure 6.7

It is important to distinguish between decreasing marginal product and decreasing returns to scale. The first one refers to the effects of a change in *a single* factor of production while the second refers to a proportional change in *all* inputs. Indeed it can very well be the case that the marginal product of any single factor diminishes even though there are increasing returns to scale

Exercise 10: *Can the production function Q = min(AL,BK), where A and B are constants, ever exhibit increasing returns to scale?*

    a. yes
    b. no
    c. it depends on the relative size of A and B

The returns to scale of an industry are technologically determined. For example, a standard engineering relationship that results in increasing returns to scale is called the cube-square rule. This rule applies to any production process that uses containers (such as cargo shipping or beer brewing). The output of the container (the gallons of beer produced, for example) is proportional to the volume of the container, while the input requirements (the combination of wood and metal used to construct the casks in which the beer is brewed, for example) are proportional to the surface area of the container. Since we know from geometry that as the surface area of an object increases, the volume of the object increases at a greater rate, production processes such as these exhibit increasing returns to scale.

Finally, as in the case of consumer demand theory, it will be useful to become familiar with some standard production functions:

- **Linear production function**, generally represented as $Q = aL + bK$, where a and b are positive constants. This production function is characterized by linear isoquants, so that the $MRTS_{L,K}$ is constant along the isoquant as we change the proportions of labor and capital used. The elasticity of substitution is infinite (so that each input is perfectly substitutable for every other input). Finally, a linear production function exhibits constant returns to scale.

- **Fixed proportions production function** (also called the **Leontief production function**), generally represented as $Q = min(aL,bK)$, where a and b are positive constants. This production function is characterized by L-shaped isoquants. The $MRTS_{L,K}$ is infinite on the vertical segment of the isoquant and zero on the horizontal segment. The elasticity of substitution is zero (so that each input is a perfect complement for the other input). The returns to scale are constant.

- **Cobb-Douglas production function**, generally represented as $Q = aL^{\alpha}K^{\beta}$, where a, α, and β are positive constants. This production function is characterized by isoquants that are convex to the origin (so that the $MRTS_{L,K}$ varies continuously along the isoquant). The elasticity of substitution is exactly one (so that each input is an imperfect substitute for the other input). Such production functions can exhibit increasing, decreasing, or constant returns to scale depending on the exponents, α and β, in the following way:

- If $\alpha + \beta > 1$, then the production function exhibits increasing returns to scale.
- If $\alpha + \beta = 1$, then the production function exhibits constant returns to scale.
- If $\alpha + \beta < 1$, then the production function exhibits decreasing returns to scale.

- **Constant Elasticity of Substitution (CES) production function**, generally represented as $Q = [aL^\phi + bK^\phi]^{1/\phi}$, where a and b are positive constants. The parameter ϕ is related to the elasticity of substitution σ according to the formula $\phi = [\sigma\text{-}1]/\sigma$. The three production functions that we have seen before are all special cases of the CES function: when σ is set to zero, we obtain L-shaped isoquants, when σ is set to infinity, we obtain linear isoquants, and when σ is set to 1, we obtain isoquants that are convex to the origin, as in the Cobb-Douglas case. The advantage of this function is that it not only has all the other special production functions as special cases, but it also has the flexibility to represent many other types of isoquants with other values of σ.

Chapter Review Questions

1. It takes three packages of cement mix, one bucket of water and a shovel-full of sand to mix a wheelbarrow-full of cement to patch a wall. If these proportions are not respected, the mixture is useless. Based on this information, which function best represents the production function for cement, where Q is the quantity of cement in wheelbarrows, P is the quantity of cement mix in packages, W is the quantity of water in buckets, S is the quantity of sand in shovel-fulls.

    a. $Q = \min (3P, W, S)$

    b. $Q = 3P + W + S$

    c. $Q = \min (P, W, S)$

    d. $Q = \min (P/3, W, S)$

    e. $Q = 3PWS$

Answer:

The best answer would be (d). Each wheelbarrow of cement requires mix, water, and sand in *fixed* proportions (3:1:1): one extra bucket of water does not increase the quantity of usable cement unless it is accompanied by an extra shovel-full of sand and three extra packages of cement. Production functions (c) and (a) and (d) all represent fixed proportions "recipes" for making cement. However, the "recipes" of production functions (c) and (a) are wrong. In the case of (c), the "recipe" says that *one* package of mix, one bucket of water, and one shovel-full of sand are required to make a wheelbarrow of cement. Recipe (a) also gets the proportions wrong: it states that we need only 1/3 package of mix per wheelbarrow, whereas we need three.

2. Suppose that a production function can be written $Q = 9KL^2 - L^3$.

   a. Graph the function for $K = 1$ with Q on the vertical axis and L on the horizontal axis. On your graph, show the regions for which the marginal product of labor is rising, constant, falling, and negative. At what value of L does Q reach a maximum?

   b. For $K = 1$, show the regions for which the average product of labor is rising, constant, falling, and negative.

   c. Calculate the formula for the average product of labor. At what level of L does the average product of labor equal the marginal product of labor?

   d. At what level of labor does the marginal product of labor become negative? How does this relate to the point at which the total product is at a maximum?

Answer:

   a. If $K = 1$, the production function becomes $Q = 9L^2 - L^3$. By plugging values into this function, we obtain the following figures:

L	Q	MP_L	AP_L
0	0	0	0
1	8	8	8
2	28	20	14
3	54	26	18
4	80	26	20
5	100	20	20
6	108	8	18
7	98	-10	14
8	64	-34	8
9	0	-64	0

And the graph below:

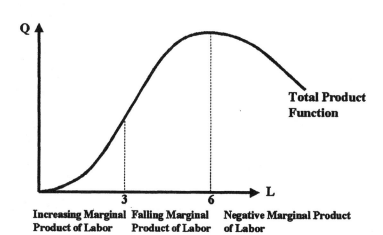

Q

Total Product Function

L

3   6

Increasing Marginal Falling Marginal   Negative Marginal Product
Product of Labor   Product of Labor   of Labor

This production function reaches a maximum at L = 6. This can be seen from the table.

b. The average product is rising for L < 4, constant at L = 4 to L = 5 and falling thereafter. The average product becomes negative at L = 9.

c. The average product of labor is the total product divided by the amount of labor or $9L - L^2$. From the table, we can see that the average product of labor equals the marginal product of labor at L = 5 (or, in other words, at the point where the average product is at a maximum).

d. The marginal product of labor becomes negative after L = 6 (or, in other words, after the point where the total product begins to fall).

3. Consider the production function $Q = 2K^2 + 3KL + .1L^2$. For this function, the marginal product of labor is $MP_L = 3K + .2L$ and the marginal product of capital is $MP_K = 4K + 3L$. Does this production exhibit increasing, decreasing, or constant returns to scale?

Answer:

We compute returns to scale by computing the amount of output we obtain by increasing all inputs by a factor, λ. If the increase in output exactly equals λ, then we have constant returns to scale. If it is less, we have decreasing returns to scale. If it is more, we have increasing returns to scale.

If K and L are both increased by λ, we have an amount of output: $Q' = 2[\lambda K]^2 + [3\lambda K\lambda L] + .1[\lambda L]^2 = (2K^2 + 3KL + .1L^2)\lambda^2 = \lambda^2 Q$. In words, multiplying all inputs by λ results in a more than proportional increase in output: there are increasing returns to scale.

Problem Set

1. In 1798, Thomas Malthus predicted that the rate of population growth would exceed that of food production because the quantity of land available for cultivation was fixed. As a result, he believed that mass starvation would occur. This has not occurred, however, despite the fact that world population has increased since Malthus' time, but the amount of land devoted to agriculture has dropped.

a. Suppose that food, Q, is produced using land, A, and labor, L, as inputs according to a production function Q = f(A, L). Using the concept of diminishing marginal product, explain Malthus' prediction of mass starvation.

b. Using the concept of technological progress, explain why Malthus' prediction has not come true.

2. The production function for an output, Q, is Q = KL.

    a. Draw some sample isoquants for this production function.

    b. Is this technology monotonic or convex?

    c. Can the isoquants for this production function cross?

3. A study of reports that the elasticity of substitution between capital and labor in the food industry is .9, while the elasticity of substitution between capital and labor in the chemicals industry is .2.

    a. Draw representative isoquants for the food and chemicals industries. Compare and contrast the two.

    b. A wage rise occurs across the board, affecting all industries. In which industry, food or chemicals, do you see more scope for firms to substitute out of labor? Justify your answer.

4. (This problem continues in chapter 7, problem 1 and chapter 8, problem 2). A firm has production function $Q = 100L^{3/4}K^{1/4}$, with $MP_L = 75K^{1/4}L^{-1/4}$ and $MP_K = 25L^{3/4}K^{-3/4}$ and faces a constant wage of w per unit for labor input and a constant rental rate of capital of r per unit.

    a. Write the equation of a sample isoquant.

    b. Derive an expression for the marginal rate of technical substitution for this production function. Give a geometric interpretation of the marginal rate of technical substitution.

    c. What is the elasticity of substitution at a point K = 1, L = 1 if we increase K by one unit?

    d. What are the returns to scale for this production function?

5. The following chart describes a production process:

L	K	Q	AP_L	MP_L	AP_K	MP_K
1	1	10	10	-	10	-
1	2	20	20	-	10	10
1	3	30	30	-	10	10
2	1	20	10	10	20	-
2	2	40	20	20	20	10
2	3	60	30	30	20	10
3	1	30	10	10	30	-
3	2	60	20	20	30	30
3	3	75	25	15	25	15

a. What is the marginal rate of technical substitution between L and K when L = 2 and K = 2? When L = 2 and K = 3? When L = 3 and K = 2?

b. What is the elasticity of substitution as we move from point (L,K) = (2,2) to (L,K) = (2,3)? What is the elasticity of substitution as we move from point (L,K) = (2,2) to (L,K) = (3,2)?

c. What can you say about the shape of the production function as we move from (L,K) = (2,2) to (L,K) =(2,3)? What can you say about the shape of the production function as we move from (L,K) = (2,2) to (L,K) = (3,2)?

6. Pigs can eat corn, soybean oil meal, or any combination of these two foods. Both these foods contain some carbohydrates and some protein, but corn has a relatively high carbohydrate content while soybean oil meal has a relatively high protein content.

a. Suppose that all that matters to weight gain is the total number of calories consumed. Further, suppose that corn contains twice the calories as the soybean oil meal food per pound. Draw an isoquant map for weight gain for pigs based on food inputs of either corn or soybean meal in pounds. What is the slope of these isoquants?

b. What matters for weight gain is still the total number of calories consumed, but the pigs must also get a good balance between carbohydrates and proteins. As long as they get these two elements in reasonable proportions, pigs thrive according to the number of calories received. However, if pigs receive too high a proportion of either proteins or carbohydrates, they die. Indeed, a diet based exclusively on either one of the two foods would be toxic. What do the isoquants for weight gain now look like?

7. Draw an isoquant map for the following production processes:

a. Suits production where trousers are on the horizontal axis and jackets are on the vertical axis.

b. Ocean shipping, which may occur either in capital-intensive but not labor-intensive "fast boats" or in labor-intensive but not capital-intensive "slow boats", but these two types of boats may not be combined in the same fleet.

c. Ocean shipping, where fast boats and slow boats, as described in part (b) of the question can be combined within the same fleet in any proportion.

Exam *(60 minutes: Closed book, closed notes)*

1. For a linear production function, must the marginal products be constant, decreasing, or increasing?

2. For the isoquant map illustrated below, answer the following questions:

   a. For what region of the isoquant map is the marginal product of labor negative? For what region is the marginal product of capital negative?

   b. For what region is the $MRTS_{L,K}$ negative? For what region is it positive?

   c. Where is the uneconomic region of production?

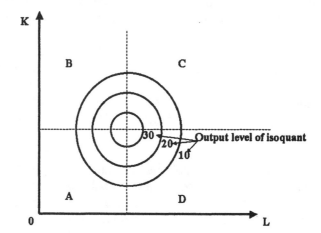

3. A firm produces q from labor L and raw materials M according to the production function $q = L^{2/3}M^{1/4}$, with marginal products $MP_L = (2/3)L^{-1/3}M^{1/4}$ and $MP_M = (1/4)L^{2/3}M^{-3/4}$.

   a. Does the production function exhibit decreasing, constant or increasing returns to scale?

   b. Derive an expression for the marginal rate of technical substitution of labor for materials as a function of L and M. Give a geometric interpretation of the marginal rate of technical substitution.

4. Suppose that a technology must use labor and capital in fixed proportions. Technology changes and allows these inputs to be substitutable, albeit not perfectly substitutable. Therefore, while the efficient combination of inputs of the original technology still produces the same amount of output as before, other combinations of labor and capital also can produce the same level of output under the new technology.

   a. Illustrate the technological change on an isoquant diagram.

b. Show the regions for which the technological change has been labor saving, capital saving, or neutral.

Answers to Exercises

1. Only statements (b) and (c) are true. W is not an input to the production function since the production function is a pure technical relationship (like a recipe, for example) for producing output. The same way as you would not include the wages of the cook in a recipe for a cake, we would not include the wages of the letter writer in the production function for a letter. Statement d is incorrect because two letters ($Q = 2$) can be produced with a minimum of 2 centimeters of pencil ($P = 2$), two sheets of paper ($S = 2$), and only 1/2 hour of work ($L = 1/2$). Therefore, the input combination of statement (d) is not an efficient way of producing two letters. It belongs to the production set, but is not on the production function. Notice that the input combination of statement (c) is even less efficient at producing two letters than the input combination of statement (d). The input combination of statement (c) is, however, a member of the production set as well.

2. The correct answers are (a), (b), and (c). (d) is incorrect because the production function is a cardinal concept. It is not the same thing to say that one unit of labor and one unit of capital produce one letter and that the same units produce a box of letters, for example.

3.

L	K	Q	AP_L	MP_L	AP_K	MP_K
1	3	30	30	30	10	---------
2	3	60	30	30	20	-----------
3	3	75	25	15	25	----------
3	2	60	20	-----------	30	15
3	1	30	10	-----------	30	30

First line: $AP_L = Q/L$ hence $30 = Q/1 \Rightarrow Q = 30 \Rightarrow AP_K = 30/3 = 10$ and $MP_L = (30-0)/1 = 30$. Second line: $AP_L = 60/2 = 30$, $MP_L = (60-30)/(2-1) = 30$ and $AP_K = 60/3 = 20$. Third line: $MP_L = \Delta Q/(3-2) = 15 \Rightarrow \Delta Q = 15$ so that the new level of output is $Q = 60 + 15 = 75$. Therefore $AP_L = 75/3 = 25$ and $AP_K = 75/3 = 25$. Fourth line: K has decreased by one unit and $MP_K = 15 \Rightarrow Q$ must have decreased by 15 to $Q = 75 - 15 = 60 \Rightarrow AP_L = 60/3 = 20$ and $AP_K = 60/2 = 30$. Fifth line: a decrease of one unit of capital has led to a decrease of $60 - 30 = 30$ units in output $\Rightarrow MP_K = 30$. Also $AP_L = 30/3 = 10$ and $AP_K = 30/1 = 30$.

4. (a) and (b) are correct. The marginal product of labor is positive for the isoquants shown on the graph since more labor for the same amount of capital (i.e., a move from point A to point B to point C) is associated with an increase in output from 10 to 20 to 25. The marginal product of capital is positive for all the

isoquants we see since, along any vertical line (where labor is constant), as we increase capital, output increases as well. The marginal product of labor is falling. This can be seen by first tracing across the horizontal line from point A to point B and calculating the increase in output (10 units) associated with the one unit increase in labor, and then tracing from point B to point C and noting that the increment of output (5 units) associated with the one unit increase in labor is less than the increment between points A and B.

5. (a) and (c) are correct. The slope of an isoquant is equal to $- MP_L/MP_K$. Therefore an isoquant can only have a positive slope if *one* of the two inputs has a negative marginal product. We are therefore in the uneconomic region of production since the firm could actually increase its output by reducing the level of the input that has a negative marginal product.

6. The correct answer to the first part of the question is (b). The correct answer to the second part of the question is (a). We know that $MRTS_{L,K} = MP_L/MP_K$. Substituting the formulas for the marginal products from the question, we obtain that $MP_L/MP_K = K/L = 4/1$. $MRTS_{K,L} = MP_K/MP_L$. Again, using the formulas for the marginal products given in the question, we obtain that $MP_K/MP_L = L/K = 9$.

7. The correct answer is (a). If we move from one point to another along the same isoquant and the MRTS does not change, it means that the slope of the isoquant is the same at these two points. This may mean that the slope of the isoquant does not change (so that it is the same everywhere). If the slope is constant everywhere, the isoquant must be linear. Therefore, (b) may be correct. It could also be the case, however, that while the MRTS is the same at these two points, it is different between these points or different in the tails. For example, either of the two following graphs might be a possibility:

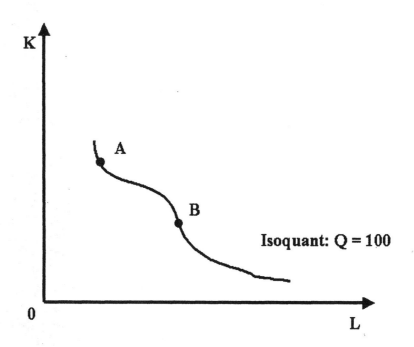

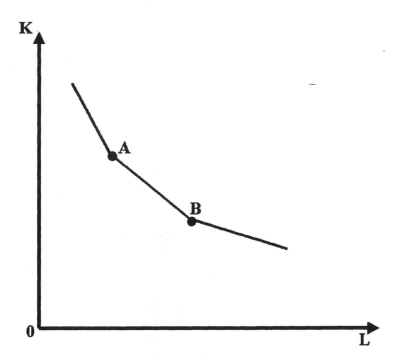

8. The correct answer to the first part of Exercise 8 is (a). The correct answer to the second part of Exercise 8 is (a). The change in the MRTS as we move from A to B is 1 - 1.1 = -.1. The change in the capital/labor ratio is 1 - 11 = -10. Therefore, using the formula for elasticity, we see that σ = (-10/-.1)(1.1/11) = 10. Figure 6.14 of the text shows isoquants for various CES production functions with different curvatures (or elasticities of substitution). From the figure, an elasticity of 10 would correspond to an isoquant that is close to linear.

9. The correct answer is (c). The $MRTS_{L,K}$ along the isoquant before the technological change is 2/2 = 1. This is the MRTS at all points along the isoquant, so along any ray from the origin, the MRTS along this isoquant is 1. The $MRTS_{L,K}$ everywhere along the isoquant after the technological change is 10/2 = 5. Hence, along any ray from the origin the MRTS has risen from 1 to 5 as a result of technological change. This is the definition of capital-saving technological progress.

10. The correct answer is (b). min(A(2L),B(2K)) = 2min(AL,BK) for any positive L and K so that this production function exhibits constant returns to scale.

Answers to Problem Set

1.

    a. Malthus' argument relies on the idea that the only possible way of increasing the production of food is to increase the amount of labor used in this sector. If the quantity of land is fixed and we have a diminishing marginal product of labor, the rate at which food production increases as we add more labor will be falling. In other words each laborer added produces less and less food. If the marginal product is always decreasing, then the average product must be falling as well. If this process continues, eventually each member of the population will fall below his or her starvation level of food.

b. Why, then, is the world *total* production of food adequate despite robust population growth and decreasing acreage devoted to the production of food? The answer is "technological progress". The "Law" of diminishing marginal returns refers to a single production function, but production functions may shift over time. As new seed varieties have become available and cultivation methods have improved, the production function for food has become more efficient so that more food can be produced with the same amount of labor and land. Even though the marginal product of labor may be falling along any single production function, it is not necessarily falling over time because the production function itself keeps shifting out. This is pictured below for the case of a fixed level of land. The average product rises over time as the total product function shifts up and the marginal product at any given labor input may rise over time as well. This is despite the fact that the marginal product diminishes along any single total product function. As a result, the marginal product of labor for $L = L_0$ measured as the slope of the initial production function can be lower than the marginal product of labor for $L = L_1 > L_0$ *at a later date*, which is measured as the slope of the new production function.

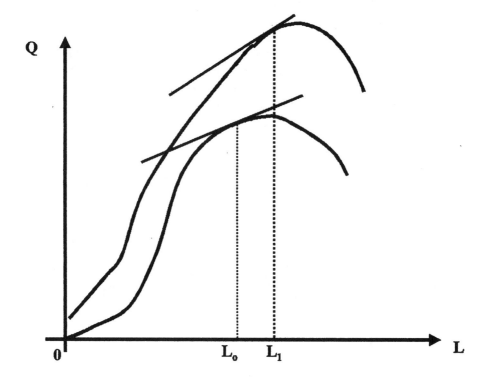

2.

a.

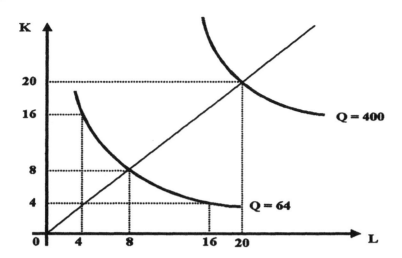

b. The technology is monotonic since an increase in either capital or labor results in an increase in Q. This corresponds to higher isoquants lying to the northeast on the graph. The technology is convex since a chord drawn between any two points on the same isoquant lies to the northeast of the isoquant. Thus, "average" input combinations result in higher levels of output than "extreme" input combinations.

c. No, since any given combination of capital and labor cannot (efficiently) yield two levels of output.

3.

b. For food, the elasticity is relatively close to 1, whereas for chemicals it is relatively close to zero, so we have a smooth curve for food, whereas the chemicals isoquant is almost L-shaped. This means that the capital and labor inputs to food are much more substitutable than those for chemicals.

c. There is more scope for substitution in food, following on answer (b). In other words, if I were to draw an isocost line in the graph, and change its slope (rotate it along the isoquant), I would move to a different capital-labor ratio for food, but would stay at almost the same capital-labor ratio for chemicals.

4.

a. A sample isoquant has the equation $Q^0 = 100L^{3/4}K^{1/4}$, where Q^0 is a fixed level of output.

b. $MRTS_{L,K} = -\Delta K/\Delta L = MP_L/MP_K = 75K^{1/4}L^{-1/4}/25L^{3/4}K^{-3/4} = 3K/L$

The marginal rate of technical substitution is the (negative of the) slope of the isoquant, as illustrated below:

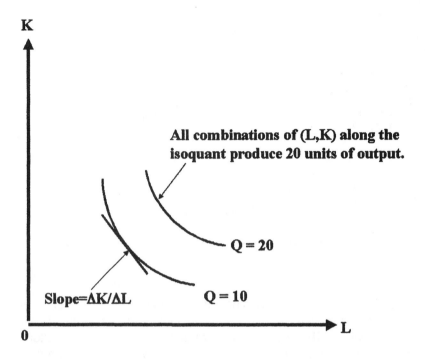

c. $\sigma = [\Delta(K/L) / \Delta (MRTS_{L,K})] \times [MRTS_{L,K}/(K/L)] = [(2-1)/(6-3)]X[3/1] = 1$

d. This is a Cobb-Douglas production function. Using the rule for adding exponents, stated in the text, we see that this function exhibits constant returns to scale since ¾ + ¼ = 1.

5.

a. $MRTS_{L,K} = 20/10 = 2$ when L = 2 and K = 2
   $MRTS_{L,K} = 30/10 = 3$ when L = 2 and K = 3
   $MRTS_{L,K} = 20/30 = 2/3$ when L = 3 and K = 2

b. $\sigma = [\Delta(K/L) / \Delta (MRTS_{L,K})] \times [MRTS_{L,K}/(K/L)] = [(1/2)/1][2/1] = 1$ when we move from (L,K) = (2,2) to (L,K) = (2,3) and $\sigma = [\Delta(K/L) / \Delta (MRTS_{L,K})] \times [MRTS_{L,K}/(K/L)] = [(-1/3)/(-4/3)][2/1] = 1/2$ when we move from (L,K) = (2,2) to (L,K) = (3,2).

c. As we move from (L,K) = (2,2) to (L,K) = (2,3) the isoquants get steeper, since the $MRTS_{L,K}$ increases. Similarly, the isoquants get flatter as we move from (L,K) = (2,2) to (L,K) = (3,2), since the $MRTS_{L,K}$ falls.

6.

a. If only the total calories consumed matter and the corn is twice as caloric as soybean oil meal, then the two foods are perfect substitutes with the corn being more productive in the proportion 2:1. Therefore, the isoquants are straight lines with a slope of -1/2 (since it takes twice as much soybean meal as corn to achieve the same output in terms of weight gain).

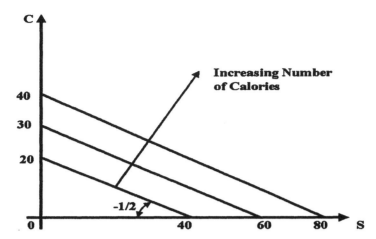

b. Pigs die if the proportion of corn in their diet is too low or if it is too high. These two limits are represented by the two rays from the origin on the graph below. Within these limits, the isoquants are as shown in part a. Outside of the cone defined by the two rays, pigs die.

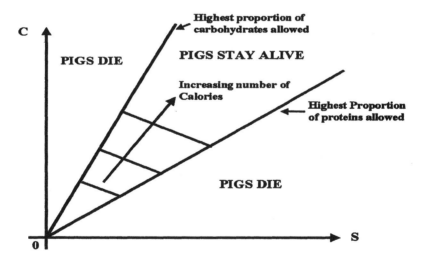

6.

a. The jackets and trousers are perfect complements. They are usually assembled in a proportion of one to one in order to make suits. Therefore the isoquants are L-shaped, with their corners lying on the 45-degree line. Some suits include two pairs of trousers for each jacket. For such suits, the isoquants are still L-shaped but their corners lie on a ray of slope 2 (with trousers on the vertical axis).

b. If the types of boats cannot be combined in the same fleet, then the isoquants look like two points corresponding to the two different technologies, as shown by points A and B, below.

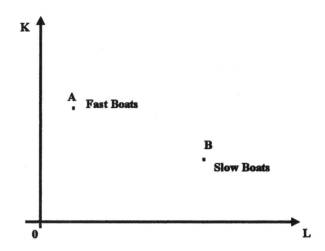

c. If the types of boats can be combined in the same fleet in any proportion, then the isoquants look like straight lines (as shown by the dotted line between points A and B, below).

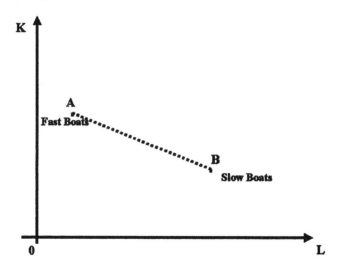

Answers to Exam

1. The marginal products must be constant for a linear production function: if Q = AL + BK, then the marginal product of labor is A and the marginal product of capital is B.

2.

a. For regions C and D, the marginal product of labor is negative since an increase in labor only (a horizontal move on the graph) causes output to fall. The marginal product of capital is negative in regions B and C since an increase in capital input only (a vertical move on the graph) causes output to fall.

b. The $MRTS_{L,K}$ is positive in regions A and C since the marginal product of both inputs is positive (therefore their ratio is positive) in region A and the marginal products are both negative in region C (so that their ratio is, again, positive). In regions B and D, the $MRTS_{L,K}$ is negative. In region B, the marginal product of capital is negative but the marginal product of labor is positive (so that their ratio is negative). In region D, the marginal product of labor is negative and the marginal product of capital is positive (so that their ratio is negative).

c. The uneconomic region of production is regions B, C, and D since, in each of these regions, at least one of the marginal products is negative. When one of the marginal products is negative, if means that an input could be reduced while still producing at least as much output, which contradicts the idea that the production function (and its isoquants) should represent only the most efficient methods of production.

3.

a. This production function exhibits decreasing returns to scale. We can see this by applying the rule that the sum of the exponents in the Cobb-Douglas production function gives us the returns to scale. In this case, the sum is $2/3 + 1/4 = 8+3/12 = 11/12 < 1$.

b. The $MRTS_{L,M} = MP_L/MP_M = (2/3)L^{-1/3}M^{1/4}/(1/4)L^{2/3}M^{-3/4} = (2/3)M/(1/4)L = (8/3)M/L$. Graphically, we can see that the MRTS falls as we move along the isoquant from large values of M and small values of L to large values of L and small values of M.

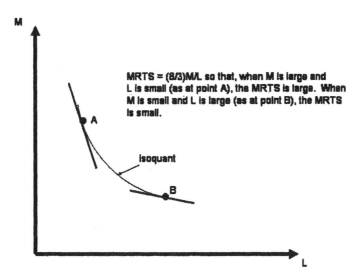

MRTS = (8/3)M/L so that, when M is large and L is small (as at point A), the MRTS is large. When M is small and L is large (as at point B), the MRTS is small.

Isoquant

4.

a.

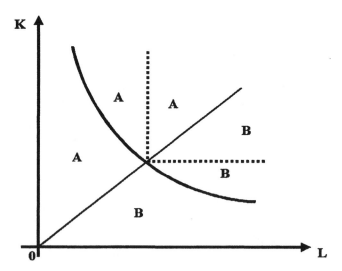

b. The technological change is labor saving in region A and capital saving in region B. This can be seen by comparing the $MRTS_{L,K}$ along the old and the new isoquants. In region A, the $MRTS_{L,K}$ falls due to the technological change (the isoquant is flatter along a ray from the origin in this region), while in region B the $MRTS_{L,K}$ rises along any ray from the origin. One could also say that, in a degenerate sense, technological progress is neutral along the ray going through the kinks of the original isoquant map.

Chapter 7: Costs and Cost Minimization

The last chapter described the technology of the firm in the same way that Chapter 3 described the preferences of consumers. Now, we wish to describe the choice problem of the firm in the same way that Chapter 4 described the choice problem of the consumer. We will begin with a presentation of the firm's cost minimization problem, which is analogous to the consumer's expenditure minimization problem that we described in Chapter 4. Next, we will derive the firm's demands for inputs in the same way that Chapter 5 derived the consumer's demands for products.

Before describing cost minimization, we need to define the economist's notion of costs. The economic cost of a resource is its **opportunity cost**, defined as the value of a resource in its best alternative use. This has several consequences:

- The only alternative we consider is the best alternative: Most choice problems involve a highly complex decision among many alternatives. Suppose, for example, that an individual must choose how to commute between home and work. Driving a car costs $3,000 a year and is nerve-racking but it is very flexible. Taking the train only costs $2,000 a year and is more relaxing but the schedule is not very convenient. Finally, using a motorbike only costs $1,000 a year but it is only fun when the weather is good. The cost of choosing to commute by train is what the individual *must give up* in order to do so. What she must give up is what she would have preferred to do if she had not decided to take the train, that is, the best alternative option between driving a car and driving a motorbike.

- Costs depend on the perspective we take: If we are evaluating a decision from a firm's point of view, we consider only those costs that a firm normally would incur. Similarly, if we are evaluating the decision from society's point of view, we must consider the (wider range of) costs that the entire society incurs due to the decision. A firm considering different production methods that imply different ways of disposing of waste will only consider its own cost of waste disposal. This may not fully take into account the social costs of the different type of (or levels of) pollution involved in the different methods. For example, the emissions from one production method may result in acid rain that falls 1,000 miles away from the plant. While the costs incurred by the landowners who occupy the areas that receive the acid rain must fully enter *society's* costs, they do not enter the *firm's* cost calculations.

- Opportunity costs often are implicit (not involving direct outlays by the firm): From a firm's perspective, the opportunity cost of using an input usually is the market price of that input. This price is an *opportunity* cost because the firm has the alternative of refraining from buying the input and keeping the cash. However a firm does not always acquire its inputs from the market. For example, a farmer uses his own labor and might be using land that he owns. Employing these two factors of production does not involve any direct outlays but it does involve opportunity costs: the farmer could use his time in another line of work and could lease his land to another farmer. In such cases, the opportunity cost of the inputs should be computed as the price that they would fetch if they were put up for sale, that is, the income that the farmer could earn in his best alternative employment and the price that the farmer could charge by selling or renting his land to the highest bidder. If there is an active market for similar goods then the opportunity cost can be obtained quite easily by observing the price that prevails on such markets. If no such market exists then evaluating opportunity costs becomes harder, as one has to evaluate the price that the inputs would fetch in a hypothetical transaction.

- <u>Costs depend on the decision being made</u>: The costs that are relevant to decision making include only the cost of foregoing alternatives *that are still available*. In other words, the concept of opportunity cost measures only cost at the time of the decision and beyond. Consider, for example, a firm that must decide whether or not to *enter* a market. The cost of *entry* (e.g., building a plant) is a relevant part of the decision since these costs can still be avoided by deciding not to enter the market. Once entry has occurred and the plant has been built the decision of whether to *continue* in the industry or get out of it for good no longer involves the cost of building the plant. The relevant cost of continuing is now the price for which the plant could be sold if the firm were to abandon the industry. Another way of stating the same principle is to say that **sunk costs** are never part of opportunity costs. A sunk cost is a cost that one can no longer recover. Such costs are not part of opportunity cost because they cannot be avoided under any of the available alternatives and should therefore not affect the choice of the agent. If a basketball team has signed a player to a guaranteed contract, then the player's salary should not affect the decision to make him a starter. Since the salary will have to be paid anyway, the decision should only be based on the player's expected contribution to the team. In other words, the total payment to the player under the guaranteed contract is a sunk cost and should be ignored.

Opportunity costs are not the only concept of costs that are used by firms. Accounting costs, for example, often differ from opportunity costs. This may be because the focus of the accountant is on keeping track of retrospective performance, or because the focus of the accountant is on costs that can be verified by an outside party (so that they generally would be as explicit and as objective as possible). The costs used by an accountant may also be determined by tax considerations or other regulatory guidelines (e.g., allowable depreciation guidelines) that would not generally affect opportunity costs.

Exercise 1: *Nuria earns a living as a receptionist at a day care center, where she earns $7 an hour. Work is often slow at the nursery, and she uses her spare time to study for a certificate in interior decoration. Her boss does not mind this use of her time since it appears not to affect the quality of her work as a receptionist. As an interior designer, Nuria could earn $12 an hour. Since she views her current job as a "dead end" and she is ambitious, this raise in earnings is appealing to her. Her courses take place in the evening at a local college. She has already paid $200 in course fees. She must pay an additional $400 to complete the entire series of courses, plus the cost of textbooks, materials, and transportation, which totals $200 for the rest of the program. She will finish the program at the end of this year if she keeps on with her studies.*

What is Nuria's opportunity cost of taking courses in interior decoration?

a. $800: the total cost of the courses, textbooks, materials, and transportation.
b. $600 plus the $12 per hour that she will earn after earning the certificate.
c. $600 plus the difference, $12-$7 between her hourly earnings with and without the certificate.
d. $7 per hour *after* the course finishes plus the $600 cost of the course that remains to be paid.

What is Nuria's opportunity cost of quitting the courses now?

a. $12 per hour, starting at the end of this year (when her studies normally would finish).
b. $12 per hour, starting at the end of this year net of $600 in course fees.
c. $12-$7 = $5 per hour, starting at the end of this year net of $600 in course fees.

Nuria's boss decides that her studying on the job lowers the quality of her work as a receptionist and informs her that she will lose her job if she continues to study during work hours. If she is fired, Nuria will not be able to find another job before she earns the certificate. What is Nuria's opportunity cost of taking courses now?

a. $800: the cost of the courses, textbooks, materials, and transportation.
b. $600 plus $7 per hour starting at the time of being fired.
c. $600 plus the difference, $12-$7 between her hourly earnings with and without the certificate, plus $7 per hour starting at the time of being fired.

We will assume that the firm's owners wish to maximize the wealth they obtain from operating the firm. This implies that they would not want to use a wasteful production process. In other words, whatever the level of output that the owners decide to produce, we can be confident that they will strive to produce this level of output at the lowest possible cost.

Suppose, then, that the firm's owners have decided to produce some output level, Q_0. The managers of the firm must minimize the cost of achieving this level of output subject to the constraint that they may only produce in technologically feasible ways. This is an example of a constrained optimization problem. Algebraically, let the technological possibilities of the firm be represented by the production function $Q = f(L,K)$. The total cost (TC) of using L units of labor at wage rate w per unit, and K units of capital at rental rate r per unit is: $TC = wL + rK$. Now, we can state the decision problem of the managers as follows:

$$\text{Min } TC = rK + wL$$
$$K, L$$

$$\text{Subject to } Q_0 = f(K,L)$$

This can be read as, "Choose the levels of capital and labor to minimize the total cost of production subject to the constraint that output be Q_0 units."

Exercise 2: *A firm wishes to produce 1000 units of output. It uses inputs of capital (K), labor (L), land (D), and materials (M). The rental rate of capital is r per unit, the market wage for labor is w, the rental rate for land is d, and the cost of materials is m. The production function is $Q = K^{1/4}L^{1/4}D^{1/4}M^{1/4}$. What is the cost minimization problem that the managers of the firm face?*

   a. $\underset{K,L}{\text{Min}}$ TC = rK + wL subject to Q_0 = f(K,L)

   b. $\underset{K,L}{\text{Min}}$ TC = rK + wL subject to 1000 = f(K,L)

   c. $\underset{K,L,D,M}{\text{Min}}$ TC = rK + wL subject to Q_0 = f(K,L,D,M)

   d. $\underset{K,L,D,M}{\text{Min}}$ TC = rK + wL + dD + mM subject to $1000 = K^{1/4}L^{1/4}D^{1/4}M^{1/4}$

This cost minimization problem should look familiar. It is analogous to the expenditure minimization problem of the consumer that we discussed in Chapter 4. In the expenditure minimization problem, the consumer chose to minimize the total expenditures, subject to attaining a given level of utility. Graphically, the consumer shifted *in* her budget line as much as possible, subject to the constraint of remaining on the target indifference curve. In the cost minimization problem, the firm minimizes expenditures necessary to attain a given level of output. As we will see shortly, this means that the firm will shift *in* her *isocost line* as much as possible subject to the constraint of remaining on the isoquant that corresponds to the target output.

As usual, we will solve this problem both graphically and algebraically. We will begin with the graphical solution. First, note that the set of combinations of labor and capital that have the same total cost, TC_0, for the firm can be written:

$$TC_0 = rK + wL$$

Rewriting this equation, we have:

$$K = [TC_0/r] - [w/r]L$$

This is the equation of a line with vertical intercept TC_0/r and slope $-w/r$ when K is measured on the vertical axis and L is measured on the horizontal axis. Such a line is called an **isocost line**. The higher the cost level associated with input levels (K,L), the farther out from the origin the isocost line is (see the left-hand panel of Figure 7.1, below). A change in the wage rate, w, or in the rental rate of capital, r, affects the slope of the isocost line. For example, if the wage rate rises, the isocost line rotates in around its vertical intercept (see the right-hand panel in Figure 7.1). In other words, the maximum number of units of labor that can be purchased at a given cost decreases while the maximum number of units of capital that can be purchased at that cost remains unchanged.

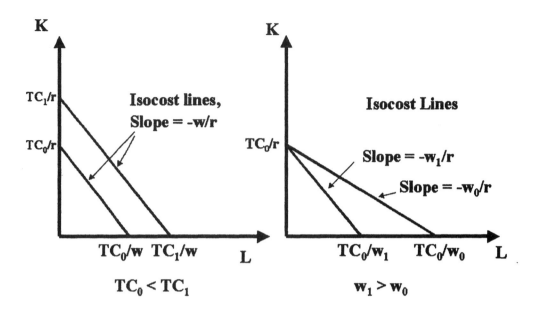

Figure 7.1

Our constraint is that we must continue to produce at least output level Q_0. Graphically, this constraint is represented by the points on the isoquant Q_0. The cheapest possible way of producing Q_0 must, then, be the point on the isoquant that lies on the lowest isocost curve. If the isoquant is a smooth curve, then the solution to the constrained optimization problem will be at the tangency point where the slope of the isoquant (the marginal rate of technical substitution) exactly equals the slope of the isocost line (the ratio of the wage to the rental rate of capital):

$$MRTS_{L,K} = -MP_L/MP_K = -(w/r)$$

Or, rewriting this equation, $MP_L/w = MP_K/r$. This is illustrated in Figure 7.2. This last condition could be interpreted as saying that the additional output per dollar spent on labor must equal the additional output per dollar spent on capital. In other words, the inputs must give equal "bang for the buck". If this were not the case, so that labor gave more additional output per dollar spent than capital, then we could lower cost and still produce the same output by reducing our expenditure on capital slightly and devoting our savings to the more productive labor input. In other words, by moving along the isoquant to a set of inputs with slightly more labor and slightly less capital, we could reach a lower isocost curve.

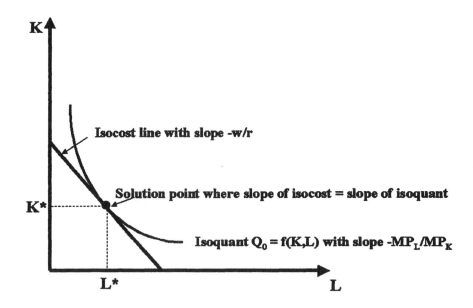

Figure 7.2

Exercise 3: *At point A in Figure 7.3, below, which of the following is true?*

a. $MP_L/w > MP_K/r$
b. $MP_L/w = MP_K/r$
c. $MP_L/w < MP_K/r$

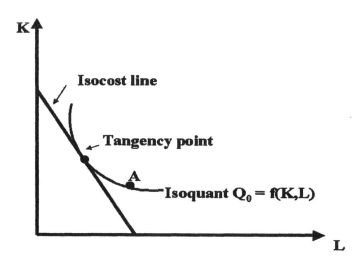

Figure 7.3

If we wanted to solve for the internal optimum algebraically, we would simply note that our solution must both lie on the target isoquant and be at a tangency point. These conditions give us two equations that we can use to solve for the two unknowns, K and L:

$$(1) \qquad Q_0 = f(K,L)$$

$$(2) \qquad MP_L/w = MP_K/r$$

Exercise 4: *Let the production function be $Q = K^{1/2}L^{1/2}$ with $MP_L = (1/2)L^{-1/2}K^{1/2}$ and $MP_K = (1/2)K^{-1/2}L^{1/2}$. Let $w = 1$ and $r = 1$. What is the cost minimizing combination of labor and capital, (L^*,K^*), that yields an output level of 100?*

  a. $L^* = 100$, $K^* = 100$
  b. $L^* = 10$, $K^* = 10$
  c. $L^* = 50$, $K^* = 50$

If the tangency condition does not hold for any positive values of capital and labor, the solution may not be an interior optimum. The easiest way to proceed is to graph the problem and see whether the solution lies at a corner point. For example, if the marginal rate of technical substitution always exceeds the ratio of the wage to the rental rate of capital, then we must check whether a corner point on the isoquant, where either L = 0 or K = 0, results in the lower cost level.

Exercise 5: *Suppose that the isoquants and isocost lines facing a firm are as pictured in Figure 7.4, below. Suppose that the firm wishes to produce output Q_0. What is the solution, (L^*,K^*), to the cost minimization problem of this firm?*

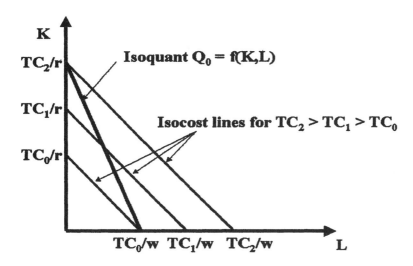

Figure 7.4

a. $K^* = TC_2/r$, $L^* = 0$
b. $K^* = TC_2/r$, $L^* = TC_2/w$
c. $K^* = 0$, $L^* = TC_0/w$
d. $K^* = TC_0/w$, $L^* = TC_0/w$

We can now examine the effect of a change in input prices on the cost minimizing choice of inputs. Suppose that we are at an interior solution. If the rental rate of capital increases, the isocost lines become flatter (w/r falls). This means that the point of tangency between the isoquant and the lowest possible isocost line must now be farther to the right. Hence the cost minimizing quantity of capital must fall and the cost minimizing quantity of labor must rise as the rental rate of capital rises. In other words, as capital becomes more expensive than labor, the firms substitutes labor for capital. This is the exact equivalent to the *substitution effect* discussed in Chapter 5. There, we analyzed the effect of a change in the price of one of the *goods* assuming that we had to remain on the same *indifference curve*.

Of course, if we are not at a tangency point (e.g., we are at a corner), a change in the price of labor or capital may not cause a change in the cost minimizing quantity of labor or capital used. For example, in Figure 7.4, it would take a very large change in slope to make the isocost line steeper than the isoquants. If such a large change in the ratio of wages to rental rate did occur, however, the change in the quantity of labor and capital used would be drastic: the solution to the constrained optimization problem would move from a point where K = 0 and only labor is used in production to a point where L = 0 and only capital is used in production!

Exercise 6: *Suppose that Q = min(K,L) is the production function of a firm. The firm wishes to minimize the cost of attaining output level 100. Let the wage rate be w = 4 and the rental rate of capital be r = 1. What is the cost minimizing combination of labor and capital, (L*, K*)?*

a. $L^* = 0$, $K^* = 100$
b. $L^* = 100$, $K^* = 0$
c. $L^* = 100$, $K^* = 100$

Suppose that the rental rate of capital doubles. What is the new cost minimizing combination of labor and capital?

a. $L^* = 0$, $K^* = 100$
b. $L^* = 100$, $K^* = 0$
c. $L^* = 100$, $K^* = 100$.

Another interesting comparative statics exercise is to ask how the cost minimizing combinations of labor and capital vary as the level of *output* changes, keeping the wage and rental rate fixed. For example, we could change the target output level from Q_0 to Q_1 in Figure 7.5 and trace out the solutions to the constrained optimization problem for each of these output levels. The path that traces out these solutions for all possible levels of output is called the **expansion path.** It is analogous to the income consumption path that we saw in consumer theory. If the quantities of labor and capital rise as we move along the expansion path to higher output levels, both labor and capital are called **normal inputs.** If the quantity of an input decreases as the firm produces more output, the input is called an **inferior input.** This is completely analogous to our discussion of normal goods and inferior goods in Chapter 5.

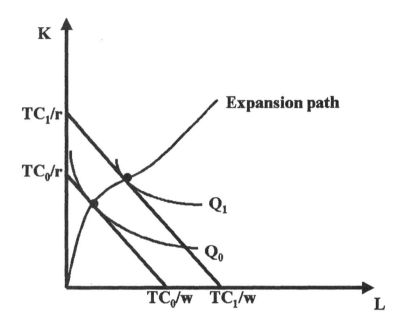

Figure 7.5

As you can see from the previous comparative statics exercises, the input combination that solves the constrained optimization problem depends on the target level of output, the wage, and the rental rate of capital. These optimal input combinations are called the **input demand functions.** These demands are sometimes called the **conditional factor demand functions,** since they are conditional on the level of output, or the **derived factor demands,** since they are demands for inputs that are derived from the consumer's demand for the final output. Since the firm's cost minimization problem is analogous to the expenditure minimization problem of the consumer, the firm's input demands are analogous to the consumer's *compensated* demand functions that were derived from the consumer's expenditure minimization problem in Chapter 5.

Algebraically, we can solve for the input demands by solving the production function and the tangency conditions for K and L as a function of Q, w, and r:

(a) $Q = f(K,L)$

(b) $MP_L/w = MP_K/r$

Exercise 7: *Suppose that the production function is Q = min(L,K). What are the input demand functions for labor, L, and capital, K, when wages are w and the rental rate of capital is r?*

    a. L = Q, K = Q
    b. L = wQ, K = rQ
    c. L = Q/w, K = Q/r
    d. L = Qwr, K = Qwr

Are K and L normal inputs?

    a. Yes
    b. K and L are inferior inputs
    c. K is normal, L is inferior

The input demand curves can be described by the appropriate elasticities. The **elasticity of demand for labor**, $\varepsilon_{L,w}$, measures the sensitivity of the cost minimizing quantity of labor to a change in the wage. Similarly, the **elasticity of demand for capital**, $\varepsilon_{K,r}$, measures the sensitivity of the cost minimizing quantity of capital to a change in the rental rate of capital. These elasticities are defined mathematically as follows:

$$\varepsilon_{L,w} = (\Delta L/L)\,(w/\Delta w)$$
$$\varepsilon_{K,r} = (\Delta K/K)(r/\Delta r)$$

where: K and L are the input demands at the relevant levels of the wage and rental rate.

The discussion up to this point has only been concerned with **long run** costs, that is, with the minimum cost of producing a given level of *output when all factors of production can be varied as much as the firm would like*. In the **short run**, as we saw in Chapter 6, at least one of the factors of production is fixed. For example, suppose that capital is fixed at level $\overline{K}$. Then the short run total cost function (written STC here) can be written as:

$$STC = wL + r\overline{K}$$

Where the **total fixed cost** (the component of the firm's cost that remains fixed as the firm's output varies) is simply $r\overline{K}$ and the **total variable cost** (the component of the firm's cost that changes as the firm's output varies) is wL. Our problem now is much simpler than before: we must choose the level of labor that minimizes the total cost of obtaining the target level of output, Q_0, with the constraint that capital must be set at $\overline{K}$:

$$\underset{L}{\text{Min }} STC = wL + r\overline{K}$$

$$\text{Subject to } Q_0 = f(L,\ \overline{K})$$

The solution to this problem gives us a **short run input demand function** for labor. For isoquants that look like a smooth curve, as in Figure 7.2, there is only a single level of labor that can be combined with this fixed amount of capital, $\overline{K}$, to efficiently produce the target level of output for this problem. This is pictured in Figure 7.6.

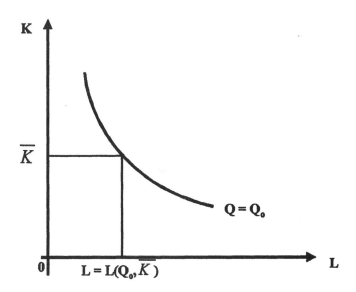

Figure 7.6

This level of capital can be substituted into the total cost to determine the attainable level of cost for the firm. The short run input demand function for labor, $L(Q, \overline{K})$, will be the single level of labor that generates each level of Q for the given amount of capital, $\overline{K}$.

Short Run Conditional Factor Demand Functions with More than Two Inputs

Suppose that there are N factors of production $K_1, K_2, \ldots K_N$ that are fixed in the short run and two that are variable, L_1 and L_2. Define w_1 and w_2 as the unit price of L_1 and L_2, respectively.

The equation of the isoquant corresponding to a level of output Q_0 is $Q_0 = F(L_1, L_2; K_1, \ldots K_N)$. From this equation we can also obtain the marginal product for each of the variable factors, $MP_{L1}(L_1, L_2, Q_0; K_1, \ldots K_N)$ and $MP_{L2}(L_1, L_2, Q_0; K_1, \ldots K_N)$. We can then express the required tangency condition as $w_1/w_2 = MP_{L1}/MP_{L2}$. Solving this equation together with the equation of the isoquant gives the short run conditional factor demands $L_1(Q_0; K_1, \ldots K_N)$ and $L_2(Q_0; K_1, \ldots K_N)$. See Exam question 2 at the end of this chapter's summary for practice.

If the firm produces at the level of output for which the short run level of capital, $\overline{K}$, equals the long run level of capital (i.e., the level that would be chosen if all inputs could be varied without restriction), then the short run level of labor demanded must also equal the long run demand of labor. In other words, if it so happens that the level of the fixed input equals the level at which the input would optimally be set if it were variable, then the fact that the input is fixed in the short run does not move the optimal level of the other variable factors away from their long run level. In some sense, the constraint that one factor is fixed does not affect the solution to the long run problem as long as it is fixed at the level that the firm would have chosen in the long run anyway.

Exercise 8: *Suppose that Q = min(K,L) and K is fixed at $\overline{K}$. What is the short run input demand for labor, L^s?*

    a. $L^s = \overline{K}$
    b. $L^s = \overline{K}$ for $Q \geq \overline{K}$ and $L^s = 0$ for $Q < \overline{K}$
    c. $L^s = Q$
    d. $L^s = Q$ for $Q \leq \overline{K}$

Chapter Review Questions

1. Suppose that average earnings of an adult in the United Kingdom are £16,000 per year. A recent policy debate has centered on waiting times for patients in the National Health System. The difficulty is that many patients must wait for operations. Suppose that these waits average three months. During this waiting time 50% of the patients are unable to work and, in addition, impose considerable burden on their families since they often are unable to care for themselves. Assume that the number of people waiting for operations is approximately 50,000. A new budget is proposed that allocates £1 billion per year to the National Health Service, with the aim of reducing the waiting time to a minimal amount, which you can assume to be zero for the purposes of this question.

    a. What is the total opportunity cost of waiting time for people who need operations?

    b. Would you vote for this budget?

Answer:

    If we use the average earnings of adults as a proxy for their opportunity cost of time, a three-month wait would result in an opportunity cost of £4000 per patient who is unable to work. The question states that 50% of the 50,000 people waiting for operations fall into this category. As a result, 25,000 x £4,000 = £100,000,000 is the opportunity cost of waiting time for these people. Regarding (b), this is considerably less than the £1 billion proposed budget. Of course, to this we would have to add any additional costs of family members who must stay at home to take care of the person who needs the operation, as well as any allowance for inconvenience that we wished to add.

2. Let $Q = 10K - K^2/2 + L$, where K is capital, L is labor, and Q is output. $MP_K = 10 - K$ and $MP_L = 1$.

    a. Derive (long run) input demand functions for this production function.

    b. Let w = 1, where w is the wage rate. Compare your input demand function for capital to the Hicksian demand function for x that you derived in Exercise 11 of chapter 5. What do you notice? Why?

Answer:

a. We must solve (a) $Q = 10K - K^2/2 + L$ and (b) $MP_K/r = (10-K)/r = 1/w = MP_L/w$, where r is the rental rate of capital. The tangency condition, (b), can be rewritten as $K^*(Q,r,w) = 10 - r/w$. Combining this with the production function, we have $L^*(Q,r,w) = Q - 10K^* + K^{*2}/2 = Q - 50 + 0.5(r/w)^2$.

b. If w = 1, then we can rewrite the input demand for K as $r = 10 - K$. This looks exactly like the Hicksian demand for good x that we derived using utility function $U = 10x - x^2/2 + y$, where $p_y = 1$. This is not surprising: the Hicksian demands are derived from the expenditure minimization problem and the cost minimization problem of the firm is analogous to the expenditure minimization problem of a consumer.

3. When we studied consumer theory, a fall in the price of good x could cause the optimal consumption of good x to decrease. Can a fall in the wage rate cause the cost minimizing amount of labor to fall? Why?

Answer:

This is not possible. In consumer theory, the total effect of a fall in the price of a good on the optimal consumption of the good could be decomposed into a substitution effect and an income effect. For the substitution effect, the consumer was constrained to stay on the same indifference curve so that a decrease in the price of a good always led to an increase in its consumption. A price decrease also increased the real income of the consumer. If the good was *inferior*, this increased purchasing power led to a decrease in the demand for the good. If that income effect was stronger than the substitution effect, then the optimal consumption of the good decreased when its price fell (i.e., this was the case of a Giffen good). When deriving the conditional factor demands of the firm, we are constrained to stay on the same isoquant. This is similar to staying on the same indifference curve in the consumer problem. In other words, conditional factor demands only capture the equivalent of a substitution effect and must, therefore, be downward sloping.

Problem Set

1. (This question builds on question 4 of chapter 6's problem set, and continues in chapter 8's problem set, question 2.) A firm has production function $Q = 100L^{3/4}K^{1/4}$, with $MP_L = 75K^{1/4}L^{-1/4}$ and $MP_K = 25L^{3/4}K^{-3/4}$ and faces a constant wage of w per unit for labor input and a constant rental rate of capital of r per unit.

   a. Derive the long run input demand functions for labor and capital.

   b. Define "normal input" and "inferior input". Which are labor and capital for this firm?

2. Let the production function of a firm be $Q = 100L + 10K$, where L is labor input, K is capital input, and Q is output. The marginal products of labor and capital are, respectively, $MP_L = 100$ and $MP_K = 10$. Derive and interpret the marginal rate of technical substitution for this firm.

   a. Let the wage rate for labor be w = $10 up to 10 man-hours of input. For any labor use in excess of 10, the wage rate doubles to w = $20. The rental rate of capital is $10 per machine hour. Illustrate the cost minimization problem of a firm wishing to produce 1000 units of output. Derive and illustrate the cost minimizing demand for labor and capital.

   b. A proposal is made to double the basic (less than 10 man-hours of input) wage rate. Describe the new cost minimization problem of the firm. As a worker, would you support this proposal? Why?

3. A university computes its annual cost per student based on the yearly cost of the salaries of all personnel employed by the college, plus food, maintenance of facilities, and student aid. It does not include the cost of the campus' land or the cost of building the existing facilities on the campus, because the university has owned the land and the facilities that have been built for many years. Does the university's annual cost per student, as computed by the university, reflect the college's true opportunity cost of providing an education to students?

4. Suppose that three technologies are available for producing sweaters: hand knitting, machine assisted knitting (individuals using small knitting machines), and large facility knitting (fully automated knitting). These different technologies use different proportions of labor and capital, as shown in the table below:

Labor and Capital requirements per sweater

	Q = 10	Q = 50	Q = 100
Hand	L=100 units K = 1 unit	L = 500 units K = 2 units	L = 1000 units K = 4 units
Machine Assisted	L = 50 units K = 2 units	L = 250 units K = 4 units	L = 500 units K = 8 units
Fully Automated	L = 1 unit K = 10 units	L = 1 unit K = 15 units	L = 1 unit K = 20 units

a. Draw isoquants for sweater production. Suppose that the cost of labor is w = $1 and the cost of capital is r = $1. Draw a family of isocost lines on the same diagram as your isoquants. What is the cost minimizing choice of labor and capital to produce 10 sweaters?

b. Now, the cost of capital rises to r = $20. What is the cost minimizing choice of labor and capital to produce 10 sweaters?

c. How much would the cost of capital have to rise in order for hand knitting to be the cost minimizing choice of labor and capital to produce 10 sweaters?

d. Answer parts (a) and (b) for a desired production of 100 sweaters. Using the same rental rate as in part (c), find the cost minimizing technology to produce 100 sweaters.

e. Why might the technology choice for producing sweaters differ in different countries?

5.

a. Let Q = min(L,K) be the production function of a firm. Trace out an expansion path for this production function.

b. Now, suppose that the quantity of labor is fixed in the short run. Draw a short run expansion path that traces out the solutions to the short run cost minimization problem at various output levels.

6. Suppose that the firm's production function is given by Q = K + L + M, where K is capital, L is labor, and M is materials. The rental rate of capital is r, the wage rate for labor is w and the price of materials is m.

   a. If the input prices are r = 2, w = 1, and m = 3, what is the solution to the firm's long run cost minimization problem given that the firm wants to produce Q units of output?

   b. What is the solution to the firm's short run cost minimization problem when the firm wants to produce Q units of output and capital is fixed at $\overline{K}$?

   c. Verify that, when Q = 10 and $\overline{K}$ = 0 the short run and the long run quantities of labor and materials are the same. Explain why this is the case.

7. In order to complete a year-long course in computer aided design (CAD), you purchase a computer and software related to CAD. The computer costs you $3,000 and the software costs an additional $500. After the course, you can resell the computer for $2,000 and the software for $200.

   a. What is the computer/software related opportunity cost of taking the course?

   b. Unfortunately, you failed the course! You are now considering whether or not you should re-take it next year. If you do, you are certain to succeed but, at the end of the year your computer will only be worth $1,100 on the resale market and your software will be worthless. What is your computer/software-related opportunity cost of re-taking the course?

8. A company operates in a small town where only 500 workers are available. On the other hand, the company can obtain any quantity of capital that it wishes in the national financial market at a fixed rental rate r = 40. Each of the 500 workers is willing to work at a daily wage of 10. Workers can also be obtained in unlimited number from the closest city but they are only willing to commute and work for a daily wage of $20. The technology available to the company can be described by the production function Q = Min(K,L/2), where L is expressed in terms of workers per day.

   a. Draw the isocost line corresponding to a total cost of $6,000.

   b. What would be the cost minimizing combination of inputs to produce an output of Q = 200 ? What is the total cost of producing this level of output?

   c. What would be the cost minimizing levels of input to produce an output of Q = 300. What is the total cost of producing this level of output?

Exam *(60 minutes: Closed book, closed notes)*

1. Suppose that you have completed four years of a doctoral program in Economics. You are considering whether to drop out of the program and take a job, or continue the program and eventually obtain a degree. When you ask your friend for advice, she says, "You have already gone so far, it would be a shame to give up now." How do you respond? Do you say "The four years that I have already spent in this program are a sunk cost and are, therefore, irrelevant"? Should the fact that you have already completed four years of the program enter into your decision of whether or not to continue?

2. A firm estimates its production function to be:

    $Q = 6KL$

    Where: Q = annual production measured in pounds
    K = machine hours (capital) per year
    L = man hours (labor) per year

    The marginal products of capital and labor are given as follows:

    $MP_K = 6L; MP_L = 6K.$

    Wages cost the firm $7.50 per man-hour. The firm estimates $30 per hour to be its rental rate on capital. The operating budget for capital and labor is $300,000 per year.

    a. State and illustrate the conditions that determine the firm's cost minimizing use of labor and capital.

    b. Determine the firm's optimal ratio of labor to capital.

    c. Given the firm's $300,000 budget, how much capital and labor should the firm employ? How much output will the firm produce?

3. Let $Q = LK$ be the production function of a firm, where L is labor and K is capital. $MP_L = K$ and $MP_K = L$. Suppose that w = $1 per unit of labor and r = $2 per unit of capital.

    a. Find the cost minimizing input combination that results in an output of Q = 200.

    b. Suppose now that a payroll tax is imposed so that the firm must pay $3 per unit of labor to the government. How does this affect the cost minimizing input combination of the firm if it still wishes to produce Q = 200?

   c. How much revenue will the government collect from the firm as a result of the tax? How much do the firm's costs rise? Why?

   d. Now suppose that $Q = L + K$ is the production function of the firm. How do your answers to (a) - (c) change? Why?

   e. Suppose that $Q = min(L,K)$ is the production function of the firm. How do your answers to (a) - (c) change? Why?

4. A steel plant's production function is $Q = 0.025LK$, where Q is the daily output rate, L is the number of workers it uses per day, and K is a unit of daily capital employment. According to this production function, the marginal products of capital and labor are, respectively,

     $MP_K = 0.025L$
     $MP_L = 0.025K$

Suppose that the price of labor is $100 per worker per day, and that the price of capital is $200 per unit per day.

   a. The firm's vice president for manufacturing hires you to figure out what combination of inputs the plant should use to produce 20 units of output per period. What advice would you give?

   b. How much would it cost per day to produce this level of output?

   c. Now suppose that the firm increases this plant's budget to $120,000 a day and instructs the plant manager to produce as much steel as possible while not exceeding this budget. Again your advice is sought. How much capital and labor would you advise employing? How much output should the firm expect from this plant?

Answers to Exercises

1. The correct answer to the first part is (d). The payoff to the best alternative to taking the course is to continue working in her current job and save the $600 fee. She need not count the $200 that she already has paid in fees since this is an unrecoverable, sunk, cost. Further, her hourly pay during her period of study for the certificate does not enter into her calculations because she would earn $7 per hour for the remainder of her time in the program whether or not she undertook the certificate.

The correct answer to the second part of the question is (c). By quitting now, Nuria saves the $600 that she would still have to spend in order to obtain her certificate (a cost of *minus* $600) but she would forego a pay increase of $5 per hour over the course of her professional life.

The correct answer to the third part of the question is (b). As in the first part of the question, the payoff to the best alternative to taking the course is to continue working in her current job and save the $600 in fees. Now, however, we need to count the $7 per hour she earns for the remainder of the program because she can only continue her studies if she quits her current job.

2. The answer is (d). The firm's total cost is the value of all resources used to produce the output. This includes the value of capital, rK, the value of labor, wL, the value of land, dD, and the value of materials, mM. All the other total cost functions in answers (a), (b), and (c) include only two of these four inputs. We are told that the constraint is that the production level must be 1000 units. Since we know that the units of output are produced from inputs K, L, D, and M is $K^{1/4}L^{1/4}D^{1/4}M^{1/4}$, we must set $1000 = Q_0 = K^{1/4}L^{1/4}D^{1/4}M^{1/4}$ as a constraint. The firm chooses the four inputs to minimize total costs subject to this constraint.

3. The correct answer is (c). The isocost line is steeper than the isoquant at point A. Therefore, $MP_L/MP_K < w/r$ or $MP_L/w < MP_K/r$.

4. The correct answer is (a). We must solve two equations simultaneously:

    (a) $100 = K^{1/2}L^{1/2}$

    (b) $[(1/2)L^{-1/2}K^{1/2}]/1 = [(1/2)K^{-1/2}L^{1/2}]/1$

    Equation (b) simplifies to K = L. Substituting this into equation (a), we obtain L = K = 100. You can check that both equations (a) and (b) hold at this point by substituting K = L = 100 into both. Notice that this answer makes some sense: the isoquants of the production function are completely symmetric (K and L enter exactly the same way into the production function) and the wage and rental rates are equal. Therefore, it is not surprising that the answer yields equal use of these two inputs.

5. The correct answer is (c). In order to minimize cost subject to the constraint that we continue to use an input combination that yields Q_0 units of output, we must be on the lowest isocost line that still touches the isoquant $Q_0 = f(K,L)$. By finding the isocost line that is closest to the origin and still touches the isoquant in the figure, we see that the point at which the isocost and the isoquant touch is at a labor input of TC_0/w and a capital input of zero. This makes sense: a straight line isoquant corresponds to the case where capital and labor are perfect substitutes in production. The relatively steep slope of the isoquant means that the marginal product of labor is relatively high compared to the marginal product of capital. Further, the isocost line is relatively flat, indicating that the wage rate is relatively low (labor is relatively cheap compared to capital). Therefore, it is not surprising that a cost minimizing firm uses labor, for which it gets a relatively high "bang for the buck".

6. The correct answer to the first part of the question is (c). In fact, since the level of output is determined by the smaller of the two input levels, it is not possible to attain an output level of 100 with either input combination (a) or (b). Further,

note that *whatever* the wage and rental rates, labor and capital will be used in equal amounts. This can be seen in the following figure, where the lowest isocost line -- whatever its slope -- touches the isoquant at its "kink". Intuitively, capital and labor are perfect complements in this case: employing a unit more of one is useless unless a unit more of the other is added as well.

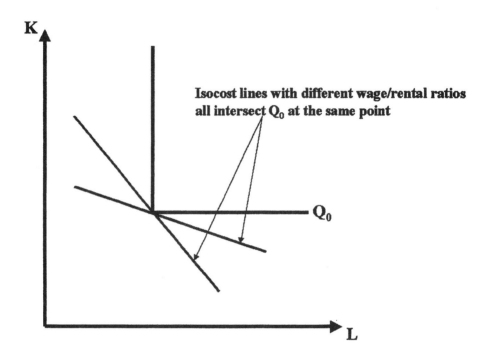

The correct answer to the second part of the question is (c). As was explained above, whatever the wage/rental rate ratio, the kink is the combination of inputs that allows the lowest cost to be attained for $Q = Q_0$, so that the optimal choice of inputs does not change.

7. The correct answer to the first part of the question is (a). As we saw in Exercise 6, both inputs must be set at a level equal to the desired amount of output in order that level of output to be attained. The wage and rental rates are irrelevant and do not affect the optimal choice of input combinations at all, as we saw in Exercise 6. Therefore, answers (b), (c), and (d), which all state that the input demands depend on the wage or the rental rate, are not the correct answers.

    The correct answer to the second part of the question is (a). The firm can only produce more output if the quantities of both labor and capital increase. Hence an increase in output will always be accompanied by an increase in both K and L.

8. The correct answer is (d). If the desired output level, Q, is less than the fixed level of capital, then the minimum amount of labor that will allow the firm to attain this level of output is $L^S = Q$. Levels of output greater than $\overline{K}$ cannot be

produced, whatever the amount of labor employed is. In this sense the conditional demand for labor is not defined for $Q > \overline{K}$.

Answers to Problem Set

1.

   a. Assume that the firm acts so as to minimize costs. The cost minimizing choice of inputs at the interior solution is characterized by: $MRTS_{L,K} = w/r$ or: $3K/L = w/r$ (tangency condition for cost minimizing firm). This gives the equation of the expansion path, the cost minimizing inputs for any output level. In addition, for any particular output level, we need to apply the constraint that output reaches the target level, Q, using the production function: $Q = 100L^{3/4}K^{1/4}$.

   Combining these two equations, we have:

   $Q = 100L^{3/4}(wL/3r)^{1/4} \Leftrightarrow L^*(Q,w,r) = (3r/w)^{1/4}(Q/100)$
   $Q = 100(3rK/w)^{3/4}K^{1/4} \Leftrightarrow K^*(Q,w,r) = (w/3r)^{3/4}(Q/100)$

   These are the input demands for labor (L*) and capital (K*). Notice that we have an interior solution to this problem for positive w and r. For this type of production function (Cobb-Douglas), the isoquants are drawn with the standard shape, so we can see graphically that the interior solution (not a corner solution) is the cost minimizing solution for this firm.

   b. If the cost minimizing quantities of labor and capital rise as output rises, labor and capital are called *normal* inputs. If the cost minimizing quantities of the input decrease as the firm produces more output, the inputs are called *inferior inputs*. We can see from the input demand functions of (b) that both labor and capital are normal inputs, since L* and K* are positive functions of Q for given w and r.

2.

   a. The marginal rate of technical substitution, $MRTS_{L,K}$, measures the amount of an input (say L, the firm would require in exchange for using a little less of another input, say K, in order to just be able to produce the same output as before. It is the (negative of the) slope of the isoquant for a constant level of output. The slope of the isoquant and the marginal products are related in the sense that $MP_L/MP_K = MRTS$. For example, in this case, $MP_L/MP_K = 100/10 = 10$. This is the (constant) $MRTS_{L,K}$ along the isoquants. In other words, the isoquants in this case are straight lines, so that labor and capital are substitutes in production at the rate of 10 units of capital being as "productive" as 1 unit of labor.

   b. Min $rK + wL$ subject to $Q^0 = f(K,L)$ is the general form of the cost minimization problem for inputs K and L and technology f(K,L). Hence, here we have:

Min 10K + 10L s.t. 1000 = 100L + 10K for up to 10 hours of labor and
Min 10K + 20L s.t. 1000 = 100L + 10K for over this amount of labor.

For labor use up to 10 hours, we have the slope of the isocost line equal to -w/r = -10/10. For labor use past this amount, we have -w/r = -20/10. In both cases, the slope is flatter than the slope of the isoquant so that the optimal solution in both cases is to hire only labor (using 10 units of labor in each case).

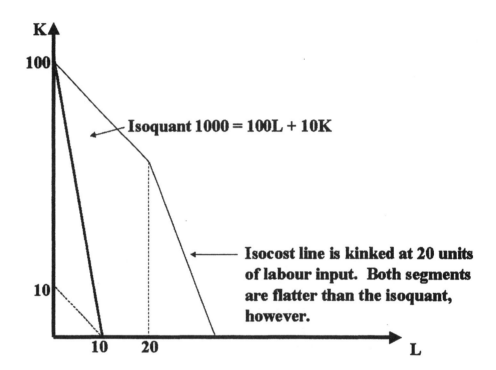

When the basic rate rises to equal the "overtime" rate, the isocost becomes straight with the slope of the lower part of the kinked line, in the graph above. Still, this is flatter than the isoquant leading to a cost minimization point where only labor is used. This means that this plan looks very good from the point of view of labor at the firm: a raise with no layoffs.

3. The fact that the money was paid for the land and facilities in the past does not mean that the *value* of the land and its facilities need not be included in the opportunity cost of providing an education, since the land and its facilities could be used for other purposes. A natural cost to assign to the land and its facilities would be the market value of renting the land and facilities for non-educational purposes (or, perhaps selling the land and razing the facilities if this results in a higher value). This implicit cost could then be allocated over the total number of students attending the university to obtain an implicit cost per student. It should be added to the explicit costs that the college already uses in calculating the cost of providing an education to the students.

4.

a. Each of the three technologies described gives us *one point* on each of the isoquants for Q = 10, Q = 50 and Q = 100. If a firm can combine these technologies in any proportion, the line segments between these three points also represent feasible combinations of capital and labor corresponding to these levels of output. Such combinations are represented by the dotted line segments on the graph below. If the technologies cannot be combined then each isoquant is just made of the three points corresponding to the exclusive use of one of the three technologies. The cost of making 10 sweaters is: (1): Hand = $101; (2) Machine Assisted = $52; (3) Automated = $11. Since fully automated technology is the cheapest it will not be combined with any of the other two so that the cost minimizing combination of inputs is L = 1 and K = 10.

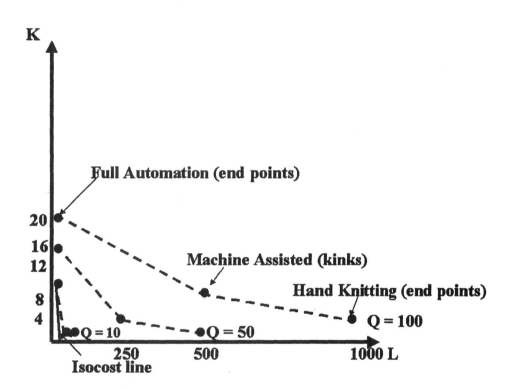

b. If the cost if capital rises to $20, then we can recompute the costs of the three different technologies as: (1) Hand = $120; (2) Machine Assisted = $90; (3) Fully Automated = $201. Therefore, Machine Assisted is the cheapest way to produce the 10 sweaters at this higher cost of capital. In terms of the graph, the isocost line has become flatter so that the lowest isocost line intersects the isoquant for Q = 10 at the "kink" instead of at the corner.

c. The cost of capital would have to rise to $50 before hand knitting would be the cost minimizing technology choice for 10 sweaters. At r = $50 we have: (1) Hand = $150; (2) Machine Assisted = $150; (3) Fully Automated = $501.

d. If we wished to produce 100 sweaters at the original wage and rental rate of $1, we have: (1) Hand = $1004; (2) Machine Assisted = $508; (3) Fully Automated = $21. Therefore, we would choose full automation in order to minimize cost. If r = $20, we have: (1) Hand = $1080; (2) Machine Assisted = $660 and (3) Fully Automated = $401. The cost minimizing choice still is full automation. If r = $50, we have: (1) Hand = $1200; (2) Machine Assisted = $900, and (3) Fully Automated = $1001 so that machine assisted technology minimizes costs.

e. Different countries might face different costs of capital or labor, as well as have different desired levels of production. Either of these could affect technology choice if the producers minimize costs.

5.

a. Whatever the wage and the rental rate of capital, the efficient production choice is $L = K = Q$. Hence the expansion path is a straight, 45° line from the origin.

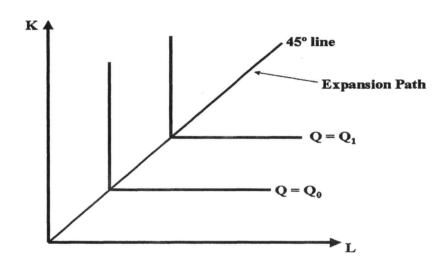

b. The expansion path is the 45° line until the fixed quantity of labor is attained. After this, no further increase in capital results in an increase in output. Therefore, the expansion path terminates at this point.

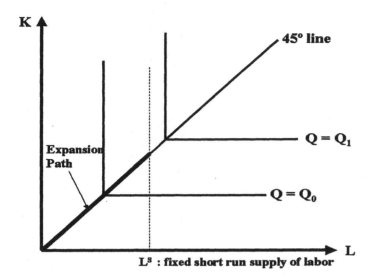

6.

    a. Since K, L, and M are all perfect substitutes in production, the firm minimizes cost by consuming only the cheapest input, which is labor. In order to produce Q units of output, it must set $L^* = Q$.

    b. If capital is fixed at $\overline{K}$, then the firm consumes $\overline{K}$ of capital as long as the desired output is less than or equal to $\overline{K}$. This is because this fixed amount of capital must be paid for anyway, that is, $r\overline{K}$ is a sunk cost. After this point, the firm adds units of labor (only) so that $L^* = Q - \overline{K}$.

    c. When Q = 10 and the amount of capital that is fixed in the short run is zero, the firm uses exclusively labor to produce the 10 units. This is the long run solution from part (a). The reason for this equivalence is that, in the short run, the level of capital happens to be fixed at exactly the level that the firm would choose if the amount of capital could be freely determined.

7.

    a. When deciding whether or not to take the course, the relevant computer and software costs are equal to the initial outlay of $3,500 minus the $2,200 that can be recovered once the course has been completed, that is, to $1,300. When deciding whether or not to take the course, the relevant comparison is between the $2,200 that can be obtained by reselling the computer and software now and the $1,100 that can be obtained by reselling this equipment one year from now.

    b. Based on the answer to (a), the computer-related cost of re-taking the course is $2,200 - $1,100 = $1,100. The initial cost of the computer, $3,500, is now irrelevant: it is a sunk cost.

8.

a.

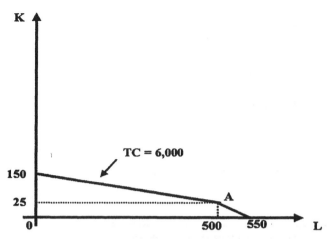

If the firm only uses capital it can purchase 6,000/40 = 150 units, which is the vertical intercept of the isocost line. The firm can then exchange one unit of capital for 40/10 = 4 units of local labor up to the point (A on the graph) where all 500 local workers are employed. Beyond this, the firm has to hire workers from out of town so that each unit of capital can only be replaced by 40/20 = 2 units of labor. There is therefore a kink at point A, where the slope of the isocost line goes from -1/4 to -1/2.

b. Labor and capital must be used in a fixed proportion of 2 units of labor to each unit of capital. Hence the cost minimizing way of producing Q = 200 is K = 200 and L = 400 (point B on the graph below). The cost of this combination is TC = 200 x 40 + 400 x 10 = 12,000.

c. The cost minimizing solution is K = 300 and L = 600 (point D on the graph below). Since L > 500, the firm must now use 100 workers from out of town. Hence the total cost is TC = 300 x 400 + 500 x 10 + 100 x 20 = 19,000. Notice that a 50 % increase in output has led to a 58% increase in total cost. In other words, the average cost of production has gone up.

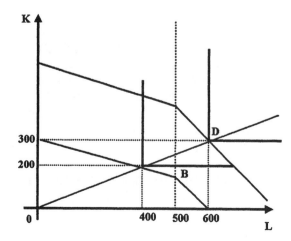

Answers to Exam

1. The only relevant aspect of the problem should be the payoff of the additional year to complete the program versus the payoff to getting a job. What your friend may be referring to is that your remaining cost of completing the program may be rather low compared to the benefit of completing the program now that you are very close to the end. After all, the period of time you must wait before earning a higher salary due to completing the degree may be quite short, and your accumulated knowledge from your studies may make completing your last-year's courses relatively easy. These considerations may affect the costs that you still have to incur and so may be relevant to your decision. In other words, the four years spent in the program *are* a sunk cost, that is, a cost that can never be recovered. The fact that you have spent these four years does, however, affect your current alternatives: if you had not spent these four years, you could not hope to finish the program relatively fast.

2.

    a. and b. We want $MP_K/P_K = MP_L/P_L$. Graphically,

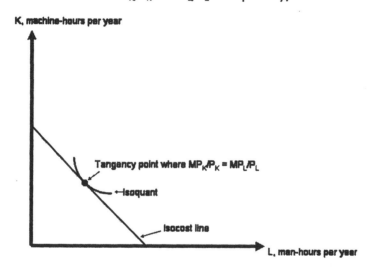

    Here, the optimality condition is $6L/30 = 6K/7.5$ or $K = .25 L$. Note that man-hours and machine hours have the same marginal productivity (at the same levels of input). However, capital is 4 times as expensive as labor. As a result we will always use 4 times more man-hours than machine hours.

    b. The budget is $300,000 or $7.5L + 30K = 300,000$. From (a) we know that $K = .25L$. Hence, we have $300,000 = 7.5L + 7.5L = 15L$ or $L = 20,000$. Plug this in to $K = .25L$ to get $K = 5000$. Total output produced is $Q = 6KL = 600,000,000$ pounds of output.

3.

    a. Tangency condition: $MP_L/w = MP_K/r \Leftrightarrow K/1 = L/2$ so that $2K = L$. Combining this with $Q = 200$, we have $2K^2 = 200 \Rightarrow K^* = 10$, $L^* = 20$.

In this case, both inputs have the same marginal productivities, but K is twice as expensive as L, so the firm optimally chooses to use twice as much labor as capital.

b. The total cost of a unit of labor is now $1 + $3 = $4. The tangency condition is K/4 = L/2 so that K/2 = L. Combining this with Q = 200, we have $K^2/2 = 200$ or K** = 20, L** = 10. In this case, the tax has made labor twice as expensive as capital for the same marginal product. Hence, the firm optimally chooses to use twice as much capital as labor.

c. Revenue = $3xL* = $30. Firm's costs before the tax are TC = rK* + wL* = $2(10) + $1(20) = $40. Firm's costs after the tax are TC = rK** + wL** = $2(20) + $4(10) = $80. The firm's costs rise, but since the firm can substitute into capital, it does not bear the entire cost of the tax on the original labor demanded. If the firm could not substitute away from labor, then it would bear an extra cost of $3 for each of the 20 units of labor that it was initially employing, that is, an extra cost of $60. However, because the firm can adjust its mixture of capital and labor, it only pays taxes of $30 and only bears a total cost increase of $80 - $40 = $40.

d. If Q = L + K, then the cost minimizing input combination at the original prices is L* = 200; K* = 0, since the firm views the inputs as perfect substitutes and capital has the higher price. After the payroll tax is imposed, labor becomes the more expensive input so that L** = 0 and K** = 200 at the cost minimizing solution. The government collects zero in tax revenues and the costs of the firm rise to 400 from 200. With this technology, K and L are perfect substitutes. The payroll tax is high enough to induce a drastic substitution away from labor, reducing the tax revenues to zero.

e. If Q = min(L,K), then the cost minimizing input combination at the original prices is L* = K* = 200 since the firm views the inputs as perfect complements in production. After the payroll tax is imposed, the optimal combination of inputs does not change since there are no possibilities of substitution between K and L. Therefore the government collects $3x200 = $600 in tax revenues and the firm's costs rise by the full amount of the tax, $600.

4.

a. MP_L/MP_K = w/r ⇔ .025K/.025L = 100/200 or K/L = .5 (tangency) Q = f(K,L) ⇔ 20 = .025LK (constraint). Putting these together, K = .5L or 2K = L and substituting into constraint, we have 20 = .025(2K²) ⇔ 20 = .05K² ⇔ 2000/5 = K² ⇔ K* = 20. Hence, L* = 40.

b. 20(200) + 40(100) = 4000 + 4000 = $8000/day

c. 120000 = K(200) + L(100). But we know that we must use the ratio 2K = L to produce with the optimal input combination. Hence, we have 120000 = K(200) + 2K(100) or K = 120000/400 or K**=300, L** = 600. At this level of input use, we can produce .025(300)(600) = 25(180) = 4500.

Chapter 8: Cost Curves

By performing comparative statics on the cost minimization problem of Chapter 7, we can derive the firm's total cost curve. In other words, we can derive the cost of producing various levels of output *assuming* that the firm will use its inputs in the cost minimizing way to produce that output.

The **long-run total cost curve** shows how the minimized total cost varies as we vary output, while keeping factor prices fixed. Algebraically, we can write total cost as:

$$TC = wL^* + rK^*$$

where L^* and K^* are the conditional input demands that we derived in Chapter 7. These input demands are functions of the input prices w, r, and of the level of output, Q, that the firm wishes to produce, that is:

$$L^* = L^*(w,r,Q)$$
$$K^* = K^*(w,r,Q)$$

Substituting these two functions into the equation for total cost gives us

$$TC = wL^*(w,r,Q) + rK^*(w,r,Q)$$

So that total cost is itself a function of w, r and Q. We can write this as

$$TC = C(w,r,Q)$$

where $C(w,r,Q)$ is the long-run cost function of the firm.

For example, in Exercise 7 of Chapter 7 in this guide, we showed that the conditional input demands of labor and capital for the production function $Q = \min(L,K)$ were $L^* = Q$ and $K^* = Q$. The total cost curve for production function $Q = \min(L,K)$ would, then, be written:

$$TC = wQ + rQ = (w+r)Q$$

This total cost curve is, then, a line starting at 0 and rising with slope $(w+r)$. This is shown in Figure 8.1:

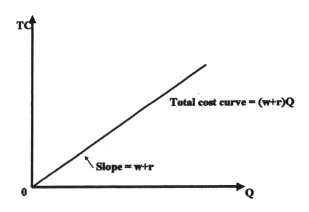

Figure 8.1

Exercise 1: *Suppose that the production function is $Q = L + K$, where L is labor and K is capital. Let the wage rate be fixed at w and the rental rate of capital be fixed at r. What is the total cost curve of the firm?*

   a. TC = wrQ
   b. TC = min(w,r)Q
   c. TC = 2Q

Since all factors of production are variable in the long-run, total cost *must* be zero when output is zero, that is, the long-run total cost curve must go through the origin of the graph. As we saw in Chapter 7, producing a higher level of output involves a higher cost: in order to reach a higher isoquant, one must move to a higher (parallel) isocost line (see Figure 8.2). This implies that the total cost function must be increasing in the level of output.

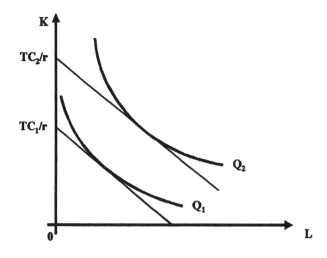

Figure 8.2

Exercise 2: *Which of the following could be a valid long-run total cost curve, where Q is the level of output?*

   a. $TC = 100 + Q^2$
   b. $TC = 100Q - 5Q^2$
   c. $TC = 100Q^2$

    Recall from Chapter 2 that the demand curve showed how output demanded was related to the price of output, all else held constant. As we changed the price, we moved *along* the demand curve. On the other hand, when one of the variables that had been held constant changed, the demand curve shifted. Similarly, the total cost curve shows how total cost relates to output, all else held constant. As we change the firm's desired level of output, we move *along* the total cost curve. For example, when we increase desired output from Q_0 to Q_1, we move along total cost curve $Q(w+r)$ from TC_0 to TC_1 in Figure 8.3, below. On the other hand, when one of the variables that had been held constant changes, the total cost curve shifts. For example, if the wage changes, the total cost curve shifts. This need not be a parallel shift, however. Let us examine how total cost curve $(w+r)Q$ changes as w changes. As w rises to w' ($> w$), the total cost curve rotates upward: it still passes through zero, but as Q rises and we use more and more labor, the total cost at the higher wage level diverges more and more from the total cost at the lower wage level. This is depicted in Figure 8.3.

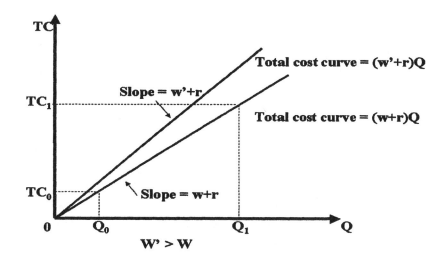

Figure 8.3

Exercise 3: *Let the production function be Q = L + K, where L is labor and K is capital. Let the wage rate be w, and the rental rate of capital be r. Derive the total long-run cost curve for this production function. How does the cost curve change when both the wage and the rental rate of capital fall by half?*

a. Total cost falls by 1/4
b. Total cost falls by 1/2
c. Total cost does not change

Now, suppose that only the wage falls by 1/2 while the rental rate of capital stays at its original level. How does the total cost curve change?

a. Total cost falls by less than 1/2
b. Total cost falls by 1/2
c. Total cost does not change
d. (a), (b), or (c), depending on the levels of w and r

The **long-run average cost curve** is the total cost curve divided by the level of output, Q. In other words,

$$AC(Q) = TC(Q)/Q$$

The **long-run marginal cost curve** is the change in the long-run total cost due to a change in output divided by the change in output. In other words, it is the additional cost of producing "one more unit" of output:

$$MC(Q) = [TC(Q+\Delta Q) - TC(Q)]/\Delta Q = \Delta TC/\Delta Q$$

Graphically, we can also think of MC(Q) as the slope of the total cost curve at point Q. AC(Q) is the slope of a ray from the origin to the total cost curve at point Q.

Exercise 4: *For the production function Q = min(L,K), where L is labor and K is capital, what are the average and marginal cost curves?*

a. AC(Q) = (w+r); MC(Q) = (w+r)
b. AC(Q) = 2Q; MC(Q) = 2
c. AC(Q) = (w+r)Q; MC(Q) = (w+r)

For most purposes here, we will assume that average cost is U-shaped and that marginal cost eventually rises as output keeps increasing. It is very important for future chapters that you understand the relationship between total, average, and marginal costs. This relationship is the same as the relationship between any "total", "average", and "marginal" magnitude (see boxed text in Chapter 6 of this Study Guide). The most important thing to understand is how average and marginal cost are related. For example, suppose that two students have handed in their tests and have received marks of 85 and 90. The average is 87.5. Now, you hand in your test and receive a mark of 95. This last, or *marginal*, test is higher than the current average of 87.5 so that it raises the average class mark to 90. On the other hand, if you had received a mark of 80, your *marginal* test would have been below the current average and would have lowered the average class mark to 80. Hence we can conclude that *when the marginal cost exceeds the average cost, the average cost must be rising but when the marginal cost is less than the average cost, the average cost must be falling.* This, in turn implies that *when marginal cost equals average cost, average cost neither rises nor falls, that is, average cost is flat.* In other words, for standard U-shaped average cost curves, the minimum of the average cost curve must be where average cost is equal to marginal cost. *We can then directly find the output level at which the average cost reaches a minimum by finding the output level at which average cost equals marginal cost.*

Exercise 5: *Let $TC(Q) = 100Q - 5Q^2 + 3Q^3$, with $MC(Q) = 100 - 10Q + 9Q^2$. At what level of output does the average cost curve reach a minimum?*

    a. $Q = 9/10$
    b. $Q = 0$
    c. $Q = 5/6$

What is the average cost at its minimum?

    a. $AC = 100$
    b. $AC = 97\dfrac{11}{12}$
    c. $AC = 98$

Exercise 6: *Graph average and marginal cost for Exercise 5 with cost on the vertical axis and output on the horizontal axis. Which of the following statements is true?*

    a. Average cost is U-shaped.
    b. Average cost is falling for all levels of Q.
    c. Marginal cost and average cost are rising for all Q.
    d. Marginal cost exceeds average cost for Q > 5/6, while marginal cost is less than average cost for Q < 5/6.

When average cost falls as output rises, we say that there are **economies of scale**. If average cost rises as output rises, we say that there are **diseconomies of scale**. In other words, the left-hand side of the "U" on a typical average cost curve is the region of economies of scale. The right-hand side of the "U" is the region of diseconomies of scale. The point at which the long-run average cost curve attains its minimum is often called the **minimum efficient scale** of production.

Where do economies or diseconomies of scale come from? Economies of scale may result from **indivisible inputs**. In other words, an input may be available only in a certain minimum size. Even if the output is small, the quantity of this input cannot be scaled down. On the other hand, diseconomies of scale may result from **managerial diseconomies**. In other words, they result when an increase in output requires a more than proportional increase in spending on managerial services.

Exercise 7: *For the average cost of Exercise 5, which of the following is true?*

    a. There are diseconomies of scale for Q < 5/6, but economies of scale for Q > 5/6.

b. There are economies of scale for Q < 5/6, but diseconomies of scale for Q > 5/6.
c. There are no economies of scale, but there are diseconomies of scale.
d. The minimum efficient scale of production for this firm is Q = 5/6.

As long as the prices of all factors of production remain constant, there is a precise relationship between the *returns to scale* defined in Chapter 6 as a characteristics of a production function and the *economies of scale* that are a characteristic of the long-run average cost curve. When the production function exhibits *increasing returns to scale*, the long-run average cost curve exhibits *economies of scale*. When the production function exhibits *decreasing returns to scale*, the long-run average cost curve exhibits *diseconomies of scale*. When the production function exhibits *constant returns to scale*, the long-run average cost exhibits *neither economies nor diseconomies of scale*. Assume, for example, that we can quadruple output by just doubling all the inputs (and, therefore, doubling the cost of production). This is the case of increasing returns to scale. The average cost per unit of output must, then, fall (since cost has doubled but output has quadrupled): there are economies of scale.

Exercise 8: *In Figure 8.4, what must Q_1 be in order for the long-run average cost curve to exhibit diseconomies of scale?*

a. Q_0
b. Any number greater than Q_0
c. Any number less than Q_0
d. Any number between Q_0 and $2Q_0$

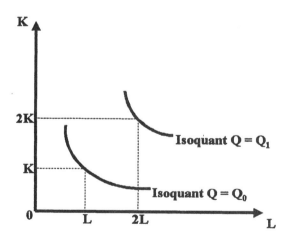

Figure 8.4

A useful way of summarizing the shape of the average cost curve is the **output elasticity of total cost**, $\varepsilon_{TC,Q}$, which measures the percentage change in total cost per 1% change in output. Using our formula for any elasticity in Chapter 2, the elasticity of total cost with respect to output is $\varepsilon_{TC,Q} = (\Delta TC/\Delta Q)(Q/TC)$. Since the second term in brackets is simply the reciprocal of average cost, and the first term is the marginal cost, the elasticity can be rewritten as MC/AC. When $\varepsilon_{TC,Q} < 1$, it must, therefore, be the case that MC < AC so that we have economies of scale. Similarly, if $\varepsilon_{TC,Q} > 1$, then it must be the case that MC > AC so that we have diseconomies of scale. If $\varepsilon_{TC,Q} = 1$, then MC = AC so that we have neither diseconomies nor economies of scale.

Exercise 9: *Your research assistant tells you that he has measured the output elasticity of total cost of a firm, and has found its value to be -1.23. You know that input prices do not change as output increases. What do you conclude?*

   a. The research assistant made an error in his calculations.
   b. The firm is not operating efficiently.
   c. The production function exhibits decreasing returns to scale.

You check the calculations of the research assistant and discover an error. You recalculate the output elasticity of total cost to be zero for the firm. What do you conclude?

   a. You made an error in your calculations.
   b. The firm is not operating efficiently.
   c. The marginal cost of production is zero.

The long-run total cost curve shows how the firm's minimized total cost varies with output when the firm is free to adjust all its inputs. The **short-run total cost curve**, STC(Q), tells the minimized total cost of producing Q units of output when some factors of production are fixed. The short-run total cost curve is the sum of two components: the **total variable cost curve**, TVC(Q), and the **total fixed cost curve**, TFC so that STC(Q) = TFC + TVC(Q). The total variable costs change as output changes, while the total fixed costs do not. For example, in the short-run total cost curve $STC(Q) = 100 + Q^2$, the total fixed costs are 100 and the total variable costs are Q^2.

Subtleties of Short-run Cost Curves

The short-run cost curve slopes upward for the same reason as does the long-run cost curve: a firm that is run efficiently cannot produce more without also using more inputs. Our example of a short-run cost curve, $100 + Q^2$, does, indeed, slope upward. In contrast to the long-run cost curve, however, our example of a short-run cost curve does not equal zero when output is zero. This may not be quite right: the short-run cost curve would generally equal zero at zero output since most fixed costs that we can imagine can be avoided by setting output to zero. As soon as *any* amount of output is produced, however small, these fixed costs can conceivably become quite large. In other words, we really should say that $STC(Q) = 100 + Q^2$ for Q > 0 and STC(Q) = 0 at Q = 0. For convenience in this summary, we will simply assume that the fixed costs remain positive at zero and will *not* force short-run cost curve to jump down to zero at zero output.

When a firm is free to vary all input levels, it can combine inputs at least as efficiently as it could if it were forced to use a fixed level of one input. In other words, the firm can combine inputs at least as efficiently in the long-run as in the short-run. This means that, for a given level of output, the firm's short-run total costs must be no less than the long-run total costs. It is only when the fixed inputs happen to be at the level that would be chosen in the long-run anyway that the firm's short-run total cost equals the long-run total. Since average cost is equal to total cost divided by output, short-run average costs lie above long-run average costs *except* when the fixed inputs are at their long-run cost minimizing level. At this level of output (Q_1 on the figure below), short-run average cost equals long-run average cost.

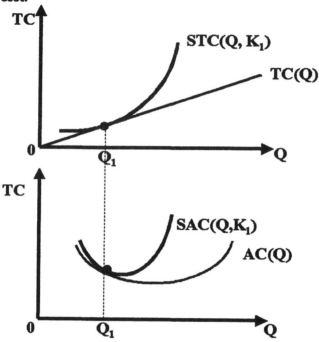

K_1 is the long run cost minimizing plant size for Q_1 units of output

Figure 8.5

Exercise 10: *Let the production function of a firm be Q = K + L. Suppose that K is fixed at level $\overline{K}$ in the short-run. What is the short-run total cost curve of the firm?*

   a. $STC(Q) = r\overline{K} + \min(w,r)(Q - \overline{K})$ for $Q \geq \overline{K}$
   b. $STC(Q) = \min(w,r)(Q - \overline{K})$
   c. $STC(Q) = \min(w,r)Q$
   d. $STC(Q) = r\overline{K} + (w+r)(Q - \overline{K})$

The long-run total cost of this firm is as given in Exercise 1. Compare STC(Q) to TC(Q). Are they ever equal? If so, at what value of Q does STC(Q) = TC(Q)?

   a. $STC(Q) > TC(Q)$ for all values of Q.
   b. $STC(Q) = TC(Q)$ for $Q = \overline{K}$ when $r \leq w$
   c. $STC(Q) = TC(Q)$ for $Q = \overline{K}$.

We can define the **short-run average cost** (SAC) of the firm and the **short-run marginal cost** (SMC) of the firm analogously to the long-run average cost and the long-run marginal cost:

$$SAC(Q) = STC(Q)/Q$$

$$SMC(Q) = [STC(Q+\Delta Q)-STC(Q)]/\Delta Q = \Delta STC/\Delta Q$$

Because the short-run total cost is the sum of total variable cost and total fixed cost, we can also express the short-run average cost as the sum of **average variable cost** and **average fixed cost**:

$$SAC = TVC/Q + TFC/Q = AVC + AFC$$

Graphically, SMC(Q) is the slope of the short-run total cost curve at Q while SAC(Q) is the slope of a ray from the origin to the short-run total cost curve at Q. At the points where the short-run total cost equals the long-run total cost, the SMC(Q) equals the long-run MC(Q) since the slopes of the short-run and long-run total cost curves are equal.

Just as the long-run marginal cost went through the minimum of the U-shaped long-run average cost curve, *the short-run marginal cost intersects the short-run average cost at the minimum of short-run average cost.* Since short-run average cost is composed of two components, we can say more, however. *Short-run marginal cost also goes through the minimum of the short-run average variable cost curve.* The reason is that the marginal cost of production is only the portion of total cost that changes as output changes. Since the average variable cost also refers only to the portion of total cost that changes as output changes, the relationship between marginal and average cost that we saw in the long-run also holds between marginal and average variable cost in the short-run. The relationship between short-run and long-run marginal and average costs can be summarized in Figure 8.6:

- MC(Q) cuts AC(Q) at its minimum.
- SMC(Q,K$_1$) cuts AC(Q,K$_1$) at its minimum
- SAC(Q,K$_1$) equals AC(Q) at the output where K$_1$ is the cost minimizing level of capital
- SAC lies above AC except at the output where K$_1$ is the cost minimizing level of capital

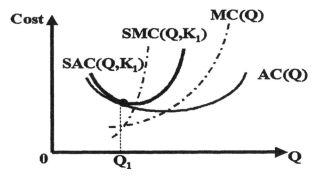

K$_1$ is the long run cost minimizing plant size for Q$_1$ units of output

Figure 8.6

Exercise 11: *Which of the following statements is true?*

    a. The average fixed costs must decrease in output.
    b. The minimum of the short-run average total cost curve may coincide with the minimum of the short-run average variable cost curve.
    c. The minimum of the short-run average total cost curve may occur at a higher level of output than the minimum of the short-run average variable cost curve.
    d. The minimum of the short-run average total cost curve may occur at a lower level of output than the minimum of the short-run average variable cost curve.

Exercise 12: *At the minimum efficient scale, it is true that:*

    a. $SAC(Q, K_{MES}) = AC(Q)$, where K_{MES} is the cost minimizing level of capital at the minimum efficient scale.
    b. $MC(Q) = AC(Q)$.
    c. $SMC(Q, K_{MES}) = SAC(Q, K_{MES})$, where K_{MES} is the cost minimizing level of capital at the minimum efficient scale.
    d. $STC(Q, K_{MES}) = TC(Q)$, where K_{MES} is the cost minimizing level of capital at the minimum efficient scale.

There are **economies of scope** when the total cost of producing given quantities of two goods in the *same* firm (or plant) is less than the cost of producing the same quantities in two *different* firms. In other words, producing a variety of goods is less expensive than specializing in the production of a single good. Mathematically, this can be written as:

$$TC(Q_1, Q_2) < TC(Q_1, 0) + TC(0, Q_2)$$

where the left-hand side represents the cost of producing Q_1 units of good 1 and Q_2 units of good 2 in the same firm, while the right-hand costs are the costs of single-product firms producing positive amounts of one good only. $TC(x, 0)$ is called the **stand-alone cost** of producing x and $TC(0, y)$ is called the stand-alone cost of producing y.

Exercise 13: *Which of the following are possible sources of economies of scope?*

    a. Workers get bored when they do the same task all the time.
    b. Workers are much more efficient if they specialize in one product.
    c. It is less costly for a firm producing good A to add production of one unit of product B to its product line than it would be for a new firm to start produce its first unit of product B from scratch.

In contrast, **economies of experience** or **learning-by-doing** refers to the cost advantages that result as *cumulative* output gets larger. The cumulative output is the total output that has been produced over the history of the product. In other words, a firm that produces 10 units in period 1 and 20 in period 2 has a cumulative output at the end of period 2 of $10 + 20 = 30$ units. Economies of experience are not the same as economies of scale, which refer to the cost advantages that result from larger scale of production *within a given time period*. For example, the firm would exhibit economies of scale if the average cost of producing 20 units in period 1 were less than the average cost of producing 10 units in period 1.

As the name indicates, the cost savings due to learning-by-doing are the result of improvements in performance that occur *over time* due to increased experience producing the products. These economies usually are described by the **experience curve**, which relates the average variable cost to the cumulative output. The **slope of the experience curve** usually is expressed as a percentage by which average variable cost falls when output doubles. In other words, a slope of 80% would indicate that average variable costs at an output of 2 are 80% of the average variable cost at an output of 1.

Exercise 14: *Which of the following statements is true?*

  a. A firm must exhibit economies of scale in order to have economies of experience.
  b. A firm that exhibits economies of experience must have economies of scale.
  c. A firm that exhibits economies of scope must have economies of scale.
  d. If a firm has both economies of scope and economies of scale, it must have economies of experience.

In order to know how the total cost of a *particular* firm varies as the factors that influence cost, or **cost drivers,** vary, we would need to collect data on that firm's total cost and that firm's cost drivers. The cost drivers we have considered so far in this summary are input prices, scale, scope, and cumulative output. We will focus on input prices and scale. The relationship between the cost drivers and the total cost is called the **total cost function**. An important property of long-run total cost functions is that doubling the prices of *all* factors of production must *exactly* double the minimum cost of producing a given level of output. This property reflects the fact that a proportional increase in input prices leaves the slope of the isocost line unchanged so that the point of tangency between the isocost line and the isoquant remains the same. If the optimal combination of inputs does not change, then total cost must increase in the same proportion as factor prices.

- One common example is the **constant elasticity cost function**. Suppose the firm has two factors of production: labor and capital. Then, a constant elasticity cost function for the firm would be:

$$TC = aQ^b w^c r^d$$

Where a, b, c, and d are constants, Q is output, w is the wage rate, and r is the rental rate of capital. The exponents are the elasticity of the total cost with respect to the corresponding cost driver (e.g., the elasticity of total cost with respect to output is b). Further, the sum of the exponents of the prices of the inputs must be constrained to equal 1. Otherwise, the function would not capture the fact that a doubling of all prices of inputs should double the total cost. Taking logs of both sides of the constant elasticity cost function, we see that the log of total cost is a *linear* function of the logs of the cost drivers:

$$\log TC = \log a + b \log Q + c \log w + d \log r$$

Since the output elasticity of total cost is constant for this function, the cost function exhibits either economies of scale (if $b < 1$), diseconomies of scale ($b > 1$), or neither economies nor diseconomies of scale ($b = 1$) for its entire range. Therefore, graphically, the average cost either falls, rises, or is constant everywhere.

- The **translog cost function** allows for the possibility that the cost function might exhibit non-constant economies of scale. This cost curve assumes that the log of total cost of the firm is a *quadratic* function of the cost drivers:

$$\log TC = b_0 + b_1 \log Q + b_2 \log w + b_3 \log r + b_4 (\log Q)^2 + b_5 (\log w)^2 + b_6 (\log r)^2 + b_7 (\log w)(\log r) + b_8 (\log w)(\log Q) + b_9 (\log r)(\log Q)$$

The constraint that a doubling of input prices doubles total cost is captured by the following restrictions that must hold for this total cost function:

$b_2 + b_3 = 1$
$b_5 + b_6 + b_7 = 0$
$b_8 + b_9 = 0$

Further, if $b_4 = b_5 = b_6 = b_7 = b_8 = b_9 = 0$, then this cost function reduces to the constant elasticity cost function.

Exercise 15: *A firm's cost drivers are output, Q, the wage rate, w, the rental rate of capital, r, and the rental rate of land, m. If you wanted to estimate a constant elasticity cost curve for this firm, which of the following equations would you estimate, where a, b, c, d, and e are constants?*

a. $TC = aQ^b w^c r^d$ subject to $c + d = 1$
b. $TC = aQ^b w^c r^d m^e$ subject to $c + d = 1$
c. $TC = aQ^b w^c r^d m^e$ subject to $c + d + e = 1$

Chapter Review Questions

1. Suppose that a firm's costs are as follows:

Output (units)	Total fixed cost (dollars)	Total variable cost (dollars)
0	1000	0
1	1000	50
2	1000	100
3	1000	140
4	1000	150
5	1000	200
6	1000	270
7	1000	350
8	1000	490

What are the firm's short-term total costs, average variable costs, average fixed costs, and short-term marginal costs?

Answer:

Output (Q)	STC= TFC+TVC	AVC=TVC/Q	AFC=TFC/Q	SMC= ΔSTC/ΔQ
0	1000	0	Infinite	0
1	1050	50	1000	50
2	1100	50	500	50
3	1140	46.67	333.33	40
4	1150	37.5	250	10
5	1200	40	200	50
6	1270	45	166.67	70
7	1350	50	142.86	80
8	1490	61.27	125	140

2. Let the production function of a firm be Q = min(L,K), where L is the quantity of labor employed, K is the quantity of capital employed, and Q is output. Let the wage rate be w = 1 and the rental rate of capital be r = 1.

   a. What is the total cost curve of this firm? What is the average cost curve of the firm? What is the marginal cost curve of the firm?

   b. What is the minimum efficient scale of the firm?

   c. Suppose that, in the short-run, $\overline{K}$ = 10. What is the short-run total cost of the firm? What is the short-run average cost? What is the short-run marginal cost?

   d. Where does short-run average cost equal long-run average cost? Where does short-run marginal cost equal long-run marginal cost? Why?

   e. Why can short-run marginal cost be less than long-run marginal cost, but short-run average cost must always lie above long-run average cost?

Answer:

a. We saw in Exercise 4 of this chapter that the total cost curve is TC(Q,r,w) = (w+r)Q. The average cost curve is AC = TC/Q = (w+r). The marginal cost curve is the change in total cost when output increases by one unit, or MC = w+r.

b. The minimum efficient scale of this firm is the minimum point on the average cost curve. Since the average cost curve is flat, any output level is equally efficient.

c. If capital is fixed at $\overline{K}$ = 10, then the lowest cost method of producing any output below 10 is to set L = Q. It will not be possible to produce more than 10 units of output since output is limited to the lesser of capital or labor. Therefore, the short-run total cost curve is STC(Q,w,r,$\overline{K}$) = r$\overline{K}$ + wQ for Q ≤ 10 and STC is infinite for Q > 10. The short-run average cost curve is SAC = STC/Q = r$\overline{K}$/Q + w for Q ≤ 10 and is infinite for Q > 10. Note that, since $\overline{K}$/Q ≥ 1, SAC always lies above AC. SMC = w for Q ≤ 10 and is infinite for Q > 10. Graphically, short-run and long-run average and marginal costs are as follows:

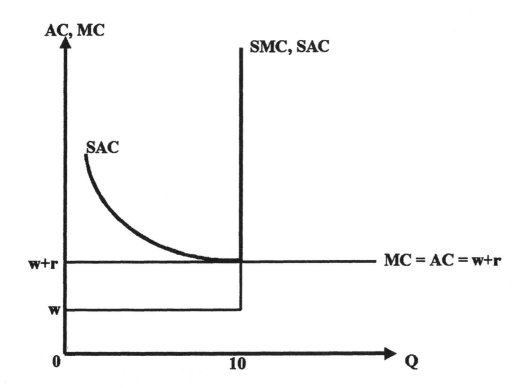

d. Using our expressions for SAC and AC from parts (a) and (c), SAC equals AC at Q = $\overline{K}$. Using our expressions for SMC and MC from parts (a) and (c), SMC equals MC at Q = $\overline{K}$ as well. This can be seen by noting that SMC lies below MC for all values of Q $\leq$ 10 and jumps to infinity at Q > 10. The two curves cross at exactly Q = 10.

e. We know that the short-run total cost curve lies above the long-run total cost curve. In other words, the *level* of STC is higher than the *level* of TC. This means that the SAC must lie above AC since the average cost depends on the level of total costs. Algebraically, STC>TC => STC/Q > TC/Q ⇔ SAC > AC. On the other hand, SMC is the *slope* of the STC curve and MC is the *slope* of the TC curve. The slopes of STC and TC have no specific relation to each other. Therefore, there is no set relation between short-run and long-run marginal costs.

3. The total cost of a firm can be written TC = a + bQ + cQ², with a, b, and c all non-zero. MC = b + 2cQ.

   a. Write down the formula for average cost for this firm and draw average cost on a diagram. Where are the regions of decreasing and increasing economies of scale?

   b. Compare this to a case where the total cost of a firm can be written TC = a + bQ with MC = b. What can you say about economies of scale for this total cost curve?

c. If you wished to estimate the cost curve for a firm, but did not know whether the function used in part (a) or in part (b) was correct, why would it be a better choice to estimate a translog cost curve than a constant elasticity cost curve?

Answer:

a. AC = TC/Q = a/Q + b + cQ. This reaches a minimum where AC = MC or where a/Q + b + cQ = b + 2cQ. Solving this equation, the minimum of AC occurs at $Q^* = (a/c)^{1/2}$. Economies of scale occur at outputs below Q^*, and diseconomies of scale occur for outputs above Q^*. At Q^*, there are neither economies nor diseconomies of scale.

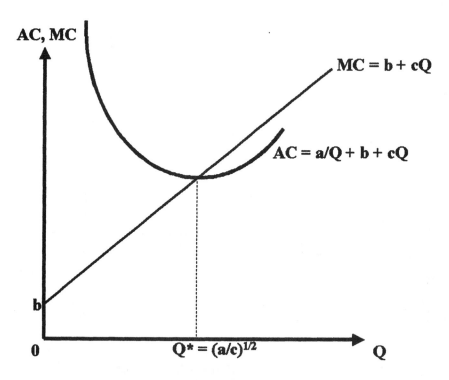

b. AC = a/Q + b. This function decreases continually so that there are economies of scale for all levels of output.

c. The translog cost function allows for varying economies of scale depending on the level of output, as in part (a). With restrictions on the coefficients, we can also obtain from the translog a constant degree of economies of scale as in part (b). Therefore, it would seem more reasonable to use the translog function since it is flexible enough to encompass both cases.

Problem Set

1. Three production methods are available to produce an output, Q. Engineers have measured the input requirements for three output levels to be the following:

	Q = 1	Q = 2	Q = 3
Process 1	L = 10 K = 1	L = 11 K = 2	L = 12 K = 3
Process 2	L = 5 K = 5	L = 7 K = 7	L = 12 K = 12
Process 3	L = 1 K = 10	L = 2 K = 10	L = 3 K = 10

Where L is labor and K is capital. Let both the wage and rental rate of capital be $1.

a. What are the total and average costs associated with each technology for each level of production? Which process exhibits increasing or decreasing returns to scale?

b. What is the firm's total cost curve for Q = 1, 2, 3? What is the firm's average and marginal cost curve for these three levels of output? Does the firm's cost exhibit economies or diseconomies of scale?

c. What can you say about the firm's minimum efficient scale?

d. Graph the average cost curves for each technology and the average cost curve of the firm. How are these curves related to each other?

2. (This problem builds on problem 4 in chapters 6 and problem 1 in chapter 7) A firm has production function $Q = 100L^{3/4}K^{1/4}$, with $MP_L = 75K^{1/4}L^{-1/4}$ and $MP_K = 25L^{3/4}K^{-3/4}$ and faces a constant wage of w per unit for labor input and a constant rental rate of capital of r per unit. Answer all the following questions:

a. Derive the long run total cost function for this firm. Illustrate the long run total cost curve as a function of Q for fixed w and r.

b. What is the minimum efficient scale of production for this firm? Explain your answer.

3. You hire a consultant from ABC Associates to make an econometric estimate of the cost of production at your firm. The consultant's estimate is STC(Q) = .5 + 2Q, where Q is output. The consultant tells you that the minimum efficient scale is infinite based on her estimates. Do you believe her?

4. The "0.6 rule" states that the increase in the total cost of production is given by the increase in capacity raised to the 0.6 power. In other words:

$$TC_2 = TC_1 \times (Q_2/Q_1)^{.6}$$

where Q_1 is the original capacity, Q_2 is the new capacity, TC_2 is the cost at capacity Q_2, and TC_1 is the cost level at capacity level Q_1. Does this rule suggest that the production process is characterized by economies of scale?

5. Suppose that the marginal product of labor is greater than the average product of labor for some level of output. Further, suppose that labor is the only input to production. How does the marginal cost compare to the average variable cost of production for this same level of output? What can you say about the output elasticity of total cost?

6. A plant hires 10 workers who can each produce 100 units per hour of output using the existing machinery (capital stock) at normal speeds. Workers are paid $10 per hour for normal working hours (an 8-hour day), but must receive double this amount for any overtime. The number of workers is fixed in the short-run. Equipment's rental rate is $10 per hour. The plant may produce 100 units of output per half hour by running its equipment harder. This method causes wear and tear equivalent to an extra $10 per hour for the equipment. Calculate and draw the total cost curve for this firm. Calculate and draw the average cost curve and the marginal cost curve of this firm.

7. A firm has a U-shaped average cost curve.

   a. Suppose that the firm must pay an output tax of t per unit. How does this affect the total, average, and marginal costs of the firm? How does the minimum of the new average cost curve compare to the minimum of the old average cost curve?

   b. Suppose that, instead, the firm must pay an up-front, fixed, franchise fee, F, in order to operate. What is the effect of this tax on the (after-tax) total, average, and marginal cost curves of the firm? How does the minimum of the new average cost curve compare to the minimum of the old average cost curve?

8. You are a manager in a firm that produces two goods at output levels Q_1 and Q_2. The cost of producing either Q_1 units of good 1 alone *or* Q2 units of good 2 alone is $10 million, and the cost of producing Q_1 units of good 1 and Q_2 units of good 2 together is $18 million.

   a. Does production at your firm exhibit economies of scope?

b. You wish to get a measure of the degree of economies of scope in the production of the two goods. The cost control section of your firm suggests the following measure, S:

$$S = \{[TC(Q_1,0) + TC(0,Q_2) - TC(Q_1,Q_2)]/TC(Q_1,Q_2)\}100$$

where the notation used is as in the summary for this chapter. What is the value of S for your firm? How would you interpret this measure in words?

9. You work for XYZ corporation and have been asked to estimate the firm's total cost curve. You present the following estimate as part of a slide presentation to the president of the company:

$$TC = .5Q^{.1}w^{.3}r^{.7}$$

a. After listening to your presentation, the president comments, "so we obtain a 10% increase in our total cost when we increase our output by 1 percent." Do you agree with him? Why or why not?

b. You notice that the president has jotted down on his note pad that your numbers imply that the firm would obtain cost savings by increasing output infinitely, since the estimate indicates economies of scale everywhere. Has the president correctly interpreted your results? Why or why not?

c. The president refers several times in his comments to the fact that your total cost curve is "linear". Since the form you have written on your slide is multiplicative, what could he be referring to?

Exam *(60 minutes: Closed book, closed notes)*

1. If the expansion path for a firm is a straight line, must the long-run total cost curve be a straight line?

2.
   a. Average costs can never rise when marginal costs are declining. True or false? Explain your answer.

   b. If the marginal costs of two firms are the same, the average variable costs of those firms must be the same. True or false? Explain your answer.

3. You have been asked to conduct a study to examine how costs have fallen over time at your firm. As a first cut, you estimate the following relationship:

$$AVC(N) = N^{.8}$$

where AVC is the average variable cost of the firm and N is the cumulative output of the firm.

    a. What does your estimate show about costs? Why?

    b. Let your estimate be AVC(N) = $N^{.8}$. What does this show about costs?

4. An engineering study of firm X finds that total cost is related to output in the following way:

Total Cost (thousands of dollars)	Output (thousands)
5	4
20	8
30	15
40	18
60	32
70	36
80	40

    a. Plot the data on a diagram with total cost on the vertical axis and output on the horizontal axis.

    b. Which total cost curve reflects the data better: TC = a + bQ or TC = a + bQ + cQ^2, with the coefficients a, b, and c different from zero?

Answers to Exercises

1. The correct answer is (b). To solve for the total cost curve, we need the input demand functions for this production function. The input demands for this production function are:

L*(Q,w,r) = Q when w < r
           = 0   w > r

K*(Q,w,r) = Q when r < w
           = 0   r > w

(See problem 6, Chapter 7 to see why.) Hence , we have TC = wL* = wQ if w < r and TC = rK* = rQ if w>r. Combining these two cases we can write TC = min(w,r)Q.

2. The correct answer is (c). Total cost curve (a) has a fixed cost that must be paid even if output is zero. This is inconsistent with the fact that the cost curve is for the long-run, where the firm can choose the level of every factor of production. Total cost curve (b) is decreasing in output for all Q > 10. This is inconsistent with the fact that the cost curve must be rising in output.

3. The correct answer to the first part of the question is (b). From Exercise 1, we know that the total cost curve is TC = min(w,r)Q. When both the wage and rental rate fall by half, the ranking of wage and rental rates does not change. For example, if w was smaller than r, this still is the case at the new wage and rental rates. If w < r, then TC = min(w,r)Q = wQ falls by half, as w falls by half. If r <w, then TC = min(w,r)Q = rQ falls by half as r falls by half.

   The correct answer to the second part is (d). If w < r, then w/2 < r and the total cost falls by half when the wage rate falls by half for the same reason as was given in the first part of the answer. If (1/2)w > r, then no labor is used either before or after the fall in wages. Since the rental rate of capital does not change, the total cost does not change in this case either. If w > r > (1/2)w, then the firm's total cost function was TC = rQ *before* the wage fall but it is TC = w'Q *after* the change in wages, where w' is the new wage rate. Therefore, the change in total cost is ΔTC = (r-w')Q. Since w > r > (1/2)w = w', it must be the case that rQ < 2w'Q so that the total cost falls by less than (1/2).

4. The correct answer is (a). We saw in Chapter 7, Exercise 7, that the conditional input demands for this production function are L = Q and K = Q so that the long-run total cost function is TC = wQ + rQ =(w+r)Q. Therefore, the average cost is TC/Q = w+r. The marginal cost is the increase in total cost for a one-unit increase in Q. This equals w+r as well.

5. The correct answer is (c). Average cost, $AC(Q) = TC(Q)/Q = 100 - 5Q + 3Q^2$. This equals marginal cost when $AC = 100 - 5Q + 3Q^2 = 100 - 10Q + 9Q^2$ or, solving for Q, when $Q^* = 5/6$. Substituting into AC, we have AC(min) = 100 - $5Q^* + 3Q^{*2} = 100 - 25/12$ or $AC = 97\frac{11}{12}$. Therefore, the correct answer to the second part of the question is (b).

6. The correct answer is that (a) and (d) are true. Graphing average and marginal costs, we have:

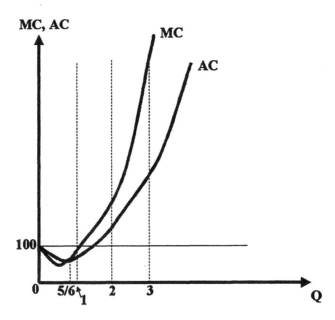

7. The correct answers are (b) and (d). From the graph of Exercise 6, we see that average cost falls until 5/6 and rises thereafter.

8. The correct answer is (d). When the production function exhibits decreasing returns to scale, the cost curve exhibits diseconomies of scale. Decreasing returns to scale implies that a doubling of all inputs less than doubles output.

9. The correct answer is (a) or (b). A negative output elasticity would imply that either marginal or average cost is negative. Marginal cost is negative when the total cost falls as more output is produced. If the firm operates efficiently and input prices do not change, this is not possible, as we saw at the beginning of the chapter. Therefore, we could conclude that either the firm was not operating efficiently or, if it was, the research assistant made an error.

   The correct answer is (a) or (c). When marginal cost is zero, the output elasticity of total cost will be zero. It certainly is possible for marginal cost to be approximately zero in some cases. For example, the marginal cost of an additional passenger on a regularly scheduled airplane flight when the plane is not full and the plane is about to leave is virtually zero. Similarly, once a piece of software has been designed, the cost of producing additional copies is negligible. This is not the case for all cost curves, however, so it would be a good idea to check your calculations to make sure that a zero marginal cost makes sense in the production activity you are studying.

10. The correct answer to the first part of the question is (a). In the short-run, the capital cost for $\overline{K}$ units of capital is fixed. Since capital and labor are perfect substitutes for this production function, the firm would minimize its cost of production by using the $\overline{K}$ units of capital to produce output when the desired

output level is less than $\overline{K}$. For any units of output that exceed $\overline{K}$, in other words for units (Q - $\overline{K}$), the firm would minimize costs by using the input that costs less per unit.

The correct answer to the second part of the question is (b). $\overline{K}$ is the long-run cost minimizing amount of capital when Q = $\overline{K}$ only if r < w. When w < r, the firm would prefer to use only labor so that the long-run cost function would be wQ < rQ, for all output level, including Q = $\overline{K}$. Notice that the short-run total cost function *equals* the long-run total cost function at output levels Q > $\overline{K}$ as well when r < w, but *must* lie above the long-run total cost function for any level of output that is less than $\overline{K}$ whatever the prices of the inputs.

11. Statements (a), (b), and (c) are correct. Since the total fixed costs are constant (by definition), TFC/Q *must* decrease in output so that statement (a) is correct. If fixed costs are zero, then average total cost is the same as average variable cost and statement (b) is true. If fixed costs are positive then average total cost is the sum of average variable cost and of average fixed costs. This implies that the minimum of average total costs must occur somewhere *between* the minimum of the average variable cost curve and the minimum of the average fixed cost curve. Since the average fixed cost curve is decreasing everywhere, this "in-between" region must be to the right of the minimum of the average variable cost curve: statement (c) is correct.

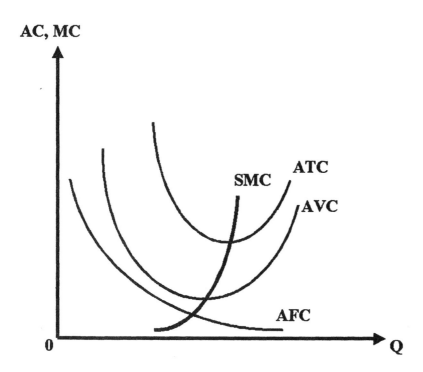

12. All of the statements are correct. At the minimum efficient scale, the long-run average cost curve reaches a minimum by definition. Therefore, (b) is correct since the marginal cost cuts the average cost curve at its minimum. The short-run average cost curve coincides with the long-run average cost curve wherever the inputs are used at their long-run cost minimizing levels. Therefore, (a) is correct. Similarly, short-run total costs equal long-run total costs whenever the inputs are used at their long-run cost minimizing level. Therefore, (d) is correct. Finally short-run marginal cost must intersect short-run average cost at its minimum, so that (c) is correct as well.

13. (c) and possibly (a) are possible sources of economies of scope. Statement (a) may or may not be associated with economies of scope, depending on the nature of the tasks performed by workers. The argument is as follows. If workers get bored when they perform the same task, it is likely that they will be less efficient than if they were given a variety of tasks to perform. If each task were associated with a different product, then economies of scope would result because more efficient workers would be those who were less bored. Of course, if a single task is associated with many different products then this is no longer the case. For example, it is conceivable that building a single product from beginning to end would involve more varied tasks than building a single stage of many different products. For economies of scope to hold, it should be the case that workers be more efficient at producing a variety of *products* (not *tasks*). Statement (b) suggests that there is no special benefit from combining several products into the same firm. This makes economies of scope less likely. Statement (c) is correct since it can be rewritten in the form of the definition of economies of scope as: $TC(Q_A,1) < TC(Q_A,0) + TC(0,1)$.

14. All the statements are false. Economies of scale, economies of experience, and economies of scope are completely distinct concepts, so they are not linked in any set way. Economies of scale refer to the production of *one good* during a *given time period*. Economies of scope refer to the production of *more than one good*. Economies of experience refer to the *cumulative* effect of production over *several time periods*.

15. The correct answer is (c). The sum of the exponents of *all* the prices must equal 1, and *all* the input prices must enter the cost function.

Answers to Problem Set

1.

   a. The total costs and average costs for each technology and each level of production are:

Total Costs, Average Costs	Q = 1	Q = 2	Q = 3
Process 1	TC = 11 AC = 11	TC = 13 AC = 6.5	TC = 15 AC = 5
Process 2	TC = 10 AC = 10	TC = 14 AC = 7	TC = 24 AC = 8
Process 3	TC = 11 AC = 11	TC = 12 AC = 6	TC = 13 AC = 4.33

Process 1 exhibits increasing returns to scale, process 2 exhibits initially increasing and later decreasing returns to scale, and process 3 exhibits increasing returns to scale (the average costs of each process are decreasing, U-shaped and decreasing, respectively).

b. The total cost curve for the firm is the cost associated with the cost minimizing use of inputs at each desired output level. The cost minimizing input combination for Q = 1 is process 2 (L = 5, K = 5). The cost minimizing input combination for Q = 2,3 is process 3 (L = 2, K = 10 and L = 3, K = 10, respectively). Therefore, the total cost curve, average cost curve, and marginal cost curve for the firm are:

TC (Q = 1) = 10   AC(Q = 1) = 10   MC(Q = 1) = 10
TC (Q = 2) = 12   AC(Q = 2) = 6   MC(Q = 2) = 2
TC (Q = 3) = 13   AC(Q = 3) = 4.33 MC(Q = 3) = 1

Note that both average and marginal cost curves are decreasing in output. From the decreasing average cost curve, we see that there are economies of scale for the firm. Marginal cost lies at or below average cost for all three levels of output shown.

c. All three output levels are below the minimum efficient scale, since average cost does not reach a minimum at any of these three output levels.

d.

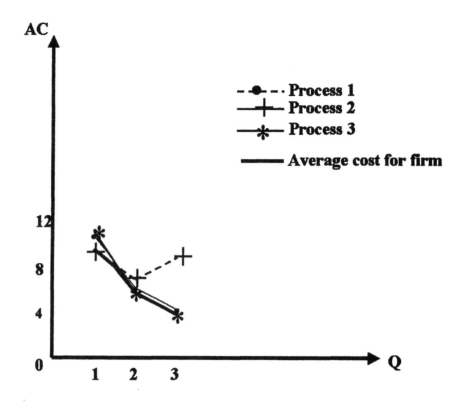

The average cost curve for the firm is the lower envelope of the average cost curves for each process.

2.

a. $TC(Q,w,r) = wL^*(Q,w,r) + rK^*(Q,w,r)$, where L^* and K^* are the labor and capital input demands. If you do not remember how to derive them, refer to chapter 7's problem 1. In other words, $TC(Q,w,r) = w(3r/w)^{1/4}(Q/100) + r(w/3r)^{3/4}(Q/100)$. For fixed w and r, we can define a constant $A = (w/100)(3r/w)^{1/4}$ and $B = (r/100)(w/3r)^{3/4}$ and re-write the total cost curve as $TC(Q) = (A+B)Q$. Hence, the total cost curve is a straight line with slope $(A+B)$:

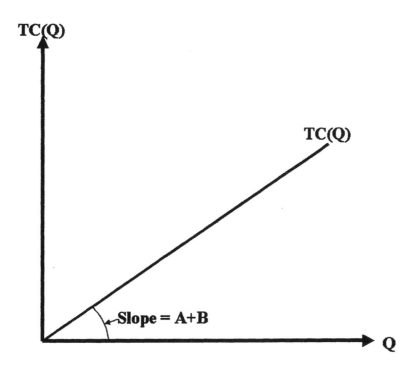

b. The average cost curve for this firm is a horizontal line, AC(Q) = TC(Q)/Q = (A+B), hence the cost curves for this firm exhibit neither economies nor diseconomies of scale. All output levels result in the same level of average cost, so that the *minimum* efficient scale is zero. In fact, all scales of operation are equally efficient. This comes from the fact that the production function is constant returns to scale, so changing output levels amounts to simply "replicating" the existing production process. If you do not remember why this is constant returns to scale, refer to chapter 6, problem set question 4.

3. The minimum efficient scale is calculated based on the *long-run* total (or average) cost function, so the consultant should derive the long-run cost function before making any statements about minimum efficient scale. For example, even though the process that the firm is using in the short-run (with its current level of fixed inputs) exhibits increasing returns to scale, another process which does not exhibit increasing returns to scale everywhere could be optimal for another output range. The lower envelope of these would be the firm's long-run average cost function. As you can see from the graph below, the minimum efficient scale based on this lower envelope is not infinite.

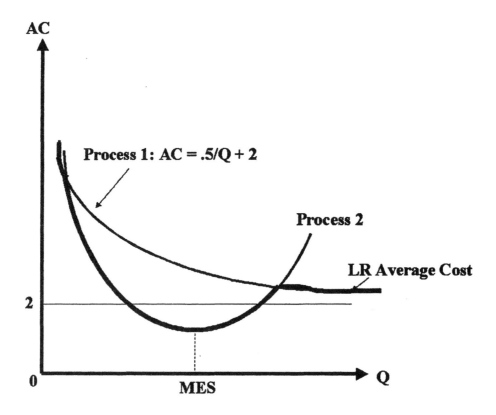

4. Yes. For example, the "0.6 rule" indicates that a doubling of output less than doubles total cost. Let $Q_2 = 200$ and $Q_1 = 100$, for example. Then $TC_2 = TC_1(2)^{.6}$ or $TC_2/TC_1 = 1.5$ (approximately). Therefore, total cost increases only 50% while output increases 100%. This means that the average cost of production must be falling. When the average cost of production falls, this means that there are economies of scale.

5. If the marginal product of labor exceeds the average product of labor, the average product must be rising. If the average product is rising, then a given increase in output must require a less than proportional increase in labor. Since labor is the only input, this means that there are increasing returns to scale. If there are increasing returns to scale, then the cost function exhibits economies of scale. In other words, average cost is falling. If average cost is falling, then marginal cost must lie below average cost. If MC < AC, then the output elasticity of total cost must be less than one.

6. It is always cheaper to produce output by running the equipment harder and using less labor. For example, by running the equipment at normal speeds, we obtain that 100 units of output costs ($10+$10) = $20. On the other hand, by running the equipment harder, we could obtain the 100 units at a cost of only $5 in labor and $10 in equipment, which sums to $15. Similarly, at all higher output levels, the method of production that uses capital intensively is cheaper than the "labor-intensive" method. You can verify that additional units of output cost $20 per 100 up to a total of 800 units per day, after which additional units cost $30 per 100 when the labor-intensive method is used. When the capital-intensive

method is used, additional units of output cost $15 per 100 up to a total of 1600 units per day, after which additional units cost $20 per 100. The maximum feasible level of production using the labor-intensive method is 2400 units per day and the maximum feasible units of production using the capital-intensive method is 4800 units (if we assume that the labor can, in fact, work 24 hours a day).

Based on the total costs of production using the capital-intensive method, the average cost of production is $.15 for the first 1600 units and rises slowly up to $.187 at the maximum of 4800 units. The marginal cost is $.15 for the first 1600 units, after which it is $.20 for additional units of to a maximum of 4800 units. As long as marginal cost is flat, so is average cost. When marginal cost rises, it pulls up average cost as well.

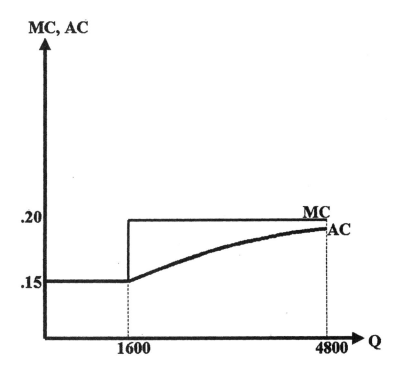

7.

    a. A tax of t per unit of output increases total cost by tQ. Therefore, the tax shifts up both the marginal cost and average cost curves by t. Because the shift of both average and marginal cost is the same for all levels of output, the minimum of average cost occurs at the same output level as before the tax. This can be seen by noting that the new average cost, AC', equals the old average cost plus t (AC + t). The new marginal cost, MC', equals the old marginal cost plus t (MC + t). The old minimum of average cost occurred where AC = MC. Adding t to each side, we obtain AC' = MC'. Therefore, equality at the old levels implies equality at the new levels.

    b. The franchise fee F is a fixed (but not sunk) cost of operation. It increases TC by F for output levels greater than zero so that TC' = TC + F, where TC' is the new level of total costs and TVC is the old level of total cost. Average cost becomes AC' = TC'/Q = (TC + F)/Q = AC + F/Q, that is, average cost shifts up, but as Q increases, the new average cost falls toward the old level of average cost. Marginal cost is not affected by the franchise fee since F is a fixed cost. Because the additional term F/Q is decreasing for all levels of output, the minimum of AC' must lie at a higher output level than the minimum of AC. This can be seen graphically by noting that MC slopes upward and has not changed due to the tax.

8.

   a. $TC(Q_1,Q_2) = \$18 < \$10 + \$10 = TC(Q_1,0) + TC(0,Q_2)$: there are economies of scope.

   b. $S = [(\$10 + \$10 - \$18)/\$18]100 = [\$2/\$18] \times 100 = 100/9$. We could think of S as the percentage cost increase when the goods are produced separately rather than together. A number greater than zero would indicate that there are economies of scope; a number less than zero would indicate that there are no economies of scope.

9.

   a. This is a constant elasticity cost function. The exponent of output is the elasticity of total cost, $\varepsilon_{TC,Q}$. A value of .1 for this exponent indicates a 0.1% increase in total cost when output increases by 1 %.

   b. When $\varepsilon_{TC,Q} < 1$, this indicates economies of scale. Further, this is constant everywhere by assumption of the constant elasticity cost function. Therefore, the president is correct that your numbers indicate that the minimum efficient scale is infinite according to your calculations.

   c. The president might be referring to the fact that, when you take logs on each side of your equation, the *log* of total cost is a linear function of the *logs* of output, the wage and the rental rate of capital.

Answers to Exam

1. If the expansion path is a straight line, then the inputs are demanded in a constant *ratio*, no matter what the output level. This does not mean that the total cost curve must be straight, however because we still do not know how much the *amount* of inputs required must increase when output increases. For example, consider the following diagram of an expansion path with isoquants for Q_0, Q_1, and Q_2. Let $Q_1 = 2Q_0$ and $Q_2 = 3Q_1$. Then a doubling of inputs just doubles output between Q_0 and Q_1, but *more* than doubles output between Q_1 and Q_2. Therefore, we have constant returns to scale between Q_0 and Q_1 but increasing returns to scale between Q_1 and Q_2. This implies that total cost is a straight line between Q_0 and Q_1 (average cost is flat), but increases at a slower rate between Q_1 and Q_2 (average cost is falling).

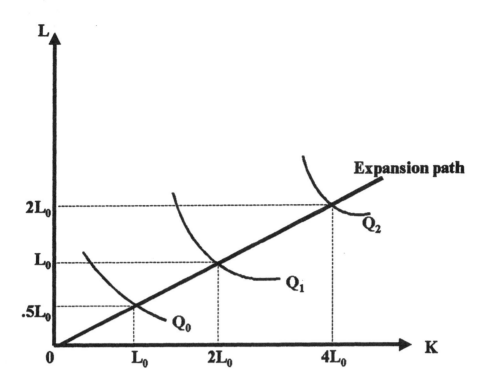

2.

   a. False. If marginal costs are *above* average costs, average costs rise. Therefore, it is possible for marginal costs to decline and average costs to rise as long as the marginal costs remain above average costs.

   b. True. If the marginal costs are the same at all levels of output, each unit of output costs the same amount to add to the existing units. When we *add up* the marginal cost of each unit produced, we obtain the total variable cost of the firm. Therefore, the total variable costs of the firms must be the same if the marginal costs are the same everywhere because the sum of these marginal costs must be the same. It follows that, if the total variable costs of the firms are the same, the average variable costs must also be the same.

3.

   a. The estimate shows that, as cumulative output increases, average variable cost falls. Specifically, the experience elasticity, or the percentage change in average variable cost for every 1% increase in cumulative output, is -.8. If the cumulative output doubles, average variable costs fall to 80% of their former level. Since average variable cost falls when cumulative output rises, the firm exhibits learning by doing or economies of experience.

   b. If the exponent is positive, it indicates *diseconomies* of experience. (In other words, average variable costs rise with cumulative output.) Unless techniques that were known before are forgotten over time, it is unclear why this would ever be the case. Perhaps some traditional crafts (such as stained-glass making and stone carving) fit into this category.

4.

a.

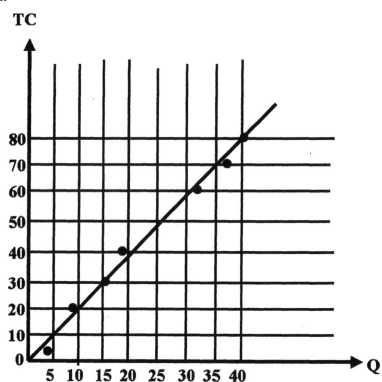

b. The linear form is probably sufficient. While there is some non-linearity in the data, it is fairly closely grouped around the 45° line. It would be reasonable to assume that the differences between the data and the straight line can be attributed to measurement error.

Chapter 9: Perfectly Competitive Markets

In Chapters 7 and 8, we examined the cost minimization problem of a producer that wanted to reach a target output level of Q_0. Now, we will assume that the producer chooses its target output to maximize the profits earned from production. Clearly, the output that a firm wants to produce depends on the price that it can get for its product. This relationship between output and price is called the **supply curve of the firm**. If we add up the output supplied by all producers for various price levels, we obtain **the aggregate supply curve** for the entire market. We can combine aggregate supply with aggregate demand to derive market equilibrium.

To put this analysis in perspective, by the end of this chapter we will be right back where we started our market analysis in Chapter 2 of this book. We will have derived aggregate demand from a set of basic assumptions on consumer behavior (Chapters 3 - 5), and we will have derived aggregate supply from a set of basic assumptions on firm behavior (Chapters 6 - 9). The advantage of deriving supply and demand from basic principles is that it allows us to understand what assumptions underlie the type of supply and demand analysis that we conducted in Chapter 2. Further, it also allows us to derive additional insights about *individual* consumers and firms that we would not have been able to deduce from the model of *aggregate* behavior. Using the map analogy of Chapter 1, our models of *individual* consumer and firm behavior gives us a "map" of economic behavior on a scale where we see all the detail. Our model of *aggregate* supply and demand give us a "map" of economic behavior on a scale where we see just the largest features of the "economic geography".

Let us now proceed with the analysis of market equilibrium, which is the subject of this chapter. The type of market we will analyze is a **perfectly competitive market**. A perfectly competitive market has four *characteristics*:

1. Each *buyer's* purchases are so **small** that he/she has an imperceptible effect on market price. Further, each *seller's* sales are so **small** that he/she has an imperceptible effect on market price. When both buyers and sellers are small in this way, we call the industry **fragmented**.

2. Firms produce **undifferentiated products** in the sense that consumers perceive the products to be identical. In other words, the products may be physically the same or, if they are not the same, the differences do not in any way affect consumers' demand (or valuation) of the product.

3. Consumers have **perfect information** about the prices all sellers in the market charge.

4. Finally, all firms (both current industry participants and potential new entrants to the industry) have **equal access to resources** (such as technology and raw materials).

The first three assumptions are necessary for the market to be perfectly competitive in the short-run. The fourth assumption must be added to define perfect competition in the long-run.

Exercise 1: *Which of the following statements is correct?*

a. Suppose that 12.6 billion barrels of crude oil were transported by sea between oil-producing and oil-consuming nations in 1977. A single supertanker could easily have a capacity of 300,000 deadweight tons, where a single deadweight ton of cargo equals approximately 7 barrels of crude oil. The large size of a single supertanker means that the market for oil tanker shipping cannot be fragmented.

b. Maple syrup is rated by quality and color. For example, one type of maple syrup might be "grade A amber." This rating system indicates that maple syrup is a differentiated product so that it would be inaccurate to characterize the maple syrup market as perfectly competitive.

c. In order to grow wheat, Tim would have to buy a farm as well as all the inputs to wheat production (farm equipment, seeds, and so on). These inputs all are costly so that Tim, as a potential new entrant to wheat production, would incur substantial costs to enter. This means that the market for wheat cannot be perfectly competitive.

These four characteristics have three important *consequences*:

1. Characteristic (1) implies that buyers and sellers take the price of the product as *given* when making their purchase and output decisions, since each decision has an imperceptible effect on market price. Because of this, sellers and buyers in such markets are termed **price takers**.

2. Characteristics (2) and (3) imply that there is a *single price* at which transactions occur: any output in this market that is priced lower than any other would immediately attract the entire market demand, since consumers view all output as exactly the same *except for price*. Similarly, any output priced higher than any other would attract no demand at all. This is implication is often called the **Law of one price**.

3. Characteristic (4) implies that all firms have identical long-run cost functions. This consequence is called **free entry**.

Exercise 2: *Which of the following statements is true?*

a. An implication of price taking is that market demand must be flat in the perfectly competitive market, since consumers do not view their purchase decisions as having any effect on market price.

b. If we observe a market where all output sells at the same price, it must be the case that the output is undifferentiated and that consumers have perfect information about price.

Next, for any level of output that a firm produces, the firm's **economic profit** is the revenue it earns from the output minus its opportunity cost of producing the output. Recall from Chapter 8 that we represent the opportunity cost of producing a level of output by the firm's total cost curve. Algebraically, then, economic profit, π, can be written as the difference between the total revenue earned from q and the total cost curve:

$$\pi(q) = TR(q) - TC(q)$$

Note that economic profit is not the same as the profit that is reported on firms' balance sheets. This latter measure of profit is termed **accounting profit** and measures the difference between total revenue and the historical (and explicit) cost of resources. When we say profit in the rest of the Study Guide, we will mean economic profit.

With these definitions of perfectly competitive markets and economic profit in hand, we can proceed to our analysis of firms' supply decisions.

We will assume that each firm sets its output so as to maximize profits. Therefore, the following maximization problem determines the firm's output choice:

$$\text{Max } \pi(q) = TR(q) - TC(q)$$
$$q$$

Where π stands for the firm's profits, q is the output *of the firm*, TR is the total revenue curve, and TC is the total cost curve. (The total revenue curve is simply the market price times the output, q.) Notice that this is an unconstrained maximization problem: all the technological constraints have been taken into account in the total cost curve and all the consumers' budget constraints have been taken into account in the total revenue curve.

The solution to this problem is that the firm wishes to set q at a level that equates **marginal revenue**, defined as the additional revenue earned when output increases slightly, to marginal cost. However, *a price-taking firm anticipates that each additional unit sold will earn the market price*. Therefore, the marginal revenue of a price-taking firm exactly equals price.

Exercise 3: *Let the market price be P. The market demand is Q = 100 - P, where Q is aggregate output of all firms in the industry. What is the total revenue of a single perfectly competitive firm for any given market price, P, and level of firm output, q?*

a. TR = Pq
b. TR = P(100 - P)
c. TR = P(100 - q)

What is the marginal revenue of this perfectly competitive firm?

a. MR = 100 - 2P
b. MR = 100 - 2q
c. MR = P

We add the requirement that marginal cost be rising at the firm's profit-maximizing, or optimal, output, q*. This requirement is important for the following reason. If marginal cost is rising at q*, then the firm has an incentive to increase output up to q* -- because P > MC for this range -- but to stop at q* -- since P < MC at higher values of output. Therefore, q* is the only level of output that can maximize profits, and so it is an equilibrium (i.e., a point where the firm has no incentive to change its behavior). If, to the contrary, marginal cost were *falling* at q*, then profit could be increased by increasing output -- since P > MC at values of output just higher than q*-- and q* could not be an equilibrium.

As a result, the perfectly competitive firm's profit maximization conditions are that the firm sets output at a level, q*, so that:

- P = MC at q*
- Marginal cost must be increasing in output at q*

This is illustrated in Figure 9.1.

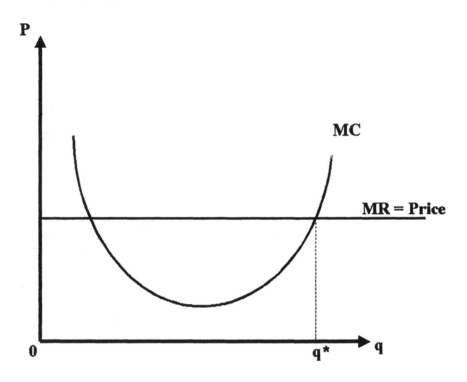

Figure 9.1

Exercise 4: *P = $7 and MC = 10 - 8q + 4q². By substituting the following values of output into the marginal cost function, at which level of output is price equal to marginal cost?*

    a. q = 1/2
    b. q = 3/2
    c. q = 1

Of the following output levels, which is the perfectly competitive firm's profit-maximizing output?

    a. q = 1/2
    b. q = 3/2
    c. q = 1

If we maintain the assumption that P = $7, what can be said about the slope of the total cost curve and the slope of the total revenue curve at an output level of q = 1, where total revenue (and total cost) are on the vertical axis and output is on the horizontal axis?

    a. The slope of total revenue curve is larger than the slope of the total cost curve at q = 1.

    b. The slope of the total revenue curve equals the slope of the total cost curve at q = 1.

    c. The slope of the total revenue curve is less than the slope of the total cost curve at q = 1.

    The **firm's short-run supply curve** tells us how the profit maximizing output, q*, changes as the market price changes in the short-run. Offhand, it appears that the firm's short-run supply curve is defined by the equation P = MC. After all, this equation does tell us how the profit maximizing output changes as the market price changes. There are two reasons why this is not the case:

- The **short-run** is the period of time in which the firm's plant size is fixed and the number of firms in the industry is fixed. Hence, the marginal cost that we would want to use in this equation is the *short-run marginal cost*, SMC.

- We have implicitly assumed in our profit maximization conditions that the firm does better producing a positive output than not producing at all. We now define P_S as the price below which the firm would prefer to shut its doors. P_s is called the **shut down price**.

Taking these two considerations into account, the firm's short-run supply curve is defined by the following equations:

    1. P = SMC, where SMC slopes upward as long as $P \geq P_S$
    2. 0 where $P < P_S$

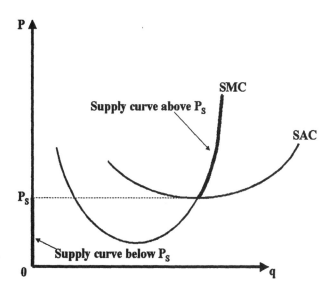

Figure 9.2

Computing the Shut Down Price

In order to determine P_s, we must compare the profits that the firm could earn if it produced such that P = SMC to the profits the firm would earn by producing nothing. What the firm could earn by producing nothing depends, in turn, on the portion of the firm's short-run total costs that are *fixed and sunk (SFC),* and the portion that are *fixed but non-sunk (NSFC).* **Sunk fixed costs** are the costs that are **output insensitive** when output is positive *and* unavoidable even if output is zero. **Non-sunk fixed costs** are the costs that are output-insensitive when output is positive, but avoidable when output is zero. If *all* the firm's fixed costs are sunk, then it must pay the same fixed costs whether its output is positive or zero. Therefore, all of the fixed costs are irrelevant to the decision of whether or not to produce a positive output. As a result, the firm chooses to produce a positive output if the total revenue from production covers its total *variable* costs, TR(q) > TVC(q). Dividing each side of this inequality by q, we have the condition P > AVC(q). The shut down price is defined, then, as the *lowest* point on the average variable cost curve: if price were to exceed AVC at any positive output, the firm could earn profit from the output and would therefore do better than producing nothing.

Exercise 5: *A firm's sunk fixed cost is $50. It has no non-sunk fixed costs. Suppose that market price is $10 and AVC(q) = 10 - 4q + q^2, where q is the firm's output. What is the firm's shut down price? You may solve either graphically or by substituting in values of q = {0, 1, 2, 3},*

   a. P_s = $6
   b. P_s = $10
   c. P_s = $7

What are the firm's economic profits at output level q = 2?

   a. $58
   b. $0
   c. $8

Should the firm produce a positive output if market price = $10?

   a. yes
   b. no
   c. need more information

Similarly, if *none* of the firm's fixed costs are sunk, the firm can avoid *all* costs by producing nothing. On the other hand, it must cover all costs, fixed and variable, if it produces a positive amount. Therefore, the firm will produce a positive output only if the total revenue from production covers its total variable *and* fixed costs or TR(q) > TC(q). Again, dividing both sides of the inequality by q, we have P > SAC(q) as the production condition. The shut down price is the lowest point on the average cost curve. Finally, if only *some* of the fixed costs are sunk, the firm chooses to produce a positive output if the total revenue from production covers its total variable costs plus the *portion* of fixed costs that are non-sunk. TR(q) > TVC(q) +

NSFC. Defining the **average non-sunk cost curve** as ANSC(q) = [TVC(q) + NSFC]/q we have P > ANSC(q) as the production condition. The shut down price is the minimum of the average non-sunk cost curve.

These conditions can be summarized as follows:

Shut Down Price

	No sunk costs	All fixed costs sunk	Some f. costs sunk
Produce if...	$P \geq SAC(q)$	$P \geq AVC(q)$	$P \geq ANSC(Q)$
P_s	Min(SAC)	Min(AVC)	Min(ANSC)

It is helpful to remember, when computing P_s, that the minimum of the SAC (or ANSC or the AVC) curve occurs where SMC equals SAC (or ANSC or AVC).

Exercise 6: *A firm's total cost function is as follows:*

TC = $25 if q = 0
   $50 - q + q² if q > 0

The associated marginal cost is MC = 2q - 1. What is the shut down condition for this firm?

a. $P \geq AC(q)$
b. $P \geq AVC(q)$
c. $P \geq ANSC(q)$

What is the shut down price for this firm?

a. $\$50^{1/2}$
b. $\$0$
c. $\$9$

The **short-run market supply curve** at any price is the sum of the quantities supplied by each firm at that price. Graphically, this is the horizontal sum of the firms' short-run supply curves since the quantities each firm supplies are measured on the horizontal axis. Let this sum be denoted $Q^S(P)$.

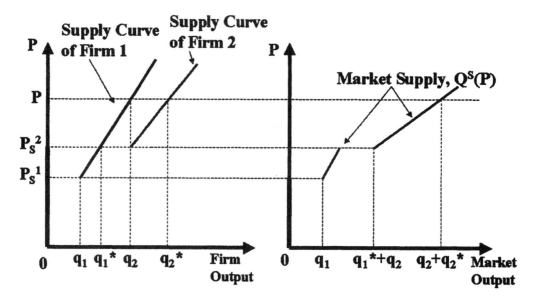

Figure 9.3

A **short-run perfectly competitive equilibrium** occurs when quantity demanded *by the market* at a given price equals the quantity supplied *by the market* at that same price. If $Q^D(P)$ is market demand at price P, then, the short-run perfectly competitive equilibrium is defined by the equation:

$$Q^S(P) = Q^D(P)$$

Graphically, the short-run perfectly competitive equilibrium occurs where market supply equals market demand. It is very important that you remember that *market* and not *firm* supply equals market demand in the market equilibrium and that the number of firms in the market is fixed in the short-run.

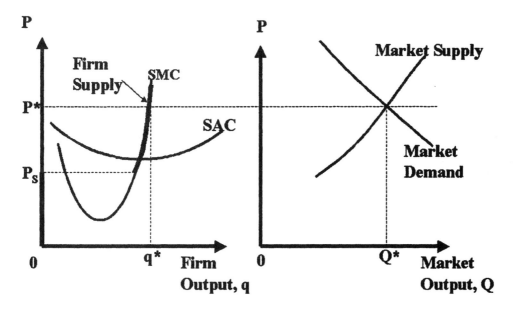

Figure 9.4

To summarize, then, the perfectly competitive equilibrium for a given number of firms, n, in the industry and a market demand, $Q^D(P^*)$, is defined as the firm output level, q*, and the price level, P* such that:

- Every firm is producing on its short-run supply curve, $P^* = SMC(q^*)$
- Industry supply equals industry demand, $nq^* = Q^D(P^*)$

Exercise 7: *Each firm in a perfectly competitive industry has the total cost curve:*

$TC(q) = 0$ *for q = 0 and* $100 + q^2$ *for q > 0, where q is the output of the firm.*

The associated marginal cost is MC = 2q. There are n = 200 firms in the industry. What is the short-run firm supply curve for this industry?

a. $P = 2q$ above $P_S = \$20$
b. $P = 2q$ above $P_S = \$10$
c. $P = 100 + q^2$ above $P_S = \$20$

What is the short-run industry supply curve for this industry?

a. $Q^S(P) = 100P$ above $P_S = \$10$
b. $Q^S(P) = 100P$ above $P_S = \$20$
c. $Q^S(P) = P/2$ above $P_S = \$20$

Market demand for this industry is given by Q = 3000 - 50P. What is the short-run perfectly competitive equilibrium price, firm output and market output?

  a. P* = $10, q* = 5, Q = 1000
  b. P* = $20, q* = 10, Q = 2000
  c. P* = $1, q* = 0, Q = 0

As in Chapter 2, we can describe the shape of the market supply curve using the **price elasticity of supply**, $\sigma_{Q,P} = (\Delta Q^S/\Delta P)(P/Q^S)$, and we can analyze market price movements by performing **comparative statics** on supply and demand. It would be worthwhile to review Chapter 2 at this point to refresh your memory on these concepts.

The **long-run** is the period of time in which all the firm's inputs, including plant size, can be adjusted. The number of firms in the industry can change as well. Therefore, while the day to day output decisions of the firm might be determined by the solution to the firm's short-run supply problem, its decisions on *target* production levels in the future would be based on the firm's long-run equilibrium output. We turn now to the solution to the firm's long-run output choice problem.

Exercise 8: *Which of the following could be a long-run decision?*

  a. A decision to shut down production, but not to exit the industry
  b. A decision to shut down production and exit the industry
  c. A decision to increase the size of a plant with no change in labor force

The firm's long-run decisions will, naturally, be based on its *long-run* total costs. This suggests that the firm's long-run supply curve will trace out the outputs at which price equals long-run marginal cost. However, the firm can decide to shut down operations, just as it could in the short-run. Since all costs are avoidable in the long-run, there are no sunk costs. Therefore, the appropriate long-run level of the shut down price is the price that just equals the minimum of the long-run average cost curve. At any price lower than this, the firm would make negative profits, since total revenue would be less than total cost. Summarizing, the **firm's long-run supply curve** is described by the two following conditions:

  - If $P \geq P_S$, the firm sets output so that P = MC, where MC is *long-run* marginal cost
  - If $P < P_S$, the firm sets output to zero.
  - P_S is the minimum price that touches the long-run AC curve.

Exercise 9: *Let a firm's long-run marginal cost be MC(q) = 50 - 2q + .75q², where q is the firm's output and its average cost be AC(q) = 50 - q + .25q². Which of the following statements is true about the firm's long-run supply curve?*

  a. The firm's long-run supply curve slopes upward.
  b. The firm's long-run supply curve is flat.
  c. The firm produces a constant output level of 2, whatever the price.
  d. The firm's long-run shutdown price is $49.

We can infer from our shut down condition and the "free entry" characteristic of perfectly competitive markets that, as long as $P > P_S$, it would pay a firm to enter the industry in the long-run. This is because free entry implies that a firm entering the industry can make positive economic profits under the same conditions as any existing firm in the industry. Therefore, if price exceeds average cost for an existing firm, this would also be true for an entering firm. The market can only be in equilibrium, however, if there is no impetus to change *any variable*. Therefore, long-run equilibrium only holds if there is no incentive to enter, as this would change the number of firms in the market. As a result, the market is in **long-run perfectly competitive equilibrium** at price P*, firm output q*, and number of firms, n*, for market demand $Q^D(P^*)$ when all of the following conditions are present:

- $P^* = MC(Q^*)$
- $P^* = AC(Q^*)$
- $Q^D(P^*) = n^*q^*$

The first condition ensures that firms are maximizing profits in the long-run so that there is no incentive for firms to change their production, taking as given the market price. The second condition ensures that existing firms are earning zero economic profits so that there is no incentive for more firms to enter. The third condition ensures that aggregate demand equals aggregate supply so that there is no pressure for market price to change.

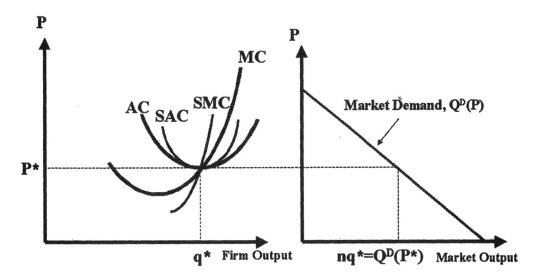

Figure 9.5

Exercise 10: *Suppose that long-run total costs of a typical firm in a competitive industry are given by: TC(q) = 0 for q = 0 and TC(q) = 100 + q² for q > 0 with MC(q) = 2q, where q is the output of a typical firm. Market demand for the industry* is Q = 3000 - 50P, where Q is the industry output. Assuming that all firms have identical cost structures, what are the long-run competitive equilibrium price, total quantity, number of firms, and the quantity produced by each firm?

    a. P* = 10, Q* = 2000, n* = 200, q* = 10
    b. P* = 20, Q* = 2000, n* = 200, q* = 10
    c. P* = 20, Q* = 1000, n* = 10, q* = 10

We can depict the long-run perfectly competitive equilibrium as the intersection of the market demand curve with the **long-run market supply curve**. The long-run market supply curve tells us the total quantity of output that will be supplied at various market prices, assuming that all long-run adjustments take place. It cannot be derived as the sum of the firms' long-run supply curves because the number of firms in the industry can vary in the long-run. This means that we do not know *how many* firms' supply curves to add up! Instead, the long-run market supply curve is derived from the following reasoning. If price exceeds the minimum of the average cost curve, then entry would occur. This entry would shift out industry supply until the market equilibrium price fell back to the minimum of average cost. If price were to fall *below* the minimum of the average cost curve, however, then firms would be earning negative profits and would exit the industry. Exit would shift back the industry supply curve until market equilibrium price rose back to the minimum of the average cost curve. Therefore, output can only be supplied so as to set price equal to the minimum of average cost in the long-run. In other words, the long-run market supply curve is flat along the line P = minimum of average cost.

Exercise 11: *For the total cost and marginal cost curve of Exercise 10, what is the equation of the long-run market supply curve for this perfectly competitive industry? (The notation is the same as in Exercise 10.)*

    a. $P = 100/Q + Q^2$
    b. P = 2Q
    c. P = 20

In fact, the conclusion that the long-run market supply is flat relies on the assumption that we have not stated explicitly: we have assumed that the average cost of production does not vary as *industry* output varies. In other words, entry of new firms into the industry does not change the cost of inputs to production. This assumption need not always hold, however. For example, the long-run market supply curve is upward-sloping when the average cost curve shifts up as input prices rise due to an increase in industry output. Such an industry is called an **increasing cost industry**. This is more likely to be the case when firms use **industry specific inputs**, which are scarce inputs that only firms in this industry use. For example, a recent boom in the worldwide sales of Tequila has driven up the price of the special type of agave plant used in the fermentation stage. In contrast, when changes in industry output have no effect on input prices, we call the industry a **constant cost industry**. Here, the long-run market supply curve is flat. An industry where input prices change as industry output expands or contracts is also called an industry with **pecuniary effects**.

Exercise 12: *For furniture makers, wood is an important input. Which of the following would give rise to pecuniary effects in the furniture-making industry?*

    a. The firms supplying wood offer quantity discounts to their customers.

    b. As demand for wood grows the price of wood remains the same but its quality decreases so that a greater proportion of the planks purchased must be discarded.

    c. As their output increases, the furniture manufacturers can use more efficient techniques of production

Under our assumption of free entry, economic profits are driven to zero. In many industries, however, entry is not "free" in the sense that we have assumed. For example, an industry that uses coal exploits a resource that is in fixed supply. If these resources are, indeed, fixed, then only a limited number of firms will be able to enter. The fact that entry is restricted does not necessarily allow us to conclude that economic profit must be positive for the firms in the industry, however. The reason relates to the concept of opportunity cost. Suppose that, if we account for all costs *except* for those of the scarce resource, a firm *appears* to be earning a profit of π. Stated otherwise, suppose that the potential economic profit due to the use of this resource in production is π. Any other firm should be willing to bid *up to* π for the right to use the scarce resource since any firm that pays price π will earn zero economic profits net of this price. But this means that the resource's *opportunity cost* to any one industry participant is exactly π (because the "market price" for the resource is π) and so true economic profit is still zero!

The amount π can be thought of as a rental rate for the scarce factor, and so is called the **economic rent** due to the factor. The economic rent is defined as the value generated from a scarce resource that is in excess of the minimum payment necessary to have that factor supplied to a particular *use*. In other words, think of π as the *extra* value generated by using the scarce resource in its most productive use (product A) rather than its next most productive use (product B). Once the owner of the resource has decided to use the resource to produce product A, she may rent this resource to various different *users* (firms). Since any one user may need to bid up to π to win the right to use the resource, any one *user* may earn zero economic profit. The economic rent is not zero, however, since its value in product A net of its value in product B is unaffected by *who* exploits the resource.

The economic rent that is paid out to (or "captured by") the factor is the *portion* of π that any one firm must actually pay in order to become the *user* of the resource to produce A. The amount of the economic rent that is captured by the firm is the portion of π that need not be paid to win the right to be the *user* of the resource. Economic rent is depicted in Figure 9.6.

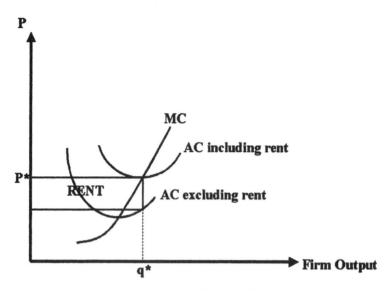

Figure 9.6

Exercise 13: *Talented programmers such as George Chip-head are in short supply. George works for a firm that earns an economic profit of $10,000 a month, without taking into account the price of George's labor. George is the only scarce resource that the firm employs. George currently charges $20 an hour for his services and works on average 50 hours a month. He realizes that he could earn much more if he really "played the market", but this does not really interest him: $20 an hour is perfectly sufficient for all his needs. What is George's economic rent? How much of the economic rent is captured by the firm as economic profits?*

    a. Economic rent = $9,000; George captures 1/9 of this rent. The firm's economic profits are $9,000.

    b. Economic rent = $10,000; George captures 1/10 of this rent. The firm's economic profits are $9,000.

    c. Economic rent = $1,100; George captures all of this rent. The firm's economic profits are $0.

As George grows older, he becomes more materialistic and more cynical about what he views as high corporate profits. He decides that he has been underpaid by the firm and solicits other job offers. When his firm gets wind of his activity, it raises his wages and a brisk bidding war ensues. The firm's final bid to George, which he accepts, is to pay him $200 per hour for 50 hours per month of work. What is George's economic rent now? What portion does George capture? What is the economic profit of the firm?

    a. Economic rent is unchanged. George captures all this rent and the firm's economic profits are zero.

    b. Economic rent falls to zero. George captures zero economic rent and the firm's economic profits are zero as well.

    c. Economic rent is $10,000. George captures zero economic rent and the firm's economic profits are $10,000.

So far, economic profit has been our main measure of producer benefit from production. However, **producer surplus** is an alternative measure of producer benefit. In other words, if we think of the supply curve as the price, p(Q), that would be just high enough to induce producers to supply Q units of output, producer surplus measures the amount by which market price exceeds this minimum. It can be thought of as the area between the supply curve and the market price. Since the supply curve is the MC curve above the minimum of average non-sunk costs, the producer surplus corresponds to the shaded area in Figure 9.7, below. Algebraically, producer's surplus is the firm's total revenue minus total non-sunk costs. In the long-run, this equals economic profit since all costs are non-sunk. In the short-run, however, producer surplus for each firm equals its economic profit *plus* its total sunk fixed costs. For the industry, producers' surplus is measured as the area between the market price and the industry supply curve.

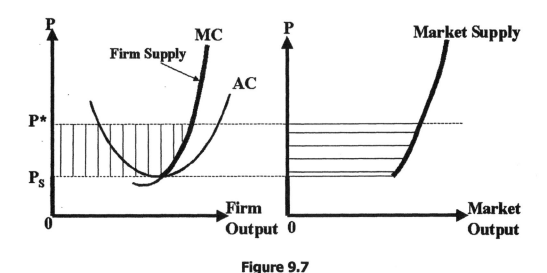

Figure 9.7

Another very useful way to think of producer surplus is as a gain from trade. In the short-run, the firm earns its total revenue minus all (sunk and non-sunk costs) if it produces so that trade occurs. If the firm shuts down, so that trade does not occur, it loses its sunk costs. The producer's surplus is equal to the gain from trading versus not trading: the profit from production minus the profit from producing zero. This difference simply equals the total revenue minus all non-sunk costs. As you recall, consumer's surplus also is a gain from trade. Producer's surplus is, then, a natural analog to the concept of consumer's surplus.

One might wonder when one measure of benefit is more appropriate than the other. One reason why we might wish to use producer's surplus rather than economic profits could be that we have information on marginal costs but not on average costs. Since producer's surplus can be measured as the area between market price and the marginal cost curve (supply curve) alone, producer's surplus is easier to compute in this case. If, on the other hand, we have information on average costs but not marginal costs, economic profit is easier to compute. The second reason is based on the gains from trade interpretation of consumer's and producer's surplus. If we wish to measure society's welfare (or benefits) from economic activity by the total gains to trade for consumers and producers, then the sum of consumer's and producer's surplus is the appropriate measure of benefit to these two groups. We will investigate this interpretation more thoroughly in Chapter 10.

In contrast to economic profit and producer surplus, economic rent is a separate concept that measures the benefit that is due to the scarceness of a valuable input. When economic rent exists, it need not be captured by firms and instead may be paid to the scarce factors of production.

Exercise 14: *Suppose that the land available that is suitable for growing cranberries is limited, but all other inputs to production are not. Without the rental price of the land, a farmer growing cranberries would earn a profit of π and produce output q^* when the market price is p^*. At this price, all available land is cultivated. The marginal and average costs of the farmer are depicted as follows:*

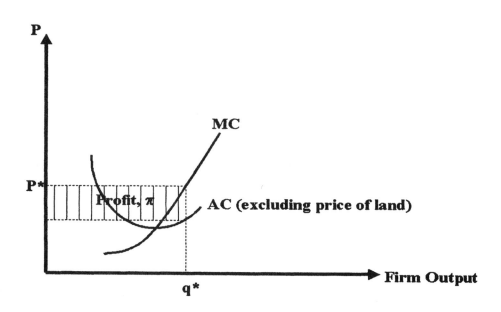

What is the effect on marginal cost of production if the owner of the land charges a rental price, π, for the land?

   a. The marginal cost shifts up by π.
   b. The marginal cost does not change.
   c. The marginal cost shifts down by π.

What is the effect on producer surplus if the owner of the land charges a rental price, π, for the land?

a. The producer surplus decreases by the portion of π above the marginal cost curve.
b. The producer surplus does not change.
c. The producer surplus decreases by π.

Suppose that the market price of cranberries rises to p**. What is the effect of this change on the economic rent due to the land if the owner continues to charge a rental price of π for the land? What happens to economic profit? Producer surplus?

a. Economic rent, economic profit, and producer surplus do not change.
b. The economic rent does not change, but the economic profit increases. Producer surplus increases
c. The economic rent increases, but the economic profit does not change. Producer surplus increases.
d. The economic rent, economic profit, and producer surplus all increase.

Chapter Review Questions

1. The following figure depicts an industry in short-run equilibrium. MC and AC are the long-run marginal and average cost curves, respectively. SMC and SAC are the short-run marginal and average cost curves. P* is the short-run market price.

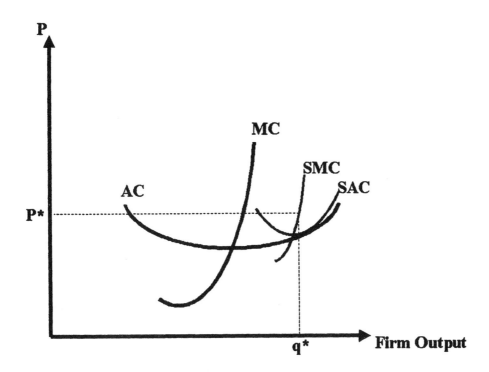

a. Illustrate short-run profits for the firm. Is the firm making economic profits or losses in the short-run?

b. What is the long-run equilibrium output for a competitive firm, given this graph?

c. Illustrate on the graph the short-run and long-run firm supply curve. Is the short-run shut down price greater or smaller than the long-run shut down price, assuming that no costs are sunk, even in the short-run?

d. Supposing that this is a constant cost industry, what is the equation for the long-run market supply curve?

Answer:

a. Short-run profits are illustrated below as $[P^*-SAC(q^*)]q^* =$ area in the box drawn with thickened lines in the figure below. These profits are positive.

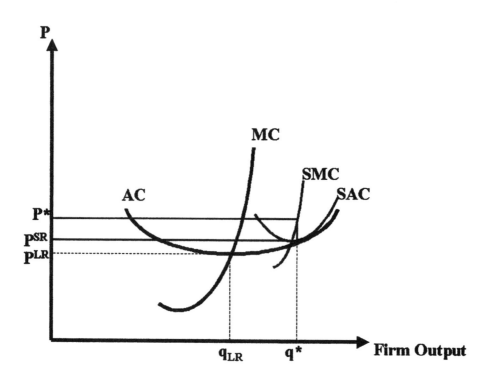

b. Long-run equilibrium output is the minimum of the long-run average cost curve, shown as point q_{LR} in the diagram.

c. The short-run supply curve is P = SMC for $P > P^{SR}$, where P^{SR} is the short-run shut down price. $P^{SR} = min(SAC)$. For $P < P^{SR}$, supply is zero.

The long-run supply curve is P = MC for $P > P^{LR}$, where P^{LR} is the long-run shut down price. $P^{LR} = min(AC)$. For $P < P^{LR}$, supply is zero.

$P^{SR} > P^{LR}$. This is not surprising since the long-run shut down price is the minimum point on the long-run average cost curve and the short-run average cost curve lies everywhere above the long-run average cost curve.

d. The long-run market supply curve is flat at the minimum point on the long-run average cost curve, P = min(AC).

2. For a typical perfectly competitive firm, let the total cost of producing output q be $TC(q) = 10 + 10q - q^2 + .25q^3$ with $MC(q) = 10 - 2q + .75q^2$. Let market price be $P^* = \$10$.

   a. Derive the short-run supply curve of a firm in this industry.

   b. How much will the firm optimally produce?

   c. Will the firm make short-run profits?

Answer:

a. All fixed costs are sunk, since $TC(0) = \$10$. Therefore, the firm's shut down price will be the minimum of the AVC curve. Since $TVC(q) = 10q - q^2 + .25q^3$, $AVC(q) = 10 - q + .25q^2$. In order to find the minimum of AVC, we set AVC = MC so that $10 - q + .25q^2 = 10 - 2q + .75q^2$ or $q^* = 2$. At $q^* = 2$, AVC = \$9. Therefore, the supply curve of the firm is:

   $P = MC$, or $P = 10 - 2q + .75q^2$ for $P \geq \$9$.
   $q = 0$ for $P < \$9$.

b. Since $P^* = \$10 > \$9$, the firm will optimally produce where $P^* = MC$ or where $10 = 10 - 2q + .75q^2$. This yields $q^* = 8/3 = 2.67$.

c. The firm makes short-run profits if $P^* > AVC(q^*)$ because all fixed costs are sunk. At q^*, $AVC = TVC(q^*)/q^* = 10 - q^* + q^{*2}/4$ or $AVC = \$82/9$. This is less than P^* so that the firm makes profits in the short-run. The profits equal $(P^*-AVC)q^* = (8/9)(8/3) = 64/27$.

3.
   a. Illustrate the optimal output when market price is P^* for the firm in the figure below. Illustrate economic profit for the firm on the same graph.

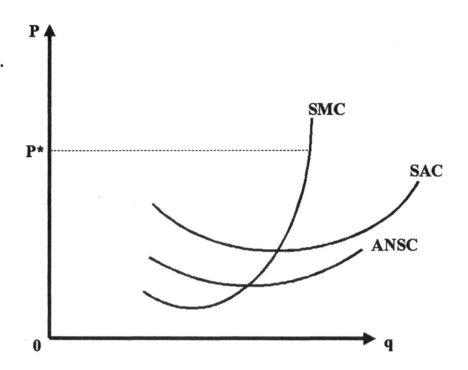

b. Illustrate producer's surplus for the firm in the graph. From your diagram, can you argue that producer's surplus must be larger or smaller than economic profit?

c. Now, suppose that market price falls to P** = min(SAC). Illustrate the producer surplus and economic profit for the firm. Why is the producer's surplus still positive? Use your answer to illustrate in a diagram why producer's surplus must equal economic profit in the long-run.

Answer:

a. The optimal output when price is P* is determined by the point P = SMC. This is output level q*. Since P* exceeds the minimum of short-run average cost, the firm will make positive economic profits in the amount [P* - SAC(q*)]q* = shaded <u>rectangle</u> in the diagram that follows part (b).

b. Producer surplus is the area between the price and the firm's supply curve. This is shown as the shaded area in the figure, below. Note that the shut down price is determined by the average non-sunk cost curve. Economic profits must be smaller than producer's surplus since the average cost curve must lie above the average non-sunk cost curve. This is as it should be: producer's surplus should be economic profits *plus* total sunk fixed costs.

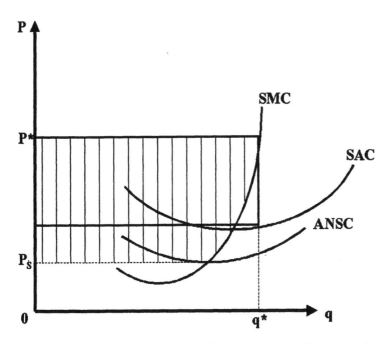

c.   Since P** equals the minimum of average cost, the optimal output is now q**
and economic profit is zero. Producer's surplus is the shaded area in the graph
below and is positive (hence, it is larger than economic profit). Producer's
surplus may remain positive even when profits are zero when total sunk fixed
costs are positive (the ANSC curve is lower than the SAC curve). In the long-
run, all costs are non-sunk so that the ANSC curve coincides with the AC curve
(not shown on the graph). Therefore, in the long-run, economic profit and
producer's surplus must be the same.

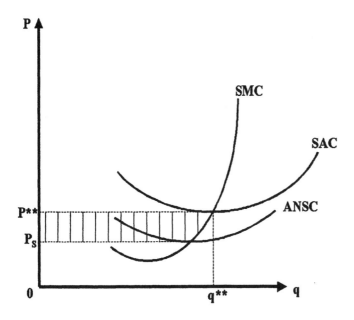

Problem Set

1. Three regions of the world are able to produce cocoa beans: Africa, South America, and Central America. In each of these regions the production of cocoa is ensured by a large number of small plantations. None of these regions has pecuniary effects in cocoa production. The cost of production varies across these three regions, however. Let the following be true:

   Africa: $MC_A = 4Q_A$; minimum of average cost = $min(AC_A) = 10$
   South America: $MC_S = 5Q_S$; $min(AC_S) = 15$
   Central America: $MC_C = 6Q_C$; $min(AC_C) = 20$

   Where: Q_A, Q_S, and Q_C are the outputs of cocoa beans in Africa, South America and Central America, respectively. MC_i and AC_i (i = A,S,C) are the long-run marginal and average costs for each region. Further, assume that no region can produce more than 30 units of cocoa, even in the long-run. The worldwide market for cocoa beans is perfectly competitive.

   a. Write the equation for a typical firm's long-run supply curve in each region.

   b. Write the equation for the long-run worldwide market supply curve. Draw this supply curve on a graph.

   c. We are told that each region does not have pecuniary effects. Does the worldwide cocoa industry exhibit pecuniary effects?

2. The short run total cost function for a typical firm in a competitive industry is:

   $$STC(q) = 0 \qquad\qquad \text{if } q = 0$$
   $$STC(q) = 100 + 10q + q^2 \quad \text{if } q > 0$$

   with short run marginal cost, $SMC(q) = 10+2q$.

   a. Define and calculate the firm's shut down price and the firm's short run supply function. Give a graphical interpretation of your answer.

   b. Let market price be p = 25. What are the firm's (short run) profits and producer's surplus at this price? How do profits change if price rises to p = 34? Explain your answer.

   c. Suppose that a subsidy of 6 per unit is provided to firms in this industry. What is the effect of this subsidy on your answers to (a) and (b)?

3. Let a firm's long run marginal cost be $MC(q) = 100 - 2q + 1.5q^2$, where q is the firm's output, and its average cost be $AC(q) = 100 - q + .5q^2$.

   a. Calculate and define in words the firm's shutdown price. Explain your answer.

b. What is the equation of the firm's (long run) supply curve? Explain your answer and illustrate the curve carefully in a diagram.

c. What is the equation of the long run market supply curve, assuming that this is a constant cost industry? Explain your answer in words, using graphs as appropriate.

4. (This question allows you to combine material from the last three chapters)

a. Illustrate and explain how one would incorporate the idea of technological change into an isoquant map.

b. Suppose that "labor saving technological change" occurs. Assuming that the factor prices remain fixed, illustrate and explain the cost minimizing choice of capital and labor used to produce a fixed level of output before and after the change.

c. Illustrate the long run cost function of the firm before and after the technological change in (b). Supposing that all firms in a perfectly competitive industry have access to the technology that generated the change, illustrate and explain the effect of the change on the long run equilibrium behavior of the firm and the market.

5. Is the short-run industry supply curve more or less elastic than the short-run firm supply curve?

6. The long run cost function for a typical firm in a competitive industry is given by:

$TC(q) = 0$ for $q = 0$
$= 100 + q^2$ for $q > 0$ with $MC = 2q$

Market demand for the industry product is given by:

$Q = 500 - 10P$

a. Assuming that all firms have identical cost structures, find the long run competitive equilibrium price, total quantity, number of firms, and the quantity produced by each firm.

b. Suppose that the government restricts entry into this market. In particular, assume that the government requires that each firm obtain a license to participate in the market, and that only 20 licenses are issued. Assuming that all firms have identical cost structures, find the long run competitive equilibrium price, total quantity, quantity produced by each firm, and profits of each firm. How much would a firm be willing to pay for a license?

7. Define and distinguish among the concepts of producer's surplus, economic profits, and economic rent. What are the arguments for or against using each as a measure of a producer's well-being?

Exam *(60 minutes: Closed book, closed notes)*

1.

a. For a perfectly competitive industry, what is the price elasticity of the firm's demand curve? How does this compare with the price elasticity of the industry's demand curve?

b. What is the price elasticity of the industry's long-run supply curve if there are no pecuniary effects? How does this compare with the price elasticity of the firm's long-run supply curve?

2. The long-run total cost curve for a firm in a perfectly competitive industry is $TC(q) = 10q - q^2 + Q^3$, where q is the output of a typical firm and Q is industry output.

a. Compute the long-run average cost for a typical firm in this industry. Graph average cost for a typical firm as a function of that firm's output for industry outputs of 10, 20, and 30.

b. Is this an increasing, constant, or decreasing cost industry?

3. The market demand for a product is $Q^D = 10,000 - 100P$, where Q^D is the aggregate demand for the market and P is the market price. The total cost of production of the product is $TC(Q) = Q^2/2$, with $MC(Q) = Q$. These functions apply to both the short-run and the long-run. The market for the product is perfectly competitive and there are 100 firms currently producing the product. If society's total welfare is measured by consumers' surplus plus producers' surplus, what is the short-run welfare loss of banning the manufacture and sale of this product?

4. Let total cost be $TC(q) = 100 + q^2$ for positive q and $TC(q) = 0$ for q = 0, marginal cost be $MC(q) = 2q$ and demand be $Q^D = 10000 - 100P$. Answer the following questions.

a. What will be the industry output in long-run equilibrium?

b. Suppose that demand is $Q^D = 5000 - 50P$. What is the industry output in long-run equilibrium? How many firms will there be in the industry?

c. Suppose that demand now shifts to $Q^D = 6000 - 50P$ but that it is not possible to manufacture more (industry) output than the long-run equilibrium output in (b). What is the new equilibrium price of output? How much profit does each manufacturer earn if each sets its output optimally given the new price and constraints in this setup?

    d. In the long-run, how many new firms will enter this industry when demand shifts as in (c)?

Answers to Exercises

1. All three statements are not correct. Let us consider them in turn.

    a. In order to violate the assumptions of perfect competition, a single producer would need to be large enough that his/her production decision has a perceptible impact on prices. We know from statement (a) that a single supertanker is large in terms of barrels, but we also know that the total market size in terms of barrels is much larger. In fact, if a single supertanker carries 7x300,000 = 2,100,000 barrels of crude oil (per voyage) 6,000 such supertanker voyages would be needed to transport all the oil in this market. If it takes a few weeks for a supertanker to make a round trip from the oil supplying countries to the oil consuming countries, a single supertanker would only be able to make (as a rough guess) 10 voyages per year if time off for maintenance is included. This still leaves room for 600 supertankers to transport the oil in this market.

       Still, we do not as yet have an answer to the question. A single firm might *own* all the supertankers in this market. If so, this firm would certainly be a large enough supplier in this market for its production decisions (e.g., how many tankers to make available) to affect the market price for oil transport. On the other hand, if each firm in the market only owns a single supertanker, then there is room for 600 firms in the market. In this case, it would be much more reasonable to assume that each firm is so small that it has an imperceptible effect on transport prices. In other words, it is not the supertanker size that matters *per se*, but rather how concentrated the ownership of the means of transport is.

    b. The statement indicates that maple syrup can be considered a differentiated product if consumers care about the rating (grade and color) of the product. On the other hand, *within a specific rating class* maple syrup may still operate in a perfectly competitive way. In other words, if the four assumptions of perfect competition continue to hold within a specific grade and color class, then the market for maple syrup of this class will be perfectly competitive.

    c. The fact that it costs something to enter this market does not necessarily mean that the market for wheat is not perfectly competitive. The fourth assumption requires only that all market participants (including potential entrants) have *equal access* to resources and not that these resources be costless. For example, it must be the case that Tim can obtain a tractor as easily as an active farmer. Since the standard method of obtaining a tractor is buying from a farm equipment store, Tim and any active farmer have equal access to these tractors (at the same price).

2. The statements are not correct. Let us consider each statement in turn:

   a. When we derived individual demands for goods in Chapter 5, we assumed that individual consumers take market prices as given. However this does not mean that consumers would not change the quantity of the good that they wished to purchase if the price of the good were to change. In fact we saw that, except for Giffen goods, both individual demand functions and market demand functions are downward sloping. Therefore, the statement is not correct.

   b. Again, in this case, the prices of output could be the same for other reasons and not because output is undifferentiated and information on prices is perfect. For example, suppose that half of the output is sold in one location and half in another location, with a cost of traveling between the two locations being quite high. Consumers would prefer to buy the output locally at the same price because they could thereby avoid the transportation cost. (Therefore, the product is differentiated by the location of sale.) If each local market has the same characteristics (the same number and type of consumers, the same production costs and so on), then the price in the two local markets could very well be the same. This would not be because the product was undifferentiated, however. It would be because the two local markets are identical.

2. The answer to the first part of the question is (a). The total revenue is simply the market price, which is taken as given, times the firm's output. The answer to the second part of the question is (c). The marginal revenue is the amount the firm earns from an additional unit of output. This is simply equal to the price that the unit will fetch when sold on the market. Since the price is taken as given, the marginal revenue of the unit is just the price.

3. The answer to the first part of the question is that the output levels in (a) and (b) are such that price equals marginal cost since $7 = $10 - $8(1/2) + $4(1/4) and $7 = $10 - $8(3/2) + $4(9/4). (c) is not correct since $7 ≠ $10 - $8 + $4 = $6.

   The answer to the second part of the question is (b): q* = 3/2. At q = 1/2, marginal cost is falling (since marginal cost at q = 1 is less than marginal cost at q = 1/2) so that profits increase if output increases. On the other hand, you can check by substituting q = 2 (and any larger value of q, in fact) into marginal cost that marginal cost is rising at q = 3/2.

   The answer to the third part of the question is (a). The slope of the total revenue curve is the market price, which equals $7. The slope of the total cost curve is marginal cost, which equals $6 at q = 1. Therefore, the slope of the total revenue curve exceeds the slope of the total cost curve.

4. The answer to the first part of the question is (a). By substituting in the values of output we are given, we find that average variable cost is minimized at q = 2. At this minimum, AVC = $6. This minimum of AVC is the shut down price when all fixed costs are sunk.

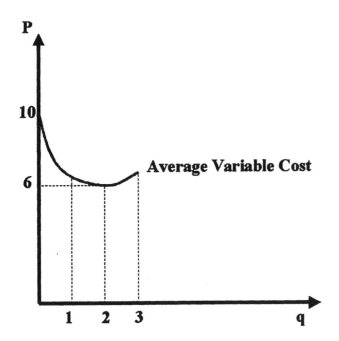

The answer to the second part of the question is (c). The firm earns a total revenue of price times output or $10(2) = $20. The total cost is equal to the total variable cost, that is, to the average variable cost times the output = $6(2) = $12. Sunk costs do not count: since they cannot be recovered anyway they are not part of the firm's opportunity cost. Profit is total revenue minus total cost (=total fixed cost + total variable cost) = $20 - $12 = $8.

The answer to the third part of the question is (c). The market price, $10, exceeds the shut down price, $6. At any price above the shut down price, the firm would do better operating than shutting down.

5. The answer to the first part of the question is (c). Since the total cost is $25 even if output is zero, $25 is the sunk cost. This leaves $25 as the non-sunk cost. Since a portion of the fixed cost is sunk, the relevant shut down condition is that price must exceed the minimum of average non-sunk cost.

   The answer to the second part of the question is (c). The average non-sunk cost curve is $ANSC(Q) = [TVC(q) + NSFC] /q = [q^2 - q + \$25]/q = q - \$1 + \$25/q$. Setting this equal to short-run marginal cost, we have $q - 1 + 25/q = 2q - 1$ or $q^* = 5$. At this output level, the average non-sunk cost curve reaches a minimum. The value of $ANSC(q)$ at $q = q^*$ is $5 - \$1 + \$25/5 = \$9$.

6. The answer to the first part of the question is (a). The firm supply curve is the marginal cost curve, $P = 2q$ for prices above the shut down price. Since there are no sunk costs, the shut down price is computed as the minimum of the average cost curve. $AC(q) = TC(q)/q = 100/q + q$. Setting this equal to marginal cost to

find the minimum of average cost we have $AC(q) = 100/q + q = 2q = MC$ or $q* = 10$. At this output, $AC(q) = 100/10 + 10 = \$20$. Therefore, $P_S = \$20$.

The answer to the second part of the question is (b). The short-run market supply curve for the industry is the horizontal sum of the firm supply curves. Denote firm supply by q^S. When $P_S < \$20$, $q^S = 0$ so that industry supply is zero as well. When $P_S \geq \$20$, $q^S = P/2$ from the answer to the first part of the question. Summing q^S over the 200 firms, we have $q^S = 200(P/2) = 100P$. Note that it is very important that you remember to solve for q first before summing the supplies!

The answer to the third part of the question is (b). Market equilibrium is where $Q^S(P) = Q^D(P)$ or $100P = 3000 - 50P$ so that $P* = \$20$. Since $P* \geq P_S$, each firm chooses a positive level of output: each firm supplies $q^S = 10$ and industry output is $200(10) = 2000 = Q^S$.

7. The correct answers are (b) and (c). (a) is a short-run decision because output is being adjusted without an accompanying optimal adjustment of all inputs: if the firm really were to decide to permanently produce zero, it should sell off all its assets. It has not done this here because it has not exited the industry. The number of firms in the industry does not change in this case. In (b), the number of firms in the industry changes and the firm changes all its inputs to their optimal level by selling off all assets (exiting the industry). In option (c), if the labor force is not already at its long-run optimal level, then this is a short-run decision. If the labor force need not adjust to attain its long-run optimal level, then this can be a long-run decision.

8. The correct answers are (a) and (d). First, we calculate the shut down price. We obtain the minimum point on AC by setting $AC = MC$. Solving this equation, we obtain that $q* = 2$. The associated level of AC is \$49 so that $P^S = min(AC) = \$49$. This is statement (d). At prices above P_S, $P = MC$ defines the supply curve. You can check by substitution that $MC(q)$ is upward sloping for these prices (i.e., quantities above $q*$). Therefore, (a) is correct as well.

9. The correct answer is (b). From Exercise 7 we know that $P* = 20$ and $q* = 10$. Adding the final condition for market equilibrium, we have $Q^D(P*) = n*Q^S(P*)$ or $3000 - 50(20) = n*(10)$ or $200 = n*$. $Q* = n*(10) = 2000$.

10. The correct answer is (c). The minimum of the average cost curve is $P* = 20$, from Exercise 7. Therefore, the long-run supply curve is flat along the line $P* = 20$.

11. (a) and (b) are correct. If the total output of the furniture industry increases, then output per firm increases. Since there are quantity discounts, this means that the price of input faced by individual furniture-makers decreases. Hence, (a) is correct. (b) is also correct, even though the price of wood remains constant. This is because the price of a <u>usable</u> piece of wood increases with output. (c) is

not correct: the fact that furniture-making technology is more efficient at higher levels of output *does* mean that the average cost of a furniture-making firm decreases as its production increases, but this decrease does not come from a change in input prices.

12. The correct answer to the first part of the question is (b). George's economic rent is the economic profit that is due to his labor: $10,000 a month. George captures what he earns: $1,000 per month, which is one-tenth of the total rent. The firm captures the remainder as profits: $9,000 per month.

The correct answer to the second part of the question is (a). George's rent does not change depending on the bidding for his services: it depends on the value he generates when working in this industry, which has not changed. On the other hand, George now captures all the rent and the firm is left with zero economic profits.

13. The answer to the first part of the question is (b). Since the rental price of land is not a variable cost, it does not affect marginal cost. On the other hand, it does affect average cost (shifts it up). Since the rent charged for the land is exactly the profit that the farmer was formerly earning, the average cost rises just to the point where its minimum is at p* so that the optimal production level stays the same. In total, economic rent is unchanged at π, economic profit of the farmer falls to zero, and output is unchanged. Since profits are still non-negative, the increase in the rental price does not induce any farmer to leave the industry.

The answer to the second part of the question is (b). Since marginal cost does not change and price does not change, producer surplus does not change.

The answer to the third part of the question is (c). First, since all available land is already occupied, the increase in p does not trigger any entry. When price rises but marginal cost is unchanged, producer surplus rises because it is the area between marginal cost and market price. Economic profit of the farmer rises since p** now exceeds the minimum of average cost including the price of land. Economic rent also increases since this is measured as the economic profit that the farmer could earn without *any* charge for the land. This has increased from π to π plus the shaded area in the graph.

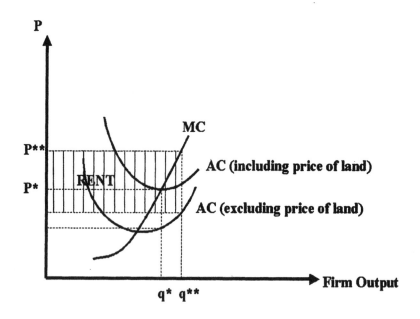

Answers to Problem Set

1.

   a. LR supply in Africa: P = 10 for Q_A < 30
      LR supply in South America: P = 15 for Q_S < 30
      LR supply in Central America: P = 20 for Q_C < 30

   b. LR worldwide supply: Q < 30: P = 10
                           $Q \in (30,60)$: P = 15
                           $Q \in (60,90)$: P = 20
                           Quantities in excess of 90 not feasible

   Note that a price of 10 is sufficient to elicit supply from Africa, only. Once
   price rises to 15, both Africa and South America produce. Only when
   price rises to 20 do all three regions produce.

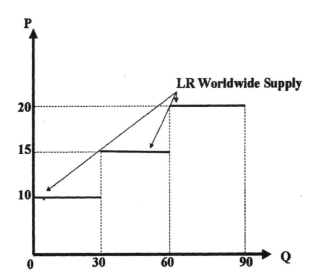

c. The worldwide industry supply curve does rise as output rises. Therefore, the worldwide industry exhibits pecuniary effects (even though each individual region does not). The reason is that, as output rises so that less productive areas of the world are used to produce cocoa, the costs of inputs effectively rise since it is more costly to farm in regions less suited to cocoa production.

2.

a. The shutdown price is the price at which the firm would prefer (make more profits by) shutting down than producing a positive output. In this problem, the shutdown price = P^S = min(AC) since sunk fixed costs are 0 and non-sunk fixed costs are 100. Hence, AC(q) is $(100+10q + q^2)/q = 100/q + 10 + q$. To calculate the minimum of this curve, let SMC = AC so that $100/q + 10 + q = 10 + 2q$ or $q = 10$ at the minimum. Hence, min(AC) = 30 = shutdown price.

The firm's short run supply function is defined by P = SMC(q) for P no less than the shutdown price. Hence, P = 10 + 2q or q^s = -5 + p/2 for P $\geq P^s$ and q^s = 0 for P < P^s is the supply curve of the firm. (SMC is always upwards sloping, so this is not a concern in this problem.)

b. Profit is total revenue minus total costs, where costs are economic costs (i.e., they exclude sunk costs). In this case, however, there are no sunk costs, as costs fall to zero when output is zero. Producer surplus for a single firm is the area above the firm's supply function and market price. Profits and producer surplus if P = 25 are zero, since the firm shuts down at this price. If the price is P = 34, the firm finds it optimal to operate at positive levels of output. Output at this price is determined by the supply function as 34 = 10 + 2q or q^s = 12. Total revenue is 34(12) = 408 and total cost is $100 + 10(12) + 12^2$ or 364. The firm makes profits of 408 - 364 = 44.

c. The firm's unit costs (marginal costs) effectively fall by 6 so that they are now $4 + 2q = SMC$. Hence, the supply curve of the firm shifts down (or out) by 6 units (but retains its shape). Average costs fall as well, becoming $100/q + 4 + q$. This lowers the shutdown price. The minimum of the AC curve still occurs at 10 units, but this corresponds to an average cost of $10 + 4 + 10 = 24$. In other words, the shutdown price also falls by 6. Now, it pays the firm to produce at both price levels in (b). At a price of 25, the firm produces 10.5 units, and earns profits of $25(10.5) - 100 - 4(10.5) - 10.5^2 (= 10.25)$. At a price of 34, the firm produces 15 units and earns profits of $15(34) - 100 - 4(15) - 15^2 = 586$.

3.

a. The shutdown price is at the minimum of the long run average cost curve. Hence, setting MC = AC to find the minimum, we have $100 - 2q + 1.5q^2 = 100 - q + .5q^2$ or $q = 1$ at the minimum. This corresponds to an average cost of 99.5, so that the shutdown price is $P^s = 99.5$. At any price below this point, it is better for the firm to exit the market than to continue to produce. At any point above this, the firm would do better continuing to produce, even if it makes short term losses, as these losses would be less than the loss suffered by exiting the market completely.

b. The firm's long run supply function is the rising portion of the marginal cost curve above the shutdown price or $P = 100 - 2q + 1.5q^2$ for all prices above 99.5.

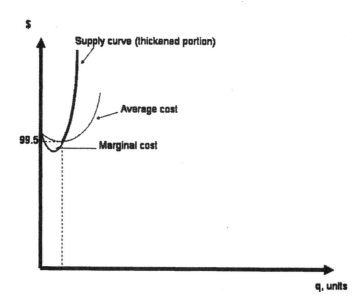

c. The long run market supply curve is flat for a constant cost industry at the minimum of the long run average cost curve, as all prices above this level would induce entry into the industry. Hence, the long run supply curve is flat at the shut down price of $P = 99.5$. This is the equation of long run supply.

4.

    a. This question provides review of chapters 6-8 as well as application to this chapter's equilibrium material. Technological change can be illustrated on an isoquant map by a shift and, perhaps, a change in shape of the isoquants. If we think of technological progress as allowing us to produce the same amount of output with less input, then the isoquant shifts in with technological progress. If the technological progress alters the substitutability of labor and capital (or whatever the inputs are) in the production function, then it changes the shape. Three cases are usually distinguished: neutral technological progress (which leaves the slope of the isoquant unchanged along any ray from the origin), labor saving technological progress (which results in a fall in the $MRTS_{L,K}$ along any ray from the origin...or makes the isoquants flatter) and capital saving technological progress (which results in a rise in the $MRTS_{L,K}$ along any ray from the origin...or makes the isoquants steeper if K is on the vertical axis). Two of the three cases are illustrated below (you can imagine the third):

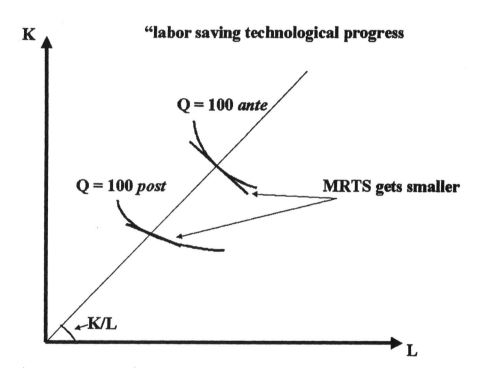

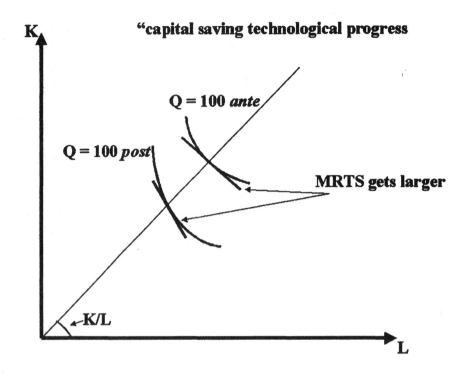

b. Since the isoquants are flatter along any ray from the origin, whatever the optimizing capital-labor ratio was before no longer is for fixed factor prices. This can be seen as follows:

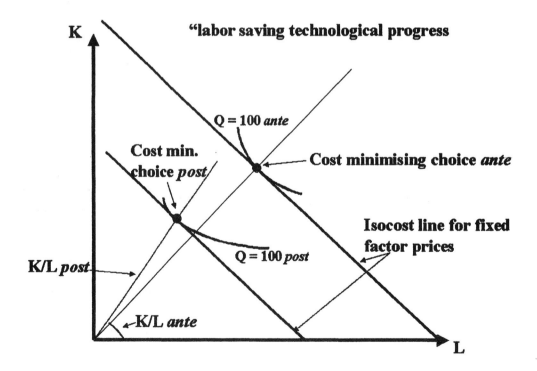

Since the isocost line slope does not change with the technological progress, the tangency must occur at a higher capital-labor ratio. It is in this sense that the technological progress is "labor saving": in the graph above, the firm saves on labor relative to capital after the change.

c. The long run cost function relates the total cost to output and the factor prices. For example, for inputs L and K, the long run cost function would be: TC(Q,w,r) = rK*(Q,w,r)+wL*(Q,w,r). The technological change in (b) changes the factor demands, not the prices of the inputs, so it affects the K* and the L*. In particular, for a given output, it cuts the inputs required to obtain this output, so it must shift the total cost curve down. The technological progress in (b) also changes the relative use of the factors, increasing the relative use of K and decreasing the relative use of L. It depends on the factor price structure how this affects the total cost curve. In the easiest case, when the factor prices are the same for the two inputs, for example, a relative shift from L to K would make no difference. A sample illustration of the effect of technological change on the total cost curve is as follows:

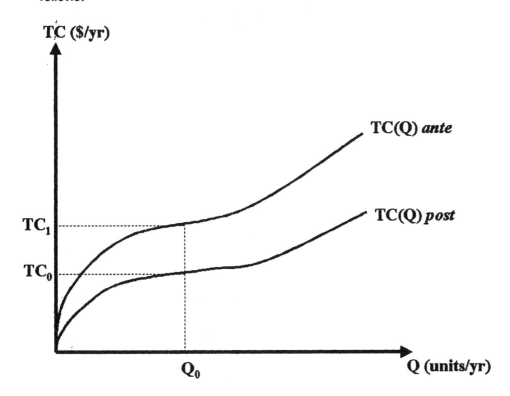

The difference between the two curves increases as output increases, as the total savings rise with the increase in the total bill for input.

If all firms have access to the new technology, then the long run marginal and average costs of all firms shift down. Assuming that the technological change does not destroy the conditions for perfect competition to make sense (such as...it still results in rising marginal and average cost after a relatively small scale), it moves the long run equilibrium output for the firm from the minimum of the old average cost curve to the minimum of the new average cost curve. This will correspond to a lower market price, as the minimum of the new curve must fall below the minimum of the old curve. On the other hand, without further information, we cannot say whether the firm produces more or less than before in equilibrium: that depends on the scale at which the minimum of average cost occurs.

Of course, the technological change could also change the shape of the average and marginal cost curves so drastically that the market structure would change: we needn't have the underlying cost conditions that would generate small firms in the market any more and this would mean that the assumptions of perfect competition were no longer fulfilled. Since this portion of the exam is not supposed to rely on knowledge of industry structures other than perfect competition, I would not require students to push this part of the answer further.

4. The short-run industry supply curve will be the horizontal sum of the firms' short-run supply curves. This makes the short-run industry supply curve flatter than the short-run firm supply curve since a given change in price will elicit a much larger change in output at the industry level than at the firm level. In other words, $\Delta Q^S/\Delta P$ is much larger at the industry level than at the firm level. More precisely, $\Delta Q^S/\Delta P = n\Delta q^s/\Delta P$, where n is the number of identical firms in the industry. Recall, however, that the price elasticity of market supply is $(\Delta Q^S/\Delta P)(P/Q^S)$, while the price elasticity of a firm's individual supply curve is $(\Delta q^s/\Delta P)(p/q^s)$. Since $Q^s = nq^s$, we have $(\Delta Q^S/\Delta P)(P/Q^S) = (n\Delta q^s/\Delta P)(p/nq^s) = (\Delta q^s/\Delta P)(p/q^s)$. We can then say that, *for any given price*, the industry supply curve will have the same elasticity as the firm's supply.

6.

   a. The long run industry supply curve with N firms in the industry is $Q^s = NP/2$ (where each firm supplies according to $q^s = p/2$). Long run equilibrium price is obtained by setting $Q^d = Q^s$ or $P = 1000/[N+20]$. The equilibrium number of firms is obtained by setting equilibrium profits to zero so that $P = LRAC$. To obtain the minimum of LRAC, set $100/q + q = MC = 2q$ so that $q = 10$. This means that, at the minimum, $LRAC = 20$. Hence, we have $P = 1000/[N+20] = 20$ or $N = 30$. The equilibrium price will be $P = 1000/[30+20] = 20$ and each firm will produce $q = p/2 = 10$. Total market output will be $10 \times 30 = 300$.

   b. The industry supply curve is $Q^s = 20q^s = 10P$ so that the equilibrium price, given by $Q^s = Q^d$ is $P = 25$. $Q = 250$, $q = 250/20 = 12.5$ The revenues of an individual firm are $R = pq = 312.5$ and costs are $TC = 100 + 156.25 = 256.25$ hence the profits of an individual firm are $312.5 - 256.25 = 56.25$

   Since these are economic profits, they represent profits over and above what the firm could get in another industry. Hence each firm should be willing to pay up to 56.25 to get a license.

7.

We defined the total producers' surplus as the area above the market supply curve and below the market price. It is a monetary measure of the benefit that producers derive from producing a good at a particular price. Note that the producer earns the price for every unit sold, but only incurs the marginal cost for each unit. This is why the difference between the price and the marginal cost curve measures the total benefit derived from production. Since the market supply curve is simply the sum of the individual supply curves, which are the rising portion of the marginal cost curves, the difference between the price and the market supply curve measures the surplus of all producers in the market. If we wished to measure this for a single firm, we would calculate the corresponding area for a single firm.

Notice that the producer's surplus does not deduct fixed costs, whereas profits do. In other words, profits are measured by the difference between the price and the average cost of each unit, multiplied by the number of units sold. Profit measures the "money in pocket" of the producer, whereas the producer surplus measures the benefit over and above what would be required to induce positive supply. Formally, economic profit is the difference between sales revenues and opportunity cost. As opportunity cost and accounting cost need not be the same, economic and accounting profit need not be the same (in fact, economic profit could be either larger or smaller than accounting profit).

Economic rent is the difference between the maximum amount that firms would be willing to pay to acquire a fixed input and the minimum amount that they have to pay for it. It is the economic return attributable to a productive scare input which is in fixed supply. Economic rent is a measure of "surplus" associated with a scarce input, whereas economic profit is associated with a firm. The two need not be the same: when a scarce input in an otherwise perfectly competitive industry lowers the average cost of production, for example, if this scarce input is priced the same as the price of the alternative input that generates the "old" level of average cost, then all the economic rent is captured by the firm as economic profit. On the other hand, the scarce input could potentially be priced so high as to drive the new and old levels of average cost to the same level, in which case the economic profit of the firm would remain zero, and the entire surplus would be captured by the input as economic rent. Hence, it is a good measure of the input source's well being in some cases, and a good measure of firm well being in others.

Answers to Exam

1.

a. The price elasticity of demand is defined as $\varepsilon_{Q,P} = (\Delta Q / \Delta P)(P/Q)$. For the firm, any change in the firm's own price, taking as given the market price for output, results in either no sales (if price exceeds market price) or sales to the entire market (if price is less than market price). This means that ΔQ in the elasticity formula remains large even if ΔP is infinitesimally small. Hence this elasticity can be taken to be infinite.

The price elasticity of the industry's demand curve is negative (if demand slopes down), but is not as negative as the price elasticity of the firm's demand since industry demand generally would not be flat.

b. The price elasticity of supply is defined as $\sigma_{Q,P} = (\Delta Q/\Delta P)(P/Q)$. Again, if there are no pecuniary effects, the long-run supply is flat at the minimum of the long-run average cost function. Therefore, the price elasticity of supply is infinite for the same reason as the elasticity of demand for the firm was infinite in part (a).

The firm's long-run supply curve traces out $P = MC$. For upward sloping marginal cost, this supply curve has positive (but not infinite) elasticity since $\Delta Q/\Delta P$ will equal the slope of the marginal cost curve and both P and firm output, Q, will be some finite numbers.

2.

    a. The average cost for a typical firm is $AC(q) = 10 - q + Q^3/q$. Graphically,

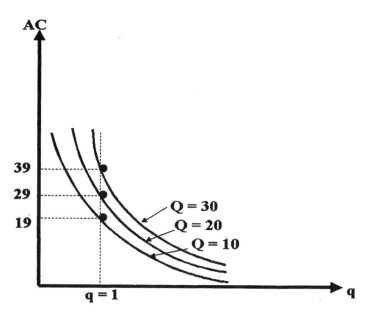

    b. This is an increasing cost industry, since the average cost for the firm shifts up as industry output increases.

3. A typical firm's supply curve in this industry is $P = MC = q$ above P^S. Note, however, that the minimum of the average cost curve occurs at $q = 0$ (and $P = 0$) so that the shut down price is zero for the firm. Summing these firm supply functions ($q = P$ for each firm) across the 100 firms, we obtain an industry short-term supply curve of $Q^S = 100P$. Setting this equal to the industry demand curve of $Q^D = 10,000 - 100P$ we have $10,000 - 100P = 100P$ or $P^* = 50$ and $Q^* = 5000$ as the industry equilibrium price and output.

Consumers' surplus in the short-run will, then, be the area of the triangle under industry demand and above equilibrium market price. This equals the base of the triangle (= $Q^* = 5000$) times the height (= the intercept of demand minus $P^* = 100 - 50$) times (1/2). This equals $5000(50)(1/2) = 125,000$. Producers' surplus equals the area of the triangle under the price and above industry supply. This equals the width of the triangle (= $Q^* = 5000$) times the height (50) times (1/2) or 125,000. The total of these is 250,000. The welfare loss of banning this product in the short-run is, then 250,000 (if the alternative to having this product is zero welfare).

4.

    a. In the long-run equilibrium, each firm will operate at the minimum point on its average cost curve. This can be found by equating marginal and average costs so that $q + 100/q = 2q$ or $q^* = 10$. The minimum point on the average cost curve is, then, $10 + 100/10$ or $P^* = 20$.

    b. If industry demand is $Q^D = 5000 - 50P$, then the equilibrium output sold will equate industry demand with long-run industry supply. Long-run industry supply is flat at P^* so that $Q^D = Q^S = 5000 - 50(20) = 4000$ in long-run equilibrium. Since each firm produces 10 units, this means that there will be 400 firms in the industry in long-run equilibrium.

    c. If no more of the product can be produced than the 4000 units currently for sale, the new equilibrium price of the product will equate the new demand and the (fixed) current supply because demand has shifted out. Therefore, the new equilibrium is at $Q^D = Q^S = 4000 = 6000 - 50P$ and $P^{**} = 40$. At this price, each firm equates price to marginal cost to determine how much to supply. If we set $P^{**} = 40 = 2q$, then we obtain $q^{**} = 20$. Total revenue for each firm is, then, $20(40) = 800$. The total cost of producing q^{**} units of output is $AC(q^{**})$ times q^{**} or $(20 + 100/20)20 = 25(20) = 500$. The difference, $800 - 500 = 300$ is the profit of each firm.

    d. In the long-run, price falls to the minimum of average cost (P^*) and each firm produces q^*, as calculated in part (a). At this price, $Q^D = Q^S = 6000 - 50(20) = 5000$ and 500 firms operate in the industry. This represents an increase of 100 firms.

Chapter 10: Competitive Markets: Applications

In Chapter 9, we learned how equilibrium was determined in perfectly competitive markets. In this chapter, we learn how to analyze the consequences of government intervention in such markets. In order to identify winners and losers, we will use the concepts of consumers' surplus (discussed in Chapter 5) and producers' surplus (discussed in Chapter 9). We will think of the total benefit to the economy -- the total surplus -- as the sum of consumers' and producers' surplus. A perfectly competitive market without intervention maximizes this total surplus. Each of the government policies that we study in this chapter creates benefits for specific economic agents (either producers or consumers). Therefore, each policy has a constituency that favors its use. On the other hand, all these policies reduce total surplus: the total welfare losses suffered by the losers outweigh the total welfare gains obtained by the winners.

Let us first show why a perfectly competitive market without intervention maximizes total surplus. A perfectly competitive equilibrium market price and quantity occur at the intersection of demand and supply, (P^*, Q^*), in Figure 10.1. Consumer surplus is the area of triangle ABC, while producer surplus is the area of triangle DBC. Total surplus is the sum of these, area ADC.

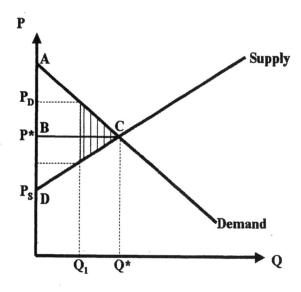

Figure 10.1

Consider now an output level, Q_1, which is lower than Q^*. At Q_1, sellers would be willing to sell an extra unit at price P_S, while consumers would be willing to buy at price P_D. P_D exceeds P_S so that any price between these two at which trade occurs, call it P^*, results in a gain in consumers' surplus of $P_D - P^*$ and a gain in producers' surplus of $P^* - P_S$. In other words, there are unrealized gains from trade. The gain in total surplus is $P_D - P_S$ (which is independent of P^*). Therefore, increasing output above Q_1 increases total surplus. This will be true as long as P_D exceeds P_S or, equivalently, as long as demand lies above supply.

Consider now a level of output that exceeds Q* (e.g., Q_2 in Figure 10.2). At Q_2 the price at which sellers would be willing to supply an extra unit, P_S, *exceeds* the price at which consumers would be willing to buy, P_D. Any price between these two at which trade occurs, say P*, results in a loss in consumers' surplus of P* - P_D and a loss in producers' surplus of P_S - P*. The loss in total surplus is P_S - P_D. Therefore, reducing output below Q_2 increases surplus. This will be true as long as P_S exceeds P_D or, equivalently, as long as supply lies above demand.

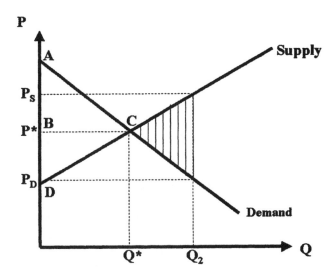

Figure 10.2

It follows that total surplus can only be maximized at the competitive equilibrium point (P*,Q*). Any other point involves a loss in total surplus called a **deadweight loss**. For example, the deadweight losses in Figures 10.1 and 10.2 are the shaded areas. In Figure 10.1, there is a deadweight loss because *too little* is produced so that there are unrealized gains to trade. In Figure 10.2, there is a deadweight loss because *too much* is produced so that there are losses to trade that occur.

Economic efficiency means that the total surplus is maximized. The perfectly competitive market is said to be efficient because it maximizes this surplus. Every consumer who is willing to pay more than the opportunity cost of the resources needed to produce the extra output is able to buy; every consumer who is not willing to pay the opportunity cost of the extra output does not buy. Stated differently, all gains from trade are exhausted at the perfectly competitive equilibrium.

Exercise 1: *You are a legislator who is asked to consider a new government policy to pass into law. According to your aides, this policy would result in a reduction in the amount of output traded in the economy; however, lobbyists for a major consumer group tell you that they would benefit from the plan. You believe that the economy currently is at the competitive equilibrium, and you wish to maximize total surplus. Should you vote for this plan?*

a. You should not since the policy must create a deadweight loss.
b. You should vote for the plan, since it increases surplus for the consumer group.

Exercise 2: *Consider the following alternative to perfect competition: a dictator sets a total output, Q*, that must be produced as well as a price P* at which consumers can acquire the good. P* and Q* are as shown in Figure 10.1. All consumers are informed of this price and output and all trades that are desired can actually occur. Is total surplus maximized in this alternative economy?*

a. Yes.
b. No.
c. More information is needed.

Government intervention in a competitive market can destroy economic efficiency and result in a deadweight loss. Intervention may take many forms. Most forms of intervention that we analyze in this chapter and their *general* effects on perfectly competitive markets are summarized in the following table.

Intervention Type:	Effect on (domestic) Quantity Traded	Effect on (domestic) Consumer Surplus	Effect on (domestic) Producer Surplus	Effect on (domestic) Government Budget	Is a (domestic) Deadweight Loss Created?
Excise Tax	Falls	Falls	Falls	Positive	Yes
Subsidies to Producers	Rises	Rises	Rises	Negative	Yes
Maximum Price Ceilings for Producers	Falls; Excess Demand	Rise or Fall	Falls	Zero	Yes
Minimum Price Floors for Producers	Falls; Excess Supply	Falls	Rise or Fall	Zero	Yes
Production Quotas	Falls; Excess Supply	Falls	Rise or Fall	Zero	Yes
Import Tariffs	Falls	Falls	Rises	Positive	Yes
Import Quotas	Falls	Falls	Rises	Zero	Yes

Table 10.1

We will now briefly consider each policy in turn.

1. Excise Tax

An **excise tax** is an amount paid by either the consumer or the producer per unit of the good at the point of sale. This is sometimes called a **specific tax**. In other words, the total amount paid by the demander exceeds the total amount received by the seller by the tax, T. Consider the effect of a tax that must be paid by suppliers, illustrated in Figure 10.3. In order to induce producers to supply the same amount as before, they must receive \$T *more* than before in order to compensate for the fact that they must pay the tax. Geometrically, this means that the supply curve shifts *up* by \$T to S'. The market equilibrium occurs at output Q_1, where S' intersects demand. At this new equilibrium, buyers pay P_D and sellers receive, for each unit of the good, an after tax revenue of $P_D - T = P_S$. The equilibrium conditions for this market are now that quantity demanded must equal quantity supplied, $Q_D = Q_S$, and $P_D - T = P_S$.

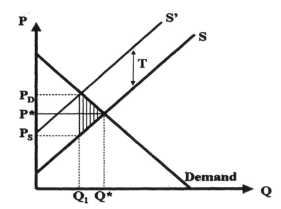

Figure 10.3

The equilibrium before the tax was at output level Q* so that the shaded area in the figure was part of consumers' and producers' surplus before the tax was imposed. (Compare Figures 10.3 and 10.1 to see this.) Now, the shaded area is a deadweight loss to society since these units are no longer produced in equilibrium.

Exercise 3: *Suppose that the same tax, T, must be paid by consumers instead of suppliers. How would Figure 10.3 change?*

  a. The figure would not change at all.
  b. Demand would shift in by T while supply would remain at its original level, S.
  c. Demand would shift out by T, while supply would remain at its original level, S.

How would the deadweight loss compare to the deadweight loss in Figure 10.3?

  a. It would be the same.
  b. It would be larger.
  c. It would be smaller.

The equilibrium price paid by buyers, P_D exceeds the original equilibrium price, P*, by *less than* the amount of the tax. In other words, P_D is less than P* + T. This is because consumers reduce their purchases as price rises. The equilibrium price received by sellers, P_S, falls short of the original equilibrium price, P*, by less than the entire amount of the tax. In other words, P_S exceeds P* - T. This is because sellers reduce their supply as the price falls. The amount by which the price paid by buyers, P_D, rises over the non-tax equilibrium price, P*, is the **incidence of the tax on consumers**; the amount by which the price received by sellers, P_S, falls below P* is called the incidence of the tax on producers. In the special case where supply is flat, the equilibrium price will rise by the *entire* amount of the tax, so that the entire tax burden falls on consumers. In the special case where supply is vertical, supply cannot shift when the tax is imposed so that the *entire* tax burden falls on producers. These cases are pictured in Figure 10.4, below.

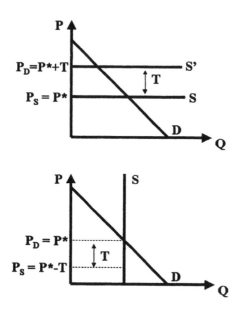

Figure 10.4

In general, as long as the demand curve slopes downward and the supply curve slopes upward, the tax raises the equilibrium price to buyers and lowers the price to sellers. Figure 10.4 suggests that the *incidence* of the tax on consumers and producers depends on the relative elasticities of demand and supply. In fact, it can be shown that the relative change in the buyers' price, P_D, and the sellers' price, P_S, due to the tax equals the relative elasiticities of supply, $\varepsilon_{QS,P}$, and demand, $\varepsilon_{QD,P}$.

$$\Delta P_D/\Delta P_S = \varepsilon_{QS,P}/\varepsilon_{QD,P}$$

Exercise 4: *What is the incidence of an excise tax in the long-run in a constant cost perfectly competitive industry?*

a. The entire burden of the tax falls on producers.
b. The entire burden of the tax falls on consumers.
c. The burden is shared between consumers and producers.

Exercise 5: *In Figure 10.4, what is the deadweight loss resulting from the tax when supply is horizontal? What is the deadweight loss when supply is vertical?*

   a. In both cases, the deadweight loss is zero.
   b. When supply is horizontal, deadweight loss is zero. When supply is vertical, deadweight loss is positive.
   c. When supply is horizontal, deadweight loss is positive. When supply is vertical, deadweight loss is zero.

2. Subsidies

A **subsidy** is a negative tax. In other words a subsidy, T, paid to producers means that the price producers receive, P_S, is the price paid by consumers, P_D, *plus* the subsidy. Not surprisingly, then, the effects are opposite from those of a tax. The subsidy shifts supply *down* by a vertical distance T and the equilibrium quantity traded *rises*. The price paid by buyers *falls* and the price received by sellers *rises* as long as supply slopes upward and demand slopes downward. Here, the deadweight loss occurs because output rises *above* the no-subsidy level. (Compare the Figure 10.5 to Figure 10.2 to see why.) The subsidy is depicted in Figure 10.5, below, where the deadweight loss is the shaded area. The equilibrium conditions in this market are now that $Q_D = Q_S$ and $P_D + T = P_S$.

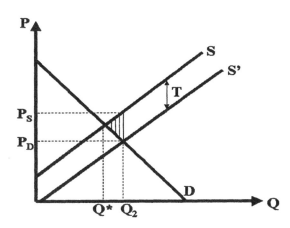

Figure 10.5

Exercise 6: *Suppose that the subsidy is a percentage applied to the price so that the amount of the subsidy is αP, where P is the market price and α is a number between 0 and 1. Therefore, suppliers actually receive a payment of $(1+\alpha)P$ for each unit of the good sold. (This type of subsidy is called an **ad valorem** subsidy.) How does the supply and demand diagram change when this type of subsidy is used rather than a per unit subsidy?*

a. The ad valorem subsidy shifts supply down (as in Figure 10.5), but the vertical distance between the old and new supply is now α.
b. The ad valorem subsidy rotates supply down so that the vertical distance between the new and old supply curves is αP_S.
c. The ad valorem subsidy rotates supply upward so that the vertical distance between the new and old supply curves is αP_S.

3. Maximum Price Ceilings for Producers

A **price ceiling** is a legal maximum on the price per unit that a producer can receive. If the price ceiling is *below* the pre-control competitive equilibrium price, then the ceiling is called **binding**. Let the price ceiling be P_{MAX} in Figure 10.6. The quantity traded in this market will be limited to the amount that producers are willing to supply at this price, Q_S, even though demanders would like to purchase a much higher quantity, Q_D. Because Q_D exceeds Q_S, there is excess demand. Because the quantity traded does not equal the pre-control competitive quantity, Q^*, there is a deadweight loss: some consumers who value the good more than its marginal cost in production are unable to purchase. If we assume that the consumers who value the good most highly are the ones who actually receive the supply that producers make available, the deadweight loss is the shaded area in Figure 10.6, below. The equilibrium conditions for this market are now that $P = P_{MAX}$; $Q_S = Q_S(P_{MAX})$ and $Q_D = Q_D(P_{MAX})$.

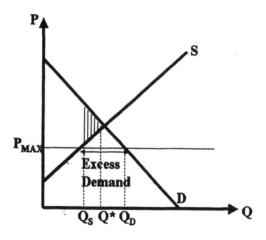

Figure 10.6

Exercise 7: *Which of the following statements is true in the long-run about a constant cost perfectly competitive industry where a binding price ceiling is imposed?*

a. All consumers' surplus is lost.
b. As the price falls, consumers' surplus increases.

   c. The amount of the deadweight loss equals the consumer's surplus before the price ceiling was imposed.

   d. Producers' surplus does not change due to the price ceiling.

4. Minimum Price Floors

A **price floor** is a minimum price that consumers can legally pay for a good. Price floors sometimes are referred to as **price supports**. If the price floor is *above* the pre-control competitive equilibrium price, it is said to be binding. The quantity traded in this market will be limited to the amount that consumers are willing to purchase at this price, Q_D, even though producers would like to supply a much higher quantity, Q_S. Because Q_S exceeds Q_D, there is excess supply. Because the quantity traded does not equal the pre-control competitive quantity, Q^*, there is a deadweight loss: consumers who value the good more than its marginal cost in production are unwilling to purchase at the inflated price. If we make the further assumption that the most efficiently produced units are the ones that actually are consumed, then the effect of the binding price ceiling is the shaded area in Figure 10.7, below. The equilibrium conditions of this market are now that $P = P_{MIN}$; $Q_S=Q_S(P_{MIN})$; $Q_D = Q_D(P_{MIN})$.

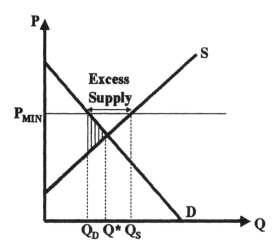

Figure 10.7

Exercise 8: *For Figure 10.7, suppose that the government both supports the price of the good at P_{MIN} and commits itself to buy up at that price any surplus (excess supply) that producers put on the market. What is the government's expense for this purchasing program?*

   a. $P_{MIN}(Q^* - Q_D)$

   b. $P_{MIN}(Q_S - Q^*)$

   c. $P_{MIN}(Q_S - Q_D)$

What is the deadweight loss of this support plus purchase program (compared to the perfectly competitive market with no intervention)? Let deadweight loss be measured as the loss in consumers' surplus, plus the loss in producers' surplus plus the government's expenditure for the program.

   a. The shaded area in Figure 10.7.
   b. The shaded area plus the area below supply between Q_D and Q_S
   c. The area below supply between Q_D and Q_S.
   d. The entire government expenditure minus the portion of government expenditure lying above both the demand and the supply curves but below P_{MIN}.

5. Production Quotas

A **production quota** is a limit on the total quantity that producers can supply to the market. Imposing a quota creates a vertical segment in the supply curve at the level of the quota: even if the price increases dramatically, firms cannot increase the quantity supplied. The new equilibrium occurs where the new supply curve intersects demand. The production quota is said to be binding if the limit on production is below the competitive equilibrium output level in the absence of the quota. A binding quota will, then, result in a deadweight loss since some consumers who are willing to pay more than the marginal cost of production cannot purchase the good. Since the *original* supply curve represents the opportunity cost (marginal cost) of resources to produce the output, the appropriate measure of welfare loss due to unrealized gains from trade is the difference between the demand curve and the *original* supply curve over the range of output curtailed by the quota. This is illustrated in Figure 10.8, below, where the deadweight loss is the shaded area. The equilibrium conditions are now that $Q = Q_{MAX}$; $P_D = P_D(Q_{MAX})$; $P_S = P_S(Q_{MAX})$.

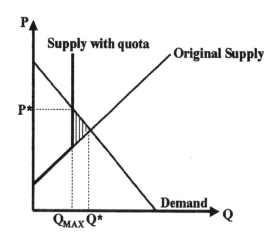

Figure 10.8

Exercise 9: *Suppose that P* in Figure 10.8 equals P_{MIN} in Figure 10.7. In other words, consider a quota program that results in the same market price as the price support program of Figure 10.7. Which of the following statements is true?*

a. The deadweight losses of the two programs are the same.
b. The consumer surpluses of the two programs are the same.
c. The producer surpluses of the two programs are the same.
d. The market output under the two programs is the same.

6. Import Tariffs and Quotas

Tariffs are taxes levied by the government on goods imported into the country. Tariffs sometimes are called **duties**. An **import quota** is a limit on the total number of units of a good that can be imported into the country. In order to examine the effects of these instruments, we must first discuss the underlying supply and demand conditions that generate imports. Imports will be observed any time the world price of a good is below the equilibrium price for the domestic market in the absence of imports. For example, suppose that the country can import as much of a good as it wants at price P_W in Figure 10.9 (i.e., foreign supply is flat at P_W). This price is below P*, the price that would prevail in the domestic market if imports were not possible. The quantity imported will equal $Q_4 - Q_1$ at price P_W and Q_1 will be produced locally. Consumers' surplus will be the area of triangle AP_WB and domestic producers' surplus will be the area of triangle DP_WC. Hence the total surplus of the country is ABCD.

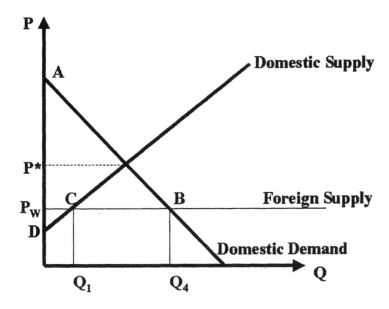

Figure 10.9

If a tariff of T per unit is imposed on imports, the effective world price increases from P_W to $P_W + T$, as shown in Figure 10.10, below. At this new price, quantity Q_3 is demanded and quantity Q_2 is supplied domestically. Imports shrink to the quantity $Q_3 - Q_2$. Since total consumption decreases from Q_4 to Q_3, there is a deadweight loss from this distortion in consumption equal to area B. There is also is a net *opportunity cost* to expanding domestic output from Q_1 to Q_2: units of output that could be obtained at a cost of P_W under free trade must now be produced at a higher cost. This "production" deadweight loss is equal to area A in Figure 10.10. Area C represents the domestic government's tariff revenue: T times the number of units imported. This is a net gain for the domestic government. But this tariff revenue is entirely paid by local consumers who must now pay T more for each of the $(Q_3 - Q_2)$ units imported. In the end, then, C is just a transfer from consumers to their government and does not affect the country's welfare. Area D was part of consumers' surplus before the tariff was imposed, but is part of the domestic producers' surplus after the tariff is imposed. Again, this is a simple transfer that does not affect the welfare of the country as a whole. Therefore, the net effect of the tariff on the country's welfare is equal to $- A - B$, which is unambiguously negative. Equilibrium conditions for this market are now that $P = P_W + T$; $Q_D = Q_D(P_W + T)$; $Q_S = Q_S(P_W + T)$.

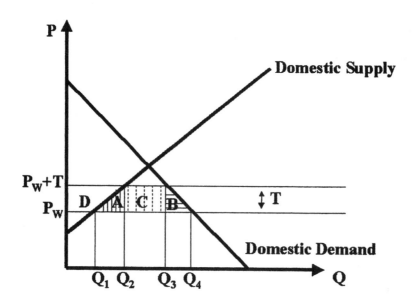

Figure 10.10

Consider now a quota that limits imports to a maximum of $Q_3 - Q_2$ in Figure 10.10. This means that, for all $P \geq P_W$, the total supply curve is represented by the domestic supply curve plus $(Q_3 - Q_2)$ so that total supply equals demand at Q_3. Therefore, both the equilibrium quantity and the equilibrium price are the same as in the case of the tariff. The deadweight loss areas A and B would still be deadweight losses for the same reason as before. On the other hand, the quota generates no government revenue. Area C is now a direct transfer from domestic consumers to foreign producers. Not surprisingly, then, a quota that achieves the same total consumption and the same total price as a unit tariff results in a larger domestic welfare loss of $-(A + B + C)$. The equilibrium condition for the market is now that $Q_D(P) = Q_S(P)+\text{Quota}$.

Exercise 10: *Let the market for a good be as shown in Figure 10.11:*

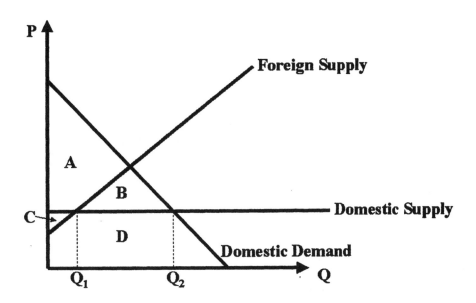

Figure 10.11

Assume that foreigners cannot supply their product to any other market than the domestic market. What is the quantity of the good that is imported and what is the quantity produced domestically under free trade (no tariffs)?

a. Q_1 is imported, Q_2 is produced domestically.
b. Q_1 is imported, $Q_2 - Q_1$ is produced domestically.
c. 0 is imported, Q_2 is produced domestically.

What is the effect of a tariff on the equilibrium price and total surplus in the home market?

a. The price rises in the amount of the tariff.
b. The price does not change.
c. The price rises, but less than the tariff.

Chapter Review Questions

1. Let demand be $Q_D = 100 - P$ and supply be $Q_S = P$.

   a. Calculate the competitive market equilibrium, consumers' surplus, producers' surplus, and total surplus.

   b. Calculate consumers' surplus, producers' surplus, and total surplus if a production quota of $Q = 45$ is set. Is this more or less than your answer to (a)? How does you answer change if the quota is set at $Q = 55$?

   c. Calculate consumers' surplus, producers' surplus, and total surplus if an excise tax of $T = 10$ is imposed on suppliers. How does your answer compare to (b)? How does government revenue compare under the quota and the tax? What if this is a subsidy for suppliers of $T = 10$?

   d. Calculate consumers' surplus, producers' surplus, and total surplus if a price ceiling of $P = 45$ is imposed in this market. Calculate consumers' surplus, producers' surplus, and total surplus if a price floor of $P = 55$ is imposed on this market. How do these surpluses compare?

Answer:

a. The competitive equilibrium is the point where demand equals supply or $100 - P = P$. Hence, $P^* = 50$, $Q^* = 50$. Consumers' surplus is the area under demand and above P^* so that $CS = (100-50)(50)(1/2) = 1250$. Producers' surplus is the area under P^* and above supply so that $PS = (50-0)(50)(1/2) = 1250$. Total surplus is the sum of consumers' and producers' surplus so that $TS = 1250 + 1250 = 2500$.

b. If $Q = 45$, then P^* becomes 55. At this new equilibrium, consumers' surplus is $(100 - 55)(45)(1/2) = 1012.5$. Producers' surplus is $(55-45)(45) + (45-0)(45)(1/2) = 1462.5$. Total surplus is $1012.5 + 1462.5 = 2475$. Therefore, the deadweight loss is $2500 - 2475 = 25$. You can verify that this is the area of the deadweight loss triangle $(50-45)(55-45)(1/2)$.

   If $Q = 55$ is the quota, then it is not binding. Therefore, consumers', producers', and total surplus are as in (a).

c. If $T = 10$, then the new supply curve is $Q_S = P - 10$. The new equilibrium price and quantity are obtained by setting this new supply curve equal to demand and solving. Hence, we have $P - 10 = 100 - P$ or $P^* = 55$, $Q^* = 45$. Consumers' surplus is $(100-55)(45)(1/2) = 1012.5$. Producers' surplus is now $(55-10)(45)(1/2) = 1012.5$. Total surplus is now $1012.5+1012.5 = 2025$ (not counting government revenues from the tax). Deadweight loss based on this total surplus measure is $2500-2025 = 475$. Tax revenues are $10(45) = 450$, so that they do not make up for the entire deadweight loss. If tax revenues are included in total surplus, then the deadweight loss is 25 (as in part (b)).

If a subsidy of 10 is given to suppliers, the new supply curve is $Q_S = P + 10$. The new equilibrium price and quantity are obtained from $P + 10 = 100 - P$ or $P^* = 45$, $Q^* = 55$. Consumers' surplus is $(100 - 45)(55)(1/2) = 1512.5$. Producers' surplus is $(45-(-10))(55)(1/2) = 1512.5$. The total surplus is, then, $1512.5+1512.5 = 3025$ (not counting government expenditure for the subsidy) so that there is a gain in surplus of $3025-2500 = 525$. Government expenditure now equals $T(Q^*) = 10(55) = 550$. Deducting this expenditure in the total surplus we have a net total surplus of 2475 and a deadweight loss of 25.

d. If a price ceiling of P = 45 is imposed, then $Q_S = 45$ is the amount sellers are willing to supply but $100-45 = 55 = Q_D$ is the amount demanded (so that there is a 10 unit excess demand). Consumers' surplus is now $(100-55)(45)(1/2) + (55-45)(45) = 1012.5+450 = 1462.5$ and producers' surplus is now $(45)(45)(1/2) = 1012.5$. Total surplus is, then, $1462.5+1012.5 = 2475$. The deadweight loss is $2500-2475 = 25$.

If a price floor of P = 55 is imposed, then $Q_D = 45$ and $Q_S = 55$ so that there is excess supply of 10 units. Consumers' surplus is $(100-55)(45)(1/2) = 1012.5$ and producers' surplus is now $45(45)(1/2) + (55-45)(45) = 1462.5$ so that total surplus is 2475 (as in the case of the price ceiling). The deadweight loss is 25, as before, as well.

2. Explain why foreign producers might prefer quotas to tariffs.

Answer:

Foreign producers might prefer the quota because it raises the equilibrium price they *receive* for the goods they are able to sell in the domestic market and, hence, raises their producer surplus. A tariff (that results in the same level of imports) would raise the price *paid by consumers* but foreign producers only receive that price minus the tariff. Even in the most favorable case (shown in the text) where world supply is horizontal, the tariff leaves the *net* price obtained by foreign producers unchanged. In all other cases, that net price actually decreases.

3. Demand is given by $Q_D = \$100 - 2P$ and supply is given by $Q_S = 2P$.

  a. Now, consumers must pay an *ad valorem* tax of .5P at the time of purchase. In other words, the consumers must pay a tax equal to 50% of the price of the good. Illustrate in a diagram the effect of the tax on the equilibrium in this market.

  b. If, instead, consumers must pay a specific tax of T = $10 at the time of purchase, what is the new equilibrium price and output level in this market? Illustrate your answer in a diagram.

  c. What is the incidence of both types of taxes on consumers and producers?

Answer:

a. The new demand curve is $Q_D' = 100 - 2(1.5)P$ so that the new equilibrium price is determined by $Q_D' = Q_S$ or $100-3P = 2P$ or $P^{**} = 20$.

b. Now, the new demand curve is $Q_D' = 100 - 2P - 20$ so that the new equilibrium price is determined by $Q_D' = Q_S$ or $80 - 2P = 2P$ or $P^{**} = 20$.

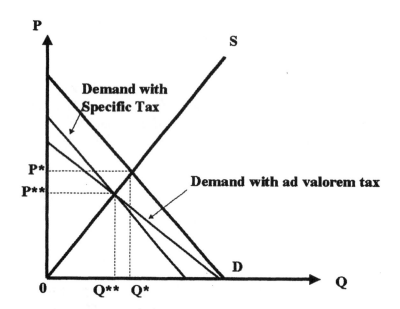

c. In order to calculate the incidence of the tax, we need to compare the old and the new equilibrium price. Before any tax is imposed, the equilibrium price is determined by $Q_D = Q_S$ or $100-2P = 2P$ or $P^* = 25$. The incidence of the *ad valorem* tax on consumers is $5 in equilibrium since the equilibrium price falls by $5, but they must pay $10 to the government with each purchase. The incidence of the *ad valorem* tax on producers is also $5 since price falls by $5, but they need pay nothing to the government. The incidence of the specific tax is the same, since the equilibrium under the tax and without the tax is the same as in the *ad valorem* case.

Problem Set

1. Let a binding price ceiling of P_{MAX} be imposed on a market, as in Figure 10.6.

    a. Now, suppose that consumers with the *minimum* willingness to pay are those who buy. What is the deadweight loss?

    b. Suppose that a *random selection* of consumers is able to buy. Suppose further that the amount supplied with the price ceiling, Q_S is exactly half the amount demanded, Q_D in Figure 10.6. What is the deadweight loss now?

2. Suppose that supply is perfectly inelastic. Do you think it likely that consumers will gain or lose from the imposition of a price ceiling? Now suppose that supply is perfectly elastic. Do you think it likely that consumers will gain or lose from the imposition of a price ceiling?

3. Suppose that, in an effort to improve the welfare of its workers, a government proposes a minimum wage that must be paid to all individuals who work in the country. Explain, using a demand and supply diagram, whether employers or workers would vote for such a proposal. Do all workers gain from this plan?

4. A new report by a major medical research group finds that aspirin, in addition to its pain-killing and anti-inflammatory properties, can help to reduce the risk of developing certain cancers. In order to prevent price-gouging by aspirin producers, the government places a limit on the price of aspirin at its pre-discovery equilibrium level. What is the effect of this policy on the market for aspirin? Are there problems with this policy?

5. Domestic demand for cars in Country A is given by $Q_D = 100 - 2P$ and domestic supply is given by $Q_S = 2P$. (You may take all prices to be in thousands.)

   a. Calculate the equilibrium price and output for this market.

   b. Now, suppose that cars are available on the world market for a price of $P_W = \$10$. What is the free trade equilibrium quantity produced domestically, imported, and demanded? Calculate domestic and foreign producers' surplus.

   c. In response to complaints by its domestic car producers, the government places a "voluntary" import quota of 40 units on foreign car producers. What is the effect of this quota on domestic price, consumers' surplus, and producers' surplus? Who benefits from the quotas? Should foreign producers welcome the policy? Who loses?

   d. What is the welfare loss due to the policy of part (c) from the point of view of the domestic country? From the point of view of the world? From the point of view of the foreign country?

6. Suppose that a payroll tax (i.e., a tax paid on wages) is imposed. The tax is shared equally between employers and employees, with each group responsible for paying $5 whatever the wage level. Employees fall into two categories: skilled and unskilled labor. There is no mobility across these two groups and their supply and demand characteristics differ, as detailed below.

   a. The demand for skilled labor is elastic, but the supply of skilled labor is completely inelastic. Illustrate the effect of the tax on the level of wages and employment in equilibrium. What is the incidence of the tax on skilled workers and their employers? Does employment fall as a result of the tax?

b. The demand for unskilled labor is elastic, and the supply of unskilled labor is infinitely elastic. Illustrate the effect of the tax on the level of wages and employment in equilibrium. What is the incidence of the tax on unskilled workers and employers? Does employment fall as a result of the tax?

Exam *(60 minutes: Closed book, closed notes)*

1. Demand is given by $Q_D = 4P^{-1}$ and supply is given by $Q_S = P$.

   a. What is the equilibrium price in this market?

   b. Suppose that a specific tax of $T = \$1$ is levied on this market. What is the incidence of tax on consumers? On producers?

   c. Answer question 1(b) for $T = \$2$.

   d. How does your answer to 1(a) and 1(b) change if $Q_D = P^{-1}$ and $Q_S = P^2$?

2. Domestic demand for extra virgin olive oil in Country A is given by $Q_D = \$40 - 5P$ and domestic supply is given by $Q_S = 3P$.

   a. Calculate the equilibrium price and output for this market.

   b. Now, let extra virgin olive oil be available on the world market for a price of $P_W = \$2$. What is the free trade equilibrium quantity produced domestically, the quantity imported, and the total quantity demanded in Country A? What is consumers' surplus and producers' surplus in Country A?

   c. Let a tariff of $3 per unit be imposed on imports of olive oil. What is the quantity produced domestically, imported, and demanded with the tariff? What is consumers' and producers' surplus at this tariff rate? What are the government's tariff revenues?

   d. Suppose that the tariff is replaced by a complete ban on imports. Which program do consumers prefer? Domestic producers? Foreign producers?

3. Let demand for wheat be $Q_D = 60 - 5P$ and the supply of wheat be $Q_S = P$. Suppose that the government currently supports the price of wheat at $P_{MIN} = \$12$ and purchases any excess supply at this price.

   a. Illustrate the current price, quantity demanded, and quantity supplied for this market. How much does this policy cost the government?

   b. The weather was very wet last year, which was bad for growing wheat. Illustrate the effect of the poor weather on the wheat market. What is the effect on consumers, producers, and government expenditures of the poor weather?

    c. This year, the weather was not a problem, but a new study indicated that more people than previously suspected had an allergy to wheat. Illustrate the effect of this new discovery on the wheat market. What is the effect on consumers, producers, and government expenditures of the study?

4. Agricultural markets often are considered to have a perfectly competitive structure; however, producer subsidies, minimum price floors, production quotas, and import tariffs are commonly observed in agricultural markets. Discuss the advantages and disadvantages of *each* of these forms of government intervention in a perfectly competitive market, supporting your answer with diagrams, as appropriate.

Answers to Exercises

1. The correct answer is (a). If the economy currently is at the competitive equilibrium, *any* move from this point will create a deadweight loss. Even if the plan creates a benefit for consumers, the losses to producers must outweigh this gain.

2. The correct answer is (a). Whether by planning or by competition, as long as the economy can trade at (P^*, Q^*) total surplus is maximized. (We are assuming here that total output Q^* is still produced at the minimum possible cost.)

3. The correct answer to the first part of the question is (b). In order to induce consumers to demand the same amount as before, they must pay $T *less* than before in order to compensate for the fact that they must pay the tax. Geometrically, this means that the demand curve shifts *down* by $T to D'. The market equilibrium occurs at output Q_1, where curve D' intersects the original supply curve, S. Q_1 is the same as when producers pay the tax because, in both cases, it occurs at the point where the vertical distance between the *original* demand and supply curves equals T.

The correct answer to the second part of the question is (a). Since Q_1 is the same in either case, and the distance P_D - P_S is also the same, the areas of the deadweight loss triangles in both cases is the same. Therefore, the deadweight loss is the same to society no matter who is responsible for actually paying the tax.

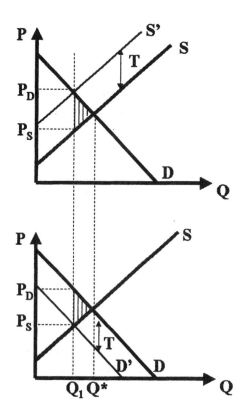

4. The correct answer is (b). Since the long-run supply curve is flat in a constant cost industry, the entire tax burden falls on consumers (as shown in the top panel of Figure 10.4).

5. The correct answer is (c). When supply is horizontal, the deadweight loss is positive since the equilibrium quantity exchanged is no longer at the original competitive output level, Q*. The deadweight loss is illustrated as the shaded triangle in the figure below. When supply is vertical, Q* continues to be traded after the tax is imposed so that there is no deadweight loss.

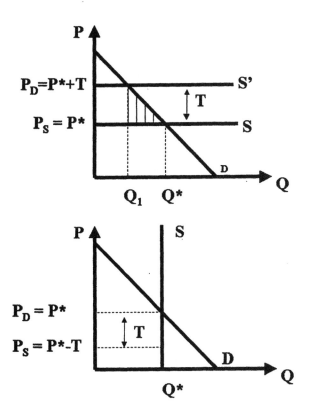

6. The correct answer is (b). In order to induce producers to supply the same amount as before, they need only receive a price $P/(1+\alpha) = P_S$. Once the subsidy is paid, this price P_S ensures that producers receive the same amount $(1+\alpha)P_S = P$ as before. From this expression we see that $P - P_S = \alpha P_S$. Graphically, the supply curve has rotated down so that the vertical distance between the curves is αP_S.

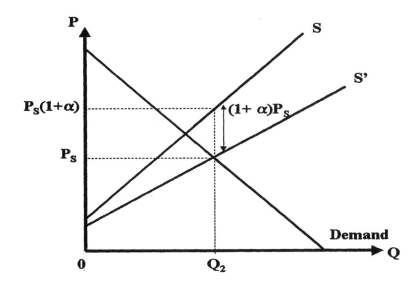

7. The correct answers are (a), (c), and (d). Since long-run supply in a constant cost perfectly competitive industry is flat at the minimum of average cost, a binding price ceiling reduces the price below the level at which firms would find it profitable to produce. As a result, they supply zero to the market. If no output is supplied, no surplus is earned by either producers or consumers after the price ceiling is imposed.

We must compare this to the situation before the price ceiling is imposed. Since the long-run supply curve is flat, producers' surplus is zero before the price ceiling is imposed. On the other hand, consumers' surplus is positive (the area between demand and market price).

Comparing the two situations, we see that all consumers' surplus is lost when the price ceiling is imposed. Further, since producers' surplus is zero both before and after the change, producers' surplus is not affected by the price ceiling. The amount of total surplus lost to society equals the loss in consumers' surplus. Therefore, the loss in consumers' surplus also equals the deadweight loss due to the price ceiling.

8. The correct answer to the first part of the question is (c). The equilibrium quantity demanded by consumers is Q_D so that the amount available to the government for purchase is $Q_D - Q_S$. The price that must be paid for this is P_{MIN}. Therefore, the expense is $(Q_D - Q_S)P_{MIN}$.

The correct answer to the second part of the question is (d). All units between Q_D and Q_S are actually purchased at price P_{MIN}. Therefore, the new producers' surplus is the area between P_{MIN} and the supply curve for all units actually sold (all units up to Q_S). This represents an *increase* of A + B + C in the figure below. On the other hand, consumers' surplus *falls* by areas A + B, since this surplus was earned by consumers before the support plus purchase program was imposed. Adding these together, the total *increase* in consumers' and producers' surplus is area C. Therefore, the total deadweight loss to society is the government expenditure minus area C.

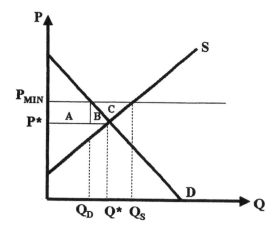

9. All of the statements are correct. If the price support is at the same level as the equilibrium price under a binding quota program, then the equilibrium output in the price support program will be the same as the binding quota (statement d). Since the prices and outputs are the same under the two programs and the deadweight loss is computed as the area under the demand curve and above the *original* supply curve, the deadweight loss must be the same. Since demand has not changed and supply has not changed for output levels below the equilibrium level, consumers' and producers' surplus will be the same under the two programs as well since the price and output are the same.

10. The correct answer to the first part of the question is (b). For units below Q_1, the foreign supply is forthcoming at the lowest price, so it is presumed to be imported. Quantities between Q_1 and Q_2 are forthcoming at a lower price from the domestic suppliers so that these units are presumed to be supplied domestically.

The correct answer to the second part of the question is (b). A tariff reduces the amount of foreign supply (potentially to zero if the tariff is high enough to shift the foreign supply curve completely above the domestic supply curve), but it does not affect the price level since enough domestic supply is forthcoming at the current price to entirely satisfy demand.

Answers to Problems

1.

    a. The amount supplied is Q_S, as in Figure 10.6. This is allocated to individuals with valuations between T and X on the demand curve. As a result, the consumers' surplus is the vertically shaded area in the figure below (D+E). The producers' surplus is the horizontally shaded area, F. The deadweight loss is the difference between the total surplus without the program and the total surplus with the program. These are calculated in the table that follows the figure:

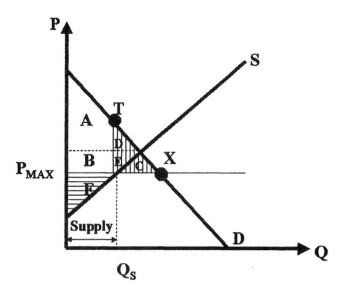

	Without Price Control	With Price Control
Consumers' Surplus	A+D	D+E+C
Producers' Surplus	B+E+F	F
Total Surplus (CS + PS)	A+D+B+E+F	D+E+F+C
Deadweight loss	None	A+B-C

b. If a random selection of consumers with valuations above P_{MAX} receives the good, then the consumers' surplus is calculated based on an average valuation of the customers that actually receive the good. If $Q_S = (1/2)Q_D$, then a random selection of half the customers with valuations above P_{MAX} actually receive the good. Therefore, the consumers' surplus earned is $(1/2)(A+D+B+E+C)$ in the figure of problem 1(a). Producers' surplus is area F. Therefore, the total surplus is $CS + PS = (1/2)(A+D+B+E+C) + F$ and the deadweight loss from the program is $(A+D+B+E+F) - (1/2)(A+D+B+E+C) - F = (1/2)(A+D+B+E-C)$.

2. If supply is vertical, then a binding price ceiling causes no change in supply and consumers gain from the price ceiling. The increase in consumer surplus is the shaded area in the first of the two figures below. If supply is horizontal, then a binding price ceiling causes supply to drop to zero and all consumers' surplus is lost. The lost consumers' surplus is illustrated as the horizontally shaded area in the second diagram below.

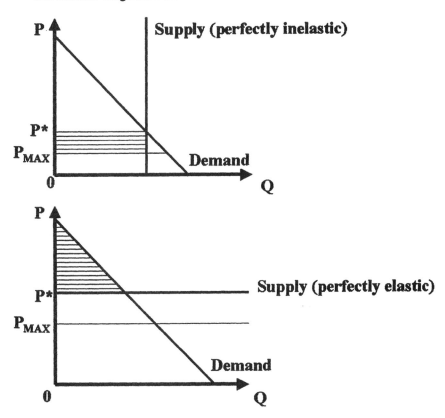

3. The minimum wage law creates an excess supply of labor: demand falls and supply rises when the market wage increases. The workers who actually obtain jobs are better off, but the workers who want to work but are no longer able to lose. If the workers who actually obtain jobs are those who are willing to work for the lowest wage, then the surplus enjoyed by employed workers is A + B after the change. The surplus enjoyed by employers is C. The deadweight loss due to the plan is area D + E. Unemployment equals $Q_S - Q_D$.

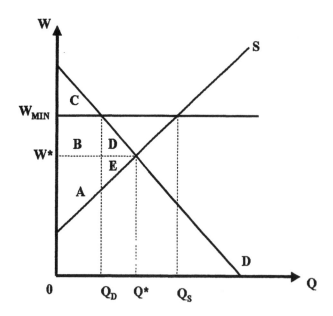

4. As a result of the new use for the product, the demand for aspirin shifts out. The effect of the policy is to create excess demand for aspirin as long as supply is not completely flat. The program causes a deadweight loss that is similar to the case of a price ceiling of Figure 10.6 and Problem 1. As in Problem 1, the welfare loss due to the unsatisfied demand (i.e., the welfare loss compared to the policy of allowing the price to adjust freely) varies depending on which individuals actually receive the limited supply of aspirin.

5.

    a. The equilibrium price is such that demand equals supply, or $100 - 2P = 2P$ or $P^* = 25$. (and $Q_S^* = Q_D^* = 50$).

    b. If $P_W = 10$, then 20 units are supplied by domestic producers (since $Q_S = 2P$ is the equation of domestic supply), $100 - 2(10) = 80$ units are demanded by domestic consumers and the difference, $80 - 20 = 60$ units are supplied by imports. Consumers' surplus is the area under demand for the units actually consumed so that $CS = 80(50-10)(1/2) = 1600$. Producers' surplus for domestic suppliers is the area below price and above the domestic supply curve or $10(20)(1/2) = 100$. Foreign producers' surplus is the area between market price and the foreign supply curve. Since the foreign supply curve is flat at the equilibrium price, foreign producers' surplus is zero.

    c. When the quota is imposed, the equilibrium price rises since the effective total supply on the domestic market is the domestic supply plus 40 units when price is above $10. Therefore, equilibrium price is calculated as $Q_S = 2P + 40 = Q_D = 100 - 2P$ or $P^* = 15$. At this price, 30 units are supplied domestically, 40 units are imported, and $100 - 2P = 70$ units are demanded. Domestic producers' surplus is now the area between the new equilibrium price and the domestic supply curve so that domestic surplus is $15(30)(1/2) = 225$. Foreign producers' surplus is the area between foreign supply and the market price on the 40 units sold or

40(15-10) = 200. Consumers' surplus is now the area under demand for the 70 units actually consumed or 70(50-15)(1/2) = 1225.

Both domestic and foreign producers' surplus has risen as a result of the plan, so both of these groups should support the plan. Consumers' surplus has fallen, so consumers' groups should not support the plan.

d. In terms of Figure 10.10, the quota generates 150 units of producers' surplus for the foreign firms (area C), 25 units of distortion in consumption (area B), 25 units of production distortion (area A), and 125 units of transfer of consumers' surplus to domestic producers (area D). The deadweight loss from the world's point of view is areas A + B or 50 units. From the domestic country's point of view, the welfare loss is A + B + C = 200 units. From the foreign country's viewpoint, there is no loss from the policy (it is a pure gain).

6.

a. If supply is vertical, the wage falls by the full amount of the tax paid by employers so that the entire wage bill for an employee stays constant at the original (pre-tax) wage level. Therefore, the incidence of the tax falls fully on labor (w'+$5 = w). Employment does not change.

b. If supply is horizontal, then the wage tax shifts supply up by the amount of the tax, while demand shifts back by the amount of the tax. The wage rises by the full amount of the tax paid by employees, but equilibrium employment drops drastically to the intersection of the new demand and supply. The incidence of the tax falls fully on employers (w' = w+$5). Employment falls.

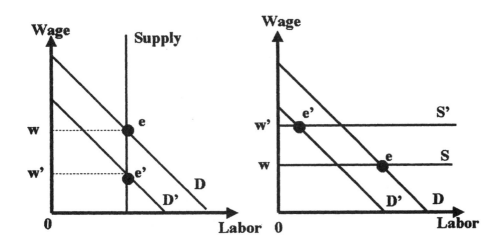

Answers to Exam

1.

   a. Setting supply equal to demand and solving, we obtain an equilibrium price of $P^* = 2$.

   b. The relative change in price for this market is the ratio of the elasticities of supply and demand $= 1/-1 = -1$. Therefore, the prices change by the same amount. For a $1 tax, this means that the price to consumers would rise by $.50 and the price received by producers would fall by $.50. The impact of the tax is equally borne by consumers and producers.

   c. If the tax is $2, then this means that the price to consumers would rise by $1 and the price received by producers would fall by $1.

   d. Now, the equilibrium price is $P = 1$, however the incidence changes. We now have the ratio of supply and demand elasticities equal to $2/-1 = -2$. Therefore, the price to consumers would rise by $.67 and the price received by producers would fall by $.33. The impact of the tax is primarily borne by consumers.

2.

   a. Equilibrium price occurs where demand and supply intersect or where $40-5P = 3P$ or $P^* = \$5$. $Q_S^* = Q_D^* = 15$.

   b. If $P_W = 2$, then the equilibrium quantity demanded will be $Q_D = 40-10 = 30$. Domestic supply will be $Q_S = 3P = 6$. 24 units are imported. Domestic consumers' surplus is $6(30)(1/2) = 90$. Domestic producers' surplus is $2(6)(1/2) = 6$.

   c. The tariff is prohibitive: no olive oil will be imported at the price including the tariff. Therefore, the equilibrium is as in part (a) of this question. Consumers' surplus is $(8-5)(15)(1/2) = 45/2$ and producers' surplus is $(15)(5)(1/2) = 75/2$. The government earns no tariff revenues since no imports occur.

   d. If a complete ban on imports were imposed, then the same equilibrium as in (c) would result. Consumers, domestic producers, and foreign producers are indifferent between the two programs.

3.

   a. The equilibrium price without the price support is $P^* = \$10$ in this market (equating demand and supply and solving). If the government actually purchases any excess supply at a price of $12, then it purchases $Q_S(12) - Q_D(12) = 12$ units (the entire amount of domestic production) at $12 each. This results in a government expenditure of $(12)(\$12) = \$144$. The welfare loss of the program is the entire government expenditure minus area C in the figure below (see Exercise 8). This equals $144 - (12)(2)(1/2) = 128$.

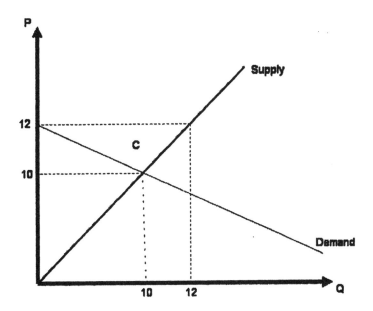

b. Suppose that supply shifts back, but not enough to drive equilibrium price above the support level. In this case, government expenditure falls but is not eliminated. Producers' surplus falls, but consumers' surplus is unchanged (since the market price does not change). The welfare cost of the policy in this market is now the new government expenditure, which is the new government purchase times the support price, minus the area above the new supply and demand but below the support price, C'. While it is not relevant here (because the support price is so high that it eliminates domestic demand), there would normally be a second case where the supply shifts back so far that the equilibrium price in the market exceeds the support price. In this case, the price support is no longer binding and equilibrium is determined by the intersection of the new supply with the old demand curve. Government expenditure is zero in this case. Both producers' and consumers' surplus falls. On the other hand, there is no deadweight loss in the new supply situation since the competitive market is free to determine price and quantity traded.

c. In this case, equilibrium price does not change since the support price is still binding. Neither does the government expenditure increase because it is already purchasing the entire domestic supply.

4.

a. A price ceiling is inefficient because it creates a deadweight loss shown as the shaded area in Figure 10.6. A price ceiling is associated with excess demand if supply is upward sloping and demand is downward sloping.

A *maximum* production quota cannot restore efficiency: either the quota does not bind (in which case it does not affect efficiency) or it does bind, in which case it reduces the number of units traded and makes the inefficiency worse. A *minimum* production quota set at Q* (in Figure 10.6) would restore efficiency provided that the individuals who value the units most highly receive these units. In that case all demand to the left of Q* is satisfied at price P$_{MAX}$. Consumer surplus is the area C +B in the figure below. Producers' surplus is area A minus area B (where area B is the triangle below supply, above P$_{MAX}$, and to the left of Q*). Consumers' surplus increases as a result of the program and producers' surplus falls; however, there is no deadweight loss. Rather, the change in surplus is a transfer from producers to consumers.

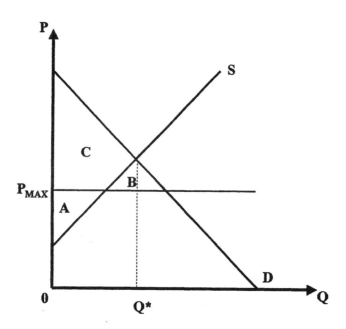

b. A price floor is inefficient because it creates a deadweight loss, which is illustrated as the shaded area in Figure 10.7. Generally, there will be excess supply with a price floor if supply is upward sloping and demand is downward sloping.

If a *minimum* production quota cannot restore efficiency: either the quota does not bind (in which case it does not affect efficiency) or it does bind (as at Q' in the figure below), in which case it makes the inefficiency worse by increasing production.

A *maximum* quota set at Q*, reestablishes efficiency provided that the producers who get to sell are the most efficient ones (i.e., the ones to the left of Q*). Area B is a loss in consumers' surplus, but a gain in producers' surplus. This creates no deadweight loss for reasons analogous to the argument in part (a) of this question.

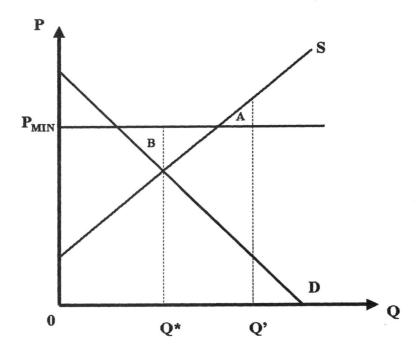

4. In each of these cases, total domestic welfare goes down (deadweight loss is created), as we move away from the unconstrained perfectly competitive market equilibrium. In each case, particular constituencies may win or lose. The table presented in the beginning of the chapter breaks down constituencies into producers, consumers and (somewhat artificially, perhaps) the government budget. When an entry says "rises", it suggests that this constituency may favor the program, and the program could be considered as an "advantage" for that group. Similarly, a "disadvantage" for each group would be represented by an entry of "falls". The details of this answer are really a summary of this chapter's discussion, so I refer you to the text for a more thorough description.

Chapter 11: Monopoly and Monopsony

Until now, we have analyzed markets characterized by many small buyers and sellers. Not all markets have these features, however. We will now examine production and pricing decisions in **monopoly markets**, which are markets with many small buyers but only a single seller. We will also analyze **monopsony markets**, which are markets with many small sellers but only a single buyer. We will also maintain the assumption that a single, undifferentiated product is produced, and full information on the existence of this product and its price is available. Clearly, since we assume that only a single seller exists, the assumption of "free entry" no longer holds.

Since the monopolist is the only seller in her market, she faces the entire market demand, which we can write as P(Q). (Recall that P(Q) was called *the inverse demand curve* in Chapter 2.) We will assume that the monopolist chooses output so as to maximize profits. As we saw in Chapter 9, a firm's profit maximization problem can be written as:

$$\text{Max } \pi(Q) = TR(Q) - TC(Q)$$
$$Q$$

where Q is the monopolist's output, TR(Q) is the total revenue of producing Q units, and TC(Q) is the total cost of producing Q units. The profit maximizing output is the output such that marginal revenue equals marginal cost. In other words, as long as an additional unit earns more than it costs, MR(Q) > MC(Q), the firm can increase profits by increasing production. As soon as the additional unit costs more than it earns, MR(Q) < MC(Q), the firm can increase profits by decreasing production. Only at the output level where MR(Q) = MC(Q) can the monopolist's profits be maximized. In other words the **profit maximization condition for a monopolist is:**

$$MR(Q) = MC(Q)$$

Exercise 1: *Consider the following depiction of marginal revenue and marginal cost facing a monopolist:*

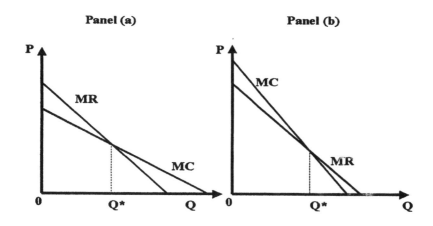

Which of the following statements is true?

a. Q* is the profit maximizing output in panel (a). The profit maximizing output in panel (b) is zero.
b. Zero is the profit maximizing output in both panels, since marginal cost is decreasing.
c. Q* is the profit maximizing output in panels (a) and (b).
d. Q* is the profit maximizing output in panel (a). The profit maximizing output in panel (b) is infinite.

For a firm in a perfectly competitive market, marginal revenue was equal to price: since each perfectly competitive firm takes the price as given, the extra revenue provided by the sale of one more unit of output is the price itself (see Chapter 9). For a monopolist, this is not true: marginal revenue does *not* equal price because the monopolist realizes that its output is so large that its supply decisions do affect price. The fact that the monopolist can influence market price by its output decisions is called **market power**. Perfectly competitive firms do not have market power. Monopolists do.

For a firm with market power, marginal revenue is less than price. When the monopolist increases production by one unit, it earns the market price for that unit. On the other hand, in order to sell the additional unit, the monopolist realizes that it must reduce price slightly. This reduction in price affects *all* units the monopolist wishes to sell and not just the last unit. All these units except the last unit are called the **inframarginal units**. Hence, the monopolist suffers a loss due to the price reduction on all the inframarginal units. Therefore, for a small increase in output, the marginal revenue from the additional unit sold has two components:

$$MR(Q) = P + Q(\Delta P/\Delta Q)$$

Since the price that demanders are willing to pay falls as consumption rises, $(\Delta P/\Delta Q)$ is negative. Therefore, $MR(Q)$ must be *less than* price.

If total revenue can be written as the output sold times the price demanders are willing to pay to consume that output, $TR(Q) = QP(Q)$, then it follows that average revenue is $TR(Q)/Q = QP(Q)/Q = P(Q)$. Therefore, the inverse demand curve is precisely the average revenue curve. Total revenue, average revenue, marginal revenue, and market demand are related as shown in Figure 11.1.

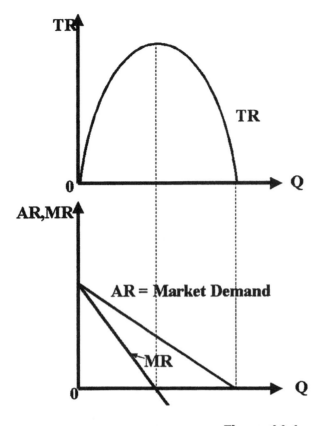

Figure 11.1

Note that the relationships among these three curves correspond to the general relationships among total, average, and marginal curves that we outlined in Chapter 6. In particular marginal revenue is the slope of the total revenue curve.

Exercise 2: *Let a monopolist face an inverse demand of P(Q) = 100 - 25Q. Which of the following statements is (are) true?*

   a. The equation of the average revenue curve is AR(Q) = 100 - 25Q.
   b. The marginal revenue curve is twice as steep as the average revenue curve.
   c. The slope of the marginal revenue curve is -50.
   d. For outputs less than Q = 4, marginal revenue is positive, while for outputs greater than Q = 4, marginal revenue is negative.

    Now that we have analyzed marginal revenue, we can return to the monopolist's profit maximization condition. We can depict the condition graphically as in Figure 11.2. The profit maximizing output, Q*, sets marginal revenue equal to marginal cost. The equilibrium price is determined by reading the price that the monopolist would have to charge in order to sell Q* units off the demand curve, P*. The monopolist's profits are calculated as the difference between P* and AC(Q*), multiplied by the number of units sold, Q*. Graphically, this is the shaded box in the figure.

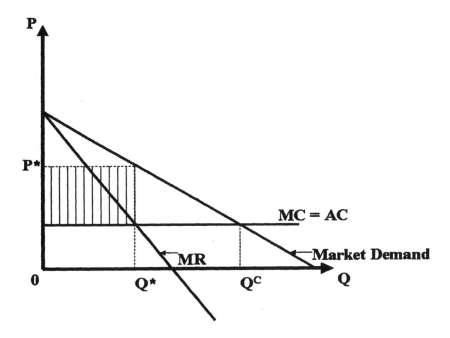

Figure 11.2

Q* is less than the perfectly competitive market output, shown as Q^C in Figure 11.2. This can be seen algebraically by recalling that, for a given quantity, marginal revenue is always less than price. Therefore, when marginal cost equals price marginal cost must exceed marginal revenue so that it pays the monopolist to reduce output. If output is below Q^C, then price exceeds marginal (and average) cost so that the monopolist must earn positive profits.

Exercise 3: *Let a monopolist face inverse demand of P(Q) = 10 - 2Q and let MC(Q) = Q while TC(Q) = 1 + .5Q². What is the monopolist's profit maximizing output? What is the market price?*

   a. Q* = 1, P* = 8
   b. Q* = 2, P* = 6
   c. Q* = 0, P* = 10

At Q, what is the monopolist's profit?*

   a. Profit = 12
   b. Profit = 9
   c. Profit = 0

Suppose that TC(Q) = 11 + .5Q² when Q > 0 and TC(Q) = 0 for Q = 0 so that no costs are sunk (and MC(Q) = Q, as before)? How does the profit maximizing output change?

   a. Q* does not change since marginal cost has not changed.
   b. Q* is now zero since average cost of positive output has risen, even if marginal cost has not changed.
   c. Q* = 1 since both average and marginal cost have changed.

Turning now to the comparative statics of the monopolist's profit maximization problem, if the market demand curve shifts up, then the monopolist's equilibrium output increases. From Figure 11.3, below, we can see that an upward shift in demand increases the price that customers are willing to pay for each level of output, Q. This increases marginal revenue. On the other hand, the second term in marginal revenue does not change since the slope of demand has not changed. Therefore, the total effect on marginal revenue is positive. Since marginal revenue rises but marginal cost does not, units that previously were unprofitable to produce now are profitable. Therefore, equilibrium output increases. In other words, the point of intersection of marginal revenue and marginal cost must move to the right. If MC is constant or increases with quantity, then equilibrium price rises as well. If MC is downward sloping, however, then equilibrium price may fall as shown in the second panel of Figure 11.3.

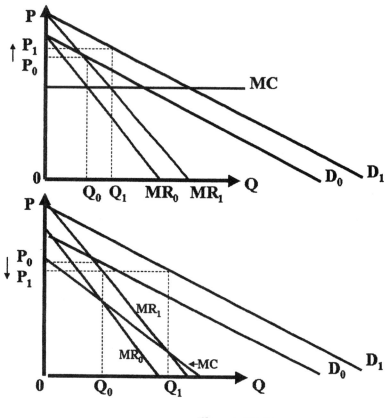

Figure 11.3

An upward shift in marginal cost will decrease the profit maximizing quantity and increase the profit maximizing price for the monopolist. The profit-maximizing quantity decreases because units that were previously just profitable are unprofitable at the new higher marginal cost. If equilibrium quantity decreases, however, then market price will rise as long as market demand slopes downward.

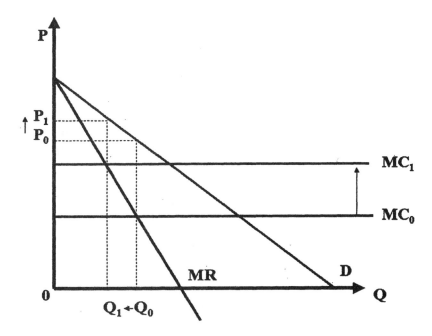

Figure 11.4

Exercise 4: *Let a monopolist face a linear demand, $P_0(Q) = 10 - 2Q$ and marginal cost $MC(Q) = 2$. Suppose that now demand shifts to $P_1(Q) = 12 - 2Q$. How does the equilibrium price change?*

    a. Equilibrium price rises.
    b. Equilibrium price falls.
    c. Equilibrium price is unchanged.

    It is sometimes useful to rephrase the profit maximization condition of the monopolist in terms of the price elasticity of demand, $\varepsilon_{Q,P} = (\Delta Q/\Delta P)(P/Q)$. (Review Chapter 2 for more information on $\varepsilon_{Q,P}$.) Manipulating our expression for marginal revenue, we have:

$$MR(Q) = P + Q(\Delta P/\Delta Q) = P[1 + (Q/P)(\Delta P/\Delta Q)] \text{ or...}$$

$$MR(Q) = P(1 + 1/\varepsilon_{Q,P})$$

Hence, we can rewrite the profit maximization condition as:

$$MR(Q) = P(1 + 1/\varepsilon_{Q,P}) = MC(Q) \text{ or...}$$

$$(P - MC)/P = -1/\varepsilon_{Q,P}$$

    The entire final expression is called the **inverse elasticity pricing rule** (or **IEPR**). It is very useful if we wish to compute the equilibrium price for a constant elasticity demand curve.

Exercise 5: *Let a monopolist face market demand $Q = 100P^{-b}$. What is the equation for the monopolist's marginal revenue curve?*

    a. $MR(Q) = P(1 + 1/b)$
    b. $MR(Q) = P(1 + 1/100)$
    c. $MR(Q) = P(1 + 1/-b)$

The left-hand side of the IEPR is the monopolist's optimal markup of price over marginal cost. This is sometimes called the **percentage contribution margin**. The left-hand side is used by itself as a measure of market power called the **Lerner Index of market power**. It ranges from 0 to 1 (zero for a perfectly competitive industry where price equals marginal cost). The markup is a measure of market power because it illustrates the degree to which a firm can force up price by restricting output.

Exercise 6: *Let a monopolist face market demand $Q = 100P^{-2}$. Calculate the percentage contribution margin for the monopolist. Suppose that market demand changes to become $Q = P^{-2}$. Does the percentage contribution margin rise or fall in equilibrium if $MC = 1/2$ and does not change?*

    a. The percentage contribution margin falls.
    b. The percentage contribution margin rises.
    c. The percentage contribution margin does not change.

Does the monopolist have more or less market power measured by the Lerner Index after the change in demand if the market is in equilibrium?

    a. The monopolist's market power rises.
    b. The monopolist's market power falls.
    c. The monopolist's market power does not change.

If marginal cost is positive, then $(1+1/\varepsilon_{Q,P})$ must be positive as well in order for IEPR to hold. This, in turn, implies that $\varepsilon_{Q,P} < -1$ must hold. Recall from Chapter 2 that the region where $\varepsilon_{Q,P} < -1$ is called the *elastic* region of the demand curve. It is for this reason that we say that IEPR implies that the monopolist will always operate on the elastic region of the market demand curve. The intuition for this result is simple. We know that, for most demand curves, the demand is less elastic at low prices than at high prices. Consider a monopolist deciding whether or not to lower its price a little. Since a decrease in price will increase the quantities sold it will also increase the total cost of production. The effect of the price decrease on revenues depends on the elasticity of demand. If demand is elastic, revenues increase. But if demand is inelastic, revenues decrease. In other words, if demand is inelastic, a decrease in price increases cost and decreases revenues! This is why the monopolist will stop cutting its price before reaching the inelastic portion of the demand curve.

Because the monopolist operates on the elastic portion of the demand curve, the price increase that the monopolist obtains as a result of a reduction in its output is relatively small. In fact, for this portion of the demand curve, a reduction in output results in a reduction in total revenue as well. This can be seen by noting that:

$$\varepsilon_{Q,P} < -1 \Leftrightarrow (\Delta Q/\Delta P)(P/Q) < -1 \Leftrightarrow \Delta QP < -\Delta PQ \Leftrightarrow \Delta QP + \Delta PQ < 0 \Leftrightarrow \Delta TR < 0$$

where TR is total revenue, which equals P x Q. This fact allows us to draw additional conclusions based on IEPR. For example, we can say that an upward shift in marginal cost must always reduce the monopolist's total revenues because it reduces the monopolist's optimal output. Similarly, a downward shift in marginal cost must always increase the monopolist's revenues.

Exercise 7: *A monopolist faces inverse demand curve P = 100 - Q. The monopolist's marginal cost is MC = $50. Calculate the monopolist's profit maximizing output and price. What is the price elasticity of demand at this point?*

   a. -1
   b. -3
   c. -1/2

Let marginal cost increase to MC = $60. Calculate the new profit maximizing output and price. What is the price elasticity of demand at this point?

   a. -3/2
   b. -4
   c. -1

Calculate total revenue before and after the change in marginal cost. Has total revenue...

   a. Increased?
   b. Decreased?
   c. Remained unchanged?

In Chapter 10, we studied the incidence of an excise tax on suppliers and demanders in perfectly competitive markets. A *similar but not identical* concept that we can study in the context of the IEPR is the **pass-through rate**. The pass-through rate is the percentage change in price per 1% increase in marginal cost. Mathematically,

$$\text{Pass-through rate} = (\Delta P/P)(MC/\Delta MC)$$

We can think of this as a measure of the burden of an increase in the monopolist's costs (due, for example, to an excise tax) passed on to consumers. Another way to think of pass-through is as an elasticity of price with respect to marginal cost.

Exercise 8: *For the change in marginal cost in Exercise 7, calculate the pass-through rate (calculated at the new price and marginal cost). Does the monopolist pass the entire change in marginal cost on to consumers?*

   a. No, the monopolist does not pass on the entire price increase to consumers.
   b. Yes, the monopolist passes on the entire price increase to consumers.

In Chapter 10, we showed that the perfectly competitive equilibrium maximized total surplus. Because the monopoly equilibrium does not correspond to the perfectly competitive equilibrium, the monopoly equilibrium generally entails a deadweight loss. For example, consider a market that is perfectly competitive. What would be the deadweight loss from converting production to monopoly? The **deadweight loss due to monopoly** is shown as the shaded area in Figure 11.5, below, where the perfectly competitive equilibrium is point e^C and the monopoly equilibrium is point e^M. The deadweight loss results because demanders who value the product at more than its opportunity cost (i.e., marginal cost) are unable to buy when the monopolist restricts supply in order to force up prices (and profits). In other words, the deadweight loss is due to unrealized gains from trade.

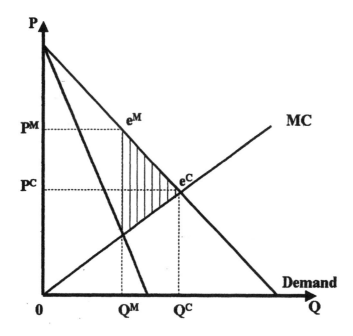

Figure 11.5

Of course, in some markets perfect competition might not possible so that the appropriate benchmark to use in calculating deadweight loss is not perfect competition. For example, suppose that the total cost incurred by a single firm to produce output is less than the combined total cost of two or more firms if they divided that output among them. More formally:

$$TC(Q) < TC(q_1) + TC(q_2) + ... TC(q_N) \text{ for all } N > 1$$

Where $Q = q_1 + q_2 + ...q_N$ is the sum of the outputs of $N \geq 2$ firms and $C(q_i)$ is the cost to firm i of producing q_i. A market with this type of underlying cost condition is called a **natural monopoly** because it is more efficient for a single firm to produce than for many firms to produce the same total quantity of output. As a result, a monopoly producer could always "drive out" a set of many small producers by pricing based on its lower cost. Therefore, it would be "natural" for monopoly to arise. Such a market is illustrated in Figure 11.6.

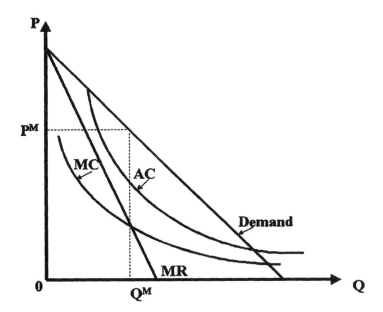

Figure 11.6

Natural monopoly can only arise if average costs are sufficiently decreasing, that is, if they are decreasing up to the point where they meet the demand curve or if they do not start increasing much before that point. We know that when average costs are decreasing marginal cost must be less than average cost. This is why this cost structure is not compatible with perfect competition: any small firm would be producing in the range where MC < AC so that the competitive rule of P = MC would leave the firm with negative profits.

Exercise 9: *Let the average cost curve for any firm in an industry be: AC(Q) = 12/Q + Q + .5Q², where Q is firm output so that the average cost for various levels of output is the following:*

Level of Output of the Firm	Average Cost of the Firm
Q = 0	AC = infinite
Q = .5	AC = 24.625
Q = 1	AC = 13.5
Q = 1.5	AC = 10.625
Q = 2	AC = 10
Q = 3	AC = 11.5
Q = 4	AC = 15

Let inverse market demand be P = 12 - Q. Is this industry a natural monopoly?

   a. Yes.

   b. No.

Suppose that market demand shifts out to P = 14.5 - Q. Is this industry a natural monopoly?

   a. Yes.

   b. No.

    Since perfect competition is not necessarily a relevant benchmark for a natural monopoly market, we must determine another benchmark in order to determine the deadweight loss that arises due to optimizing behavior of a monopolist. One such point of comparison is the case where the monopolist is forced to produce at a point where price equals average cost so that profit is equal to zero. This comparison is illustrated in Figure 11.7, below, as a comparison of points e^C and e^M. The deadweight loss due to monopoly is the loss from moving from point e^C to e^M (in other words, from moving away from marginal cost pricing). It is the shaded area in the figure, that is, the sum of the difference between the willingness to pay of consumers and marginal cost.

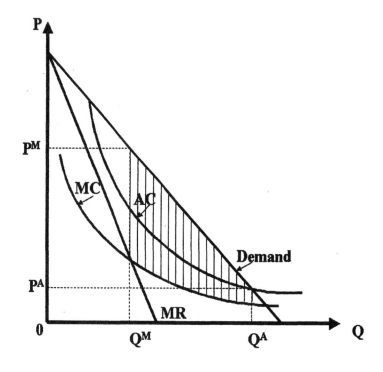

Figure 11.7

Exercise 10: *Suppose that, instead of forcing the monopolist to produce at the point where average cost equals demand in the figure above, the monopolist is forced to produce at a point where marginal cost equals demand or close its doors. Will the monopolist agree to produce at this point or will it shut down?*

a. The monopolist finds it more profitable to shut down than to produce at this point.
b. The monopolist finds it more profitable to produce at this point than to shut down.
c. We cannot say, since we do not know average variable cost.

Finally, we consider a monopolist that may operate many different production facilities (plants) in order to produce output. We answer two questions: "How will the monopolist allocate production across these plants?" and "How does the monopolist determine how much to produce in total?" For the purpose of comparison, recall that under perfect competition market output was composed of the sum of outputs from many small, independent, producers. Each producer's output was such that the marginal cost of that producer equaled price. Total market output was such that the horizontal sum of all the individual producers' output equaled market demand. In contrast, the market output under monopoly is composed of the output of a sole producer; however, this producer may operate many different production facilities. The monopolist allocates output across production facilities so as to equate the marginal cost of each facility. In other words, the monopolist maximizes the profitability of each unit of output by producing it at the facility where it has the lowest marginal cost. As a result, output will be reallocated across facilities until no facility has a lower marginal cost than any other. Further, the total amount that this monopolist wishes to supply to the market is determined by equating marginal revenue to the horizontal sum of these individual production facilities' marginal cost curves. This horizontal sum is called the **multi-plant marginal cost curve**. It represents the aggregate amount the monopolist can produce with all its plants, at each level of marginal cost. Summarizing:

- How does the monopolist optimally allocate output across plants? Such that $MC_1 = MC_2 = ... = MC_i = ... = MC_N$ where MC_i represents the marginal cost of plant i.

- How much does the monopolist optimally produce? Such that $MC_T = MR$, where MC_T is the horizontal sum of the individual plants' marginal cost curves.

These rules only apply to situations where plant-specific marginal costs are constant or increasing. With decreasing marginal costs, production will tend to be concentrated in a single plant. This is illustrated in the following exercise.

Exercise 11: *Suppose that a monopolist operates two plants with marginal cost schedules:*

$MC_1 = 10 - .5Q_1$ *for* $Q_1 \leq 20$ *and 0 for* $Q_1 > 20$
$MC_2 = 15 - Q_2$ *for* $Q_2 \leq 15$ *and 0 for* $Q_2 > 15$

where Q_1 is the output of plant 1 and Q_2 is the output of plant 2. Market demand is $P = 25 - Q$, where $Q = Q_1 + Q_2$. How much output should the monopolist produce in each of the two plants?

a. $Q = Q_1 = 10$ units should be produced in plant 1.
b. $Q = Q_2 = 10$ units should be produced in plant 2.
c. Output should be split across the plants, $Q_1 = Q_2 = 5$.
d. Either (a) or (b): both result in the same level of marginal cost.

Suppose that demand shifts in to P = 20 - Q. How much output should the monopolist produce in each of the two plants?

    a. $Q = Q_1 = 5$, no output is produced at plant 2.
    b. $Q = Q_2 = 5$, no output is produced at plant 1.
    c. $Q = Q_1 = 6.67$, no output is produced at plant 2.
    d. $Q = Q_2 = 6.67$, no output is produced at plant 1.

Now, let's look at the opposite of monopoly. A monopoly market has a single seller and many buyers. A **monopsony market** has a single buyer and many sellers. We will consider the case where the monopsonist is a firm that is the sole buyer of an input, which is supplied by many sellers. We will derive the profit maximizing equilibrium for the monopsonist, derive the equivalent of IEPR for this type of market, and analyze the welfare consequences of monopsony. You will see that it is analogous to our analysis of monopoly.

The basic profit maximization condition for the monopsonist can be expressed:

$$MRP_L = ME_L$$

where L is the input of which the monopsonist is the sole buyer. If L represents labor, then MRP_L is called the **marginal revenue product of labor**. It is the additional revenue that the monopsonist gets from using one more unit of labor input. In other words, it is the benefit of increasing the use of labor slightly. More precisely, the MRP_L will be the marginal product of labor times the revenue earned from this marginal product. In the simple case where the monopsonist sells its product in a competitive market, the marginal revenue product is, then:

$$MRP_L = P \times MP_L$$

where P is the price of the output and MP_L is the increase in units of output when input L is increased slightly.

Exercise 12: *Suppose that a monopsonist's production function satisfies the law of diminishing marginal returns in all its inputs. What is true about the monopsonist's marginal revenue product of labor if it sells output in a competitive market?*

    a. The marginal revenue product of its inputs is decreasing.
    b. The marginal revenue product of its inputs is increasing.
    c. The marginal revenue product of its inputs is a straight line.

ME_L is the **marginal expenditure on labor**. It is the increase in the firm's total cost when it employs an additional unit of labor. If labor is supplied at an increasing price (so that, for example, the labor supply curve, $w(L)$, slopes upward), then the marginal expenditure on labor is composed of two terms. The first term is the market wage. The second is the increase in wages that occurs due to the unit increase in employment times the total labor force (since the increase in wages applies to all employed persons). Hence, we have:

$$ME_L = w + L(\Delta w / \Delta L)$$

The two terms in ME_L are equivalent to the two terms we had in marginal revenue for the monopolist. The first term reflects the expenditure on the marginal unit, and the second term reflects the increase in expenditure on the *inframarginal* units. In the same way as marginal revenue lay below price for the monopolist, marginal expenditure on labor lies above the supply curve for labor for the monopsonist. This can be seen algebraically by noting that $\Delta w / \Delta L$ is positive when the supply curve for labor is upward sloping and can be seen graphically in Figure 11.7, below.

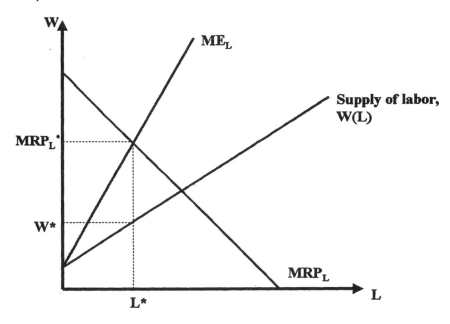

Figure 11.7

We can also see from the figure that the equilibrium wage, W*, paid to the input will be *less than* the marginal revenue product of labor, MRP_L^*. In other words, analogous to the output restriction of the monopolist, the monopsonist reduces its inputs because it takes into account the fact that this will reduce the price of the input. In contrast, a firm that is a perfect competitor on the input market would be so small that its own increased labor demand would not affect the market price. In other words, the firm would be a price taker on the input market. Hence, $ME_L = W^*$ and the firm would set the marginal revenue product of labor *equal to* the market wage, as shown in Figure 11.8.

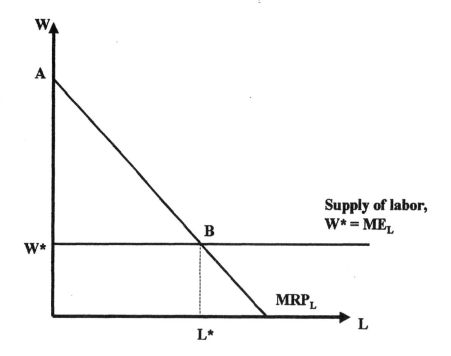

Figure 11.8

Exercise 13: *Suppose that a monopsonist in the labor market has a production function given by Q(K,L) = K + 2L, where Q is output, K is capital, and L is labor. Let the supply of labor be W(L) = 4L. The monopsonist sells its output on a perfectly competitive market at a price of P = $8. Find the marginal revenue product of labor curve. Which of the following statements is true?*

- a. The law of diminishing marginal returns holds for this production function.
- b. The MRP_L curve slopes downward.
- c. The MRP_L curve is flat.

Which of the following is the equation for the marginal expenditure for labor curve?

- a. $ME_L = 8L$
- b. $ME_L = 8$
- c. $ME_L = K + 2$

Find the monopsony equilibrium wage and labor demand. What is the difference between the marginal revenue product and the wage in equilibrium?

- a. 16.
- b. 0.
- c. 8.

The fact that the monopsonist can influence its input prices is called **buyer power**. Firms in perfectly competitive input markets do not have buyer power. Monopsonists do. In fact, we could measure this buyer power by rewriting the monopsony equilibrium condition, $MRP_L = ME_L$ in the form of an **inverse elasticity pricing rule for monopsony** in the same way as we developed an IEPR for monopoly. Hence, defining the elasticity of labor supply, $\sigma_{L,w}$, as $\sigma_{L,w} = (w/L)(\Delta L/\Delta w)$ we have:

$$ME_L = w + L\Delta w/\Delta L = w[1 + (L/w)(\Delta w/\Delta L)] \text{ or...}$$

$$ME_L = w(1 + 1/\sigma_{L,w})$$

So that the profit maximization condition for the monopsonist becomes:

$$MRP_L = ME_L = w(1 + 1/\sigma_{L,w}) \text{ or...}$$

$$(MRP_L - w)/w = 1/\sigma_{L,w}$$

This final expression is the IEPR for the monopsonist. In other words, the percent deviation between the marginal revenue product and the wage depends, in equilibrium, on the elasticity of supply of labor in the same way as the percentage deviation between the marginal cost and the price of the monopolist depended on the price elasticity of demand. We can use this equation, in turn, to express the amount of buyer power in the input market.

Exercise 14: *In Figure 11.8, which of the following statements is (are) true at point (L*,W*)?*

    a. The monopsonist has no buyer power.
    b. The percentage deviation between MRP_L and W is zero.
    c. Even though $MRP_L = W$ in equilibrium, IEPR holds because the supply of labor is flat.

    The monopsonist's surplus is measured as the area under the MRP_L curve and above the equilibrium wage. In other words, it is the benefit earned on each unit of input net of the input's price. Since the monopsonist is the buyer of the input, this surplus is equivalent to consumers' surplus in our model of monopoly. The surplus earned by labor is measured as the area under the equilibrium wage and above the supply curve of labor. In other words, it is the benefit earned by each "unit of labor" net of the wage that would be required to induce each "unit of labor" to work. Since labor is the input that is supplied in this model, this surplus is equivalent to producers' surplus in our model of monopoly. By comparing the monopsony solution, (L*,W*), to the competitive solution, (L_C, W_C), we can deduce that the monopsony results in a deadweight loss of area B + C in Figure 11.9. This represents the loss due to the input restriction of the monopsonist: there are unrealized gains from trade since units of labor that would be willing to work at a wage that is less than their marginal revenue product go unemployed.

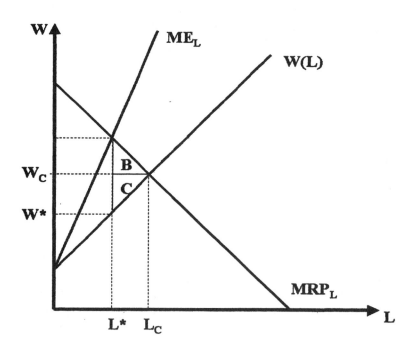

Figure 11.9

Exercise 15: *In the following graph (taken from the answer to Exercise 13), what is the deadweight loss to monopsony? What is consumers' surplus? What is producers' surplus?*

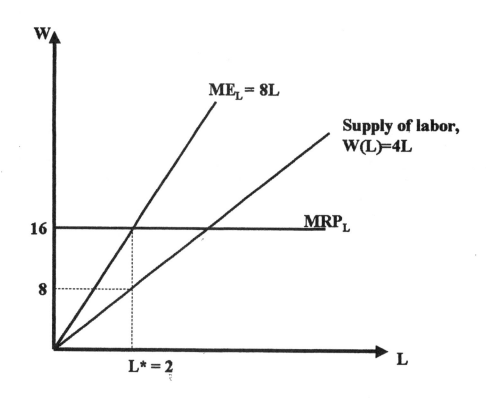

a. DWL = 16, CS = 16, PS = 16
b. DWL = 32, CS = 0, PS = 8
c. DWL = 8, CS = 16, PS = 8

What is the deadweight loss of monopsony in Figure 11.8? What is consumers' surplus? What is producers' surplus?

a. DWL = 0, CS = AW*B, PS = 0
b. DWL = 0, CS = AW*B, PS = W*L*
c. DWL = 0, CS = AW*B, PS = W*L*/2

Chapter Review Questions

1. Let a monopolist face inverse demand $P(Q) = 100 - Q$ and marginal cost $MC(Q) = 20$.   What is the profit maximizing price and quantity for the monopolist? Use IEPR to derive the price elasticity of demand at the profit maximizing price.

Answer:

The profit maximization condition of the monopolist is $MR(Q) = MC(Q)$. Calculating $MR(Q)$, we have $MR(Q) = P + Q(\Delta P/\Delta Q) = 100 - Q + Q(-1) = 100 - 2Q$. Note that marginal revenue has the same intercept as inverse demand, but twice the slope. This will generally be true for linear demand. $MC(Q)$ is given at 20 so that $MR(Q) = MC(Q) \Leftrightarrow 100 - 2Q = 20$. Solving, we have $Q^* = 40$. Substituting into inverse demand, we have $P^* = 100 - 40 = 60$.

IEPR says that $(P - MC)/P = -1/\varepsilon_{Q,P}$ must hold at the profit maximizing price and quantity. Hence, using our calculation of P^*, we have $(60 - 20)/60 = -1/\varepsilon_{Q,P}$. Therefore, we can solve to obtain $\varepsilon_{Q,P} = -3/2$. As a cross-check of this figure, we can verify that the monopolist is, indeed, operating on the elastic portion of the demand curve since elasticity is less than -1.

2. Let a monopolist have total cost $TC(Q) = 2Q$ and face an inverse demand of $P(Q) = 20 - Q$.

    a. What is the profit maximizing output and price? At this point, what is the profit of the monopolist? How does it compare to producer's surplus?

    b. Now, suppose that $TC(Q) = 2 + 2Q$. What is the profit maximizing output and price? How do profit and producer's surplus compare at this point?

Answer:

a. As in the first review question, we solve for the profit maximizing output and price by setting $MR(Q) = MC(Q)$. In this case, $MR(Q) = 20 - Q + Q(-1) = 20 - 2Q$. Recalling from Chapter 8 that $MC(Q) = \Delta TC/\Delta Q$, we have $MC(Q) = 2$. Hence, $MR(Q) = MC(Q) \Leftrightarrow 20 - 2Q = 2 => Q^* = 9$. Substituting into the formula for inverse demand, we have $P^* = 11$. Profit for the monopolist is $\pi^* = TR(Q^*) - $

$TC(Q^*) = P^*Q^* - TC(Q^*) = 9(11) - 2(9) = 81$. Producer's surplus is the area under equilibrium price and above the marginal cost curve for all units sold. Hence, $PS = (11-2)(9) = 81$. Therefore, profit and producer's surplus are the same.

b. If $TC(Q) = 2 + 2Q$, then marginal cost is still $MC(Q) = 2$ and $MR(Q)$ is unchanged as well (since demand has not changed). Therefore, the profit maximization condition is the same and $Q^* = 9$, $P^* = 11$. $\pi^* = 9(11) - 2 - 2(9) = 79$. Producer's surplus is the same at $(11-2)(9) = 81$. Hence, producer's surplus is greater than profit. Since producer's surplus should differ from profit by the (sunk) fixed cost of production, this is reasonable: $PS - \pi^* = 2 = FC$.

3. Suppose that an employer is a monopsonist in a labor market. The monopsonist's demand for labor is $w(L) = 500 - 4L$. The supply of labor is given by $w(L) = 20 + 4L$.

   a. What is the monopsonist's profit maximizing quantity of labor and what is the equilibrium wage rate?

   b. Suppose that the monopsonist is required by the government to pay the perfectly competitive wage rate. By how much would the monopsonist's wage bill increase?

Answer:

a. In order to find the monopsonist's profit maximizing quantity of labor, we must set $MRP_L = ME_L$. The MRP_L is the monopsonist's demand for labor, and is given as $w(L) = 500 - 4L$. $ME_L = w(L) + L(\Delta w/\Delta L) = 20 + 4L + L(4) = 20 + 8L$. Hence, we have $500 - 4L = 20 + 8L \Leftrightarrow 480 = 12L$ so that $L^* = 40$. The equilibrium wage rate is $20 + 4(40) = 180$.

b. The perfectly competitive wage would be the wage at which demand and supply are equal in the labor market or $500 - 4L = 20 + 4L$ so that $480 = 8L$ or $L^C = 60$. Equilibrium wage at this point is $w^C = 20 + 4(60) = 260$. The wage bill increases by $L^C w^C - L^* w^* = 60(260) - 40(180) = 8400$.

Problem Set

1. Let a monopolist face inverse demand in the output market of $P(Q) = 10 - Q$, where Q is output and P is the price of output.

   a. Derive the equation of the marginal revenue curve of the monopolist.

   b. Suppose that the monopolist is also a monopsonist in the labor market. Suppose that the production function of the firm is $Q = 2L^{1/2}$, with $MP_L = L^{-1/2}$. What is the equation of the marginal revenue product of labor of the monopolist?

2. Suppose that the monopolist faces a demand curve of the following form: If $P > 10$, $Q(P) = 0$. If $P \leq 10$, $Q(P) = 20$.

   a. What is the price elasticity of demand for $P < 10$? What is the price elasticity of demand at $P = 10$?

   b. Let marginal cost be constant at $MC = 1$. What is the monopolist's profit maximizing price and quantity? Does IEPR hold at this point?

3. Suppose that a monopolist faces an inverse demand curve in the output market of $P(Q) = 20 - Q$, where Q is output and P is the price of output.

   a. Calculate the equation of the marginal revenue curve of the monopolist. What is the difference between this curve and the inverse demand curve?

   b. Using your answer to (a), calculate $MR(1)$, $MR(2)$, and $MR(3)$. Now, calculate the change in total revenue of increasing output from 1 to 2 units. Calculate the change in total revenue of increasing output from 2 to 3 units. Are these the same as $MR(1)$, $MR(2)$, and $MR(3)$? Why?

   c. Let $TC(Q) = 10 + 10Q$ for this monopolist. Calculate $MC(Q)$, $AC(Q)$ and $AVC(Q)$. Calculate the profit maximizing output and price for the monopolist.

   d. Suppose that $TC(Q) = 30 + 10Q$ and the entire fixed cost is not sunk. What is the profit maximizing output for the monopolist? If the entire fixed cost is sunk, what is the profit maximizing output? Why?

   e. Suppose that the monopolist produces an output level of $Q = 8$. Calculate the price elasticity of demand at this point. Does IEPR hold at this point if $TC(Q) = 10 + 10Q$? Why?

4. (This problem gives you practice with applications of the idea of marginal revenue.)

   There are two countries, country 1 and country 2. The total capital invested in country 1 is $K_1 = (1 - t_1 + t_2)$, where t_1 is country 1's tax rate and t_2 is country 2's tax rate. Suppose that country 2's tax rate is fixed and constant.

   a. Country 1's revenue from capital taxation is $t_1 K_1$. What is the marginal revenue that country 1 earns from an increase in its own tax rate?

   b. Suppose that country 1 wishes to maximize the revenues from capital taxation. Using marginal reasoning, write the conditions that determine the optimal level of taxation for country 1. What is country 1's optimal tax rate?

5. Consider a monopolist who is faced with the inverse demand function $P = 200 - 0.5Q$, where P is the price and Q is the output. The marginal cost of production is $50.

a. Find the profit maximizing quantity and price that the monopolist would choose.

b. What is the total welfare (i.e. the sum of consumer surplus and producer surplus) at the monopoly outcome?

c. Explain what you understand by the term 'Dead Weight Loss' and calculate it for this case. Why is it positive?

d. Suppose the government gives the monopolist a subsidy, s, per unit of output produced and sold. Explain how this would affect the level of total welfare.

6. Suppose that any firm that produces output, Q, for a market has total cost of $TC(Q) = aQ$. Is this industry a natural monopoly? Suppose now that the government imposes a lump sum franchise fee of T on any firm that enters the industry. Is the industry a natural monopoly now?

7. Consider a firm that produces a single product Q using only one type of input: labor (L). The firm is a perfect competitor in the output market (i.e. takes the price of Q given) but is a monopsonist in the labor market.

a. Determine the profit-maximizing level of employment and show that the monopsonist under-employs labor relative to the competitive equilibrium.

b. What is the effect of a minimum wage (set by the government) on the level of employment?

8. Suppose that a monopolist faces inverse demand of $P(Q) = a-bQ$, and a total cost of $TC(Q) = cQ$.

a. Calculate the monopolist's profit maximizing price and quantity. What is profit at this point?

b. Suppose that a profit tax, which requires the monopolist to pay 10% of any profits earned to the government, is imposed on the monopolist instead of the excise tax. In other words, the monopolist's profit is now $\pi(Q) = [TR(Q) - TC(Q)].9$. What is the new equilibrium price? Why?

Exam *(60 minutes: Closed book, closed notes)*

1. Suppose that the price elasticity of demand is constant at $\varepsilon_{Q,P} = -5$. A monopolist currently sets its profit maximizing price at $P^* = 50$.

a. What is the monopolist's marginal cost?

    b. Assuming that marginal cost is constant at the level you derived in (a), would you recommend that the monopolist sell additional output at half-price if it does not affect the price and sales of the monopolist's existing units?

2. Suppose that the minimum efficient scale of an industry is at 100 units of output. At this point, average cost equals 50. Inverse demand for this industry is $P(Q) = 300 - 2Q$, where Q is industry output. Is this industry a natural monopoly? Suppose that demand shifts to $P(Q) = 150 - 2Q$. Is the industry a natural monopoly now?

3. A monopolist faces inverse demand of $P(Q) = 18 - 2Q$, where Q is output. The monopolist can produce output in two plants, with marginal cost curves of $MC_1(Q_1) = 5 + Q_1$ and $MC_2(Q_2) = 2 + 2Q_2$, respectively, where Q_1 is the output produced in plant 1 and Q_2 is the output produced in plant 2.

    a. Calculate the profit maximizing output to produce in plant 1, plant 2, and in total. What is the firm's profit maximizing price and profit?

    b. Suppose that labor costs increase at plant 2 so that $MC_1(Q_1) = 6 + 2Q_1$ so that MC_1 lies everywhere above MC_2. Is it optimal to shut down plant 1? Why?

4. Let $w(L) = a + bL$. What is the equation of the marginal expenditure for labor curve? How does its slope compare with the slope of the labor supply curve?

Answers to Exercises

1. The correct answer is statement (a). We can see from panel (a) that the reasoning in the text results in the monopolist increasing output to Q*. This is an example of a case where marginal cost need not be rising for the monopolist to maximize profits by setting marginal revenue equal to marginal cost. Therefore, statement (b) is incorrect. In panel (b), all output levels below Q* result in a higher marginal cost than marginal revenue. Therefore, it cannot be profit maximizing for the monopolist to produce Q* in panel (b)! This means that statement (c) is incorrect. On the other hand, if output is increased beyond Q*, the additional units become profitable. As drawn, the region for which marginal revenue exceeds marginal cost is very small. This suggests that the monopolist cannot make a positive profit by producing positive Q. Therefore, statement (d) cannot be correct. The best that the monopolist can do in panel (b) is, then, to produce zero and statement (a) is correct.

We can generalize from this case to say that when marginal cost falls faster than marginal revenue, the profit maximization condition does not have an interior solution, and so we must check for corner solutions.

2. Statements (a), (b), and (c) are correct. The inverse demand curve is the same as the average revenue curve for a monopolist, so statement (a) is correct. Calculating marginal revenue and noting that $(\Delta P/\Delta Q)$ is the slope of the inverse demand curve, we have $MR(Q) = P + Q(\Delta P/\Delta Q) = 100 - 25Q + Q(-25) = 100 - 50Q$. Therefore, statements (b) and (c) are correct since the marginal revenue curve slope is -50, which is twice as steep as the inverse market demand slope of -25. Finally, at $Q = 2$, $MR(Q) = 100 - 50(2) = 0$. At any higher level of Q, $MR(Q)$ is negative and at lower levels of Q, $MR(Q)$ is positive. Therefore, statement (d) is incorrect.

3. The correct answer to the first part of the question is (b). If $P(Q) = 10 - 2Q$, then $MR(Q) = 10 - 2Q + Q(-2) = 10 - 4Q$. Setting this equal to marginal cost, we have $10 - 4Q = Q$ or $Q^* = 2$. At this output, $P^* = 10 - 2(2) = 6$.

   The correct answer to the second part of the question is (b). Profit = $TR(Q^*) - TC(Q^*) = P^*Q^* - TC(Q^*) = 6(2) - (1+.5(2^2)) = 12 - 1 - 2 = 9$.

   The correct answer to the third part of the question is (b). While the marginal cost is the same (since the portion of total cost that changes with Q is still $.5Q^2$), the average cost is now $TC(Q)/Q = 11/Q + .5Q = AC(Q)$. This is higher than it was before. At this higher average cost level, we can calculate profits for the monopolist at the profit maximizing output of Q^* as Profit = $TR(Q^*) - TC(Q^*) = 2(6) - 11 - .5(2^2) = 12 - 11 - 2 = -1$. Therefore, the monopolist would do better to produce zero.

4. The correct answer is (a). For inverse demand curve $P_0(Q)$, we have $MR_0(Q) = 10 - 4Q$. Setting this equal to marginal cost, we have $10 - 4Q = 2 \Rightarrow Q_0 = 2$ and $P_0 = 10 - 2(2) = 6$. For inverse demand curve $P_1(Q)$, we have $MR_1(Q) = 12 - 4Q$. Setting this equal to marginal cost, we have $12 - 4Q = 2 \Rightarrow Q_1 = 2.5$ and $P_1 = 12 - 2(2.5) = 7$. Therefore, $P_1 > P_0$ and so equilibrium price has risen.

5. The correct answer is (c). Recall from Chapter 2 that demand that is of the form $Q = aP^{-b}$ has a constant elasticity of -b. Hence, $MR(Q) = P(1+1/\varepsilon_{Q,P}) = P(1 + 1/-b)$.

6. The correct answer to the first part of the question is (c). The percentage contribution margin is $-1/-2 = 1/2$ in both cases. In other words, the *percentage* contribution margin does not change in equilibrium -- even if demand *shifts* a great deal -- as long as the elasticity does not change. Note, however, that the absolute contribution, P - MC, may change quite a bit when demand shifts even if the percentage contribution does not change.

   The correct answer to the second part of the question is (c). The Lerner Index equals $-1/\varepsilon_{Q,P}$ in equilibrium. We know that this does not change with the change in demand, so that the Lerner Index does not change as well.

7. The correct answer to the first part of the question is (b). The profit maximizing output is determined by MR = 100 - 2Q = 50 = MC. Solving, we have Q* = 25 and P* = 100 - Q* = 75. Elasticity equals $\varepsilon_{Q,P} = (\Delta Q/\Delta P)(P/Q) = -1(75/25) = -3$.

   The correct answer to the second part of the question is (b). Using the same method as in part (a), we have MR = 100 - 2Q = 60 = MC. Solving, we have Q** = 20 and P** = 80. $\varepsilon_{Q,P} = (\Delta Q/\Delta P)(P/Q) = -1(80/20) = -4$.

   The correct answer to the third part of the question is (b). Total revenue before the change is Q*P* = 25(75) = 1875. Total revenue after the change is Q**P** = 20(80) = 1600. Total revenue has decreased when output has decreased.

   Notice that the monopolist operates on the elastic portion of the demand curve in both cases.

8. The correct answer is (a). The pass-through rate at the new price is $(\Delta P/P)(MC/\Delta MC) = 5/80(60/10) = 3/8$, which is less than one. Therefore, the monopolist will pass along only a portion of the increase in marginal costs to consumers.

9. The answer to the first part of the question is (a). The industry is a natural monopoly since average cost intersects demand at Q = 2, where average cost is at a minimum. In other words, average cost is falling everywhere at all relevant levels of demand. If average cost is decreasing at all relevant levels of demand, the total cost of any given quantity of output is minimized if a single firm produces all output. This is the definition of a natural monopoly.

   The answer to the second part of the question is (b). The industry is no longer a natural monopoly when demand shifts out since average cost rises significantly before intersecting demand. In fact, demand equals average cost at Q = 3. Here, a single firm producing 3 units incurs an average cost of 11.5 while two firms producing 1.5 units each incur average costs of 10.625 each. Therefore, we have TC(3) = 3(11.5) > TC(1.5) + TC(1.5) = (10.625) (1.5 + 1.5). Hence, the industry is no longer a natural monopoly at this higher level of demand.

10. The correct answer is (a). When marginal cost is falling, it lies below average variable cost so that it is unprofitable for the monopolist to produce any positive level of output at this point. The monopolist will shut down.

11. The correct answer to the first part of the question is (d). Since marginal cost is decreasing at both plants, the cost-minimizing way to produce is to allocate all production to a single plant, whichever can produce the output most inexpensively. The two marginal cost curves are decreasing and intersect at an output level of 10: at less than 10 units of output, plant 1 is cheaper and at more than 10 units of output, plant 2 is cheaper.

   At an output of 10, both plants generate a marginal cost of 5. Marginal revenue at an output of 10 is MR = 25 - 2(10) = 5 as well. As a result, either allocating all output to plant 1 (and producing 10 units total) or allocating all output to plant 2 (and producing 10 units total) is optimal since both strategies equate marginal revenue to marginal cost and produce the output in the least-cost way.

The correct answer to the second part of the question is (c). It is still the case that the optimal strategy for the monopolist is to allocate all production to only a single plant, since marginal cost is decreasing. We must just determine which plant has the lower cost at the profit maximizing market output. Setting marginal revenue equal to marginal cost, we find that the profit maximizing output with all production in plant 1 is $20 - 2Q_1 = 10 - .5Q_1$ or $Q_1 = 6.67$. If all production is concentrated in plant 2, we have $20 - 2Q_2 = 15 - Q_2$ or $Q_2 = 5$. At either of these output levels, plant 1 produces the output at a lower marginal cost so that the profit maximizing decision is to produce all output in plant 1. 6.67 units are produced in total.

12. The correct answer is (a). The law of diminishing marginal returns summarizes the fact that the marginal product of each input is decreasing as output increases when all other inputs are held constant. This means that, as output increases, the marginal revenue product decreases since the (constant) price times the marginal product will decrease. The marginal product need not decline in a straight line, so the marginal revenue product need not be a straight line either.

13. The correct answer to the first part of the question is statement (c). The marginal product of labor for this production function is $\Delta Q/\Delta L = 2$, which is constant. Therefore, statement (a) is incorrect. Further, $MRP_L = P \times MP_L = 8 \times 2 = 16$ so that MRP_L is flat, not declining. Therefore, statement (c) and not statement (b) is correct.

The correct answer to the second part of the question is (a). The marginal expenditure on labor is $ME_L = w + L(\Delta w/\Delta L) = 4L + L(4) = 8L$.

The correct answer to the third part of the question is (c). In equilibrium $MRP_L = ME_L$ or $16 = 8L$. Therefore, $L^* = 2$. At this labor demand, the equilibrium wage is found from the labor supply equation: $W(L^*) = 4L^* = 4(2) = 8$. Therefore, the difference between MRP_L and $W(L)$ in equilibrium is $16 - 8 = 8$. Graphically, we have:

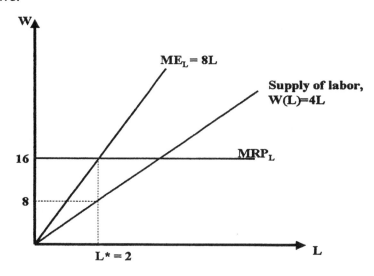

14. All the statements are correct. When the labor supply curve is flat, the marginal expenditure curve equals the wage. Hence, there is no difference between the point where MRP_L equals the ME_L and the point where MRP_L equals the wage. As a result, there is no buyer power because MRP_L equals the wage in equilibrium (statements (a) and (b)). If the labor supply function is flat, then the elasticity of labor supply, $\sigma_{L,W}$, is infinite. Hence, the percentage deviation between W and MRP_L is zero (the left-hand side of IEPR). The inverse of the elasticity is also zero ($1/\sigma_{L,W} = 1/\infty = 0$) so that IEPR holds.

15. The correct answer to the first part of the question is (c). The deadweight loss is area A, below or $(16-8)(4-2)(1/2) = 8$. The consumers' surplus is $(16-8)(2) = 16$, which is area C. The producers' surplus is $(8-0)(2)(1/2) = 8$ or area B.

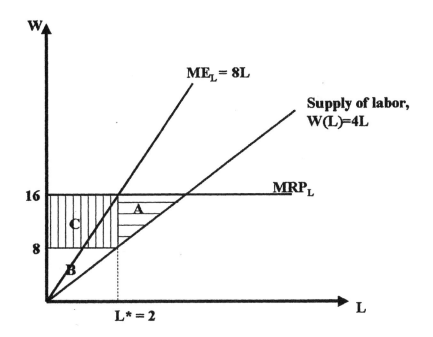

The correct answer to the second part of the question is (a). The deadweight loss is zero because the monopsony and competitive solutions coincide. Consumers' surplus is the entire triangle above the wage and below the MRP_L curve. Producers' surplus is zero, since the labor supply function is constant at the equilibrium wage.

Answers to Problem Set

1.

    a. $MR(Q) = P + Q(\Delta P/\Delta Q) = 10 - Q + Q(-1) = 10 - 2Q$.

    b. $MRP_L = MP_L(MR(Q)) = L^{-1/2}(10-2Q) = L^{-1/2}(10 - 2(2L^{1/2})) = 10L^{-1/2}-4$.

2.

  a. If P < 10, then demand is completely inelastic at Q(P) = 20. More precisely, $\varepsilon_{Q,P} = (\Delta Q/\Delta P)(P/Q) = 0 \times P/20 = 0$. At P = 10, for an increase in price, we have $\varepsilon_{Q,P} = (\Delta Q/\Delta P)(P/Q) = (-20)(10/20) = -10$. For a decrease in price, we have $\varepsilon_{Q,P} = (0/-1)(10/20) = 0$.

  b. If MC = 1, then the monopolist maximizes profit by setting P* = 10 and selling 20 units. This can be seen by simply calculating profit at different prices. For all prices above P = 10 the monopolist cannot sell anything and makes zero profits. For all prices P ≤ 10 the monopolist sells exactly 20 units. Since the quantity sold is not affected by the price charged, profits are maximized by setting the highest possible price over this range, that is, by setting p = 10.

  IEPR at the point P = 10 would say that $(10 - 1)/10 = -1/\varepsilon_{Q,P}$. At P = 10, however, elasticity is either 0 or -10. This suggests that IEPR does not hold at this point. This is not surprising, since elasticity does not change continuously at this "corner" point the same way as the marginal revenue jumps at this corner point. In other words, since IEPR is derived from MR = MC and since marginal revenue does not equal marginal cost at the profit maximizing point, there is no reason for IEPR to hold either.

3.

  a. $MR(Q) = P + Q(\Delta P/\Delta Q) = 20 - Q - Q = 20 - 2Q$. The marginal revenue curve has the same intercept as inverse demand, but twice the slope.

  b. MR(1) = 18; MR(2) = 16; MR(3) = 14. $\Delta TR(1 \rightarrow 2) = 17$. $\Delta TR(2 \rightarrow 3) = 15$. The change in revenue for each one unit change in output is the midpoint between the marginal revenue at the old and new output levels. This is because the formula we have for marginal revenue is true for very small changes in output. A one unit change in output is already a "large" change, so it is not quite the marginal revenue at either the old or the new output level. Instead, it is an average of the two.

  c. MC(Q) = 10. AC(Q) = 10/Q + 10. AVC(Q) = 10. The profit maximizing output and price for the monopolist are derived as follows: MC = MR => 20 − 2Q = 10 or Q* = 5. P* = 15 (from the equation for inverse demand). Note that price covers average cost at this point, so the monopolist prefers to produce a positive quantity than to shut down operations.

  d. If the total cost rises to 30 + 10Q, and if the fixed cost is not sunk, the firm would prefer to shut down and not produce since its price when it operates does not cover the average cost, but it makes a profit of zero if it shuts down. If the entire fixed cost is sunk, then the firm prefers to produce at the point Q*,P*, since it earns a price that is higher than its average variable cost, but loses the entire fixed cost even if it shuts down operations.

  e. $\varepsilon_{Q,P} = (\Delta Q/\Delta P)(P/Q)$. At Q = 8, we have P = 12 and $\varepsilon_{Q,P} = -1(12/8) = -1.5$. IEPR says that $(P - MC)/P = -1/\varepsilon_{Q,P}$ so that $(12 - 10)/12 = -1/-1.5$ or

$1/6 = 2/3$. IEPR does not hold at this point. This is not surprising, since IEPR was derived for the equilibrium point and $Q = 8$ is not the equilibrium.

4.

a. The marginal revenue from the increase in taxation will be the baseline rate of capital investment, K_1, plus any decrease in investment that occurs when the taxation increases or $\Delta K_1/\Delta t_1$ times whatever the rate of taxation is, t_1. Summarizing, then, the formula for the marginal revenue would be $K_1 + t_1 \Delta K_1/\Delta t_1$ In this case, a small increase in, say, one unit of t_1 would cause K_1 to decrease by one unit since $K_1 = 1 - t_1 + t_2$ (and t_2 is fixed). We have, then, $\Delta K_1/\Delta t_1 = -1$. Hence, $MR = (1 - t_1 + t_2) + (-1)t_1 = 1-2t_1 + t_2$.

b. The maximization conditions are that the benefit from increasing the tax has to equal the cost from the increase. In this case, we do not have a marginal cost term on the right hand side, as the government cares only about revenues: the marginal cost is effectively zero in this case. We have, then, $1 - 2t_1 + t_2 = 0$. This can be solved for t_1^* so that $t_1^* = (1+t_2)/2$. Notice that this result implies that an exogenous increase in taxation in country 2 will result in an *increase* in the optimal tax rate in country 1.

5.

a. The profit maximizing price and quantity are determined by the condition $MR = MC$. Using the formula for marginal revenue, we see that $MR = 200 - .5Q - .5Q = 200 - Q$. Setting this equal to marginal cost, we have $200 - Q = 50$ or $Q^* = 150$. Substituting back into the equation for demand we have $P^* = 125$.

b. Consumers' surplus is the area of the triangle formed by the choke price (200), the current price (125), and the output (150). Hence, we have CS $= (1/2)(150)(200-125)=5625$. Producer's surplus is the area of the square formed by the current price (125), the marginal cost (50), and the output (150). Hence, we have $(125-50)(150)=11250$. Total welfare is the sum of these numbers, or TW $= 5625 + 11250 = 16875$.

c. The deadweight loss is a measure of inefficiency in the monopoly market. The total welfare under perfect competition in this market would be the area of the triangle formed by the choke price (200), marginal cost (50) and the output that would be produced if it were priced at marginal cost (300). Hence, total welfare under competition would equal $(1/2)(200-50)(300) = 22500$. The difference between this and the total welfare under monopoly should be the deadweight loss, DWL $= 5625$.

d. When a subsidy is given per unit produced, the monopolist will choose his output such that $MR + s = MC$. This will increase the optimal output and the equilibrium price will decrease. Hence, consumers' surplus rises, as does total surplus (not taking into account the funding of the subsidy).

6. If TC(Q) = aQ, then AC(Q) = a = MC(Q). Since average and marginal costs are flat (and not falling), a single firm's cost of producing a given amount of output is no lower than many firms' costs of producing the same total amount among them. Hence, this is not a natural monopoly. On the other hand, if we introduce a lump sum franchise fee of T, we have TC(Q) = T + aQ so that AC(Q) = T/Q + a. This is falling over all levels of Q, so that the industry is now a natural monopoly.

7.
   a. Referring to figures 11.7 and 11.8, reproduced below, we have seen that the monopsonist restricts its use of inputs in the same way as the monopolist restricts its production of output: since the monopsonist takes into account the effect of its own hiring on the prevailing wage, it hires less than a firm in a perfectly competitive labor market. Graphically, the marginal expenditure on labor is rising for the monopsonist, whereas it is flat for the perfect competitor. Both types of firm set the marginal expenditure on labor input equal to the marginal revenue product of the input in order to hire so as to maximize profits. This is based on the same type of "marginal reasoning" as we have seen several times in optimization problems throughout the book. The wage paid by the monopsonist is less than the marginal revenue product of labor, while the wage paid by the perfect competitor is equal to the marginal revenue product of labor.

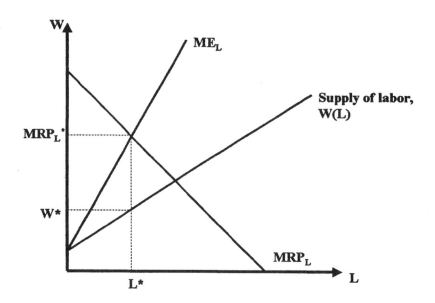

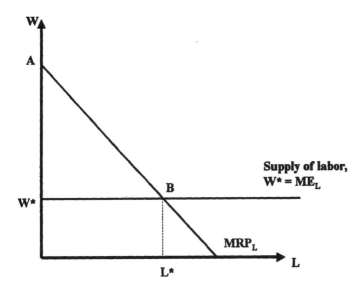

b. The effect of a minimum wage set by the government on the monopsonist is illustrated in the diagram, below. In this case, the monopsonist sets the wage at w^M and hires L^M workers. Imposing a binding minimum wage, w^{min}, causes hiring to *increase* to L^{min}, as the monopsonist now perceives that wage is no longer sensitive to its hiring decision. The wage, then, will be set equal to the marginal revenue product in order to maximize profits.

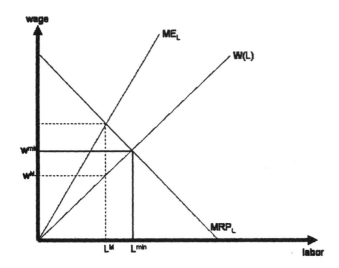

8.

   a. Setting marginal revenue equal to marginal cost, we have MR = a - 2bQ = c or Q* = (a-c)/2b and P* = (a+c)/2. Profit = TR - TC = [(a+c)/2](a-c)/2b - c(a-c)/2b = (a-c)²/4b

   b. The profit tax reduces total profits earned, but does not affect the comparison of marginal revenue and marginal cost. In other words, the monopolist maximizes .9π(Q) the same way as it maximizes π(Q) since the profit curve has simply shifted down by 10%, but has not changed shape. This is shown graphically below.

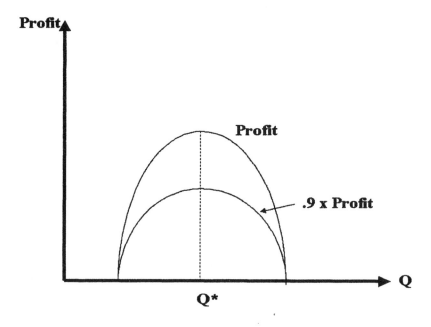

Answers to Exam

1.

    a. If the monopolist is currently maximizing profits, then IEPR must hold at the profit maximizing point. Hence, $(P - MC)/P = -1/\varepsilon_{Q,P}$. We have $P = 50$ and $\varepsilon_{Q,P} = -5$ so that, substituting, we have $(50 - MC)/50 = -1/-5$ or $MC = 40$ (at the equilibrium point).

    b. Half of $P*$ is 25. This is below marginal cost so that it is not profitable to sell these units even if these sales do not affect the price and sales of the monopolist's existing units.

2. The industry is a natural monopoly if the total cost of producing a given amount of output is lower when a single firm produces it than when many firms divide the output among them. Graphically, falling average cost over the relevant output range for demand satisfies this condition. Average cost that rises very slightly over the relevant output range may also satisfy this condition.

From the equation of demand, we know that when price equals 50, demand equals 100. From the information in the problem we also know that average cost falls continually as output increases to 100, at which point average cost is 50. Hence, we can say that average cost intersects demand at $P = AC = 50$ and this is also the minimum point on the average cost curve. As a result, we know that average cost falls continually until it intersects demand. This means that for all relevant output levels, the industry is a monopoly. The average cost and demand are pictured in the graph below.

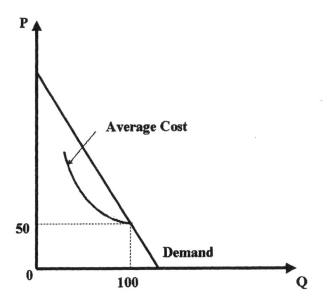

If demand shifts in to $P(Q) = 150 - 2Q$, then at a price of 50, demand is only 50. The shift is parallel and inward, so from the graph it can be seen that average cost falls over the entire relevant range of output. On the other hand, if demand shifts out to, say, $P(Q) = 500 - 2Q$, then we need to know how average cost behaves at output levels higher than 100 in order to answer the question. If average cost is flat or rises very slightly for output levels higher than 100, then the industry is a natural monopoly. If average cost rises sharply, however, the industry is no longer a natural monopoly.

3.

    a. First, we solve for output as a function of marginal cost so that:

$$Q_1 = MC_1 - 5$$
$$Q_2 = MC_2/2 - 1$$

Summing these expressions for $MC_1 = MC_2$, we have $Q = MC_T(3/2) - 6$, where MC_T is the common level of marginal cost in the two plants and $Q = Q_1 + Q_2$ is the total output of the firm. Inverting this expression to obtain MC_T, we have $MC_T = (2/3)Q + 4$.

Marginal revenue can be derived from inverse demand as $MR(Q) = 18 - 4Q$. Therefore, the profit maximization condition of the monopolist is $18 - 4Q = (2/3)Q + 4$ or $Q^* = 3$.

In order to decide how much to allocate to each plant, we recall that the marginal costs of the plants must be equal, and furthermore must equal the aggregate marginal cost, MC_T. At $Q^* = 3$, $MC_T = 6$. Therefore, $Q_1^* = 1$ and $Q_2^* = 2$.

b. If $MC_2 = 6 + 2Q_2$, then it is not necessarily better to concentrate all output in a single plant since the firm may still obtain lower costs overall by splitting output between the two plants, as illustrated below. Suppose, for example, that the firm desires to produce 10 units of output. The aggregate cost may be reduced by making the last unit that is produced in plant 1 the first unit produced at plant 2. This is because the marginal cost of producing a single unit at plant 2 is only 6, while the marginal cost of producing the tenth unit is plant 1 is $2 + 2(10) = 22$.

4. $ME_L = w(L) + L(\Delta w/\Delta L) = a + bL + L(b) = a + 2bL$. This is twice the slope of the labor supply curve. Recall that, in the case of a monopolist facing linear demand, marginal revenue had twice the slope of demand but the same intercept. In other words, for $P(Q) = a - bQ$, we had $MR(Q) = a - 2bQ$. The case of marginal expenditure is exactly analogous for the monopsonist in the case of linear labor supply.

Chapter 12: Capturing Surplus

In Chapter 11, we studied the monopolist's pricing decision under the assumption that the monopolist could set only a single, **uniform price** for its product. In other words, the monopolist had to charge the same price for every unit of output sold. We saw how a uniform pricing monopolist could use market power to capture more surplus than a perfectly competitive firm. In this chapter, we will examine how a monopolist can do even better than this by pursuing price and non-price strategies. First, we will suppose that the monopolist may charge more than one price for the product. This is called **price discrimination**. For example, the firm may charge different prices for different units of the same good, or it may charge different prices for the same good to different consumer groups. We will also examine how firms may capture more surplus by selling two related goods as a package, rather than separately. This is called a strategy of **bundling** or **tying**. Finally, we will examine how **advertising** can be used to increase the surplus captured by the firm.

In Chapter 11, we saw that a uniform pricing monopolist's profit maximization condition is to set output such that marginal revenue equals marginal cost. For the monopoly depicted in Figure 12.1, this results in an amount of consumer's surplus, triangle AP^Me^M, an amount of producer's surplus, area $0P^Me^MB$, and a deadweight loss equal to the shaded area in the figure.

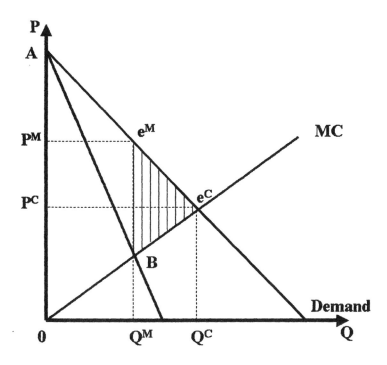

Figure 12.1

First, we wish to know how the monopolist might capture even more surplus by following a strategy of price discrimination. We will analyze three traditional types (or "degrees") of price discrimination:

1. First Degree Price Discrimination or "Perfect" Price Discrimination

First degree price discrimination means that the monopolist sells different units of a product for different prices. Since different units of the good may be purchased by different individuals, these prices may differ from consumer to consumer.

In order to derive the *optimal* price for the monopolist to charge for each unit, we recall from Chapter 5 that we can interpret the demand curve for a product as a "willingness to pay" curve. The market demand curve depicted in Figure 12.2 can be interpreted in two ways. If each consumer purchases at most one unit of the good, then the demand curve shows that one consumer is willing to pay 10 for that unit, another consumer is willing to pay 9, and so on. Alternatively, we could suppose that all consumers buy many units of the product. Under this interpretation, the figure would say each consumer is willing to pay 10 for the first unit she consumes, but only 9 for the second and so on up to the total units purchased by each consumer. Either way, the demand curve represents the maximum willingness to pay for each unit. Another way to say this is that the demand curve represents consumers' **reservation price** for each unit. If the firm knows this maximum willingness to pay for each unit, then a first degree price discriminating monopolist's profit maximizing strategy is to charge the maximum willingness to pay for each unit. For example, the consumer who values a unit at 10 would be charged 10, while the consumer who values a unit of the good at 9 would be charged 9 and so on. Alternatively, a consumer wishing to buy 3 units would be charged 10 for the first, 9 for the second, and 8 for the third.

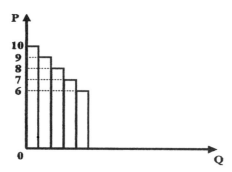

Figure 12.2

With first degree discrimination, the marginal revenue generated by each unit sold is exactly the price of that unit. Because the monopolist is now able to charge a *different* price for each unit of the good, an additional unit of the good can be sold without having to decrease the price of the other *(inframarginal)* units. The sale of the additional unit can be secured by setting the price *for this* unit equal to the consumer's willingness to pay. As a result, the monopolist continues to sell units as long as the *price* of that unit exceeds the marginal cost of producing the unit. This occurs at the point where demand exactly equals marginal cost since, at this point, the maximum willingness to pay for the last unit placed on the market is exactly equal to marginal cost. Hence, the price discriminating monopolist maximizes profits by selling Q* units in Figure 12.3.

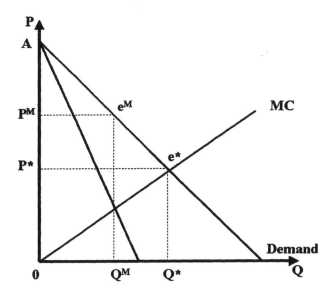

Figure 12.3

Exercise 1: *Let inverse market demand be P = 10 - .75Q. What is the equation of marginal revenue for a first degree price discriminating monopolist facing this demand curve?*

    a. MR = 10 - .75Q
    b. MR = 13.33 - (4/3)P
    c. MR = 10 - 1.5Q

Suppose that the equation of marginal cost for this monopolist is MC = 1 + .25Q. What is the first degree price discriminating monopolist's optimal output?

    a. Q* = 36/7
    b. Q* = 4
    c. Q* = 9

As usual, we calculate producer's surplus as the difference between the market price and the marginal cost for every unit sold. When the monopolist price discriminates, however, market price is traced out by the demand curve for every unit sold. Hence, at output level Q*, producer's surplus is the entire area below the demand curve and above marginal cost for all units up to Q*. This is the area of triangle Ae*0 in Figure 12.3. Consumer's surplus is zero, since each consumer pays a price equal to his maximum willingness to pay. Moreover, the deadweight loss is zero because output is sold up to the point where the willingness to pay is just equal to the opportunity cost of resources. In other words, at Q* every consumer who is willing to pay at least the opportunity cost of the resources needed to produce the extra output is able to buy. Further, every consumer who is not willing to pay the opportunity cost of the extra output does not buy. In fact, Q* is exactly the same output level as the perfectly competitive equilibrium output level: total surplus is maximized and deadweight loss is zero at this point. Comparing Figure 12.3 with Figure 12.1, however, it is clear that the surplus is distributed very differently. In the competitive equilibrium (Q^C in Figure 12.1) consumer's surplus is area Ae^Cp^C and producer's surplus is area $0e^Cp^C$. With perfect price discrimination, consumer's surplus is zero and producer's surplus is $0Ae^*$ in Figure 12.3, which exactly equals the total surplus in Figure 12.1. In other words, the perfectly discriminating monopolist manages to capture the whole consumer surplus.

Exercise 2: *Let the market for a product be composed of two types of consumers, each of which can be easily distinguished by the monopolist on sight. Let the demand for any individual in the two groups be depicted as follows:*

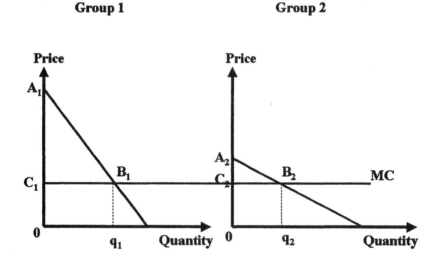

When a consumer from group 1 approaches the monopolist to purchase the good, what is the profit maximizing offer for a first degree price discriminating monopolist to make? Suppose that the offer is made on a "take it or leave it" basis.

    a. The monopolist would offer to sell q_1 units of output at price C_1
    b. The monopolist would offer to sell q_1 units of output at a price equal to the area of triangle $A_1C_1B_1$
    c. The monopolist would offer to sell q_2 units of output at a price equal to the area of triangle $A_2C_2B_2$

If the monopolist conducts first degree price discrimination and sells to both groups, what is the surplus captured by the monopolist from each group if it makes the profit maximizing offer to each member of each group?

    a. The monopolist captures surplus $A_1C_1B_1$ from each member of group 1 and $A_2C_2B_2$ from each member of group 2.
    b. The monopolist captures surplus $A_2C_2B_2$ from each member of both groups 1 and 2.
    c. The monopolist captures surplus $A_1C_1B_1$ from each member of both groups 1 and 2.

2. Second Degree Price Discrimination

If a seller does not know each consumer's exact willingness to pay for each unit of the good, then it is not possible to pursue a policy of first degree price discrimination: all consumers would have an incentive to claim that their willingness to pay is very low so as to obtain the product cheaply! On the other hand, the monopolist may still be able to follow a policy of **second degree price discrimination**. Second degree price discrimination means that the monopolist sells different units of the product for different prices, but every consumer who buys the same quantity of output pays the same price. In other words, prices vary across units of the product, but not across people. For example, a monopolist may offer quantity discounts for larger purchases. The monopolist need not know the "type" of any particular customer in order to offer this form of discount: only the quantity transacted must be known.

Even though the monopolist cannot identify the willingness to pay of any single consumer, the consumer's purchasing behavior in the face of price discrimination reveals something about the consumer's willingness to pay. Low-willingness-to-pay customers may choose one package of quantity and price while high-willingness-to-pay customers may choose another package. Sometimes this is referred to as a price schedule that allows consumers to **"self-select"**. All customers of a particular "type" choose -- on their own -- to consume one package, while all customers of a different "type" choose to consume another package.

Second degree price discrimination allows the monopolist to capture more surplus than uniform pricing when it knows that different willingness-to-pay groups exist but cannot identify any single consumer as coming from one group or the other. We will illustrate this with the following example. Suppose that there are high- and low-willingness-to-pay consumers in the economy, who are represented by the demands in Figure 12.4. Demand$_1$ is the demand of "type 1" customers, with a low willingness to pay, and Demand$_2$ is the demand of "type 2" customers, with a high willingness to pay. These demands are known to the monopolist, but it is impossible to tell by simple inspection which consumer belongs to which group. Suppose for simplicity that the marginal cost of production of the monopolist is zero. Further, assume that the monopolist wishes to sell to both groups: assume that there are enough type 1 customers that it is not in the monopolist's interest to simply set a price that only appeals to type 2.

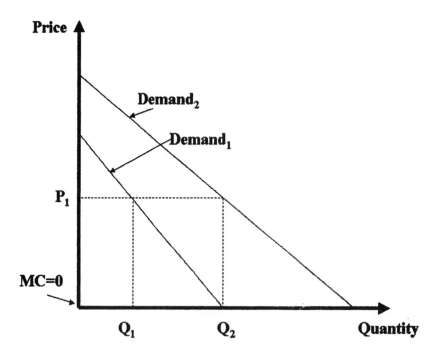

Figure 12.4

If the monopolist announces any two prices, P_1 and P_2, where $P_1 < P_2$, all consumers have an incentive to simply purchase their demanded quantities at the low price. The monopolist effectively can only obtain a single price for all units sold under this scheme and captures surplus equal to the difference between P_1 and marginal cost (= rectangle P_1Q_1 from group 1 and rectangle P_1Q_2 from group 2). Now, suppose that the monopolist can sell different quantities of output for different prices. Specifically, suppose that the monopolist offers only two packages: consumers can purchase Q^0_1 units of output at price (A+E) or Q^0_2 units of output at price (A+C+E) in Figure 12.5. If a consumer from group 2 buys Q^0_1 units, she obtains B+D units of consumer surplus, whereas she also obtains B+D if she buys Q^0_2. Hence, she has no incentive to lie about her type and may as well purchase Q^0_2 units of output. Customers from group 1 do better consuming Q^0_1 units of output. Hence, the monopolist obtains A+E units of surplus from group 1 and A+C+E units from group 2. Comparing this surplus to the surplus captured in Figure 12.4, the monopolist gains from this second degree price discrimination.

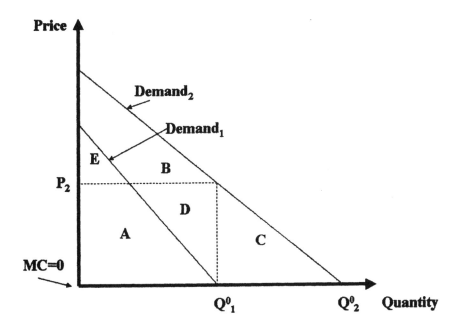

Figure 12.5

Exercise 3: *The paragraph preceding Figure 12.5, above, considered the case where there were many type 1 customers. Now, suppose that very few type 1 customers and very many type 2 customers exist. Would the second degree price discrimination scheme proposed above increase the surplus captured by the monopolist compared to a uniform pricing scheme where a single price, P, is set for a package of Q_2^0 units of output?*

   a. Yes.
   b. No.

A common example of second degree discrimination is a **block tariff**, which is a particular type of quantity discount. To illustrate, a block tariff with two "blocks" means that a consumer pays a price for the first x units consumed and a different price for any additional units consumed. For example, suppose that all consumers have demand as shown in Figure 12.2. Interpret this figure as meaning that consumers demand multiple units of output, but have decreasing marginal utility of the good as their consumption increases. Let marginal cost be zero for simplicity. A block tariff with two blocks might charge a price of 8 for the first 3 units and a price of 6 for the next 2. This allows the firm to capture a surplus of (8x3 + 6x2 = 36) units, whereas a single price of 6 for all units would only capture a surplus of (6x5 = 30). This is second degree price discrimination because different quantities of output are priced differently, but all consumers face the same price schedule.

More generally, if we consider any downward sloping demand, a block pricing schedule will leave a consumer's surplus equal to area B to customers and will capture a surplus of area A for the monopolist.

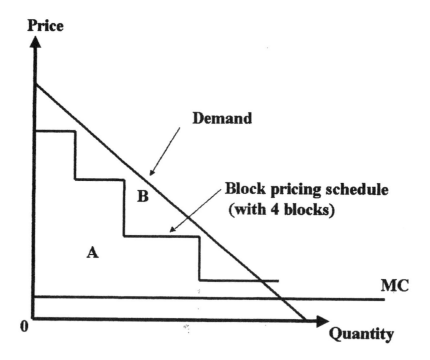

Figure 12.6

Clearly, the more blocks are added, the closer block tariffs gets to capturing all the consumer's surplus.

Exercise 4: *Let there be two types of customers in the market for a good; type 1 has a low demand for the good and type 2 has a high demand, as shown in Figure 12.7, below.*

Compare two pricing schemes. In the first scheme, suppose that all customers are charged price P_1 for the good. Call this the uniform pricing scheme. In the second, all customers are charged P_1 for the first Q_1 units consumed and P_2 for any additional units. Call this the block pricing scheme. Which of the following statements is true?

    a. Type 1 will consume Q_1^* under uniform pricing. Type 2 will consume Q_2^* under the uniform pricing scheme.
    b. Type 1 will consume Q_1^* under the block pricing scheme. Type 2 will consume Q_2^* under the block pricing scheme.
    c. Type 1 will consume Q_1^{**} under the block pricing scheme. Type 2 will consume Q_2^* under the block pricing scheme.
    d. Type 1 prefers the block pricing scheme.
    e. All customers prefer the uniform pricing scheme.

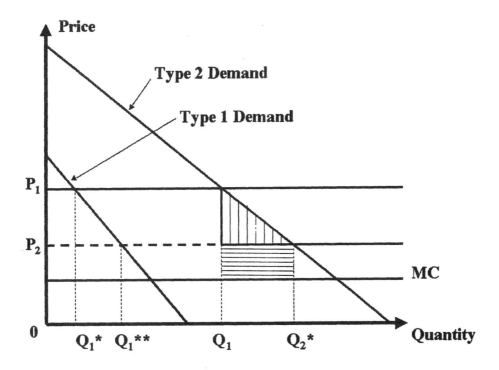

Figure 12.7

Exercise 5: *Suppose that a monopolist has a constant marginal cost of producing a good. Consumers all have downward sloping demand, but the demand differs across customers. If the monopolist sets a usage fee equal to its marginal cost of production, but a different subscription charge for each customer, is it conducting first degree price discrimination or second degree price discrimination?*

   a. First degree price discrimination
   b. Second degree price discrimination
   c. Either type of price discrimination is possible.

3. Third Degree Price Discrimination

A seller may know how the willingness to pay for each unit varies across broad customer groups, even if the seller does not know the exact willingness to pay of each consumer. For example, it may be possible to find out that students and senior citizens are less willing to pay for certain goods (like movies) than other people. In such a case, the monopolist sells output to different consumers for different prices, but each unit sold to any one consumer group carries the same price. This type of price discrimination typically requires each consumer to be easily identifiable as belonging to a certain group. For example, it may be possible to identify a student by requiring a student identification card to be shown at the time of purchase.

Since each consumer can be identified as a member of a particular group, the profit maximizing price will be chosen to equate marginal revenue to marginal cost *for that group's demand curve.* For example, suppose that output is sold in two markets, Germany and the United States, and that consumers cannot exchange goods (arbitrage) across the two countries. Demand in the two markets is represented in Figure 12.8 below. If the marginal cost is the same for each market, as depicted in the figure, the optimal price will set the marginal revenue for each market equal to the (same) marginal cost. This yields price P_1 in market 1 and price P_2 in market 2 with a surplus of area P_1Q_1 + area P_2Q_2 captured by the price discriminating monopolist. Note that this raises the surplus captured by the producer compared to the case where the same price must be charged to the two groups. For example, suppose that the price that sets marginal revenue equal to marginal cost in market 1 is used in both markets. Hence, under uniform pricing, the monopolist captures surplus of only area P_1Q_1 + area P_1Q'. It can be seen from the figure that area P_1Q' is smaller than area P_2Q_2 so that the monopolist captures less surplus under this scheme.

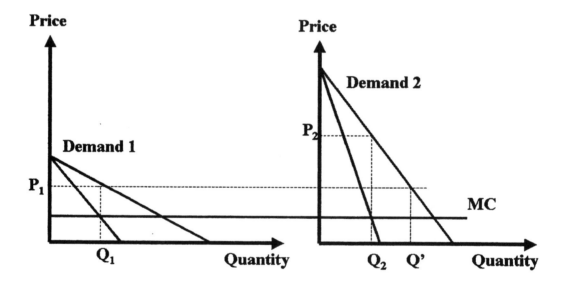

Figure 12.8

If the marginal cost differs across the two markets, the profit maximizing price will be chosen to equate each market's marginal revenue equal to each market's marginal cost ($MR_1 = MC_1$ and $MR_2 = MC_2$, where MR_I and MC_I are the marginal revenue and marginal cost in market I).

Exercise 6: *Suppose that a monopolist supplies a good to its home market at a marginal cost of 10. It also supplies the good to a foreign market, but since all its production facilities are in the home market, it must add a transportation cost of 5 per unit to the production cost in order to sell the units in the foreign country. Inverse demand at home is $P_H = 40 - .5Q$. Inverse demand in the foreign country is $P_F = 60 - .25Q$. What is the profit maximizing price for the monopolist in each country if the monopolist must charge a uniform price in each country?*

a. $P_H = 10$; $P_F = 15$
b. $P_H = 25$; $P_F = 25$
c. $P_H = 25$; $P_F = 37.5$

In an effort to conduct price discrimination, firms may **screen** customers. In other words, a firm may attempt to identify which group customers come from. The monopolist may do this either by direct methods (such as demanding proof of age) or indirect methods that allow customers to **self-select** into groups that reflect their different willingness to pay. If direct methods are possible, then it permits the firm to use third degree price discrimination. For example, if identification cards show whether an individual is a student or not, different prices can be charged to students than to others. If only methods that induce self-selection are possible (such as quantity discounts), then they allow the firm to practice second degree price discrimination. In either case, screening allows the uniformed party to a transaction (in this case, the firm) to gather information on the hidden characteristics of the informed party (in this case, the customers).

It should be emphasized that all three degrees of price discrimination can only work when certain underlying conditions are fulfilled. First, the firm that conducts the price discrimination must have market power: it must face a downward sloping demand. If it is a price taker, then consumers will flock to the lowest priced supplier and it is impossible for any firm to raise price above this level. Second, it must not be possible for consumers to resell the product. In other words, it must not be possible for a customer who buys the product for a low price to resell the product to another customer with a higher willingness to pay. If such resale were possible, the surplus would be captured by the customers who bought the product for the low price and not by the monopolist.

Exercise 7: *Would you expect price discrimination to be more prevalent in services or in goods?*

a. services
b. goods

Finally, while price discrimination is commonly defined in terms of differences in *prices*, it would be more accurate to say that price discrimination refers to differences in *mark-ups* (i.e., price-cost margins) across customers, customer groups, or quantities. In other words, if the marginal cost of production differed across markets but the same mark-up were charged in the separate markets, this would not really qualify as price discrimination. In Exercise 7, above, for example, the mark-up differs across the home and foreign markets since at home the mark-up is 25-10 = 15 and in the foreign market the mark-up is 37.5-15 = 22.5. Hence, the exercise does illustrate price discrimination between the markets. If the optimal prices in this exercise were $P_H = 25$ and $P_F = 30$, then the mark-up would be 15 in both markets and it there would be no real price discrimination despite the apparent differences in price charged to the customer.

4. Tying

Tying (or **tie-in sales**) refers to a case when customers may buy one product only if they agree to buy another product as well. There are two types of tie-in sales. The first, the **requirements tie-in sale**, requires that customers who make a purchase of one product from a firm make all their purchases of *another* product from a firm. For example, a customer who buys a fax machine from a firm might be required to buy paper for the fax machine from the same firm. The second, **bundling** (sometimes referred to as pure bundling), is a sale in which many units of the same good -- or two (or more) goods -- are sold in a package. Customers cannot buy these products (or units) separately. For example, most new cars are bundles of products that could theoretically be sold separately such as a tires, a heating system, a radio, seats, and so on. If these different products are available either as a package or as separate "options", the firm practices **mixed bundling**.

If one product is essentially useless without the other (such as a fax machine and paper), a requirements tie-in sale allows the firm to meter demand of the products and thus practice second degree price discrimination. For example, if the firm has a fixed price, F, for the fax machine and a price, p, for each sheet of paper used, then it can charge the equivalent of a subscription fee (F) plus a usage charge (p) for the machine and its use. Low-level users would choose contracts with a low subscription fee and a relatively high usage charge while high-level users would select plans offering high subscription fees but low usage charges

Under bundling, a package is offered for a single price to all customers. Consider the simplest case where only a single good is offered for sale and all customers have the same downward sloping demand, as shown in Figure 12.9. If the monopolist wishes to capture the most possible surplus, then it should offer the bundle of Q* units for a price equal to area A. In this way, the monopolist can always capture the entire consumer's surplus by means of bundling since this policy is equivalent to our reinterpretation of first degree price discrimination in Exercise 2.

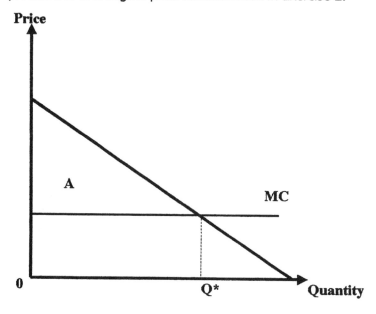

Figure 12.9

Bundling can also be used to capture surplus when several *different* goods are packaged together in the bundle. In order to understand why, let us return to our discussion of marginal revenue in Chapter 11. Recall that a profit maximizing monopolist must balance off the gain it receives from selling one more unit of a good (the price) against the loss it incurs on all inframarginal units of the good when it lowers price enough to induce the additional unit to be purchased. Clearly, the monopolist would prefer to minimize this loss. In other words, the monopolist would prefer to have to lower price only slightly in order to pick up the extra sale. This occurs when the willingness to pay for the good is rather similar across customers (or, equivalently, when demand is rather flat).

Bundling is therefore a profitable strategy when it makes the willingness to pay rather similar across customers. One case where this is true is when the willingnesses to pay for the different goods in the bundle are **negatively correlated** (i.e., when a person who values good 1 highly tends to value good 2 very little). In the table below, we see an example of negative and positive correlation in demand for a goods 1 and 2. Each consumer wants at most one unit of each good. The willingness to pay for a bundle consisting of one unit of good 1 and one unit of good 2 is shown as well.

Positive Correlation (Unprofitable Bundle)

Customer: Willingness to Pay:

	Good 1	Good 2	Bundle
Customer 1	$1000	$600	$1600
Customer 2	$ 750	$250	$1000

Profit maximizing price:	$ 750	$ 600	$1000
Quantity sold:	2	1	2
Revenue	$ 1500	$ 600	$ 2000

Negative Correlation (Profitable Bundle)

Customer: Willingness to Pay:

	Good 1	Good 2	Bundle
Customer 1	$1000	$250	$1250
Customer 2	$ 750	$600	$1250

Profit maximizing price:	$ 750	$ 600	$ 1250
Quantity sold:	2	1	2
Revenue:	$ 1500	$ 600	$ 2500

We will assume that the marginal cost of production of the goods is zero. Now, let us review the profits the firm could earn from selling the goods separately and as a bundle in the cases of negative and positive correlation, respectively. In both tables, the profit maximizing price for good 1 is $750 (earning a profit of $1500 since both customers buy at this price) and the profit maximizing price for good 2 is $600 (earning a profit of $600 since only customer 1 buys at this price). The total profit is $1500 + $600 = $2100. If the firm were to bundle and demands for the two goods are positively correlated (top table), the profit maximizing price for the bundle would be $1000 (for a profit of $2000). Hence, it is more profitable to sell the goods separately. If the demands are negatively correlated, as in the bottom table, then the profit maximizing prices for goods 1 and 2 are the same as before (for a profit of $2100). The profit maximizing price for the bundle has risen to $1250, however, for a profit of $1250 + $1250 = $2500! Hence, it is more profitable to sell the goods in a bundle.

The intuition for this result is that the firm must lower price to the lowest aggregate willingness to pay in order to increase sales from one to two units. When demands are negatively correlated, the aggregate willingness to pay of all the customers is very similar so that price need not be lowered much in order to pick up the extra sale. Therefore, the price of the bundle is relatively high. When demands are positively correlated, the aggregate willingness to pay of the low valuation customer is far below that of the high valuation customer so that price must be lowered a lot to pick up the extra sale. This tends to depress the price of the bundle and makes bundling unprofitable. In fact, it is not negative or positive correlation *per se* that is important here: what is important is that bundling is profitable when it reduces the spread in valuations and is not profitable when it does not reduce this spread.

Mixed bundling can improve on this further. It involves offering each product for sale individually *and* as part of a bundle. At its most basic level, we can think that mixed bundling can always do at least as well as pure bundling because the components that are offered for sale separately can always be priced so high as to make their purchase prohibitive. Hence, the only relevant price is the bundle price, and mixed bundling is equivalent to pure bundling. Mixed bundling may be better than pure bundling in a stricter sense, however, in that it allows the monopolist to segment customers into more groups, with prices tailored to each group. Hence, in the same way that block pricing with more blocks enables a monopolist to capture more surplus, mixed bundling allows the monopolist to capture more surplus than either pure bundling or than selling the goods separately.

For example, suppose that there are many customers in the market, some with high valuations for both goods, some with low valuations for both goods, and some customers with a high valuation for one good and a low valuation for the other good. Hence, we cannot say that all demands are either positively or negatively correlated (as we could in the case of only two customers) so that neither bundling nor selling the products separately clearly reduces the variance in the willingness to pay of all the customers. Further, if a pure bundling strategy were followed, some customers who have a high valuation for only a single good would not buy since their value for the two goods might not be high enough to equal to bundle price. A mixed bundling strategy that charges a high price for each component separately and a moderate price for the bundle would induce these consumers to purchase. Those with a high valuation for a single good will buy that good alone, those with a moderate to high valuation for both buy the bundle, and those with a low valuation for both goods buy nothing. Hence, mixed bundling allows the firm to both increase the number of customers who purchase and to price discriminate among those who do purchase.

Exercise 8: *Consider the following willingnesses to pay (reservation prices) for one unit of each of two goods in a market with four customers. The market is supplied by a monopolist with zero marginal cost of production of both goods.*

Customer	Reservation price: good 1	Reservation price: good 2	Reservation price: bundle
Customer 1	900	100	1000
Customer 2	800	600	1400
Customer 3	600	600	1200
Customer 4	100	900	1000

What is the monopolist's profit maximizing (uniform) price for good 1 separately, P_1, good 2 separately, P_2 under a strategy of selling the goods separately? What is the price of a bundle consisting of one unit of each good, P_B if only the pure bundle will be offered?

    a. $P_1 = 900$; $P_2 = 900$; $P_B = 1000$
    b. $P_1 = 600$; $P_2 = 600$; $P_B = 1200$
    c. $P_1 = 600$; $P_2 = 600$; $P_B = 1000$

What is the optimal price to set for each good and the bundle if a strategy of mixed bundling is followed ?

    a. $P_1 = 100$; $P_2 = 100$; $P_B = 1000$
    b. $P_1 = 600$; $P_2 = 600$; $P_B = 1200$
    c. $P_1 = 900$; $P_2 = 900$; $P_B = 1200$

Is pure bundling a more profitable strategy than selling the goods separately?
Is mixed bundling a more profitable strategy than pure bundling?

    a. Pure bundling is better than separate sale and mixed bundling is better than pure bundling.
    b. Mixed bundling is equivalent to pure bundling. Both are better than separate sale of the goods.
    c. All three strategies do equally well.

5. Advertising

One of the important functions of advertising is to shift out demand. Supposing, then, that this is the only effect of advertising, we can depict demand with and without advertising as in Figure 12.9. While we have drawn demand as rotating out, we could also suppose that the effect of advertising is to cause a parallel shift out in demand.

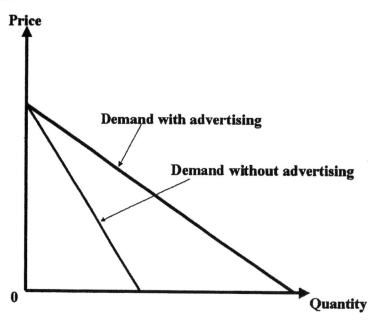

Figure 12.9

While the shift clearly increases the profit that can potentially be earned by the firm, advertising is also costly. As usual, the profit maximizing amount of advertising must balance this cost against the potential benefits that can be earned. Suppose that advertising is a pure fixed cost. The profit maximizing conditions of a monopolist who can control both the output level and advertising expenditures are as follows:

1. Output is chosen optimally, as before, by setting $MR_Q = MC_Q$, *holding constant the level of advertising*. This is what we did in Chapter 11 for the monopolist who could only control the output level: advertising was implicitly held constant. Accordingly, MR_Q is defined as the change in revenue due to a change in output, *holding the level of advertising constant.* MC_Q, similarly, is defined as the change in total cost due to a change in output *only*.

2. Advertising is chosen optimally by setting the marginal revenue due to an increase in advertising *holding output constant* equal to the marginal cost of increasing advertising *also holding output constant*. We can express this as $MR_A = MC_A$. The marginal revenue from an increase in advertising *holding output constant* is the change in revenues that occur as demand is shifted out due to a small increase in advertising expenditures. Similarly, the marginal cost from an increase in advertising *holding output constant* is the change in total cost that occurs when advertising increases slightly.

By manipulating these two profit maximization we can obtain the expression that summarizes these two profit maximizing conditions for the advertising monopolist:

$$A/(PQ) = -E_{Q,A}/E_{Q,P}$$

$E_{Q,A}$ is the elasticity of output with respect to advertising, $(\Delta Q/\Delta A)(A/Q)$ and $E_{Q,P}$ is the price elasticity of demand, $(\Delta Q/\Delta P)(P/Q)$. This expression must hold at the profit maximizing advertising expenditure and output. The expression says that the ratio of advertising expenditure to sales revenues (the left-hand side of the equation) must vary according to the relative responsiveness of demand to advertising expenditure (the right-hand side of the equation).

Exercise 9: *Let a monopolist face inverse demand curve $P = 10Q^{-1/2}A^{1/4}$, where P is price, Q is output, and A is advertising expenditure. Define advertising intensity as the share of revenues that is spent on advertising. If the monopolist chooses P and A to maximize profits, then its advertising intensity is*

a. 0.5
b. 1/8
c. 1/4

Chapter Review Questions

1. As we noted in the summary, price discrimination is not the only reason why prices might differ across individuals, groups of individuals, or quantities. Knowing whether or not price discrimination is the cause of observed price differences has some importance, however, since some types of price discrimination are illegal.

   Suppose a monopolist sells a certain electronic component in two countries, the United States and Japan. Suppose further that all of the components are manufactured in Japan and then must be shipped to the United States at a cost of 4 per unit. Further, suppose that the monopolist charges a price of $P_U = 15$ for the component in the United States and a price of $P_J = 11$ for the component in Japan.

   a. Do the underlying conditions exist for the monopolist to conduct price discrimination in the sale of its electronic component? Explain.

   b. What degree of price discrimination would be most likely in the sale of this electronic component?

   c. Given the facts of this case, do you think that price discrimination can explain the difference in prices across these two markets?

Answer:

a. In order to price discriminate, the monopolist first must be able to prevent arbitrage. If the component cannot be easily traded across these two countries or among individuals, then arbitrage can be prevented. If no developed secondary market for the component exists, or if the buyers are small consumers (as opposed to large firms, for example), or if the component is large and difficult to ship, arbitrage is unlikely. Since there are transportation costs of 4 per unit, a price difference equal to 4 or less would not be arbitraged away. Second, the monopolist must have market power. If no close substitute for this component is sold in the two countries, then this is likely.

b. The monopolist charges different prices in Japan and the United States but, within each of these two markets, all units are sold at the same price. Hence (unless all consumers have identical inelastic demands) this cannot be first degree discrimination. Second degree discrimination involves self selection. There is no self-selection here: all U.S. consumers are offered the same uniform price and all Japanese consumers are offered the same uniform price. On the other hand, different groups of consumers (U.S. versus Japanese) are charged different prices: this could be third degree price discrimination.

c. The prices differ by exactly the difference in marginal costs across the countries (the transportation cost per unit is 4). This means that the mark-up in the two countries actually is identical. We argued in the summary that the distinguishing feature of price discrimination as opposed to other reasons why prices might differ is that the mark-ups differ under price discrimination. Hence, an argument could be made that it is merely the difference in marginal cost of getting the good to market and not price discrimination per se that is causing prices to differ across these two markets.

2. A monopolist currently charges a uniform price for a good, depicted as P^M in the figure below. A new economist hired into the strategic planning unit suggests that the company has enough information to pursue first degree price discrimination.

    a. Show on the graph how much the monopolist will benefit from such a change.

    b. Illustrate on the graph which consumers would be made better off by the change in policy, which would be made worse off, and which would be indifferent between uniform pricing and first degree price discrimination.

    c. If the regulatory authority that oversees the monopolist cares only about maximizing total surplus, should it condemn or welcome the change in policy?

    d. Suppose now that the regulatory authority has a mandate to balance consumer and producer interests. Can you tell whether the authority will condemn or welcome the change in policy?

Answer:

a. Monopolist will gain areas A and C in the graph so that it earns total surplus A+B+C. Under the uniform pricing policy, the monopolist earns B.

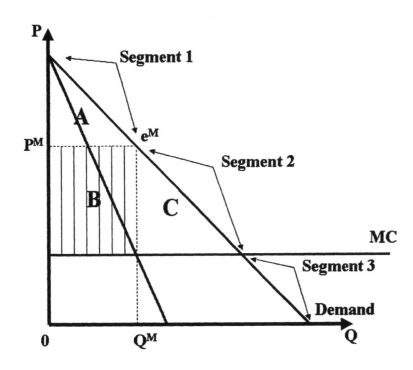

b. Consumers on segment 1 of the demand curve lose since they no longer earn surplus A. Consumers on segment 2 and on segment 3 of the demand curve are no better and no worse off: Segment 2 did not purchase the good before. Now the segment purchases, but earns no surplus from the purchase. Segment 3 continues not to purchase the good.

c. The regulatory authority should welcome the change, since total surplus increases from area A + B to area A+B+C in the figure accompanying part (a).

d. The monopolist will argue for the policy of price discrimination, while consumers in area A will argue against it. It is unclear which group will win out so the regulatory body's decision is unclear.

3. Suppose that a monopolist can sell in two markets. Demand in market 1 is $Q_1 = 100 - 2p_1$ while demand in market 2 is $Q_2 = 20 - p_2$. Marginal cost is 10 in both markets.

   a. What is the profit maximizing price and quantity to provide in the two markets if the monopolist can conduct third degree price discrimination?

   b. What is the profit maximizing price and quantity to produce if the monopolist must charge a uniform price in the two markets? Will both markets be served?

   c. If the price discrimination scheme for the two markets has an administrative fixed cost of 30, will the profit maximizing monopolist pursue this scheme?

Answer:

a. With third degree price discrimination, the monopolist sets marginal revenue for each market equal to marginal cost. $MR_1 = 50 - Q_1 = MC = 10 \Rightarrow Q_1^* = 40$ and $P_1^* = 30$. $MR_2 = 20 - 2Q_2 = MC = 10 \Rightarrow Q_2^* = 5$ and $P_2^* = 15$. Profits under this scheme are $(30-10)(40) + (15-10)(5) = 825$.

b. With uniform pricing, the monopolist may sell to both markets. Alternatively, the monopolist may decide to sell to a single market if including the market with the lower demand forces the uniform price down too far. We must, then, consider two cases:

   1. The monopolist sells only to the high demand market (market 1): $MR = 50 - Q = MC = 10 \Rightarrow Q^* = 40$ and $P^* = 30$ for a profit of $(30-10)(40) = 800$.

   2. The monopolist sells in both markets: Total demand $= Q = Q_1 + Q_2 = 120 - 3P$. Inverting demand to obtain inverse demand, we can obtain marginal revenue of $MR = 40 - 2Q/3 = MC = 10$ so that $Q^{**} = 45$ and $P^{**} = 25$. At this price, however, demand is zero in market 2 since price is larger than the highest price consumers are willing to pay!

Hence, it is more profitable to sell to the market 1 only at uniform price P* = 30.

c. If the fixed cost of using the price discrimination system is 30, then the total profits from using price discrimination are 825 - 30 = 795, which is less than the total profits from using uniform pricing so the profit maximizing firm should charge a uniform price.

Problem Set

1. A profit maximizing monopolist has two types of customers (young and old). The demand function for the old customers is given by $P_o = 100 - 0.5Q_o$ and the demand function for the young customers is given by $P_y = 160 - Q_y$ where P and Q refer to price of the good and the level of output that is produced and sold respectively. The production cost per unit is constant at $10.

    a. Under what conditions could the monopolist price discriminate between these two markets? Assuming that the monopolist *can* discriminate on prices, what price will he charge in each market? What are the quantities that will be sold in each market?

    b. Suppose that the monopolist cannot price discriminate between the two markets. What price would he choose? Now how much can he sell in each market?

2. Tinytown has two distinct parts: the wealthy people live at the top of the hill and the poor people live at the bottom of the hill. Joe, the only local painter, paints houses for anyone who lives in the town. For the same size of house, he charges much more to paint a house at the top of the hill than at the bottom of the hill. Using the concept of price discrimination, explain why this might be true. What type of price discrimination might Joe be conducting?

3. It costs a large amount, call it R, to conduct research into an important new drug. The drug is patentable and would be very useful for both industrialized countries and less developed economies. Assume that the drug company that potentially would develop this drug knows a lot about the potential demand for the drug in both types of countries. Assume that market demand for this drug is downward sloping and linear and marginal and average cost is constant at MC. The only difference between an industrialized country and a less developed country is that the market demand of the latter has a lower vertical intercept, as shown below:

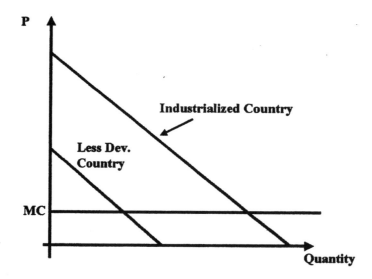

a. Illustrate in a diagram the profit a price discriminating monopolist could earn in these two markets. Under what conditions would the drug company decide to conduct research?

b. Suppose that contraband makes it impossible to sustain any price difference between the two countries. Under what conditions would the drug company decide to conduct research now?

4. A monopolist faces inverse demand $p = 200 - 4Q$ in the market for a good. The marginal (and average) cost is constant at MC = 80. The monopolist wishes to offer a block tariff for the good with two blocks: for units purchased up to Q_1, the price will be $p_1 = 200 - 4Q_1$. For units purchased between Q_1 and Q_2, price will be $p_2 = 200 - 4Q_2$. This is depicted in the following figure:

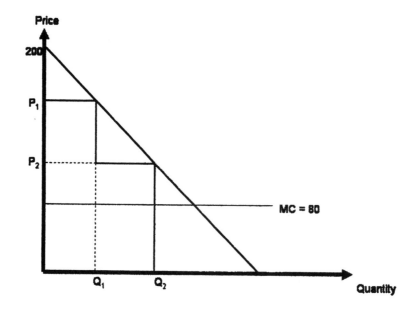

a. Write down the profit of the monopolist that uses these two blocks. What is total revenue? What is total cost?

b. What is the marginal revenue due to an increase in Q_1 *holding Q_2 constant*? What is the marginal cost of an increase in Q_1 *holding Q_2 constant*? Explain your answer.

c. What is the marginal revenue due to an increase in Q_2 *holding Q_1 constant*? What is the marginal cost of an increase in Q_2 *holding Q_1 constant*? Explain your answer.

d. Using your answers to (b) and (c), write down the profit maximization conditions of the monopolist if it may set both Q_1 and Q_2 so as to maximize profits. What are the optimal levels of Q_1 and Q_2? What is profit at this point?

5. A monopolist produces two goods, goods 1 and 2. Consumers in this market have reservation prices r_1 and r_2 for these goods. Each consumer, then, can be represented as a point on the following graph. For example, consumer A would have reservation prices r_1^a and r_2^a for the two goods. This is depicted below with some points representing consumers B-F.

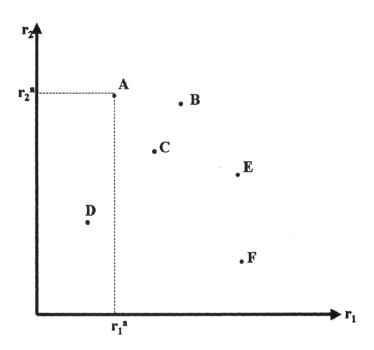

a. Suppose that the monopolist sells the two goods separately (i.e., follows a pure components strategy) at prices p_1 and p_2. Illustrate these two prices on the reservation price graph (i.e., illustrate all the reservation prices for good 1 that equal p_1 and all the reservation prices for good 2 that equal p_2). Illustrate which consumers buy which goods at these two prices.

b. Suppose that the monopolist sells the goods only as a bundle (or follows a pure bundling strategy) at price p_B. Illustrate this price on the reservation price graph. (i.e., illustrate all the reservation prices for which $r_1 + r_2 = p_b$.) Illustrate which customers buy at this price.

c. Suppose that the monopolist sells the goods under a mixed bundling strategy, so that the components are available separately at prices p_1 and p_2 as well as in a bundle. Illustrate the three prices on a reservation price graph. Illustrate which consumers buy which goods at these prices.

d. Using your graphs, illustrate why mixed bundling may be a desirable policy.

Exam *(60 minutes: Closed Book, Closed Notes)*

1. A firm wishes to hire a hard-working employee.

   a. Can you propose a direct screening device to allow the firm to distinguish between the hard-workers and the lazy employees before the individual has been hired?

   b. If no direct pre-hire screening is possible, the firm would like to offer a contract that would encourage only hard-working employees to apply for the job. In other words, the firm would like to establish conditions of employment such that only hard-workers would wish to accept the contract. Suppose that all other firms offer a flat wage rage (in other words, a remuneration contract that does not vary with the effort put into the job). Now, suppose that our firm offers a flat wage rate that is higher than the going wage. Could this contract encourage self-selection by only hard- workers into the job? Could a piece rate (in other words, a contract that paid employees per unit of output that they produced) induce self-selection by hard-workers into the job?

2. The Bums and Tums fitness club is deciding on how to price admission to the club. Suppose that all consumers have identical, linear, downward sloping demand for the number of hours they use the facilities at the club in a given year. Further, the marginal cost and average cost of providing an hour of service to any user is, for simplicity, constant. There are no other fitness clubs in the town where Bums and Tums is located.

   a. What type or types of price discrimination might be possible for the club?

   b. Using a graph and words, explain why the club might wish to charge an annual entrance fee that allows free access to the facility rather than a uniform charge for each use.

   c. Now, suppose that Bums and Tums is considering opening a new club in another town (that is isolated from the first town). Building the club will involve a significant fixed cost, F. Should the entry decision depend on whether or not Bums and Tums can offer the annual entrance fee scheme?

3. Consider a market where the demand is $Q = P^{-1/2}A^{1/2}$.

   a. Referring back to the discussion of constant elasticity demand curves in Chapter 2, state the price elasticity of demand for this market.

   b. Using your answer for (a) as a guide, state the advertising elasticity of demand for this market.

   c. Explain why the advertising elasticity of part (b) is a positive number.

   d. What is a monopolist's profit maximizing advertising-sales ratio for this market? Would the advertising-sales ratio change if the cost structure of the firm changed?

4. Show that a subscription fee plus a usage charge results in a quantity discount for high-use consumers.

Answers to Exercises

1. The correct answer to the first part of the question is (a). The marginal revenue curve and the demand curve are exactly the same for a monopolist that can conduct first degree price discrimination.

   The correct answer to the second part of the question is (b). The monopolist will increase output up to the point where MR = MC. Since MR is the same as demand, however, we obtain that optimal output occurs where MR = 10 - .75Q = MC = 1 + .25Q. Solving, we obtain Q* = 9. The optimal price will be to charge each customer exactly his reservation price for the unit(s) he buys.

2. The correct answer to the first part of the question is (b). The monopolist clearly wants to capture entire surplus of each consumer. Further, the monopolist wishes to maximize the size of the surplus captured, which is equal to the surplus obtained from the consumer minus the cost of producing the goods. The monopolist maximizes surplus by fixing output at the level where the consumer is willing to pay at least the marginal cost of production for each unit consumed. This occurs at point q_1 for group 1 (and, incidentally, at point q_2 for group 2). The group 1 consumer will accept to pay any price up to the entire consumer's surplus generated by the purchase of q_1. This is triangle $A_1C_1B_1$.

   The correct answer to the second part of the question is (a). The profit maximizing monopolist charges any group 1 customer triangle $A_1C_1B_1$ for q_1 units and so captures this entire triangle as surplus from each group 1 customer. The monopolist charges $A_2C_2B_2$ to each group 2 customer for q_2 units and so captures this entire triangle as surplus from each group 2 customer.

3. The answer is (b). The pricing scheme in the text allows type 2 customers to keep B+D in surplus while it captures all surplus from type 1 customers. If there are very few type 1 customers, then this scheme may be dominated by a scheme that charges a single price of (A+B+C+D+E) for packages of Q_2^0 units of output. In this case, type 2 customers keep no surplus, and type 1 customers do not buy at all. While this scheme loses surplus (A+E) from each type 1 customer, it gains surplus (B+D) from each type 2 customer. If there are many type 2 customers and few type 1 customers, then this may be a better plan.

4. The correct statement is (b). The other statements are not fully correct. Under uniform pricing at a price of P_1, each type of consumer simply purchases at the point where P_1 touches the demand curve. In the case of type 1, this is as point Q_1^* and in the case of type 2, this is the point Q_1. Hence, (a) is incorrect. Under the block pricing scheme, the price schedule is traced out by the thick line at level P_1 until quantity Q_1 and falls to P_2 thereafter. The two types will consume at the points where this line touches their demand curve. In the case of type 1, this is still at point Q_1^*. In the case of type 2, the price schedule touches at two points: Q_1 and Q_2^*. The type 2 consumer captures an additional triangle of consumer's surplus (the vertically shaded area) if she consumes at point Q_2^*, however, so it Q_2^* is the optimal point for any type 2. Hence, (b) is correct and (c) is incorrect. Type 1 consumers purchase the same amount and capture the same amount of consumer's surplus under both schemes, so type 1 consumers are indifferent between the two schemes. Hence, (d) is incorrect. Finally, type 2 captures additional consumer's surplus (the vertically shaded area) under block pricing so that statement (e) is incorrect. Note that the monopolist also captures additional surplus when block pricing is used so that, in fact, block pricing represents a Pareto improvement for all agents in this market.

5. The correct answer is (a). Even though it is a subscription fee plus a usage charge, the monopolist is charging a different price both by number of units consumed and by customer. This makes the scheme first degree price discrimination and not second degree price discrimination.

6. The correct answer is (c). At home, the monopolist sets marginal revenue at home equal to marginal cost at home so that $MR_H = 40 - Q = 10 = MC_H$ so that $Q^*_H = 30$. Substituting into home demand, $P_H = 25$. Abroad, the monopolist sets marginal revenue abroad equal to marginal cost abroad so that $MR_F = 60 - .5Q = 15 = MC_F$ so that $Q^*_F = 90$. Substituting into foreign demand, $P^*_F = 37.5$.

7. To the extent that services are harder to re-sell, one would expect more price discrimination in services than in goods.

8. The correct answer to the first part of the question is (c). The demand when the price of either good 1 or 2 is 100 is 4 so that the monopolist earns 400 + 400 = 800 from setting this price and selling the goods separately. If the price is 600,

only three units of each good will be sold, resulting in profits of 1800 + 1800 = 3600. If the price rises further to 800, profits will be 1600 + 800 = 2400. Finally, if price rises to 900, profits are 900 + 900 = 1800 since only a single unit of each good will be demanded. Hence, the profit maximizing price for the goods when they are only sold separately is $P_1 = 600$ and $P_2 = 600$ for a profit of 3600.

The profit maximizing price for the bundle is 1000. Here, demand is 4 so that profits are 4000. If the price of the bundle rises to 1200, only two units will be bought, resulting in profits of 2400. If price rises further to 1400, only a single unit is bought and profits are 1400. Hence, the profit maximizing price for the bundle when pure bundling is conducted is 1000 for a profit of 4000.

The correct answer to the second part of the question is (c). The correct answer to the third part of the question is (a). The profit maximizing price for goods 1 and 2 sold separately under a strategy of mixed bundling is 900 for each good. The profit maximizing price for the bundle when mixed bundling is used is 1200. At these prices, customers 1 and 4 consume their high valuation good only and customers 2 and 3 consume only the bundle. Profits are 900 + 900 + 1200 + 1200 = 4200. Comparing this to the profits of pure bundling and selling the goods separately (sometimes referred to as a "pure components" strategy), we can see that both forms of bundling dominate a pure components strategy, and mixed bundling does even better than pure bundling.

9. The correct answer is (c). From the inverse demand we get $Q = 100A^{1/2}P^{-2}$ so that $E_{Q,A} = 1/2$ and $E_{Q,P} = -2$. The advertising intensity is $A/PQ = -E_{Q,A}/E_{Q,P} = 1/4$.

Answers to Problems

1.

    a. There can be price discrimination if it is allowed legally and if the buyers cannot trade among themselves. If they could, then those buying cheaper can always sell them at a higher price (but what is less than what the monopolist charges). In order to calculate the prices for the two markets, we have the following calculations. In market "o", we have, then, $P_o = 100 - 0.5Q_o$ → $MR_o = 100 - Q_o$ → $100 - Q_o = 10$ or $Q_o^* = 90$ → $P_o^* = 55$. In market "y", we have $P_y = 160 - Q_y$ → $MR_y = 160 - 2y$ → $160 - 2y = 10$ → $Q_y^* = 75$ → $P_y^* = 85$.

    b. If the monopolist cannot price discriminate, we must add the demands (not the inverse demands) to get total demand, $Q = Q_o + Q_y = 200 - 2P + 160 - P = 360 - 3P$. Hence, calculating the inverse demand based on this, we have $P = 120 - Q/3$. Marginal revenue based on the inverse demand is $MR = 120 - 2Q/3$ so that our profit maximization condition becomes $120 - 2Q/3 = 10$ or $Q^* = 165$ and $P^* = 65$. The optimal quantity, Q^*, will be divided between the markets such that $Q_o = 200 - 130 = 70$ and $Q_y = 160 - 65 = 95$. At this equilibrium, the price is less than the P_y^* and more than P_o^* in part a. The young market buys more and the old market buys less.

2. It is likely that Joe's marginal costs are the same whether the house is located on the top of the hill or the bottom of the hill, so any difference in price we see for the same paint job is likely to be due to price discrimination. Painting a house is a service that would be difficult to trade, so arbitrage is unlikely. Further, Joe is the only house painter so he likely has some market power. We do not know whether Joe charges a different price to each customer for the same size job, only that he charges more to the wealthy people as a group. If he were to be charging a different price for each equivalent job to each customer, then he would be practicing first degree price discrimination. If he charges a higher price to the wealthy people as a group, he is conducting third degree price discrimination, using the location of the house as an identifier of the wealth of the individual requesting the paint job.

   A third degree price discriminating monopolist would charge a higher price to a group with a less elastic demand. If the wealthy people have less time or willingness to paint their houses themselves, it might be likely that their demands would be less elastic.

3.

   a. If the drug is patentable and important, it is a reasonable assumption that the drug company will be a monopolist for a number of years. As the two countries have different demand curves, the company will use third degree price discrimination, charging PI in the industrialized country and PL in the less developed country. The firm's profits are area PIABMC in the industrialized country and area PLDEMC in the less developed country, as shown below.

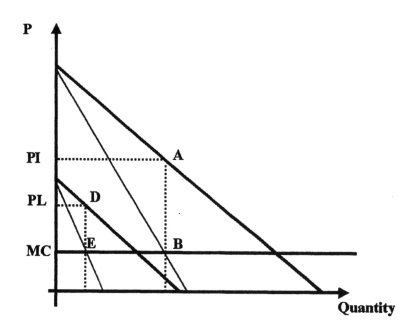

Hence, if the cost of developing the drug, R, is less than total profits, then the drug company should proceed with the research since the net profit will be positive from the venture.

b. If third degree price discrimination is not feasible, then the monopolist would charge a single price P*. If demand in the less developed country is not too low, then the optimal price will occur where MC is equal to the MR curve corresponding to the total demand for the drug. This total demand is obtained as the horizontal sum of the demand in the two countries. This is represented on the graph below. If demand in the less developed country is sufficiently low, then the drug company would set P = PI, as in the graph above so that consumers in the industrialized country would be the only ones who could afford the drug. In either case the total profits of the firm are lower than when third degree price discrimination was possible. It is therefore possible that the drug would only be developed if the drug company were reasonably sure that contraband would not be tolerated.

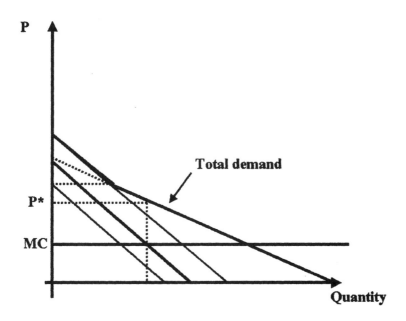

4.

a. Profit is $P_1Q_1 + P_2(Q_2-Q_1) - 80Q_2$. Total revenue is $TR = P_1Q_1 + P_2(Q_2-Q_1)$ and total cost is $TC = 80Q_2$ (80 per unit times the total number of units, which is Q_2).

b. $MR_1 = \Delta TR/\Delta Q_1 = \Delta(P_1Q_1)/\Delta Q_1 + \Delta(P_2(Q_2-Q_1))/\Delta Q_1$. Since Q_2 is held constant, this boils down to $\Delta(P_1Q_1)/\Delta Q_1 - \Delta(P_2Q_1)/\Delta Q_1 = P_1 + \Delta P_1/\Delta Q_1 - P_2 = P_1 - 4Q_1 - P_2 = (200 - 4Q_1 - 4Q_1 - (200 - 4Q_2)) = 4Q_2 - 8Q_1$. $MC_1 = \Delta TC/\Delta Q_1 = \Delta(80Q_2)/\Delta Q_1$. Since we assume that Q_2 is constant, $MC_1 = 0$. This makes sense. If we increase Q_1, keeping Q_2 constant, it means that we are keeping total production constant but switching output between two pricing categories. Since we have kept total production constant, the marginal cost of production is zero!

c. $MR_2 = \Delta TR/\Delta Q_2 = \Delta(P_1Q_1)/\Delta Q_1 + \Delta(P_2(Q_2-Q_1))/\Delta Q_2$. Since we assume that Q_1 is constant, the first term is zero. The second term is $\Delta(P_2Q_2)/\Delta Q_2 - Q_1\Delta P_2/\Delta Q_2 = P_2 + \Delta P_2/\Delta Q_2 - Q_1\Delta P_2/\Delta Q_2 = P_2 - 4Q_2 + 4Q_1 = 200 - 4Q_2 - 4Q_2 + 4Q_1 = 200 - 8Q_2 + 4Q_1$. In other words, marginal revenue is the usual expression plus a term (Q_1) that takes account of the fact that the loss in revenue on inframarginal units when P_2 is changed only occurs over $(Q_2 - Q_1)$. $MC_2 = \Delta TC/\Delta Q_2 = \Delta 80Q_2/\Delta Q_2 = 80$.

d. The profit maximization conditions are, then: (1) $MR_1 = MC_1$ and (2) $MR_2 = MC_2$. Rewriting these, we have (1) $4Q_2 = 8Q_1$ and (2) $200 - 8Q_2 + 4Q_1 = 80$. Solving these by substituting $2Q_1 = Q_2$ into the second condition we have $Q_1^* = 10$ and $Q_2^* = 20$. Prices are $P_1^* = 200 - 4(10) = 160$ and $P_2^* = 200 - 4(20) = 120$. Profit is $(160-80)(10) + (120-80)(20) = 800 + 800 = 1600$.

5.

a. The points where r_2 equals the price p_2 form a straight line, as do the points where r_1 equals p_1 (since price is a constant number in both cases). Consumers, such as A, who have a reservation price for good 2 that exceeds p_2 buy this good. Consumers, such as C, who have a reservation price for good 1 that exceeds p_1 buy this good. Consumers, such as B, whose reservation prices for both goods exceed both prices buy both goods. Consumers, such as D, whose reservation prices for both goods are less than price do not purchase anything. Hence, a "pure components" strategy segments the market of consumers into four purchasing blocks.

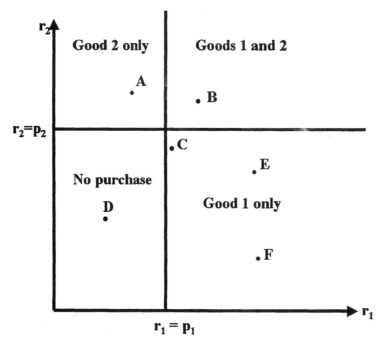

b. The points where the sum of the reservation prices equal p_b is a diagonal line with slope -1 since p_b is a constant. (Think of how we drew the budget constraint for consumers. In that case, the weighted sum of two prices equaled a constant, income.) Consumers, such as A or E, with reservation prices that total to more than p_b purchase the bundle while consumers, such as D, with reservation prices that total to less than p_b do not purchase. Hence, bundling divides consumers in this market into two segments.

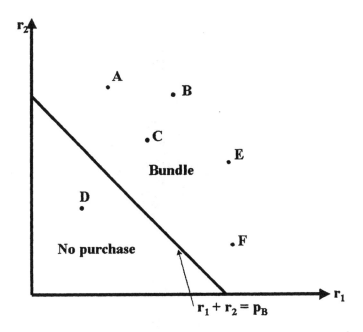

c. If mixed bundling is used, the market is segmented according to the graph below into 6 purchasing blocks.

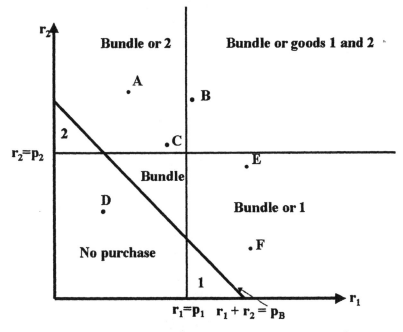

d. Mixed bundling increases the market size compared to the pure components strategy by the triangle labeled "bundle", since these consumers would buy nothing if the bundle were not offered. In other words, consumers with a relatively even and relatively low valuation of the two goods are lost under the pure components strategy. Similarly, it increases the market size compared to the pure bundling strategy by the triangles labeled "1" and "2", since these consumers would buy nothing if the pure components were not offered. In other words, consumers with a high valuation of only a single good are lost under the pure bundling strategy.

Answers to Exam

1.

a. One possible direct screening device might be a university or high school degree. Such a degree might be evidence that the person interviewing for the job might be persistent and hard-working enough to obtain a significant achievement.

b. If the job offers a flat wage rate regardless of the amount of work put in, then lazy and hard-working employees face the same rewards from working. It is not possible, then, for this contract to induce self-selection. On the other hand, if the job offers a piece rate, then lazy employees (who presumably would have low output levels) would receive a lower reward from working than hard-working employees since the total remuneration from work is the piece rate times the output produced. The piece rate could, then, work as a self-selection device in the following way. A hard-working employee would be more tempted to work in the firm rather than elsewhere if the piece rate is high enough that the worker's own anticipated output times the piece rate results in a higher overall remuneration than the competing flat wage rate.

2.

a. If Bums and Tums can ask for a picture identification card at the door, then it can prevent arbitrage across customers. Further, if Bums and Tums is the only gym in town, it has some market power. Hence, price discrimination is possible.

If Bums and Tums knows each customer's reservation price, then it can conduct first degree price discrimination. In fact, since all customers are identical in this market, Bums and Tums could charge the entire amount of consumer's surplus (if it knows demand) by setting a yearly membership fee equal to consumer's surplus for the amount of usage, Q*, that maximizes consumer's surplus (i.e., the point at which marginal cost intersects demand). Under such a scheme members could use the gym for up to Q* hours a year. Equivalently, Bums and Tums could charge the same membership fee and an hourly price equal to marginal cost. In this case, there is no need to restrict the number of hours per year as members would choose on their own to come for only Q* hours a year.

b. By setting profit maximizing uniform charge for each use, the monopolist would capture the profits that are shaded below. By setting an entrance fee equal to the entire consumer's surplus for the quantity of use that maximizes consumer's surplus, the firm can capture the entire triangle below demand and above marginal cost.

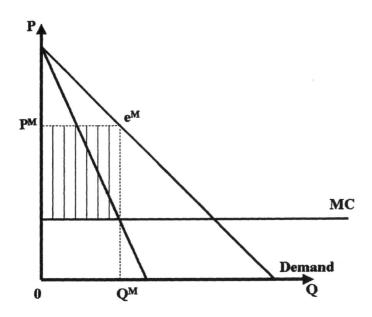

c. The entry decision should depend on the pricing scheme, since the uniform pricing scheme results in lower profits than the annual entrance scheme. If the uniform pricing scheme must be used and results in profits that are less than F, then entry should not occur. If the annual fee may be used and results in profits that are more than F, then entry should occur.

3.

    a. The price elasticity of demand is −½.

    b. By analogy, the advertising elasticity of demand is ½.

    c. The advertising elasticity is positive since an increase in advertising tends to increase demand. As long as we assume that there is no bad advertising and advertising actually has a positive effect, this will be the case.

    d. We know from the summary that the profit maximizing monopolist will set the advertising sales ratio equal to $-E_{Q,A}/E_{Q,P} = -(1/2)/(-1/2) = 1$. In other words, for this demand function, the advertising sales ratio is constant and equal to 1 (whatever the output or advertising level).

4. The subscription fee, F, plus a usage charge, p, results in a total expenditure of a consumer of F + pq, where q is the number of units consumed. The average expenditure per unit is, then, F/q + p. Therefore, as q increases, the average expenditure per unit sold falls. Hence, the average expenditure per unit is lower for high use customers than for low use customers. This is equivalent to saying that there is a quantity discount for higher use customers.

Chapter 13: Market Structure and Competition

The **structure of a market** -- the number of firms that compete with each other, the ease with which firms enter or leave the market, and the extent to which firms' products are differentiated from competitors' products -- affects how intensely firms compete with each other. As shown in Table 13.1, market structures differ along two important dimensions: the number of sellers and the nature of **product differentiation** (i.e., the extent to which products sold in the market differ on important characteristics while remaining demand substitutes).

Number of firms (sellers):

Degree of Product Differentiation:	Many	Few	One Dominant	One
Firms produce identical products	Perfect Competition	**Oligopoly with homogeneous products**	**Dominant firm**	Monopoly
Firms produce differentiated products	**Monopolistic Competition**	**Oligopoly with differentiated products**	------------	------------

Table 13.1

So far, we have studied perfect competition and monopoly. These are extreme market structures in the sense that they refer only to the cases of very many or a single seller. Many markets cannot be classified into one of these extremes.   For example, the U.S. market for colas has a *few* sellers and many buyers. In this chapter, we will study several models of such intermediate market structures. They are indicated in bold in the table. We will begin with **oligopoly** (i.e., markets characterized by few sellers and many buyers). There are many different models of oligopoly. We will study three: the **Cournot model**, the **Bertrand model** and the **Stackelberg model**. For markets where a firm with a large market share coexists with many small firms, we introduce a model of **dominant firm** competition. We will also interpret the Stackelberg model as a "dominant firm" model. Finally, we study markets that have many buyers and sellers but where differentiated products are sold by using the model of (**Chamberlinian**) **monopolistic competition**.

Unless specifically mentioned, we will assume that marginal and average costs are the same and constant. The problems at the end of the chapter investigate how our conclusions change when this is not the case.

Cournot Oligopoly

The simplest version of this model is a case with only two sellers. Markets with two sellers are called **duopoly markets**. We will start by assuming that the two firms sell homogeneous products. One of the main distinguishing characteristics of the Cournot model is that we assume that the only decision that the two firms must make is *how much to produce*. Further, this decision is made simultaneously and non-cooperatively so that the firms do not communicate or collude with each other when making their decision. Rather, each firm chooses its output so as to maximize its own profits, taking into account its guess about the amount of output that will be supplied by the other firm.

Exercise 1: *Let (inverse) market demand be P(Q) = 100 - Q, where Q is market output and equals the sum of the outputs of firms 1 and 2 (i.e., Q = q_1 + q_2). The firms sell a homogeneous (identical) product. Firm 1's total cost of production equals TC(q_1) = 10q_1. Which of the following expressions is the profit function of firm 1?*

   a. Profit of firm 1 = (100 - q_1)q_1 - 10q_1
   b. Profit of firm 1 = (100 - q_1 - q_2)q_1 - 10q_1
   c. Profit of firm 1 = (100 - q_1 - q_2 - 10)q_1
   d. Profit of firm 1 = (100 - Q)Q - 10Q

Recall that the monopolist chose its output level by producing at the point where marginal revenue equaled marginal cost. The marginal revenue curve was obtained from the market demand curve. Our two Cournot duopolists behave in a similar way. The only difference is that the marginal revenue is now obtained from each firm's **residual demand curve.** Firm 1's residual demand curve is the demand left over once the other firm has sold its output of q_2. If, for example firm 1 expects that firm 2 will produce 10 units of output then firm 1's residual demand curve is equal to the market demand curve minus the 10 units that firm 2 is anticipated to sell. In other words, the residual demand curve facing firm 1 is simply the market demand curve shifted back 10 units, as shown in Figure 13.1, below.

Price

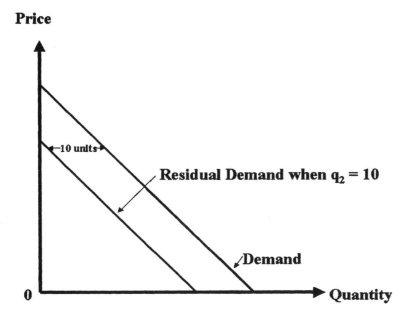

Figure 13.1

Exercise 2: *Let the (inverse) market demand be as in Exercise 1. Suppose that firm 2 is anticipated to sell 20 units. What is the equation for firm 1's residual demand curve?*

a. $P = 100 - q_1 - 20$
b. $P = 100 - q_1 - 10$
c. $P = 100 - Q - 20$
d. $P = 100 - q_1 - q_2 - 20$

Now, suppose that firm 2 is anticipated to sell q_2 units. What is the equation for firm 2's residual demand curve?

a. $P = 100 - q_1 - 20$
b. $P = 100 - Q - 20$
c. $P = 100 - q_1 - q_2$
d. $P = 100 - Q - q_2$

Firm 1's residual demand curve can be interpreted as the demand that is left unfilled if all the units produced by firm 2 actually sell. Hence, firm 1 can be thought of as a monopolist for this unfilled portion of demand since no other producer has output to sell to this group! The profit maximizing behavior for firm 1 is, then, to calculate marginal revenue based on its residual demand curve and set output so that this "residual marginal revenue" equals marginal cost. This is pictured in Figure 13.2 as point q_1^* when firm 2 is anticipated to produce 10 units.

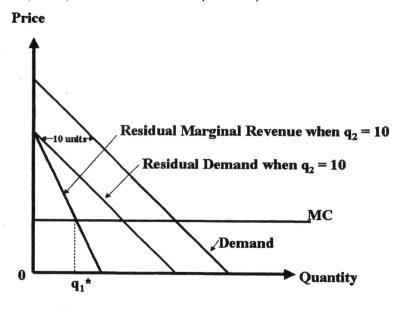

Figure 13.2

The general equation for the residual marginal revenue of firm 1 when firm 2 produces some output, q_2, is $MR_{q2} = P + q_1(\Delta P/\Delta q_1)$. In other words, the marginal revenue for firm 1 is the price its extra unit of output can command plus the loss on all its *own* inframarginal units, q_1, due to the decrease in price that results when q_1 *only* increases.

Exercise 3: *Let inverse market demand and firm 1's total cost curve be as in Exercise 1. What is the equation of firm 1's residual marginal revenue curve when firm 2 is anticipated to produce 20 units of output?*

    a. $MR_{20} = 100 - q_1 - 20$
    b. $MR_{20} = 100 - q_1 - q_2 - 20$
    c. $MR_{20} = 100 - 2q_1 - 20$

What is the profit maximization condition of firm 1 when firm 2 is anticipated to produce 20 units of output?

    a. $100 - 2q_1 - 20 = 10q_1$
    b. $100 - 2q_1 - 20 = 10$
    c. $100 - q_1 - 20 = 10$

What is the profit maximization condition of firm 1 when firm 2 is anticipated to produce q_2 units of output?

    a. $100 - 2q_1 - q_2 = 10q_1$
    b. $100 - 2q_1 - q_2 = 10$
    c. $100 - q_1 - q_2 = 10$

The intersection of "residual marginal revenue" and marginal cost gives firm 1's profit maximizing *response* to a given output level by firm 2. For example, point $q_1*(20)$ in Figure 13.3 gives firm 1's profit maximizing response to an output level of 20 by firm 2. Consequently, the point where residual marginal revenue equals marginal cost is often called the **best response** of firm 1 to firm 2. If we could plot the best response of firm 1 to *any* anticipated level of output of firm 2, then this set of points would form the **best response function** or the **reaction function** of firm 1. This is pictured in Figure 13.3. Algebraically, the best response function of firm 1 is simply the profit maximization condition (residual marginal revenue = marginal cost) when firm 2's anticipated output is q_2. The reaction function is written, however, putting q_1 on the left-hand side of the equality.

Exercise 4: *What is the best response of firm 1 to an output of $q_2 = 20$ when demand and cost are as in Exercise 1?*

    a. $q_1 = 80$
    b. $q_1 =$ (approximately) 2.8
    c. $q_1 = 35$

What is the equation of the reaction function of firm 1 when demand and cost are as in Exercise 1?

    a. $q_1 = 90 - q_2/2$
    b. $q_1 = 45 - q_2/2$
    c. $q_1 = 45 - q_2$

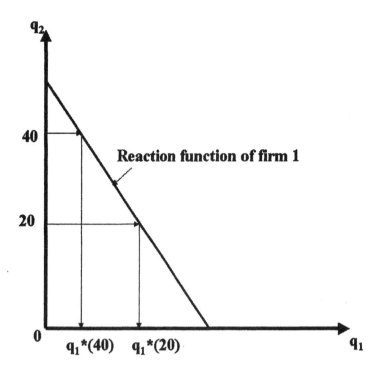

Figure 13.3

We can derive the reaction function for firm 2 using exactly the same reasoning. In other words, we need to calculate the residual demand of firm 2 for any output level, q_1, produced by firm 1. We must then calculate the (residual) marginal revenue corresponding to this residual demand and set it equal to marginal cost. Finally, we rewrite this profit maximization condition with q_2 on the left-hand side of the equality to get firm 2's reaction function (see Exercise 5 to calculate a reaction function for firm 2).

Equilibrium in the Cournot market must satisfy the condition that each firm must be producing its best response to the other firm's anticipated output. In other words, each firm must be producing at a point on its reaction function. Graphically, this means that the equilibrium point is the point where the reaction functions cross. This is depicted in Figure 13.4, below.

---

4 Steps to Finding a Cournot Equilibrium

1. Find the equation of the residual demand curve for each firm.
2. Find the equation of the "residual marginal revenue" curve for each firm.
3. Set the residual marginal revenue curve equal to marginal cost for each firm.
4. Solve the set of equalities in step 3 simultaneously to obtain the equilibrium output for each firm. These equilibrium output levels are the Cournot equilibrium outputs for the market.

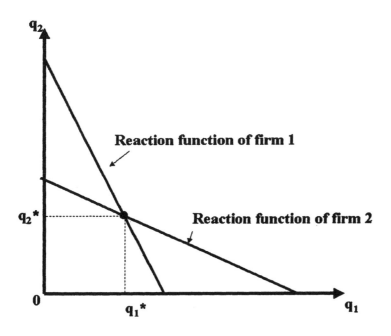

Figure 13.4

Exercise 5: *For the demand and cost in Exercise 1, and assuming that firm 2's costs are the same as firm 1's, what is the Cournot equilibrium set of outputs, (q_1^*, q_2^*)?*

    a. $q_1^* = 30$; $q_2^* = 45$
    b. $q_1^* = 45$; $q_2^* = 30$
    c. $q_1^* = 30$; $q_2^* = 30$

What is the profit of each firm in the Cournot equilibrium?

    a. profit of firm 1 = 900; profit of firm 2 = 900
    b. profit of firm 1 = 0; profit of firm 2 = 0
    c. profit of firm 1 = 900; profit of firm 2 = 0

Bertrand Oligopoly

In the Cournot model, each firm selects a *quantity* to produce and the resulting total output determines market price. In contrast, the Bertrand model assumes that each firm selects a *price* to charge and simply produces the quantity required to satisfy the demand that comes its way. In the simplest case we consider here, we will derive equilibrium in a market with two firms (duopoly) and a homogeneous product. Each firm chooses its price to maximize its profits given the anticipated price of the other firm. The choice of price occurs simultaneously and non-cooperatively.

In order to derive the Bertrand equilibrium, note that a firm in a Bertrand market that has set its price *higher* than its competitor's will sell no output: all consumers flock to the low price supplier since the product is assumed to be homogeneous. On the other hand, a firm that has set its price *lower* than its competitor's will capture all market demand. Hence, firm 1's residual demand curve is composed of two segments: whenever $p_1 > p_2$, residual demand is zero. Whenever $p_1 < p_2$, residual demand equals market demand. At the point where $p_1 = p_2$, consumers are indifferent as to which firm's output they buy, so we assume for simplicity that the firms split market demand equally. Hence, the residual demand for firm 1 looks as follows:

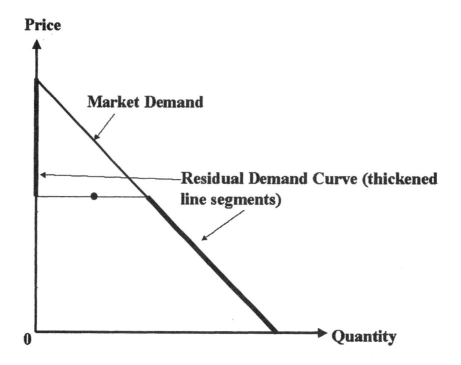

Figure 13.5

The equation for the Bertrand residual demand for firm 1 when market demand is Q is, then:

$$q_1 = 0 \qquad \text{if } p_1 > p_2$$
$$(1/2)Q(p_1,p_2) \qquad \text{if } p_1 = p_2$$
$$Q(p_1,p_2) \qquad \text{if } p_1 < p_2$$

Now, we wish to determine the equilibrium price for the Bertrand market. For any anticipated price, p_2, what would firm 1's profit maximizing best response be? If it charged $p_1 > p_2$, it would earn nothing. If it charged $p_1 = p_2$, then it would earn profits based on serving half of industry demand. As long as price exceeds marginal (and average) cost, this would clearly yield higher profits than charging $p_1 > p_2$. On the other hand, suppose firm 1 lowered its price just a tiny bit more so that $p_1 < p_2$. While this is a *tiny* decrease in price, it would drastically increase the number of customers who wished to purchase from firm 1, from $(1/2)Q$ to Q! As long as price exceeds marginal (and average) cost, then, this price cut is profitable. Hence, we can say that the best response to any price, p_2, which exceeds marginal (and average) cost is to charge p_1 *slightly less* than p_2. Formally, the reaction function of firm 1 is:

$$p_1 = p_2 - \varepsilon \text{ (with } \varepsilon \text{ very small) when } p_2 > MC$$
$$p_1 = p_2 \qquad \ldots \qquad \text{when } p_2 = MC$$

This is illustrated below:

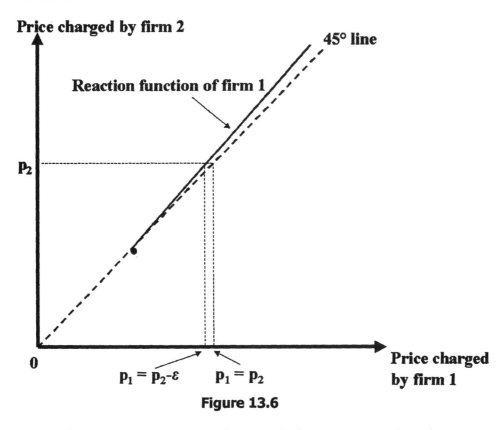

Figure 13.6

The reaction function of firm 2 is derived in exactly the same way and can be expressed as:

$$p_2 = p_1 - \varepsilon \text{ (with } \varepsilon \text{ very small) when } p_1 > MC$$
$$p_2 = p_1 \qquad \ldots \qquad \text{when } p_1 = MC$$

Graphically, firm 2's reaction function is a line that lies slightly to the right of the 45° line in Figure 13.6. The Bertrand equilibrium is the point that lies on both reaction functions, where each firm is choosing its profit maximizing price given the anticipated price charged by the rival firm. Let us think about where this equilibrium point must lie. If it is in the interest of each firm to undercut the price of the other as long as price exceeds marginal (and average) cost, but it is in the interest of neither firm to price below marginal (and average) cost, then the equilibrium point must be where each firm is pricing exactly *at* marginal (and average) cost. Here, each firm has no incentive to raise price (since it would lose all its customers) or to lower price (since it would earn negative profits). Graphically, the intersection of the reaction functions occurs at the lower left-hand point on the reaction functions, below:

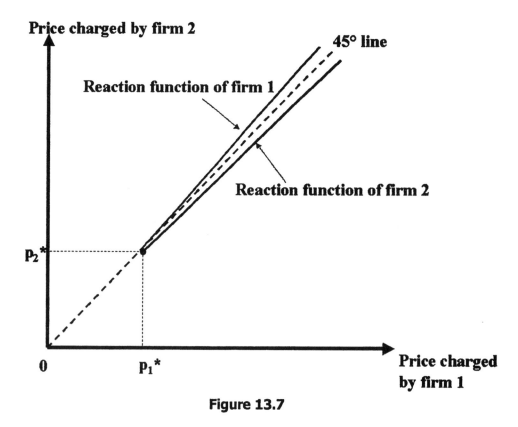

Figure 13.7

Exercise 6: *For the demand and costs given in Exercises 1-5, above, what are the Bertrand equilibrium prices?*

    a. $p_1^* = 30$; $p_2^* = 30$
    b. $p_1^* = 30$; $p_2^* = 10$
    c. $p_1^* = 10$; $p_2^* = 10$

Since the Bertrand equilibrium occurs at the point where price equals marginal (and average) cost for both firms, profits are zero for the firms in Bertrand equilibrium. This was not true for the Cournot equilibrium (e.g., see Exercise 5). We have seen, then, that the basic *reasoning* of the Bertrand model is the same as that of the Cournot model, but the *characteristics* of the Bertrand equilibrium differ *drastically* from those of the Cournot equilibrium. We turn now to an explanation of this difference.

The assumptions and conclusions of our two simple versions of the Cournot and Bertrand models are summarized in the table below. Note that "static" in the table refers to the fact that the firms make their decision on price or quantity only once.

ASSUMPTIONS

Simplified Version of COURNOT	Simplified Version of BERTRAND
2 firms	2 firms
Constant marginal and average cost	Constant marginal and average cost
Simultaneous and noncooperative	Simultaneous and noncooperative
Homogeneous product	Homogeneous product
Static	Static
Choice variable: QUANTITY	Choice variable: PRICE

CONCLUSIONS

Simplified Version of COURNOT	Simplified Version of BERTRAND
Reaction functions SLOPE DOWN	Reaction functions SLOPE UP
Price EXCEEDS marginal cost for less than an infinite number of sellers	Price EQUALS marginal cost for any number of sellers greater than one
Profits POSITIVE for less than an infinite number of sellers	Profits ZERO for any number of sellers greater than one

Table 13.2

The assumptions of the two models are the same with the exception that the Cournot model assumes that firms set quantities and the Bertrand model assumes that firms set prices. The conclusions differ drastically, however. In the Cournot duopoly, both firms make positive profits and market price is above marginal cost. In the Bertrand model, both firms make zero profits and market price equals marginal cost. Recalling from Chapter 11 that it did not matter to the equilibrium profit whether a *monopolist* set quantity or price, it is surprising that changing the decision variable makes such a difference when we move from one to two sellers. This can be understood as follows. In the Cournot model, firm 1 chooses its level of output taking the level of output of its rival, q_2, as *given*. In other words, firm 1 assumes that, however much it decides to produce, it cannot expect to steal *any* customers away from its rival. Hence, because business stealing is not an option, firms do not behave very aggressively. On the other hand, a firm that lowers its price even infinitesimally steals *all* the customers of its rival in the Bertrand model. Because business stealing is so easy, it makes firms behave very aggressively. This drives down price and profits much farther than in the Cournot case.

We can see another contrast between the models in their predictions about the number of firms required in the industry to drive industry profits to zero. Consider first the Cournot case. The two firms together in a Cournot duopoly produce more output than they would if they acted together as a monopolist (see Exam question 4 to explore this). This is not surprising. Because each firm maximizes its own profit, it *only* takes into account the fact that when it expands its output it reduces the price it earns on its *own* units. The firm does not care about the fact that it reduces the earnings of its rival at the same time. Hence, each firm underestimates the cost to the *industry* due to an increase in output. As the number of firms in the Cournot industry increases, this overproduction gets worse because each firm takes into account the effect of the loss in earnings over a smaller and smaller output *relative* to total market size. Hence, the industry output grows as the number of Cournot competitors grows. When the number of competitors becomes infinite, in fact, the Cournot equilibrium market output attains the perfectly competitive equilibrium market output, price falls to the perfectly competitive equilibrium price, and profits fall to zero. In contrast, the Bertrand model predicts that prices fall to marginal cost and profits fall to zero as soon as *at least* two firms are in the industry. Prices and profits fall no farther no matter how many other competitors are added. Formally, the percentage contribution margin at the equilibrium price, $(P*-MC)/P*$, falls in the Cournot model as the number of competitors in the industry, N, rises:

$$(P* - MC)/P* = - (1/N)(1/\varepsilon_{Q,P})$$

where $\varepsilon_{Q,P}$ is the price elasticity of market demand. In the Bertrand model, the percentage contribution margin is zero no matter what N is (as long as N is no less than 2).

Exercise 7: *Suppose that demand and cost are the same as in Exercise 1, but now there are <u>three</u> firms competing in the market. To get started, compute the residual demand facing firm 1 when firm 2 produces q_2 and firm 3 produces q_3. What is the Cournot equilibrium quantity supplied by each firm in this market?*

   a. $q_1* = q_2* = q_3* = 30$
   b. $q_1* = q_2* = q_3* = 22.5$
   c. $q_1* = q_2* = q_3* = 45$

What are the industry output and the profit level of each firm in the Cournot equilibrium?

   a. $Q* = 90$; Profit of each firm $= 900$
   b. $Q* = 67.5$; Profit of each firm $= 506.25$
   c. $Q* = 135$; Profit of each firm $= 0$

Again, supposing that demand and cost are as in Exercise 1, but three firms compete in the market, what is industry output level and profit level for each firm in the Bertrand equilibrium?

   a. $Q* = 90$; Profit of each firm $= 0$
   b. $Q* = 67.5$; Profit of each firm $= 506.25$
   c. $Q* = 70$; Profit of each firm $= 300$

Stackelberg Oligopoly

The Cournot and Bertrand models can accommodate some asymmetry among market participants. For example, the levels of marginal cost can differ across firms (see Exam problem 3 at the end of this summary for an example of this). These two models do not, however, accommodate a case where one firm plays a dominant role over the other. Two cases that interpret what "dominance" means slightly differently will be considered here. The first is the **Stackelberg model** of oligopoly. This model assumes that dominance translates into the ability to choose output *first*, before the rival. In other words, rather than acting simultaneously, as in the Cournot and Bertrand models, the firms act sequentially with one firm choosing its output first and the other choosing second, taking the first firm's choice as *given*. The first firm to choose is called the **leader** and the second to choose is the **follower**. Not surprisingly, perhaps, leadership will translate into higher profits and market share.

Now, let's look at how to work out the equilibrium output choices in this model. Consider the follower's decision first. The follower must observe the leader's (irrevocable) output decision and choose its own optimal response. The behavior, then, looks very much like the Cournot firm's: taking the output of the leader as given, the follower selects its best response so as to maximize profits. Hence, the follower's behavior in the Stackelberg model can be summarized by the Cournot best response function.

Exercise 8: *Let firm 2 face demand and cost as in Exercise 1. Suppose that firm 2 is a Stackelberg follower, facing rival firm 1. Which of the following functions summarizes firm 2's behavior?*

  a. $100 - 2q_2 - q_1 = 10q_2$
  b. $100 - 2q_2 - q_1 = 10$
  c. $100 - q_2 - q_1 = 10$

Given that the follower will be behaving according to the "rule" that the best response function gives us, what is the best choice of the Stackelberg leader? The leader takes as a "constraint" on its own choice that the follower will behave according to its (Cournot) best response function. The leader then maximizes its own profits subject to this "constraint". Mathematically, in place of the follower's output in the demand equation, the leader uses the *output equation* given by the best response function. First, we calculate the revenue of the leader substituting the output equation for output of the follower. This gives us the "effective" or "residual" demand, taking into account the way that the follower will behave. Based on this we can calculate an "effective" marginal revenue and set it equal to marginal cost to obtain the profit maximizing solution.

Exercise 9: *Firm 2 is a Stackelberg follower whose behavior is summarized by the best response function $q_2 = 45 - q_1/2$. Demand and cost for the leader and follower are as given in Exercise 1. What is the leader's "effective" demand?*

  a. $55 - q_1/2$
  b. $55q_1 - q_1^2/2$
  c. $(55 - q_1/2)(45 + q_1/2)$

Now, using the revenue you have calculated, what is the effective marginal revenue for the leader, firm 1?

a. $55 - q_1/2$
b. $55 - Q$
c. $55 - q_1$

The leader uses its priority in setting quantity to choose a point that is *better* for it than the Cournot equilibrium. As the leader is constrained to choose some point along the follower's reaction function it could, of course, choose the Cournot equilibrium point. In general, however, the leader can do better by grabbing a larger part of the market. Using the same type of reasoning we developed for the Cournot model the follower, knowing that it can do nothing to steal these customers away from the leader, does best to retreat into a smaller market share.

Exercise 10: *For the firms in Exercise 9, calculate the Stackelberg leader's equilibrium output. Using the follower's best response function, calculate the follower's Stackelberg equilibrium output. What are the output levels of the two firms?*

a. Leader's output = 45; Follower's output = 22.5
b. Leader's output = 55; Follower's output = 35
c. Leader's output = 30; Follower's output = 30

Dominant Firms with "Fringe" Competitors

We assumed in the Stackelberg model that there were a small number (two) of firms in the market, with one firm being "dominant". We could also have an alternative concept of dominance that does not fit the Cournot, Bertrand or the Stackelberg model well: In this case, one firm produces an overwhelming share of the market output (a "dominant firm") while many other firms have such small market shares that they act like perfectly competitive firms (the "competitive fringe"). The reason is that the Cournot, Bertrand and Stackelberg firms are assumed to act as if they had some degree of market power *no matter what their market share*. Hence, these models cannot truly reflect industries where a "fringe" of small firms acts as price takers. Another way to put this is that the Cournot, Bertrand and Stackelberg firms always maximize profits by setting *marginal revenue* (different from price) equal to marginal cost. Fringe firms assume they are so small that they assume that their own output decisions cannot affect market price. Hence, they maximize profits by setting *price* equal to marginal cost.

Suppose, then, that there is a fringe of many small firms that choose their output levels so as to maximize profits taking market price as *given*. If the number of firms in the fringe is fixed, the horizontal summation of the fringe marginal cost curves (above the shut-down price) yields a short-run fringe supply curve, S_F. Let us assume that the dominant firm, on the other hand, wishes to set a price that maximizes its profits *taking into account* both market demand, D_M, and how its price affects the competitive fringe's supply. In other words, the reasoning of the dominant firm is similar to that of our oligopoly firms: it calculates its residual demand and then equates residual marginal revenue to marginal cost in order to determine its profit maximizing price. The only difference lies in how the residual demand is computed. Instead of taking the (single) quantity or price of the other firm as given, the dominant firm computes the *total* output of the competitive fringe *for each possible price level.*

We first calculate the dominant firm's residual demand curve. This curve tells us how much the dominant firm can sell at different prices, taking into account the quantity that the fringe will be placing on the market. This residual demand is, then, the market demand *minus* the fringe supply, S_F, at each price. This is the *horizontal* difference between the D_M and the S_F curve. For example, if price is below the fringe's shut-down price, no fringe firm will supply output and the residual demand equals the entire market demand. For prices above the shut-down price, the fringe supplies positive quantities so that the residual demand lies to the left of market demand. An example is shown in Figure 13.8, below. At price P_A in the figure, the fringe sells enough output that there is no residual demand left for the dominant firm. At price P_B, the fringe shuts down so that the dominant firm faces the entire market demand.

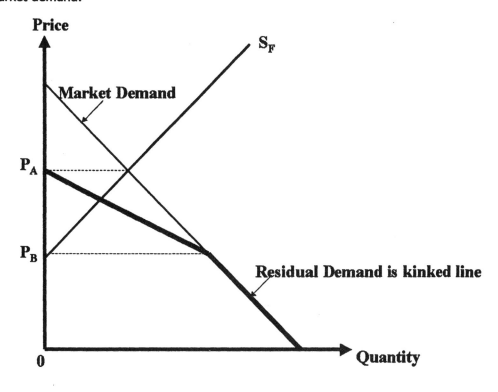

Figure 13.8

Exercise 11: *Let a competitive fringe of 30 small firms each have marginal cost equal to $10q_i$ and average cost equal to $5q_i$, where q_i is the output of firm i (and i = 1, 2, ...30). Let market demand be $P(Q) = 100 - Q$. All firms produce a homogeneous product so that market output is simply the sum of the outputs of all firms in the market. Suppose we now introduce a single, dominant firm into this market in addition to the 30 fringe firms.*

What is the shut-down price of the fringe firms?

a. $P^S = 0$
b. $P^S = 10$
c. $P^S = 20$

What is the equation of the residual demand faced by the dominant firm, where q_{DF} stands for the output of the dominant firm?

a. $P = 100 - 4/3q_{DF}$
b. $P = 25 - .25q_{DF}$
c. $P = 100 - 11q_{DF}$

As before, the dominant firm maximizes profits by setting residual marginal revenue equal to marginal cost. For prices so low that the fringe supply is zero, the residual marginal revenue simply equals the market marginal revenue. In other words, the dominant firm solves the same problem as a monopolist over this region. As price rises so that fringe supply is positive, residual marginal revenue must be based on the residual demand (that lies below market demand). This equilibrium point is a **short term equilibrium**, assuming that the number of fringe firms is fixed. The profits of the fringe firms may be positive at this point. A case where profits are positive for both the fringe and the dominant firm at the short term equilibrium is illustrated in Figure 13.9, below.

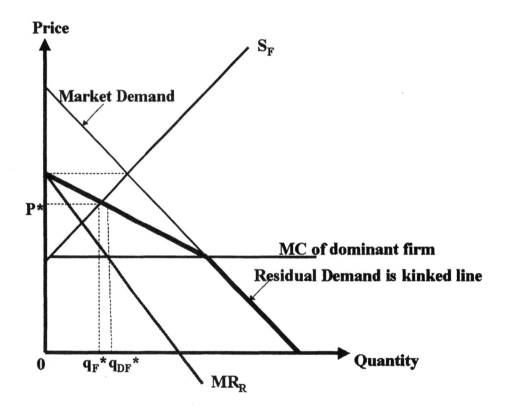

Figure 13.9

Exercise 12: *For the industry described in Exercise 11, what is the equation of the residual marginal revenue curve faced by the dominant firm, where q_{DF} is the output of the dominant firm?*

a. $MR_R = 25 - .5q_{DF}$
b. $MR_R = 100 - 8/3q_{DF}$
c. $MR_R = 100 - 22q_{DF}$

Supposing that the marginal (and average) cost of the dominant firm is constant and equal to MC = 5, what is the dominant firm's profit maximizing price and output? How much does the fringe supply (in total) at this price?

a. $P_{DF}^* = 5$; $q_{DF}^* = 40$; $S_F^* = 15$
b. $P_{DF}^* = 15$; $q_{DF}^* = 40$; $S_F^* = 45$
c. $P_{DF}^* = 15$; $q_{DF}^* = 40$; $S_F^* = 1.5$

   If the short-run price is above the shut-down price of the competitive fringe, entry will occur in the long-run (since the fringe is assumed to be competitive). If entry is *unlimited* in the long-run, then the fringe's long-run supply curve will be flat at the shut-down price (analogous to the perfect competition long-run industry supply curve). As a result, the residual demand curve for the dominant firm follows up the market demand curve until price reaches the fringe's shut-down price. At this point, residual demand becomes flat. For any price above this level, residual demand is zero. Residual marginal revenue equals residual demand for the segments where residual demand is zero and where it is flat at price. Elsewhere, marginal revenue is based on market demand.

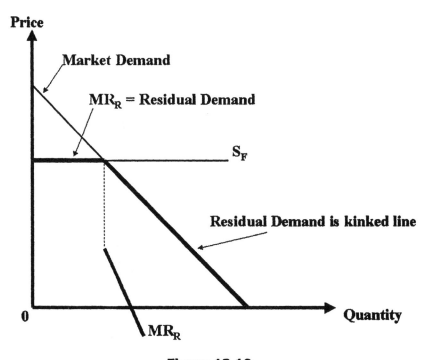

Figure 13.10

Exercise 13: *Let the market demand be P(Q) = 120 - Q. The sellers in the industry are composed of a dominant firm, with marginal cost of MC = 10q$_{DF}$ and average cost of AC = 5q$_{DF}$, as well as fringe firms. Each fringe firm has a shut-down price of P$_S$ = 80. There is no limit to the potential number of entrants to this industry. What are the long-run equilibrium price, output, and profit level of the dominant firm?*

    a. P* = 110; q*$_{DF}$ = 10; Profit = 100
    b. P* = 80; q*$_{DF}$ = 8; Profit = 0
    c. P* = 80; q*$_{DF}$ = 8; Profit = 320

Oligopoly with Differentiated Products

Economists distinguish between two types of product differentiation. Two products, 1 and 2, are **vertically differentiated** if, at the same price, all consumers prefer to purchase 1 rather than 2. In other words vertical differentiation refers to a pure quality differences between goods 1 and 2. In contrast, products 1 and 2 are **horizontally differentiated** if, at the same price, *some* customers prefer to purchase 1 rather than 2 at an equal price while others prefer to purchase 2 rather than 1. For example, while certain individuals would purchase Coke over Pepsi at the same price, others would purchase Pepsi over Coke. In this summary, we ignore quality differences and analyze the Cournot and Bertrand in the presence of horizontal differentiation only.

If a market contains products that are horizontally differentiated, then these products can sell for different prices. Because these products are still (imperfect) substitutes for each other, the demand for each product depends on the prices of all the products in the market. For example, if products 1 and 2 are horizontally differentiated, then the demand for product 1 decreases when its price increases but rises as the price of product 2 increases. Hence, an example of demands for products 1 and 2 might be the following:

$$Q_1 = 100 - P_1 + .5P_2$$
$$Q_2 = 100 - P_2 + .5P_1$$

In other words, as the price of 1 rises, less of 1 and more of 2 is consumed while as the price of 2 rises, less of 2 and more of 1 is consumed. By treating the two equations above as a system of equations in two unknowns, P$_1$ and P$_2$, and solving it, we can obtain the corresponding inverse demands:

$$P_1 = 200 - (4/3)Q_1 - (2/3)Q_2$$
$$P_2 = 200 - (2/3)Q_1 - (4/3)Q_2$$

Exercise 14: *In the demands for substitute products 1 and 2 given in the paragraph above, what is the formula for the own price elasticity of demand of good 1?*

    a. $\varepsilon_{Q1,P1}$ = -1(P$_1$)/Q$_1$
    b. $\varepsilon_{Q1,P1}$ = -(4/3)Q$_1$/P$_1$
    c. $\varepsilon_{Q1,P1}$ = 1(P$_1$/Q$_1$)

What is the formula for the cross price elasticity of demand for good 1?

a. $\varepsilon_{Q1,P2} = -1(P_2/Q_1)$
b. $\varepsilon_{Q1,P2} = (1/2)(P_2/Q_1)$
c. $\varepsilon_{Q1,P2} = -(2/3)(P_2/Q_1)$

Introducing product differentiation changes the equilibrium in both the Cournot and Bertrand models. However, the *qualitative* results of the Cournot model remain the same in the sense that profits still remain positive, and price remains above marginal cost. Also, the reaction functions remain downward sloping. On the other hand, the qualitative results of the Bertrand model change in the sense that the firms generally price *above* marginal cost, and make *positive* profits. The reaction functions are upward sloping, but they no longer lie very close to each other on each side of the 45° line (compare to Figure 13.6 of this summary). This change in the Bertrand reaction functions is the difference that you should focus on. The reason for this difference is that when firm A cuts its price slightly, it does *not* capture the entire market: product differentiation implies that some customers have a preference for product B that a small price change would not overcome. As a result, the business stealing incentive to cut price is much weaker when the products are differentiated. Hence, the Bertrand competitors are less aggressive. Consequently, prices and profits remain higher than under Bertrand competition with homogeneous products. A sample set of reaction functions for a Bertrand industry with product differentiation is shown below.

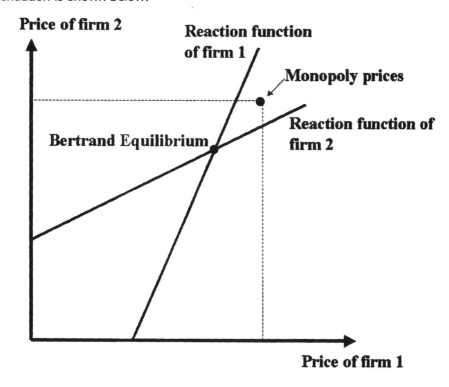

Figure 13.11

Exercise 15: *The shape of the Bertrand reaction functions in Figure 13.11 indicates that:*

a. When the price of product 1 rises, the best response of firm 2 is to raise its price as well.
b. When the price of product 1 rises, the best response of firm 2 is to lower its price.
c. When the price of product 1 is zero, the best response of firm 2 is to charge a positive price.
d. When the price of product 1 is zero, the best response of firm 2 is to charge zero as well.

The Bertrand equilibrium price will generally be below the price a monopolist would charge for the two goods. The reason is analogous to the reason why Cournot competitors tend to overproduce compared to the monopoly solution. Recall that a Bertrand competitor sets its price to maximize its own profits *only.* The competitor's profits are not its concern. Hence, when a Bertrand competitor lowers its price, it takes into account the positive effect the price cut will have on its *own* profits, but not the negative effect it will have on its competitor's profits. This means that a Bertrand competitor has a larger incentive to cut price than a monopolist since the monopolist would take into account the negative effect of a price cut for product 1 on the profits it earns from product 2. The monopoly price is indicated in Figure 13.11.

The algebraic steps to follow to solve for the Cournot and Bertrand equilibria under product differentiation are the same as the four steps for the homogeneous good case. Two problems in at the end of this summary (Problems 1 and 3) help you through the mechanics of these steps.

Monopolistic Competition

A market that is monopolistically competitive has three features. First, it consists of many buyers and sellers. Second, there is free entry and exit. Third, firms produce horizontally differentiated products. Hence, this model is just like the perfectly competitive model except that firms sell horizontally differentiated products rather than homogeneous products. Because the products are horizontally differentiated, each firm's demand curve for its own product is *downward sloping* rather than flat as in the case of perfect competition. In other words, if all other prices are fixed, a single firm's price cut generates *some* extra demand, but it does not necessarily allow the firm to capture *all* the demand in the market.

Because each firm faces downward sloping demand, each firm operates much like a monopolist on its demand despite the existence of many competitors. In other words, each firm sets marginal revenue (not equal to price) based on its own ("perceived" or "residual") demand equal to marginal cost in order to maximize profit. Equilibrium for a typical firm is represented in Figure 13.12.

This looks very much like the behavior of the differentiated product oligopolists of the previous section. In fact, one can think of the short-run equilibrium of the monopolistic competition model as analogous to the differentiated product oligopoly equilibrium. This analogy is explored in Problem 2 at the end of this summary. The real difference comes not in the short-run behavior but in the long-run behavior of this market. Recall that, even in the long-run, the oligopoly models assumed that entry is restricted. In the monopolistic competition model, however, we have free entry in the long-run. Hence, new entry occurs in response to a short-run price that exceeds average cost. When new entry occurs, the (residual) demand facing any one firm shifts in. This is because each firm captures a smaller share of the market at any given price when the substitutes available in the market proliferate. This is shown graphically in Figure 13.13. Note that we have depicted an average cost in Figure 13.13 that is not equal to marginal cost. The reason why this is important will become clear in a moment.

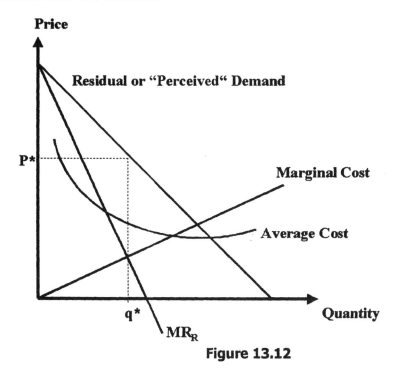

Figure 13.12

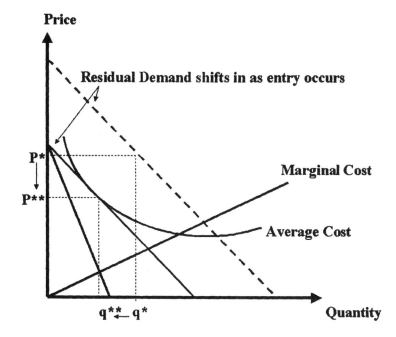

Figure 13.13

Entry will continue until each firm in the market earns zero profit. In other words, when demand has shifted back to a point where equilibrium price just covers both the fixed and variable costs of the firm, entry will stop. In other words, the long-run equilibrium conditions in this market are:

1. marginal revenue = marginal cost for each firm, based on its own (residual) demand
2. price equals average cost for each firm, based on its own (residual) demand

Graphically, this occurs at the point where demand has shifted back until it is just tangent to the firm's average cost curve at the output level where marginal revenue equals marginal cost for each firm. This is the point (q^{**}, P^{**}) illustrated in Figure 13.13. It is now clear why average cost could not equal marginal cost for monopolistic competition. If average and marginal cost had been the same (either flat or rising), then we could not obtain a long-run equilibrium satisfying both conditions (1) and (2), above.

Exercise 16: *Let each firm in an industry have marginal cost $MC = 10q_i$, and average cost $AC = 600/q_i + 5q_i$. Let demand be $P_i = 120 - q_i$ for each firm. What is the long-run monopolistically competitive equilibrium price for each good and firm output for this market?*

    a. $P_i^* = 110$; $q_i^* = 10$
    b. $P_i^* = 100$; $q_i^* = 20$
    c. $P_i^* = 95$; $q_i^* = 15$

The name of this market structure, "monopolistic competition", illustrates the fact that this market structure has both "monopolistic" and "competitive" behavior: in the short-run, firms behave as monopolists on their residual (or so-called "perceived") demand curves. In the long-run, free entry occurs, driving profits to zero.

Chapter Review Questions

1.
    a. Suppose that a government decides to terminate the monopoly position of a firm by breaking up that monopoly into two, identical, companies. Which of the models of market structure we have discussed so far would best describe competition in this industry?

    b. Now, suppose that instead of breaking up the monopoly, the government decides to terminate the monopoly by allowing free access to the patents upon which the monopoly was based. These patents allow any firm to produce the products that are identical to the monopolist's. The additional entry cost (besides patent access) for this industry is negligible. Which of the models of market structure we have discussed so far would best describe competition in this industry?

Answer:

a. While we do not know whether price or quantity is the decision variable in this industry, we can infer that the industry will be composed of a duopoly (at least, initially) with two identical competitors. If the firms can be assumed to produce identical products, then either the homogeneous product Bertrand model or the homogeneous product Cournot model would be appropriate. The dominant firm with fringe model would probably not be a very good descriptor of this industry, since we do not have any evidence that entry would be easy. Similarly, monopolistic competition and perfect competition can be ruled out if we have no reason to believe that there is free entry in this industry in the long-run.

b. If many firms can freely enter this industry upon receiving patent access and produce identical products, then perfect competition model could be an appropriate descriptor of this industry. On the other hand, perfect competition assumes that all sellers are small. This might not be a good assumption if the monopolist continues to have a cost advantage over the entrants or if it maintains a large market share for other reasons. Hence, the dominant firm with fringe model might be a better descriptor. Because there is free entry, the Cournot and Bertrand models probably would not be the best choice. Monopolistic competition assumes horizontal product differentiation, which is ruled out in the question.

2. A market for a homogeneous good has inverse demand $P = 120 - 2Q$. The marginal (and average) cost of production of the good is $MC = 20$.

a. Suppose that a monopolist produces this good. What is the profit maximizing output of the monopolist? Call the optimal output level q^M.

b. Now, two Cournot competitors produce the good. Compute the reaction functions of the two firms. What is the best response of firm 1 to an output level of zero by firm 2? How does this compare to your answer in (a)?

c. What is the best response of firm 1 to an output level of q^M by firm 2? What is the best response of firm 1 to an output level of $q^M/2$ by firm 2?

d. Suppose that the two Cournot competitors decide to increase profits by cooperating in the following way: each agrees to produce $q^M/2$ so that the industry generates monopoly profits. What does your answer to (c) suggest about whether the firms will have an incentive to "cheat" on this agreement by producing more than $q^M/2$?

Answer:

a. A monopolist sets marginal revenue (based on market demand) equal to marginal cost so that $120 - 4Q = 20$ or $q^M = 25$.

b. Let the output of firm 1 be q_1 and the output of firm 2 be q_2. Then the residual demand of firm 1 is $(120 - 2q_2) - 2q_1 = P$. The marginal revenue based on residual demand is $(120 - 2q_2) - 4q_1 = MR_R$. Setting this equal to marginal cost we have $120 - 2q_2 - 4q_1 = 20$ or $q_1* = 25 - .5q_2$. This is the reaction function of firm 1. Similarly, the reaction function of firm 2 is $q_2* = 25 - .5q_1$.

Using the reaction function, we see that the best response of firm 1 to $q_2 = 0$ is $q_1* = 25$. This is the monopoly output of part (a). Hence, if firm 2 decides to not operate, firm 1 simply operates as a monopolist on market demand.

c. If firm 2 produces output q^M, firm 1's best response (based on the reaction function of part (b) is $q_1* = 25 - .5(25) = 12.5$). In other words, while firm 1 operates as a monopolist in the industry when firm 2 produces zero it is *not* true that firm 1 produces zero if firm 2 produces as a monopolist. This is not surprising: if firm 1 produces zero it earns zero profits. On the other hand, we know that a monopolist restricts output so as to earn positive profits. By restricting output in this way, firm 2 leaves room for firm 1 to produce *some* output and earn positive profits.

If firm 2 produces half of monopoly output, firm 1's best response is $q_1* = 25 - .5(12.5) = 18.75$. In other words, if firm 2 produces half of the monopoly output, it is not optimal for firm 1 to produce half of monopoly output as well (even though responding with $q^M/2$ would mean that the two firms together would maximize the *industry* profits). The reason is that firm 1 chooses its best response to maximize its *own* profits only. As such, firm 1 does not take into account that by increasing its output beyond $q^M/2$ it depresses firm 2's profits to below half the monopoly profits. The fact is that by taking a larger share of the market firm 1 can increase its own profits, so it does so even if it hurts firm 2 in the process.

d. The answer to (c) suggests that this agreement would break down since $q^M/2$ would neither be firm 1's best response to an output of $q^M/2$ by firm 2, nor would it be firm 2's best response to an output of $q^M/2$ by firm 1. Both firms would have an incentive to increase their output beyond $q^M/2$ to a point where they would each be on their best response (or reaction) function. A point where each is on its reaction function is, of course, the Cournot equilibrium.

3. You are a consultant who has been hired to analyze the future of a certain industry. You have gathered some preliminary data that indicate the following. The industry is currently composed of 30 small firms. Each firm produces a product that is imperfectly substitutable for the other firms' products; however, no clear quality differences exist across products. The number of buyers of each of these substitute products is large. All industry participants (including new entrants to the industry) appear to have equal access to the resources necessary to produce and sell for this market. Further, you have estimated that, at current production levels, the marginal cost of each firm is 5, the marginal revenue of each firm is 5 as well, and the average cost of each firm is 10. The market price of each version of the product is 12.

a. What market structure do you think most appropriately describes this industry? What are the (long-run) equilibrium conditions for this market structure?

b. Would you expect the current price and output per firm to change in the short-run?

c. Would you expect long-run changes in number of industry participants and price for this industry?

Answer:

a. This industry appears to be monopolistically competitive. A large number of buyers and sellers exist, there is free entry, and the products sold are horizontally differentiated. The equilibrium conditions for this industry structure are (1) MR = MC for each firm and (2) P = AC for each firm.

b. The short-run equilibrium condition is condition (1) that MR = MC. This is satisfied at current output levels, so there is no reason to expect a change in the short-run.

c. At current production levels, price exceeds average cost, so the second condition for long-run equilibrium is violated. If price exceeds average cost, there is an incentive for firms to enter this industry so that we can say that we expect the number of market participants to rise. As entry occurs, each firm's residual demand will shift back. Whether this means that equilibrium price will rise or fall depends on the shape of average cost as well as on the shape of demand, so we would need further information to obtain a prediction of the direction of future price movements. We can, however, predict that there will be forces putting pressure on price to change.

Problem Set

1. Let the demands for two products, 1 and 2, be written:

$q_1 = 100 - P_1 + .5P_2$
$q_2 = 100 - P_2 + .5P_1$

Product 1 is produced by firm 1 at a marginal and average cost of 10. Product 2 is produced by firm 2 at the same marginal and average cost. Each firm wishes to set its price so as to maximize its own profits.

a. Compute the residual demand of firm 1. Illustrate the residual demand on a graph with the price of good 1 on the vertical axis and the quantity of good 1 on the horizontal axis. What is the vertical intercept of this residual demand? What happens to residual demand of good 1 as the price of good 2 increases?

b. Compute the residual demand for firm 2. Compute the marginal revenue curve of firm 1 and of firm 2 based on residual demand.

c. Calculate and illustrate the reaction functions of the two firms. Using your answer to part (a), explain the slopes of the reaction functions.

d. Calculate the Bertrand equilibrium prices, outputs, and profits for this market.

2. Let the demands for two products, 1 and 2, be written as:

$$q_1 = 100 - P_1 + .5P_2$$
$$q_2 = 100 - P_2 + .5P_1$$

Product 1 is produced by firm 1 and product 2 is produced by firm 2. Each firm has a total cost of production of $TC(q_i) = 2322.22 + 10q_i$, where i = 1,2. Assume that the firms are monopolistic competitors.

a. What is the short-run equilibrium in this market? Calculate the profit of each firm at the short-run equilibrium. How does this compare to your answer for problem (1d)?

b. Calculate the long-run monopolistic competition equilibrium in this market. Is there an incentive to enter in this market?

3. Let the demands for two products, 1 and 2, be written as:

$$P_1 = 200 - (4/3)q_1 - (2/3)q_2$$
$$P_2 = 200 - (2/3)q_1 - (4/3)q_2$$

Product 1 is produced by firm 1 and product 2 is produced by firm 2. Each firm has a marginal and average cost of 10. Each firm sets output so as to maximize its own profits.

a. Compute the residual demand of firm 1. Illustrate the residual demand on a graph with the price of good 1 on the vertical axis and the quantity of good 1 on the horizontal axis. What is the vertical intercept of this residual demand? What happens to residual demand of good 1 as the output of good 2 increases?

b. Compute the residual demand for firm 2. Compute the marginal revenue curve of firm 1 and of firm 2 based on residual demand.

c. Calculate and illustrate the reaction functions of the two firms. Using your answer to part (a), explain the slopes of the reaction functions.

d. Calculate the Cournot equilibrium prices, outputs, and profits for this market.

e. Compare your answer to (3d) to your answer to (1d). What do you notice?

4. Two firms compete as Bertrand competitors in a market for a homogeneous good. Each firm can produce the good at a marginal and average cost of 10.

Market demand is $Q = 100 - P$. Assume that, when the firms charge the same price, they each receive half of market demand.

a. Suppose that firm 2 sets a price of $P_2 = 40$. What is the best response of firm 1 to this price? How much would each firm sell if these prices were to prevail?

b. Now, assume that each firm has a capacity constraint of 30 units. In other words, each firm may produce a maximum of 30 units of output at a MC of 10. Suppose that firm 2 has set a price of $P_2 = 40$. Is there any incentive for firm 1 to set its price below 40?

c. Under the assumptions of part (b), what is the residual demand that firm 1 faces if it sets $P_1 > 40$?

d. Under the assumptions of part (b), what is the best response of firm 1 to $P_2 = 40$? Compute the outputs of the two firms and their profits at this point.

e. Compare your answer in part (d) to your answer to the Cournot equilibrium derived in Exercises 1-5 of the summary. What do you notice? Can you explain your result?

5. The demand for product 1 is written as follows:

$q_1 = A + BP_1 + CP_2$

where q_1 is the quantity of good 1, P_1 is the price of good 1, and P_2 is the price of good 2. A, B, and C are constants. The demand for good 2 falls as the price of good 2 rises.

a. For each of the parameter values that follow, state whether you think that goods 1 and 2 are substitutes, complements or, perhaps, neither. State your reasons.

   i.   A is positive, B is negative, and C is positive.

   ii.   A is positive, B is negative, and C is negative.

   iii.   A is positive, B is negative, and C is zero.

b. When would it be reasonable to assume that B has a larger absolute value than C?

6. Suppose that an industry is composed of many buyers and sellers. Each seller produces a horizontally differentiated product. There is free entry in the long-run. Each firm faces a downward sloping demand curve for its product.

a. If marginal costs are $MC = 10q_i$ and average costs $AC = 5q_i$, where q_i is the output of each firm, illustrate the short-run monopolistically competitive equilibrium for this industry.

b. Write down the conditions for long-run equilibrium in this industry. Can these conditions be satisfied? Why?

Exam *(60 minutes: Closed book; Closed notes)*

1. A and B are the only goods sold in a market. Consumers have diminishing marginal utility for the consumption of each of these two goods. Good A is identical to good B except that product A is of higher quality. Let the prices of goods A and B be P_A and P_B, respectively. Drawing the inverse demand of good B on a graph with P_B on the vertical axis and Q_B on the horizontal axis,

   a. What can you say about the slope of the demand for product B for prices $P_B > P_A$?

   b. What can you say about the slope of the demand for product B for prices $P_B = P_A$?

   c. What can you say about the slope of the demand for product B for prices $P_B < P_A$?

2. Let the inverse demand for a homogeneous good be written $P = 90 - (4/3)Q$. A perfectly competitive fringe of firms have supply curve $P = 60 + 4Q$. A single, dominant firm can produce this good at a marginal and average cost of $MC_D = 10$.

   a. Solve for the profit maximizing price and output of the dominant firm. What is the equilibrium output of the fringe at this point? Illustrate your solution on a graph.

   b. Suppose that the marginal cost of the dominant firm rises to $MC_D = 30$. What is the profit maximizing price and output of the dominant firm? What is the equilibrium output of the fringe at this point?

   c. Answer part (c) for $MC_D = 40$.

   d. Answer part (c) for $MC_D = 85$.

3. Let the inverse demand for a homogeneous good be $P = 100 - Q$. There are only two firms in the market. The firms are Cournot competitors.

   a. The two firms have marginal and average cost of $MC = 10$. Solve for their reaction functions and illustrate them on a graph.

   b. Now, suppose that firm 1 can produce the good at a marginal and average cost of 10, while firm 2 can produce the same good at a marginal and average cost of 20. Solve for the reaction functions of the two firms. Illustrate the reaction functions on a graph. What has changed?

c. Solve for the Cournot equilibrium in parts (a) and (b). What has changed?

4. Suppose that a market for a homogeneous product has demand $P = 200 - 2Q$. Each firm that operates in the industry has a constant marginal cost of production of 40, but also a fixed cost of production of 20 if any output is produced. The fixed cost of production is zero if output is zero, however.

   a. Suppose that a monopolist operates in this industry. What is the equilibrium price and output level? Does the monopolist make positive profits?

   b. Suppose that the industry is composed of two (identical) Cournot duopolists. What is the equilibrium price and output for each of the firms in this industry? Do the firms make positive profits?

   c. How would your answer to (b) change if the firms were Bertrand duopolists?

   d. Now, suppose that the firms behave as Stackelberg competitors. What are the equilibrium price, output levels, and profit levels of the firms? Compare the answer to your previous answers. What do you notice?

Answers to Exercises

1. The correct answers are (b) and (c). The profit of firm 1 equals total revenue (Pq_1) minus total cost ($10q_1$). Substituting the expression we are given for inverse market demand into profit, we obtain: profit of firm 1 = $\pi_1 = (100 - Q)q_1 - 10q_1$. Since $Q = q_1 + q_2$, this can be rewritten in either of two ways: $\pi_1 = (100 - q_1 - q_2)q_1 - 10q_1$ or, equivalently, $\pi_1 = (100 - q_1 - q_2 - 10)q_1$. As an aside, expression (d) of this exercise is industry profit (i.e., the profit of a monopolist operating in this industry).

2. The answer to the first part of the exercise is (a). We obtain residual demand by substituting $q_2 = 20$ into inverse demand to obtain $P(q_1) = 100 - q_1 - 20$. To fix ideas, note that if q_2 were equal to 10, then the correct answer would be (b). Note that answers (c) and (d) both double count firm 2's output by subtracting both q_2 *and* 20 from market demand.

   The correct answer to the second part of the exercise is (c). In other words, using our expression for inverse market demand, we obtain $P(q_1) = 100 - q_1 - q_2$, where q_2 is the fixed amount of output that firm 2 is anticipated to sell. Note that if $q_2 = 20$ is substituted into this expression, we obtain expression (a) of the first part of the question. Note that (b) and (d) double count firm 2's output.

3. The correct answer to the first part of the question is (c). Residual demand when $q_2 = 20$ is $P(q_1) = 100 - q_1 - 20$ (see Exercise 2). Using the formula for residual marginal revenue, then, we have $MR_{20} = P(q_1) + q_1(\Delta P/\Delta q_1)$. We can see from residual demand that $\Delta P/\Delta q_1 = -1$. By substitution, we obtain: $MR_{20} = 100 - q_1 - 20 + q_1(-1) = 100 - 2q_1 - 20$. Note that answer (a) is residual demand, not residual marginal revenue!

The correct answer to the second part of the question is (b). The profit maximization condition sets $MR_{20} = MC$. Since $TC(q_1) = 10q_1$, $MC = 10$. Hence, we have $100 - 2q_1 - 20 = 10$. Expression (a) sets MR_{20} equal to total cost, while expression (c) sets residual demand equal to marginal cost.

The correct answer to the third part of the question is (b). The profit maximization condition sets $MR_{q2} = MC$. Using our formula for residual marginal revenue, we have $MR_{q2} = 100 - q_1 - q_2 + q_1(-1) = 100 - 2q_1 - q_2$. Hence, we have $100 - 2q_1 - q_2 = 10$.

4. The correct answer to the first part of the question is (c). From Exercise 3, we know that the profit maximization condition of firm 1 when $q_2 = 20$ is $100 - 2q_1 - 20 = 10$. Solving this for q_1, we obtain that $70 = 2q_1$, or, $q_1*(20) = 35$.

   The correct answer to the second part of the question is (b). We know from Exercise 3 that the profit maximization condition for firm 1 when firm 2 produces any output, q_2 is $100 - 2q_1 - q_2 = 10$. Putting q_1 on the left-hand side and solving, this expression can be rewritten as $2q_1 = 90 - q_2$ or $q_1 = 45 - q_2/2$.

5. The correct answer to the first part of the exercise is (c). We know from Exercise 4 that firm 1's reaction function is $q_1 = 45 - q_2/2$. Using exactly the same reasoning as in Exercises 1-4 for firm 2, we can state that the profit maximization condition for firm 2 is $100 - 2q_2 - q_1 = 10$. Hence, firm 2's reaction function is $q_2 = 45 - q_1/2$. The Cournot equilibrium is the set of points, (q_1*, q_2*) that satisfy these two reaction functions simultaneously so that we must solve simultaneously:

   $$q_1 = 45 - q_2/2$$
   $$q_2 = 45 - q_1/2$$

   We substitute from the second equation into the first to obtain $q_1 = 45 - (45 - q_1/2)/2$. Solving this, we obtain $q_1 = 22.5 + q_1/4$ or $\frac{3}{4}q_1 = 22.5$. This yields $q_1* = 30$. Substituting $q_1 = 30$ into the second equation, we obtain $q_2 = 45 - 30/2$ or $q_2* = 30$. Hence, the Cournot equilibrium is $q_1* = 30$; $q_2* = 30$.

   The correct answer to the second part of the exercise is (a). At the Cournot equilibrium, market price equals $P(Q) = 100 - 30 - 30 = 40$. Hence, total revenue for each firm is $40(30) = 1200$. Total cost for each firm is $10(30) = 300$. Therefore, profits for each firm are $1200 - 300 = 900$.

6. The correct answer is (c). We know from the summary that the Bertrand equilibrium price equals marginal cost. In this problem, the marginal cost for each firm is 10.

7. The correct answer to the first part of the exercise is (b). Starting with firm 1, the residual demand facing firm 1 is $P = 100 - q_1 - q_2 - q_3$. Firm 1's residual marginal revenue is $MR = P + q_1(\Delta P/\Delta q_1) = 100 - q_1 - q_2 - q_3 + q_1(-1) = 100 -$

$2q_1 - q_2 - q_3$. Hence, firm 1's profit maximization condition is $100 - 2q_1 - q_2 - q_3 = 10$. The reaction function of firm 1 is $q_1 = 45 - q_2/2 - q_3/2$. Similarly, the reaction functions of firms 2 and 3 are $q_2 = 45 - q_1/2 - q_3/2$ and $q_3 = 45 - q_1/2 - q_2/2$. To solve these three reaction functions simultaneously for the Cournot equilibrium, rewrite firm 2 and 3's reaction functions as, respectively, $q_1 = 90 - 2q_2 - q_3$ and $q_1 = 90 - q_2 - 2q_3$. Setting these equal, we obtain that $q_2 = q_3$ must hold at the equilibrium. Now, setting the reaction function of firm 1 equal to the rewritten version of the reaction function of firm 2, we have $90 - 2q_2 - q_3 = 45 - q_2/2 - q_3/2$. Using our condition that $q_2 = q_3$, however, we can solve this equation to obtain $q_2^* = q_3^* = 22.5$. Substituting this solution into firm 1's reaction function, we see that $q_1^* = 22.5$ as well.

The correct answer to the second part of the exercise is (b). Total output is $Q^* = q_1^* + q_2^* + q_3^* = 22.5 + 22.5 + 22.5 = 67.5$. Each firm earns total revenue ($= Pq_i^* = (100 - 67.5)22.5 = (32.5)(22.5)$) minus total cost ($=10q_i^* = 10(22.5)$) so that total profit for each firm is $(32.5)(22.5) - 10(22.5) = (22.5)(22.5) = 506.25$.

The correct answer to the third part of the exercise is (a). Each firm in the Bertrand equilibrium charges $p_i^* = MC$. Hence, $p_1^* = p_2^* = p_3^* = 10$. At a price of 10, we can solve inverse market demand to obtain that $Q^* = 100 - 10 = 90$. Since each firm prices at marginal (and average) cost, the profit of each firm is zero.

8. The correct answer is (b). Refer back to Exercise 5 to see the calculation of the Cournot best response function for firm 2. As the follower's behavior in the Stackelberg model is effectively the same (whatever the level of output of firm 1, firm 2 simply calculates its best response and acts accordingly) it is calculated in exactly the same way.

9. The correct answer to the first part of the problem is (a). Referring back to Exercise 1, demand is given by $P = 100 - Q$, where $Q = q_1 + q_2$. Now, we have an equation for q_2 that captures how we anticipate the follower to behave: $q_2 = 45 - q_1/2$. Notice what this comes from: if we solve the equation in Exercise 8 for q_2 as a function of q_1 we obtain exactly this equation. This was done in Exercise 5 as well. In any case, we can substitute this into the equation for demand to get the "effective" or "residual" demand facing firm 1: $P = 100 - q_1 - [45 - q_1/2] = 55 - q_1/2$.

The correct answer to the second part of the problem is (c). We know that the equation for marginal revenue of firm 1 is $P + q_1(\Delta P/\Delta q_1)$. Hence, using the "effective" demand we have Marginal revenue $= (55 - q_1/2) + q_1(-1/2) = 55 - q_1$. Make sure that you use only q_1 and not Q when calculating marginal revenue: it is only firm 1's revenue that counts, so total revenue is Pq_1, not PQ.

10. The correct answer is (a). The leader's behavior is captured by setting its marginal revenue from Exercise 9 equal to marginal cost or $55 - q_1 = 10$. This means that the leader's optimal output choice is $q_1^* = 45$. The follower uses this value of q_1 in its reaction function to obtain the best response $q_2^* = 45 - q_1^*/2 = 45 - 45/2 = 22.5$. We could compare these to the Cournot equilibrium outputs of 30 for each firm. Notice that the leader's output has risen and the follower's output has fallen. In order to work out whether profits have risen or fallen, let

us calculate profits for the Stackelberg case. Price at the Stackelberg equilibrium is $P = 100 - q_1^* - q_2^* = 100 - 45 - 22.5 = 32.5$ so that profit for the leader is Revenue − Total Cost = $32.5(45) - 10(45) = 22.5(45) = 1012.5$ while profit for the follower is Revenue − Total Cost = $32.5(22.5) - 10(22.5) = 22.5(22.5) = 560.25$. Using the numbers from Exercise 5 for comparison, we see that the leader's profits have risen compared to the Cournot case while the follower's profits have fallen.

11. The correct answer to the first part of the question is (a). Average and marginal cost are minimized at zero. As long as price is positive, firms can make positive profits by producing positive output levels.

    The correct answer to the second part of the exercise is (b). The equation of S_F is the horizontal sum of the individual fringe supply functions. Each fringe firm has supply function $P = MC$ or $P = 10q_i$ as long as price is not less than zero (the shut-down price). We can solve for q_i as a function of P so that each firm supplies $q_i = P/10$. We then sum over the 30 firms to obtain S_F: $Q = 30q_i = 30(P/10) = 3P$. Hence, $P = Q/3$ is the equation of S_F. Next, we obtain residual demand by taking the horizontal difference between demand and S_F. Solving both demand and S_F for Q as a function of P, we have $Q = 100 - P$ (demand) and $Q = 3P$ (S_F). Hence, the difference is $100 - P - 3P = 100 - 4P$. Therefore, the equation of the dominant firm's residual demand is $q_{DF} = 100 - 4P$ or $P = 25 - .25q_{DF}$.

12. The correct answer to the first part of the exercise is (a). We know from Exercise 11 that the dominant firm's residual demand is $P = 25 - .25q_{DF}$. Using the formula for residual marginal revenue, we have $MR_R = P + q_{DF}(\Delta P/\Delta q_{DF})$ so that $MR_R = P + q_{DF}(-.25)$ or $MR_R = 25 - .25q_{DF} - .25q_{DF} = 25 - .5q_{DF}$

    The correct answer to the second part of the exercise is (b). The profit maximization condition of the dominant firm is $MR_R = MC$. Using the answer from the first part of this exercise, then, we have $25 - .5q_{DF} = 5$ or $q_{DF}^* = 40$. Tracing up to the residual demand curve, we obtain $p_{DF}^* = 25 - .25(40) = 15$. At this price, $S_F^* = 3(15) = 45$. We can check that total output satisfies industry demand by noting that market demand at a price of 15 is $100 - 15 = 85$. 85 equals the sum of q_{DF}^* and S_F^*.

13. The correct answer is (c). The price cannot rise above the shut-down price of the fringe firms in the long-run, since this would attract entry. Hence, $P^* = 80$. At this price, the residual demand curve is flat and marginal revenue equals price. Setting $P = MC$ for the dominant firm, we have $80 = 10q_{DF}$ so that $q^*_{DF} = 8$. Profit equals total revenue minus total cost or $80(8) - 5(8)(8) = 320$.

14. The correct answer to the first part of the question is (a). The formula for own price elasticity of demand is $\varepsilon_{Q,P} = (\Delta Q/\Delta P)(P/Q)$. From the equations of demand, we have $\Delta Q_1/\Delta P_1 = -1$. Hence, by substituting this into the formula for elasticity, we obtain $\varepsilon_{Q1,P1} = -1(P_1/Q_1)$.

The correct answer to the second part of the question is (b). The formula for the cross price elasticity of demand is $\varepsilon_{Q1,P2} = (\Delta Q_1/\Delta P_2)(P_2/Q_1)$. From the equations of demand, we have $\Delta Q_1/\Delta P_2 = .5$. By substituting this into the formula for elasticity, we obtain $\varepsilon_{Q1,P2} = (1/2)(P_2/Q_1)$.

15. The correct answers are (a) and (c). The reaction functions have positive slope so that a rise in the price of one good causes the best response price of the rival to rise as well. (This is in contrast to the Cournot model where the rise in output of one firm causes the best response output of the rival to *fall*.) The intercept of firm 2's reaction function is positive, indicating that when the price of good 1 is zero, the best response of firm 2 is to charge a positive price. This makes some sense. If there are some consumers who would prefer to buy good 2 at a price that exceeds marginal cost even if good 1 is available for free, then it certainly would be better for firm 2 to charge a positive price than to charge zero (and be guaranteed to make zero profits).

16. The correct answer is (a). The long-run equilibrium conditions are that marginal revenue equals marginal cost and that price equals average cost for each firm. In other words, we need to find a quantity and price that satisfy:

(1) $120 - 2q_i = 10q_i$
(2) $120 - q_i = 600/q_i + 5q_i$

From (1), we see that $q_i = 10$ equates marginal revenue and marginal cost. Substituting this into equation (2), we see that 10 also satisfies this equation. Hence, $q^*_i = 10$ and $P^*_i = 110$ form a long-run equilibrium for this industry. You can check this by noticing that, at this price and output, all firms earn zero profit.

Answers to Problem Set

1. a. The residual demand of firm 1 is firm 1's demand taking as given firm 2's price: $P_1 = (100 + .5P_2) - q_1$. The vertical intercept is the term in brackets. When the price of good 2 rises, the demand for good 1 shifts up. This is what one would expect if the goods are demand substitutes.

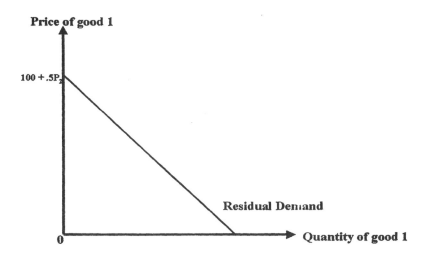

b. Similarly, the residual demand for good 2 is $P_2 = (100 + .5P_1) - q_2$. The marginal revenue curves for firms 1 and 2 are, respectively, $MR_{R1} = 100 + .5P_2 - 2q_1$ and $MR_{R2} = 100 + .5P_1 - 2q_2$. These two marginal revenues are symmetric (in the sense that they are the same functions with the subscripts reversed). This is not surprising since the demands for the two products are symmetric as well. The marginal revenue curves also shift up when the competitor's price rises, reflecting the increase in demand that occurs when a competitor raises its price.

c. Setting marginal revenue equal to marginal cost for firm 1, we have $100 + .5P_2 - 2q_1 = 10$. Hence, $45 + .25P_2 = q_1$. Using our equation for demand, then, we have $P_1 = (100 + .5P_2) - (45 + .25P_2) = 55 + .25P_2$. Hence, the reaction function of firm 1 is $P_1^* = 55 + .25P_2$. Similarly, the reaction function of firm 2 is $P_2^* = 55 + .25P_1$. These are upward sloping in the space of prices. For example, the best response of firm 1 to a price rise by firm 2 is to raise its price as well. To explain this, recall from parts (a) and (b) that the residual demand (and marginal revenue) of firm 1 shifted out when the price of firm 2 rose. When P_2 rises, firm 1 faces an increased incentive to raise its own price because consumers are less inclined to buy firm 2's product at the higher price. Hence, the gain on firm 1's inframarginal units when it increases price is balanced against a smaller loss in revenue because fewer consumers defect to product 2. This means that firm 1's best response to a price increase by firm 2 is a price *increase* as well.

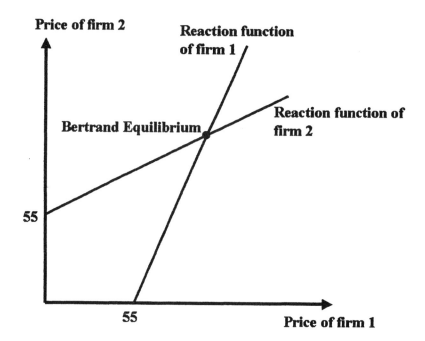

d. Substituting from firm 2's reaction function into firm 1's reaction function, we obtain $P_1 = 55 + .25(55 + .25P_1)$ or $P_1^* = 73.33 = P_2^*$. Using demand, we obtain $q_1^* = 100 - 73.333 + .5(73.333) = 36.667 = q_2^*$ and profits of both firms are total revenue minus total cost or 73.33(36.667) - 10(36.667) = 2322.22

2.

a. The short-run equilibrium requires that each firm set marginal revenue equal to marginal cost. However, notice that the marginal cost and marginal revenue are the same here as in Problem 1. Hence, the short-run equilibrium in this market is the same as the differentiated products Bertrand equilibrium in Problem 1.

b. In the long-run, price must equal average cost and marginal revenue must equal marginal cost as well. Average cost here equals $2322.22/q_i + 10$. Using our short-run equilibrium solution from (a), we have P = 73.33 and AC = 2322.22/36.67 + 10 which is indeed, equal to 73.33. Hence the short-run solution coincides with the long-run solution so that there is no incentive for additional firms to enter in this industry.

3.

a. Residual demand for firm 1 is $P_1 = [200 - (2/3)q_2] - (4/3)q_1$. The vertical intercept is the term in square brackets. Note that this shifts down as q_2 increases.

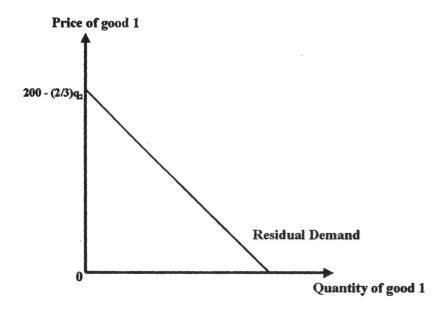

b. Similarly, the residual demand for good 2 is $P_2 = [200 - (2/3)q_1] - (4/3)q_2$. The marginal revenue of each firm is, respectively, $MR_{R1} = [200 - (2/3)q_2] - (8/3)q_1$ and $MR_{R2} = [200 - (2/3)q_1] - (8/3)q_2$. These two curves are symmetric so that they are mirror images of each other with the subscripts switched. This is not surprising since the demands also are mirror images of each other. The marginal revenue curve of each firm shifts down when its competitor's output rises.

c. The reaction function of firm 1 is obtained from the profit maximization conditions of firm 1, $MR_{R1} = MC$, so that $200 - (2/3)q_2 - (8/3)q_1 = 10$. Solving, we have $q_1^* = 91.25 - .25q_2 = q_1$. Similarly, $q_2^* = 91.25 - .25q_1$. These are both downward sloping functions in quantity space.

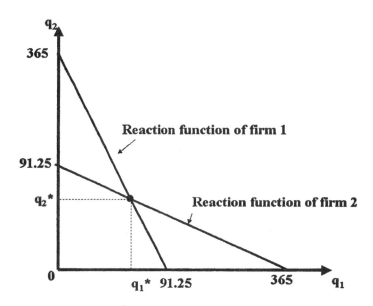

As the output of firm 2 increases, the residual demand and marginal revenue of firm 1 shifts in. Hence, any given quantity increase by firm 1 earns less compared to the marginal cost of production and so it is less tempting to increase output. This makes the best response to an increase in output by firm 2 a *decrease* in output by firm 1.

d. Substituting from the reaction function of firm 2 into the reaction function of firm 1, we have $q_1 = 91.25 - .25(91.25 - .25q_1)$ or $q_1^* = 73 = q_2^*$. From demand, then, we obtain that $P_1^* = P_2^* = 54$ and profits are $54(73) - 10(73) = 3212$ for each firm.

e. Problem 3's demands are simply the inverse demands that are obtained from the direct demands in Problem 1. However, we find that price is lower, output is higher, and profits are higher under Cournot than under Bertrand.

4.

a. If $P_2 = 40$, the best response of firm 1 is to set price slightly below 40 since this still exceeds marginal cost. Firm 1 produces output for the entire market demand so that $q_1 = 100 - P_1 = 100 - 40 + \varepsilon = 60 + \varepsilon$, where ε is a small number. Firm 2 sells nothing, since it receives no demand.

b. If firm 1 cuts price below 40, it receives the entire market demand, but can only satisfy 30 units of this demand. At a price of exactly 40, firm 1 receives half of market demand so that it receives $q_1 = (100 - 40)/2 = 30$ units of demand. Hence, there is no incentive to lower price below 40 since it merely lowers the price firm 1 charges on units it would sell in any case.

c. If firm 1 sets price above 40, then the entire market demand goes to firm 2. Firm 2, however, can satisfy only 30 units of this demand. Hence, any remaining individuals who wish to purchase at the price firm 1 is offering but cannot obtain the product from firm 2 will purchase from firm 1. Since firm 2 sells 30 units the residual demand facing firm 1 when it prices above 40 is $P_1 = 100 - q_1 - 30 = 70 - q_1$.

d. The marginal revenue based on residual demand for P_1 above 40 is $70 - 2q_1 = MR_R$. Setting this equal to marginal cost, we have $70 - 2q_1 = 10$ or $q_1{}^* = 30$. Substituting this back into residual demand, we have $P_1{}^* = 40$.

e. The solution to this problem is the same as the Cournot solution for the same demand and marginal cost. Hence, by imposing the Cournot equilibrium capacity constraints on the Bertrand problem, we can obtain the same equilibrium price and output as under the Cournot model. The point is that the capacity constraint greatly reduces the ability of firms to steal business from each other so that equilibrium price can remain above marginal cost, as it did in the simple Cournot model, despite the fact that competitors set prices.

5.

a. (i) Parameter C determines the degree of substitutability or complementarity between the goods since it shows how the demand for good 1 changes as the price of good 2 changes. If C is positive, so that a rise in the price of good 2 causes the demand for good 1 to rise as well, then it means that the goods are substitutes.

(ii) If C is negative, then a rise in the price of good 2 causes a fall in the demand for good 1. This suggests that the goods are complements.

(iii) If C is zero, then a change in the price of good 2 has no effect on the demand for good 1. Hence, the goods are neither substitutes nor complements. (The demands are *independent* of each other.) In fact, in general one would expect that the weaker is the substitutability/ complementarity between goods 1 and 2, the smaller is the absolute value of C relative to B.

b. As long as the goods are *imperfect* substitutes and complements, one would expect that the price movements of good 2 would have a weaker effect on the demand for good 1 than the price movements of good 1 itself. On the other hand, for goods that are *perfect* substitutes or complements, the price movements of good 2 would be expected to have an equally strong effect on the demand for good 1 as the price movements of good 1 itself. If the absolute value of C equals that of B, then it means that price movements of good 2 affect the demand for good 1 as much as the price movements of good 1. Hence, only if the goods are perfect substitutes or complements would we expect the absolute value of C and B to be the same.

6.

a.

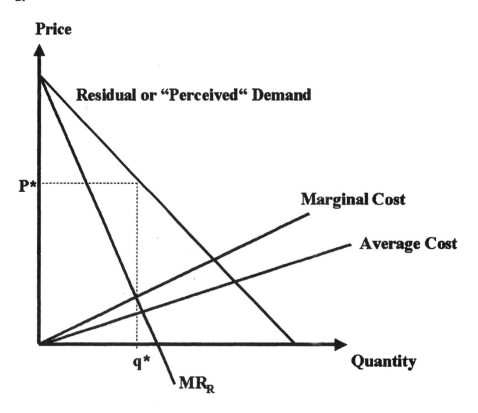

Point (q*,P*) is the short-run equilibrium for this industry. Note that price exceeds average cost at this point, so all firms make positive profits.

b. The long-run equilibrium conditions are (1) $MR_R = MC$ and (2) $P = AC$. Clearly, these are not satisfied at the short-run equilibrium since P* is above average cost at output q*. If entry occurs in the long-run, the residual demand shifts back, and both q* and P* fall. However, average cost falls as q* falls as well. This means that profits remain positive and further entry occurs! In fact, average cost continues to fall as residual demand shifts back farther. As a result, the long-run equilibrium conditions can never be satisfied with this cost and demand structure. To see this formally, notice that, as we know from Chapter 10, MR is always smaller than price. But since P = AC and MR = MC we must have MC < AC in long-run equilibrium, which is impossible since MC > AC for all $q_i > 0$.

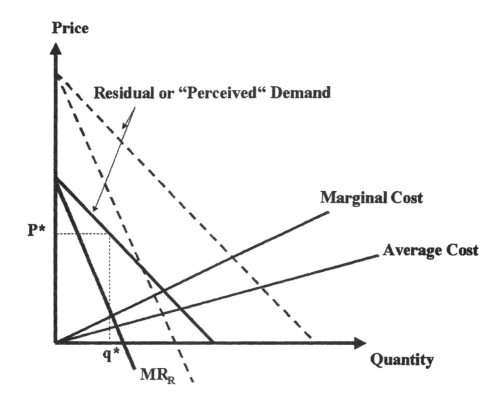

Answers to Exam

1.

    a. If P_B exceeds P_A, then the demand for good B should be zero. This is because goods A and B are identical except that A's quality is higher. Hence, all consumers prefer A to B at the same price and certainly prefer A to B when B's price is higher. The slope of demand should be vertical at zero.

    b. As explained in part (a), good A is preferable to B at equal prices so the demand for good B should still be zero at this point. The slope of demand is vertical at zero.

    c. If the quality of good A is discretely higher than that of B, it is unlikely that any consumers would switch from consuming A to B if the price of B is only slightly less than that of A. However, there will be a threshold price, $\underline{P}$, at which consumers are indifferent between consuming the lower quality good for the lower price and consuming the higher quality product at the higher price. If P_B drops below this threshold, all consumers should prefer to consume product B, since the utility value of the product net of the price is higher for price below this point. Hence, the slope of demand should be (1) vertical as long as P_B is above the threshold, (2) once $P_B = \underline{P}$, consumers are indifferent between the two goods (we can assume that they split their demand between the two), and (3) for prices $P_B < \underline{P}$, the demand for good B has the same slope as the market demand for the good. Graphically, the demand for good B should look as follows:

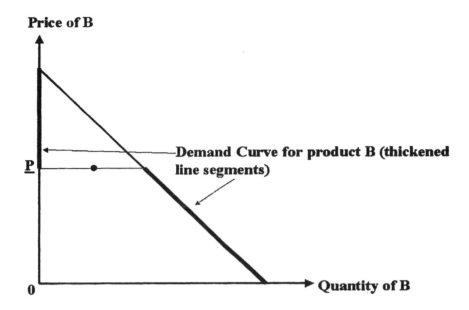

2.

a. If the dominant firm completely ignores the fringe and sets marginal revenue based on market demand equal to marginal cost, the optimal output is obtained as follows: $90 - (8/3)q_{DF} = 10$ or $q^*_{DF} = 30$ and $P^* = 50$. This price is so low that the fringe would not supply any output, so the dominant firm can price as a monopolist with no worry about entry. This is illustrated in the figure below:

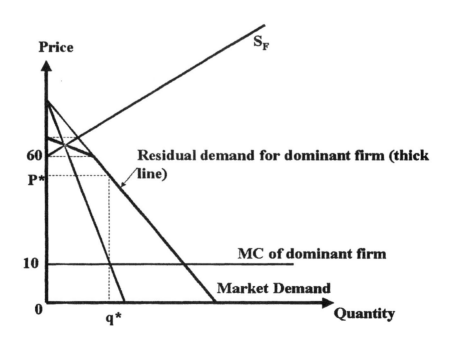

b. At a marginal cost of 30, a dominant firm that completely ignores the fringe would produce at a point where the marginal revenue based on market demand equaled marginal cost. Hence, $90 - (8/3)q_{DF} = 30$ or $q_{DF}* = 22.5$ and $P* = 60$. At this point, the fringe just supplies zero output. Graphically, the point $(q*, P*)$ occurs just at the "kink" in the residual demand curve for the dominant firm.

c. The flatter portion of the dominant firm's residual demand occurs between prices of 82.5 (where the fringe supply intersects the market demand) and 60 (where the fringe supply drops to zero). Over this range, the equation of residual demand is given by the horizontal difference between market demand and the fringe supply curve. Market demand can be written $Q_M = 270/4 - .75P$ and the fringe supply curve can be written $Q_F = -60/4 + P/4$ so that $Q_M - Q_F = 270/4 - .75P + 60/4 - .25P = 330/4 - P$. Solving this for price as a function of quantity, the residual demand curve is $P = 330/4 - Q$. Marginal revenue based on residual demand is $MR_R = 330/4 - 2Q$. Setting this equal to marginal cost, we obtain the profit maximization conditions of the dominant firm as $330/4 - 2Q = 40$ or $q_{DF}* = 21.25 = 170/8$. Substituting $q_{DF}*$ into residual demand, $P* = 330/4 - 170/8 = 61.25$. Substituting this price into the fringe supply curve, we obtain that the fringe supplies $q*_F = 5/16$.

d. If the dominant firm's marginal cost rises above $P* = 82.5$, then we saw in part (c) that the fringe firm supplies the entire market output and residual demand drops to zero. Hence, the dominant firm's output drops to zero and the fringe supplies at the point where S_F crosses market demand or at the point where $q_F* = 5.625$.

3.

a. The residual demand of firm 1 is $(100 - q_2) - q_1 = P$. Marginal revenue for firm 1 based on this residual demand is $(100 - q_2) - 2q_1 = MR_R$. Setting this equal to marginal cost, we have the profit maximization condition of firm 1: $(100 - q_2) - 2q_1 = 10$. Hence, solving for q_1, we have the equation for firm 1's reaction function: $q_1 = 45 - q_2/2$. Similarly, $q_2 = 45 - q_1/2$ is the reaction function of firm 2. By substituting from the reaction function of firm 2 into the reaction function of firm 1, we have $q_1 = 45 - (45 - q_1/2)/2$ or $q_1* = 30$. Similarly, $q_2* = 30$. The reaction functions and equilibria are illustrated as the solid lines on the graph below.

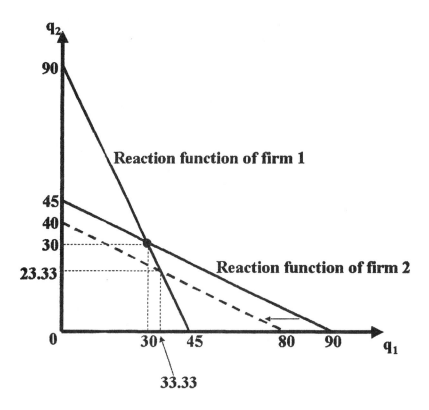

b. Neither marginal cost nor marginal revenue has changed for firm 1; however, marginal cost has risen for firm 2. Since marginal revenue is unchanged for firm 2, its new profit maximization conditions are $(100 - q_1) - 2q_2 = 20$. Solving this for q_2 we have a new equation for firm 2's reaction function of $q_2 = 40 - q_1/2$. This is illustrated as the dashed line in the figure of part (a). The reaction function of firm 2 has shifted in when the marginal cost of firm 2 rises. The reaction function of firm 1 remains unchanged, since neither its marginal revenue nor its marginal cost has been affected by the change.

c. Substituting firm 2's new reaction function into firm 1's (old) reaction function, we can solve for the new Cournot equilibrium as $q_1 = 45 - (40 - q_1/2)/2$ so that $q_1^* = 33.33$. The new Cournot equilibrium output of firm 2 is, then, $q_2^* = 40 - 33.33/2 = 23.33$. This is illustrated in the figure of part (a) as the intersection of the dotted reaction function with the original reaction function of firm 1. At these new output levels, price is $P^* = 100 - 33.33 - 23.33 = 43.33$. The profit of firm 1 is, then, $43.33(33.33) - 10(33.33) = 1110.89$ and the profit of firm 2 is $43.33(23.33) - 20(23.33) = 544.29$. Hence, firm 2 loses from the rise in its costs, but firm 1 gains.

4.

a. The monopolist's marginal revenue is $MR = 200 - 4Q$. Setting this equal to marginal cost, we have $200 - 4Q = 40$ or $Q^* = 40$. At this output, price is $P^* = 200 - 80 = 120$. This price exceeds average cost at Q^* so that profits are positive.

b. The residual demand of firm 1 is $P = (200 - 2q_2) - 2q_1$. Marginal revenue based on this residual demand is $P = (200 - 2q_2) - 4q_1$. Setting this equal to marginal cost, we have firm 1's profit maximization conditions: $(200 - 2q_2) - 4q_1 = 40$. Solving for q_1, we obtain the reaction function of firm 1: $q_1 = 40 - q_2/2 = q_1$. Similarly, $q_2 = 40 - q_1/2$. Substituting the reaction function of firm 2 into the reaction function of firm 1, we can obtain the Cournot equilibrium outputs as $q_1 = 40 - (40 - q_1/2)/2$ or $q_1^* = 26.67 = q_2^*$. At this output, price is $P^* = 93.33$. This is above average cost for both firms at their optimal output levels since average cost at $q_1^* = 20/26.67 + 40 < 93.33$. Hence, both firms make positive profits at the Cournot equilibrium.

c. If the firms are Bertrand competitors, each firm's best response to any price above marginal cost is to undercut this price slightly. This tends to drive equilibrium price down to $MC = 40$. Any firm operating in this industry would, then, earn zero profits minus the fixed cost of production, 20. Since the fixed cost is zero for an output of zero, the two firms would do better leaving the industry. If the two firms are out of the industry, however, then we have the following difficulty: if either firm anticipates that the other would stay out of the industry, we know from (a) that the rival firm would want to enter and act as a monopolist. Hence, we need to know more about the conjectures of these firms concerning which will stay out and which will stay in before we can derive the industry equilibrium price, quantity, or number of firms.

The basic difficulty here is that the fixed cost transforms this industry into a natural monopoly, rather than a natural oligopoly.

d. The Stackelberg equilibrium can be computed by characterizing one firm's reactions by the Cournot best response function and then calculating the best response of the rival by substituting the best response function into demand and setting marginal revenue based on this new demand equal to marginal cost. Let firm 2 be follower, then, and take the best response function from (b), above so that $q_2 = 40 - q_1/2$. Substituting this into demand, we have $P = 200 - 2Q = 200 - 2q_1 - 2(40 - q_1/2) = 120 - q_1$. Marginal revenue based on this will be $MR = 120 - 2q_1$. Setting this equal to marginal cost, we have $120 - 2q_1 = 40$ or $q_1^* = 40$. Using the best response function to obtain firm 2's reaction, we have $q_2^* = 40 - 40/2 = 20$. Price is now $200 - 2(40+20) = 80$ and profit is Revenue − Total Cost, which for firm 1 yields $\Pi_1 = 80(40) - 40(40) - 20 = 1580$ and for firm 2 yields $\Pi_2 = 80(20) - 20(40) - 20 = 760$. While the Stackelberg leader produces the monopoly output, the follower produces a positive quantity, and so price (and profit) is lower than the monopoly level.

Chapter 14: Game Theory and Strategic Behavior

Game theory is the study of optimal decision making in a situation where the actions of each decision maker have a significant impact on the fortunes of other decision makers. In this chapter, we will review the basics of game theoretic models and will derive various types of equilibria within those models. While game theory has wide applications, we will focus here on how game theory can be used to understand microeconomic problems. The reasoning of the models will look familiar to you. In fact, we will see that the Cournot and Bertrand models that we studied in Chapter 13 can be recast as game theoretic models. We will also see that Cournot and Bertrand equilibria are examples of a particular type of equilibrium commonly used in game theory (the "Nash" equilibrium). Game theory allows us to do more than just re-derive our earlier results, however. It gives us a framework for analyzing more complex settings than we have seen until now.

Consider the following example, where two firms produce a homogeneous product. Each firm must decide whether to set a high price or a low price for its output. If both firms price high, each will earn a profit of 20. If both price low, each will earn a profit of 10. On the other hand, if firm 1 prices low while firm 2 prices high, firm 1 obtains the entire market demand at the low price. Hence, firm 1 earns a profit of 30 while firm 2 earns nothing at all. Similarly, if firm 2 cuts price while firm 1 prices high, all demand will accrue to firm 2 and firm 1 will earn nothing. We can summarize the decisions that the firms must take and the payoffs to each decision in the following **payoff matrix**:

Firm 2

	Price high	Price low
Price high	(20,20)	(0, 30)
Price low	(30, 0)	(10,10)

Firm 1

Game Matrix 1

This game, like *all* games, has the following elements:

1. *Players:* These are the agents who participate in the game. In our game matrix 1, firms 1 and 2 are the only players.
2. *Strategies:* These are actions that each player may take under any possible circumstance. Here, "price high" and "price low" are the only possible strategies.
3. *Outcomes:* These are the various possible results of the game. Here, there are four outcomes, corresponding to the four cells of the matrix.
4. *Payoffs:* These are the benefits that each player gets from each possible outcome of the game. Here, the payoffs are the profits listed in each cell of the matrix. By convention, we will list the payoff of the "horizontal player" first and the

payoff of the "vertical player" is second so that the payoffs are listed as (profit of firm 1, profit of firm 2) in each cell.

5. *Information:* This is a full specification of who knows what when.
6. *Timing:* We must know who can make what decision when. Here, the pricing decisions are taken simultaneously and the pricing game is played only once.

Exercise 1: *Which of the following statements is true about the game of chess?*

    a. There are three possible outcomes of the game.
    b. There are two players.
    c. Decisions are taken sequentially.
    d. There are two strategies for each player.

These six elements completely specify the game. However, we also wish to know which are the likely outcome(s) of the game. Game theorists use the concept of equilibrium in the same way as we have used equilibrium to predict the outcome of all the economic situations we have considered so far (i.e. as a state of rest, where economic agents do not have any reason to modify their behavior). One commonly used type of equilibrium is the **Nash equilibrium**. At a Nash equilibrium, each player chooses a strategy that gives the highest payoff *to that player*, given the strategy chosen by each other player in the game. In other words, each player does the best he or she possibly can without taking into consideration the consequences for the other player(s). For this reason, Nash equilibrium is often called an equilibrium of "rational self-interest".

The way to calculate the Nash equilibrium for Game Matrix 1 is the following.

1. Take a particular strategy as given (and fixed) for firm 2 and calculate the response that gives the highest payoff to firm 1.

    • If firm 2 prices high, the response that yields the highest payoff to firm 1 is to price low (since it yields 30 rather than 20). Hence firm 1's best response to "price high" is "price low".
    • If firm 2 prices low, the response that yields the highest payoff to firm 1 is also to price low (since it yields 10 rather than 0). Hence, firm 1's best response to "price low" is "price low".

Summarizing, the "best response function" or "reaction function" of firm 1 is:

<u>Firm 2</u>   <u>Firm 1</u>

Price high → Price low
Price low → Price low

2. Take a particular strategy as given (and fixed) for firm 1 and calculate the response that gives the highest payoff to firm 2.

    • If firm 1 prices high, the response that yields the highest payoff to firm 2 is to price low (since it yields 30 rather than 20). Hence firm 2's best response to "price high" is "price low".

- If firm 1 prices low, the response that yields the highest payoff to firm 2 is also to price low (since it yields 10 rather than 0). Hence, firm 2's best response to "price low" is "price low".

Summarizing, the "best response function" or "reaction function of firm 2 is:

Firm 1   Firm 2

Price high → Price low
Price low → Price low

3. Using your results from steps (1) and (2), find the combination of strategies such that *each* player's strategy is a best response to the other's. These strategies form a Nash equilibrium.

For a simple two-by-two matrix, the easiest way to see where the Nash equilibrium lies is to illustrate the reaction functions that we have listed above on the game matrix itself. We will do this by *underlining* the best response of firm 1 for every move by firm 2 and typing in *bold* the best response of firm 2 to every move by firm 1.

Firm 2

	Price high	Price low
Price high	(20,20)	(0, **30**)
Price low	(<u>30</u>, 0)	(<u>10</u>,**10**)

Firm 1

Best Responses for Game Matrix 1

The Nash equilibrium is the cell where each player is making his/her best response to the move by the other player. This occurs in cells with *both* an underlined and a bold number. The only payoffs that are underlined *and* in bold are those in the lower right-hand corner. We can check by reasoning that this cell is a Nash equilibrium. The strategy "price low" by firm 1 is a best response to the strategy "price low" by firm 2. The strategy "price low" by firm 2 is a best response to the strategy "price low" by firm 1. Hence, a Nash equilibrium is that both firm 1 and firm 2 play the strategy "price low". The Nash equilibrium outcome of this game is (10,10).

Exercise 2: *Which of the following statements is true about Game Matrix 1?*

a. The cell in the upper left-hand corner ("Price high, Price high") could *also* be a Nash equilibrium for this game since both the players do better in this cell than in the lower right-hand corner cell.

b. "Price high" could not be a Nash equilibrium strategy because the best response of either firm to "price high" is "price low".
c. There is no incentive to deviate from a strategy of "Price high".
d. If either firm prices low, the best response to this strategy is to "price low".

The reasoning we have used to find the Nash equilibrium should look familiar to you from Chapter 13. In the Cournot and Bertrand equilibrium, firms pursue rational self-interest in the sense that each firm maximizes its own profits without concerning itself about its rivals' profits. For every possible move by the rival (where actions are *output* levels in the Cournot model and *price* levels in the Bertrand model), we obtained the best response of the firm. The set of best responses to all possible moves of the rival formed the "reaction" function of the firm. The Cournot and Bertrand equilibria were the points where these reaction functions intersected. At that point, each firm's choice of output (or price) maximized its profits given the output (or price) chosen by the other firm. Hence, Cournot and Bertrand equilibria are, in fact, also Nash equilibria. The main difference between these models and the simple two-by-two matrices that we have analyzed here is that the Cournot and Bertrand models have a continuum of possible actions that the players can take (i.e., *any* output level or *any* price level is possible). In Game Matrix 1, there are just two possible price levels so that Game Matrix 1 recasts Bertrand competition as a simple game where the equilibrium has the same price-cutting characteristic as the Bertrand equilibrium.

Exercise 3: *What is the Nash equilibrium for the following game matrix?*

<u>Firm 2</u>

		Low output	High output
Firm 1	Low output	(625,625)	(468.75,703.125)
	High output	(703.125,468.75)	(555.61,555.61)

a. (Low output, Low output)
b. (Low output, High output)
c. (High output, Low output)
d. (High output, High output)

Game Matrix 1 illustrates the important point that the Nash equilibrium does not necessarily maximize the collective interest of the players. For example, both players would be better off if they could agree to price high: each would receive a payoff of 20, not 10. However, the very fact that each player pursues his or her own self-interest *without* taking into account any negative impact this might have on the rival means that the players do not necessarily act in the collective good. Games where the players choose a set of payoffs that do not maximize the aggregate payoffs of the players (the "collective good") are called **Prisoner's Dilemmas**. Game Matrix 1 has the structure of a Prisoner's Dilemma. The Prisoner's Dilemma should look familiar from Chapter 13: the Bertrand and Cournot equilibrium yielded lower profits to the firms than the point where each firm priced or produced at the joint monopoly solution. In other words, while the joint monopoly solution was the point that maximized collective self-interest in the Cournot and Bertrand games, it did not coincide with the Nash equilibrium.

Exercise 4: *Which of these statements is true about the following game matrix?*

<u>Firm 2</u>

		Low output	High output
		Low output	High output
Firm 1	Low output	(555,555)	(500,650)
	High output	(650,500)	(625,625)

a. The game is a prisoner's dilemma
b. The game is not a prisoner's dilemma
c. The Nash equilibrium is (Low output, Low output)
d. The Nash equilibrium is (High output, High output)

Game Matrix 1 has another feature that we should mention. For each player in this game, "price low" was a strategy that was better than any other strategy *no matter what strategy* the rival followed. Such a strategy is called a **dominant strategy**. A **dominant strategy equilibrium** occurs when *each and every* player uses a dominant strategy. All dominant strategy equilibria are Nash equilibria as well. In contrast, Nash equilibria are *not necessarily* dominant strategy equilibria. For example, consider the following game between two players. The players have at their disposal two strategies, labeled A and B. The payoffs to each of the four possible outcomes are listed in each cell of the matrix.

<u>Player 2</u>

		Strategy A	Strategy B
		Strategy A	Strategy B
Player 1	Strategy A	(10, 5)	(10,10)
	Strategy B	(15,20)	(15,15)

Game Matrix 2

Let us look for the Nash equilibrium of Game Matrix 2 using the three steps we described above. We will also check that there is no dominant strategy equilibrium.

1. Take a particular strategy as given (and fixed) for Player 2 and calculate the best response of Player 1. Repeat this for every possible strategy by Player 2. The best response function of Player 1 is, then:

<u>Player 2</u>   <u>Player 1</u>

Strategy A → Strategy B (because 15 > 10)
Strategy B → Strategy B (because 15 > 10)

2. Take a particular strategy as given (and fixed) for Player 1 and calculate the best response of Player 2. Repeat this for every possible strategy by Player 1. The best response function of Player 2 is, then:

<u>Player 1</u>   <u>Player 2</u>

Strategy A → Strategy B (because 10 > 5)
Strategy B → Strategy A (because 20 > 15)

3. Using the results of steps (1) and (2), find the combination of strategies such that *each* player's strategy is a best response to the other's. These strategies form a Nash equilibrium.

<u>Player 2</u>

	Strategy A	Strategy B
Strategy A	(10, 5)	(10,**10**)
Strategy B	(<u>15</u>,**20**)	(<u>15</u>,15)

Player 1 (Strategy A, Strategy B rows at left)

Best Responses for Game Matrix 2

The only cell with both underlining and bold is the lower left-hand corner. Hence the Nash equilibrium for this game is that Player 1 uses Strategy B and Player 2 uses Strategy A. The Nash equilibrium outcome is (15, 20).

There is no dominant strategy equilibrium for Game Matrix 2. Player 1 has a dominant strategy of Strategy B, since this is Player 1's best response *no matter which* strategy Player 2 follows. Player 2, however, does *not* have a dominant strategy: the best response of Player 2 changes depending on which strategy Player 1 follows. Hence, no dominant strategy equilibrium exists because not all players have a dominant strategy. On the other hand, a Nash equilibrium exists, as steps (1)-(3) show.

Exercise 5: *Which of the following statements is true?*

a. The game matrix in Exercise 3 has a dominant strategy equilibrium
b. The game matrix in Exercise 4 has a dominant strategy equilibrium
c. In a dominant strategy equilibrium the aggregate payoffs of the players is never maximized.
d. In any game, there are always at least as many Nash equilibria as there are dominant strategy equilibria.

In contrast to a dominant strategy, a **dominated strategy** is a strategy that gives a *lower* payoff than an alternative strategy no matter what the other player does. In Game Matrix 2, Strategy A is a dominated strategy for Player 1 since Strategy B gives a higher payoff to Player 1 no matter what Player 2 does. Since a dominated strategy will never be chosen by a player, the cells associated with this strategy can be eliminated from the game matrix as a way of simplifying the game. For example, we can safely eliminate the entire top row of Game Matrix 2 because we know that these outcomes will never occur: Player 1 will never choose to play Strategy A. Hence, we have a simpler matrix to analyze. While this makes little difference in a very simple game such as Game Matrix 2, it can make solving for the equilibrium much easier in complex games. An example of this is given in Exercise 6.

Exercise 6: *Consider the following game matrix:*

Player 2

Player 1	Strategy A	Strategy B	Strategy C
Strategy A	(5,8)	(15,10)	(10,5)
Strategy B	(10,15)	(20,9)	(15,0)
Strategy C	(20,20)	(10,10)	(10,8)

Which of the following statements is true for this matrix?

a. Neither player has a dominant strategy in the 3x3 matrix, above.
b. Both players have a dominated strategy in the 3x3 matrix, above.
c. The Nash equilibrium for this game is (Strategy A, Strategy A).
d. The Nash equilibrium for this game is (Strategy C, Strategy A).

Both Game Matrix 1 and Game Matrix 2 have a single Nash equilibrium. Even simple games may, however, have multiple Nash Equilibria or, alternatively, may have no equilibrium at all. For example, you should verify using our three step procedure that the best responses of the players in the following two games are represented by the underlining and bold on the following game matrices:

	Player 2	
	Left	Right
Up	($\underline{20}$, **20**)	(5,10)
Down	(10,5)	($\underline{15}$, **15**)

Player 1

Game Matrix 3A

	Player 2	
	Left	Right
Up	($\underline{1}$,-1)	(-1,**1**)
Down	(-1,**1**)	($\underline{1}$,-1)

Player 1

Game Matrix 3B

Game Matrix 3A has two Nash equilibria: in the first, Player 1 plays "Up" and Player 2 plays "Left". In the second, Player 1 plays "Down" and Player 2 plays "Right". We can check by reasoning that each of these is a Nash equilibrium. For example, the best response of Player 1 to "Left" is, indeed, "Up" since 20 is greater than 10. The best response of Player 2 to "Up" is, indeed, "Left" since 20 is greater than 10. Hence, both players are on their best response function when they are at the upper left-hand cell so that this is a Nash equilibrium.

Game Matrix 3B has no Nash equilibrium: no cell has a set of payoffs that is both underlined *and* in bold. We can check by reasoning that no equilibrium exists: Suppose that Player 2 plays "Left". The best response of Player 1 is to play "Up" since 1 is greater than -1. But if Player 1 plays "Up", the best response of Player 2 is now to play "Right". If Player 2 plays "Right", however, the best response of Player 1 is to play "Down". Finally, since the best response to "Down" is "Left", we get right back to the cell where we started! The reasoning is completely circular so that no equilibrium, or stable point, exists.

Exercise 7: *Suppose that we change the payoff in the lower left-hand corner of the game in Exercise 6 to obtain the following game matrix:*

<u>Player 2</u>

	Strategy A	Strategy B	Strategy C
<u>Player 1</u> Strategy A	(5,8)	(15,10)	(10,5)
Strategy B	(10,15)	(20,9)	(15,0)
Strategy C	(20,5)	(10,10)	(10,8)

What is/are the Nash equilibria of this game?

a. (Strategy C, Strategy A) is the unique Nash equilibrium.
b. There is no Nash equilibrium.
c. (Strategy B, Strategy B) is the unique Nash equilibrium.
d. Both (Strategy C, Strategy A) and (Strategy B, Strategy B) are Nash equilibria.

There is a caveat to what we have said about games where there is no Nash equilibrium. Until now, we have considered cases where the players may make only specific choices among the possible moves in the game. For example, in Game Matrix 3B, we have assumed that Player 1 may only choose *either* "Up" *or* "Down" and Player 2 may only choose *either* "Left" *or* "Right". When we limit ourselves in this way, we are looking at what are called **pure strategies**. By contrast, we could assume that a player may choose among two or more moves according to pre-specified probabilities (i.e., by throwing dice or by picking moves out of a hat). This is called a **mixed strategy** or a **randomized strategy**. While many games do not have a Nash equilibrium in pure strategies, virtually *every* game you are likely to encounter has at least one Nash equilibrium in mixed strategies. In fact, even games with multiple Nash equilibria in pure strategies have equilibria in mixed strategies as well.

The way we check that a candidate set of probabilities forms a mixed strategy equilibrium for a game is to see whether the expected payoff to each player for each pure strategy is the same. For example, suppose that we claim that a Nash equilibrium in mixed strategies for Game Matrix 3B is that each player uses each of the strategies at his disposal with probability $1/2$. Now, Player 1 obtains expected payoff $(1/2)(1) + (1/2)(-1) = 0$ by moving "Up" and expected payoff $(1/2)(1) + (1/2)(-1) = 0$ by moving "Down". Player 2 obtains expected payoff $(1/2)(1) + (1/2)(-1) = 0$ by moving "Left" and expected payoff $(1/2)(1) + (1/2)(-1) = 0$ by moving "Right". Hence, each player obtains the same expected payoff to each of their pure strategies. As a result, we have found a Nash equilibrium in mixed strategies for this game.

Exercise 8: *Consider the following game matrix:*

<u>Player 2</u>

	Strategy A	Strategy B
Strategy A	(9,6)	(3,3)
Strategy B	(3,3)	(6,9)

<u>Player 1</u> (Strategy A / Strategy B rows, left side)

Which of the following statements is true?

a. There is a unique Nash equilibrium in pure strategies.
b. There are two Nash equilibria in pure strategies.
c. The mixed strategy equilibrium puts probability (1/2) on each strategy for each player.
d. The mixed strategy equilibrium of Player 1 puts probability (2/3) on Strategy A and probability (1/3) on Strategy B and Player 2 puts probability (1/3) on Strategy A and probability (2/3) on Strategy B.

A five-step approach to identifying the Nash equilibria of a simultaneous-move game involving two players

1. If both players have a dominant strategy, these constitute their Nash equilibrium strategies (and their dominant strategy equilibrium, as well).

2. If one player has a dominant strategy, then this constitutes the Nash equilibrium strategy for this player. We then find the rival player's best response to the dominant strategy in order to find the rival's Nash equilibrium strategy.

3. If neither player has a dominant strategy, then we may search for and eliminate any dominated strategies in order to simplify the game.

4. By using the "underlining and bold" technique, we can identify all the Nash equilibria in pure strategies for the simplified game.

5. After finding the equilibria in pure strategies, we can look for the mixed strategy equilibria by finding the probabilities to apply to each set of payoffs so that the pure strategies yield the same expected payoffs for the players.

Exercise 9: *Find all the Nash equilibria (in pure and mixed strategies) for the following game matrix:*

Player 2

	Strategy A	Strategy B
Strategy A	(10,9)	(5,5)
Strategy B	(5,5)	(9,10)

Player 1 (Strategy A, Strategy B rows)

Which of the following are the probabilities applied by each player to Strategy A and Strategy B in the mixed strategy equilibrium?

a. (1/2, 1/2)
b. (1/3, 2/3)
c. (1/4, 3/4)
d. (5/9, 4/9)

Up to now, we have only analyzed one-shot games (i.e., games where each agent must only decide on an action once). However, many real life strategic situations involve repeated interaction among economic agents. Such situations can be analyzed in **repeated games** (i.e., in games where a given one-shot game is played several times by the same players). For example, suppose that the pricing game in Game Matrix 1 is played out daily between two firms over a number of years. What would the equilibrium of such a repeated game between these two players look like?

When interaction is repeated, it opens the possibility for contingent strategies of the type "If you do action A, I will do action B". This greatly *increases* the number of possible strategies open to the players, since many possible contingencies can be imagined for even simple games. Not surprisingly, with this increase in possible strategies comes an increase in the number of possible equilibria.

Exercise 10: *Suppose that the game described by Game Matrix 1 is repeated twice. All payoffs are evaluated as if they were received immediately (so that a payoff of 20 received tomorrow is worth 20 today). If firm 1 follows a strategy of "always price high", what is the best response of firm 2?*

a. "Price high unless a low price is observed, in which case price low next period".
b. "Always price high".
c. "Always price low".

Now, suppose that firm 1 follows a strategy of "Price high unless a low price is observed, in which case price low". What is the best response of firm 2?

 a. "Price high unless a low price is observed, in which case price low next period".
 b. "Always price high".
 c. "Always price low".

To simplify our study, we will focus on a single type of repeated game (a repeated Prisoner's Dilemma) and a particular type of contingent strategy called a "Grim Trigger" strategy. The general idea behind such strategies is to ensure that players pursue the "common good" by "punishing" any player who does not. More precisely, a "Grim Trigger" strategy is a strategy that inflicts a severe punishment on a rival player as soon as a rival player is observed to make a particular move. This punishment lasts from the time the move is observed until the final repetition or "period" of the game. For example, consider a game that repeats Game Matrix 1. The following would be a Grim Trigger strategy for firm 1: "As long as firm 2 prices high, I will price high. The first time firm 2 is observed to price low, I will price low in all remaining periods of the game." Hence, by pricing high, firm 2 can ensure itself of a payoff equal to 20 each period that the game is played. On the other hand, if firm 2 ever prices low, it receives a payoff of 30 in the period when this "cheating" occurs followed by 10 in every period thereafter. Hence, a single incidence of "cheating" is punished by a low payoff for the entire remainder of the game.

The optimal response of firm 2 to the Grim Trigger strategy depends on how much firm 2 cares about its future payoffs. If it values payoffs in future periods highly compared to its payoff today, it would do better to price high. If it values payoffs in the future very little compared to its payoff today, it would do better to price low. Hence, if the two firms care a great deal about future payoffs, a Grim Trigger strategy has the appealing feature that it can induce both firms to price high. This allows the firms to achieve the collective profit-maximizing solution to the game and so "solves" the Prisoner's Dilemma.

Exercise 11: *Suppose that Game Matrix 1 is repeated twice. Suppose that each firm must commit to a strategy at the beginning of the game (before any play has occurred). Suppose that a payoff received tomorrow is worth only half the value of that payoff if it were received today (so that a payoff of 10 today and 10 tomorrow has the same value as a payoff of 15 today). Let Firm 1 follow the Grim Trigger strategy of "Price high until a low price is observed, after which price low." What is the best response of firm 2?*

 a. "Always price low."
 b. "Always price high."
 c. "Price high until a low price is observed, after which price low."
 d. Player 2 receives the same payoff under (a), (b), and (c) so any of these is an equally good response.

A second feature of the simple games that we have analyzed is that all players have been assumed to make their decisions simultaneously. This assumption does not hold in many real life situations, where one player often can move before the others. A game where one player moves before the other(s) *and* that player's move is observed by the other player(s) before they make their decisions is called a **sequential-move game**. We depict sequential-move games with a **game tree**, which shows the different "moves" that each player can make and the order in which those moves get chosen. For example, suppose that in Game Matrix 3A, Player 1 gets to make his decision first and Player 2 makes her decision second after observing Player 1's move. We can, then, rewrite Game Matrix 3A as the following game tree:

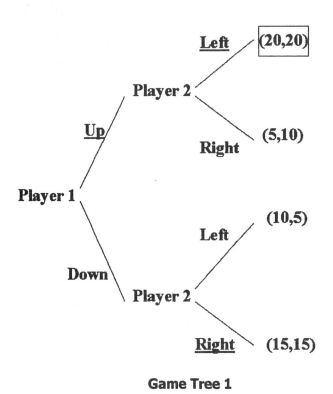

Game Tree 1

The tree is read from left to right. First, Player 1 chooses between the top branch of the tree ("Up") and the bottom branch ("Down"). Next, Player 2 chooses between "Left" and "Right", each represented by another branch on the tree. After all firms have made their decisions, each receives the payoff listed at the right-hand side of the tree. The payoff to Player 1 is listed first and the payoff to Player 2 is listed second in each set of brackets. The players, possible strategies, and payoffs are exactly as in Game Matrix 3A, but this time they are represented as a tree rather than as a matrix, and Player 1 gets to choose first.

Sequential games are often solved by using a technique called **backward induction**. This technique helps us determine the optimal decision of each player *at each point in the game*. Backward induction solves for the equilibrium from right to left, starting with the last set of branches on the tree. The last set of branches represents Player 2's decision problem, taking into account the decision that was already made by Player 1. For example, suppose that Player 1 has decided to play

"Up" so that we are at the top set of branches on the tree. Now, Player 2 must decide between "Left" and "Right" *given* that Player 1's choice of "Up" is irrevocable. Player 2 can obtain a payoff of 20 by choosing "Left" and a payoff of 10 by choosing "Right", so the optimal move is "Left". This best response is underlined on the tree. Similarly, once Player 1's choice of "Down" is given and irrevocable, Player 2 faces a choice between moving "Left" and obtaining a payoff of 5 and moving "Right" and obtaining a payoff of 15. Clearly, it is now better to move "Right". This best response is underlined on the tree.

Now we move left on the tree to analyze Player 1's choice. Player 1 need only compare the payoffs to each of his possible moves under the assumption that Player 2 will make her best response. Hence, Player 1 may move "Up" -- and receive the payoff that will result when Player 2 follows with her best response of "Left" -- or may choose "Down" -- and receive the payoff that will result when Player 2 follows with her best response of "Right". This means that Player 1 faces a choice between receiving 20 (if he chooses "Up") or 15 if he chooses "Down". Player 1 prefers, then, to move "Up". This best response is underlined on the tree.

Now, we can state that the equilibrium of the game is the path that we can trace from one end of the tree to the other by following an unbroken string of underlined moves. The only unbroken path that we can trace out is the path of "Up" followed by "Left".   Hence, the equilibrium outcome of this game is (20,20). This is indicated by the boxed payoffs. Comparing this equilibrium to that of Game Matrix 3A, we see that by allowing one player to move before the other, we have eliminated the second Nash equilibrium of the simultaneous game. Stated differently, by committing *irrevocably* in advance to a particular strategy, Player 1 has improved his payoff (and, in this case, Player 2's payoff as well). Comparing these two games illustrates the strategic value to inflexibility. In general, such a commitment early in a game that alters later behavior of any or all players is called a **strategic move**, and has many uses in real life game situations.

Exercise 12: *Suppose that Player 1 can move before Player 2 in the game matrix of Exercise 7. What is the Nash equilibrium of this game?*

a. (Strategy A, Strategy B)
b. (Strategy B, Strategy B)
c. (Strategy B, Strategy A)
d. (Strategy C, Strategy B)

Suppose that, instead, Player 2 moves first. What is the Nash equilibrium of this game?

a. (Strategy A, Strategy B)
b. (Strategy B, Strategy B)
c. (Strategy B, Strategy A)
d. (Strategy C, Strategy B)

Chapter Review Questions

1. Find all the Nash equilibria of the following game matrix:

<u>Player 2</u>

	Strategy A	Strategy B	Strategy C
Player 1 **Strategy A**	(10,10)	(5,15)	(-5,5)
Strategy B	(15,0)	(10,5)	(0,0)
Strategy C	(5,-5)	(0,0)	(5,10)

Answer:

First, note that Strategy A is a dominated strategy for both Player 1 and Player 2. For example, in each column Player 1's payoff from playing Strategy B is higher than her payoff from playing Strategy A. Similarly, in each row, the payoff to Strategy B is higher than the payoff of Strategy A for Player 2. By eliminating these strategies from the matrix, we are left with the following game:

<u>Player 2</u>

	Strategy B	Strategy C
Strategy B	(<u>10</u>, **5**)	(0, 0)
Player 1 Strategy C	(0, 0)	(<u>5</u>, **10**)

The best responses are underlined or written in bold. Since both the upper left-hand corner and the lower right-hand corner contain a best response for each player, these are Nash equilibria in pure strategies.

There is also a Nash equilibrium in mixed strategies, which we solve for by finding the probability that makes each player indifferent between his two pure strategies. In other words, we must find the probability, pr, with which *Player 1* uses Strategy B that makes *Player 2* just indifferent between his two pure strategies:

$$pr \times 5 + (1 - pr) \times 0 = pr \times 0 + (1 - pr) \times 10$$

Solving this, we find that pr = 2/3. The probability that Player 1 uses Strategy C must, then, be 1 - 2/3 = 1/3. Similarly, we must find the probability, pr, with which *Player 2* uses Strategy B that makes *Player 1* just indifferent between his two pure strategies:

pr x 10 + (1- pr) x 0 = pr x 0 + (1 - pr) x 5

Solving this, we find that pr = 1/3. The probability that Player 2 uses Strategy C must, then be 1 - pr = 2/3.

2. State whether each of the following strategies is (1) a (pure) strategy, (2) a mixed strategy, (3) a Grim Trigger strategy, (4) a Nash equilibrium strategy. (Several may apply to any one strategy.) Explain your answer.

   a. Always move right.

   b. Move right with probability .5 and move left with probability .5.

   c. If Player 1 moves right, I move left. If Player 1 moves left, I move right.

   d. Move right unless Player 1 moves left, in which case move left at the next opportunity.

Answer:

a. This is a pure strategy since the player moves right with certainty. It is not a Grim Trigger strategy because no trigger is specified at which a punishment phase begins. It is a (degenerate) mixed strategy because the probability with which "right" is played is 1. This may also be a Nash equilibrium strategy if it forms a part of a set of best responses of all players.

b. This is a mixed strategy since it applies a probability to two pure strategies. It may also be a Nash equilibrium strategy if it is a strategy that is part of a set of best responses of all players. It is not a Grim Trigger strategy since no trigger is specified at which a punishment phase begins.

c. This is a pure strategy (and thus a degenerate mixed strategy) since the probability with which each move is made is one, given the move of the other player. It is not a Grim Trigger strategy because no trigger is specified at which a punishment phase begins. It may be a Nash equilibrium strategy if it is a part of a set of best responses of all players.

d. This is a Grim Trigger strategy if moving left does, indeed, inflict punishment on the rival. It may be a Nash equilibrium strategy if it is part of a set of best responses of all players. Finally, it is a degenerate mixed strategy (and thus a pure strategy) in the sense that the probability with which each move is made is one, given the move of the other player.

3. TyranoCo. and Rex Corporation are the only two makers of toy dinosaurs. While neither firm currently serves the U.K. market, significant unmet demand exists there. Hence, both firms are currently in the process of deciding on how much capacity to build to serve the market. Strict antitrust laws prevent the firms from colluding or communicating in any way during their decision process, but each firm is aware that the other is planning new capacity. Further, the technology for making toy dinosaurs is well-known (as these two firms have been competing together in several other markets for a number of years) and the U.K. customers have characteristics similar to those of customers in other markets. Hence, the general production and marketing conditions of the product hold essentially no secrets for these firms. It is rumored that a decision is expected from both firms near the end of this calendar year.

The main difficulty that each firm is facing in making its decision is the following. The nature of technology in this industry is that, once a plant is built, it is very expensive for the firm to run the plant at less than capacity. Hence, the capacity will essentially determine the output level that the firm will produce. Further, the technology dictates that only two sizes of plant: "large" or "small" are cost-effective. If both firms produce at the low output level, both make rather high profits. Unfortunately, if both firms produce at a high output level, the price in the market will fall drastically and each firm will make very low profits. On the other hand, given that either firm restricts its capacity, the rival would do better building a large capacity plant and serving a large market share than restricting its output as well. This leaves the firm with restricted capacity worse off as it produces little, but the large quantity produced by its rival still drives price down considerably. In other words, each firm would like the other to restrict its output, but would not like to do so itself.

   a. Write down the elements of this game.

   b. Would you depict this game as a game matrix or a game tree? What do you observe about the structure of this game?

   c. What do you think is the likely outcome in this industry? What does your answer depend on?

Answer:

a. *Players:* TyranoCo. and Rex Corporation.
   Strategies: Each firm may choose to build a large or a small plant.
   Outcomes: There are four: each firm may build a large plant, one may build a large plant and the other a small plant, or both may build a small plant.
   Payoffs: These are the profits earned under each of the four outcomes.
   Information: Each firm knows who can do what and when as well as the payoffs associated with each possible outcome.
   Timing: Simultaneous (both firms are deciding on capacity this year).

b. Since the game is simultaneous, a game matrix is more appropriate, because there is no need to show the order in which actions are taken. The last few lines of the problem suggest that some fictitious numbers that would mimic the characteristics of the problem might look like the following:

Rex Corporation

	Large Plant	Small Plant
Large Plant	(<u>25</u>, **25**)	(<u>50</u>, 10)
TyranoCo.		
Small Plant	(10 , **50**)	(40, 40)

The Nash equilibrium is indicated in the upper left-hand corner. This is not the point that maximizes the collective interest of the firms. Hence, the game has the structure of a prisoner's dilemma.

c. A good guess for the likely outcome is the Nash equilibrium derived in part (b). However, this depends on whether or not the game is repeated. If the game were to be repeated, then the firms might be able to devise Grim Trigger strategies to enforce the lower right-hand corner outcome. We are not given any information on repetition, except that this is the second market where the firms have had a capacity choice decision. If the U.K. entry is part of a general worldwide expansion by both firms, repetition could be possible.

Problem Set

1. Refer back to problem 4 of chapter 11 in this guide. In the same set up, now suppose that each country sets its own tax rate to maximize its own revenues (so that country 1 sets t_1 to maximize $t_1 K_1$ and country 2 sets t_2 to maximize $t_2 K_2$).

   a. Suppose that the countries set their tax rates simultaneously. Find the unique Nash equilibrium of this game.

   b. Now suppose that country 1 sets its tax rate and then, after observing the tax rate set by country 1, country 2 sets its tax rate. Derive the unique equilibrium of this game by solving backwards.

   c. Compare your results. How do you interpret them?

2. Two firms compete in the breakfast cereal market. GC Corp. has to decide whether or not to introduce a new variety of cereal. After that decision is made, the rival firm, Big Q, can decide whether or not to introduce its own new cereal. Once both firms have made their product introduction decision, GC Corp., which is the industry leader, must decide whether to price aggressively ("be tough") or price cooperatively ("be soft"). The firms' profits are as follows, with the first number standing for GC Corp.'s profits:

- Both firms introduce a new product and GC Corp. plays tough (0,0)
    GC Corp. plays soft (3,3)
- Only GC Corp. introduces a new product and GC Corp. plays tough (4,1)
    GC Corp. plays soft (7,2)
- Only Big Q introduces a new product and GC Corp. plays tough (1,2)
    GC Corp. plays soft (2,7)
- Neither firm introduces a new product and GC Corp. plays tough (1,1)
    GC Corp. plays soft (5,5)

a. Represent this problem in a game tree.

b. Using backward induction, what is the equilibrium of this game?

c. Now, suppose that GC Corp. can commit to playing "tough" or "soft" in advance (i.e., after its product introduction decision but before the product introduction decision of Big Q). This commitment is irrevocable. Represent the new problem as a game tree. What is the equilibrium of this new game?

3. Suppose that an industry cartel wishes to keep a new entrant out of an industry. Cartel members can conduct "predatory pricing", where the cartel lowers its price until the entrant leaves, after which it returns its price to the cartel's optimal (monopoly) level. Let the alternative pricing strategy be "accommodation", where the cartel simply acknowledges the entry of the new firm and prices as a duopolist against the entrant. Suppose that the payoffs of predatory pricing versus accommodation are as follows:

New Entrant

		Enter	Stay Out
	Predate	(-50, -10)	(-25, 0)
Cartel			
	Accommodate	(75, 25)	(100, 0)

a. What is the likely outcome of this game?

b. If the cartel threatens to predate, should the entrant believe the threat?

4. You are asked to find the Nash equilibrium of the following game matrix by following the steps in parts (a) - (c), below:

	Player 2			
	Move 1	Move 2	Move 3	Move 4
Move A	(5,10)	(8,15)	(3,8)	(1,10)
Move B	(20,8)	(10,10)	(10,5)	(25,0)
Move C	(30,5)	(20,10)	(15,5)	(20,3)
Move D	(10,10)	(15,15)	(10,20)	(30,10)

(Player 1 labels the rows; Player 2 labels the columns)

a. First, look at the moves available to Player 1. Do you see any dominated strategies? If so, eliminate them from the matrix.

b. Now, look at the moves available to Player 2 in the revised matrix. Do you see any dominated strategies? If so, eliminate them from the matrix.

c. Repeat steps (a) and (b) until no more dominated strategies remain. What is the Nash equilibrium of this simplified matrix?

5. Consider a two-player simultaneous-move game where the players' strategies and payoffs are described by the following matrix:

	Player B	
	Left	Right
Up	(3,3)	(1,0)
Down	(1,0)	(x,2)

(Player A labels the rows)

Where x is some positive number and the first entry in each cell represents player A's payoff, while the second entry is player B's payoff.

a. Derive the Nash equilibrium/equilibria when x = 0.

b. Derive the Nash equilibrium/equilibria when x = 2. Briefly discuss which of the two is relatively more plausible.

6. Consider the following sequential game between a government, G, and a firm, F. The government announces the rate of taxation, t, where $0 \leq t \leq 1$, and tax is paid by the firm per unit of output it produces. After observing the government's choice, the firm then chooses the quantity q of a good to be sold in order to maximize its profits. The marginal revenue of the firm when it sells output is MR = 1-2q. The tax paid to the government is the firm's only marginal cost.

 a. Derive the optimal output of the firm as a function of the tax rate set by the government.

 b. The benefit from increasing the tax by one the increase earned on all units sold. The cost of increasing the tax is the reduction in output induced by the increase times the tax rate. Using this information, show that when the government only wishes to maximize the tax revenue it collects from the firm, the equilibrium rate of taxation is ½.

 c. Suppose that the government cares only about consumers' surplus, which we will assume for this question can be written as $(q^2/2)$, where q is the output of the firm. What is the equilibrium rate of taxation now?

 d. What can you deduce about the change in equilibrium rate of taxation if the government puts more and more weight on consumers' surplus and less and less on its tax revenues from the firm?

Exam *(60 minutes: Closed book; Closed notes)*

1.
 a. Is it possible to have more than one dominant strategy equilibrium in a game? Explain your answer.

 b. Can more than one Grim Trigger strategy support the same equilibrium outcome?

 c. Is it possible to have more than one mixed strategy equilibrium in a game? Explain your answer.

2. Two firms, A and B, compete as duopolists in an industry. The firms produce a homogeneous good at marginal and average cost of MC = 10. The (inverse) market demand for the product can be written as P = 100 – Q. Each of the firms chooses an output level so as to maximize its own profits; however, firm A makes its decision before firm B. Hence, firm B sets its output so as to maximize its own profits given whatever output level was set initially by firm A. Firm A, on the other hand, sets its output level taking into account the fact that firm B will react to this. To make matters less complicated, assume that firm B may set output at one of only two levels: 30 or 22.5. Firm A may also set its output at one of only two levels, 30 or 45. The competition occurs only once and is not repeated.

a. Depict the game in a game tree, making sure to calculate the payoffs on each branch of the tree correctly.

b. Find the Nash equilibrium solution to this game, using backwards induction to solve for the equilibrium.

c. Comparing your answer to the Cournot game in Chapter 13, Exercise 5, explain why firm A makes higher profits than firm B in equilibrium in this game.

d. Interpret this game as a Stackelberg game. How much would firm A be willing to pay for the right (or the ability) to choose first in this game? Can you think of a governmental or firm-level policy that would allow a firm to move earlier than a competitor?

3. Two firms, Zap Corporation and ElectroCo., have different technologies for their new DVD players. Both firms would gain by having a single standard emerge in the industry, since consumers are currently hesitant to buy due to the lack of a standard. However, each firm would do better if its own technology was chosen as the industry standard. The resulting payoff matrix for the two companies' standardization decision is as follows:

ElectroCo.

		Produce Own System	Adopt Rival's System
Zap	Produce Own System	(10, 10)	(100, 50)
	Adopt Rival's System	(50, 100)	(0, 0)

a. Does either firm have a dominant strategy?

b. What is/are the Nash equilibrium for this game?

c. Now, suppose that the government of the country of BigMarket says that it will only allow DVD players with the ElectroCo. standard to be marketed within its borders. This changes the game matrix to the following:

ElectroCo.

	Produce Own System	Adopt Rival's System
Produce Own System	(10, 75)	(100, 50)
Adopt Rival's System	(50, 150)	(0, 0)

Zap

How do your answers to (a) and (b) change with these new payoffs?

d. How much would ElectroCo. be willing to spend in lobbying effort in order to get BigMarket to approve its standard as in (c)?

4. Consider an industry with two firms. Each firm may either "cooperate" with its rival or it may "cheat" in each period of play. If both firms cooperate, they earn $50 in that period. If only firm A cheats, it earns $75 in that period, but firm B earns $25. If only firm B cheats, it earns $75 in that period, but firm A earns $25. If both firms cheat, then each earns $30 in that period.

   a. Write down the payoff matrix for a single period of this game.

   b. Assume that the game is played for only a single period. What is the likely outcome of this game? Are the firms able to attain their best preferred outcome?

   c. Suppose that the firms can sign an explicit agreement that says: any firm that cheats will be fined $100. How does this change the payoffs of the game? Will collusion become more likely?

   d. Suppose that now explicit agreements between the firms are illegal. Also assume that the game is repeated twice. Suppose that firm A commits to a strategy of cooperating in the first period, after which it will make whatever move firm B made in the first period. What is the likely outcome of the game if firm A plays this strategy? Does this "tacit collusion" resolve the problem of part (c)?

Answers to Exercises

1. The correct answer is that statements (a), (b), and (c) are correct. There are three possible outcomes: player 1 wins, player 2 wins, and the two players agree to a draw. Generally, chess has only two players (not counting referees). Decisions are made sequentially: one player moves after the other. The incorrect statement is (d): each player has a very large number of strategies open to her.

These strategies include various rules of thumb (such as "always open by moving the pawn that stands in front of the right-hand knight forward two spaces"), contingent strategies ("if the opponent plays aggressively, I will too") and other "gambits".

2. Statements (b) and (d) are correct. Statement (a) is wrong because what matters for the Nash equilibrium is only that a move be a best response to a rival's move. It is irrelevant to each player whether the *rival* does better when this best response is taken. Statement (c) is wrong because each firm does better pricing low rather than pricing high (no matter what the rival does). Hence, there is an incentive to deviate from pricing high to pricing low.

3. The correct answer is (d). The best responses for this game matrix are shown by underlining and bold below:

Firm 2

		Low Output	High Output
	Low Output	(625,625)	(468.75,**703.125**)
Firm 1			
	High Output	(<u>703.125</u>,468.75)	(<u>555.61</u>,**555.61**)

Hence, the Nash equilibrium is that firm 1 and firm 2 both set a high level of output.

4. Statements (b) and (d) are correct. (c) is incorrect because the Nash equilibrium is for each firm to produce high output, as shown by the best responses below:

Firm 2

		Low Output	High Output
	Low Output	(555,555)	(500,**650**)
Firm 1			
	High Output	(<u>650</u>,500)	(<u>625</u>,**625**)

Since the Nash equilibrium also maximizes the joint payoffs of the firms, the game is not a Prisoner's Dilemma. Hence, (a) is incorrect.

5. Statements (a), (b), and (d) are correct. It can be seen from the answers to Exercises 3 and 4 that the firms always play a single move, whatever the rival's move. This means that each firm has a dominant strategy in each of these exercises. Statement (d) is correct because any dominant strategy equilibrium also is a Nash equilibrium; however, the opposite is not necessarily true. Hence, while there are at least as many Nash equilibria as dominant strategy equilibria, the opposite is not true. An example of why statement (c) is wrong is given by the game matrix in Exercise 4: here, the dominant strategy equilibrium also maximizes the collective good.

6. Statements (a), (b), and (d) are correct. In the original matrix, neither firm has a dominant strategy since each player's best move changes depending on what the rival does. For example, If Player 2 chooses Strategy A, the best response of Player 1 is Strategy C. On the other hand, if Player 2 chooses Strategy B, the best response of Player 1 is Strategy B. Similarly, if Player 1 chooses Strategy A, the best response of Player 2 is Strategy B, while if Player 1 chooses Strategy B, the best response of Player 2 is Strategy A.

Both firms have dominated strategies in the original matrix, however, since Strategy A is always dominated by Strategy B for Player 1 and Strategy C is always dominated by Strategy B for Player 2. This can be seen by noting that all the payoffs for Strategy A are lower than the payoffs for Strategy B for Player 1 in each column. All the payoffs for Strategy C are lower than the payoffs for Strategy B for Player 2 in each row.

If we eliminate the dominated strategies from the 3x3 matrix, we obtain a new matrix that looks like the following:

Player 2

	Strategy A	Strategy B
Player 1 Strategy B	(10, 15)	(20, 9)
Strategy C	(20, 20)	(10, 10)

In this new matrix, Strategy B is dominated for Player 2 by Strategy A and so can be eliminated from the game matrix. This leaves only the first column of the matrix, where Player 2 plays Strategy A and Player 1 can respond with either Strategy B or C. Clearly, Strategy C is the best response. Hence, the Nash equilibrium for this entire game matrix is that Player 1 uses Strategy C, Player 2 uses Strategy A, and each of the players receives a payoff of 20.

7. The correct answer is (b). Solving for the Nash equilibrium of this matrix, we first note that Strategy C is a dominated strategy for Player 2 by comparing the payoff in each row of Strategy C to the payoff to Strategy B for the same row. With Strategy C eliminated from the game matrix, we see that now Strategy A is dominated for Player 1 by Strategy B. This is true since, in each column, Strategy B yields a higher payoff than Strategy A for Player 1. The remaining 2x2 matrix is as follows with the best responses shown by underlining and bold:

Player 2

		Strategy A	Strategy B
Player 1	Strategy B	(10, **15**)	(<u>20</u>, 9)
	Strategy C	(<u>20</u>, 5)	(10, **10**)

Since no pair of moves is a pair of best responses for both players, there is no Nash equilibrium to this game.

8. Statements (b) and (d) are correct. The best responses for this game matrix are shown by underlining and bold in the following matrix:

Player 2

		Strategy A	Strategy B
Player 1	Strategy A	(<u>9</u>,**6**)	(3,3)
	Strategy B	(3,3)	(<u>6</u>,**9**)

Hence, there are two pure strategy Nash equilibria in the upper left-hand corner and the lower right-hand corner, respectively. There is also a mixed strategy equilibrium as in statement (d). We can check this by noting that the payoff to Strategy A equals the payoff to Strategy B for Player 2 when Player 1 uses the given probabilities:

Expected payoff to Strategy A for Player 2: $(2/3)(6) + (1/3)(3) = 5$
Expected payoff to Strategy B for Player 2: $(2/3)(3) + (1/3)(9) = 5$

By a similar calculation, Player 1 is also indifferent between her two available strategies. Note that (c) cannot be correct since:

Expected payoff to Strategy A for Player 2: (1/2)(6) + (1/2)(3) = 4.5
Expected payoff to Strategy B for Player 2: (1/2)(3) + (1/2)(9) = 6

Since the expected payoff to Strategy A for Player 2 is higher than that of Strategy B it never makes sense for 2 to play B with any positive probability. Hence, given that Player 1 plays A with probability 1/2 and B with probability 1/2, Player 2's best response is to play A for sure. The same reasoning applies to Player 1.

9. The correct answer is (d). The Nash equilibria in pure strategies are shown in the following matrix using underlining and bold:

Player 2

	Strategy A	Strategy B
Strategy A	(**10**,**9**)	(5,5)
Strategy B	(5,5)	(**9**,**10**)

Player 1

The mixed strategy equilibrium can be obtained by solving for the probabilities that Player 1 applies to Strategies A and B that leaves Player 2 indifferent between Strategies A and B:

pr x 9 + (1 - pr) x 5 = pr x 5 + (1 - pr) x 10

where: pr is the probability that Player 1 uses Strategy A.

The solution to this equation is that pr = 5/9. Hence, (1-pr) = 4/9. This set of probabilities also leaves Player 1 indifferent between Strategies A and B when it is used by Player 2.

10. The correct answer to the first part of the question is (c). If firm 1 always prices high, only the top row of the matrix is relevant to firm 2's decision. Firm 2 clearly earns more by responding with Price Low.

(a), (b), and (c) all yield the same payoff and are all best responses by firm 2. By always pricing high, firm 2 earns 20 in each period for a total payoff of 40. On the other hand, if firm 2 always prices low, it obtains 30 in the first period and 10 in the second period for a total payoff of 40. If it follows the contingent strategy of (a), it receives 20 each period for a total payoff of 40 (since both firms price low *only if* the rival initiates a price cut).

11. The correct answer is (a). Recall from Exercise 10 that any of these strategies was a best response to the Grim Trigger strategy proposed for firm 1 in this matrix when the game is repeated twice and when all future payoffs are worth the same as the same payoff received today. When we make firms "discount" (or care less about) the future, we see that these strategies no longer yield the same payoff. The strategy of always pricing high yields $20 + (1/2)(20) = 30$. The strategy of always pricing low, however, yields $30 + (1/2)(10) = 35$. The contingent strategy of (c) results in the same payoff as the strategy of always pricing high. In any case, the strategy of pricing low does best. Hence, when the period during which the punishment is to be inflicted is discounted, the same Grim Trigger strategy becomes less effective (since, in effect, the punishment is weakened).

12. The correct answer to the first part of the question is (a). The game tree is now:

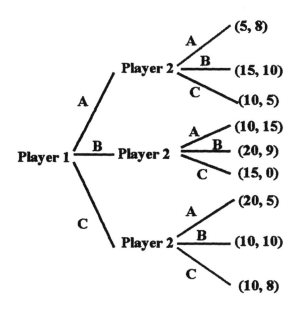

Hence, If Player 1 uses Strategy A, Player 2's best response is Strategy B (yielding payoff pair (15, 10)). If Player 1 uses Strategy B, Player 2's best response is Strategy A (yielding payoff pair (10, 15)). If Player 1 uses Strategy C, Player 2's best response is Strategy B (yielding payoff pair (10, 10)). Knowing Player 2's best response, then, Player 1 can see that its best choice is to use Strategy A since this will eventually yield a payoff of 15 rather than 10 under the other two strategy choices. The Nash equilibrium is, then, that Player 1 chooses Strategy A, Player 2 responds with Strategy B, and the players receive payoff pair (15, 10).

The correct answer to the second part of the question is (b). If Player 2 moves first, the game tree becomes:

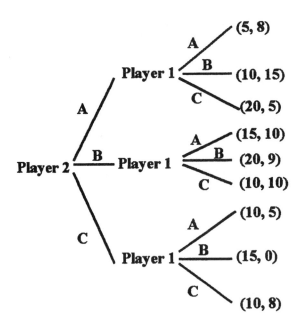

Now, we see that the best response of Player 1 to Strategy A is Strategy C (for a payoff of (20, 5)). The best response of Player 1 to Strategy B is Strategy B (for a payoff of (20, 9)). The best response of Player 1 to Strategy C is Strategy B (for a payoff of (15, 0)). Hence, knowing these best responses, Player 2 chooses Strategy B which yields a payoff of 9 to Player 2 after Player 1 has followed with her best response of Strategy B.

Answers to Problem Set

1.

    a. Recall from chapter 11, problem 4 that country 1's optimal tax rate is determined by MR = 0 or $1 - 2t_1 + t_2 = 0$ for any fixed tax rate set by country 2. If we think of this as a game between the two countries, each of which sets its own tax rate, then we have a similar condition for country 2: $1 - 2t_2 + t_1 = 0$, which determines its optimal tax rate for any given tax level set by country 1. Now we have two conditions that must be solved simultaneously to obtain the optimal tax rates of this game: $1 - 2t_1 + t_2 = 0$ and $1 - 2t_2 + t_1 = 0$. From the first of these conditions, we know that $(1+t_2)/2 = t_1$. Substituting this into the second condition, then, $1 - 2t_2 + (1+t_2)/2 = 0$ or $3/2 - (3/2)t_2 = 0$ or $t^*_2 = 1$. Similarly, $t^*_1 = 1$. Not surprisingly, as the two countries are identical except for the number that labels them, the Nash equilibrium tax rates are identical across the two countries.

    b. The second of the two countries to move, country 2, views country 1's tax rate as fixed and unchanging according to this new game. As a result, we can calculate its optimal tax rate as a function of country 1's tax rate just as before: $t_2 = (1+t_1)/2$ for whatever tax rate country 1 sets. Country 1 can take this information into account in calculating its own tax, rate, however. Its revenue from taxes now can be re-written solely as a function of its own tax rate: $t_1K_1 = t_1[1-t_1+(1+t_1)/2]$. For every one unit increase in t_1, the marginal revenue generated is the baseline level of capital investment, K_1 plus t_1 times the effect that a small (one unit) increase in t_1 has on K_1, $\Delta K_1/\Delta t_1$. Now, $K_1 = [1-t_1+(1+t_1)/2]$ once we have taken country 2's future behavior into account. A one unit increase in t_1 decreases K_1 by one unit, but also *increases* t_2 by half a unit. Net, then, the one unit increase in t_1 decreases K_1 by much less than before: only a half unit! We now have a new marginal revenue for our increase in t_1, then, MR $= K_1 + t_1\Delta K_1/\Delta t_1 = 1 - t_1 + (1+t_1)/2 + t_1(-1/2) = 3/2 - t_1$. This must be set equal to zero to obtain the optimal level of t_1: $3/2 - t_1 = 0$. Hence, the new optimal level of t_1 has increased to $3/2$. The optimal response of country 2, substituting $t_1 = 3/2$ into its optimal response is $t_2 = (1+t_1)/2 = 5/4$.

c. When country 1 takes into account that an increase in its own tax rate will cause an increase in country 2's tax rate, it realizes that it will suffer less decrease in its own investment when it increases its tax rate than in the simultaneous Nash equilibrium. Since there is less "cost" to an increase in tax rate, country 1's optimal tax rate rises above that of part (a). Even though country 2 takes country 1's tax rate as fixed and given -- just as in part (a) -- it raises its optimal tax rate because country 1's tax rate is higher than it was in part (a). Equilibrium tax rates are higher all around and both countries' tax revenues increase. Notice the similarity between the reasoning in this problem and that in chapter 13's comparison of Cournot to Stackelberg equilibrium. In that case as well, we moved from simultaneous quantity setting to sequential moves. There is a difference in the set-ups, however: in the Cournot-Stackelberg case, the first mover did better but the second mover did worse than the Cournot case. The case considered in this problem has the structure that *both* players do better when the moves are sequential.

2.

   a. A game tree that reflects this game is as follows:

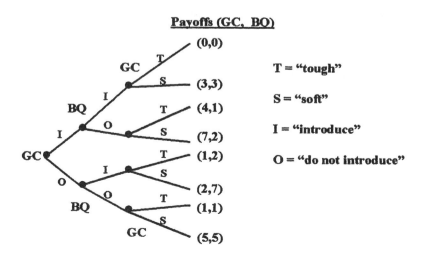

Payoffs (GC, BQ)

T = "tough"

S = "soft"

I = "introduce"

O = "do not introduce"

b. First, consider the last decision ("tough" or "soft"). Notice that GC's payoff if it plays "soft" always is higher than its payoff to playing "tough", given the previous introduction decisions. For example, if both have introduced a new product, GC obtains 3 by playing "soft" and only 0 if it plays "tough". Hence, GC always plays soft in the last set of branches of the tree.

Now, working backwards, we can see that if GC has introduced a product and knowing that GC will always play "soft" at the end of the tree, Big Q obtains a payoff of 3 from introducing a product and only 2 from not introducing. Hence, Big Q's best response when GC introduces is to introduce a product as well. If GC does not introduce a product, Big Q obtains a payoff of 7 if it introduces a product and 5 if it does not. Hence, Big Q's best response is to introduce if GC does not introduce.

Finally, we can consider GC's decision at the beginning of the tree. If GC introduces a product, it knows that the best response of Big Q will be to follow after which it will play soft. This results in a total payoff of 3 to GC. If GC does not introduce a product, Big Q will and GC will play soft afterwards. This results in a payoff to GC of 2. Hence, it is better to introduce a product.

The Nash equilibrium obtained by backwards induction is, then, that both firms introduce a product and price "soft".

c. If GC can commit to "tough" or "soft" at the beginning of the game, the game tree becomes the following:

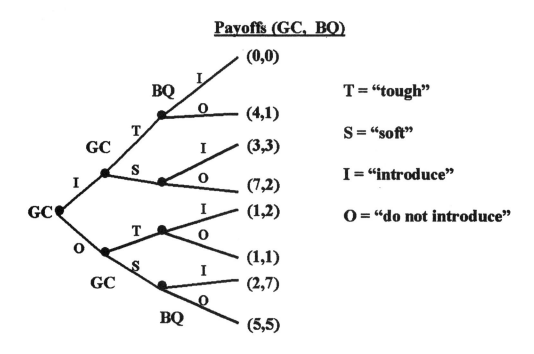

Payoffs (GC, BQ)

T = "tough"

S = "soft"

I = "introduce"

O = "do not introduce"

Working backwards, we start by solving for the best responses at the last set of branches, where BQ decides whether or not to introduce a product. If we are on the top set of branches, where GC has decided to both introduce and play tough, BQ receives 0 if it introduces and 1 if it does not. Hence, the best response is to introduce. On the other hand, if we move down to the next set of branches, where GC has introduced and decided to play soft, BQ receives 3 if it introduces and 2 if it does not. Hence, the best response for BQ here is not to introduce. If GC has not introduced and plays tough, then BQ receives 2 if it introduces and 1 if it does not. The best response here is, then, to introduce. Finally, if GC has not introduced and plays soft, then BQ receives 7 by introducing and 5 by not introducing. The best response here is to introduce.

If GC introduces, then, it faces the choice of playing tough (and receiving a payoff of 4) or playing soft (and receiving a payoff of 3). Hence, once GC has introduced, its best strategy is to play tough. Similarly, if GC has not introduced, it receives 1 if it plays tough and 2 if it plays soft. It is better to play soft, then, if it has not introduced a product.

Finally, GC must decide whether or not to introduce a product in the first place. If it introduces, it knows that it will play tough afterward and BQ will not introduce. This yields a payoff of 4. If GC introduces, it knows it will play soft afterward and BQ will introduce. This yields a payoff of 2. Hence, GC does better by introducing the product.

Hence, the Nash equilibrium we obtain by solving backwards is the GC introduces a product and prices "tough", after which BQ decides not to introduce a product.

3.

    a. The best responses are illustrated by the "underline and bold" technique in the matrix below. (Note that the Cartel has a dominant strategy of accommodation.) The only Nash equilibrium (in pure strategies) is that the New Entrant enters and the Cartel accommodates the entry. The Cartel receives a payoff of 75 and the New Entrant receives a payoff of 25.

New Entrant

	Enter	Stay Out
Predate	(-50, -10)	(-25, **0**)
Accommodate	(<u>75</u>, **25**)	(<u>100</u>, 0)

Cartel

    b. If the Cartel claims that it will predate, the New Entrant should not believe the claim, as this is not the equilibrium that would emerge if the entrant disregarded the threat to predate and actually entered. In other words, predation is an incredible (or empty) threat.

4.

a. Examining first the payoffs to Player 1, we see that Move B always yields a higher payoff than Move A for Player 1. For example, if Player 2 makes Move 1, then Player 1 receives 20 if she makes Move B while she receives only 5 if she makes Move A. Similarly, if Player 2 makes Move 2, Player 1 receives 10 if she makes Move B while she receives only 8 if she makes Move A. Hence, we can eliminate Move A since it is a dominated strategy. Cross out the first row to obtain the revised matrix.

b. Now, in our revised matrix (without the first row), we see that Move 2 always dominates Move 1 for Player 2. For example, if Player 1 makes Move A, then Player 2 receives 15 if he makes Move 2 and only 10 if he makes Move 1. Similarly, if Player 1 makes Move B, Player 2 receives 10 if he makes Move 2 while he receives only 8 if he makes Move 1. Hence, we can eliminate Move 1 since it, too, is a dominated strategy. Cross out the first column to obtain the revised matrix.

c. Now, we have a matrix without the first row or column to consider. In this matrix, we see that Move 4 is dominated by Move 3 because, for each row, the payoff to Player 2 is higher with Move 3 than with Move 4. Hence, Move 4 is a dominated strategy and we can eliminate the last column of the matrix.

In the new matrix (without Move 1, Move 4, or Move A), we see that Moves B and D for Player 1 are dominated by Move C. We can eliminate both B and D from the matrix.

This leaves only Move C and Moves 2 and 3. In this two-cell matrix, it is always better for Player 2 to make Move 2 since it receives 10 rather than 5 by doing so. Hence, the Nash equilibrium of the entire matrix is the last remaining cell where Player 1 makes Move C, Player 2 makes Move 2, and the payoffs to Players 1 and 2 are 20 and 10, respectively.

5.

a. The unique equilibrium is that B plays left while A plays right. As can be seen from the payoffs, up is a dominant strategy for A. For B, if A plays up, B prefers to play left while if A plays down, B prefers to play right.

Player B

	Left	Right

	Left	Right
Up	(3,**3**)	(1,0)
Down	(1,0)	(0,**2**)

Player A

b. Now, we have two Nash equilibria: the upper left hand corner and the lower right hand corner (Up, left) and (Down, right). In this case, there is no longer a dominant strategy for A.

Player B

	Left	Right
Up	(3,**3**)	(1,0)
Down	(1,0)	(2,**2**)

Player A

The more plausible of the two is arguably the upper left hand corner (Up, left), as this leaves both players with a higher payoff than the other equilibrium (Down, right). This is a concept we will return to in Chapter 16 when we discuss equilibria where all players are made better off and none worse off.

6.

a. Solving the game backwards, we first need to set the firm's marginal revenue equal to its marginal cost in order to maximize profits. In this case, then, we have $1-2q = t$ or $q^* = (1-t)/2$. In other words, the higher the tax rate, the lower the output of the firm.

b. If the government equates the marginal benefit and marginal cost of any tax increase, then (using the information in the question) it equates the revenue it earns from increasing the tax slightly (say, by \$1) on all the units sold to the cost of a slight tax increase: the reduction in units sold times the amount of the tax. Hence we have $1(q^*) = t(\Delta q^*/\Delta t)$ or $(1-t)/2 = t(-1/2)$. Solving this, we have $\frac{1}{2} = t^*$. This can also be seen by graphing the revenue obtained from the tax, tq*, and noticing that it reaches a maximum at t = ½ .

c. If the government is concerned only about consumers' surplus, then it will set the tax equal to zero, as consumers' surplus is $(q^2*/2) = (1-t)^2/8$. Clearly, this decreases as t increases when t is between 0 and 1.

d. If the government cares about both tax revenues and consumers' surplus, it will set the tax rate at some level *below* t= ½ because this maximum was calculated not taking into account the consumers' surplus cost of raising the tax. Hence, we can deduce that the higher the weight on consumers' surplus in the government's payoff function, the lower the equilibrium tax rate.

Answers to Exam

1.

a. A dominant strategy is better than *any other* whatever the opponent's strategy. Hence, there can be only one dominant strategy per player. A dominant strategy equilibrium is an equilibrium where each player is using a dominant strategy. Hence, there can be only a single dominant strategy equilibrium because each player can have only a single dominant strategy.

b. Many different levels of punishment are sufficient to enforce the desired equilibrium. Hence, any Grim Trigger strategy with a punishment sufficiently large to induce the desired behavior in equilibrium would support the same equilibrium outcome. For example, it might be enough to induce desirable behavior to have six periods of punishment. Any Grim Trigger strategy with at least six periods of punishment (seven, eight, and so on) would support the same equilibrium outcome.

c. Several mixed strategy equilibria may exist for the same game. In the simplest possible case, imagine a game matrix with the same payoff to one of the players under two possible moves. For example, suppose that regardless of whether Player 1 uses Strategy A or Strategy B, Player 2 obtains a payoff of 5. Hence, any set of probabilities Player 1 applies to Strategies A and B would yield the same payoff as any other set of probabilities to Player 2.

2.

a. The game can be depicted as follows:

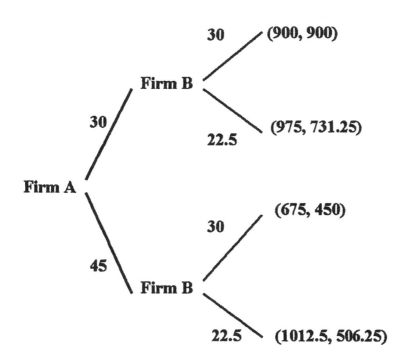

b. The Nash equilibrium calculated by backwards induction is the following. At the last branch, if firm A has chosen to produce 30, firm B's best response is to produce 30 as well since it earns profits of 900 rather than 731.25 by doing so. If firm A has chosen to produce 45, firm B's best response is to cut production back to 22.5 since it earns 506.25 rather than 450 by doing so.

Now, moving backwards to firm A's decision, it knows that if it produces 30, firm B will respond with 30 and it will earn 900. On the other hand, if it produces 45, Firm B will respond with 22.5 and firm A will earn 1012.5. This means that the better move for A is to produce 45. Hence, the Nash equilibrium obtained by backwards induction is that firm A produces 45 and firm B produces 22.5 for a payoff of 1012.5 for firm A and 506.25 for firm B.

c. Notice that an output level of 30 for each firm is the Cournot equilibrium for this demand and marginal cost, as we saw in Chapter 13. The Cournot equilibrium occurred when the firms chose output levels simultaneously. In the game, however, one of the firms moves first. Recall from Chapter 13 that in the quantity setting game, firm B's best response to an increase in output is to *decrease* its own output. Firm A can take advantage of this fact by committing to the higher output of 45 and inducing firm B to cut its output.

d. This game, like the Stackelberg game, allows Firm A an advantage because it can commit to a level of output before Firm B. Notice, too, that we solved the Stackelberg game in Chapter 13 by considering the follower's response first and then working backwards to the leader's problem. This is like the backwards induction we have discussed here.

If the alternative to choosing first were to choose second, Firm A would be willing to pay the difference in payoff between these two alternatives: $1012.5 - 506.25 = 506.25$ for the right to move first. If the alternative were to move simultaneously, then we would have to work out the equilibrium in this case. If the payoffs and possible moves are those given in this problem, then we can construct a 2x2 matrix where there are, in fact, two Nash equilibria:

Firm B

	30	22.5
Firm A 30	(<u>900</u>, **900**)	(975, 731.25)
45	(675, 450)	(<u>1012.5</u>, **506.25**)

How much Firm A would be willing to pay would depend on which of these it thought more likely. If it thought that the upper left hand corner were the outcome of this simultaneous game, then it would be willing to pay $1012.5 - 900 = 112.5$. If it thought that the lower right hand corner were the outcome, then it would be willing to pay nothing.

3.

a. Neither firm has a dominant strategy. For example, if Zap chooses to adopt ElectroCo's system, then ElectroCo does better sticking to its own system as well. On the other hand, if Zap sticks to its own system, ElectroCo does better adopting Zap's system as well.

b. The Nash equilibria in pure strategies are that both adopt Zap's system or both adopt ElectroCo's system, as shown by the underlining and bold in the matrix below.

ElectroCo.

	Produce Own System	Adopt Rival's System
Zap — Produce Own System	(10, 10)	(<u>100</u>, **50**)
Zap — Adopt Rival's System	(<u>50</u>, **100**)	(0, 0)

Hence, this game has the character of a "coordination problem" where each firm would do better coordinating with the other on a single standard, but each would prefer its own standard. The Nash equilibrium in mixed strategies is that Zap plays "own system" with probability 5/7 and "adopt" with probability 2/7 while ElectroCo plays "own system" with probability 5/7 and "adopt" with probability 2/7. These can be obtained by solving for the probability that makes each firm indifferent about which (pure) strategy it plays. In other words, for each firm we solve the equations:

pr x 10 + (1 - pr) x 100 = pr x 50 + (1 - pr) x 0

where: pr is the probability that a firm plays "own" and (1 - pr) is the probability that each firm plays "adopt". The solution of this equation is pr = 5/7.

c. ElectroCo. Now has a dominant strategy of keeping its own system. Given this, Zap would do better adopting ElectroCo's system as well so that the new (unique) Nash equilibrium in pure strategies is for both firms to use ElectroCo's system. The payoffs to the firms are that Zap earns 50 and ElectroCo earns 150.

d. ElectroCo's payoffs are 150 in the revised game. In the original game, it earned either 100 or 50, depending on which equilibrium occurred. Hence, the range of payments it is willing to make are between 50 (=150 - 100) and 100 (=150 - 50). If we simply state which of the two pure strategy equilibria will occur in the matrix of parts (a) and (b), we can resolve which of these two ElectroCo. would be willing to pay.

Another way to resolve the problem would be to look for the mixed strategy equilibrium in the matrix of parts (a) and (b). In part (b), the probability that each firm placed on keeping its own system was 5/7 in the mixed strategy equilibrium. Using this probability for each firm, in the mixed strategy equilibrium the upper left-hand cell occurs with probability (5/7)(5/7), the upper right hand cell (and the lower left-hand cell) occur with probability (5/7)(2/7), and the lower right-hand cell occurs with probability (2/7)(2/7). Hence, the expected payoff in the first matrix for each firm is:

(5/7)(5/7)(10) + (5/7)(2/7)(100) + (5/7)(2/7)(50) + (2/7)(2/7)(0) = 1750/49 = 35.71

The gain to obtaining the lower left-hand corner of the new matrix for sure rather than being in this mixed strategy equilibrium is, then, 150 − 35.71 = 114.29.

4.

  a. The payoff matrix is as follows:

Firm 2

	Cooperate	Cheat
Cooperate (Firm 1)	(50, 50)	(25, **75**)
Cheat	(<u>75</u>, 25)	(<u>30</u>, **30**)

  b. If this game is played for only a single period, the likely outcome is that both firms will cheat, as is indicated by the underlining and bold in the matrix of part (a). However, both firms would be better off is they could "collude" (i.e., if they could agree to cooperate). The problem is that it is in the selfish interest of each player to cheat as long as the rival cooperates.

  c. The new game matrix is:

Firm 2

	Cooperate	Cheat
Cooperate (Firm 1)	(<u>50</u>, **50**)	(<u>25</u>, -25)
Cheat	(-25, **25**)	(-70, -70)

The new Nash equilibrium is that both firms cooperate, as is indicated in the matrix.

  c. If firm A cooperates in the first period, after which it will mimic whatever firm B did in the first period, then B faces the following decision. It may cheat in the first period and earn 75, followed by a payoff of 30 if it makes its best response to cheating by firm A. Alternatively, it could cooperate in the first period and earn 50, after which it can earn a payoff of 75 by cheating when A cooperates. Hence, firm B does better by cooperating in the first period after which it cheats. This does not fully resolve the problem of part (a). The difficulty is that firm A cannot punish firm B for its cheating in the last period so that it cannot alter B's incentives to cheat in this period.

Chapter 15: Risk and Information

Many economic decisions are made in the face of uncertainty.   For example, we invest in stocks without knowing the value that those stocks will have in the future. For the majority of this chapter, we will be interested in analyzing decision making by economic agents in situations where the uncertainty about future events is quantifiable: where the possible outcomes are known and where the likelihood of each outcome is known or can be estimated. Situations of quantifiable uncertainty are sometimes referred to as situations of **risk**. Notice that this *event risk* is distinct from the *strategic risk* that agents faced in Chapter 14. There, each individual's best choice depended on other individuals' choices. Here, in contrast, we will focus on decision-making under uncertainty that occurs *even in the absence of* strategic interaction. For example, going outside without knowing what the weather will be is a decision subject to event risk (as we analyze here) but not strategic risk (as we analyzed in Chapter 14).

We will first describe risky outcomes using the concepts and terminology of probability theory. Next, we will analyze how a decision-maker evaluates risky outcomes using the concept of **expected utility**. This includes a discussion of when an individual will choose to *undertake* a risky project and when he will buy insurance in order to *eliminate*, or at least reduce, the associated risk. We can then use these insights to examine how a decision-maker might choose a plan of action in the face of risk. As part of this analysis, we derive the value that the decision-maker would place on obtaining information that would resolve the uncertainty she faces *before* she makes her decision.   Finally, we wrap up the analysis of Chapter 14 and Chapter 15 with an introduction to auction theory, where event risk and strategic risk interact.

A **lottery** is an event that has an uncertain outcome. Nevertheless, all the *possible* outcomes of the lottery are known, and the **probabilities** (or **likelihoods**) with which each outcome occurs are known as well. For example, I might buy a lottery ticket that gives me a 33% chance of winning $100 and a 67% chance of winning $25. In this case, there are two (known) outcomes and a known likelihood of each outcome.

A lottery is fully described by the **probability distribution** that shows all the possible outcomes in the lottery and their associated probabilities. It is a way of (fully) describing the lottery. The following probability distribution describing our example lottery is shown in Figure 15.1.

For any lottery, the probability of *each outcome* must be between 0 and 1 and the *sum* of the probabilities of *all outcomes* equals 1. In our example, .67 and .33 are both between 0 and 1 and .67 + .33 = 1. If the probabilities of a lottery reflect the subjective beliefs of the decision makers about how events might unfold, they are called **subjective probabilities.** For example, I might "feel lucky" on the day of the lottery and believe that my chance of winning is closer to 50% than to 33%. Even if the probabilities of lottery outcomes are subjective, they must still lie between 0 and 1, and must also sum to 1. Hence, if I think that my chance of winning has increased to 50%, I must also think that my chance of losing has fallen to 50%.

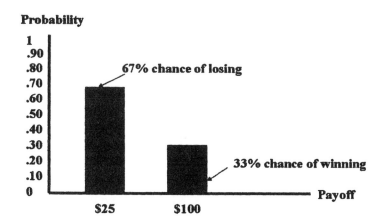

Figure 15.1

While the probability distribution describes the lottery completely, it is also a bit cumbersome. We might, then, want some summary statistics that describe the lottery incompletely, but are easier to use. One such statistic is the **expected value** of a lottery. The expected value is a measure of the average (or probability-weighted) payoff of the lottery. In other words, the expected value sums all the possible payoffs, where each payoff is multiplied by its probability of occurring. For example, if there are three possible outcomes, A, B, and C, of a lottery, the expected value of the lottery is:

Expected Value = {probability of outcome A x payoff if A occurs} +
                     {probability of outcome B x payoff if B occurs} +
                     {probability of outcome C x payoff if C occurs}

In our example lottery, which pays $25 with probability .67 and $100 with probability 0.33, the expected value is .67 x $25 + .33 x 100 = $50. Notice that the expected value need not be one of the outcomes of the lottery. Instead, it is the average payoff you would expect *per play* if you played the lottery many times.

Exercise 1: *Three possible investment projects, A, B, and C, yield the following payoffs in "bad times", "normal times", and "good times". The probabilities of each of these three states of nature are given as well:*

Probability:	.6	.2	.2
Project:	Bad times	Normal times	Good times
A	0	0	20
B	4	4	4
C	0	9	16

Calculate the expected value of each project. Which of the following is true?

a. The expected value of A is the same as the expected value of B.
b. The expected value of A is 4.
c. The expected value of A is less than the expected value of B.
d. The expected value of A is less than the expected value of C.

If you only cared about maximizing the expected value of your investment, which project would you undertake?

a. A
b. B
c. C
d. Either A or C

A second summary statistic we could use to describe the lottery is the lottery's **variance**. The variance measures the average deviation between the possible outcomes of the lottery and the expected value of the lottery. The same way that expected value is a measure of the lottery's average payoff, variance is a measure of the lottery's risk: the higher the variance, the higher the risk.

Computing the Variance of a Lottery

1. Find the expected value of the lottery, $E(X)$.

2. For each possible outcome, $x_1, x_2,...x_N$, take the difference between the lottery's payoff at that outcome and the lottery's expected value. Square this result to obtain $(x_i - E(X))^2$ for $i = 1$ to N. This is called the **squared deviation**.

3. Average the squared deviations over all possible outcomes by multiplying each squared deviation by the probability, p_i, of the associated outcome and summing over all squared deviations. This yields the variance:

$$VAR(X) = p_1(x_1 - E(X))^2 + p_2(x_2-E(X))^2 +.....+ p_N(x_N - E(X))^2$$

Our example lottery has an expected value of $50. Hence, the squared deviation for winning is $(\$100 - \$50)^2 = 50^2 = 2500$. The squared deviation of losing is $(\$25 - \$50)^2 = 25^2 = 625$. Hence, the variance is $(2500 \times .33)+ (625 \times .67) = 1250$. The **standard deviation** is the square root of the variance. In our example, the standard deviation is the square root of 1250.

Exercise 2: *For the projects in Exercise 1, which statement is true?*

a. Project A has the highest variance.
b. Projects A and C have the same variance, but different expected values.

c. Project B's variance is zero.

If you only cared about minimizing the variance of your investment, which project would you undertake?

a. A
b. B
c. C

In what follows, we will *only* use the expected value and the variance to describe the characteristics of different lotteries. For many simple lotteries, in fact, this is all the information we *need* to know in order to determine our optimal behavior in the face of uncertainty.

Lotteries can differ in their expected values and in their variance (degree of risk). In order to analyze an individual's choice between lotteries with different degrees of risk and different expected values, we need to modify our concept of utility from Chapter 3. Suppose that we depicted the relationship between utility and the level of income of an individual as in Figure 15.2:

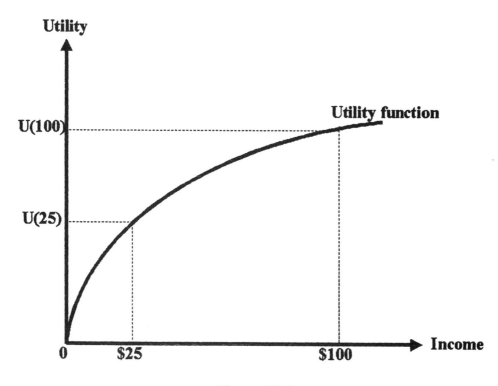

Figure 15.2

In other words, the utility of $100 is U(100) and the utility of $25 is U(25). Now, suppose that we wished to calculate the utility value of the example lottery and represent it on this graph. In the same way as we measured the average payoff of the lottery by expected value, we measure the average payoff of the lottery in terms of utility as **expected utility**. The expected utility is an average utility: it sums the utilities of each outcome, where each utility is multiplied by its probability of occurring. For example, if utility were to take the specific functional form U = (income)$^{1/2}$, we would have:

Expected utility = .67 x U(25) + .33 x U(100) = .67 x 5 + .33 x 10 = 20/3 = 6.67

Graphically, we could depict the expected utility of the lottery as the utility of point A, EU, on Figure 15.3, below:

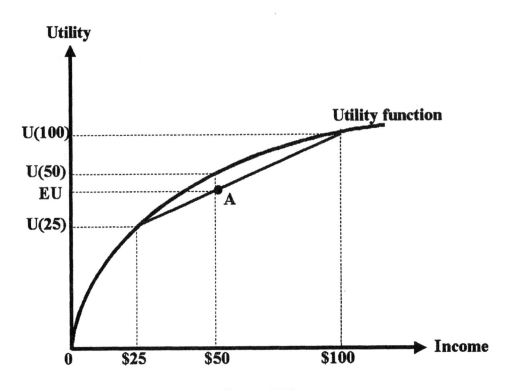

Figure 15.3

We can notice something interesting about the expected utility of this individual, however. From the figure, we see that, because the utility function is concave, EU is less that U(50). Hence, the expected utility value of the lottery is less than the utility value that the individual would get from receiving $50, the expected value of the lottery, *as a sure thing*. In other words, this individual would prefer a sure thing to a lottery of *equal* expected value. This means that the shape of the utility function indicates something about the attitude of this individual toward risk. Because the individual of Figure 15.3 prefers a sure thing to a lottery *of equal expected value* we say that she is **risk-averse**. Any utility function that exhibits diminishing marginal utility implies that the individual is risk-averse. We can see that the individual of our example does exhibit diminishing marginal utility since the same increase in income, ΔI, results in a lower increment in utility, (ΔU_1) at low income levels than at high income levels (ΔU_2). This is illustrated in Figure 15.4, below.

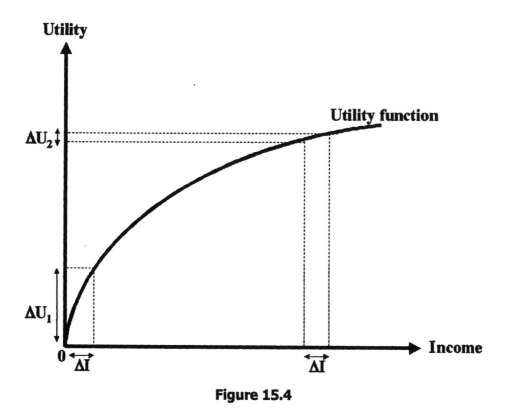

Figure 15.4

Exercise 3: *A shareholder of the company making the investment choice between the projects outlined in Exercise 1 obtains a utility from his shares in the company that equals the income the shares earn. Hence, his utility of the investment projects equals the payoffs from the projects. Graph the shareholder's utility function with utility on the vertical axis and the investment payoff on the horizontal axis. What is true about this graph?*

    a. The shareholder's utility is a linear function of the investment income.
    b. The shareholder's expected utility of each project is a point that lies on the utility function.
    c. Project A has the highest expected utility for the shareholder.
    d. The shareholder's expected utility of project A equals the utility of the expected value of project A.

The manager in charge of making the investment decision of Exercise 1 obtains a utility from making the investment equal to the square root of the payoff of the investment. Graph the manager's utility function in the same way as you did the shareholder's utility. What is true about this graph?

    a. Marginal utility is a decreasing function of the investment income.
    b. The manager has a decreasing marginal utility of income.
    c. Project C has the highest expected utility for the manager.
    d. The expected utility of project A is less than the utility of the expected value of project A.

A new manager replaces the old manager. This manager has a utility of making the investment that equals the square of the payoff of the investment. Graph the new manager's utility function in the same way as you have graphed the shareholder's utility. What is true about this graph?

   a. Utility is an increasing function of the investment income.
   b. The manager has increasing marginal utility of the payoff.
   c. Project C has the highest expected utility for the new manager.
   d. The expected utility of project A is greater than the utility of the expected value of project A.

Hence, both expected value *and* riskiness affect the expected utility of a lottery. Of course, while many people are risk-averse, some people are *indifferent* between a sure thing and a lottery with the same expected value. Such people are called **risk-neutral**. They have a constant marginal utility. Graphically, a risk-neutral person's utility function is a straight line. Other people *prefer* a lottery to a sure thing that is equal to the expected value of the lottery. This final group is called **risk-loving**. These people have an increasing marginal utility. Their utility functions curve upwards. Risk-neutral and risk-loving preferences are shown in Figure 15.5, below, where utility is a function of income:

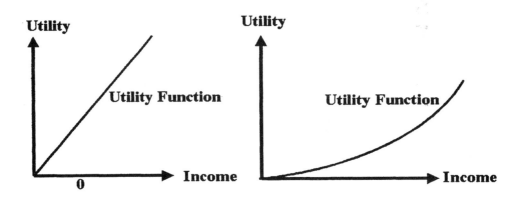

Figure 15.5

Exercise 4: *Refer back to your calculations and graphs for Exercise 3. Which of the following is true?*

   a. The shareholder is risk-neutral; both managers are risk-averse.
   b. The shareholder is risk-neutral; only the first manager is risk-averse.
   c. The risk attitude of the shareholders and managers affects their preferred investment choice.

While we know that a risk-averse individual would always choose a sure thing over a lottery of equal expected value, a risk-averse person *may* choose a lottery over a sure thing if the lottery has a *greater* expected value. The increase in expected value that the risk-averse person would require to just be indifferent between the lottery and the sure thing is called the person's **risk premium**. Consider our example lottery with the utility function $U = (income)^{1/2}$. Recall from the discussion preceding Figure 15.3 that the expected utility that the individual obtains from this lottery is 6.67 or 20/3. Suppose now that the individual is offered a sure thing. The sure thing that would yield the same utility as the lottery is the amount, $X, which solves:

$$U(\$X) = \text{Expected utility of lottery} \quad \text{or...} \quad X^{1/2} = 20/3$$

Solving this, we obtain X = 400/9 or 44.44. Hence, this person is indifferent between sure payoff of $44.44 and a lottery with expected value of $50. This means that the risk premium that induces the individual to accept the lottery is ($50 - $44.44) = $5.56. Graphically, the risk premium is shown in Figure 15.6 is the difference in income between points A and D, where A corresponds to the lottery and D is the amount of income obtained for sure that yields the same expected utility as the lottery (i.e., D and A are on the same horizontal line).

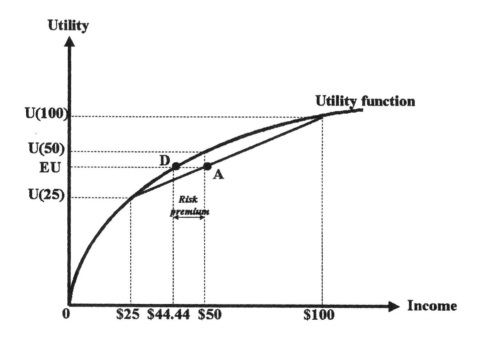

Figure 15.6

Exercise 5: *Refer to your calculations in the exercises so far. Calculate the risk premium for the preferred project of each of the three decision makers in Exercise 3. Which of the following statements is true?*

   a. The risk-averse decision maker has a positive risk premium.
   b. None of the decision makers has a positive risk premium.
   c. The risk premium of the "new" manager (see Exercise 3) is –4.

We used the concept of a risk premium to see when a risk-averse person would choose to *accept* risk. We can use the same concept to determine how much a risk-averse person would be willing to pay for insurance that would eliminate (or reduce) the risk associated with a lottery. Consider the following example. An individual expects his future earnings to be worth $100. If he falls seriously ill, however, the individual's expected future earnings are only $25. The individual believes that his chance of falling ill is 67%, while the chance of remaining in good health is 33%. The individual's utility as a function of the value his earnings equal to $U = (\text{earnings})^{1/2}$. This situation should look familiar: the individual faces a lottery with the same probabilities and payoffs as our example lottery in Figure 15.6. Hence, with no insurance, the individual obtains expected utility EU associated with point A in Figure 15.6.

Now, let us imagine that an insurance company offers to **fully insure** the individual against illness. Full insurance is insurance that eliminates all risk (i.e., it eliminates all variance in the value of his earnings). In our example, then, a full insurance policy might pay out nothing in the case of good health, but pay out $75 to the individual if he becomes incapacitated due to illness. In that case, the individual obtains earnings equal to $100 regardless of his health (and so faces zero variance in his earnings). The insurance policy is **fairly priced** if the insurance **premium** -- the price the individual pays for the insurance policy -- equals the expected value of the promised insurance payment. Because there is a .67 chance that the policy pays $75 and a .33 chance that it pays nothing, the expected value of the promised payment is .67 x $75 + .33 x $0 = $50. If such a fairly priced insurance is offered, the individual faces the following choice:

- Buy the insurance policy at a price of $50 and receive $100 - $50 = $50 regardless of his state of health or,

- Don't buy insurance and receive $100 if he is in good health and $25 if he is in bad health. The expected value in this case is .33 x $100 + .67 x $25 = $50.

Since the individual is risk-averse, he prefers a sure thing to a lottery with the same expected value. Hence, *a risk-averse individual would always purchase a fairly priced insurance policy.* In fact, a risk-averse individual might buy the insurance policy even if it were not fairly priced. To see this, refer back to Figure 15.6. From our discussion of the risk premium, we know that this individual is indifferent between getting $44.44 for sure (point D) and not getting any insurance (point A). But this means that the individual is willing to pay up to $5.56 for the full insurance policy, since paying such a premium would leave him with $44.44 whether or not he is in good health. In other words, the risk premium also measures how much the individual is willing to pay above and beyond a "fair price" for a full insurance policy.

Exercise 6: *Insurance is now available for Project C. The insurance costs $11, which must be paid regardless of the state. The insurance pays $0 in good times, $7 in normal times, and $16 in bad times. Is this insurance fairly priced?*

a. Yes
b. No

How does the insurance affect the choice of preferred project by each of the decision makers in Exercise 3?

    a. The first manager switches to project C and buys insurance on the project.
    b. The new manager does not change his choice of project if insurance is offered on project C.
    c. Only the first manager strictly prefers to buy insurance.
    d. The shareholder is indifferent between buying insurance or not with project C.

    Real insurance markets are complicated by the presence of **asymmetric information**. There is asymmetric information whenever one party to a transaction knows something that is relevant to the value of the transaction and that is unknown to the other party or parties. There are two types of asymmetric information. There is **moral hazard** when one of the parties cannot observe all of the relevant *actions* undertaken by the other(s). For example, there is moral hazard if an employer cannot accurately check how hard her employees work. In insurance markets, moral hazard refers to the fact that the insurance provider cannot verify whether the insured party exercises "due care": does the insured driver drive carefully? Does the purchaser of health insurance follow a healthy lifestyle? The concern is that insurance actually reduces the individual's incentives to behave cautiously: a party who has fully insured her car might take less care in driving than a party who is not insured for the simple reason that she would not suffer any direct financial loss in the case of accident. In other words, the probability that a bad event might actually happen is not independent of the amount of insurance purchased: the more complete the coverage, the less careful the insured person and the more likely a bad event will occur. It is because of moral hazard that insurance companies rarely offer full coverage. They prefer to force their clients to bear at least part of the cost of "accidents" (e.g., by paying a "deductible") to make sure that they at least exercise a minimum amount of care.

    There is **adverse selection** when one of the parties knows more than the other party about some fixed *characteristic* of the transaction. For example, an employer might not know whether or not the person that she is about to hire is honest. In insurance markets, the concern is that insurance providers might not be able to perfectly distinguish between "high risk" and "low risk" customers. For example, a health insurance company might not have all the relevant information about the medical history of the customer's family. If the insurance provider cannot tell different "types" of customers apart (i.e., it can not apply third degree price discrimination; see Chapter 11), it can charge a higher price to high-risk clients. That, in turn, might force the insurer to set a price that many low-risk clients are not willing to pay, leading to a higher proportion of high-risk individuals in the client base of the company than in the population at large. One way to minimize the adverse selection problem is for the insurer to rely on *second degree* price discrimination (see Chapter 11). This could be achieved, for example by offering a low-priced basic health insurance package plus a high-priced package covering more illnesses and procedures. Low-risk individuals would likely select the first plan, while high-risk individuals might opt for the second one.

    So far, we have limited our attention to situations where the individual faces a simple choice between two or more lotteries. For more complex decisions, where we wish to identify the optimal plan of action in the face of risk, a more structured analysis is useful. For such decisions, we can describe the options available to a decision maker, as well as the risky events that can occur at each point in time, with a **decision tree.** For example, Figure 15.7 illustrates the options available to our worker who could purchase fairly priced health insurance.

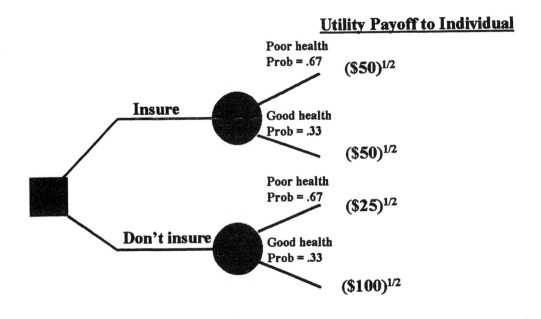

Figure 15.7

The elements of the decision tree are:

- *Decision Nodes,* denoted by ☐ in the diagram. A decision node is a point at which the decision maker must decide between several alternatives, denoted by branches extending from the node.

- *Chance Nodes,* denoted by ◯ in the diagram. A chance node is a lottery that the decision maker faces. Each branch extending from the node corresponds to a possible outcome of the lottery.

- *Probabilities.* Each branch extending from the chance node has a probability of occurring. The sum of the probabilities across *all* branches of a *single* chance node must equal 1.

- *Payoffs.* Each branch at the right-hand side of the tree has a payoff associated with it, measured in the units the decision maker cares about: utility in our example but (perhaps) profits for a firm.

Once the decision has been laid out as a decision tree, the decision maker can evaluate the alternatives. If there is a sequence of decisions to be made, the decision maker evaluates the alternatives by solving the tree backwards, as we did for game trees in Chapter 14. However, in the case shown in Figure 15.7, there is only one decision to be made: to insure and reach node B or to not insure and reach node C. At node B, the expected payoff to the decision maker is $.67(\$50)^{1/2} + .33(\$50)^{1/2} = (\$50)^{1/2} = \$7$ (approximately). At node C, the expected payoff is $.67(\$25)^{1/2} + .33(\$100)^{1/2} = .67 \times \$5 + .33 \times \$10 = \$6.67$. Hence, the individual prefers to be at node B so that the optimal decision is to insure.

Up to now we have assumed that the uncertainty faced by the decision maker is *exogenous*. However, there are situations where the decision maker can take actions that reduce the degree of uncertainty with which he is confronted. In particular, the individual can *invest* in the gathering of information. The increase in expected utility resulting from obtaining better information is called the **value of information**.

A risk-neutral individual can undertake a physical exam before deciding to purchase insurance. Suppose, for simplicity, that the physical exam is a precise reflection of the individual's future state of health so that the exam completely resolves the uncertainty. If the outcome of the exam is that the individual is in good health, he has no reason to purchase insurance and can earn $100 for sure. If the outcome of the exam is that he is in poor health, he can purchase insurance and obtain $50 for sure. While his outcome is the same as before if he is discovered to be in poor health, he earns significantly more if he is in good health because he saves the cost of insurance. This increase in value is called the value of information or, in this case, the **value of perfect information** because the exam reduces the uncertainty to zero. The value of (perfect) information to our individual is the new expected payoff assuming he conducts the physical exam ($.67 \times 50^{1/2} + .33 \times 100^{1/2} = \$8$, approximately) net of the old expected payoff without the exam and assuming he makes the optimal choice ($7). Hence, the value of information is $8 - $7 = $1 in this case. The individual should, in principle, be willing to pay up to $1 to conduct the physical exam (i.e., obtain information) that resolves his health uncertainty before the insurance decision. As a matter of terminology for future courses, the value of information is sometimes referred to as the *option* value of information. The analysis of situations -- like this one -- where a decision maker can tailor his decision to information that he may receive in the future is called the analysis of **real options**.

Exercise 7: *Suppose that the decision makers of Exercise 3 can wait before making their decisions about projects A, B, and C. If the decision maker waits, he or she receives full information about the state of the world (good times, normal times, or bad times) before choosing the project. Draw the decision tree facing the decision makers and calculate the value of perfect information in utility terms for each decision maker. Would all three decision makers do better waiting than investing immediately if the cost of waiting is zero?*

Finally, we turn to the theory of auctions. Auctions typically involve several (often, very few) players making decisions under uncertainty. The uncertainty may be either event uncertainty or strategic uncertainty or both so that this theory draws both from the techniques we have presented here and the game theory we presented in Chapter 14. The common types of auctions analyzed in auction theory are as follows:

- **English auctions**: Each participant cries out his/her bid. Each bidder can raise his/her bid whenever he/she wants. When nobody wants to enter a higher bid, the individual who entered the last (i.e., the highest) bid wins the object and pays a price equal to that last bid.
- **First-price sealed-bid auctions**: Each bidder submits one bid, not knowing the other bids. The highest bidder pays his/her bid and wins the object.
- **Second-price sealed-bid auctions**: Each bidder submits one bid, not knowing the other bids. The highest bidder pays the second highest bid and wins the object.
- **Dutch descending auction**: The seller announces a bid, which is then lowered until a buyer announces a desire to buy the item at that price.

In a **private value** auction, each potential bidder has his or her own valuation of the object. These valuations are personal in the sense that, for me, knowing other players' valuations would not change my idea of what the item auctioned is worth *to me*. In a **pure common value** auction, the true value of the item is the same for all bidders but each bidder has her own idea of what that true value might be. Each of the four bulleted types of auctions listed above could potentially be either private value or common value auctions. Auctions involve strategic interaction (and strategic risk) in the sense that each participant's best choice of bid usually depends on the other participants' bids. Consider for example a first-price sealed-bid auction where you and I bid for an object that I value at $15. If I know that you have bid $10 then my best bid is $10.01. If, on the other hand, you have bid $16, then I should not enter a bid higher than $16 since this would make me pay more than $16 for an object which is only worth $15 to me. Since the true value of the item to each bidder is not necessarily known, auctions can also involve event risk. We can use auctions, then, to illustrate how strategic risk and event risk interact to determine optimal behavior.

Here, we will only examine two types of auctions: first-price sealed-bid auctions with private values and first-price sealed-bid auctions with a common value. The other combinations are left to your future courses. Our examination will be very brief: we will only present here the intuition for two general results for these types of auctions:

1. In a first-price sealed-bid auction with private values, a bidder's optimal strategy is to submit a bid that is less than her true valuation of the item. Let's think about this. By submitting a bid exactly equal to her true valuation of the item, the bidder could do no better than earning a *net* value of zero since she would be paying exactly what she thinks the item is worth! In other words, if she loses she earns a payoff of zero, but if she wins she *also* earns a payoff of zero. By reducing her bid, the bidder reduces her chances of winning, but *if she wins* she obtains a *positive* net value since she pays less than she thinks the item is worth. Hence, if she loses she obtains a payoff that is no worse than before, but if she wins she earns a positive net value. It can be shown (not here) that the precise bid she submits in the Nash equilibrium strategy is, in fact, $(N-1)/N$ times her own true valuation of the object. Notice that, as N gets larger and larger, the bidder's Nash equilibrium strategy is to submit a bid that is closer and closer to her own true valuation of the object. Hence, the amount by which each bidder reduces her bid *decreases* as the number of participants in the auction *increases*. In other words, as the number of participants rises, the equilibrium bid approaches the bidder's true valuation.

2. In a first-price sealed-bid auction with common values, a winning bidder might bid an amount that exceeds the bidder's valuation of the item. To see this, imagine that many individuals are bidding to win an unknown sum of money that is hidden in a bag. Suppose that the money is worth the same amount to all bidders so that this is a common value auction. Now, if everyone submits a bid, the winning bid will be the *most optimistic* estimation of the actual sum that is hidden in the bag. Hence, the person who wins will be the individual who is most likely to have *overestimated* the amount of money in the bag. *On average,* then, this individual will pay more for the bag than it is worth.

When a winning bidder tends to bid an amount that exceeds her valuation for the item, the winner suffers what is called the **winner's curse**. The solution to the winner's curse is, not surprisingly, for each bidder to shade *down* her bid. In contrast to the result outlined under point (1), however, the amount by which each bidder reduces her bid *increases* as the number of participants in the auction *increases* because the winner's curse becomes more severe. To see this, consider two common value auctions, one with two bidders and the other with 1000 bidders. To win the first auction, one only needs to be more optimistic than one other bidder, meaning that the winner will tend to overestimate the value of the item but not by all that much *on average.* To win against 999 other bidders, on the other hand, means that one is the most optimistic among a very large group. This can (on average) only be true if the one overvalues the object quite drastically.

These auctions illustrate the interaction of strategic and event risk. In the first case, when there is no uncertainty as to who places the highest value on the item, it is easy for an individual to bid an amount that is sure to win the item. In the second case, when there is no uncertainty as to the value of the item to be sold, there is no winner's curse because each player is sure to bid no more than her value. The problems were created by *event risk.* Given the event risk, however, *strategic interaction* determines exactly how much the bids should be shaded since each player must have a conjecture about the other players' bids in order to determine by how much shading affects her probability of winning the auction.

Exercise 8: *The three investment projects of Exercise 1 are the only projects that a company may undertake. The company is for sale to two possible buyers: the two managers of Exercise 3. The sale will be conducted by inviting public bids for the shares of the company, to be submitted to the current shareholders. Bidders can raise their proposed price at any time. The shares will be awarded to the party whose bid is not raised by anyone else. If that bid does not exceed the value placed by existing shareholders on the shares, the shareholders will remain in control of the company. Assume that the managers know their own utility functions and know about the investment projects available to the company, but do not know each others' utility functions. Which of the following statements is correct?*

a. This is a common value auction.
b. This is a private value auction.
c. This is an English auction.
d. This is a sealed-bid auction.

Chapter Review Questions

1. You have been following the prices of a share of stock in three different companies for the past year: HighTech Co., BigOil Co., and JumpStart Co. For HighTech, you find that, 20% of the year, a share was worth $30. 20% of the year, it was worth $40, 20% of the year it was worth $70, 20% of the year it was worth $90, and 20% of the year it was worth $120. A share of BigOil stock was worth $50 one quarter of the year, $60 another quarter of the year, $80 one quarter of the year, and $90 one quarter of the year. A share of JumpStart stock was worth $0 half the year and $140 the other half of the year.

    a. Draw a probability distribution for the prices of a share of this stock, based on your research. Find the expected value and the variance of this distribution.

    b. Do risk-averse investors prefer one of these stocks over the other? What about risk-neutral investors? Risk-loving investors?

Answer:

a. If we use the observed frequencies as approximations of the true probabilities of the value of the stock, then the probability distributions would look as follows for the three stocks:

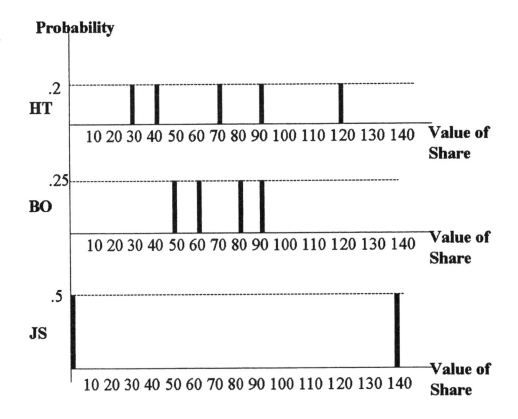

The expected value and variance of each of the stocks is as follows:

	Expected Value	Variance
HighTech	70	1080
BigOil	70	250
JumpStart	70	4900

For example, the expected value for HighTech would be computed as EV = .2(30) + .2(40) + .2(70) + .2(90) + .2(120) = 70 and the variance would be calculated as Var = $.2(30\text{-}70)^2$ + $.2(40\text{-}70)^2$ + $.2(70\text{-}70)^2$ + $.2(90\text{-}70)^2$ + $.2(120\text{-}70)^2$ = 1080.

b. A risk-neutral investor would be indifferent between these stocks, as they all have the same expected value. On the other hand, a risk-averse investor would prefer BigOil, as it attains the same expected value as the others with the least variance. A risk-loving investor would prefer JumpStart, as it attains the same expected value as the others with the most variance.

2. Suppose that John's utility function is the following, where I is income:

U(I) = I^2 for I ≤ 10
$\quad\quad$ $(I\text{-}10)^{1/2}$ + 100 for I > 10

a. Draw a graph of John's utility function with income on the horizontal axis and utility on the vertical axis. Is John risk-averse, risk-neutral or risk-loving?

b. Kate offers John the following choice: he may play a game of chance where he would receive an income of zero with 25% probability and $14 with 75% probability. Alternatively, he may receive an assured income of $10. Is the expected value of the game of chance the same as the assured income? Will John accept this bet? Why?

c. Now, Kate offers John the following choice: he may play a game of chance where he would receive an income of zero with 25% probability and $4 with 75% probability. Alternatively, he may receive an assured income of $3. Is the expected value of the game of chance the same as the assured income? Will John accept this bet? Why?

d. Does John's behavior help to explain why some people refuse to make small bets, but buy lottery tickets (for large bets)?

Answer:

a. John is risk-loving for income levels less than 10 and risk-averse for income levels greater than 10.

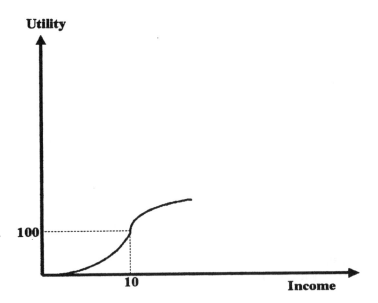

b. The expected value of the bet is EV = .25(0) + .75($14) = $10.5. Hence, its expected value exceeds the sure thing of $10. On the other hand, the expected utility of the bet is EU = .25U($0) + .75U($14) = .75(2+100) = 76.5, whereas the utility of the sure thing is U($10) = 100. Hence, John will not accept the bet, even if its expected value exceeds that of the sure thing, as the bet's payoff falls into the range for which John is risk-averse.

c. The expected value is the same as the sure thing, as EV = .25($0) + .75($4) = $3. The expected utility of the bet is now EU = .25U($0) + .75U($4) = .75(16) = 12. The utility of the sure thing is U($3) = 9. Hence, John accepts this bet, even though it has the same expected value as the sure thing. This is because, over the range of payoffs of the bet, John is risk-loving.

d. No. John's behavior is the opposite: he likes small bets more than buying a lottery ticket (participate in a lottery with a possible large payoff), at a fair price for the lottery ticket.

3. Suppose that a state has only individuals with utility function $U = I^{1/2}$, where I is income. The state is subject to periodic hurricanes that reduce the income of the residents of the state to $0. Hurricanes occur with probability 50%. If no hurricane occurs, residents of the state have income $100.

    a. Illustrate in a diagram the lottery faced by uninsured individuals who inhabit this state. Now, suppose that insurance is available at a price of $36, to be paid whether or not a hurricane occurs, and pays out $61 in the event of a hurricane. Illustrate the utility of an insured individual on the same diagram.

    b. Who will buy insurance in this state?

c. Now, suppose that the state receives federal disaster relief in the case of a hurricane. If a hurricane occurs, all uninsured individuals in the state receive a grant of $25. How does this program affect the demand for insurance in the state? What if the grants are awarded regardless of whether the individual is insured?

Answer:

a. We have:

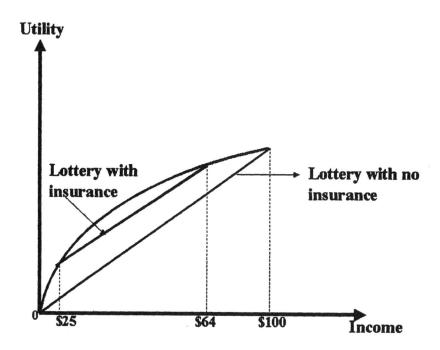

b. The lottery faced by an uninsured individual yields a payoff of $100 with 50% probability and a payoff of $0 with 50% probability. The expected value of this lottery is $50 and the expected utility of this lottery is .5U($0) + .5U($100) = .5(10) = 5. The lottery faced by an insured individual yields a payoff of $64 with 50% probability and $25 with 50% probability. The expected value of this lottery is .5($25) + .5($64) = $12.5+$32 = $44.5 and the expected utility of this lottery is .5U($25) + .5U($64) = .5(5) + .5(8) = 6.5. Hence, the expected utility under insurance is larger, so that all individuals in this state purchase insurance.

c. The state grant yields a lottery for uninsured individuals of $25 with 50% probability and $100 with 50% probability. The expected utility of this lottery is .5U($25) + .5U($100) = .5(5) + .5(10) = 7.5. Now, the expected utility of remaining uninsured exceeds that of becoming insured so that the demand for insurance drops to zero in this state (the federal grant substitutes completely for private insurance). If this grant is available to all individuals, then an individual who both receives the grant and purchases insurance receives a lottery with a payoff of $64 if there is no hurricane and $50 if there is a hurricane. The expected utility of this lottery is .5U($50) + .5U($64) = 7.525. Hence, the utility of purchasing private insurance is higher than that of remaining uninsured.

Under this scheme, the demand for the private insurance remains as high as without the federal grant.

Problem Set

1. Fred is a farmer who grows vegetables on land that is close to a river. The river occasionally floods in the spring, with disastrous consequences. If there is no flood, the production will be high and the vegetables will sell for $2500. If there is flood, then what is left of the vegetables will be worth only $100. Fred can buy flood insurance at a cost of $ 0.1 for each $1 worth of coverage. Fred thinks that the probability that there will be a flood is 0.1. Letting I denote income, Fred's utility function is $U(I) = I^{1/2}$.

   a. Can we say anything about Fred's preference towards risk? Illustrate your answer in a diagram.

   b. What is Fred's expected income if he doesn't buy insurance? What is his expected utility?

   c. Now suppose Fred wishes to buy flood insurance: he will pay the insurance premium (0.1 of the coverage) and will receive £K coverage in the event of a flood. What level of coverage will Fred optimally select? With this level of coverage, what is Fred's income going to be if there is a flood? What will his income be if there is no flood?

2. A trucking firm pays its drivers based on how quickly they deliver goods from one point to another. Unfortunately, to obtain the higher payoff, the truck drivers must break the speed limit. Suppose that a driver who makes a fast delivery obtains a payoff of $100 and a driver who makes a slow delivery obtains a payoff of $81 per shipment. A slow driver has no chance of getting a ticket for speeding, but a fast driver receives a ticket with probability 50%. A driver who receives a ticket is responsible for paying the fine himself. Two types of drivers are employed at the firm: type A drivers with utility $U(I) = I^2$ and type B drivers with utility $U(I) = I^{1/2}$, where I is income.

   a. If the fine for speeding is $36, which type of driver speeds?

   b. If the fine for speeding rises to $51, which type of driver speeds?

   c. If the fine remains at $36, but the probability of receiving a ticket rises to 75%, which type of driver speeds?

   d. Show graphically that either a rise in the amount of the fine or the probability of receiving a ticket can be used to deter speeding.

3. An investor with a total wealth of $100 is faced with the two following opportunities. First, he may invest the $100 now and receive $144 if there are

good times, but receive only $64 if there are bad times. The investor estimates that good times happen with 50% probability. He can also buy an investor newsletter that tells him whether good times or bad times will occur.

    a. Draw the decision tree that illustrates the options available to the investor and the payoffs to the different options. Define p as the price of the newsletter.

    b. If the investor is risk-neutral with $U(I) = I$, where I is income, how much would he be willing to pay for the subscription to the newsletter?

    c. If the investor is risk-averse with utility $U(I) = I^{1/2}$, where I is income, how much would this investor be willing to pay for the subscription to the newsletter?

    d. Suppose that the owner of the newsletter estimates that there are 75 risk-averse investors like those of part (c) and 25 investors like those of part (b). If it costs zero to produce the newsletter, how should the newsletter be priced assuming (1) that the owner wishes to maximize the profits of the newsletter and (2) that this is the only newsletter available to investors?

4. Mr. Clever wishes to sell his house. Two neighbors, both of whom are very familiar with the house, are interested in buying. Mr. Clever sets up an auction whereby the two neighbors are called to Mr. Clever's house on a Saturday afternoon. The neighbors are invited to bid for the house, with the highest bid winning.

    a. What type of auction has Mr. Clever designed for his house?

    b. Suppose we define Pareto Efficiency of the auction as requiring that the good to be sold be awarded to the person with the highest valuation. Has Mr. Clever designed a Pareto Efficient auction for his house?

    c. Suppose that Mr. Clever, because he is so clever, knows the valuations placed by the neighbors on his house. If he sets a minimum bid equal to the valuation of the higher bidder, will his auction still be Pareto Efficient in the sense defined in (b)?

5. Draw a set of axes where expected value of income received is on the vertical axis and standard deviation of income is on the horizontal axis. Carla prefers a higher expected income for the same degree of risk, and requires a positive risk premium to undertake more risk for the same expected income.

    a. Draw a representative set of indifference curves for Carla on these axes. Is Carla risk-averse, risk-neutral or risk-loving?

    b. Suppose that the only bets that Carla can undertake are those along the 45° line. Illustrate Carla's utility-maximizing bet when these choices are offered to her. Does Carla choose to undertake a positive amount of risk?

6. Draw a set of axes where income received in "good times" is on the vertical axis and income received in "bad times" is on the horizontal axis.

   a. Let income in good times be $60,000 and income in bad times be $0. Illustrate this point on the axes if no insurance against losses of income is available.

   b. Now, insurance is available. The insurance costs $30,000 whether there are good or bad times. If bad times occur, the individual receives $60,000 with insurance. If good times occur, the individual receives $0. Bad times occur with 50% probability. Draw the individual's new point on the same set of axes. What interpretation does this graph suggest for the insurance contract?

   c. Using your graph in (b), can you think of a way of representing the preferences of an individual who prefers to insure than not? Interpret your illustration, referring to our description of preferences in Chapter 3.

7. Police officers are supposed to wear their bullet-proof vests whenever they are on patrol. As these vests are uncomfortable, many officers do not follow the rule and leave their vests at home. A recent study of a large police department has shown that police officers who comply with regulations and wear their vests are engaged in more shooting incidents than the rest of their colleagues. Using the concepts of moral hazard and adverse selection, can you provide some explanations for this observation?

Exam *(60 minutes: Closed book; Closed notes)*

1. Suppose that Ian has utility function $U = I^{1/2}$, where I is income. Ian's current income is $100. Anders, a friend, offers Ian a gamble where Anders will pay Ian $4 with a 50% chance and $0 with a 50% chance. The gamble costs $1, payable to Anders, to play.

   a. Illustrate Ian's utility function and the gamble he is offered on a graph. What is Ian's risk preference?

   b. Do you think that Ian will accept this gamble? Explain your answer.

   c. Must Anders be risk-loving in order to offer this gamble to Ian?

2. Professor Pete needs to hire a part-time secretary to help him with his administrative work. He has two options. First, he may hire the secretary privately, using a $48,000 fund he has for his personal use. The secretary's salary will cost $12,000 out of this fund. Unfortunately, if the secretary is injured on the job, Pete is liable for damages and has a .1 chance of losing the entire fund. Second, he may hire the secretary through the personnel office of the university where he works. If he follows this second option, the university

collects a $4,000 overhead charge to the secretary's salary, so that the salary will cost Pete $16,000 total; however, in the case of injury, Professor Pete is not liable for any damages. Professor Pete's utility function is $U = I^{1/2}$, where I is income. Which option should he choose?

3. Suppose that an employer cannot observe an employee's effort, but is able to observe the final output produced. Discuss the problem of moral hazard in the context of this employer-employee relationship under the two following situations, below. Do you think that the employer can design an employment contract that eliminates the moral hazard problem in each case?

   a. Only the level of effort exerted by the employee influences how much output is obtained. (For example, an employee at his work station can work harder and make more widgets or he can be lazy and make fewer widgets.)

   b. The level of effort exerted by the employee affects the quantity produced, but also random exogenous factors influence the final outcome. (For example, while the employee may work hard, his machine also may randomly quit working, which reduces his output.)

4. Two potential buyers bid for a painting. Buyer A values the painting at V_A and buyer B values it at V_B. Each potential buyer knows his own valuation but not the valuation of his rival. The auction begins with each buyer raising his hand. The price of the painting is then increased progressively by the auctioneer. To remain in the bidding a buyer must keep his hand up at all times. As soon as one of the two buyers lowers his hand, the painting is awarded to the remaining bidder at the price that prevailed when the other bidder dropped out.

   a. Is this a private value auction or a common value auction?

   b. Show that the optimal strategy of each bidder is to keep his hand up until the price reaches his valuation or until the other bidder drops out, whichever event comes first. Is the auction efficient?

Answers to Exercises

1. (a), (b), and (d) are true. The expected value of project A is .6(0) + .2(0) + .2(20) = 4. The expected value of project B is .6(4) + .2(4) + .2(4) = 4. The expected value of project C is .6(0) + .2(9) + .2(16) = 5.

   The correct answer to the second part of the question is (c). If the investor only cared about maximizing the expected value of the investment, she would choose project C since the expected value of this project is 5, while the other projects have an expected value of only 4.

2. (a) and (c) are true. Project A has variance $.6 \times (0\text{-}4)^2 + .2 \times (0\text{-}4)^2 + .2 \times (20\text{-}4)^2 = .8 \times 16 + .2 \times 256 = 12.8 + 51.2 = 64$. Project B has variance $.6 \times (4\text{-}4)^2$

+ .2 x (4-4)^2 + .2 x (4-4)^2 = 0. Project C has variance .6 x (0-5)^2 + .2 x (9-5)^2 + .2 x (16-5)^2 = 34.4.

The correct answer to the second part of the question is (b). If the investor only cared about minimizing variance, she would choose project B since the variance is zero. This is less than the variance of project A or C.

3. The correct statements for the first part of the question are (a), (b), and (d). The utility equals the income from the shares, so that we can write U = I, where I is the income and U is the utility from the income. Hence, if we graph utility as a function of income, utility is linear. In fact, it is a 45° line extending northeast from the origin. Hence, statement (a) is correct. The expected utility of the project would equal the probability of each outcome times the utility from the outcome. The expected utility of project A is, then, the probability of each income possible income level (0, 0, or 20) when project A is undertaken times the utility of each of these three income levels. Since the utility of income simply equals the income level, we can then write expected utility of A = EU(A) = .6 x U(0) + .2 x U(0) + .2 x U(20) = .6 x 0 + .2 x 0 + .2 x 20 = 4. But 4 is simply the expected value of project A. Hence, statement (d) is correct. Since the expected utility of a project is simply the expected income from the project, project A's expected utility equals 4, which equals the expected value of A. This is a point on the 45° line so that the expected utility does, in fact, lie on the utility function. This means that statement (b) is correct. The investor's utility of A is shown in the graph below.

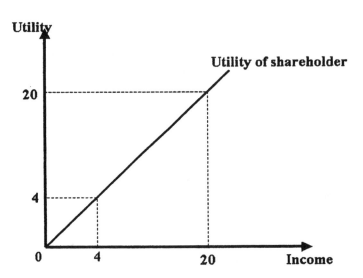

Since the expected utility equals the expected value of the projects, the project with the highest expected value has the highest expected utility for the shareholder. We know from Exercise 1 that the project with the highest expected value is project C. Hence, statement (c) is false.

Note that the marginal utility of income is constant for the shareholder since the utility gain for any change in income (say, an increase in $1 of income) is worth the same in terms of utility no matter what the initial income level was. For example, an increase of $1 in income is worth 1 to the shareholder whether his initial income level was $0 or whether it was $40.

The correct answer to the second part of the question is that (a), (b), and (d) are correct. The manager in the second part of the question has utility function $U = I^{1/2}$, so that the utility function is concave, as shown in Figure 15.2 of the summary. Hence, the marginal utility is a decreasing function of the income from the investment so that (a) is correct. The marginal utility of the income is decreasing. For example, the marginal utility of increasing income by $17 at income level zero is $17^{1/2} - 0^{1/2} = 4.1$ (approximately), whereas the marginal utility of increasing income by $17 at income level 64 is $81^{1/2} - 64^{1/2} = 1$. This can also be seen graphically since the utility function is concave in income. Hence, statement (b) is correct. The expected utility of project A is EU(A) = .6 x U(0) + .2 x U(0) + .2 x U(20) = .6 x $0^{1/2}$ + .2 x $0^{1/2}$ + .2 x $20^{1/2}$ = .2 x $20^{1/2}$ = .9 (approximately). The utility of the expected value of project A is U(4) = $4^{1/2}$ = 2. Hence, statement (d) is correct.

The expected utility of each project for the manager of the second part of the question is EU(A) = .9 (as calculated above). EU(B) = $4^{1/2}$ = 2. EU(C) = .6 x U(0) + .2 x U(9) + .2 x U(16) = .6 x 0 + .2 x 3 + .2 x 4 = .6 + .8 = 1.4. Hence, project B has the highest expected value for the manager. Statement (c) is, then, false.

The correct answer to the third part of the question is also (a), (b), and (d). Here, $U = I^2$, so that the utility function is convex. Hence, the utility is an increasing function of the income from the investment so that (a) is correct. The marginal utility of income is increasing. For example, the marginal utility of increasing income by $1 at zero income is $1^2 - 0^2 = 1$, whereas the marginal utility of increasing income by $1 at $2 of income is $3^2 - 2^2 = 9 - 4 = 5$. This can also be seen graphically since the utility function is convex in income. Hence, statement (b) is correct. The expected utility of project A is EU(A) = .6 x U(0) + .2 x U(0) + .2 x U(20) = .6 x 0^2 + .2 x 0^2 + .2 x 20^2 = .2 x 400 = 80. Since the expected value of project A is 4, the expected utility is larger than the utility of the expected value = EU(4) = 4^2 = 16. Hence, statement (d) is correct. The utility of the manager is illustrated below.

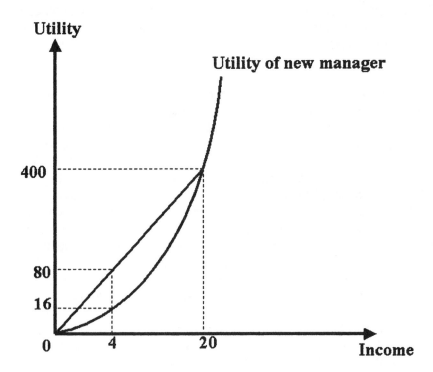

The expected utility of each project for the manager of the third part of the question is EU(A) = 80 (as calculated above). EU(B) = 4^2 = 16. EU(C) = .6 x U(0) + .2 x U(9) + .2 x U(16) = .2 x 9^2 + .2 x 16^2 = .2 x 81 + .2 x 256 = 67.4. Hence, project A has the highest expected utility for the new manager.

4. Statements (b) and (c) are correct. Recall from the answer to Exercise 3 that the marginal utility of income is constant for the shareholder, decreasing for the first manager and increasing for the new manager. Hence, the shareholder is risk-neutral, the first manager is risk-averse and the new manager is risk-loving. We see from this that statement (b) is correct and statement (a) is false. Recall, too, that the shareholder obtains highest expected utility from project C, the first manager obtains highest expected utility from project B and the new manager obtains highest expected utility from project A. Hence, the risk preference affects the preferred investment choice. Hence, statement (c) is correct.

5. Statements (b) and (c) are correct. Statement (a) is false. The risk premium for the shareholder is zero since the shareholder is risk-neutral: the shareholder cares only about the expected value of the investment so that the sure thing that would yield the same value as any lottery is simply the expected value of the lottery. In other words, U(expected value of lottery) = Expected utility of lottery. The risk premium for the first manager is the sure thing that yields the same expected utility as project B (the preferred project of the first manager). In Exercise 3, we calculated the expected utility of project B as 2 for this manager. Hence, we need to find the amount, $X, such that U(X) = 2. Since U(X) = $X^{1/2}$, we have $X^{1/2}$ = 2 or X = 4. Hence, the risk premium for the first manager also is

zero. This is not surprising since project B has no variance (and hence, no risk). Therefore, no premium is required to induce even the risk-averse manager to undertake this project. The risk premium for the new manager is the sure thing that yields the same expected utility as project A (the preferred project of the new manager). Recall from Exercise 3 that project A yields expected utility 80 for the new manager. Hence, we need to find the amount $X such that U(X) = 80. The utility function for the new manager is $U(X) = X^2$ so that we need to find X such that $X^2 = 80$. Solving, we find that X is (approximately) 9. The risk premium for the new manager is the difference between the expected value of the lottery and the sure thing that would yield the same utility is approximately (5 − 9) = -4. This means that the manager actually requires a premium to *avoid* risk. This is not surprising since this manager is risk-loving.

6. The correct answer to the first question of this exercise is (a). The insurance is fairly priced if the expected payout equals the price. Using the probabilities in Exercise 1, the expected payout is .2($0) + .2($7) + .6($16) = $1.4 + $9.6 = $11 = price.

   All the statements for the second part of the question are correct. First, note that the variance of project C with insurance is zero, as the insurance results in a payout of $16, whatever the state of nature. The expected value of project C remains $5, as the $11 price of the insurance must be paid whatever the state (hence, the net payoff for the project with insurance is $16 - $11 = $5.) A risk-neutral or a risk-averse agent will accept this insurance, certainly, as it leaves the expected value of the project unchanged and lowers the variance to zero. Now, project C with insurance has a higher expected value and lower variance than either of the other two alternatives. Hence, the risk-averse manager will switch to project C and buy the insurance. Further, the shareholder prefers project C with insurance to any other because the expected payoff is higher than either project A or project B. On the other hand, since the insurance does not change the expected value of project C, the shareholder is indifferent between buying insurance or not with project C. Finally, the second manager still prefers to invest in project A, since the expected utility of this project is still 80, while the expected utility of project C with insurance is now $5^2 = 25 (since the net payoff of the project in each state of the world is now $5).

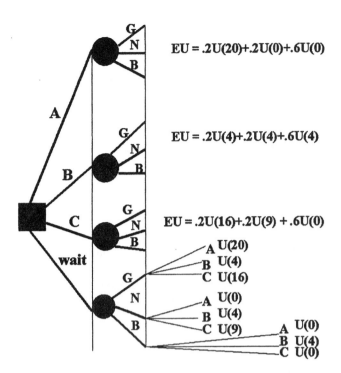

EU = .2U(20)+.2U(0)+.6U(0)

EU = .2U(4)+.2U(4)+.6U(4)

EU = .2U(16)+.2U(9) + .6U(0)

A U(20)
B U(4)
C U(16)

A U(0)
B U(4)
C U(9)

A U(0)
B U(4)
C U(0)

7.

The tree represents the choice of investing immediately in project A, B, or C on the top three branches (after which the state of nature is determined) or waiting for the state of nature to be determined on the bottom branch, after which the investment decision is made. In the case of investing immediately, the payoff in utility terms are the payoffs calculated in Exercise 3 for the three agents. The expected utility of waiting is the probability of each state of nature times the utility of the best investment choice *given* that the state of nature is known. For example, if times are good, investment A gives the highest payoffs in utility terms (=U(20)), while if times are normal, investment C gives the highest payoff (=U(9)) and if times are bad, investment B gives the highest payoff (=U(4)). The expected utility is the average of these payoffs, weighted by the probability that each state occurs so that EU(wait) = .2U(20) + .2U(9) + .6U(4). Hence, for each of the three agents, we have:

	Shareholder	Manager 1	Manager 2
EU(A)	4	0.9	80
EU(B)	4	2	16
EU(C)	5	1.4	67.4
EU(wait)	8.2	2.7	105.8

The value of the information, if there is no cost to waiting to get it, is the increase in (utility) value to the agent of waiting rather than choosing the next best alternative. For the shareholder, then, this is the difference 8.2 - 5 = 3.2. For the first manager, the value of waiting is 2.7 - 1.4 = 1.3. For the second manager, the value of waiting is 105.8 - 80 = 25.8. Hence, all three decision makers would do better waiting than investing immediately if the cost of waiting is zero.

8. Statements (b) and (c) are correct. This is a private value auction in the sense that the different managers would, in fact, choose to do different investment projects so that the value of the company is not the same for the two managers. (Further, the utility derived from the company is not the same in any case, as the utility functions differ.) This is an English auction if the bids are ascending, with the highest bidder winning the company and all parties knowing the bids submitted.

Answers to Problem Set

1.

    a. Fred is risk averse. We can see this because his marginal utility is decreasing (or, alternatively, the utility function is concave to the horizontal axis). In other words, Fred prefers the average outcome to the extreme outcomes, weighted by their probabilities. This will imply that he prefers to fully insure at fairly priced insurance, as he will *always* do better at the utility of the average to the average of the extreme utilities.

    b. If Fred doesn't buy insurance, he gets $.9(2500) + .1(100) = 2250+10=2260$. His expected utility is $.9(2500)^{1/2} + .1(100)^{1/2} = .9(50) + .1(10) = 46$.

    c. Fred will fully insure, as he is risk averse and as the insurance is fairly priced. In other words, the insurance is priced so that the premium is equal to the expected payout. This is the case, as the premium is equal to 10% of the coverage, and the risk of payout is also equal to 10%. Hence, he will equate his income in the two states so that 2500-premium $= 2250 + $ coverage - premium or $2500-.1K = 2250+K-.1K \Leftrightarrow 2500-.1K = 100+.9K \Leftrightarrow K = 2500-100$ or $K = 2400$. Hence, he obtains coverage of 2400 in exchange for a premium of 240. This means that he earns $2500-240 (=2260)$ in the good state and $100+2400-240=2260$ in the bad state as well. He bears no risk.

2.

    a. If the fine is $36, then the expected utility of speeding is EU(fast) = $.5U(\$100-\$36) + .5U(\$100)$. The expected utility of driving slowly is EU(slow) = $U(\$81)$. Hence, for type A drivers, we have EU(fast) = $.5(\$64)^2 + .5(\$100)^2 = 2048 + 5000 = 7048$ and EU(slow) = $(\$81)^2 = 6561$. Hence, type A drivers prefer to speed. For type B drivers, we have EU(fast) = $.5(\$64)^{1/2} + .5(\$100)^{1/2} = 9$ and EU(slow) = $(\$81)^{1/2} = 9$. Hence, the type B drivers are indifferent between speeding and not speeding. Any slight increase in the fine would make them prefer not to speed, in fact.

    b. If the fine rises to $51, we can recompute the above expected utilities to obtain for type A: EU(fast) = 6200.5 and EU(slow) = 6561 so that the type A drivers do not wish to speed. For type B we have: EU(fast) = 8.5 and EU(slow) = 9 so that the type B drivers do not wish to speed, either.

c. If the probability of receiving the fine increases to 75%, we can recompute the above expected utilities to obtain for type A: EU(fast) = 5572 and EU(slow) = 6561 so that type A does not wish to speed. For type B, we obtain EU(fast) = 8.5 and EU(slow) = 9, so that type B does not wish to speed either.

d.

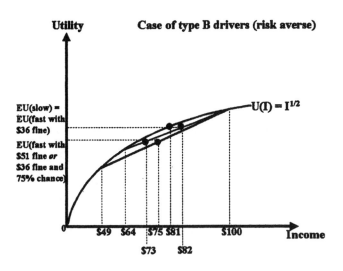

3.

a. Define the price of the newsletter as P.

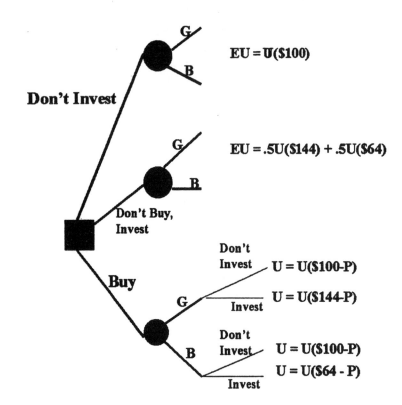

b. For this type of investor, the expected utility from not buying the newsletter but investing is .5($144) + .5($64) = $104. The expected utility from buying the newsletter is the chance that the newsletter reveals that times are good, in which case the individual invests and receives $144-P, and the chance that the newsletter reveals that times are bad, in which case the individual does better not investing and ends up with $100 - P. Hence, the value of the newsletter is .5($144 - P) + .5($100 - P) = $122 - P. Hence, the individual is willing to pay up to P = 122 – 104 = $18 in order to get the newsletter.

c. For this type of investor, the expected utility from not buying but investing is $.5(144)^{1/2} + .5(64)^{1/2} = 10$. The utility obtained from buying is the chance that the newsletter reveals that times are good times, resulting in the utility from investing $(144-P)^{1/2}$ plus the chance that the newsletter reveals that times are bad times, resulting in the utility from not investing $(100 – P)^{1/2}$. Hence, the value gained due to the newsletter is $.5(144 – P)^{1/2} + 0.5(100 – P)^{1/2} – 10$. For P = 0, this value is equal to 11 – 10 = 1. The highest value of P for which that value is positive is approximately P = $20. Comparing this to the answer in (b) we see that, not surprisingly, a risk-averse individual is willing to pay more for the newsletter than a risk-neutral individual.

d. If there are 75 investors like those discussed in (b) and 25 like those discussed in (c), then the profit maximizing choice must be either (1) to charge $20 for the newsletter and obtain a total revenue of $20 times the 25 investors who find this a price worth paying or (2) to charge $18 and obtain a total revenue of $18 times all 100 investors, who would find this price worth paying. Since 20x25 = 500 < 100 x 18 = 1800, it is more profitable to charge $18 and sell only to both types of investors.

4.

a. Mr. Clever has designed an English auction for his house: Each participant will cry out his or her bid and the highest bidder will win the house. This is a private value auction in the sense that each neighbor has his or her own valuation of the house, corresponding to his or her idiosyncratic tastes.

b. Mr. Clever's auction is Pareto Efficient, as the highest bidder will also be the individual with the highest valuation. It cannot be otherwise, as the bidders will offer up to (but no more than) their own valuations for the house (so as to not decrease their utility by buying). Hence, the individual with the higher true value will win the house.

c. Mr. Clever's auction still is Pareto Efficient, but the surplus from the sale is divided differently. In the case of the minimum bid, Mr. Clever collects the entire surplus from the auction. In case (b), the winning bidder collects the entire difference in value between her valuation and the valuation of the other neighbor.

5.

a.

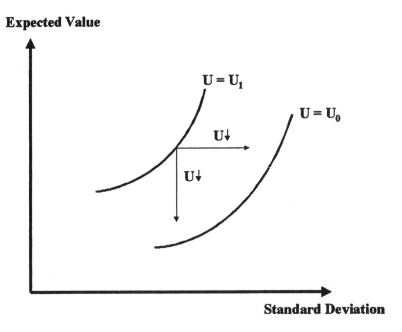

Utility falls along a horizontal line, as shown, as the standard deviation increases for the same expected value. It also falls along a vertical line as the expected value falls for a given standard deviation. Carla is risk-averse, since she prefers less variance for the same expected value. The information given in the problem only implies that the indifference curves have a positive slope: a larger standard deviation must be compensated by a higher expected value in order to yield the same level of utility. The indifference curves need not have the illustrated curvature.

If Carla were to be risk-neutral, her indifference curves would be horizontal: the same expected value would yield the same utility, regardless of variance. If she were a risk lover, the indifference curves would have a negative slope and increase to the right: for the same expected value, higher variance would yield higher utility and a higher expected value would require less variance to yield the same level of utility.

b. If Carla can undertake bets along the 45° line, then for the indifference curves illustrated above, Carla maximizes utility with a positive amount of risk. If Carla were to have straight-line indifference curves with a positive slope, and if the slope were to exceed that of the 45° line, then she would maximize utility by choosing zero risk, as illustrated below.

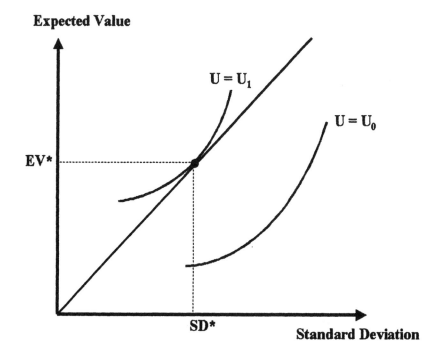

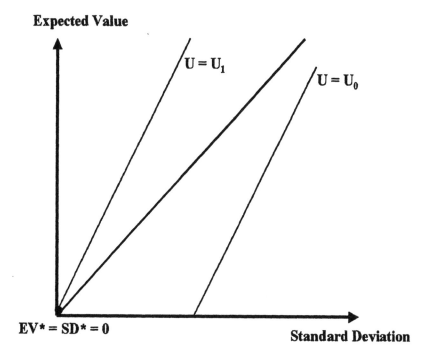

6.

a.

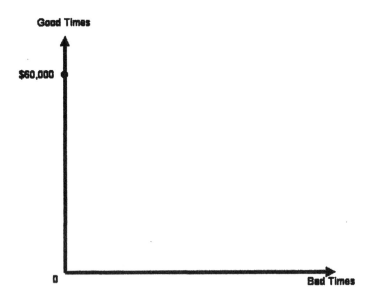

b.

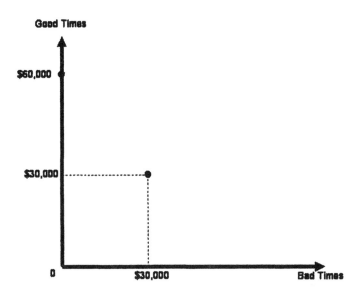

Hence, we can represent insurance as a reallocation of consumption across two states of the world: good and bad times. The insurance contract represents full insurance, since it equalizes consumption across the two states (i.e., the variance of income is zero).

c. We could think of preferences for income in the two states as standard preferences across two goods, with a preference for variety leading to a preference for insurance. In this case, IC_2 represents a higher level of preference, for example.

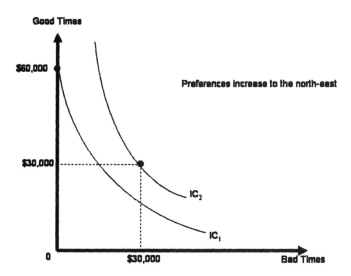

7. One possibility is that officers wearing their vests are less reluctant to confront criminals because they know that the vest provides some protection. This is a "moral hazard" explanation: wearing the vest (a form of "insurance") modifies the actions of the police officers (they are less "cautious"). Another possibility is that police officers who know that they have a better chance of finding themselves in dangerous situations (either because of the neighborhood they patrol or because of their adventurous nature) make a point of wearing their vests. This is an "adverse selection" explanation: police officers of the "adventurous" type choose to wear the vest.

Answers to Exam

1.

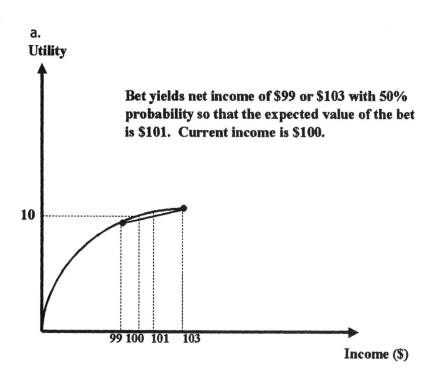

a.
Utility

Bet yields net income of $99 or $103 with 50% probability so that the expected value of the bet is $101. Current income is $100.

10

99 100 101 103

Income ($)

Ian is risk-averse since the marginal utility decreases as income increases.

b. Ian will accept this gamble, even though it raises the variance of his income, because the utility from the gamble is greater than his utility of keeping his current level of income. He currently has utility level of 10 $(10 = (100)^{1/2})$. The gamble gives him expected utility of $.5U(99) + .5U(103) = .5(99)^{1/2} + .5(103)^{1/2} \cong .5(9.95) + .5(10.14) = 4.975 + 5.07 = 10.045$. Hence, his utility rises ever so slightly by accepting the gamble. In other words, the increase in expected value compensates him for the increase in variance.

c. Anders has a negative expected value of offering the gamble, as he earns $1 with 50% probability and loses $3 with 50% probability. Hence, he could be risk-loving to offer this gamble: a risk-neutral person would never offer it because the expected value is negative. Alternatively, perhaps Anders is a very generous person who likes to give money to his friends, even if the gift is disguised as a bet.

2. Professor Pete starts out with $I = \$48,000$. He has two options. If he does not use the personnel office to do his hiring, he obtains an income net of the secretary's salary of $36,000 with probability .9 and a net income of $0 with a probability of .1. If he hires through the personnel office, he obtains a net income of $32,000 with a probability of 1. Hence, he must compare expected utility of $.9U(36,000) + .1U(0)$ to the utility of 32,000. Computing this, we have $.9U(36,000) = .9(60)(10)^{1/2} \cong 54(3.15) = 170.1$. $U(32,000) \cong 178.9$. Hence, Pete should not use the personnel office in his hiring.

3.

a. Although the effort may not be observable to the employer, the employer can deduce the level of effort from the firm's output, as the output is perfectly correlated with effort (i.e., output depends on effort only). While there is a potential moral hazard problem in this case that the employee may behave in a lazy way, hence, decreasing the output of the firm, the employer can use the employment contract to control the moral hazard. For example, the employer can impose a punishment in the wage contract if output falls below the level that a hard-working employee would produce.

b. In this case, the employer cannot deduce the level of effort put in by the worker just by looking at output, as the output depends on other factors as well that are not under the control of the employee. In other words, high output can be the result of hard work or good luck. Similarly, low output can be the result of laziness or bad luck.

The firm can still influence the worker's effort by means of the labor contract, though. If the firm wants the worker to exert high effort, it needs to make the wage when high output is observed large enough that, even if the worker is unlucky (and so would receive a lower wage corresponding to the lower output), the worker would prefer to work hard than to be lazy. In other words, the worker's *expected* wage when he works hard has to outweigh the *expected* wage when he is lazy, of course taking into account any psychological cost the worker suffers when he works hard. The wage would also need to be such that the worker would agree to work in the first place and that the firm would not find it too costly to induce high effort.

4.

a. This is a private value auction. A's valuation of the good is personal. Knowing B's valuation would not lead A to revise his own valuation.

b. By keeping his hand up, a bidder is only saying that he is still willing to buy the painting at this price. It is, therefore, a *dominant strategy* for A to keep his hand up as long as the price, p, is below his valuation V_A. By dropping out before that, say at a price $p_o < V_A$, A loses the opportunity to obtain some surplus if the other player still has his hand up at p_o but would quit the bidding at p_q such that $p_o < p_q < V_A$. Since the same reasoning applies for B, both players are willing to stay in the bidding as long as the price is below their private valuation of the painting. Hence, the outcome of this auction is that the bidder with the highest valuation wins at a price equal to the valuation of the losing bidder. Since the bidder with the highest valuation wins, the auction is efficient.

Chapter 16: General Equilibrium Theory

A **partial equilibrium analysis** studies the determination of price and output in a single market, taking as given the prices in all other markets. This is the type of equilibrium analysis we have conducted so far. In this chapter, we will study **general equilibrium analysis**, where we determine price and output in more than one market at the same time. A general equilibrium analysis has three main advantages over a partial equilibrium analysis. First, the answers that we obtain from a partial equilibrium analysis are not correct when there are significant linkages between different markets. In fact, many markets in the economy are linked: the equilibrium of the market for corn undoubtedly depends on the characteristics of the market for a substitute, such as soy. Further, equilibrium in a goods market (such as corn) would usually depend on the characteristics of the market for inputs, such as labor services. The second advantage of a general equilibrium analysis is that it makes the notion of "opportunity cost" endogenous. So far, the opportunity cost of a resource has been defined as the price that it can command in its best alternative use, but that alternative use was defined exogenously. In general equilibrium, all prices are determined endogenously so that the price that a resource can obtain in any market, and therefore its opportunity cost, is also endogenous. Finally, general equilibrium also allows us to determine where consumers' incomes come from: instead of being given exogenously, a consumer's income will now depend on the value of the factors of production (e.g., labor and capital) that she owns.

Let us start with equilibrium determined in two linked markets, corn and soy. Let demand and supply in the two markets be the following:

$$Q_c^D = 12 - 2p_c + p_s \qquad Q_c^S = 4 + p_c$$
$$Q_s^D = 6 - 4p_s + p_c \qquad Q_s^S = 4 + p_s$$

From the equations, you can see that the linkage between the markets occurs on the demand side only. Since a rise in the price of soy increases the demand for corn, we can see that soy and corn are substitutes in consumption. This can be seen in the demand for soy as well. The supply of corn depends only on corn's price and the supply of soy depends only on the price of soy. The general equilibrium level of prices and outputs for these two markets occurs where demand equals supply in the two markets simultaneously, or where the following two equations hold simultaneously:

1. $Q_c^D = Q_c^S$
2. $Q_s^D = Q_s^S$

For the demands and supplies we have above, equation 1 requires that $12 - 2p_c + p_s = 4 + p_c$ and equation 2 requires that $6 - 4p_s + p_c = 4 + p_s$. We can solve for p_c from equation 1 and substitute this into equation 2 to obtain $p^*_c = 3$ and $p^*_s = 1$. The equivalent equilibrium quantities traded are $Q^*_c = 7$ and $Q^*_s = 5$.

Now, suppose that demand were to shift in the market for corn to $18 - 2p_c + p_s$. If we were to conduct only a partial equilibrium analysis of the market for corn, we would take the price of soy as given (at $p_s = 1$) and solve $18 - 2p_c + 1 = 4 + p_c$ or $15 = 3p_c$ or $p^{**}_c = 5$ and $Q^{**}_c = 9$. However, assuming that p_s remains unchanged is incorrect; the rise in the price of corn will tend to drive demand toward soy, resulting in an increase in p_s. A general equilibrium analysis accounts for these simultaneous changes in p_c and p_s by solving equation 1 and equation 2 again, using the new equation of demand for corn. Hence, we would solve $18 - 2p_c + p_s = 4 + p_c$ and $6 - 4p_s + p_c = 4 + p_s$ simultaneously. This would yield $p'_c = 5.14$ and $p'_s = 1.43$ and $Q'_c = 9.14$ and $Q'_s = 5.43$. The partial equilibrium analysis would have underestimated the price of corn and soy as well as the quantity traded of both goods. The price of corn is *underestimated* because we have *overestimated* the substitution into soy: as the price of soy rises, demand shifts to corn, causing a rise in its price.

Graphically, the general equilibrium at the original levels of demand and supply is shown as point e_0 in the diagrams below. When demand shifts out in the market for corn, it causes a shift out in the demand for soy as well, which means that both markets experience a rise in price and output. This new general equilibrium is shown as e_2. The partial equilibrium analysis would result in an estimate of equilibrium e_1 in the two markets.

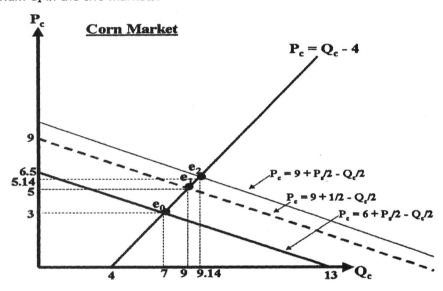

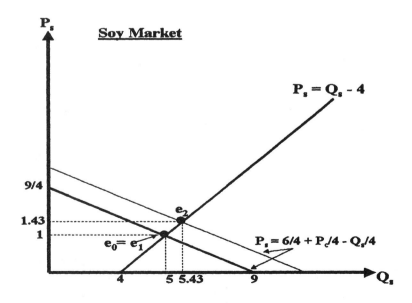

Figure 16.1

Exercise 1: *Suppose that the equations for demand and supply in the markets are as shown in the example, above. Now, let the* <u>*supply*</u> *of corn shift out to* $Q_c^S = 6 + p_c$ *while all other equations stay the same. Which of the following is true?*

a. The new equilibrium prices are $p^*_c = 16/7$ and $p^*_s = 6/7$.
b. The equilibrium in the market for soy does not change, as there is no linkage on the supply side across these markets.
c. The price rises in both the corn and soy markets because the two products are demand substitutes.

Our partial equilibrium analysis of competitive markets in Chapter 10 showed us that a single competitive market maximizes the net economic surplus that can be generated in that market. However, suppose that now we consider a *general* equilibrium analysis of perfect competition. Can we still say that perfect competition is desirable once a firm's costs and a consumer's income are determined endogenously? In fact, the efficiency results we derived earlier can both be maintained and made more precise once income and costs are endogenous.

A pattern of consumption and input usage for an economy is called an **allocation** of goods and inputs. For example, an allocation of goods between consumers A and B might be that A has 2 apples and B has 3 oranges. An allocation of labor inputs between two firms, A and B, might be 10 units of labor for firm A and 5 units of labor to firm B. An allocation of goods and inputs is **economically efficient** if there is no feasible allocation of goods and inputs that would make some economic agents better off without hurting others. To achieve overall economic efficiency, three types of efficiency conditions must be satisfied:

1. **Exchange Efficiency:** For given amounts of goods available for consumption, we cannot reallocate these *goods* among consumers without making at least some consumers worse off.

2. **Input Efficiency:** For given amounts of inputs available in the economy, we cannot reallocate these *inputs* among firms without reducing the output of at least one of the goods that is produced in the economy.

3. **Substitution Efficiency:** For given amounts of inputs available in the economy, we cannot alter the *mix of products* available for consumption in a manner that makes all consumers better off.

Exchange Efficiency

We will explore each type of efficiency in turn. In order to do so, we will introduce the tool of an **Edgeworth Box**. An Edgeworth Box shows all the possible allocations of goods that are possible in an economy, given the total available supply of the goods. The Edgeworth Box is usually drawn for two economic agents and two goods, to keep the picture simple. The length of the side of the box measures the total amount of the good available. For example, the width of the box in Figure 16.2 reflects the total amount (8 units) of good X available and the height of the box reflects the total amount (10 units) of good Y available. Initially, we assume that each individual in the economy holds a fixed allocation of the goods. This is called the individual's **endowment**. If person A's allocation is measured from the lower left-hand corner and person B's allocation is measured from the upper right-hand corner of the box, then A's endowment of, say, 5 units of good X and 3 units of good Y would be represented by point E in the box. As person B holds the remainder of the two goods (3 units of good X and 7 units of good Y), then point E also represents B's endowment of the goods. Any other *feasible* consumption allocation must lie in the box. In other words, any other allocation that does not allocate, in total, more of good X or good Y than is *available* must lie somewhere in the box.

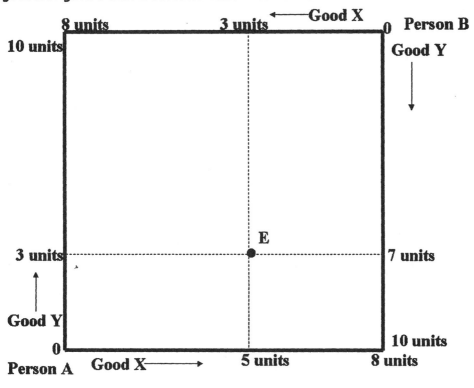

Figure 16.2

Exercise 2: *Suppose that a social planner proposes an alternative allocation of goods for Figure 16.2 where person A has 1 unit of good X and 4 units of good Y and person B has 7 units of good X and 7 units of good Y. Is this allocation feasible?*

   a. Yes.
   b. No.
   c. We need more information to decide.

     We can draw standard indifference curves of the two individuals between the two available goods in the usual way. The difference between the Edgeworth Box and the usual diagram is that we must measure the utility of the individuals from the appropriate corner. If person A's consumption of goods is measured from the lower left-hand corner, then we must draw the indifference curves and measure utility from the lower left-hand corner as well. If we measure person B's consumption of goods from the upper right-hand corner, we must draw the indifference curves and measure utility from the upper right-hand corner as well. In other words, IC_0^A represents a lower level of utility than IC_1^A for consumer A and IC_0^B represents a lower level of utility than IC_1^B for consumer B. Sample indifference curves, including those that represent the utility of the consumers at the endowment point, E, are shown in Figure 16.3, below.

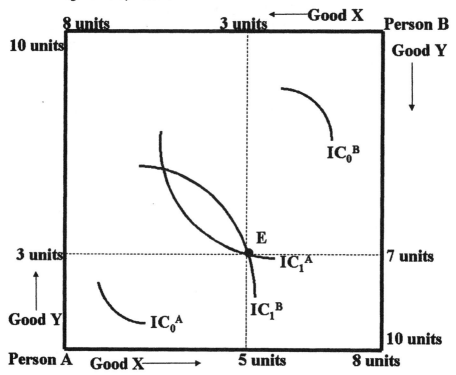

Figure 16.3

Notice that, at point E, there is a reallocation of goods that would make at least one consumer better off and neither worse off. For example, suppose that the consumers reallocate the goods so that A has 4 units of each good and B has 6 units of good Y and 4 units of good X, as in Figure 16.4, below. At the new point, both consumers would be on a higher indifference curve than they were at the endowment point. Hence point E is not exchange efficient: there are potential gains from barter or gains from exchange. In fact, any point, such as A, that lies within the "lens" formed by IC_1^A and IC_1^B represents an allocation that would make at least one party better off without making either worse off. This "lens" is shaded in Figure 16.4.

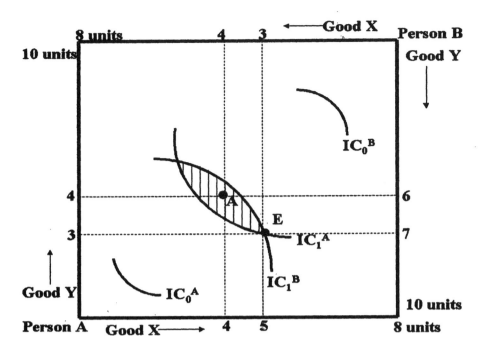

Figure 16.4

In order for an allocation to be efficient, the indifference curves passing through that allocation must not define any "lens". This is only possible if the two indifference curves are tangent at the point representing the allocation. This is illustrated by point M in Figure 16.5. At point M, the allocations that make person A no worse off are shown in the vertically shaded area, while the allocations that make person B no worse off are shown in the horizontally shaded area. You can see that no lens exists: at point M, person A could only be made better off by making B worse off and person B could only be made better off by making A worse off. Hence, M is exchange efficient.

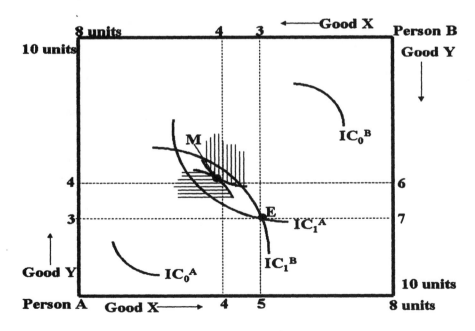

Figure 16.5

Exercise 3: *Will the following allocation be attained through voluntary bargaining from point E between persons A and B?*

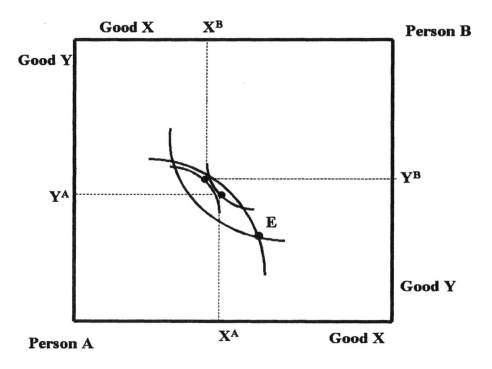

a. Yes. The allocation lies in the "lens" formed by the indifference curves through E and is feasible
b. No. The allocation lies in the "lens" but is infeasible.
c. No. The allocation does not use all units of Y, so it must be possible to make both parties better off by changing to a different allocation.
d. Both (b) and (c) are correct.

Of course, M is not the only exchange efficient point. In fact, any point of tangency between the indifference curves – anywhere in the Edgeworth Box – is exchange efficient. The *full* set of tangency points within the box is called the **contract curve**. The contract curve is illustrated in Figure 16.6, below. While all points on the contract curve are exchange efficient, not all of them can be said to dominate a particular allocation that is not on the contract curve. In Figure 16.6., for example, allocation B is exchange efficient but it does not dominate allocation E because person A's welfare is lower at B than at E. In other words, we would not expect two persons starting at allocation E to agree to move from E to B. On the other hand, these same persons would agree to move to a point such as M that is both on the contract curve and within the "lens" defined by the indifference curves passing through the initial allocation E. Such a move would benefit both consumers. Once at M, however, there would be no scope for any other mutually beneficial move. In other words, the *portion* of the contract curve that lies within the original lens represents the exchange efficient points that are bargaining outcomes *attainable* from endowment point E.

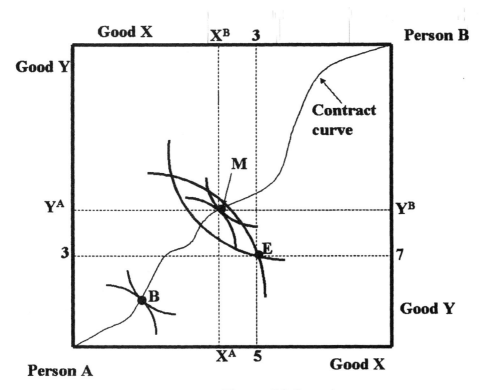

Figure 16.6

In algebraic terms, the equation of the contract curve is simply the set of points within the box where the indifference curves of the two individuals have the same slope (i.e., the set of points for which the marginal rates of substitution of the two individuals are equal). Hence, if the total amount of X in the box is X* and the total amount of Y in the box is Y*, the equation of the contract curve in Figure 16.6 is the set of allocations of X and Y where the following equations hold simultaneously:

$$1. \ MRS^A_{X,Y} = MRS^B_{X,Y}$$

$$2. \ X^A + X^B = X*$$
$$Y^A + Y^B = Y*$$

Equation (1) states that both consumers have the same relative valuation of the two goods. Equation (2) states that aggregate demand must equal aggregate supply for all goods.

Exercise 4: *Let $U^A = X^A Y^A$ and $U^B = X^B Y^B$, with marginal utilities $MU^A_X = Y^A$ $MU^A_Y = X^A$ and $MU^B_X = Y^B$, $MU^B_Y = X^B$. Let 100 units of goods X and Y be available for exchange so that $X* = Y* = 100$. What is the equation of the contract curve?*

    a. $X^B = Y^B$
    b. $X^A = Y^A$
    c. $X^B = (1/2)Y^B$
    d. Either (a) or (b)

Which of the following statements is true about this contract curve?

a. It is a straight line drawn from person A's corner to person B's corner.
b. It is a straight line drawn from the lower right-hand corner (X*) to the upper left-hand corner Y*

The key question is whether competitive markets will lead the economy to an efficient allocation of resources. In other words, would individual consumers, producers, and factor owners pursuing their own self-interest and relying solely on market prices reach an efficient equilibrium? For exchange efficiency, at least, the answer is yes. To see this, recall that in a competitive equilibrium, each consumer chooses a combination of goods such that her marginal rate of substitution is equal to the price ratio. Since both consumers face the same market prices, this also implies that, in the competitive equilibrium, all consumers will have the same MRS:

$$MRS^A_{X,Y} = MRS^B_{X,Y} = P_X/P_Y$$

Hence, at the competitive equilibrium, the agents must be at a point along the contract curve. In other words, all gains from exchange are exhausted even though consumers do not necessarily bargain with each other face-to-face. Graphically, suppose that person A and person B begin at endowment E, and face prices P_X and P_Y for the two goods. As we saw in Chapter 5, the budget constraint of each consumer is a line of slope $-P_X/P_Y$ going through point E. Each consumer will choose a combination of goods corresponding to the point of tangency between that budget constraint and her indifference curve. If both consumers do not choose the same point, then their demand for each of the two goods does not add up to the quantity supplied (i.e., to the corresponding side of the box). To have a market equilibrium, then, prices must be such that the independent choices of the two consumers actually occur at the same point in the box. Such an equilibrium is represented by point M in Figure 16.7. In equilibrium, each consumer's income is endogenously determined as the value of their initial endowments, where the value depends on the equilibrium prices of the two goods.

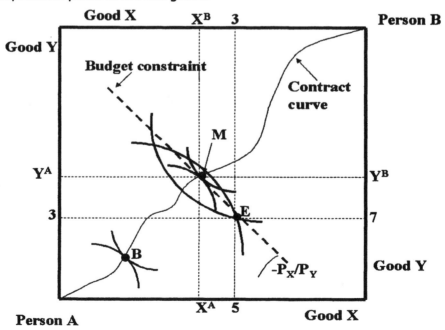

Figure 16.7

Algebraically, we can derive the "exchange" equilibrium prices as the prices for which the following hold simultaneously:

1. $MRS^A_{X,Y} = MRS^B_{X,Y} = P_X/P_Y$

2. $X^A + X^B = X*$
   $Y^A + Y^B = Y*$

Equation (1) states that all agents must be maximizing utility at the market prices. Equation (2) states that aggregate demand must equal aggregate supply for all goods.

Exercise 5: *Consider the individuals of Exercise 4. Recall from Chapter 5 that the individual demands for X and Y based on utility maximization are: $X^A = I^A/2P_X$; $Y^A = I^A/2P_Y$; $X^B = I^B/2P_X$; $Y^B = I^B/2P_Y$, where I^A is the income level of person A and I^B is the income level of person B. Recall that these demands satisfy the condition that the MRS must equal the price ratio. Now, let person A be endowed with 25 units of X and 75 units of Y. Person B is endowed with 75 units of X and 25 units of Y. Suppose that the price of X is $P_X = 1$. Let the price of Y be P_Y.*

Derive the income of person A and person B at the endowment point. Which of the following is true?

a. $I^A = 100$
b. $I^A = 25 + 75P_Y$
c. $I^B = I^A$
d. $I^B = 75 + 25P_Y$

Derive individual demands for X and Y using the income levels at the endowment point. Sum the individual demands to obtain aggregate demand. Which of the following is true about aggregate demand?

a. $X^A + X^B = 75$
b. $X^A + X^B = 50 + 50P_Y$
c. $Y^A + Y^B = 100 + 100/P_Y$
d. $Y^A + Y^B = 50/P_Y + 50$

What is the price of Y, $P*_Y$, at the "exchange" equilibrium given that the price of X, $P_X = 1$?

a. $P*_Y = 1/2$
b. $P*_Y = 1$
c. $P*_Y = 2$

What is true about the level of utility of persons A and B at these equilibrium prices?

a. $U*^A = X^A Y^A = 2500$
b. $U*^B = U*^A$
c. $U*^A = 1000 < U*^B = 2500$

Note that any point on the contract curve can be achieved by allowing competition, given an appropriate endowment. For example, if a new endowment, E', were given to these individuals, point M' could be attained at prices P_X and P_Y. This highlights a role for the government in such an economy: by redistributing the initial allocation to the "desired" endowment, the economy can attain different distributions of well-being across individuals but maintain exchange efficiency at all the resulting outcomes.

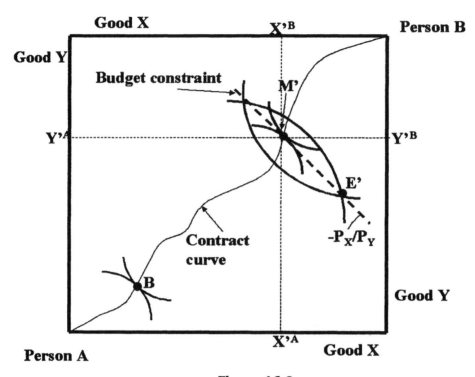

Figure 16.8

Exercise 6: *Consider the individuals of Exercise 4. Now, suppose that person A's endowment is 10 units of X and 10 units of Y, while person B's endowment is 90 units of X and 90 units of Y. For price $P_X = 1$, calculate the utility levels at the new "exchange" equilibrium. What is true now?*

a. $U^{*A} = 100$; $U^{*B} = 8100$.
b. U^{*A} has fallen from the level of Exercise 5; U^{*B} has risen from the level of Exercise 5.
c. The change in endowment from the level in Exercise 5 has changed the equilibrium point along the contract curve.

If we were to illustrate the utility of the two individuals along the contract curve in a diagram where the utility of person A is depicted on the horizontal axis and the utility of person B is depicted on the vertical axis, we would have drawn the **utility possibilities frontier**. This is the maximum utility person A could obtain, given the available resources, for each possible level of utility of person B. Because it represents allocations that are exchange efficient, the utility possibilities frontier must be downward sloping (i.e., one can only increase one person's utility by decreasing the other person's welfare).

<u>Input Efficiency</u>

When discussing exchange efficiency, we took the amount of each good available for consumption as given. We now turn to the question of whether the production of these goods is itself efficient. In the same way as we can draw an Edgeworth Box for goods, we can draw an Edgeworth Box for inputs, with a fixed amount of two inputs (labor and capital, say) to be allocated between two industries, one that produces X and the other that produces Y. Typical producers in these two industries will be called producer X and producer Y, respectively. We represent the total quantity of labor by the width of the box and the total quantity of capital as the height. Let producer X's quantity of each input be measured from the lower left-hand corner and producer Y's quantity of each input be measured from the upper right-hand corner. Any point in the box represents an allocation of inputs to the producers. Using a box analogous to the one we used for consumers, note that at point E, producer X uses 5 units of labor and 3 units of capital, while producer Y uses 3 units of labor and 7 units of capital. Instead of indifference curves, we can represent isoquants of the two producers, measured from the lower left-hand corner for producer X and from the upper right-hand corner for producer Y. For example, output level $Q^X_0 < Q^X_1$ and output level $Q^Y_0 < Q^Y_1$. The inputs in the economy will be efficiently allocated between X and Y if there is no feasible reallocation of inputs that allows one firm to produce more output without reducing the output attainable by the other firm. The entire set of efficient input allocations is called the **input contract curve** and includes all the points of tangency between the isoquants of producer X and the isoquants of producer Y that fall within the box. Since an isoquant's slope equals the (negative of the) marginal rate of technical substitution between the two inputs, the equation of the input contract curve is the set of capital and labor allocations for which the following equations hold simultaneously for a box where L* units of labor are available and K* units of capital are available:

1. $MRTS^X_{L,K} = MRTS^Y_{L,K}$

2. $L^X + L^Y = L*$
   $K^X + K^Y = K*$

Again the key question is whether competitive markets can achieve input efficiency on their own accord. Call the two inputs labor and capital and the prices of these inputs w and r. Recall that, in competitive equilibrium, each firm uses a combination of inputs that minimizes its cost of production given the prices of the inputs. This cost-minimizing combination of inputs occurs at the point of tangency between an isoquant and an isocost line of slope -w/r. Since firms in sectors X and Y face the same market prices for labor and capital, they must also have the same slope, that is,

$$MRTS^X_{L,K} = MRTS^Y_{L,K} = w/r$$

so that the resulting allocation does indeed satisfy input efficiency.

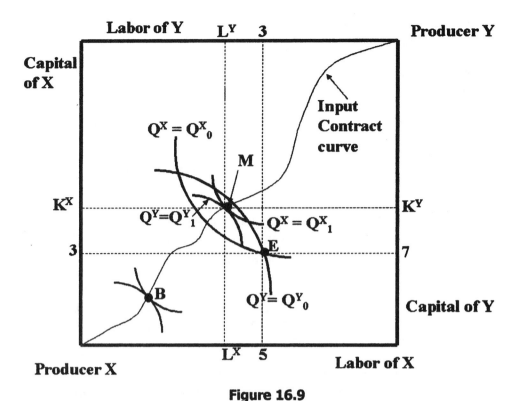

Figure 16.9

The equilibrium will, then, be at a point where the following equations hold simultaneously:

1. $MRTS^X_{L,K} = MRTS^Y_{L,K} = w/r$

2. $L^X + L^Y = L*$
   $K^X + K^Y = K*$

Exercise 7: *Suppose that the production function for good X is $X = K^{0.5}L^{0.5}$, with $MRTS^X_{L,K} = K^X/L^X$, and the production function for good Y is $Y = Min(L, K/2)$, where K is the number of units of capital and L is the number of units of labor. Let the total amount of capital be 100 units and the total amount of labor be 100 units. Suppose that the wage rage is w = 1 and the rental rate of capital is r = 2. Which of the following is true?*

  a. The input contract curve is a straight line.
  b. In the competitive allocation $100 \times 2^{0.5}/3$ units of X are produced.
  c. The demand equals the supply of inputs in equilibrium.

Substitution Efficiency

The **production possibilities frontier** (PPF) describes the maximum feasible combinations of consumption goods (X and Y) that can be produced in the economy with the economy's available supply of inputs (L and K) when inputs are used efficiently. A PPF for goods X and Y is illustrated in Figure 16.10. Since input efficiency implies that if more of X is produced, then less of Y is produced, the PPF slopes downward. Points, such as A, lying beneath the PPF, are points where inputs are used inefficiently: more of X *and* Y can be produced with the available inputs.

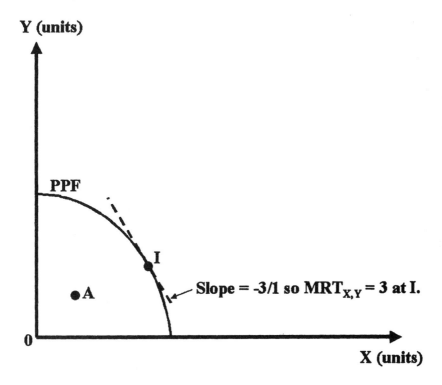

Figure 16.10

The production possibilities frontier is just another way of representing the input contract curve that we discussed in the previous section. Each point on the input contract curve determines a combination of outputs X and Y corresponding to the two isoquants that are tangent to each other at that point. That combination of X and Y is a point on the production possibilities frontier. This is not surprising. The input contract curve gives us the set of efficient combinations of inputs, while the production possibilities frontier shows the efficient combinations of outputs. Clearly, one cannot have an efficient combination of outputs if the inputs required to produce them are not, themselves, used efficiently.

The slope of the PPF gives the amount of Y that the economy must give up in order to gain one additional unit of X. This (negative of the) slope is called the **marginal rate of transformation of X for Y** or $MRT_{X,Y}$. In other words,

$$MRT_{X,Y} = -\Delta Y/\Delta X$$

For example, at point I, in Figure 16.10, the slope of the PPF is the slope of the tangent line, which is -3. Hence, the $MRT_{X,Y}$ at this point is 3: by sacrificing 3 units of Y, we can produce one more unit of X.

The $MRT_{X,Y}$ can be expressed in terms of the marginal cost of production of goods X and Y. Since we cannot increase our total resource use as we move from one point to the next along the PPF, we must have the value of resources used in any additional production of X (ΔX) exactly equal to the value of resources freed up when we reduce our production of Y (ΔY). If the cost of an increment of X is MC_X and the cost of an increment of Y is MC_Y, the following equation must hold along the PPF:

$$0 = MC_X(\Delta X) + MC_Y(\Delta Y)$$

Rearranging terms, we have:

$$-\Delta Y/\Delta X = MC_X/MC_Y$$

or:

$$MRT_{X,Y} = MC_X/MC_Y$$

Exercise 8: *The production possibility frontier for an economy is shown on the graph below. Which of the following is true about this production possibility frontier?*

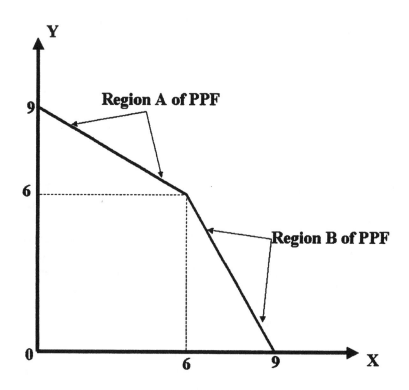

a. The $MRT_{X,Y}$ changes along the PPF.
b. The $MRT_{X,Y}$ is 1/2 for region A of the PPF and 2 for region B.
c. The $MRT_{X,Y}$ is 2 for region A of the PPF and 1/2 for region B.
d. The $MRT_{X,Y}$ is -1/2 for region A of the PPF and -2 for region B.

Substitution efficiency requires that:

$$MRT_{X,Y} = MRS^A_{X,Y} = MRS^B_{X,Y}$$

If it were not so, it would be possible to increase the well-being of all consumers by producing a different amount of goods X and Y. For example, suppose that $MRT_{X,Y} = 1$ and $MRS^A_{X,Y} = MRS^B_{X,Y} = 3$. In other words, consumers are willing to give up 3 units of X to get 1 unit of Y, whereas the producers require a reduction of only 1 unit of X to produce one more unit of Y. In this case, if firms were to reduce production of X by 1 unit and increase production of Y by 1 unit, all consumers would be better off (and firms would be no worse off). Such beneficial reallocations of production are feasible whenever the MRT differs from the common MRS of the consumers. Graphically, we can imagine indifference curves over the same two goods as those for which we have illustrated the PPF, increasing to the northeast in the usual way. The point that maximizes the well-being of consumers subject to the constraint that the total goods consumed be feasible to produce (i.e., lie on the PPF) is the point of tangency between the PPF and the highest possible indifference curve. At this tangency, the slope of the PPF is equal to the slope of the indifference curve (i.e., MRT = MRS). This is illustrated in Figure 16.11, below:

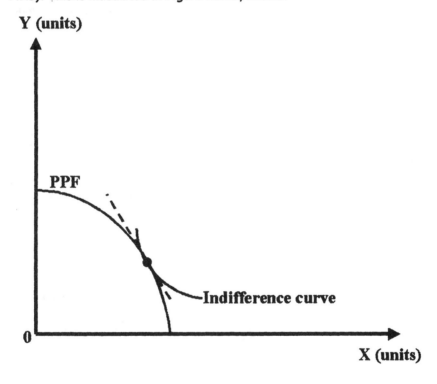

Figure 16.11

Do perfectly competitive markets ensure that substitution efficiency is achieved? Yes, for the following reasons:

1. All consumers maximize utility in the competitive equilibrium so that $MRS_{X,Y} = P_X/P_Y$.
2. Profit maximization in competitive equilibrium implies that $P_X = MC_X$ and $P_Y = MC_Y$.
3. Hence, $MRT_{X,Y} = MC_X/MC_Y = P_X/P_Y$.
4. Therefore, we have $MRS_{X,Y} = P_X/P_Y = MRT_{X,Y}$.
5. We can conclude, then, that MRS = MRT for all consumers and substitution efficiency is satisfied.

Exercise 9: *The three types of efficiency, taken together, show that the competitive (general) equilibrium is:*

a. desirable
b. equitable
c. a point at which no improvement in well-being is possible for any agent

The First and Second Fundamental Theorems of Welfare Economics

The **First Fundamental Theorem of Welfare Economics** states, in essence, that the competitive equilibrium satisfies all three types of efficiency. Formally, the theorem states:

> *The allocation of goods and inputs that arises in a general competitive equilibrium is economically efficient. That is, given the resources available to the economy, there is no other feasible allocation of goods and inputs that could simultaneously make all consumers better off.*

As we noted when we described the Edgeworth Box (see discussion of Figure 16.8), changing the endowment points changes the distribution of well-being across economic agents. In fact, we saw that any efficient point within the Edgeworth Box could be attained with the appropriate allocation of the endowments of agents. The **Second Fundamental Theorem of Welfare Economics** states this formally:

> *Any economically efficient allocation of goods and inputs can be attained as a general competitive equilibrium through a judicious allocation of the economy's scarce supplies of resources.*

Exercise 10: *Which of the following statements is true?*

a. The First Fundamental Theorem of Welfare Economics states that any competitive general equilibrium is economically efficient.
b. The First Fundamental Theorem of Welfare Economics implies that consumers need not know anything about the production of goods for efficiency to hold in competitive equilibrium.
c. The Second Fundamental Theorem of Welfare Economics implies that distributional issues can be separated from efficiency issues in the sense that endowments of goods can be redistributed to determine how much wealth agents have and then prices can be used to indicate relative scarcity.

Gains from Free Trade and Comparative Advantage

Suppose that two countries produce agricultural goods ("food") and manufactured goods ("machines"). These two countries' production possibility frontiers for food and machines are shown below in Figure 16.12:

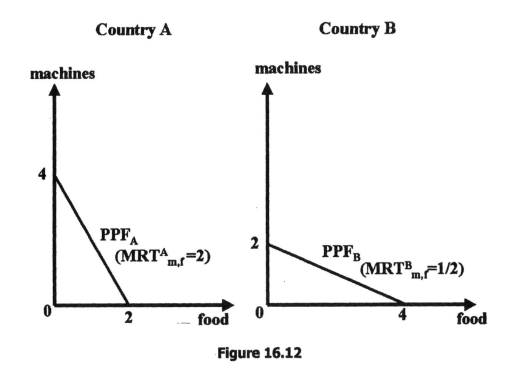

Figure 16.12

In Figure 16.12, Country A can produce an additional unit of machinery if it foregoes 1/2 unit of food, while Country B must forego 2 units of food in order to produce the additional unit of machinery. Country B can produce one more unit of food if it foregoes 1/2 unit of machinery, but Country A must forego 2 units of machinery in order to produce an additional unit of food. In this case, then, Country A has a **comparative advantage** over Country B in the production of machines while Country B has a comparative advantage over Country A in the production of food. This means that Country A has a lower opportunity cost of producing an additional unit of machinery (in terms of foregone units of food) than Country B. Similarly, Country B has a lower opportunity cost of producing an additional unit of food (in terms of foregone units of machinery) than Country A.

Exercise 11: *For the production possibility frontiers of the three individuals below, what can be said about the comparative advantage of each individual in the production of two goods, R and A?*

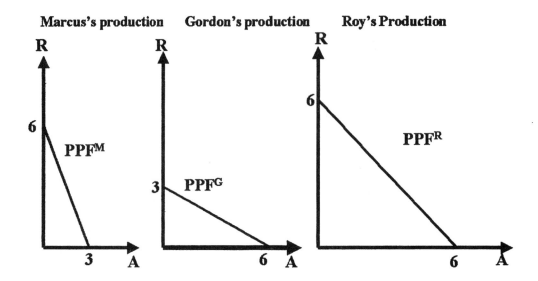

Marcus's production   Gordon's production   Roy's Production

a. Roy has no comparative advantage.
b. Gordon has a comparative advantage in production of A over Marcus.
c. Roy has a comparative advantage in the production of A over Marcus and Gordon.
d. Roy has a comparative advantage in the production of R over Gordon, but not over Marcus.

Suppose there is no trade between A and B. Each country, in competitive equilibrium, will produce at a point along its PPF where an indifference curve for a consumer in that country is tangent to the PPF for that same country. Consumers are limited to consuming what their own country can produce. This "autarky" equilibrium occurs at point A in Country A and at point B in Country B (see Figure 16.13, below). The relative price of food, P_F/P_M is 2 in A and ½ in B. Now, suppose that trade between A and B occurs. If the relative price of food falls between the autarky prices of 2 and ½, then each country will specialize in the production of the good for which it has a comparative advantage. In Figure 16.13, Country A produces at point C while Country B produces at point D. The budget constraint faced by A's consumers is now the line going through C with a slope equal to the international relative price of food (between ½ and 2). This budget constraint lies higher than the autarky equilibrium A, ensuring that A's consumers can now reach a higher level of utility. Similarly, B's budget constraint also lies higher than the autarky equilibrium B. In other words, by specializing, each country can now reach a point *outside* its individual PPF.

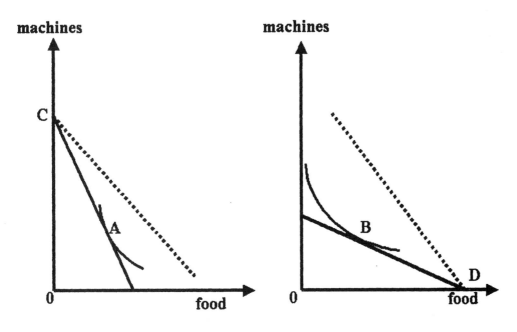

Figure 16.13

It is important to understand that the benefits of trade rely crucially on comparative advantage. It is the difference in marginal rates of transformation that allow the countries to do better by specializing in the good in which they have comparative advantage than by producing on their own. When the MRT's differ, the countries can increase the feasible set by allocating production to the "low opportunity cost" producer in the same way as the multi-plant monopolist of Chapter 11 improved its well-being by allocation production to the low cost plant.

In fact, there can be gains from trade even if one country has an **absolute advantage** over the other. A country has an absolute advantage over another country in the production of a good if production in the first country requires fewer units of a scarce input than it does in the second country. For example, in Figure 16.14, Country A has an absolute advantage in the production of both food and machinery over Country B since both the vertical and the horizontal intercept of PPF^A are greater than the intercept of PPF^B. There are, however, gains from trade as *each* country still has a *comparative* advantage in the production of a different good. If Country A specializes completely in the production of machinery and B specializes completely in the production of food, both countries can attain a point outside of their original production possibility frontiers. Hence, both have increased their feasible set, leaving the two jointly potentially better off than without trade.

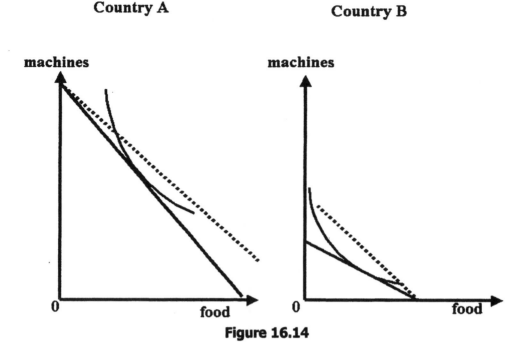

Figure 16.14

Exercise 12: *For the individuals in Exercise 11, which partners could gain from trade (compared to no trade at all)?*

a. All could gain from trading with each other.
b. Roy cannot gain from trading with either Marcus or Gordon.
c. Gordon and Marcus can gain from trade with each other, but not with Roy.

General Equilibrium Analysis with Many Markets

We are now ready to conduct a full general equilibrium analysis of many markets, including both input and output markets. This will allow us to derive an equilibrium for the entire economy, taking into account that opportunity cost comes from input market interactions and income is derived from supplying those inputs to the production process. In order for us to have equilibrium for all economic agents (producers and consumers), we need to have several conditions satisfied at the equilibrium prices and outputs for the economy:

1. The total demand for inputs must equal the total supply of inputs.
2. Firms must be maximizing profits at the equilibrium, given the price of scarce resources (such as labor input), the prices of goods, and the technology available in the economy.
3. Given the prices of goods and their income derived from the ownership of factors of production, consumers must be maximizing utility at the equilibrium (so that their individual demands for goods must be derived from utility maximization and based on the income they earn from supplying their labor).
4. The total demand for goods must equal the total supply of consumption goods.

First, we will describe the general equilibrium in a graph. Then we will derive a general equilibrium for an algebraic example.

We saw in our discussion of substitution efficiency that consumers' well-being is maximized at the point where the indifference curve for a typical consumer is just tangent to the feasible set of production possibilities for the economy, the PPF. Is this point also the bundle of goods that maximizes profits for firms? The answer is yes. The reason is that, if we imagine an *isoprofit* line, representing the profit level associated with various product mixes of goods that a typical firm could produce at given market prices, we would draw a sloped line, as in Figure 16.15 with profit increasing as output increases to the northeast. Each line represents a different profit level. For example, for profit level Π we have:

$$\Pi = P_X X + P_Y Y - C^*$$

where: C^* is the cost of production, and we will suppose that this is fixed whatever the optimal output mix (so that we just want to know how to *employ* the factors of production we have contracted, not change the amount of those factors).

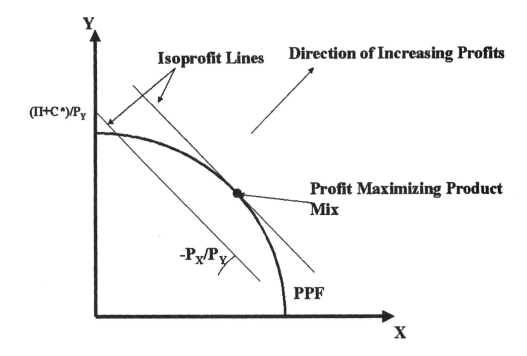

Figure 16.15

The slope of this line is $-P_X/P_Y$, so it is tangent to the PPF where the slope of the PPF $= -P_X/P_Y$. This is just the point that we derived for consumer utility maximization in Figure 16.11. Hence, the utility maximization point we derived before also corresponds to the product mix that satisfies profit maximization. This point represents, then, the aggregate demand over all consumers for the goods as well as the aggregate supply for all firms. In other words, this point (X^*, Y^* in Figure 16.16) determines the volume of goods X and Y available to be traded in the economy. We can think of this point, then, as determining the width and height of an Edgeworth Box. This is illustrated in Figure 16.16, below. Further, in equilibrium, the individual demand of each consumer for each good falls at a point within the Edgeworth Box that occurs on the contract curve. In other words, for our economy to be in equilibrium, there must be no trades that could occur and would make all agents better off. Finally, the equilibrium must be on the portion of the contract curve that lies within the "lens" formed by the incomes each consumer is endowed with due to his or her endowment of labor resources. This general equilibrium point is illustrated in Figure 16.16 as the point M* within the Edgeworth Box.

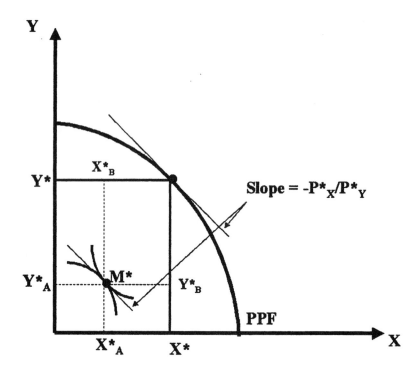

Figure 16.16

Let us re-analyze this general equilibrium with an algebraic example. Suppose that there are two goods, X and Y, which may be produced in the economy. There is only a single input, labor, that is used to produce these goods. The total amount of labor available is L*. This labor is supplied by two individuals, A and B, who also are the consumers in the economy. Each individual is endowed with an amount of labor, L^A or L^B, and the total available labor equals the sum of these two endowments so that $L^* = L^A + L^B$. The technology available to produce the goods is the following: the production function for good X is $X = L^{1/2}$ and the production function of good Y is $Y = L$. Finally, each consumer has a utility function $U = XY$, with marginal utilities $MU_X = Y$ and $MU_Y = X$. The only income available to consumers is derived from their labor income. Let the wage rate be $w = 1$. For all of the following, "*" will indicate the equilibrium.

1. Input Demand equals Input Supply and Deriving the PPF

   The *labor demand* functions of the two production processes can be obtained by inverting the two production functions so that the labor required to produce X, L^X, and the labor required to produce Y, L^Y, can be written as:

   $L^X = X^2$
   $L^Y = Y$

   We also know that the total labor demanded, $L^X + L^Y$, must not exceed total *labor supply*, L^*. Hence, we also have:

   $L^X + L^Y = L^*$

   Equating labor demand and labor supply, we have:

   $X^2 + Y = L^* \Leftrightarrow$

   $Y = L^* - X^2$

   This is the equation of the PPF: it gives the feasible trade-off between producing X and Y given the amount of the scarce resource available in the economy and the available technology.

2. Profit maximization (along the PPF)

   We saw that the point of profit maximization along the PPF occurs where the (negative of the) slope of the PPF (the MRT) equals the price ratio. Hence, the equilibrium prices must be such that MRT = P_X/P_Y.

   Since the MRT equals the (negative of the) slope of the PPF, it equals the slope of $Y = L^* - X^2$. The slope (change in Y over change in X) equals $-2X$. (This must be obtained using calculus for this example.) Hence, at the profit maximization point, we have:

   $2X^* = P^*_X/P^*_Y$

3. Utility Maximization

   Utility maximization along the PPF occurs where the slope of the indifference curve equals the price ratio so that $MRS_{X,Y} = P_X/P_Y$ must hold at point X^*,Y^*. For this utility function, the marginal rate of substitution is $MRS_{X,Y} = MU_X/MU_Y = Y/X$. Hence, we have:

   $Y^*/X^* = P^*_X/P^*_Y$

4. Aggregate Supply of Goods equals Aggregate Demand

   a. We are now ready to combine conditions derived in steps 1, 2, and 3 to derive X^* and Y^* in terms of the scarce input, labor, only. Using the conditions from steps 2 and 3 to obtain the point where MRT = MRS, we have:

$2X^* = Y^*/X^* \Leftrightarrow Y^* = 2X^{*2}$

Substituting for Y in the condition from step 1 (the equation of the PPF), we have:

$2X^{*2} = L^* - X^{*2} \Leftrightarrow X^* = (L^*/3)^{1/2}$
$Y^* = 2L^*/3$

These are the total volumes of X and Y traded in the economy (or the dimensions of the Edgeworth Box).

b. From utility maximization subject to the budget constraint for each consumer, we can obtain the individual demand functions for the two goods for each consumer. Note that individual demands for this type of utility function were derived in Chapter 5 and are:

$X^D = I/2P_X$
$Y^D = I/2P_Y$

where I is income. We know that, in this general equilibrium model, the income for each consumer is derived purely from wage earnings. Hence, the total income for the entire economy is wL^* so that the total market demand for X and Y are:

$X^D = wL^*/2P_X$
$Y^D = wL^*/2P_Y$

Recall, too, that $w = 1$ for this model. The total market demand for each good must equal the total supplied, X^*, Y^*. X^* and Y^* were derived in step 4a. Setting aggregate demand equal to aggregate supply we have, then:

$L^*/2P_X = (L^*/3)^{1/2} \Leftrightarrow P^*_X = (3L^*)^{1/2}/2$
$L^*/2P_Y = 2L^*/3 \quad \Leftrightarrow P^*_Y = 3/4$

These are the equilibrium prices.

c. If we wish to know the amount consumed by each individual, we must substitute these equilibrium prices back into our equations for individual demands. Recall that person A is endowed with L^A units of labor (so that wL^A is his income) and person B is endowed with L^B units of labor (so that wL^B is her income). Hence, each person's individual demand is:

$X^{*A} = L^A/2P^*_X$
$X^{*B} = L^B/2P^*_X$

$Y^{*A} = L^A/2P^*_Y$
$Y^{*B} = L^B/2P^*_Y$

In other words, we have derived equilibrium quantities and prices in terms of *only* the underlying scarce resource and technology at which (1) all agents maximize and

(2) all markets clear. This defines the general equilibrium for the economy. All three types of efficiency hold for this solution.

Walras' Law

In the above calculations, notice that one price was set to equal 1. For example, in the example of many markets, the wage rate was set to 1 but the prices of the goods were determined endogenously in the model. In our earlier analyses, (Exercises 5, 6, and 7), we also set one price equal to 1 each time. Now, try to solve Exercise 5 *without* setting one price equal to 1. (This is part of chapter review question 1, so you can refer to the answer to this question to help you solve.) You will find that you cannot obtain explicit values of prices as a solution: you can only solve for the *price ratio* that must hold in equilibrium, P^*_Y/P^*_X. In other words, our general equilibrium model only determines the relative prices of the goods and inputs, not the absolute level of these prices. This is an illustration of **Walras' Law**. By setting one price equal to 1 ($P_X = 1$ in Exercise 5), we essentially use that good (or input) as the "unit" in which the value of the other goods will be counted. We can then obtain an explicit solution for the other prices (i.e., for P_Y).

Chapter Review Questions

1. Re-work Exercise 5 of the summary without setting $P_X = 1$ so that it is determined endogenously. Show that you can only obtain a solution for the *relative* prices of the goods. (This is the calculation that supports the review of Walras' Law in the summary, above.)

Answer:

At the endowment point, person A has $25P_X + 75P_Y$ in income and Person B has $75P_X + 25P_Y$. Hence, the aggregate demand for X is $(25P_X + 75P_Y + 75P_X + 25P_Y)/2P_X = (100P_X + 100P_Y)/2P_X = 50 + 50P_Y/P_X$. Aggregate demand for Y is $(25P_X + 75P_Y + 75P_X + 25P_Y)/2P_Y = (100P_X + 100P_Y)/2P_Y = 50 + 50P_X/P_Y$. Hence, the equations for equilibrium are:

(1') $Y^A/X^A = Y^B/X^B = P_X/P_Y$

(2') $X^A + X^B = 100$
     $Y^A + Y^B = 100$

Or... $50 + 50P_Y/P_X = 100$
     $50 + 50P_X/P_Y = 100$

Since both aggregate demands equal 100, we have $50 + 50P_Y/P_X = 50 + 50P_X/P_Y$ or, canceling terms, $P_X/P_Y = P_Y/P_X$. Any P_Y and P_X that equal each other satisfy this equation and also satisfy (1'). Hence, P_Y cannot be assigned a single number unless we choose a value for P_X.

2. Let the markets for soy, corn, and peanut oil be described by the following equations for demand and supply:

$$Q_s^D = 3 - 2P_s + P_c + P_p \qquad Q_s^S = P_s$$
$$Q_c^D = 2 - 2P_c + P_s + P_p \qquad Q_c^S = P_c$$
$$Q_p^D = 1 - 2P_p + P_c + P_s \qquad Q_p^S = P_p$$

where: Q^D represents demand and Q^S represents supply. The subscripts s, c, and p refer to soy, corn, and peanut, respectively.

   a. Find the general equilibrium of this economy.

   b. Suppose that, because of new production techniques, the supply curve for soy oil shifts to:

   $$Q_s^S = 2P_s$$

   How does the new technique affect the general equilibrium of the economy?

   c. A $1 tax is imposed on the production of corn oil, so that the supply of corn oil is now:

   $$Q_c^S = P_c - 1$$

   How does the tax affect the general equilibrium of the economy?

Answer:

a. Setting the demand equal to the supply in each market, we have:

$$3 - 2P_s + P_c + P_p = P_s$$
$$2 - 2P_c + P_s + P_p = P_c$$
$$1 - 2P_p + P_s + P_c = P_p$$

or...

(1) $3 - 3P_s + P_c + P_p = 0$
(2) $2 - 3P_c + P_s + P_p = 0$
(3) $1 - 3P_p + P_s + P_c = 0$

Substituting from equation (1) into equation (3) and from equation (2) into equation (3), we have:

$$1 + P_s + P_c - 3(3P_s - 3 - P_c) = 0$$
$$1 + P_s + P_c - 3(3P_c - 2 - P_s) = 0$$

Solving these for P_s, we have $P_s = 9/4$. Hence, $P_c = 2$. Substituting these values back into equation (3), we have $P_p = 7/4$.

b. Our new set of equilibrium conditions for the economy is:

$3 - 2P_s + P_c + P_p = 2P_s$
$2 - 2P_c + P_s + P_p = P_c$
$1 - 2P_p + P_s + P_c = P_p$

Performing the same substitutions as before, we have:

$1 + P_s + P_c - 3(4P_s - P_c - 3) = 0$
$1 + P_s + P_c - 3(3P_c - P_s - 2) = 0$

Hence, $P_s = 3/2$; $P_c = 13/8$; $P_p = 11/8$

The new technique has caused all prices to fall in this economy, then, as the fall in the price of soy causes substitution away from corn and peanut oil. This shift in demand causes corn and peanut oil prices to fall as well.

c.

Now, the equilibrium in the economy can be represented as follows:

$3 - 2P_s + P_c + P_p = P_s$
$2 - 2P_c + P_s + P_p = P_c - 1$
$1 - 2P_p + P_s + P_c = P_p$

Performing the same substitutions as before, we have:

$1 + P_s + P_c - 3(3P_s - P_c - 3) = 0$
$1 + P_s + P_c - 3(3P_c - P_s - 3) = 0$

Hence, $P_s = 5/2$; $P_c = 5/2$; $P_p = 2$

The tax has caused the prices of all three oils to rise. As the price of corn oil rises because of the tax, demand shifts to peanut and soy oil, causing price to rise in these markets as well.

3. Can the utility possibilities frontier ever be upward sloping? Why?

Answer:

The utility possibilities frontier cannot slope upward for the same reason as the production possibilities frontier cannot slope upward: if it were so, then it would be possible to make all agents better off without making anyone worse off. Hence, we could not have been on the contract curve because, along the contract curve, we cannot shift out the utility of one individual without shifting back the utility of another.

Problem Set

1. Consider an economy where the only input is labor. Two goods can be produced. It takes 2 units of labor to produce each unit of food and 1 unit of

labor to produce each unit of manufactures. The country is endowed with 100 units of labor.

    a. What is the production possibilities frontier of the economy?

    b. Assume that all consumers have preferences represented by $U = \text{Min}(F,M)$, where F is the quantity of food consumed and M is the quantity of manufactures consumed. How much of each good will be produced? What is the relative price of food and manufactures?

    c. How does your answer to (b) change if preferences are represented by $U = FM^2$?

2. Consider the algebraic example given in the summary for equilibrium in many markets. Now a (binding) quota on the production of Y is imposed so that exactly $Y^{\#}$ units of Y must be produced in the economy. How does this policy affect the general equilibrium of the economy?

3. Firms may produce one of two products, X or Y. A firm that produces X with current technology has production function $X = 2(KL)^{1/2}$ with $MP_L = K^{1/2}L^{-1/2}$ and $MP_K = L^{1/2}K^{-1/2}$. A firm that produces Y with current technology has production function $Y = (KL)^{1/2}$ with $MP_L = .5K^{1/2}L^{-1/2}$ and $MP_K = .5K^{-1/2}L^{1/2}$. Currently, firms producing X are using 100 units of K and 100 units of L, while firms producing Y are using 300 units of K and 100 units of L. The firms currently are using all available labor and capital in the economy.

    a. Draw an Edgeworth Box that illustrates the current production of the firms.

    b. Is the current production point economically efficient? If not, identify the allocations that would allow both firms to increase output.

    c. Can the current production point be on the production possibilities frontier? Why or why not?

    d. Solve for the input contract curve for these firms.

4. The first welfare theorem of economics states that competitive equilibrium allocations are economically efficient. Under what conditions does this theorem hold? Give an example of an economy in which the first welfare theorem does not hold.

5. Suppose Country A and Country B both have 50 units of labor to devote to production of either food or manufactured goods. Country A can produce 10 units of food or 20 units of manufactured goods per day (or any linear combination thereof) with its 50 units of labor. Country B can produce 2 units of food or 1 unit of manufactured goods per day (or any combination thereof) with its 50 units of labor.

a. Sketch a production possibility frontier for each of the two countries. Does either country have a comparative advantage in the production of either good? Does either have an absolute advantage?

b. Should these two countries trade?

c. In an economy formed by 10 countries like Country A and 10 countries like Country B, what is the production possibility frontier for the entire economy?

d. Suppose that, due to population growth, Country A's level of labor increases to 100 units. What happens to Country A's production possibilities frontier?

6. Consider the following exchange economy. There are two goods, 1 and 2, and two individuals, A and B, with endowments and utility functions respectively as follows:

$$W^A = (2,1), \; w^B = (1,2), \; U^A = x^A_1 x^A_2 \text{ and } U^B = x^B_1 x^B_2.$$

Where x^i_j denotes the amount of good j (j=1,2) consumed by individual i (i = A,B) and W^i is the endowment of individual i. The marginal utilities of the goods for individual i are $MU^i_{x1} = x_2$ and $MU^i_{x2} = x_1$.

a. Draw the Edgeworth box for this economy, indicating the total dimensions, the endowment point and the indifference curves of the two individuals.

b. Find and explain the contract curve for this economy.

c. Find the competitive equilibrium price ratio and allocation, assuming that we hold $P_{x1} = 1$.

Exam *(60 minutes: Closed book, closed notes)*

1. Let the marginal cost of producing a unit of X be constant at $.50 and the marginal cost of producing a unit of Y be constant at $.25.

a. What is the slope of the production possibility frontier for this economy?

b. Let consumers purchase X and Y with a marginal rate of substitution between the goods of $MRS_{X,Y} = 1/2$ at the current levels of purchase. Does this economy satisfy substitution efficiency?

2. What do economists mean when they claim that perfectly competitive markets are "efficient"?

3. Country A wishes to maintain a consumption level of 50 units of food and 50 units of housing for its citizens. Country A currently can produce food and housing using its only input, labor, with production functions $F = 5L$ and $H = 2L$, where L is labor, F is food, and H is housing. Country A has 35 units of labor available.

    a. Must Country A fully employ its labor in order to reach its target consumption level?

    b. If Country B can also produce food and housing at rates $F = 2L$ and $H = 5L$ and wishes to maintain its citizens at the same consumption level as the citizens of Country A, must it fully employ its labor if it has 35 units of labor available?

    c. Suppose that Country A and Country B trade. Must they employ labor fully in order to reach their consumption targets?

    d. Suppose that Country A and Country B wish to double their level of consumption of both goods. Can they attain this level of consumption through trade alone?

4. The demand and supply for goods X and Y are as follows:

    $Q^D_X = 500 - 5P_X$ $Q^S_X = 200 + 4P_X - 2P_Y$
    $Q^D_Y = 400 - 2P_Y$ $Q^S_Y = 150 + 2P_Y - P_X$

    a. How does supply of X change when the price of Y changes? Can you think of a reason why this would be so?

    b. Solve for the general equilibrium outputs and prices of the goods.

Answers to Exercises

1. Statement (a) is correct. The new equilibrium prices are calculated by setting demand equal to supply in both markets simultaneously or:

    $12 - 2p_C + p_S = 6 + p_C$
    $6 - 4p_S + p_C = 4 + p_S$

    $\Leftrightarrow$

    $6 - 3p_C + p_S = 0$
    $2 - 5p_S + p_C = 0$

    Multiplying the second equation through by 3 and adding it to the first, we obtain:

    $12 - 14p_S = 0$ or $p^*_S = 6/7$.

Substituting this into the equilibrium condition for the soy market, we obtain $p^*_c = 16/7$.

Hence, both prices have fallen. Note that supply has shifted out, resulting in a lower price of corn. This causes consumers to transfer consumption into corn, lowering the price of soy. Hence, both prices fall. (c) is incorrect, then, because prices fall, not rise. (b) is incorrect because, while there is no linkage on the supply side, the change in corn price affects soy *demand*, changing the equilibrium price in that market.

2. The correct answer is (b). The allocation is not feasible because it requires 11 units of Y whereas the total available is only 10 units. The allocation of X is not problematic, as the total required units is 8 and the total available number of units is also 8.

3. The correct answer is (d). The allocation is not feasible, as it requires a greater amount of X than is available (X^A, measured from the lower left-hand corner, plus X^B, measured from the upper right-hand corner, sums to more than the total width of the box). The allocation also does not use all available units of Y as Y^A, measured from the lower left-hand corner, plus Y^B, measured from the upper right-hand corner, sums to less than the total height of the box. For the same allocation of X, it is possible to make both parties better off by allocating the remaining units of Y to the two parties.

4. The correct answer to the first part of the question is (d). By using the expressions for the marginal utilities in the exercise, we have $MRS^A_{X,Y} = MU^A_X/MU^A_Y = Y^A/X^A$. Similarly, $MRS^B_{X,Y} = MU^B_X/MU^B_Y = Y^B/X^B$. Hence, equations (1) and (2) can be written:

$$(1')\ Y^A/X^A = Y^B/X^B$$

$$(2')\ X^A + X^B = 100$$
$$Y^A + Y^B = 100$$

Combining these, we have

$$Y^A/X^A = (100-Y^A)/(100-X^A) \Leftrightarrow 100Y^A - X^AY^A = 100X^A - X^AY^A$$

$$\Leftrightarrow Y^A = X^A$$

Equivalently, we could have combined (1') and (2') in the following way:

$$Y^B/X^B = (100-Y^B)/(100-X^B) \Leftrightarrow Y^B = X^B$$

The correct answer to the second part of the question is (a). Graphically, both of these ways of writing the contract curve result in a straight line drawn from the lower left-hand corner to the upper right-hand corner of the Edgeworth Box. Hence, they represent the same contract curve and are both legitimate ways of expressing it.

5. The correct answers to the first part of the question are (b) and (d). At the endowment point, each individual has the value of his initial holdings of the goods. Hence, person A has a holding valued at $XP_X + YP_Y = 25P_X + 75P_Y = 25 + 75P_Y$, since $P_X = 1$. Similarly, person B has a holding valued at $XP_X + YP_Y = 75 + 25P_Y$.

   The correct answers to the second part of the question are (b) and (d). Using the incomes derived in the first part and the expressions for individual demand in the exercise, we have:

   $$X^A + X^B = (25 + 75P_Y + 75 + 25P_Y)/2P_X = (100 + 100P_Y)/2 = 50 + 50P_Y$$
   $$Y^A + Y^B = (25 + 75P_Y + 75 + 25P_Y)/2P_Y = (100 + 100P_Y/2P_Y = 50/P_Y + 50$$

   The correct answer to the third part of the question is (b). If $P_X = 1$, then we have equations for equilibrium:

   $$(1')\ Y^A/X^A = Y^B/X^B = 1/P_Y$$

   $$(2')\ X^A + X^B = 100$$
   $$Y^A + Y^B = 100$$

   From Exercise 4, we know that (1') and (2') imply that $X^A = Y^A$ and $X^B = Y^B$. Hence, we have $1/P_Y = 1$ so that $P^*_Y = 1$.

   The correct answers to the last part of the question are (a) and (b). The level of income at the equilibrium prices is $I^A = XP^*_X + YP^*_Y = 25 + 75 = 100$ so that the demand for X is $X^A = 100/2P_X = 50$. Similarly, we can derive the individual demands for Y^A, X^B, and Y^B as 50, each. At this level of demand $U^{*A} = X^A Y^A = 50(50) = 2500$. $U^{*B} = X^B Y^B = 50(50) = 2500$.

6. All the statements are correct. For the new endowment, $I^A = 10 + 10P_Y$ and $I^B = 90 + 90P_Y$. Aggregate demand is $X^A + X^B = (10 + 10P_Y + 90 + 90P_Y)/2 = 50 + 50P_Y$ and $Y^A + Y^B = (10 + 10P_Y + 90 + 90P_Y)/2P_Y = 50/P_Y + 50$. At $P_X = 1$, and knowing that $Y^A = X^A$, $Y^B = X^B$ and $Y^A/X^A = Y^B/X^B = 1/P_Y$, we have $P^*_Y = 1$. At this equilibrium price, we have $X^{*A} = I^A/2 = (10 + 10)/2 = 10$. $Y^{*A} = I^A/2 = (10+10)/2 = 10$. $X^{*B} = I^B/2 = (90+90)/2 = 90$. $Y^{*B} = I^B/2 = (90+90)/2 = 90$. Hence, $U^{*A} = X^{*A}Y^{*A} = 10(10) = 100$. $U^{*B} = X^{*B}Y^{*B} = 90(90) = 8100$. Comparing these to the levels in Exercise 5, we see that the utility of A has fallen and the utility of B has risen. Further, from the equilibrium demands of X and Y, we see that the change in endowment has changed the equilibrium point along the contract curve.

7. All the statements are correct. The isoquants for good Y are L shaped. The kink of the L is on a line of equation $K^Y = 2L^Y$ or, equivalently, $(100 - K^X) = 2(100 - L^X)$. The points of tangency between the two sets of isoquants must occur at that kink. Hence the equation of the input contract curve is $K^X = 2L^X - 100$ and (a) is correct. At the competitive equilibrium, the (negative of the) slope of both isoquants must be equal to $w/r = \frac{1}{2}$. The (negative of the) slope of X's isoquant

is MRTS = K^X/L^X. Therefore we have $2K^X = L^X$. We also know that the equilibrium must be at the kink of Y's isoquant so that $K^Y = 2L^Y$. Combining these two equations with $L^X + L^Y = 100$ and $K^X + K^Y = 100$ yields $L^X = 200/3$ and $K^X = 100/3$ so that $X = (20000/9)^{0.5} = (100/3)2^{0.5}$ and (b) is correct. Finally, for the allocation to be an equilibrium the demand for each factor of production must be equal to the supply of the corresponding input. So (c) is correct.

8. The correct answers are (a) and (b). The slope of the PPF in region A is $-3/6 = -1/2$. Hence, the $MRT_{X,Y}$ over this region is $1/2$. The slope of the PPF in region B is $-6/3 = -2$. Hence, the $MRT_{X,Y}$ over this region is 2.

9. None of the answers is correct. The three types of efficiency say that there is no way to make one agent better off without making another worse off, given the current state of technology, preferences of consumers, and endowments of resources. Whether this point is desirable or equitable depends, however, on a judgment over *distributions* of well-being across agents. Distributional issues go beyond efficiency questions and are not addressed by any of the three types of efficiency we have discussed. The final statement is incorrect: even if an allocation is economically efficient it is still possible to make *some* agent better off by making other agents worse off.

10. All three statements are correct. Indeed, one of the advantages of the competitive equilibrium is that the informational requirements are so low: efficiency is attained by the "invisible hand" of many decentralized market transactions, coordinated through the price mechanism.

11. Statements (b) and (d) are correct. The opportunity cost of producing a unit of A for Gordon is 1/2 unit of R, while the opportunity cost of 1 unit of A for Marcus is 2 units of R. Hence, (b) is correct. Roy's opportunity cost of producing 1 unit of R is 1 unit of A. Gordon's opportunity cost of producing 1 unit of R is 2 units of A. Hence, (d) is correct (and (a) is incorrect). Roy's opportunity cost of producing a unit of A is 1 unit of R. Hence, Roy has a comparative advantage over Marcus but not Gordon in the production of A. Therefore, (c) is incorrect.

12. Statement (a) is correct. Even though Roy has an absolute advantage over Marcus and Gordon, he can gain from trading with both. Conversely, both Marcus and Gordon can gain from trading with Roy (and with each other). For example, say Marcus and Gordon both specialize in their comparative advantage (A for Gordon and R for Marcus) while Roy produces R and A equally. The three can all reach points beyond their current production possibility frontier: Roy could have 4A and 3R, Marcus could have 3A and 3R, and Gordon could have 2A and 3R. If Marcus and Gordon trade with each other, they could each obtain 3A and 3R (again, beyond their existing PPF) by specializing completely.

Answers to Problem Set

1.

a. In order to produce as much output as possible, labor must be fully employed. The supply of labor is 100. As it takes 2 units of labor to produce each unit of food, the demand for labor coming from the food sector is $L^f = 2F$. Similarly, the demand of labor from the manufacturing sector is $L^m = M$. Setting labor supply equal to total labor demand we get $100 = 2F + M$. This is the PPF. It can be rewritten as $M = 100 - 2F$, showing that the PPF is a line with vertical intercept 100 and a slope of -2.

b. Consumers want to purchase equal quantities of the two goods (i.e., $F = M$). The point on the PPF where this is true is obtained by substituting $F = M$ in the equation of the PPF. This yields $100 = 2F + F$ so that $F = 100/3$ and $M = 100/3$. This corresponds to point E on the graph below. At point E the indifference curve is tangent to the PPF. For point E to be a competitive equilibrium, producers must want to produce this combination of output. If P^f/P^m is greater than 2, producers only want to produce M. If P^f/P^m is smaller than 2, producers only want to produce food. Hence point E can only be supported as a competitive equilibrium if $P^f/P^m = 2$, a relative price that makes producers indifferent between any point on the PPF.

manufactures

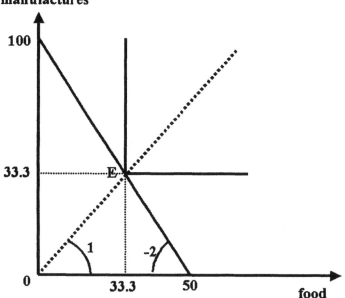

c. From Chapter 5 we know that, with this kind of preferences, consumers always want to consume positive amounts of the two goods. In equilibrium, then, producers must be willing to make both types of goods. From (b) we know that this implies $P^f/P^m = 2$. Let us set $P^m = 1$ so that $P^f = 2$. From Chapter 5 again, we know that the demand functions corresponding to these preferences are $F = I/3P^f$ and $M = 2I/3P^m$, where I is the level of consumers' income. Hence $F = I/6$ and $M = 2I/3$. I is simply the income that consumers get by selling their labor. Since firms make zero profits, total labor costs must be equal to the total value of production. At the equilibrium prices, the value of production is the same everywhere on the PPF (since producers are indifferent between all points on the PPF). In particular, it is equal to the value of the production when only M is produced (i.e., to 1 x 100 = 100). Inserting I = 100 into the consumer demands yields F = 100/6 and M = 200/3.

2.

Given that $Y = Y^\#$ and L is fixed at L^*, we must have $X^* + Y^\# = L^*$ from the labor market equilibrium condition. Hence, $X^* = L^* - Y^\#$. In other words, given the quota on Y, we trace over to the production possibility frontier to read off the maximum X we can produce given this level of Y. This gives us the "size" of the Edgeworth Box. The profit maximization condition does not hold as a tangency since the quota is binding (i.e., the firms do not *choose* to produce $Y^\#$). Consumers still maximize utility given these new outputs so that $Y^*/X^* = P_X^*/P_Y^*$ and aggregate demand is still derived from utility maximization. Hence, $X^D = L^*/2P_X$ and $Y^D = L^*/2P_Y$, as before. Setting aggregate demand equal to aggregate supply, we have $X^D = L^*/2P_X = L^* - Y^\#$ and $Y^D = L^*/2P_Y = Y^\#$ so that the new equilibrium prices are $P_X^* = L^*/2X^* = L^*/2(L^*-Y^\#)$. $P_Y^* = L^*/2Y^\#$. Notice that the equilibrium price of Y has risen and the equilibrium price of X has fallen because $Y^\#$ is less than the former ("unconstrained") equilibrium output since the quota is binding. X is correspondingly larger.

3.

a, b, and c.

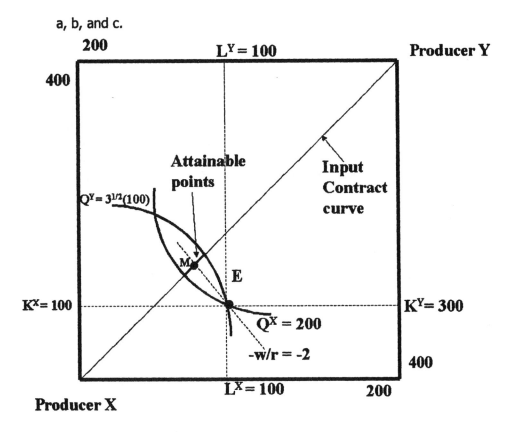

The endowment point is where firm X is using 100 units of labor and capital and firm Y is using 100 units of labor and 300 units of capital. At this point, the marginal rate of technical substitution of X is $MP_L^X/MP_K^X = K^X/L^X = 100/100 = 1$. The marginal rate of technical substitution of Y is $MP_L^Y/MP_K^Y = K^Y/L^Y = 300/100 = 3$. Hence, the isoquants do not have the same slope and the endowment point has intersecting isoquants running through it as shown above. At these levels of input usage, firm X is producing $Q^X = 2[100(100)]^{1/2} = 200$ and firm Y is producing $Q^Y = [300(100)]^{1/2} = 3^{1/2} \times 100$. The current level of production is not efficient, as the firms could each increase their well-being without decreasing the well-being of the other party. Graphically, there is a lens formed by the isoquants that pass through the endowment point. Any point within this lens represents an improvement for at least one firm. Similarly, since the endowment is not efficient, it cannot lie on the production possibilities frontier.

d. The equation of the input contract curve is the set of points for which the marginal rates of technical substitution are equal and for which the inputs used do not exceed the supply. Hence, we have $K^X/L^X = K^Y/L^Y$ (tangency condition) and $L^X + L^Y = 200$, $K^X + K^Y = 400$ (feasibility constraints). Substituting the feasibility constraints into the tangency condition, we have:

$$K^X/L^X = (400 - K^X)/(200 - L^X) \Leftrightarrow 200K^X - K^XL^X = 400L^X - K^XL^X \text{ or } K^X/L^X = 2.$$

The input contract curve is, then, a straight line with slope 2 running from the lower left-hand corner to the upper right-hand corner of the Edgeworth Box in the diagram above. The points on this curve attainable through exchange are those within the lens formed by the isoquants passing through the endowment point.

4. We have drawn our graphs in this chapter for the "standard" type of preferences. Indeed, the "standard" assumptions we have made throughout are sufficient to allow this theorem to hold. Recall that one of the standard assumptions in Chapter 3 was that preferences must be such that indifference curves are "thin". This stems from the assumption that more is better so that, for any point that we draw on an indifference map, a point – even one very close by – with more of either one of the goods and no less of the other must be strictly preferred. In fact, if indifference curves are "thick", the first welfare theorem would not hold. For example, in the graph, below, a competitive equilibrium allocation is dominated in terms of efficiency by any other allocation on A's "thick" indifference curve that puts individual B on a higher indifference curve.

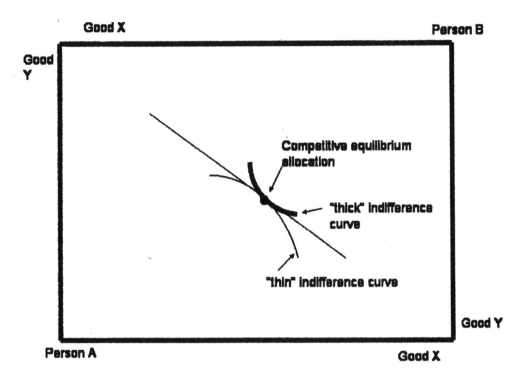

5.

    a. Country A has a comparative advantage in the production of the manufactured good, since its opportunity cost of 1 unit of manufactured good is 1/2 unit of food while the opportunity cost of Country B for each unit of manufactured good is 2 units of food. Conversely, Country B has a comparative advantage in the production of food since its opportunity cost per unit of food is 1/2 unit of manufactured goods while the opportunity cost of food in Country A is 2 units of manufactured goods. Country A has an absolute advantage over Country B, as it can produce more of both goods with the same resources.

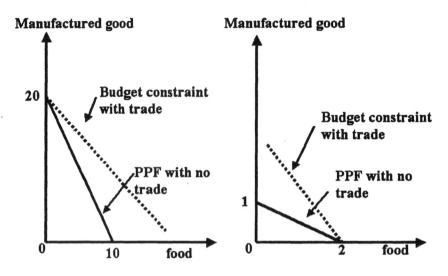

b. If the countries trade at prices such that they specialize according to their competitive advantages, they can attain points outside their original production possibility frontiers. An example point is shown in the graph above, where Country A specializes completely in the production of manufactured goods while Country B specializes completely in food.

c. The joint production possibility frontier of all the countries would look like the following. The two types of countries' production possibility frontiers are simply added up. The vertical intercept equals the production of the two types of countries if they both specialize completely in manufactured goods and the horizontal intercept equal to the production of the two types of countries if they specialize completely in the production of food.

Joint Production Possibility Frontier

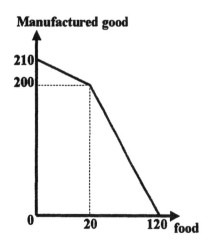

d. Country A's production possibilities frontier shifts out in a parallel way if the level of input rises and there is no change in technology. Since the size of the labor force has doubled and the production functions for both goods exhibit constant returns to scale, both the vertical and horizontal intercepts of the PPF have also doubled.

6.

a.

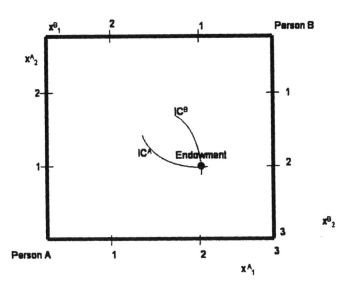

b. The equation of the contract curve is determined by the set of allocations where the marginal rates of substitution for the two individuals is equal and where all goods are allocated. In this case, we have three units of each good so that the three equations that must be satisfied are:

$$MRS^A_{x1,x2} = MRS^B_{x1,x2} \ ... \ or... \ x^A_2/x^A_1 = x^B_2/x^B_1$$
$$x^A_1 + x^B_1 = x_1 \qquad ... \ or... \ \ x^A_1 + x^B_1 = 3$$
$$x^A_2 + x^B_2 = x_2 \qquad ... \ or... \ \ x^A_2 + x^B_2 = 3$$

Combining these, we have $(3-x^A_2)/(3-x^A_1) = x^A_2/x^A_1$ ...or...
$x^A_1 = x^A_2$. Similarly, we have $x^B_1 = x^B_2$. These both represent straight lines in the Edgeworth box running from the lower left hand corner to the upper right hand corner.

c. We now require the ratio of the marginal utilities to equal the price ratio, P_{x1}/P_{x2}. Hence, we have that $x_1^A = x^A_2 = 1/P_{x2}$ or $P_{x2} = 1$. As each individual has an "income" of 3 that she must split equally between x_1 and x_2, we have that the exchange equilibrium has $x^i_1 = x^i_2 = 3/2$ for i =A,B. This point is right in the middle of the box, on the contract curve, and the indifference curves of the individuals just touch at this point.

Answers to Exam

1.

    a. The slope of the production possibility frontier is $-MC_X/MC_Y = -.5/.25 = -2$.

    b. The economy satisfies substitution efficiency if the marginal rate of transformation equals the marginal rate of substitution. Here, MRT = $MC_X/MC_Y = 2$, but $MRS_{X,Y} = 1/2$, so the two are not equal and the economy does not satisfy substitution efficiency.

2.   We have talked about efficiency mainly in two chapters: 10 and the current one, 16. In chapter 10, we defined economic efficiency as meaning that total surplus was maximized. In other words, every consumer who is willing to pay more than the opportunity cost of the resources needed to produce extra output is able to buy; every consumer who is not willing to pay the opportunity cost of the extra output does not buy. Another way of putting this is that all gains from trade are exhausted at the efficient point. We made a diagrammatic argument that the perfectly competitive equilibrium attains economic efficiency by arguing that the deadweight loss is zero at the perfectly competitive equilibrium. Deadweight loss is the reduction in net economic benefits resulting from an inefficient allocation of resources. The gist of the argument was that the perfectly competitive equilibrium point occurred at the intersection of supply and demand. Our optimization framework that generated the demand curve showed that demand measures the willingness to pay of consumers for a good. Our optimization framework for generating the supply curve showed that supply measures the opportunity cost of resources to produce extra output. Hence, the competitive equilibrium allows every consumer to buy when the willingness to pay (the vertical height of demand) exceeds or equals the opportunity cost of resources (the vertical height of supply) and does not induce anyone to buy for whom the willingness to pay is less than the opportunity cost of resources. In fact, chapter 10 explored a series of policies that changed output from the competitive equilibrium and showed that total surplus fell in each case, even though particular groups (such as consumers or producers) might gain from such a change.

We have revisited the issue of efficiency in this chapter and have gone into somewhat more detail of what efficiency can be taken to mean, as well as justifying why the definition in the previous paragraph is appropriate. We defined an economic situation as efficient if there is no way to make any person better off without hurting somebody else. When consumers only buy if their willingness to pay exceeds the opportunity cost of resources, then we are, in effect, in precisely the case where no one could be made better off without making someone else worse off. Consider the alternative of consumers buying when they are not willing to pay as much as the opportunity cost. Hence, consumption at a price that covers the opportunity cost actually makes consumers worse off! By reducing consumption and reallocating resources away from the product, we would increase the overall well-being of agents. As an aside, recall that in Chapter 14's problem 5 we used this concept of efficiency to argue that one equilibrium in a game was more compelling than another.

In this present chapter, we have obtained the results that a perfectly competitive market produces an efficient amount of output (production efficiency) and a competitive market allocates goods in a way that is efficient (allocative efficiency) because it equalizes the marginal rates of substitution across consumers. We obtained these results in a stronger framework than in chapter 10 because we obtained them when allowing the income and costs of goods as endogenous (rather than exogenous, as they were in chapter 10). As you will note from this chapter's treatment, our results on allocative efficiency were derived from an Edgeworth Box analysis, where we showed that agents in a competitive (exchange) economy would trade to an efficient point. We augmented our earlier analysis of productive efficiency to include the fact that not only would productive efficiency be achieved in each market, but the product mix across markets would be efficient. We showed this by using a production possibility frontier to show that profit maximization would achieve such an efficient product mix. We put all the types of efficiency together in a complete general equilibrium analysis of a simple economy, showing that there was efficiency in exchange (the agents were on the contract curve), efficiency in the use of inputs (the firms produced on the production possibility frontier) and there was efficiency in the product mix (the equilibrium was a tangency point with the production possibility frontier.

3.

    a. In order to reach its targets with its technology, Country A must employ 10 units of labor in making food and 25 units of labor in making housing. This totals to 35 units of labor, which is all that Country A has.

    b. Similarly, Country B must employ 10 units of labor making housing and 25 units of labor making food to reach its targets. Hence, it must fully employ its labor as well.

    c. If A specializes in food, it must only employ 25 units to produce enough food for both countries. If B specializes in housing, it must employ only 25 units to produce enough housing for both countries. Hence, both countries can reach their targets with 10 units of labor unused.

    d. No. By fully specializing in the good in which the country has a comparative advantage, we can attain at most 5(35) = 175 units of food from Country A and 5(35) = 175 units of housing from Country B. Hence, by trading alone, we cannot attain a total consumption of 100 units of food and housing in the two countries.

4.

    a. As the price of Y increases, the supply of X falls. This might be because some producers can shift their capacity into the production of the more valuable good. For example, if a farmer can plant his field with either wheat or corn, then if the price of corn rises, we would expect acreage of corn to increase and acreage of wheat to decrease.

    b. Setting demand equal to supply in both markets, we have:

$$500 - 5P_X = 200 + 4P_X - 2P_Y$$
$$400 - 2P_Y = 150 + 2P_Y - P_X$$

or...

$$300 - 9P_X + 2P_Y = 0$$
$$250 + P_X - 4P_Y = 0$$

multiplying the first equation by two and adding the two together we have:

$$850 - 17P_X = 0 \text{ ... or... } P^*_X = 50$$

Substituting into the equations of supply (or demand) we have, then,

$$P^*_Y = 75$$

And using these prices in either supply or demand we obtain:

$$Q^*_X = 250; Q^*_Y = 250$$

Chapter 17: Externalities and Public Goods

In Chapters 10 and 16, we argued that a competitive market, left on its own, would allocate resources in a Pareto optimal way. In this chapter, we study conditions under which competitive markets may *not* allocate resources efficiently, making the argument for intervention stronger than it was in Chapters 10 and 16. The first case we examine is that of markets with externalities. An **externality** arises when the actions of any consumer or producer affect the costs or benefits of other consumers or producers in some way that is not transmitted by market prices. An externality is positive if it helps other producers or consumers; it is negative if it hurts others. The bandwagon effect of Chapter 5 is an example of a positive externality, the snob effect of Chapter 5 is an example of a negative externality. The second case we examine is that of public good markets. A **public good** has two characteristics: (1) the consumption of the good by one person does not reduce the quantity that can be consumed by others, and (2) a consumer cannot be excluded from consuming the good. An air defense system for a country is an example of a public good: if one person is effectively protected, then all the people in that person's geographic area also must be protected, however numerous they are.

Negative Externalities

Suppose that a firm (a paper mill) produces a negative externality (water pollution) when it manufactures a good (paper). For example, for each unit of paper produced, let the firm produce a unit of pollution and dump it in the nearby river. If this market is organized competitively, it will not generate an efficient amount of paper or pollution. The reason is that, if the paper mill does not have to pay for the pollution, it will base its production decisions on a cost of production that is *too low* from society's point of view. The paper mill will only take into account the costs that it bears. These include the opportunity cost of labor, capital, materials, and any other inputs that it must use but *it will not include the opportunity cost of the river:* from the firm's point of view the river has a value of zero in its best alternative use. From the point of view of society, however, polluting the river decreases its value for other uses, such as fishing. Hence, the social cost of paper production is higher since it includes the cost of the other uses of the river that are sacrificed when paper production takes place. Because the private cost of paper production is lower than the social cost, too much paper (and pollution) gets produced in the competitive equilibrium.

Graphically, the marginal social cost, MSC, lies above the marginal private cost, MPC when the marginal external cost of the pollutant, MEC, is positive. This is shown in Figure 17.1, below. Now, recall from Chapter 9 that the MPC curve is also the supply curve for the perfectly competitive industry. The market equilibrium will be at the point where the market supply curve intersects demand, at e_1. The social optimum occurs at the point where the only units produced are those for which the valuation of consumers (the demand curve) lies above the marginal social cost of the resources that go into production (the marginal social cost curve). This is at point e_0. Hence, the market equilibrium results in overproduction of amount $Q_1 - Q_0$. It results in a deadweight loss because, for all units between Q_0 and Q_1, the marginal social cost exceeds the willingness to pay (the demand curve).

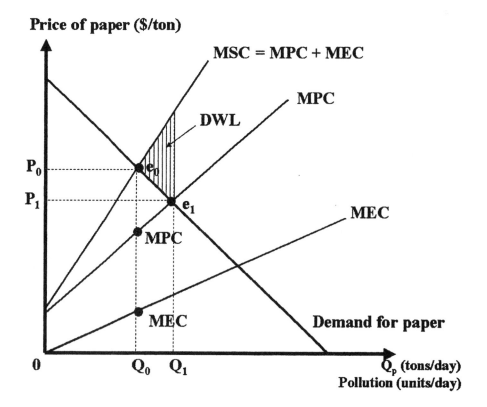

Figure 17.1

Exercise 1: *Define the net social benefit of production as the consumer surplus plus the private producer surplus minus the externality cost of production. (Consumer surplus and private producer surplus are measured gross of the externality cost.) Which of the following statements is correct about Figure 17.1?*

a. The Net Social Benefit at the market equilibrium is the area above the MSC curve and below demand up to output level Q_1 *minus* the deadweight loss.
b. The Net Social Benefit at the social optimum is the area above the MSC curve and below demand up to output level Q_0.
c. The Net Social Benefit at the market equilibrium is the area above the MPC curve and below demand up to output level Q_1.

In order to eliminate this inefficiency, the government has several options. First, it can impose a quota, or limit, on production called an **emissions standard**. For example, it can require that the industry produce no more than Q_0 units of paper (and pollution) in order to attain the social optimum of e_0. Unfortunately, the information requirements for such a quota are very high: the government must know demand, the marginal private cost, and the marginal externality cost of production in this market in order to compute Q_0 accurately.

A second option is to impose a tax on the firm's output or on the quantity of emissions. The term that refers to a tax imposed on pollutants is called an **emissions fee**. If the tax is a fixed amount per unit, T, imposed on firms, then it has the effect of shifting up the MPC curve by the amount of the tax. By choosing such a specific tax, $T, to be the vertical distance between the MPC and MSC curve at the output level Q_0, the new equilibrium can be shifted to exactly point e_0. This is illustrated below in Figure 17.2.

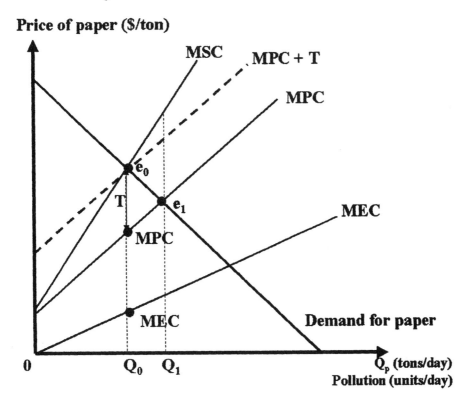

Price of paper ($/ton)

Figure 17.2

Exercise 2: *Suppose that a tax, T, is imposed as in Figure 17.2. Which of the following statements is true about the new equilibrium?*

   a. Private producer surplus falls compared to the market equilibrium, e_1.
   b. Consumer surplus falls compared to the market equilibrium, e_1.
   c. All economic agents can be made better off with the tax than they were at the market equilibrium by imposing the appropriate set of transfers among agents.

Alternatively, a tax, t(Q), which varies with the quantity produced, may be applied. If such a tax equals precisely the vertical distance between MPC and MSC at each output level, then the MPC curve is shifted up to precisely the MSC curve. Under this solution, as well, the social optimum e_0 is attained. This type of tax is illustrated in Figure 17.3, below.

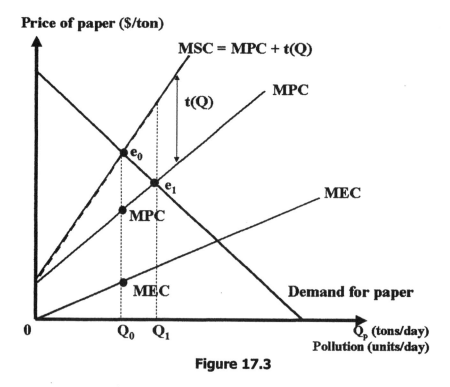

Figure 17.3

Both types of tax require detailed information on the MPC and the MEC. The first type of tax requires this knowledge only at the social optimum, e_0, since the size of the tax is determined by the distance between MSC and MPC at this point only. The tax that varies with quantity requires information on MPC and MEC at all levels of output if it is to truly reflect the MSC, as in Figure 17.3.

While the examples used so far refer to negative externalities that occur with production, we can also have cases where negative externalities occur with use of a facility (consumption). For example, commuters using their cars contribute to air pollution and consumers buying extravagantly-packaged items contribute to the congestion of landfills. The analysis of such consumption-related externalities is exactly the same as for production-related externalities.

A special case of negative externality arises from the use **common property**. A common property is a resource to which all (or, at least, many) people have free access. Consider a lake in a public park that can be used for fishing. Anyone can fish at the lake, and no one has property rights on any one fish until it is caught. One could imagine that, when very few people fish from the lake, the presence of others does not diminish the chances that any one fisherman catches a fish (now or in the future). As the number of fishermen grows, however, they deplete the number of fish in the lake so that it is harder to catch a fish today (and tomorrow). When deciding whether or not to fish, each fisherman takes into account his own cost and benefit from fishing, but not the cost that he imposes on others by reducing their chances of landing a fish. This last effect can be interpreted as an added "social cost" of fishing: as the number of fish in the lake decreases, each fisherman must spend more time to hook a fish. Hence, when fishing exceeds some minimum level, a negative "congestion" externality sets in. This situation is illustrated in Figure 17.4. The "congestion" externality is represented as a MEC curve that is zero for low usage levels, but non-zero after some minimum, Q*, is exceeded. Hence, the MSC curve ("the marginal cost of using the facility") exceeds the MPC curve for usage exceeding Q*.

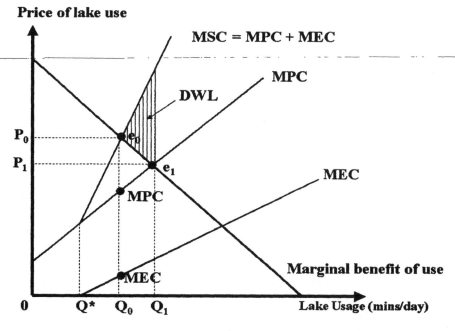

Figure 17.4

Suppose that we measure the marginal benefit from lake usage as a decreasing curve. In other words, an additional unit of "use" of the lake has less benefit than the first unit of usage. This marginal benefit curve reflects the demand, or the willingness to pay, for fishing. In the absence of any intervention, the private market will result in an equilibrium level of usage where the private marginal cost of using the lake equals the private marginal benefit from using the facility. This occurs at e_1. This results in a deadweight loss, however, as the social marginal cost exceeds the marginal cost so that, for all usage levels between Q_0 and Q_1, the marginal social cost exceeds the marginal benefit of using the lake. This can be corrected by imposing a usage fee (or a toll) for using the lake. A usage fee set at the vertical distance between MSC and MPC at the optimum, Q_0, would result in the socially optimal use of the lake. Alternatively, the government could restrict access to the common property (on, for example, a first-come-first-serve basis) in order to limit usage to a total of Q_0. This is sometimes imposed by issuing licenses (for fishing, in our example).

Exercise 3: *Parking at the University of Flatland is priced using a fixed, yearly fee with no additional fee for using the parking lot at particular times of day or particular days of the week. In fact, on Wednesdays the parking lots exhibit a great deal of congestion, forcing people to spend significant time looking for a spot or leading them to park (illegally) on sports fields, which causes significant damage. Which of the following statements is correct?*

a. The parking lots exhibit a "common property problem". The people using the parking lots do not internalize the external cost their usage imposes on others (in terms of making others take the bus).

b. The parking lots do not exhibit a "common property problem". A fee is charged to use the lot, making it possible to limit the number of users. This means that the parking lots are not common property and so cannot have a "common property problem".
c. Raising the fee sufficiently should resolve any congestion problems.
d. Raising the fee will not solve the congestion problems.

Positive Externalities

When one person becomes vaccinated against a communicable disease, she creates a positive externality because she reduces both her own chance of catching the disease and the chance that any other person catches the disease as well. We could conduct a graphical analysis to compare the market's production of goods that are associated with positive externalities (or the market's usage of a resource that is associated with positive externalities) in the same way as we have just done with negative externalities. When an individual consumer decides whether to obtain a new vaccine, for example, she takes into account her own benefit but not the benefit she imparts to others. Hence, the marginal social benefit (MSB) exceeds the marginal private benefit (MPB) of consuming the vaccine by the marginal externality benefit of MEB. We could depict this as shown in Figure 17.5 as the vertical distance between the MSB and the MPB curves, if the marginal benefit of consuming additional units falls for both MSB and MPB. The supply of vaccines can be represented by the increasing curve, reflecting the marginal cost of provision of the vaccine. Hence, the social optimum occurs at the intersection of this marginal cost curve with the MSB curve, e_0, and the market optimum occurs at the intersection of the marginal cost curve with the MPB curve, e_1. In other words, the market equilibrium results in excessively low use of the vaccine so that a deadweight loss occurs from underproduction.

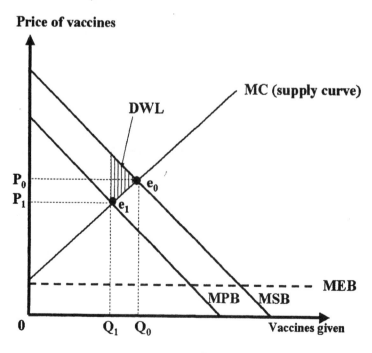

Figure 17.5

A subsidy to the production (or the consumption) of vaccines could eliminate this deadweight loss by shifting down the marginal cost curve so that it intersects the MPB curve precisely at Q_0. This is shown in Figure 17.6, below, as equilibrium e_2 for a fixed subsidy of $S.

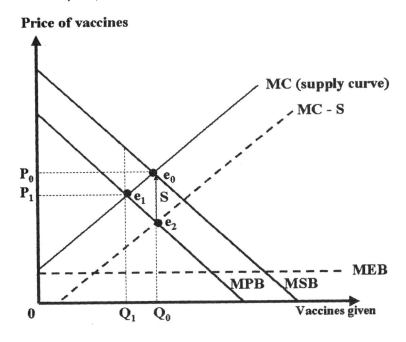

Figure 17.6

Exercise 4: *Are the externalities positive or negative for the following cases?*

    a. Wind chimes that are audible from several different houses.
    b. Smoking in a restaurant.
    c. Using bleach to clean a hospital ward.

The Coase Theorem

    We have discussed fees and quotas as means of correcting for the effect of externalities. Another means is assigning a **property right**, that is, the exclusive control over the use of an asset or resource, without interference by others. The **Coase Theorem** states that, regardless of how property rights are assigned with an externality, the allocation of resources will be efficient when the parties can bargain costlessly with each other. Put differently, the Coase Theorem states that the social optimum can result from bargaining between the parties producing and receiving an externality if property rights are clearly defined. Consider our original example of the paper mill and the fishermen. We can interpret this example as saying that the market does not attain the social optimum because there are no property rights assigned on the river: it costs nothing for the paper mill to use to dump effluent and, similarly, it costs nothing for the fishermen to use to fish. On the other hand, if the fishermen have the property rights to the river ("they own the river"), then they can force the paper mill not to dump. Of course, the paper mill can offer to compensate the fishermen for the damage they suffer as a result of the water pollution. If this compensation is sufficient to outweigh the damages, then the fishermen may very well allow the paper mill to pollute, and pocket the compensation. In other words, the property rights force the paper mill to take into account the opportunity cost of the river (the lost ability to fish in the river) in its private cost calculations. This makes the marginal private cost coincide with the marginal social cost and so restores optimality.

What is surprising is that efficiency is attained regardless of how the property rights are allocated. This can be seen from Figure 17.7, which shows the marginal benefit that the paper mill gets out of using the river as a dump (MBP) as well as the marginal benefit that fishermen obtain from fishing in the river (MBF). The horizontal axis shows the amount of river pollution. Consider the case where the paper mill has the right to the river. One might think that the firm would end up polluting the river completely since it does not bear any cost from this pollution. However, pollution does have an opportunity cost for the firm: the money that fishermen are willing to pay to induce the firm to pollute less. It is, therefore, in the paper mill's interest to stop polluting at the point where its marginal benefit from pollution is lower than the fishermen's willingness to pay to avoid more pollution. This corresponds to point E on the graph. Consider now the case where fishermen have property rights to the river. The opportunity cost of having crystal-clear water is the price that the paper mill is willing to pay in order to dump a moderate amount of discharge in the river. It is, therefore, in the fishermen's interests to let the mill pollute up to P* (i.e., up to the point where the mill's willingness to pay for polluting is just equal to the fishermen's disutility from further pollution). In other words, the resource of the river will be allocated through trade to the party that values it more highly no matter whether the fishermen or the mill receives the initial property rights on the river. Of course, the division of surplus may vary depending on which party receives the property rights, but total surplus will be maximized and will be the same under the two alternative property rights allocations.

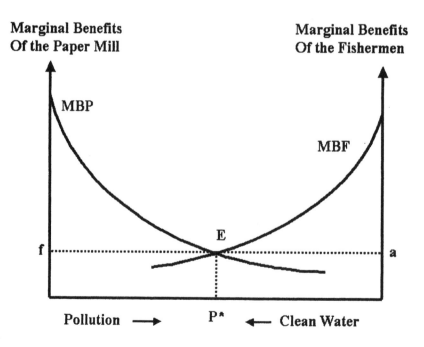

Figure 17.7

The Coase Theorem relies on the assumption that bargaining is costless. If the bargaining process itself is costly enough, then the parties may not find it worthwhile to negotiate to allocate the resource to the party that values it most highly.

Exercise 5: *Nighttime landings at the Boomtown Airport cause residents to lose sleep and have reduced milk production at the local farms by creating stress for the cows. Which of the following would best solve this problem?*

   a. Tax nighttime landings at \$T per landing.
   b. Shut down the airport at night.
   c. Set a limit on nighttime landings.
   d. Give Boomtown residents the right to determine the number of allowable nighttime landings.

Public Goods

Public goods have two characteristics: they are nonrival and nonexclusive. **Nonrival goods** are those for which consumption by one person does not reduce the quantity that can be consumed by others. Public broadcasting is an example of such a good, since the fact that one person views or listens to a broadcast does not prevent another person from doing so. A concert is another example of a nonrival good, as many people (up to a point at least) can listen to the concert at the same time. In contrast, an apple is a **rival good**, since consumption of the apple by one person prevents any other person from consuming the same apple. A **nonexclusive good** is one that is accessible to all consumers once it has been produced. For example, public highways and public parks are nonexclusive goods. An exclusive good is one to which consumers may be denied access. Cable television is an example of an exclusive good, as only consumers who obtain permission from the cable television provider have access to viewing cable programming. Any combination of rivalry and exclusivity is possible. Examples of these different possibilities are shown Table 17.1.

Goods with...	**Rivalry**	**No rivalry**
Exclusion	Apples Clothing	Cable television Club facilities
No Exclusion	Use of public resources that are depletable (public games parks, public universities...)	Public defense Public Broadcasting Air

Table 17.1

The bottom right-hand box of the table represents (pure) public goods.

Exercise 6: *Which of the following statements is true?*

a. A public university campus is a nonrival good and an exclusive good.
b. A private university campus is a nonrival good and an exclusive good.
c. Public police protection is a nonrival and a nonexclusive service.
d. A security guard hired to protect a single store at a mall (and stationed inside the store) is a rival and exclusive service.

Public goods may be undersupplied in the market. The argument is the following. To maximize total surplus, the public good should be produced up to the point where the marginal (social) benefit of an additional unit is at least as great as the marginal (social) cost of that unit. The marginal cost of a public good is the opportunity cost of the resources used to produce the good. This is represented as MC in Figure 17.7, below. The marginal benefit is the sum of the benefits of every person who values the additional unit. For example, suppose that there are two "consumers" who may benefit from police protection. The marginal benefit of the good for consumer 1 is labeled MB_1 in Figure 17.8, and the marginal benefit of the good for consumer 2 is labeled MB_2. The vertical sum of these curves gives the marginal social benefit, MSB. In other words, since the good is nonexclusive, both consumers will have access to each unit produced and will derive benefits according to their MB curve from those units. The efficient level of production for the public good is the level at which the MSB curve intersects the MC curve, at e_0.

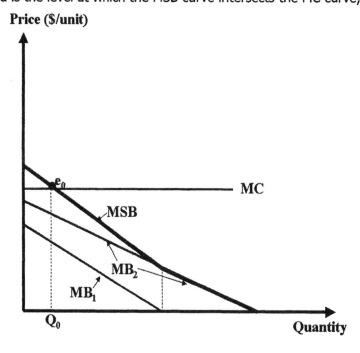

Figure 17.8

Attaining the socially efficient level of provision of the public good may be difficult, however, because public goods are nonexclusive. Consequently, individuals have no incentive to pay for the good if others contribute sufficiently to induce its provision. An individual who benefits from the good without paying is called a **free rider.** If individuals cannot be forced to pay for the public good, they would be expected to attempt to free ride, benefiting from the provision of the good without paying for it. For example, suppose that, as in Figure 17.9, the marginal cost of the public good intersects the marginal benefit curve of consumer 2, but not consumer 1. Even if consumer 1 declines to pay for the service, consumer 2 will still find it privately optimal to pay for Q* units to be provided. At this level of provision, however, consumer 1 also enjoys a benefit from these units, as the marginal benefit is positive over this range of provision. Hence, consumer 1 can free ride on consumer 2's demand for the good. The level of provision is far below the social optimum of e_0, however.

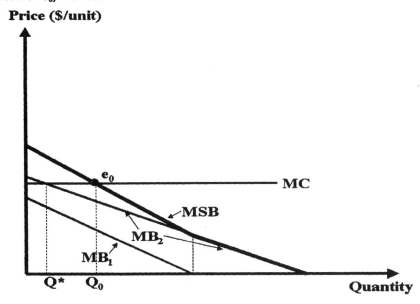

Figure 17.9

In order to avoid the free-rider problem and the consequent under provision of the public good, various measures can be undertaken. First, all persons who would potentially benefit from the good can be compelled to pay an amount such that the socially optimal quantity is produced. Second, the government can subsidize production of the good, shifting the marginal cost of production to the point that efficient provision will occur. The government can also undertake provision of the good itself. Both of these remedies rely on a government's ability to coerce (to extract payment or to raise taxes to finance the subsidy).

Exercise 7: *For which of the following marginal cost curves is there a potential free-rider problem that would reduce the provision of a public good below the social optimum?*

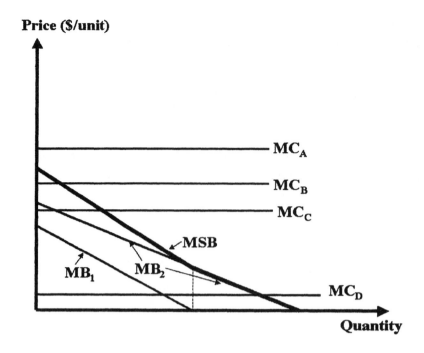

a. All marginal cost curves.
b. Only MC_B and MC_C.
c. MC_B, MC_C and MC_D.

Chapter Review Questions

1. Let the inverse market demand for paper be $P = 120 - Q$, where P is the price of paper and Q is the market output of paper. The industry inverse supply curve of paper is $P = 2Q$. The industry emits one unit of pollution for each unit of paper produced, with a marginal external cost of pollution equal to $MEC = Q$.

   a. What is the market equilibrium price and output of paper? What is the socially optimal price and output of paper for this industry? What is the deadweight loss at the market equilibrium?

   b. What is the level of specific tax, T, imposed on producers, that would make this market attain the social optimum?

   c. What is the quantity tax, $t(Q)$, imposed on producers, that would make this market attain the social optimum? What is the industry emissions standard that attains the same outcome as the optimal quantity tax?

Answer:

a.

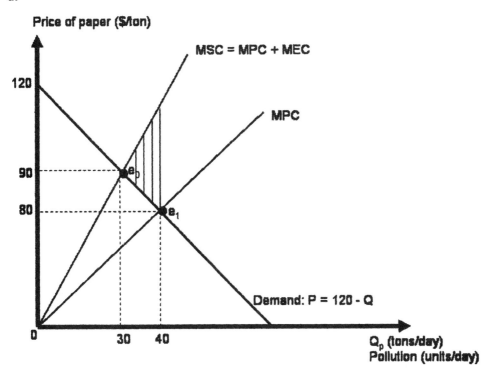

Price of paper ($/ton)

MSC = MPC + MEC

MPC

Demand: P = 120 - Q

Q_p (tons/day)
Pollution (units/day)

The market equilibrium occurs where the MPC curve intersects the demand curve or where $2Q = 120 - Q$ so that $Q_1 = 40$ and $P_1 = 80$. The social optimum occurs where the vertical sum of the MPC and MEC curves (the MSC curve) intersects demand or where $2Q + Q = 120 - Q$ so that $Q_0 = 30$ and $P_0 = 90$. The deadweight loss is, then, the area of the shaded triangle in the figure. The level of MSC for an output level of $Q = 40$ is 120 because the equation of MSC is $MSC = 2Q + Q = 3Q$, so that the height of MSC at $Q = 40$ is $MSC = 120$. Hence, the area of the deadweight loss triangle equals $(40-30) \times (120-80) \times (1/2) = 200$.

b. The specific tax, T, that would result in the market's attaining the social optimum is the vertical distance between MSC and MPC at the social optimum of $Q_0 = 30$. Since MPC at $Q = 30$ is $MPC = 2Q = 60$ and the MSC at $Q = 30$ is $MSC = 3Q = 90$, we have $T = 30$. We can verify that this level of tax does, indeed, result in the social optimum by equating MPC+T to inverse demand and working out the equilibrium price and output. For $T = 30$, we have $MPC+T = 30+2Q = 120-Q = P$ or $Q = 30$. This is the same as the social optimum of part (a).

c. The quantity tax, $t(Q)$ that results in the social optimum is $t(Q) = Q$ since, when this tax is added to MPC we have $MPC + t(Q) = 2Q + Q = MSC$. Hence, the tax makes the private and the social marginal costs of production identical so that the market attains the social optimum. The emissions standard that attains the social optimum is $Q = 30$, as this is the level that maximizes net social benefits (consumer surplus plus producer surplus net of the externality cost).

2. A firm that produces honey from bees is located next to a firm that produces apples from an apple orchard. The orchard requires pollination of the trees by bees in order to produce apples. Currently, the bees are allowed to collect pollen from any source, including the apple trees, at no fee. This leaves some of the trees unpollinated, however, imposing a loss on the apple grower. This could be corrected by increasing the number of hives in the beekeeper's operation. On the other hand, the honey firm recognizes that the apple blossoms make their honey very tasty, giving them an edge on their competition.

   a. What are the externalities present in this problem?

   b. Is there an argument, based on externalities, for merging the operations of these two separate firms?

   c. After the merger, is there an externality?

   d. Relate this discussion to the Coase Theorem.

Answer:

   a. The bees exert a positive externality on the apple orchard by pollinating the trees. The apple orchard exerts a positive externality on the beekeepers because alternative pollen sources would not produce equally tasty honey.

   b. In this case, the full benefit of bees is not reflected in the decisions of the honey producer and the full benefit of the apple blossoms is not reflected in the decisions of the orchard. On the other hand, each producer takes into account the full cost of its decisions. If the two firms were to merge, then the benefit of the bees for apple production would be taken into account in the decision of how to manage the honey operation and the benefit of the apple blossoms for honey production would be taken into account in the decision of how to manage the orchard. In other words, the full benefit to the two firms of apple and honey production would be taken into account as well as the full cost. This "internalization of the externality" would be expected to result in a decision that increased the total surplus to be divided between the two producers.

   c. An externality arises when the actions of any consumer or producer affect the costs or benefits of other consumers or producers in some way not transmitted by market prices. If the firms have merged, then there is only a single producer, so the externality no longer exists: all the costs and benefits are taken into account.

   d. The merger reassigns property rights in the sense of giving a single authority the right of making production decisions for the two former firms' operations. This can be thought of as either giving the right of pollination to the apple orchard or giving the right of apple tree planting to the honey operation.

3. Cartier produces watches that consumers cannot distinguish, at the point of sale, from cheap "knockoff" copies produced by other firms. Cartier watches are of higher quality than the knockoffs, though. The knockoffs are much cheaper to produce, having a marginal cost of production of 1 while Cartier watches have a

marginal cost of production of 10. Suppose that Cartier knows that 19 firms other than itself produce knockoffs. All producers make 1 "unit" of watches a year.

a. Assume that consumers value the watches at their *expected* marginal cost and the consumers know the marginal cost of different qualities of watch as well as the number of firms producing each type of watch. What is the most consumers are willing to pay for a watch in this market?

b. Should Cartier continue to produce high quality watches or switch to producing low quality watches?

c. Is there a public good that affects the functioning of this market? Explain.

d. Referring back to the concepts of this chapter, how do trademarks affect the level of quality provided in this industry?

Answer:

a. The expected marginal cost of watches in this market is $(19/20) \times 1 + (1/20) \times 10 = 19/20 + 10/20 = 29/20$. This is the most a consumer is willing to pay for a watch.

b. If Cartier produces high quality watches, it will earn at most 29/20 for each watch sold, but incurs a marginal cost of 10 per watch made. Hence, it loses $10 - 29/20 = 171/20$ on each watch. If Cartier produces a low quality watch, the expected marginal cost of watches in the market drops to 1, as does the value consumers place on the watches. Hence, Cartier makes no loss on the watches. Lowering the quality is the best decision for Cartier.

c. Cartier's high quality is a good that all firms in this industry benefit from, while only Cartier pays the cost of increasing the average industry quality (and, hence, the value consumers place on the industry's product). In other words, in the absence of effective trademark protection, Cartier's investment in high quality is a non-exclusive good. No firm can be excluded from the general quality reputation of the "Cartier" watches, because there is no means of identifying the origin of any single watch. Quality is a common property resource that will be underprovided by this market. On the other hand, the reputation of Cartier watches is not a non-rivalrous good: the greater the number of firms producing fake Cartier watches, the lower the reputation of the Cartier label *for everyone*. In other words, a firm's benefits from using the Cartier label definitely depends on how many other firms are using it.

d. If an effective trademark system is introduced, each watch can be traced to a particular manufacturer. Hence, consumers would be willing to pay 10 for a watch known to be manufactured by a firm of high quality and 1 for a watch traceable to a manufacturer known to have lower quality. This means that, if Cartier raises its quality, it can obtain a price for the watch that covers its marginal cost. In this case, of course, Cartier just covers its cost whether it produces low or high quality. The point is that by instituting trademarks, Cartier can capture the full benefit of increasing its quality as well as shouldering the full cost. The trademark makes it possible to exclude other firms from any one firm's quality reputation.

Problem Set

1. With no fishing, Lake Bonanza has a stock of 100 fish. The benefit earned by a fisherman who fishes at Lake Bonanza depends on her probability of catching a fish, which decreases as the stock of fish is depleted. As an approximation of this, suppose that the benefit earned by any one fisherman from sitting down and fishing at the lake is B = .25(100-a), where a is the number of other fishermen at the lake. The cost borne by any one fisherman of sitting down to fish is C = 1.

   a. If each person decides to fish if the benefits of fishing exceed the cost, how many people will decide to fish at the lake?

   b. What is the reduction in benefits to the first fisherman if a second fisherman comes to the lake? What is the reduction in benefits of the first two fishermen if a third comes to the lake? Use this information to calculate the external cost of one fisherman coming to the lake to fish.

   c. Use your answer to (b) to calculate the number of fishermen who should fish at the lake at the social optimum. Compare your answer to (a). Why do they differ?

   d. If the lake is a common resource to which access is free, what is the number of fishermen who will fish at the lake? If the lake is now managed by a profit maximizing private company that is allowed to limit the number of fishermen using the lake and charge a fee equal to the total net benefits of fishing, what is the number of fishermen who will be allowed to fish at the lake?

2. Consider the case of the paper mill and the other users of the river ("fishermen") discussed in the summary. A water treatment plant can be built by either the fishermen or the paper mill at a cost of $10M in order to obtain pollution-free water. If the water is left untreated, the fishermen suffer a loss of $20M.

   a. If the right to the river is assigned to fishermen, will the treatment plant be built? If it is assigned to the mill, will the treatment plant be built? Discuss whether the outcome is economically efficient in both cases.

   b. How does the distribution of surplus depend on the allocation of property rights?

   c. How costly would the *exercise* of property rights have to be for the *assignment* of property rights not to result in any benefit to the parties? (Costs of the exercise of property rights might include, for example, hiring lawyers to discuss the pollution problem, hiring analysts to evaluate the feasibility of the treatment plant, and so on.)

3. A restaurant may have two possible policies toward smoking. It may prohibit smoking entirely or it may allow smoking to occur throughout the restaurant. Suppose that there are two clients to the restaurant, Tim and Kate. Tim likes to smoke and Kate does not. Tim and Kate each have $10 to spend (in addition to the money needed to eat).

   a. Illustrate the preferences of these two individuals over "smoke" and "money" on the following set of axes, where the total amount of smoke consumed by Tim is measured vertically from the lower left-hand corner of the box and the amount of money for each is measured along the horizontal axes. In this diagram, why is smoke measured only one way, while money is measured in two ways? How can you tell that smoke exerts a negative externality on Kate in this diagram?

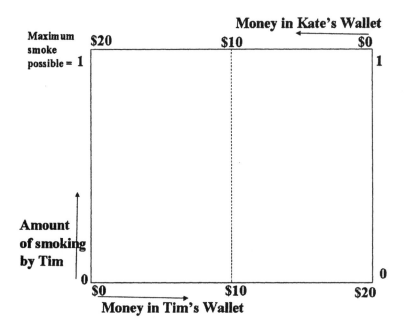

   b. Where is the endowment point if the restaurant has a no smoking policy? Where is the endowment point if the restaurant has a smoking permitted policy?

   c. Suppose that the restaurant has a no smoking policy, but the clients can bargain with each other about how much smoking they would wish to allow. Illustrate the set of possible trades of smoking for money that they could agree to. Are they Pareto Efficient?

   d. Perform the same analysis as in (c) for the case where the restaurant has a smoking permitted policy. How do these allocations differ from those in (c)?

   e. Relate your answers to the Coase Theorem.

4. "In the presence of an externality, welfare may be greater with monopoly than with competition." Do you agree? Explain your answer.

5. Apartment building A has a single water meter for the entire building and 100 residents (in 100 apartments). Each month the total bill is split evenly among the residents. Apartment building B has a water meter for each apartment and 100 residents (in 100 apartments). Each month, residents pay a bill reflecting their own usage only.

   a. Explain why apartment building A might have higher total water usage than apartment building B.

   b. Would the difference in water usage increase or decrease with the number of residents in the buildings (i.e., would this difference be greater if 200 people lived in each building rather than 100)?

   c. Discuss whether water in these two buildings is a resource with rivalry and exclusion. Is the difference in water usage due to free riding?

6. Suppose that firm 1 finds it inexpensive to reduce emissions of a toxin while firm 2 finds it more expensive. No other firms are in this industry. Let the marginal cost of emissions reduction by firm 1 be .5x, where x is the amount of reduction. On the other hand, firm 2's marginal cost of emissions reduction is .75x. The marginal social benefit of each unit of reduction is the same whichever firm conducts the reduction and can be written MB = 10 - x (decreasing because the primary health benefits are a reduction in death rates that occur only for high levels of toxins).

   a. Illustrate the marginal cost curves and the marginal benefit curves in a suitable diagram. Now, add up the two marginal cost curves horizontally. What does this sum represent?

   b. Suppose that, following an analysis of emissions of this toxin, the government decides to reduce emissions by 8 units. Using your diagram from (a), argue that a government that wishes to minimize the cost of reaching this goal will wish to impose emissions reductions x_1 on firm 1 and x_2 on firm 2 such that $MC_1(x_1) = MC_2(x_2)$.

Exam *(60 minutes: Closed book; closed notes)*

1. The individual demand curves for the only two consumers in a market are as illustrated below:

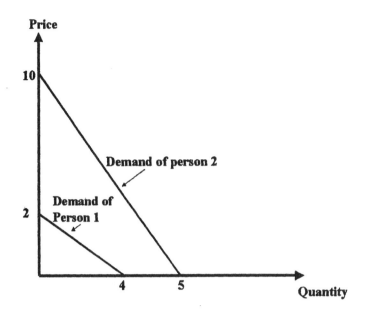

Draw the market demand for the good if it is a private good. Draw the market demand for the good if it is a public good. Explain any differences.

2. A patent grants property rights on an invention for a long period of time. Suppose that a single innovation is possible that could lower the cost of producing cars. The innovation can only be obtained by investing significant resources in research and development. If no patent were granted, would the socially optimal amount of innovation occur? Why?

3. Let the marginal private cost of production of a good be MPC = 10 and the marginal external cost be MEC = Q. The inverse market demand for the good is P = 40 - Q.

   a. If this market is organized competitively, what are the market equilibrium output, price, consumer's surplus, producers' surplus, externality cost, and net social benefit? What is the size of the deadweight loss?

   b. Calculate the marginal social cost of production. Now, calculate the same equilibrium quantities as in (a) for the social optimum.

   c. Calculate the emissions standard that would correct the difference between the social optimum and the market solution.

4. Let the marginal private cost of production of a good be MPC = 10. The marginal private benefit of the good is MPB = 40 - Q, while the marginal social benefit is MSB = 50 - Q.

   a. If this market is organized competitively, what are the market equilibrium output, price, consumer's surplus, producers' surplus, externality cost, and net social benefit? What is the size of the deadweight loss?

   b. Calculate the marginal social cost of production. Now, calculate the same equilibrium quantities as in (a) for the social optimum.

   c. Calculate the subsidy that would correct the difference between the social optimum and the market solution.

   d. How would your answers change if the marginal social benefit were MSB = 60 − Q?

Answers to Exercises

1. The correct statements are (a) and (b). At the market equilibrium, the consumer surplus is the area below demand and above P_1 for all units up to Q_1: it is the amount of benefit that the consumers obtain net of the price they must pay for the good. The private producer surplus at the market equilibrium is the area below P_1 and above the *private* marginal cost for all units produced (up to Q_1): it is the amount by which price exceeds the marginal cost of production for all units produced. The cost of the externality for these units produced is the total of the marginal externality cost for all units produced. In other words, it is the height of the MEC curve added up over all units produced (the MEC for unit 1 plus the MEC for unit 2 plus...the MEC for unit Q_1). In other words, it is the area under the MEC curve. This area is the same as the area between the MSC and the MPC curve for all units up to Q_1, as the MSC curve is simply the sum of the MPC and the MEC curves. Subtracting this area from the sum of consumer surplus and private producer surplus, we obtain the area of statement (a). Similarly, at the social optimum, consumer surplus is the area below demand and above P_0, while the private producer surplus is the area above MPC and below P_0 up to Q_0 units. The externality cost is now the area under the MEC curve up to Q_0 units of output, which is the vertical difference between the MSC and the MPC curves up to Q_0 units of output. Subtracting the externality cost from the sum of consumer surplus and private producer surplus yields the area of statement (b). Statement (c) would be correct for the case of no externalities, as the MEC would be zero so that the marginal private cost and the marginal social cost would coincide. The surpluses are illustrated and summarized in table form below.

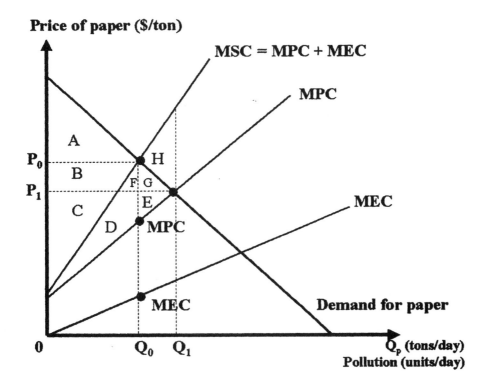

	Market Equilibrium	Social Optimum
Consumer Surplus	A+B+F+G	A
Private Producer Surplus	C+D+E	B+C+D+F
Externality Cost	D+E+F+G+H	D+F
Net Social Benefit	A+B+C-H	A+B+C

2. All the statements are correct. The reason is the following:

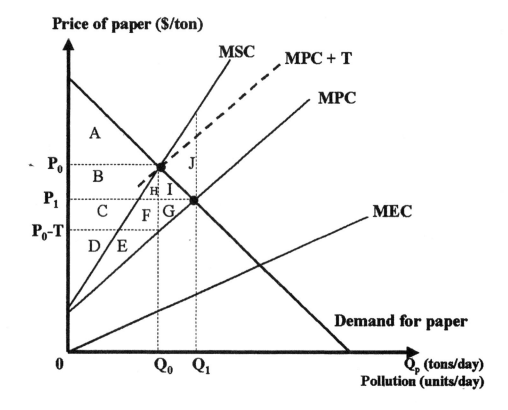

Price of paper ($/ton)

	Market Equilibrium	Optimum with Tax
Consumer Surplus	A+B+H+I	A
Private Producer Surplus	C+D+E+F+G	D+E
Externality Cost	E+F+G+H+I +J	E+F+H
Tax Revenues	0	B+C+F+H
Net Social Benefit	A+B+C+D-J	A+B+C+D

From the table, it is clear that consumer surplus falls with the tax. Private producer surplus also falls. The net social benefit is now the consumer surplus, plus the private producer surplus, net of the externality cost and including tax revenues paid to the government. This net social benefit rises, so that it should be possible to mete out the tax revenues in such a way as to make all agents better off than they were in the original market equilibrium, even though consumer surplus and private producer surplus has fallen. This is possible because the externality cost has fallen at the new equilibrium as well.

3. Statements (a) and (c) are correct. The parking lot exhibits a common property problem because the number of approved users is still large enough that, on Wednesdays at least, significant congestion costs arise. Hence, statement (a) is correct and (b) is incorrect. Raising the fee sufficiently to force usage to fall below the number of available spots can solve this problem, as the external cost falls to zero when usage is in this range (since all permit holders can find spots). Ideally, though, one would want to have a special "Wednesday permit" that would only be available to those willing to pay an additional yearly fee. One could then appropriately reduce the number of Wednesday users without ending up with half-empty parking lots on other days of the week.

4. In all cases, the externalities can be both positive and negative. In the case of wind chimes, it depends on whether those who can hear them like the sound or not. If the chimes keep many residents awake who would prefer to sleep, then even if they are soothing to the purchaser, they have a negative externality. If all the residents find them soothing, then the externality is positive. Similarly, if smoking in a restaurant bothers other diners, it has a negative externality. If smoking adds to the ambience of the restaurant by giving a "swagger" to the clientele, then it has a positive externality. Finally, the externalities of bleach are quite complex: it prevents the transfer of infection both within the hospital and outside the hospital by reducing the probability that "super infections" will develop. On the other hand, bleach is a major pollutant when it is disposed of after cleaning and when it is manufactured. The point is that the same good may have different externalities depending on the particular receiving group we focus on. Clearly, this complicates the use of instruments such as quotas and taxes to obtain the optimal use of the good or resource.

5. Solutions (a), (c), and (d) should solve the problem. The landings are creating a negative externality for local residents. Since this problem presumably gets worse as the number of landings increases, and a certain "unit" of noise is associated with each landing, the diagram representing the problem should look very similar to that of Figure 17.1. Hence, an appropriately chosen specific tax or a limit on nighttime flights would be possible solutions to the problem. Banning all nighttime flights is unlikely to be the best solution, as there is still significant benefit to having flights land at night and the marginal cost of "a little" noise is likely to be low. Allocating the decision power to local residents should also solve the problem since, according to the Coase Theorem, allocating the rights to "noise" *either the* residents or the users of the airport should allow bargaining to

an efficient solution. This assumes that bargaining has a sufficiently low cost, of course.

6. (b), (c), and (d) are correct. A public university campus is, in theory, open to all people and so is non-exclusive. It is also nonrival in the sense that many people can enjoy its benefits at the same time. A private university campus has the right to exclude certain people, but it is nonrival in the same way as the public university campus. If police presence discourages crime, then everyone benefits from crime reduction: the fact that Mr. Smith benefits from crime reduction does not prevent Mr. Jones from benefiting from it as well. In that sense, police protection is nonrival. Note, however, that if police numbers are small compared to the number of crimes committed, the fact that Mr. Smith needs immediate assistance might prevent Mr. Jones from getting immediate assistance at the same time. Police protection would then be a rival good. As public police protection is (in principle) available to all, it is also a non-exclusive good. Finally, if the security guard truly acts purely to protect the store, then this service is exclusive and rival: those who do not pay do not benefit.

7. The correct answer is (b). If marginal cost is at MC_A, the optimal production of the public good is zero, so there is no free-rider problem that would reduce production below the social optimum. If marginal cost is at MC_B, the socially optimal provision of the public good is positive, even though no single consumer would be willing to pay the marginal cost of the good. Hence, this level of marginal cost could create a problem of under provision due to free riding. Similarly, if the marginal cost is MC_C, there is potential under provision for the reasons outlined in the argument accompanying Figure 17.8 of the summary. If the marginal cost is MC_D, then the marginal social benefit coincides with a single consumer's benefit curve so that the market provision of the public good will be optimal (as consumer 2 will not "free ride on herself"). Hence, under provision only occurs with marginal costs MC_B and MC_C.

Answers to Problem Set

1.

a. As long as $.25(100-a) \geq 1$, it pays a fisherman to join the crowd and fish in the lake. This will be true as long as $a \leq 96$.

b. The first fisherman earns a benefit of $.25(100)$ if she remains alone. If one other joins, she earns $.25(100-1) = .25(99)$. Hence, she suffers a reduction of $.25$ in her benefits. If a third joins them, then each earns $.25(100-2) = .25(98)$, another $.25$ reduction in benefits. Hence, the external cost of increasing lake "usage" is $.25a$.

c. If fishermen are allowed to fish as long as the benefit exceeds the social cost, then "a" should be set such that $.25(100-a) \geq 1 + .25a$. Hence, the maximum number of fishermen should be set such that $25 - .25a = 1 + .25a$

or 24 = .5a so that a = 48. This is much lower than the level in part (a). This is because the individual fishermen compare only their private costs of fishing to their private benefit.

d. If the town operates the lake as common property, 96 fishermen will use the lake, as each individual will compare his own costs and benefits in choosing whether or not to fish. If the private company manages the lake and charges a fee equal to the total net benefits of fishing, it will allow only 48 fishermen to come to the lake. The company takes into account the fact that adding a fisherman decreases the net benefit of the other fishermen using the lake and hence decreases the fishermen's willingness to pay. To see this, notice that a fisherman's willingness to pay is equal to $0.25(100\text{-}a) - C = 24\text{-}.25a$ when a total of "a" fishermen are allowed on the lake. The profits of the private company are then $24a\text{-}.25a^2$, which is maximized at a = 48.

2.

a. If the rights to the river are assigned to the mill, then the fishermen can either suffer the $20M in damages or pay $10M for the treatment plant and suffer no damages. They opt for the treatment plant, and the mill pollutes as before. If the rights to the river are assigned to the fishermen, then the mill can either compensate the fishermen for the $20M in damages and continue to pollute, or it can pay $10M to build the treatment plant. It opts for the treatment plant, and the fishermen receive no damages. In the first case, the loss of fishermen is $10M, rather than $20M, as it would be without property rights. In the second case, the loss to the mill is $10M, rather than $20M, as it would be without property rights. Hence, building the treatment plant is the efficient solution and is chosen regardless of the allocation of property rights.

b. The party that does not receive property rights must pay $10M, while the party that receives the rights can continue using the river as they would prefer. Hence, the rights are valuable in the sense that each does better if it receives the rights than if the other party receives the rights.

c. If the exercise of property rights ("the bargaining process") costs more than $10M, then neither party will exercise the property rights, and assigning rights makes no difference to the original outcome of the problem. In other words, pollution simply continues and the fishermen suffer $20M in damages, as they did before the assignment of property rights.

3.

a. Tim and Kate must breathe the same air, with the same amount of smoke in it, so there is only one amount of smoke that both must consume at any one time. On the other hand, they each have separate wallets with money in them. Hence, the money in their wallets is measured separately. Since Kate's well-being decreases with the amount of smoking by Tim, but Tim's well-being increases, Tim's consumption of smoke has a negative effect on Kate. This illustrates the fact that the externality is negative.

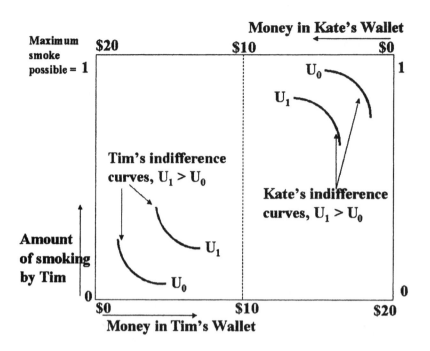

b. If there is no smoking, then the endowment is at point A, below (no smoke, $10 in each wallet). If there is a smoking policy, the endowment point is at point B, below (Tim's preferred level of smoke, $10 in each wallet).

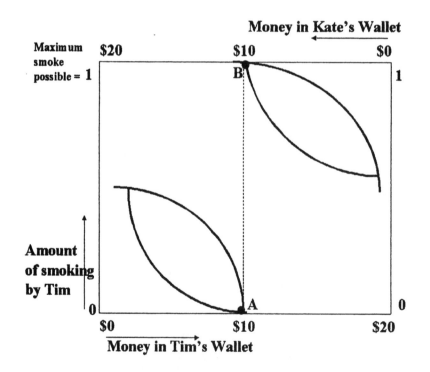

c. and d. Tim and Kate will be willing to trade to any point within the "lens" that their indifference curves form through the endowment points. In particular, they will continue bargaining until they reach some point on the contract curve that lies within this lens. These points occur where the indifference curves of the two individuals are tangent. (For a refresher on contract curves, see Chapter 16.)

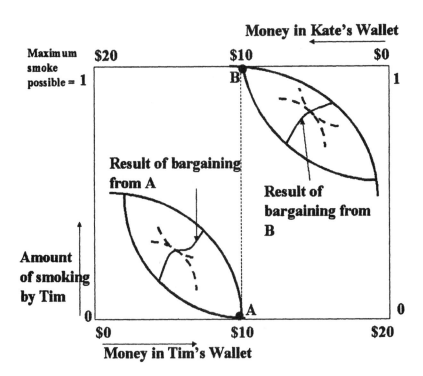

e. This analysis is a graphical way to illustrate that two parties can achieve an efficient allocation of resources by bargaining. In this case, the parties will bargain to a point on the contract curve that lies within the lens formed by their initial utility levels. The property rights regime establishes the endowment point of the parties and so changes the distribution of smoke and money (and, hence, well-being) in the outcome. This does not prevent the bargaining solution from being at an efficient point (a point on the contract curve) whatever the endowment.

4. Net Social Benefit is greater under competition than under monopoly when externalities are not present. This is because the monopoly under produces compared to the social optimum. However, if *negative* externalities are present, this underproduction can have the advantage of limiting the negative externalities. Hence, the net social benefit can be bigger under monopoly than under competitive production. In fact, if a specific tax equal to the externality cost in the monopoly equilibrium were imposed on the monopolist, it would decrease welfare! Since the monopoly equilibrium already is lower than the social optimum, this represents a reduction in welfare.

5.

a. In apartment building A, each resident obtains the entire benefit of one unit of additional water usage (since the water is used by that resident only), but shoulders only 1/100th of the cost of that usage (since the water bill is split evenly among the 100 residents). In apartment building B, each resident obtains the entire benefit of one additional unit of water usage, and shoulders the entire cost of that usage (since the water bill is paid by the same person as the water user). Hence, the residents of apartment building A face the same benefits as those of B for a much lower cost. This leads to a higher equilibrium water usage.

b. If the number of residents (one per apartment) increased, then the residents in building A would shoulder an even smaller cost of usage (1/200th), raising their usage relative to those of apartment building B. Hence, the higher the number of residents, the greater the difference.

c. Water is a common property resource in apartment building A, with no exclusion but rivalry (since a unit of water consumed by one resident cannot be consumed by another). It is a private good in apartment building B (with rivalry and exclusion), as each unit is metered separately. Since the residents of apartment building A are able to obtain the full benefits of the water without paying the full price, there is a free-riding effect.

6.

a. The horizontal sum of the marginal cost curves represents the total emissions reduction that can be produced at each level of marginal cost. The government will wish to reduce emissions as long as the benefit exceeds this sum of the marginal cost curves, as each unit of emissions reduction below this intersection represents a level at which the benefit of further reductions outweighs the cost.

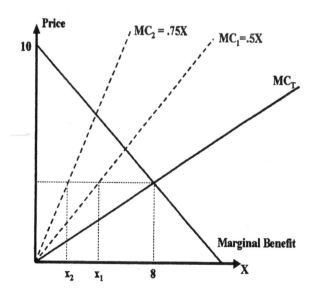

b. Quotas x_1 and x_2 that equalize the marginal cost of the reductions across firms are illustrated in the diagram accompanying part (a). If any other quotas were imposed, then the marginal cost would be lower in one firm than in the other. The government could then obtain the same total reduction for lower cost by reallocating the reduction to the lower cost firm. Note that this reasoning is very similar to that of the multi-plant monopolist of Chapter 11, which allocated production across plants so as to equalize marginal costs.

Answers to Exam

1. If the good is private, the market demand is the *horizontal* sum of the individual demand curves because the demand gives the total number of units that would be demanded at each price. Hence, at a price of 1, person 1 would demand 2 units and person 2 would demand 4.5 units, giving a market demand of 6.5. If the good is public, the market demand is the *vertical* sum of the individual demand curves, because demand gives the willingness to pay for any given number of units. Hence, person 1 would be willing to pay 1 for 2 units of the good, while person 2 would be willing to pay 6, yielding a total willingness to pay of 7.

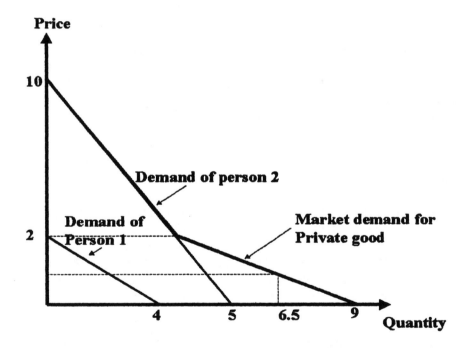

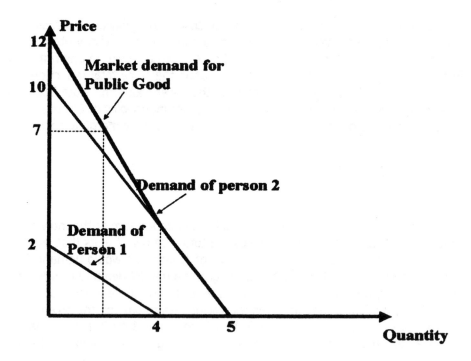

2. If no property rights are granted to an innovation, it is possible for the socially incorrect amount of innovation to occur because the benefit to the innovation can be obtained by other firms that may imitate the innovation, while the inventor shoulders the full cost of innovation. By granting property rights, the government allows the innovator to capture the full benefits of the innovation.

3.

    a. The market equilibrium occurs where MPC intersects market demand or where $10 = 40 - Q$. Hence, $Q_1 = 30$ and $P_1 = 10$. Consumer surplus is $30(30)(1/2) = 450$; producer surplus is 0 (as private marginal cost is flat); the externality cost is $30(30)(1/2) = 450$; Net Social Benefit is $CS + PS - EC = 0$. (The externality cost completely eliminates the consumer surplus from this activity!) Deadweight loss is $(30-15)(40-10)(1/2) = 225$.

    b. The social optimum occurs where the MSC intersects market demand. MSC is the vertical sum of MEC and MPC or $MSC = Q + 10$. Hence, the social optimum is the level of Q such that $Q + 10 = 40 - Q$ or $Q_0 = 15$ and $P_0 = 25$. Consumer surplus is $(15)(15) = 225$ (notice that this is the area of a rectangle, since marginal private cost is still flat); producer surplus is $(15)(15)(1/2) = 112.5$; the externality cost is $15(15)(1/2) = 112.5$; Net Social Benefit is $CS + PS - EC = 225$. There is no deadweight loss. By cutting back production to the social optimum, the deadweight loss of part (a) has been converted into social benefit in part (b)!

    c. The emissions standard that would correct this is a quota of 15 units for the market.

4.

a. The market equilibrium occurs where the marginal private benefit intersects the marginal private cost of production or where $40 - Q = 10$ so that $Q_1 = 30$ and $P_1 = 10$. Consumer surplus is the area below the marginal social benefit curve and above the market price, or $(40-10)(30)(1/2) = 450$. Producer surplus is the difference between market price and marginal private cost or 0. The deadweight loss is 50.

b. The social optimum occurs where the marginal social benefit intersects the marginal private cost of production or where $50 - Q = 10$ so that $Q_0 = 40$ and $P_0 = 10$. Consumer surplus is $(50-10)(40)(1/2)=800$; producer surplus remains zero. This is because marginal private cost is flat and equal to price in both cases: while the social benefit of production has shifted out -- so that a higher quantity is produced in equilibrium, -- there is an incentive to increase production up to the point where this benefit is driven down to the marginal private cost. There is no deadweight loss.

c. The subsidy that would correct this difference is the amount, S, such that the marginal private benefit equals the marginal (private) cost at exactly $Q = 40$ or $40 - Q = 10 - S$ at $Q = 40$. Hence, $40 - 40 = 10 - S$ or $S = 10$. In other words, the subsidy must cover the marginal private cost in its entirety to obtain the social optimum.

d. If the marginal social benefit were higher than $50 - Q$, then even with a subsidy that covered marginal private cost in its entirety -- as in part (c) – the socially optimal quantity would not be produced. In fact, in order for this to occur, the subsidy would have to be so large that the firm would be *paid* to produce, on balance, rather than incur a positive cost!